KING EDWARD VII

A BIOGRAPHY

THE MACMILLAN COMPANY
NEW YORK · BOSTON · CHICAGO · DALLAS
ATLANTA · SAN FRANCISCO

MACMILLAN & CO., LIMITED
LONDON · BOMBAY · CALCUTTA
MELBOURNE

THE MACMILLAN CO. OF CANADA, LTD.
TORONTO

George Richmond R.A. del.   Francis Holl sculpsit

King Edward VII in his eighteenth year
1858

Emery Walker ph. sc.

KING EDWARD VII

A BIOGRAPHY

BY

SIR SIDNEY LEE

VOL. I

FROM BIRTH TO ACCESSION

9TH NOVEMBER 1841 TO 22ND JANUARY 1901

New York

THE MACMILLAN COMPANY

1925

PRINTED IN THE UNITED STATES OF AMERICA

Norwood Press
J. S. Cushing Co. — Berwick & Smith Co.
Norwood, Mass., U.S.A.

PREFACE

IT is at the request of King George V., King Edward VII.'s son, that this biography has been undertaken.

The work, while it incorporates much information which has already been published, is based on documents in the royal archives to which King George has given me access, and on numerous collections of letters addressed by the late King to personal friends and to men of prominence in official life, which I have consulted with His Majesty's sanction. His Majesty has also permitted the reproduction in facsimile of the two specimens of the late King's handwriting which appear in this volume and illustrate the marked change in its character in the course of forty years.

Beyond this assistance King George is in no way responsible for the book. For its plan and execution, to which I have devoted four years of thought and labour, I am alone responsible. I have pursued to the best of my ability the lines which my previous experience as a biographer dictated. I have sought to give practical application to principles which I defined twelve years ago in these terms: "Biography is of no genuine account unless it make for thoroughness and accuracy of statement, for an equitable valuation of human effort, and above all for honest independence of judgement."

My account of Kaiser William II.'s character and conduct is my own unaided interpretation of tested evidence drawn from very varied sources both published and unpublished. The co-ordination of the *pièces justificatives* in chronological order renders imperative, I believe, the conclusions which I have reached.

In the case of a great historic figure like King Edward VII., no less than in that of one of smaller prominence in the world's affairs, sympathy with one's theme is essential to

v

justice in biography. To that credential I modestly think that I may fairly lay claim. In a work of such multiplicity, I cannot expect, whatever my efforts, to escape all error in fact or inference, but the investigations which I have long pursued into the career of King Edward have developed my faith in the generosity of his disposition as well as in his shrewdness of judgement. I trust that without sacrifice of candour or of any other fundamental principle of the biographer's art, I have drawn my portrait so as to convey to the present and to future generations a signally humane and human personality very rare among princes.

To the intensity and range of King Edward's interest before he came to the throne, in politics, and more especially in foreign politics, this book bears constant witness. It is therefore inevitable that the various changes in the political situation at home and abroad during nearly forty years of his adult life should fill a large space of my canvas. I believe that I have been able to throw new light on many vexed issues which now belong to history.

Besides the unpublished material at my disposal, I have made full use of all the information which, as far as I know, is already in print. I have examined newspapers (notably *The Times*) and periodicals of the epoch as well as the comprehensive and illuminating collections of diplomatic archives published by the French and German Governments and memoirs of leading statesmen of this and other countries. I have given in my footnotes precise references to all the published sources which I have consulted.

Of my indebtedness to King George I have already spoken. Warm thanks are at the same time due to many who have helped me with the loan of original letters of the late King, with personal reminiscences of him and with very varied suggestions. To my regret, several of those who have rendered me efficient aid have not lived long enough to acquaint themselves with the uses to which I have put their assistance.[1]

To the late Viscount Morley and the late Viscount Knollys I owe much advice and encouragement in the initial stages of the work. The Right Hon. Sir Frederick Ponsonby, Keeper of

[1] So as not to prolong unduly the list on the opposite page I have reserved for my footnotes acknowledgements to various persons who have assisted me on specific points.

the King's Privy Purse, has from first to last rendered me in all directions help which it would scarcely be possible for me to overestimate. He has also lent me a few interesting and pertinent memoranda of his father, the late General Sir Henry Ponsonby. My searches in the Windsor Archives have been facilitated by Viscount Stamfordham, Keeper of the King's Archives and King George's Private Secretary, and by the Rev. Albert Lee, Clerk of the Archives. The late Sir Arthur Davidson, formerly Equerry and Assistant Private Secretary to King Edward, who showed the liveliest interest in the undertaking up to the time of his death, was especially helpful in enabling me to consult the papers of the late King which still remain in Queen Alexandra's care at Marlborough House. With the Marquis of Lincolnshire, the late Viscount Chaplin, and Colonel Gerald Ellis, son of the late Colonel Sir Arthur Ellis, I have enjoyed the advantage of personal conversation on many points in the late King's career. The Earl of Rosebery has kindly allowed me to print a few extracts from letters written by him as Prime Minister.

To the following persons I am indebted for the loan of original letters and papers in their possession from the late King's pen: The Earl of Elgin for the papers of the late Major-General Bruce and Mrs. Bruce; Colonel Wilfrid Ashley, M.P., for letters to Viscount Palmerston; the representatives of the late Earl Russell for letters to that statesman; the Earl of Derby for letters to his grandfather, Edward Geoffrey, fourteenth Earl of Derby, Prime Minister, and to his uncle Edward Henry, fifteenth Earl of Derby; Mr. Henry Gladstone for letters to the late Right Hon. W. E. Gladstone; Lord Beaconsfield's Trustees for letters to the late Earl of Beaconsfield (by the courtesy of Mr. G. E. Buckle); the Dowager Countess of Granville for letters to the late Earl Granville, K.G.; Major Cadogan for letters to the late Earl Cadogan; Sir Arthur Leetham for letters to the late Viscount Wolseley; Sir Bartle Frere for letters to his father and mother, the late Sir Bartle and Lady Frere; the Marquis of Salisbury for letters to his late father, the Prime Minister; Lady Spring Rice for letters to her father, the late Sir Frank Lascelles; Mr. Ernest Law, C.B., for letters to his uncle, the late Mr. Alfred Montgomery; Earl Spencer for letters to the fifth Earl Spencer; the Marquis of Londonderry for

letters to his mother, the late Marchioness ; the late Sir Reginald
Acland for letters to his father, Sir Henry Acland ; Sir Frederick
Liddell, K.C.B., for letters to his father and mother, the Dean
of Christ Church and Mrs. Liddell ; the late Lady Beresford for
letters to her husband, Lord (Charles) Beresford ; the Marquis
of Lansdowne, and the Earl of Midleton for letters addressed
to themselves.

Mr. Stephen Gaselee, Librarian of the Foreign Office, has
kindly sent me, at my request, some extracts from the Foreign
Office Archives by permission of the Secretary of State. I have
derived, too, much benefit from the Archives of the Russian
Embassy in London by the courtesy of M. Eugène Sabline,
formerly *chargé d'affaires*, and until October 1924 in charge of
the liquidation of the former Russian Embassy.

In the choice of portraits, I have had the advantage of the
counsel of my friend Mr. Lionel Cust, Surveyor of the King's
pictures and works of art. To the Benchers of the Middle
Temple I am indebted for permission to reproduce the portrait
in their possession by Frank Holl, R.A.

The second and concluding volume of the work, which will
cover King Edward's reign, is in active preparation, and will, it
is hoped, be issued before the end of the present year.

SIDNEY LEE.

January 1, 1925.

CONTENTS

ILLUSTRATIONS

IN PHOTOGRAVURE BY EMERY WALKER

xi

MAPS

FACSIMILE AUTOGRAPH LETTERS

The letter runs: "*Homburg, August 19th, 1900.* MY DEAR FRANK
LASCELLES—I have just received enclosed most satisfactory telegram from
the Emperor. I have answered that I shall arrive at Cassel on Wednesday,
at 1 o'clock, for luncheon, and that I will ask you as well as Clarke to accompany me. You shall hear in due time the hour of departure. Please return
me the telegram and believe me, yours very sincerely, ALBERT EDWARD.
"Will you lunch with me at Ritter's at 1 to-morrow? A.E."

KING EDWARD VII

A BIOGRAPHY

CHAPTER I

PARENTAGE AND BIRTH

I

KING EDWARD VII. was born at twelve minutes before eleven on the morning of Tuesday, 9th November 1841, at Buckingham Palace.[1] His mother, Queen Victoria, had continued to "write notes, sign her name, and declare her pleasure up to the last moment as if nothing serious was at hand."[2] Sir Robert Peel, the Prime Minister, had already accepted an invitation to dine with her on the evening of the eventful day.

At the birth there were present not only the boy's father, Prince Albert, and his maternal grandmother, the Duchess of Kent, but also the chief officers of State whom Prince Albert had hurriedly summoned to make formal attestation of the fact that the new-born babe was lawful heir to the Crown of the United Kingdom with its colonies and dependencies beyond the seas. Conspicuous among these witnesses were the two men who excited at the time the country's liveliest interest—Sir Robert Peel, the Conservative Prime Minister, who had held office for a bare two months, and the veteran hero, the Duke of Wellington, who, having in the evening of his days exchanged a soldier's life for that of a politician, had joined Peel's cabinet without a portfolio. Just after the birth there hurried on the scene William Howley, Archbishop of Canterbury, a type of rigid ecclesiastical

---

[1] The Official Bulletin ran: "The Queen was safely delivered of a Prince this morning at forty-eight minutes past ten o'clock. Her Majesty and the Infant Prince are going on well."

(Sgd.) JAMES CLARK, M.D.
CHARLES LOCOCK, M.D.
ROBERT FERGUSON, M.D.
RICHARD BLAGDEN, M.D.

[2] Sir James Graham, *apud Croker Papers*, ii. 408.

Toryism whom King Edward well remembered in later life as the last Primate to conform to the dying habit of wearing a wig.

II

The new-born Prince was, in due time, justly proud of the long line of Kings from which he descended. The blood of many strains—Saxon, Norman, Scottish, Welsh, German—mingled in his veins. In the remote distance, his direct progenitors included the historic figures of King Alfred, William the Conqueror, Edward I. (justly reckoned the ablest of English rulers), Henry VII., and James I. The chequered fortunes of the royal house of Stuart, which derived from James I., always moved in him an especially tender sentiment. His more immediate ancestors were the three Hanoverians, George I., George II., and George III. King George III., a belated champion of personal sovereignty and a shining example of domestic virtue, was King Edward's great-grandfather. From him the descent of the Crown had taken an unusual turn. Although King George III. was father of nine sons and six daughters, yet when he died, blind and imbecile, on the 29th January 1820, at the age of eighty-two, his family was lawfully represented, in the third generation, only by an infant granddaughter scarcely eight months old.

This infant was Victoria, the only child of the aged sovereign's fourth son, Edward, Duke of Kent, who had married late in life avowedly for dynastic reasons. His choice had fallen on a homely German princess, the youngest daughter of the reigning Duke of Saxe-Coburg and Saalfeld, who was widow of a reigning Prince of Leiningen, and sister of Prince Leopold of Saxe-Coburg, subsequently first King of the Belgians. The Duchess of Kent's shrewd and well-informed brother Leopold was long the oracle alike of his niece, Princess Victoria, and of his grand-nephew the future King Edward, through his early years.[1]

[1] On 2nd May 1816 Prince Leopold married as his first wife Princess Charlotte, sole child and heiress of the Prince Regent, George III.'s eldest son, and, at that time, George III.'s only grandchild. The Princess Charlotte's premature death on 6th November 1817 left Prince Leopold a childless widower and threatened for the moment George III.'s family with early extinction. Prince Leopold remained in England till 1831, when he accepted the offer of the throne of Belgium.

The sudden death of Princess Victoria's father eight months after her birth was followed at no long interval by the deaths, without legitimate issue, of her father's three elder brothers who came before her in the succession. Two of these brothers enjoyed short and inglorious spells of kingship as King George IV. and King William IV. respectively. The death, on the 20th June 1837, of King William IV., to whom Princess Victoria stood in relation of heir-presumptive, made her Queen of England just after she had celebrated her eighteenth birthday.

Despite her youth, Queen Victoria showed, from the opening days of her long reign, a surprising aptitude for the responsibilities of her high station. Under the wise guidance of her first Prime Minister, Lord Melbourne, she rapidly familiarised herself with affairs of State. Her will was always strong, and a quick intuition rather than any force of intellect or conscious exercise of reasoning faculty soon enabled her to form decided and often sagacious opinions on the vast variety of questions which came to her notice. At the same time her instincts were very womanly; her domestic affections were strong, and her sympathies with suffering and misfortune alert. A girlish zest, which she long retained, for simple pleasures and for the lighter sides of life added to her charm. She rode, danced, played games, and displayed a lively interest in music, drama, and art. The English people welcomed with immense enthusiasm the new sovereign, whose artless promise favourably contrasted with the forbidding traits of her immediate predecessors—men far advanced in middle life whose personal failings forfeited respect. The chivalric devotion which the young Queen awoke in her subjects strengthened amazingly the position of the monarchy in England.

It was primarily at the suggestion of her uncle Leopold, now King of the Belgians, the family counsellor, that the Queen chose for her husband her first cousin Albert, second son of the reigning Duke of Saxe-Coburg and her mother's and her uncle Leopold's eldest brother. The young man, her junior by three months, moved in her, as soon as they met, a passionate attachment which grew in strength with fuller knowledge. Their marriage, which was celebrated at St. James's Palace on the 10th February 1840, proved throughout its twenty-one years' duration one of the happiest unions in recorded history.

Prince Albert played a somewhat pathetic part in the annals

of his adopted country. Carefully educated at the University of Bonn, he remained for life an earnest student of books. Of unexceptionable morals he was scrupulously conscientious in his devotion to duty, applied himself assiduously to works of philanthropy and industrial welfare, and developed a faculty for business and organisation. But the fibre of his thought was essentially German, and despite his strenuous and well-intentioned endeavours, he failed to assimilate the less deliberate and less searching view of life habitual among English people. To the Queen's chagrin her subjects never adopted her exalted estimate of his disposition and abilities. In their eyes his shy and ungenial manner was always reminiscent of his German birth and affinities. By the Queen's desire he shared her public and political responsibilities, and his intellectual power and cautious temper gave value to the political assistance which he rendered her. Some qualified praise came his way, but there was more sour censure. All his activities were jealously scrutinised by the English press and society. In course of time the Queen's intense faith in her husband and his profound earnestness exerted a perceptible influence on her character. She lost much of her early blitheness and buoyancy. Unfriendly critics were constant in complaint of the German proclivities with which Prince Albert infected the Queen and her Court.

III

King Edward's entry into the world was the signal for impressive demonstrations of national joy. A first child, Victoria, "Princess Royal of England," had been born to the youthful parents, Queen Victoria and Prince Albert, also at Buckingham Palace, on 20th November 1840, less than a year before. But popular interest in the domestic and dynastic fortunes of the young Queen was vastly stimulated by the birth of a second child and first son. No heir had been born to a reigning sovereign for some seventy-nine years. Few were alive to recall the 12th August 1762 when Queen Charlotte, wife of King George III., gave birth at St. James's Palace to the last preceding Prince of Wales, whose career, first as Prince of Wales, then as Prince Regent on behalf of his incapacitated father, and finally, for a last ten years as King George IV., cost the Crown much dignity.

The nation regarded King Edward's birth as promising the monarchy, which his mother had lately rescued from national scorn, an honourable stability.

On the evening of the Prince's day of birth the customary banquet took place at the Guildhall on the admission to office of the new Lord Mayor of London, John Pirie. Sir Robert Peel and his fellow-Ministers were guests of the City, and gave fervid expression to the national enthusiasm. William Ewart Gladstone, the future apostle of Victorian liberalism, who was as yet an unbending Tory, was present by virtue of his ministerial office of Vice-President of the Board of Trade. He was to come into personal relations with the new-born Prince in infancy, and was to maintain an uninterrupted intimacy until his death near the end of the century. On the 9th November 1880 Mr. Gladstone, then at the zenith of his political career, described to the Prince in his usual letter of birthday congratulation how he attended the Lord Mayor's Banquet thirty-nine years before, "when 'God Save the Prince of Wales,' in illuminated letters reaching across the end of the Guildhall, announced to the company the birth of your Royal Highness and the sentiment which it awoke in the heart of every loyal citizen and subject."

The press of the country faithfully echoed the general exhilaration. *The Times* next morning described in exuberant terms "the one universal feeling of joy which ran throughout the kingdom." The comic weekly, *Punch*, which was less than five months old, and was to follow with close and frankly critical attention every turn in King Edward's future career, reflected the popular excitement. In its issue after the Prince's birth (November 13) it regaled its readers with some rollicking stanzas, of which the first ran:

> Huzza! we've a little Prince at last,
> A roaring Royal boy;
> And all day long the booming bells
> Have rung their peals of joy.

The event was straightway set as a theme for the English poem at Cambridge University. The successful competitor, Sir Henry Maine, afterwards eminent as a jurist, looked forward in rather tame couplets to the time when the infant might become "the perfect man" and so develop into "the perfect king."

IV

"O how happy, how grateful did I feel to that Almighty Providence who has blessed me so peculiarly," wrote the Queen in her *Journal* on the birth of her heir, whose physical condition fully satisfied the parental pride. "Our little boy is a wonderfully large and strong child," she informed her beloved uncle and mentor, Leopold, King of the Belgians (November 29, 1841), "with very large dark-blue eyes, a finely formed but somewhat large nose, and a pretty little mouth." [1]

From his first hours of life Queen Victoria reiterated with wifely adoration the hope that in career and character her son should be a copy of his father. Her letters to her uncle abound in such phrases as these: "I hope and pray he may be like his dearest papa"; [2] "You will understand how fervent are my prayers, and I am sure everybody's must be, to see him resemble his father in *every, every* respect, both in body and mind." [3] Through the child's infancy, boyhood, and early manhood Queen Victoria clung tenaciously to such wifely aspirations. Lord Melbourne who, after retirement from the office of her first Prime Minister, remained the recipient of the Queen's domestic confidences, cautiously approved her conjugal ardour: "Your Majesty cannot offer up for the young Prince a more safe and judicious prayer than that he may resemble his father. The character, in Lord Melbourne's opinion, depends much upon the race, and on both sides he has a good chance." [4]

As the event proved, it was from his high-spirited, shrewd, and quick-witted mother in the early pride of Queen and wife, rather than from his grave and reserved father, that King Edward drew many traits as boy and man. In course of time, too, her example taught him how to reconcile free play of personal will in the ways of political criticism and suggestion, with a full recognition of the constitutional principles of ministerial responsibility and the disqualification of the Crown for the personal exercise of political power. From his father he may have derived something of his organising aptitude, of his philanthropic activity, and his zest for foreign politics. Very few distinctive features of his character seemed to throw back to earlier progenitors. To his grandfather,

[1] *Letters of Queen Victoria, 1837–61*, i. 457.   [2] *Ibid.* i. 460.
[3] Martin, *Life of Prince Consort*, i. 21.   [4] *Letters*, i. 458.

the Duke of Kent, who was both a military martinet and a patron 1841
of experiments in social reform, may perhaps be traced his Ætat. 1
almost pedantic insistence on correctness in dress and uniform,
as well as a sympathetic interest in schemes of social better-
ment. He was not in the direct line of descent from King
Henry V., King Henry VIII., or King George IV.—proverbial
examples of pleasure-loving princes to whom, at one or other
period of his career, he was popularly likened. Heredity indeed
throws imperfect light, despite Lord Melbourne's forecast, on his
matured personality. It is not easy to trace to the influence
of either parent or of any forefather, the frank *joie de vivre*, the
charm of address, the captivating *bonhomie*, the cosmopolitan
touches, the sympathy with the French outlook on life, and the
zeal for sport, which his nature soon developed. It is plain that
he inherited little of his father's austerity or cautious reticence
and nothing at all of those studious and academic predilections
which spoke eloquently of Prince Albert's German temperament.

V

The child "is to be called *Albert* and Edward is to be his
second name," wrote the Queen to her uncle Leopold, 29th
November 1841 [1]—Albert after his father and Edward after the
Queen's father, the Duke of Kent. Lord Melbourne, when
acknowledging the like intimation, guardedly questioned the right
of the name Albert to priority:

Lord Melbourne supposes that Your Majesty has determined
yourself upon the relative position of the two names, but *Edward*
is a good English appellation, and has a certain degree of popularity attached to it from ancient recollections. Albert is also
an old Anglo-Saxon name—the same, Lord Melbourne believes,
as Ethelred—but it has not been so common nor so much in use
since the Conquest. However, Your Majesty's feelings, which
Lord Melbourne perfectly understands, must determine this
point. [2]

The Queen was unmoved by Lord Melbourne's reasonable
comment. "Albert Edward" became the Prince's appellation
in all relations, save in the family circle where through life
he was called "Bertie"; in letters to his kindred he invariably
used that signature instead of his full name. It was only on

---

[1] *Letters of Queen Victoria, 1837–61,* i. 457.   [2] *Ibid.* i. 458.

his accession to the throne, more than fifty-nine years after his birth, that he abandoned his first Christian name Albert. In substantial agreement with Lord Melbourne's suggestion he then assumed the sole name of Edward, which embodies the purest English tradition.

The title of Prince of Wales, by which the new prince was to be publicly known for the greater part of his life, was not, strictly speaking, inherited. In accordance with custom, it was by Letters Patent that Queen Victoria created her son Prince of Wales when barely a month old. With that honour was linked the Earldom of Chester.[1] At the same time the heir to the throne of the United Kingdom assumed at birth and without legal formalities an imposing series of other prescriptive titles. The infant prince at once became Duke of both Cornwall and Rothesay, Earl of Carrick, Baron of Renfrew, Lord of the Isles, and Great Steward of Scotland. Save the Duchy of Cornwall, which was the gift of King Edward III. in 1337 to Edward the Black Prince and was then entailed on all heirs-apparent of English sovereignty, the inherited titles of the infant Prince were legacies from Scotland, conveyed to the Crown of England on the accession of the Scottish King James I. in 1603.[2] (Before he came to the throne King Edward, while travelling *incognito* abroad, habitually employed his Scottish title of Baron of Renfrew, only substituting for it on rare occasions his English title of Earl of Chester.)

An additional title was inherited by the infant from his father. According to the law of German heredity Prince Albert shared, with a large number of princes of Saxon descent, the title of Duke of Saxony, and Prince Albert's son was heraldically entitled to that honour. The Queen was anxious for her heir to enjoy the paternal distinction. By her direction there was at once designed for the new-born prince an armorial shield which quartered the Royal Arms of Saxony with the Royal Arms of England. The

[1] These joint dignities had, since the time of the Black Prince, the eldest son of King Edward III., invariably been conferred by the sovereign on the heir-apparent, in Letters Patent soon after his birth.

[2] A more imposing hereditary Scottish title—Prince of Scotland—which was long enjoyed by heirs to the Scottish Crown before 1603, was borne from birth by King James I.'s son, Charles I., and by his grandson, Charles II., but was ignored after the revolution of 1688, and was dropped in the case of subsequent Princes of Wales. Cf. *The Times*, February 22-23, 1924, for a proposal to revive the dignity.

procedure provoked adverse criticism in social and political
quarters, where there was fear of the influence on the new heir-
apparent of Prince Albert's German sympathies and sentiments.
Lord Palmerston and the Whigs of Holland House talked frankly
of the fresh proof which the Queen was giving of the German
leanings of the Court.[1]

VI

The Queen's vigorous health made recovery from her confinement rapid.   In December she removed with her infant heir
to Windsor Castle, where a great part of his boyhood was to be
spent.   There the christening ceremony took place.

The choice of sponsors exercised the mind of the Queen and
her husband as soon as the boy was born.   She wished to satisfy
evenly the claims of her heir's English and German kinsfolk.
As English sponsors she selected two of the few surviving children
of King George III.—her uncle, the Duke of Cambridge, King
George's seventh son, and her aunt, Princess Sophia, his fifth
daughter, a spinster.   With them she associated two of Prince
Albert's German relatives—his step-mother, the Duchess of
Saxe-Coburg, and the Duchess of Saxe-Gotha, a widowed cousin.
A third German sponsor, Duke Ferdinand of Saxe-Coburg, next
brother of the reigning Duke, stood in the same relation of uncle
to both the Queen and Prince Albert.

But to these five lineally related godparents the Queen and
Prince Albert, with an eye on international policy, added a
reigning monarch of the European continent.   Reluctantly the
Queen repressed a wish to invite her uncle, King Leopold.   Her
dead father's surly and unfriendly brother, King Ernest of
Hanover, threatened to make trouble if the Belgian sovereign
were preferred to himself.   Bickerings within the domestic
circle led her to "set her heart" on Frederick William IV., King
of Prussia, who had ascended his throne the year before.   She
ignored mutterings of discontent at the rival Courts of Paris,
Vienna, and St. Petersburg; and at the persuasion of the Prussian
Minister in London, Baron Christian von Bunsen, a scholar and
theologian as well as a diplomatist, who was one of Prince
Albert's few intimate friends, the Prussian King accepted the
flattering invitation.

[1] *Greville Memoirs, 1837–52*, ii. 63–5.

1842
Ætat. 1
The Prince of Wales was baptised with befitting pomp on the 25th January 1842, some ten weeks after his birth. The scene was St. George's Chapel, Windsor. Archbishop Howley of Canterbury, attended by Archbishop Vernon Harcourt of York, Bishop Blomfield of London, Bishop Edward Stanley of Norwich, Bishop Sumner of Winchester, and Bishop Bagot of Oxford conducted the ceremony, which Sir George Hayter commemorated in a notable painting. Prince Albert, who settled every detail, declined an original anthem which had been specially written by Sir George Elvey, the organist of St. George's, and substituted Handel's "Hallelujah Chorus." The Queen was arrayed in "the cumbrous robes of the Garter." The child, whom an eye-witness credited with "fierce stout features," was carried to the font by the Mistress of the Robes, the Duchess of Buccleuch. By the Queen's special invitation the Duke of Wellington bore the Sword of State in the procession. "You will have heard," wrote the Queen to the King of the Belgians after the ceremony (February 1), "how perfectly and splendidly everything went off on the 25th. Nothing could have done better, and *little* Albert (what a pleasure that he has that *dearest* name!) behaved so well."

VII

Of the six sponsors, only two—the Duke of Cambridge and the King of Prussia—attended in person.[1] The Prussian King was the sole German sponsor present, and this single visit of his to England provoked the liveliest curiosity, not only in St. George's Chapel but in the country at large. His imposing suite of civilians and soldiers included the eminent German naturalist, Baron Alexander von Humboldt.[2] An elaborate gold shield adorned with figures cut in onyx, which the royal godfather brought from Berlin, loomed largest among the christening

---

[1] Princess Sophia was absent through illness, and was represented by the Duke of Cambridge's elder daughter Augusta, afterwards Grand Duchess of Mecklenburg-Strelitz, who also represented the absent Duke Ferdinand of Saxe-Coburg. The Duchess of Kent represented the Duchess of Saxe-Coburg, and the Duchess of Cambridge the Duchess of Saxe-Gotha.

[2] Heinrich Abeken, who accompanied the King as chaplain, was subsequently a prominent member of Bismarck's clerical staff, acquiring the sobriquet of "Bismarck's pen." For his account of the King's experiences at the Prince of Wales's christening, see *Bismarck's Pen: Life of H. Abeken from his Letters and Journals* (English translation), 1911.

gifts. Another present to his godson was the insignia of the great Prussian Order of the Black Eagle, the first of the numerous foreign Orders of which the Prince was to be the recipient.

There was a touch of irony in the prominence of the Prussian King at the christening of an English prince, who was to figure in many scenes of coming history as Prussia's critic or adversary. At the moment, that kingdom's star was scarcely rising in the European firmament, and the Prince's godfather promised Prussia no accession of prestige for all his affability of manner and superficial interests in theology and letters as well as in politics, soldiership, and statecraft. His godson was to discover later that a stronger head and a stronger hand than his godfather's could alone make Prussia powerful and formidable.

Prince Albert welcomed the King to his son's christening in the sanguine conviction that Prussia was England's fittest ally in Europe. The paternal faith was not shared by Sir Robert Peel's Ministry, which was exploring the possibility of a French *entente*. Yet the Prussian King's sponsorship, although it fulfilled few of Prince Albert's expectations, was not without influence on the Prince of Wales's career. It proved a first link in the domestic chain which soon bound the English and Prussian Royal families together. The eldest sister of the Prince of Wales was before long to marry the nephew and heir of his Prussian godfather, and that marriage was to bring the Prince into near and early touch with Prussian life, from many phases of which he was before long instinctively to recoil.

When the Queen opened Parliament on the 3rd February 1842, the King of Prussia, who was reluctant to abridge his stay, was among her companions. In the Speech which she delivered from the Throne in the King's presence, the Queen described the birth of her son as "an event which has completed the measure of my domestic happiness." Great as was the station and the destiny to which her son was born, maternal feeling predominated in her heart when she first spoke of him in public. To her friend, the Duchess of Gordon, she had lately written: "Domestic happiness like mine sweetens all the cares and fatigue of a high station, and is the only true one."

CHAPTER II

CHILDHOOD

I

THE little Prince and his elder sister were not long the sole occupants of the royal nursery. Before the Prince was five years old two more sisters and a brother became his companions there. A second daughter, Alice, was born to the Queen on the 25th April 1843; a second son, Alfred, on the 6th August 1844; and a third daughter, Helena, on the 25th May 1846. The Queen's family of nine children—four sons and five daughters—was completed by the birth of Louise, a fourth daughter, on the 18th March 1848; of Arthur, a third son, on the 1st May 1850; of Leopold, a fourth and youngest son, on the 7th April 1853; and of Beatrice, the fifth daughter and youngest child, on the 14th April 1857.

For all his brothers and sisters the Prince cherished an affection, which they warmly reciprocated. His eldest sister, Victoria, who showed in childhood an intellectual precocity superior to his own, won from nursery days till her death his confidence and admiration. The nearness of age linked him closely, too, through childhood and boyhood with his brother Alfred and with his two younger sisters, Alice and Helena. His sister Alice proved a much-favoured comrade in later days. On his younger brothers and sisters he lavished in the nursery and schoolroom the protecting solicitude of superior years. Of the seven christening ceremonies in the royal household which succeeded his own the Prince was an interested witness. At the baptism of his sister Helena at Buckingham Palace on the 23rd July 1846, Lord Broughton noticed how the Prince of Wales "held his father's hand by the middle finger and walked about very gently with him." "Pretty but delicate looking" was the comment of the historian Macaulay, another guest on the occasion. "If that boy knew his destiny!" he added somewhat tritely.[1]

II

Queen Victoria, an only child of parents well stepped in years, lacked English kinsfolk of her own age. Her English domestic circle mainly belonged to her parents' generation, and she taught her children to imitate all the filial attention which she scrupulously paid her mother, her aunts and uncles. Elderly sedate relatives of a passing epoch loomed large in the memories of the Prince's infancy.

Very solicitous for his welfare was his grandmother, the rather pragmatical Duchess of Kent, in whose behoof he made his earliest experiments in handwriting. Devoted grand-aunts were the motherly Queen-Dowager Adelaide, King William IV.'s widow, and the pious Duchess of Gloucester, George III.'s fourth daughter, also a widow. Children's parties of an exemplary decorum were often given by these veteran ladies for the Prince and his little brothers and sisters.

More vivacious was the hospitality offered them by a grand-uncle and grand-aunt—the Duke of Cambridge, King George III.'s youngest son, and his genial wife (by birth a German of the Hesse-Cassel family [2])—at their house at Kew. The Prince specially delighted from childhood in the society of the son and two daughters of the Cambridge family, his mother's first cousins. The bluff, good-humoured son, George, was a young man of twenty-two at the Prince's birth, by two months Queen Victoria's senior. In feature and temper he preserved until his death in 1904 (at the advanced age of eighty-five) many distinctive characteristics of King George III.'s sons.[3] To the Prince he was known alike in boyhood and manhood as "Uncle George,"

---

[1] Lord Broughton's *Recollections*, vi. 181.

[2] The Duchess remained till death in 1889, at the advanced age of ninety-two, the centre of the royal family's affection; she survived her husband nearly forty years.

[3] At the age of twenty-one Prince George of Cambridge, while still living with his parents, made a morganatic marriage with a well-known actress four years his senior. The act in no way prejudiced his career. He proved an exemplary husband and father, and the Prince of Wales was in adult years on excellent terms with his sons.

1846

Ætat. 4

and their mutual relations remained for life those of an affectionate uncle and nephew. The Prince owed to his "uncle,"
whose profession was the army, his youthful enthusiasm for
that service, and after "Uncle George" succeeded his father
in the Dukedom (in 1850) and became Commander-in-Chief of
the Army (in 1856), there was much confidential intercourse
between him and his "nephew" on controverted questions of
military organisation in regard to which the Duke was stubbornly
loyal to antiquated standards. The sisters of "Uncle George,"
Augusta (born in 1822), afterwards wife of the Duke of Mecklenburg-Strelitz, and Mary (born in 1833), afterwards wife of the
Duke of Teck and mother of Queen Mary, shared their brother's
buoyant temperament. The genial heartiness of the Cambridge
household pleasurably contrasted in the Prince's boyish eyes
with the serious demeanour of the rest of Queen Victoria's English
kinsfolk.

1847

Ætat. 5

There was a substantial foreign leaven in the society of which
the Prince had earliest cognisance. Queen Victoria's and Prince
Albert's numerous German relatives of various generations were,
through the Prince's childhood, his parents' frequent guests, and
among these he laid while very young the seeds of many later
intimacies. Prince Albert was often visited by his only brother
—the Prince's sole rightful uncle—Prince Ernest (afterwards
Duke) of Saxe-Coburg-Gotha, who was a friendly companion
of the royal children, less sedate and more playful than their
father. Queen Victoria's oracular uncle, King Leopold I., often
brought with him from Brussels to Windsor his sons and daughters,
none much older than the Prince. (Their mother, King Leopold's
second wife, was daughter of King Louis Philippe.) With the
heir to the Belgian throne, the Duke of Brabant, afterwards the
astute King Leopold II. (the Prince's senior by no more than
six years), the Prince was from youth upwards on very familiar
terms, although time was to develop in King Leopold II. equivocal
traits which were ultimately to alienate the Prince's youthful
regard. He also knew well in boyhood the Duke of Brabant's
next brother, the Comte de Flandre (father of the future King
Albert of Belgium), and his sister, Princess Charlotte, whose
tragic fate as wife and widow was in a coming epoch profoundly
to stir the Prince's emotion. At the same time a trio of young
Germans, of no close kinship and by some years his seniors, who

became naturalised British subjects at his mother's invitation,
moved in the Prince strong boyish attachments which never lost
their force. His grandmother, the Duchess of Kent, by her
first marriage with the Hereditary Prince of Leiningen, was
mother of a son and daughter, step-brother and step-sister
respectively of Queen Victoria. The eldest son of the step-
brother—Prince Ernest of Leiningen (*b.* 1830)—and the youngest
son of the step-sister—Prince Victor of Hohenlohe-Langenburg,
for a time known as Count Gleichen (*b.* 1833)—both joined the
British Navy as midshipmen, and became comrades of the Prince
as soon as he left the nursery. Prince Victor accompanied him
on many of his early foreign tours. A third German prince of
somewhat maturer years, with whom the Prince began early a
lifelong friendship, was the sociable Prince Edward of Saxe-
Weimar (*b.* 1823), nephew of the Dowager-Queen Adelaide, who
joined the British Army as a subaltern in the year of the Prince's
birth, and subsequently rose to high military rank. There was
no obtrusive foreign sentiment about these family connections—
all in British service—with whom the Prince fraternised at the
opening of his youthful career.

Amid the foreign influences environing his childhood there
was only one to whom the Prince never quite reconciled himself.
The solemn figure of Baron Stockmar, his father's former tutor
and present mentor, hovered over the Prince's childhood and
boyhood, to the frequent disturbance of his equanimity. In all
matters touching the Prince's upbringing he was the royal
parents' first and last court of appeal. Rigid in his standards of
discipline, stern in rebuke of childish faults, overflowing in
cautious counsel, the Baron watched the young Prince's physical
and intellectual development with a disconcerting seriousness.

III

The appointment of a governess to the royal nursery exercised
the parents' and Baron Stockmar's thought soon after the
Prince's birth, and in June 1842 the choice fell on a Lady of the
Bedchamber to the Queen, Sarah, Lady Lyttelton.[1] Her father

[1] Lady Lyttelton died 13th April 1870. Her experiences as governess of
the Prince and the Queen's other children are recorded in *Letters from Sarah,
Lady Lyttelton, 1797–1870*, privately printed for the family in 1873, and edited
by Mrs. Horace Wyndham for publication in 1912.

was the second Earl Spencer, and her brother the third earl, had, as Lord Althorpe, led the Liberal party in the House of Commons. She was now the widow, with grown-up children, of the third Lord Lyttelton. Until the Prince turned seven, Lady Lyttelton was in chief charge of him. Her maternal tenderness mingled with shrewd common sense. The Prince, who was from infancy very sensitive to kindness, was devoted to her. She watched with generous but discerning sympathy his early growth. When he was six months she discovered intelligence lurking in "his large, clear, blue eyes." [1] Later, his governess judged the growing boy to be "very small every way," [2] and she deplored "a few passions and stampings"—fits of impatience or ill-temper which increased rather than diminished with the years. But more memorable were Lady Lyttelton's repeated intimations of the infant Prince's "politeness of manner." She recorded that, at three years old, "he bows and offers his hand beautifully, besides saluting *à la militaire*—all unbidden." At seven she noticed "a childish dignity very pretty to witness, characterising all his movements in public."

Among the royal governess's personal visitors early in her term of office were a young couple whom the Prince always reckoned in his mature years among his best friends. The future statesman, William Ewart Gladstone, had recently wedded Catherine Glynne, whose sister became on the same day and at the same place wife of the fourth Lord Lyttelton, Lady Lyttelton's eldest son. The Gladstones, who frequently visited Lady Lyttelton at Buckingham Palace, saw much of the royal children, and Mrs. Gladstone confided to her diary numerous impressions of the infant Prince. When she and her husband saw him for the first time, at barely a month old, Mrs. Gladstone made record of the query, which Macaulay echoed later: "Who could look at him and think of his destiny without mixed emotion?" In subsequent entries she noticed the Prince's diminutiveness, his unbecoming "long trousers tied below the ankles and very full," "his manners very dear and not shy." [3] The Gladstones, by the Queen's desire, soon brought their own young children with them. Their eldest son, William Henry, who was of the Prince's

[1] *Lyttelton Letters* (May 7, 1842), p. 329.   [2] *Ibid.* p. 340.
[3] Miss Lee's *Wives of the Prime Ministers, 1844–1906*, pp. 176–8; and Mrs. Gladstone's *Journal* in Mrs. Drew's *Catherine Gladstone*, 1921.

own age, was thus the first boy outside his own family whom the Prince came to know, and with characteristic fidelity to early friends he cherished for him a lifelong attachment.

The Prince's faculty as a linguist developed early under the guidance of three special governesses—English, French, and German—whom Baron Stockmar soon engaged for Lady Lyttelton's nursery establishment.[1]   The Prince's speech from babyhood was bi-lingual.   German as well as English was habitual in the royal nursery.   According to Lady Lyttelton, he was "backward in language" as compared with his eldest sister. At first he took more kindly to German than to English, and he never quite lost traces of a German accent.   "His defect is the burr . . . in pronouncing R," wrote one who knew him in later life.[2]   The Prussian Minister, Bunsen, who was freely admitted to the Queen's domestic circle while the children were very young, remarked that "they all spoke German like their native tongue, even to one another." [3]   Bunsen presented the Prince on his fifth birthday with German books, and the boy was able to read them.[4]   He retained through life a full mastery of the intricacies of the language.   To his Belgian relatives he spoke German preferably to French.   The French tongue he acquired more slowly, but he ultimately spoke it with a perfect accent and a wide vocabulary which few Englishmen have equalled.   From early manhood he took pride in his command of colloquial French. For many years after he came of age, there lived under his roof a French tutor, M. Brasseur, with whom his relations were always most cordial.

The boy's parents, while he was still in the nursery, attached great importance to his handwriting.   The conscientious Baron Stockmar wrote to him, while he was yet a child, that one in his position "should write a firm, large, and legible hand." From early days to middle age the Prince's penmanship, in spite of his parents' not infrequent complaints of carelessness, fully deserved the Baron's epithets even if little elegance or individuality could be assigned it.   In later life his handwriting lost its early legibility, and the characters were cramped, illformed, and difficult to decipher.

[1] Miss Hildyard was appointed English governess; Mme. Rollande de la Sange, French governess; and Fraulein Grüner, German governess.
[2] *Lady Rose Weigall: a Memoir* (1923), p. 115.
[3] Baron Bunsen, *Memoirs*, 1868, ii. 229-30.   [4] *Ibid*. ii. 121.

IV

1846
Ætat. 4

The Prince's parents sedulously fostered domestic affection in the nursery by means of observances to which the Prince and the other children were faithful through life. Anniversaries of their parents' wedding-day and of their parents' and their own birthdays were celebrated with much elaboration. Gifts, congratulatory letters, and festivities were profuse. Christmas, again, was for the children and their elders a season of well-organised festivity on the German pattern. Each member of the family had his or her Christmas tree decorated with candles and gifts.

The Queen was never quite happy away from her children. Despite the incessant calls of official life, she kept on them an ever-watchful eye. They were wont from infancy to accompany their parents to public ceremonies. At the age of two the Prince indeed joined the Queen and his father at a great military review in Windsor Park and valiantly suppressed an outbreak of tears when the firing began. The Queen personally trained the Prince and his brothers and sisters in strict habits of obedience and in simple religious worship. She firmly set her face against spoiling them by over-indulgence. Yet much of the leisure which the Queen commanded she devoted to supervising her children's games and to providing for them an amplitude of cheerful amusement. For their delight in their tenderest years she summoned to Buckingham Palace General Tom Thumb, the American dwarf, from the show of Barnum, the American king of showmen, and she engaged Wombwell's menagerie to perform in the Quadrangle of Windsor Castle.

1847
Ætat. 5

The Queen encouraged the Prince and the other occupants of her nursery in all the recreative accomplishments from which she had herself derived youthful pleasure. The Prince readily emulated his mother's zeal as a dancer, and soon developed a grace and an energy which defied fatigue. From an early age the Prince was taught painting and drawing, which formed a large part of his mother's early recreations. The artist, Henry Edward Corbould, gave him instruction while a boy, and as a draftsman he showed boyish promise. But it was under somewhat pedestrian influences that the Prince's artistic tastes were formed. Neither Queen Victoria nor Prince Albert showed much refinement of æsthetic feeling. In art, Prince Albert set chief value on the rather stolid realism of contemporary German painting, while the Queen's favourite English painter during the Prince's boyhood was Sir Edwin Landseer, whose technical skill was mainly confined to depicting dogs and horses.

Queen Victoria was always an ardent lover of the play, and the Prince readily assimilated his mother's enthusiasm in this regard. Recitations were encouraged in the nursery, and soon gave way to acting. George Bartley, a well-known actor, was engaged to give the Prince lessons in elocution. The royal children often performed, in the presence of their parents, short pieces in English, French, and German.[1]

From his fourth year the Prince was to his immense delight permitted by his parents to pay occasional visits to Astley's famous circus. That was his avenue of approach to the regular play-houses. From his seventh year he enjoyed ample opportunity of witnessing the best theatrical performances of the day. He was a spectator of the long series of renderings by well-known actors and actresses which were given at Windsor at the Christmas season from 1848 till his father's death, some thirteen years later. The repertory at Court ranged from Shakespeare—as many as fourteen of whose plays were included—to popular farces of passing fame. But the Prince's boyish experience of the drama was not confined to Windsor. Charles Kean, who was the first director of the Windsor performances, was through the same period producing Shakespearian and other drama with much spectacular embellishment at the Princess's Theatre in London. That playhouse, the first which the Prince visited, became a frequent resort. Interest in other serious theatrical effort was encouraged. A famous manager and actor, Samuel Phelps, whose histrionic powers were higher than those of Kean, was at the same time popularising Shakespeare and the classic drama with truer success at the theatre in Sadler's Wells, an

---

[1] The Prince's repertory came to include scenes from Racine's *Athalie*, in which he took the part of Abner, and his sister, the Princess Royal, that of Athalie, as well as a dramatised version of extracts from Thomson's *Seasons*, in which "the Prince of Wales represented Winter, with a white beard and a cloak with icicles (or what seemed such)." On the thirteenth anniversary of their parents' wedding-day (February 10, 1853) the royal children acted before Queen Victoria and Prince Albert a part of Schiller's *Wallenstein*, in which the Prince played the part of Max Piccolomini (cf. Baron Bunsen's *Memoirs*, vol. ii. p. 328).

unfashionable quarter of London.   A rendering of Shakespeare's
Henry V. by Phelps and his company specially celebrated at
Windsor the boy's twelfth birthday.   In his mature days the
Prince continued to Sir Henry Irving, the chief Shakespearian
actor and producer of the last quarter of the nineteenth century,
the same favour which his parents had shown Charles Kean and
Phelps in his youth.   But perhaps a surfeit of Shakespeare in
his early theatrical experiences accounts for a marked diminution
of his enthusiasm for the national dramatist as his career came
to a close.   A pantomime or a farce proved from the first rather
more attractive.   Yet a lifelong devotion to the theatre, even
if it soon focussed itself on the lighter phases, sprang from the
familiarity with the drama which his mother freely encouraged
in his boyhood.

His parents likewise imbued him and their other children
in early years with their own liking for music.   The Queen sang
well, and Prince Albert was a composer with serious aims.   The
Prince of Wales was taught as a child to play on the piano without
much result, but he became an enthusiast for Italian and French
opera in all its range from the date of his first visit, on 8th April
1851, to Covent Garden to hear Auber's *Massaniello* under Sir
Michael Costa's direction.   He watched with especial enthusiasm
the rise to fame of the French composer Gounod.   At the same
time he enjoyed an early introduction to the lighter musical work
of Offenbach and other French composers of comic opera.   His
taste in music remained more catholic than in drama.   He found
pleasure in concerts where classical pieces were rendered, and in
oratorios.   Serious German music appealed to him, and he was
subsequently among the first Englishmen to recognise the merits
of Wagnerian opera.   But musical comedy always remained
high in his favour.

V

Buckingham Palace and Windsor Castle were the chief homes
of the Prince's infancy and youth, but his parents invariably took
their children with them on frequent migrations to other parts
of the country, and while yet a child the Prince wandered over
large areas of his future kingdom.

The Prince's travels began within a few weeks of his birth,
when he went with his parents and sister to the Pavilion at

Brighton, the royal residence which King George IV.'s fantastic
taste had called into being.   A month was spent there, but public
demonstrations of goodwill proved so obtrusive that the Pavilion
was abandoned as a royal residence at the end of the stay.   Two
years later (1845) a more sequestered seaside retreat was acquired
by the Queen in Osborne House, near Cowes, in the Isle of Wight,
which became the young Prince's chief holiday resort in England.
In the grounds of Osborne House Prince Albert soon set up a
Swiss cottage as a workshop and playhouse for the Prince and
his brothers, and the Prince tried his youthful hand at carpenter-
ing and gardening.   Another country residence nearer London to
which the infant Prince was often taken for a week or two at a
time was Claremont House, near Esher, which had been granted
for life to King Leopold on the death of his first wife, Princess
Charlotte.[1]   There the Queen had spent, she wrote, the happiest
days of her own childhood.[2]

A great concourse of guests—foreign potentates and their
families, English leaders in State and Church, foreign diplomatists,
and English men and women of rank or distinction, besides
members of her own and her husband's families—thronged
Windsor Castle or Buckingham Palace during the Queen's
married life, and the Prince as a boy was brought by his parents
to the notice of the varied company.   Well-nigh from his cradle,
as Lady Lyttelton noticed, he showed signs of a social instinct.
He was not shy in the presence of strangers.   Almost as soon as
he could speak he plied his parents' guests with questions—
a habit which grew with his years.

In June 1844 the Tsar, Nicholas I. of Russia, arrived at
Windsor with the "dear, good King of Saxony," Frederick
Augustus II.   Both sovereigns delighted in the Prince, and the
Tsar bestowed on him the Grand Cross of St. Andrew, of which,
in his mother's words, "the boy was quite proud."[3]   Later in

---

[1] Claremont House, on King Leopold's death, reverted to the Crown.
The Queen purchased it privately in 1866, and presented it to her youngest
son, Leopold, Duke of Albany, on his marriage, 27th April 1882.   His widow
resided there after Prince Leopold's death.   The property was sold in 1918.

[2] At times the Queen took her elder children with her when she and her
husband were the guests of distinguished subjects.   Hardly had the Prince
completed his first year before the Duke of Wellington entertained him and his
mother at Walmer Castle, the Duke's official residence as Warden of the Cinque
Ports.

[3] Foreign sovereigns, emulating the example of the Prussian King and the

1845
Ætat. 3

the year, Louis Philippe, King of the French, arrived at Windsor, and on the French King's return to St. Cloud he forwarded to the Prince a little gun—"un très modeste fusil de munition adopté à sa taille"—to replace a similar toy which the child had confided to the affable King that he had lost.

At the baptism of his brother Alfred in September 1844 the Prince, who was not yet three, excited general attention by audibly asking Archbishop Howley, "What is that you have got upon your head?" Great laughter greeted the Archbishop's reply, "It is called a wig."[1] While still under eight he took a long walk at Balmoral with a scientific guest of his father, the geologist, Sir Charles Lyell, and "gave an animated account" of a recent conjuring entertainment which had been given for the royal children's benefit by John Henry Anderson, "the Wizard of the North." "Papa (the boy added) knows how all these things are done."[2] The little Prince eagerly asked the great naturalist the names of plants and begged for permission to look at spiders under his magnifying glass.

1849
Ætat. 7

VI

1848
Ætat. 6

Excursions by sea from Cowes with his parents were among the most pleasurable and instructive experiences of the Prince's childhood. They well satisfied his innate love of movement and gave him a lasting zest for yachting and for yacht-racing. From the deck of the royal yacht *Victoria and Albert* he witnessed as a lad of nine the finish of the first race for the American Cup which was run off the Isle of Wight on 23rd August 1851.[3] Each summer or autumn long cruises from Cowes were made in the royal yacht, and thus the child extended his geographical knowledge and formed his first acquaintance with Wales, Scotland, and Ireland.[4] Great popular enthusiasm greeted the boy, dressed

Russian Tsar, offered the infant Prince foreign orders in profusion. But his parents discouraged their premature acceptance "on account of his being too young and not even having any of the English orders." Arrears were rapidly made up when the infant reached manhood.

[1] *Letters of Sarah, Lady Lyttelton,* pp. 348–9.

[2] Lyell's *Life, Letters and Journals,* 1881, vol. ii. p. 157.

[3] Commodore Steven's schooner *America* won the race from the English competitors by the narrow margin of 8½ minutes (see A. E. T. Watson's *King Edward as a Sportsman,* 1911, p. 295).

[4] A. M. Broadley's *Boyhood of a Great King, 1841–58* (1906) collects from contemporary periodicals very full details of the Prince's youthful cruises.

F. Winterhalter pinxit   Emery Walker ph. sc.

At six years old
1847

in sailor's costume, wherever the royal yacht touched land—occasions which his father improved by moralisings on the duties which a Prince owed the people.[1]

In the autumn of 1847 an unusually extended cruise from Cowes abounded for the boy in impressive incidents. It brought him by way of the Welsh coast, the Firth of Clyde, and the Caledonian Canal for the first time to the Highlands, where he stayed with his parents for four weeks at Ardverichan Lodge, a hired shooting lodge on Loch Laggan. "Our two eldest children who are here," wrote the Queen to her friend the Duchess of Gordon from Ardverichan on 4th September 1847, "enjoy the Highlands as much as their parents do." Now, for the first time, the boy donned Highland dress. Thenceforth the kilt, which he constantly wore in England as well as in Scotland, won even more popular acceptance than his sailor's dress.

The cruise to Scotland was repeated next autumn by a different route—by the east coast to Aberdeen. Balmoral House, on Deeside, another shooting lodge, was now first hired by the Queen for a short term. "A fair little lad of rather a slender make with an intelligent expression," was the description given of him on his first visit to the annual Highland gathering at Braemar (September 15, 1848), when the future Archbishop of Canterbury, Edward White Benson, happened to catch sight of him.

The contact with Scotland into which the Prince was brought in childhood was unbroken through the rest of his career. Every year he revisited Deeside, where the scenery fascinates by its combination of river, burn, moor, mountain, and pine forest. Balmoral House, which was purchased by the Queen in 1852, was soon converted into a gleaming granite castle, and each autumn the Queen's family gathered round her there, either staying under her roof or in neighbouring houses.[2]

A personal introduction to Ireland also fell within the Prince's childish lot. In August 1849 he and his parents all paid a first

---

[1] A portrait of the Prince in sailor's costume, painted in 1847 by his parents' favourite artist, Winterhalter, is reproduced from the original at Buckingham Palace on the opposite page. An engraving enjoyed at the time a vast vogue. John Leech's cartoon in *Punch* of the Prince as a sailor boy, which was entitled "Every inch a sailor" (September 1846) stimulated public interest.

[2] The boy's grandmother, the Duchess of Kent, hired as her holiday quarters the neighbouring Abergeldie Castle, where he was a familiar visitor. After her mother's death the Queen herself leased Abergeldie Castle, and through many later years lent it to the Prince of Wales for his own autumn occupation.

1848
Ætat. 6

visit to that part of the Queen's dominions. Twenty-eight years had passed since any royal personage had traversed St. George's Channel, and the Irish people showed an auspicious exhilaration of spirit. Southern, Eastern, and Northern Ireland—Cork, Dublin, and Belfast—came within the yachting itinerary. In his sailor's dress the youth fascinated Irishmen and Irishwomen of the South and the North alike by his boyish charm of manner. The perennial disaffection with English rule seemed on the surface to

1849
Ætat. 7

yield to royal smiles. The Queen, at the suggestion of the Liberal Prime Minister, Lord John Russell, acknowledged the show of Irish loyalty in a way which identified her son with the hope of Irish contentment. She conferred upon the Prince a new title—that of Earl of Dublin. The honour had been enjoyed by his grandfather, the Duke of Kent, but had become extinct at the Duke's death. Letters Patent, which formally re-created the extinct earldom on 10th September 1849, associated the chief city of Ireland with the heir-apparent and his successors. It was a friendly gesture which seemed an equitable complement to the Prince's many Scottish titles, and if it failed to touch Irish grievances, it created between the Prince and Ireland a personal tie which was proof against much of the future political strain between the two countries. The Prince paid a second visit to Dublin with his parents four years later in order to inspect an exhibition of Irish industries, and there followed during his boyhood a private tour in the south of Ireland when he was unaccompanied by his parents. In adult life he crossed the Irish Channel several times in a sincere desire to assuage Irish disaffection. His personal popularity was acknowledged to the last by all classes of Irish society, and was not wholly lost upon the irreconcilable political leaders who vowed in his later years to sever the last link which bound Ireland to England.

VII

1848
Ætat. 6

Home and foreign politics, which were constantly in their parents' minds and on their lips, formed part of the air which the royal children breathed. In the spring of 1848, when the Prince was no more than six, echoes of the revolutionary storm which menaced the rulers of all western Europe, and especially the Queen's and Prince Albert's princely German kinsfolk, reached the royal nursery, and the boy learnt dimly of the anxieties which hover about thrones. There were fears—happily baseless—of a popular rising against monarchy in England. The Queen was on the point of confinement with her fourth daughter, Louise, and at the bidding of Lord John Russell, the Prime Minister, the royal children hurriedly removed at the end of March from Buckingham Palace to what was deemed the secure haven of Osborne. The royal governess, Lady Lyttelton, who was in charge of the Prince and his brothers and sisters, prognosticated gloomily. She wondered if the Prince of Wales would be still a prince ten years hence, or if "any Prince" would be "left in those days." In the event the peace of England was scarcely disturbed, and at the end of April the royal children returned safely to London. The main sign there of the European ferment was the crowd of Royalist refugees who were seeking asylum from rebellious republicanism abroad. The Queen was genuinely alarmed by the dangers which beset her German relatives. For the moment she cherished Lady Lyttelton's doubts of her own and her children's destiny. "When one thinks of one's children, their education, their future—and prays for them," she wrote to the King of the Belgians on the 11th July, "I always think and say to myself : 'Let them grow up fit for *whatever station* they may be placed in—*high or low*'— this I never thought of before, but I *do* always now." [1] But monarchy in England was too firmly rooted in popular sentiment to warrant the Queen's misgivings, and her children's future was not in peril. In Europe, too, save in France, the revolutionary triumph was short-lived.

Only the expulsion of the French King, Louis Philippe, proved irrevocable. The chief effect of the revolutionary movement of 1848 on the English royal circle came indeed from the permanent settlement in England of the exiled King of the French and his large family of Orléanist Princes and Princesses. Their misfortune touched the heart of the Queen. Her uncle, King Leopold, offered them Claremont, of which he was owner for life, for their residence, and her own hospitable attentions were unceasing. The Prince, loyal to his mother's example, added in his youth to the roll of his foreign acquaintance the whole of that notable company of French Royalists who from 1848 onwards made England their home.

[1] *Letters of Queen Victoria*, ii. 218.

CHAPTER III

PRINCE ALBERT'S EDUCATIONAL CODE

I

FOR the first seven years of his life the Prince remained in the nursery, and most of his experiences were shared by his brothers and sisters. But from his birth his father thought to dedicate him apart to his inherited mission. It was on the special training of his eldest son, who, in the normal course of things, was destined for his mother's throne, that Prince Albert's thought centred from the first.

The Queen's youth and health gave every promise of a long life. There was a reasonable assurance that the Prince of Wales's accession would be postponed to a distant day. But Prince Albert deemed it his urgent duty to perfect the infant heir in all the qualities which his future responsibilities theoretically required. The conscientious scrupulosity with which the father investigated the theory and practice of princely education tended to confuse his aim.

While the boy was still in his cradle Prince Albert took counsel with his trusted mentor, Baron Stockmar, who at once set to work on voluminous memoranda. The Baron had studied in his own fashion recent English history, and discovered disaster in King George III.'s neglect of sound principle when he educated his eldest son. It was the Baron who first paraded before Queen Victoria's and Prince Albert's eyes the bogey of the Prince Regent who became King George IV., and the ugly reminiscence made an abiding impression on Queen Victoria's mind. The Queen and her husband were alarmed by the memories alike of the Prince Regent's profligacy and of his comradeship with the politicians who were in opposition to his father's Government. Prince Albert and Baron Stockmar bent their energies towards devising a system of education which, while it might be calculated, at any rate on paper, to promise a rich crop of virtues and accomplishments, should make his son "understand his real position and its duties," and so counter any likelihood of political partisanship which might embarrass his parents or the country. Prince Albert's attitude of mind is illustrated by an early apophthegm of his which runs : "Upon the good education of Princes, and especially of those who are destined to govern, the welfare of the world in these days greatly depends" (April 10, 1849). A little later Prince Albert gave a slightly different turn to his creed in the remark that "the Prince's life" was "a *public matter* not unconnected with the present and prospective welfare of the State."[1]

1849
——
Ætat. 7

Public opinion was justly alive to the importance of training with care the future ruler of the country. History supplied instances even more convincing than George IV.'s career of the moral ruin overtaking royal heirs who were left in youth at the mercy of flatterers seeking favour by pandering to vice and self-indulgence. As early as 1843 there was dedicated to Queen Victoria an anonymous pamphlet of warning entitled "Who should educate the Prince of Wales?" which enjoyed a vast vogue.[2] The pamphleteer repeated well-worn platitudes from Fénelon's *Télemaque*, and quaintly urged that the Prince's tutor should be neither a statesman nor a churchman, "but a man of letters who has passed through the alembic of adversity." It was essential that a sovereign's religious views should be broad. It was prejudicial to a young Prince's character for the press to give publicity "to his sayings, doings, and whereabouts." Mr. Punch ridiculed with spirit much of this sententious counsel, but Prince Albert and the Baron studied the pamphlet with respectful attention. Lord Melbourne, whose advice to the Queen teemed with a common sense beyond the range of her husband or of Baron Stockmar, wrote to the Queen at the time : "Be not over-solicitous about education. It may be able to do much, but it does not do so much as is expected from it. It may mould and direct the character, but it rarely alters it."[3]

In the result Prince Albert, with Baron Stockmar's aid and

[1] Lord Esher, "The Character of King Edward," *Quarterly Review*, July 1910 (republished in *The Influence of King Edward*, 1915, p. 28).

[2] The author, who did not give his name, seems to have been the publisher, Mr. Effingham Wilson, who wrote much on public questions.

[3] *Letters of Queen Victoria*, i. 458.

Queen Victoria's wifely approval, formulated an educational discipline to which the Prince was rigidly subjected until he reached manhood.   Nothing was to be left to chance.   Unceasing surveillance by carefully chosen tutors who should answer Stockmar's definition of "persons morally good, intelligent, well-informed and experienced who fully enjoyed the parental confidence" was to check undesirable tendencies of adolescence.   He was to be kept aloof from companions of his own age.   Habits of mental concentration were to be fostered under fitting direction by unremitting study of literature, science, history, archæology, and art.   Sport and amusement of a sober kind were permitted, but were to be strictly rationed and supervised.   Freedom in any relation of life was to be sternly denied the youth.

The system, however well-intentioned, was obviously vitiated by its scorn of the idiosyncrasies of a normal boy whatever his station in life.   The repression of independence or originality, the incessant study of books, the tireless guidance of father or tutor—these were the main clauses of the Prince of Wales's educational charter as formulated by his father.   To the native temperament of the Prince the greater part of the system was peculiarly unsuited.   Although his affections were easily won, he was as impatient as other boys of restraint and dictation.   Lacking any marked intellectual strength or imaginative faculty, he had a distaste for reading.   At the same time his mind was alert and mobile and his memory was vivacious and retentive.   Life and action appealed to him, and he had a quick eye for practical affairs.   Prince Albert's scheme was consequently ill-calculated to develop rapidly his son's real gifts.

There were fortunately compensations for the defects of Prince Albert's system in the tours about the country which the Prince continued to make with his parents; in his participation with them in public functions; in his uninterrupted intercourse at Court with well-known persons of varied interests, and in the Queen's encouragement of his taste for the theatre and music. In course of time Prince Albert accepted the advice of wise counsellors and sanctioned subsidiary changes in his original scheme.   He acknowledged the advantage of foreign travel under appropriate tutelage.   The relaxations and alleviations were beneficial, but the essential features of restraint and reading were never abandoned.   King Edward looked back with pain on his educational ordeal. Happily his practical aptitudes were not crushed by the weight of the grim discipline, and matured despite discouragements. Nor did he harbour any rooted resentment against his father for the chains in which he sought to bind him. Filial respect and indeed affection were not extinguished, although they mingled with fear and with an awe-inspiring faith in paternal omniscience and omnipotence.

1849
Ætat. 7

II

The first step in the Prince's early training for kingship was his withdrawal when little more than seven years of age from the royal nursery which Lady Lyttelton controlled, and his transference to the exclusive care of a tutor who should take his cue in every detail from the boy's father. Prince Albert spent immense energy in selecting the first occupant of this new post. The name of Dr. Liddell, then Headmaster of Westminster, was first considered, but the choice fell on Henry Birch, who impressed Prince Albert at an early interview as "a young, good-looking, amiable man to whom the child was likely to be attached." Birch, who was just thirty years of age, had distinguished himself as a classical scholar at Cambridge, and, now in holy orders, was an assistant master at Eton, his old school. He assumed office in the spring of 1849 and readily won his pupil's affection. Under Birch's guidance the Prince began to keep a diary and to write regularly to his kinsfolk. To these practices his father and mother attached great moment, and they eagerly scrutinised the boy's style. His English style, if simple and direct, never lost its original baldness. The grammar was never very exact. Its most distinctive feature was the habit of weaving appositely into the text, between inverted commas, familiar colloquial phrases or proverbs.

1851
Ætat. 9

Prince Albert, who watched the tutor as closely as the pupil, soon found fault with Birch's religious teaching. He judged the tutor to attach undue importance to the Church catechism.[1] Within two years of his appointment Birch resigned his post, greatly to the boy prince's sorrow. Lady Canning, one of Queen Victoria's ladies-in-waiting, wrote of the parting with Birch: "It has been a trouble and sorrow to the Prince of Wales, who has done no end of touching things since he heard that he was to

---

[1] Disraeli's *Correspondence with his Sister, 1832–52* (1886).

lose him, three weeks ago. He is such an affectionate dear little
fellow; his notes and presents which Mr. Birch used to find on his
pillow were really too moving." Birch was rewarded for his
services with the Crown living of Prestwich in Lancashire.

Birch's successor, Frederick Waymouth Gibbs, was a man of
stronger character and exerted a better defined influence. He was
recommended to Prince Albert by Sir James Stephen, Professor
of Modern History at Cambridge, who had come to know Prince
Albert in the capacity of Chancellor of Cambridge University.
Of humble parentage, Gibbs had been brought up with Sir James
Stephen's sons, James FitzJames Stephen, the future judge, and
Leslie Stephen, the future author. His intellectual promise had
been rewarded by a Fellowship at Trinity College, Cambridge.
Joining the Bar, he was making small progress there when the
tutorship to the Prince was offered him. Precise in manner, he
was a firm believer in decorum, but lacked all trace of sycophancy.
His ability and character proved an advantage to his charge,
whose complete confidence he gained in spite of his prim bearing.
Gibbs was the Prince's inseparable companion for seven impressionable years—from his tenth to his seventeenth birthday.

The new tutor soon advised some revision of the literary
curriculum which Prince Albert prescribed. He discerned in his
charge an objective faculty for acquiring miscellaneous knowledge
in spite of an aversion to books. But Prince Albert, who
anxiously studied Gibbs's reports, deprecated any material
departure from the bookish plan.

A classical tutor and chaplain was added to the Prince's
tutorial establishment in 1855 in the person of Charles Feral
Tarver, who, like Birch, was an Etonian, and a Fellow of King's
College, Cambridge.[1] Tarver painfully sought to initiate the
Prince in the classics and in theology.

At the same time the boy's attention was turned more
insistently to natural science. In January 1856 he and his
brother Alfred attended Faraday's lectures on metals at the
Royal Institution. The experiments proved a relief from books,
and the Prince wrote appreciatively of them to the lecturer.
Near the same date William Ellis was summoned to the Palace

---

[1] He was the son of a French master at Eton who had taught French to the
Duke of Cambridge, and made a wide reputation as an Anglo-French lexico-
grapher.

to teach the Prince, along with his eldest sister, political economy.   1851
Ellis noted the superior quickness of the girl, and his failure to   Ætat. 9
move much interest in the boy.

III

Probably among the many defects in the Prince's regimen the   1852
gravest was his isolation from boys of his own age other than his   Ætat. 10
brothers and the foreign cousins who were from time to time his
parents' guests. The Prince always hungered for the society of
his fellows. Through life, he disliked solitude, and was never
happy without a congenial companion. A marked responsive-
ness to friendly sympathy and an instinct of fidelity in friendship
were notable features of his maturity. But there was nervous
fear on Prince Albert's part of the contaminating influence of men
or boys of ordinary clay. The Queen set rather less store than
her husband on social exclusiveness, and Prince Albert so far
relaxed his principle as to invite a few Eton boys whose parents
were of high character and good position to pay the Prince brief
and occasional visits at Windsor. Accordingly, there came over
from Eton for a few hours of an afternoon William Henry Gladstone, who had visited him in his nursery; Charles Carrington
(afterwards first Earl Carrington and Marquis of Lincolnshire);
Frederick Stanley (the Earl of Derby's second son and a successor
to his father's title); Charles Lindley Wood (afterwards second
Viscount Halifax); Lord Hinchingbrooke (afterwards eighth
Earl of Sandwich); George Cadogan (afterwards fifth Earl
Cadogan), and the son of the Belgian Minister in London, M.
Sylvain Van de Weyer, a man of literary tastes whose acquaintance
Prince Albert valued. The opportunities of intercourse were
restricted. Prince Albert was always present, and inspired the
boy visitors with a sense of dread. But the young Prince's good
humour and charm of manner endeared him to these Eton boys
and made them his close friends for life.

With Eton, the great public school adjoining Windsor, Prince
Albert also brought his son into formal touch by taking him to the
speech-days (on the 4th June) from 1847 onwards. But the visits
were too ceremonial to give him real knowledge or appreciation
of public-school life. The rival public school, Harrow, was likewise visited in similar conditions, and at a Speech-day there on

the 29th June 1854, the Prince of Wales first caught sight of "Chaplin Major" (afterwards Lord Chaplin), who, at Oxford a little later, was to become one of his lifelong friends.

1857
Ætat. 15

Owing to the Prince's practical seclusion from boys' society and to his enforced application to study, he took small part in outdoor games. Cricket and football were virtually unknown to him, and no athletic sport made much appeal. He went at least once to Mr. Hawtrey's house at Eton to practise in the fives' court and took some interest in croquet, but for outdoor games in general he showed little aptitude. He was taught to ride at an early age, and when, shortly before his sixth birthday, his pony ran away with him, he faced the peril with a surprising courage which foretold a future characteristic.[1] As a young man he rode well and hard, possessing good hands and nerve. Under his father's tuition he occasionally skated at Windsor in early years. Prince Albert, whose German bringing-up scarcely fostered in him the English zest for shooting and hunting, engaged in such recreations as a duty rather than as a pleasure. He encouraged his eldest son to join him in pursuit of them when his studies permitted. From his thirteenth year the Prince of Wales regularly shot over the Windsor coverts, and each autumn engaged in deer-stalking as well as shooting at Balmoral. He did not excel as a shot in spite of assiduous practice. Of hunting he had a first experience before he completed his sixteenth year, going out with the royal buckhounds at Windsor (October 1857), and he on occasion joined in the run of a pack of harriers kennelled at Cumberland Lodge, Windsor, which was, in name only, under his father's control. A genuine love of horses and dogs grew with his years. From youth to age a dog was his constant companion. But his early training rather tardily developed in him interest in the sports of the country-side. Owing to his seclusion, he learned little in youth of the exhilarating camaraderie which comes of indulgence in games or sporting recreation.

IV

The Prince Consort's educational code happily permitted his son to play some small part in current public events, many of which proved of historic import. The youth retained vivid

[1] *Lady Lyttelton's Letters.*

1851
—
Ætat. 9

memories of such experiences, which provided welcome relief from the rigid discipline of study. The opening of the Great Exhibition in Hyde Park in 1851 left a profound impression on the boy's mind. The enterprise, which aimed at promoting universal peace by encouraging the industrial arts and sciences, was mainly Prince Albert's design. Its organisation had occupied his thought continuously for some two years, and the Prince of Wales heard much of his parent's anxious wish for the success of the ambitious venture. The young Prince, in Highland costume, walked on the opening day in the royal procession, holding his mother's hand (May 1, 1851). Frequently during the summer did the Prince revisit the Exhibition under the guidance of his tutor, and numerous references to the Exhibition appear in his juvenile correspondence. Writing to Baron Stockmar of his interest in some waxwork models of the murderous Thugs of India, he received in reply the characteristic reminder that "he is born in a Christian and enlightened age in which such atrocious acts are not even dreamt of."

When the Great Exhibition building of Hyde Park was re-erected at Sydenham as the Crystal Palace the Prince attended in June 1854 the inauguration of that institution, and followed with deep concern its chequered fortunes through later days. Much energy did the Prince devote in his mature years to the promotion, in the interests of industrial progress, of exhibitions which took their cue from his father's design of 1851.

Other events of the Prince's boyhood left indelible memories. On the 14th September 1852, there died the old Duke of Wellington, the hero of Waterloo, an old-world figure very familiar to the Prince's youth. Despite his incursions into party politics, the Duke retained to the last the veneration due to a national hero. To the Queen and her little heir he had shown much paternal kindness, and the boy grieved for the old General as he watched, from the balcony of Buckingham Palace, the funeral procession wending its way in military pomp from Chelsea Hospital to St. Paul's Cathedral on November 18, 1852.

V

Of the historical episodes contemporary with the Prince's boyhood, the two most stirring were the Crimean War of 1854–56

1854
—
Ætat. 12

and the Indian Mutiny of 1857, and memories of both helped to
mould in manhood the Prince's views of some large imperial,
military, and international problems.

The Crimean War roused national feeling to its depths, and
the Prince, like all members of his family, proved responsive
to the patriotic excitement. It was as protector of Turkey
against Russia's threats of Turkish integrity that England sent her
soldiers into action in 1854, for the first time in Europe since she
had crushed Napoleonic France nearly forty years before. The
English people had resented the delay of Lord Aberdeen's Government in challenging Russia, and they had assigned the procrastination to Prince Albert's foreign affinities and sympathies.
The ill-founded charge greatly perturbed the Queen and her
household. When, on 27th February 1854, the war was at length
declared, largely owing to Lord Palmerston's persistence, the
Prince of Wales at once joined his parents in active demonstrations of identity with the national will. With the Queen he
inspected the first detachment of troops which passed through
London on the eve of embarkation for the seat of war. He was
present with his mother in the royal yacht *Fairy* when she led
out to sea the great fleet under Admiral Sir Charles Napier
which was destined for the Baltic. With his brother Alfred he
was soon constructing miniature fortifications in the grounds of
Osborne House.

The Crimean campaign proved more trying than had been
anticipated, and the break-down of the army medical service
before the end of the first year roused a storm of public grief
and indignation. A special session of Parliament was summoned
on the 12th December 1854 in order to reassure public opinion.
On that day the Prince made his first appearance in the House
of Lords. He sat by the Queen as she read from the throne
her speech in which the situation of affairs was described
as more critical than any the country had faced since 1815,
and as requiring of Government and people the most strenuous
exertions.

Visits to wounded soldiers in London and Portsmouth were
among the Prince's new experiences. To an art exhibition and
sale in Pall Mall, on behalf of the Patriotic Fund which was
opened to benefit soldiers' families in the spring of 1855, the
Prince contributed a pencil drawing by himself, called "The

Knight," which fetched 55 guineas.[1] While the royal family was at Balmoral in the autumn there arrived the long-expected news of the fall of Sebastopol after a siege of nearly a year, and the Prince helped his father to light a bonfire, by way of celebration, on the top of a neighbouring cairn (September 10, 1855). Five days later the Prince wrote to his Eton friend, Charles Wood, of a special holiday at the school to be given in honour of the victory : "The Queen and Prince have allowed the whole school a holiday, on the condition that you will all give three cheers for the success of the army."

Until the conclusion of peace in March 1856 the Prince attended an almost continuous series of military functions, and his early thought took a military turn. He watched his mother distribute medals to returning soldiers at the Horse Guards in May 1855, and paid with her his first visit to the newly established camp at Aldershot on the 14th July. After the war ended he witnessed, again at Aldershot, a great review of the Guards and other regiments from the front, and he attended the first distribution by the Queen of the newly devised Victoria Cross in Hyde Park (June 26, 1857).

With several officers who distinguished themselves in the war the young Prince was soon on terms of intimacy, and he listened with eager attention to their campaigning memories. The Prince, in spite of his youth, learned from the Crimean struggle much that was serviceable. The war, for all its heroic episodes, revealed critical defects in the country's military equipment. The revelation never quite faded from the Prince's mind. Throughout the struggle Queen Victoria urged on her Ministers the obligation of waging war, when once it was begun, with the utmost rigour, and the Prince readily assimilated, in later days, his mother's resolute temper. It was Palmerston's spirited foreign policy which had chiefly led to the war. The Palmerstonian creed, which embraced a thoroughgoing distrust of Russia, was to become, through a long period of the Prince's life, his political faith, which was only to be modified after many years.

[1] A coloured drawing by his eldest sister, entitled "The Battlefield," brought the larger sum of 250 guineas.

VI

The most striking influence on the young Prince's career, which may be assigned to the Crimean War, was the association into which it incidentally brought him for the first time with the pleasant land of France. No characteristic was more distinctive of the Prince's mature life than his sympathy with France and with the French people, and it was the Crimean War which first stirred into life his French proclivities.

It was a curious tangle which brought about the Prince's personal introduction to England's nearest continental neighbour.

Napoleon III.'s creation, by *coup d'état*, of the Second French Empire had been warmly resented by the Queen and Prince Albert. The new ruler of France was credited, in England, with his great uncle's hostile designs. During the first years of Napoleon III.'s reign the Prince of Wales learned much of the military precautions which it was deemed needful to take against the peril of French aggression. In 1853 he accompanied his mother to the newly formed camp at Chobham (July 23) and attended at Spithead (August 11) a naval review which was intended to demonstrate England's strength. But next year the Anglo-French situation completely changed. The English Ministry sought friendly relations with the Emperor of the French, and the Queen, with constitutional correctness, abandoned, although with reluctance, her personal misgivings. The dispute with Russia gave the opportunity of cementing an Anglo-French understanding. France offered to join England in the Crimean War. Her offer was accepted. The Emperor thereupon proposed to celebrate the new alliance by an exchange of hospitalities between himself and the Queen and her family.

As early as July 1854 Prince Albert let it be confidentially known that he was ready to pay the French Emperor a visit, and it was his eldest son's heedless exclamation, "Papa is going to France," at a children's party given by his great-aunt, the Duchess of Gloucester, that made public property of his parents' changed attitude to Napoleon III.[1] The boy was premature in his announcement of his father's intention. There

[1] Buckle, *Life of Disraeli*, vol. iii. p. 546.

was delay in the fulfilment of the French Emperor's wish to make the Prince Consort's acquaintance. Queen Victoria claimed the right to entertain her new French ally before he entertained her husband or herself. Accordingly, in April 1855, Napoleon III. and his lately married wife, the Empress Eugénie, paid a State visit to Windsor and Buckingham Palace as Queen Victoria's guests. They were accorded a brilliant reception. The young Prince joined in the festivities and won the hearts of the imperial guests.

In the following August the Queen and Prince Albert set foot in the French capital on a return visit, and with them went the Prince and his eldest sister. The Prince's first visit to Paris stamped itself on his mind more forcibly than any other of his youthful adventures.

It was not the Prince's first experience of continental travel. He had already crossed the Channel, for the first time three years before, on a six days' visit with his parents to his grand-uncle, King Leopold, at the royal palace of Laeken, near Brussels. On the journey back he caught his first glimpse of France off Calais, towards which the royal yacht steered by the Queen's direction. Of historic import were the conditions which attached to the Prince's introduction to France and the French capital in August 1855. Stuart pretenders to the English throne had sought asylum in Paris, but no acknowledged English sovereign had visited that city for more than four centuries— since the infant king, Henry VI., went thither to be crowned King of France in 1430.

The visit to Paris of Queen Victoria and the heir-apparent lasted a week, from the 20th to the 27th of August. The boy, clad in Highland costume, fascinated the Parisian populace from the moment that he figured in the Queen's processional entry. His bearing at the dazzling entertainments which were provided by the Imperial Court in the Queen's honour, was credited with a singular social charm. Commendation of his graceful dancing ran high at a great ball at Versailles. Queen Victoria found an opportunity of visiting, during her stay, the chief sights of the French capital, and her son was her companion. Still in Highland costume, he visited with her the tomb of the great Napoleon at the Hôtel des Invalides, and she bade him pay homage to the hero on his knees. A thunderstorm broke out at the moment, and the notable scene moved to tears the French Generals who were present.[1]

The imperial hosts were unremitting in their attentions to their guests. The Emperor, with his low voice and air of mystery, interested the boy, and the buoyant Empress caught his affection. A year later he was overjoyed to receive from the Empress a locket, enclosing a slip of her own hair entwined with one of the Emperor's and a wisp of the scanty hair of the new-born Prince Imperial. Numerous were the notable Frenchmen and Frenchwomen at the gay Imperial Court with whom the Prince came, on this occasion, into initial contact. One of the longest lived of these was Marshal Canrobert, who was soon to take chief command of the French armies in the Crimea. Half a century later the old Marshal recalled to the Prince the delight which the first sight of him evoked. With truth did Prince Albert write to Stockmar, in an unusually light-hearted vein, how his son, "qui est si gentil," contrived to make himself a general favourite.[2]

The mutual impression, although it had its vicissitudes, proved in the long run imperishable. Frenchmen of every class and political creed soon thronged the ranks of the Prince's admirers. "Le petit bonhomme est vraiment charmant," wrote Louis Blanc, a French communist exile in England, who as he wandered about London caught frequent sights of the boy; "il a je ne sais quoi qui plaît, et, aux côtés de ses parents, il apparaît comme un vrai personnage de féerie."[3] This early understanding between the Prince and the French people strangely defied the German prepossessions of his family. As it matured it became a factor of significance in the history of the two countries and of Europe.

"We have returned delighted with our visit," wrote the Queen to the Duchess of Gordon from Osborne, 2nd September 1855, "which we can never forget and which by strengthening the alliance promises to be of lasting benefit to the countries as well as to all the world." But the Queen was in too sanguine a mood. The old jealousy between England and

---

[1] The Prince of Wales figures prominently in the picture by E. M. Ward, R.A., depicting the episode, which is at Windsor Castle.

[2] Martin, *Life of Prince Consort*, iii. 60.

[3] Louis Blanc, *Lettres sur l'Angleterre* (1865–66).

France was not to be exorcised so early in the Prince of Wales's life. The *entente cordiale* with Napoleon III. proved a fleeting scene in the drama of Anglo-French relations. Nearly half a century was to pass before that familiar phrase was to acquire under the auspices of King Edward any lasting significance. The view of an Anglo-French understanding, which long persisted in England, was reflected in Lord Palmerston's remark to Lord Clarendon, on 20th September 1857: "In an alliance with France we are riding a runaway horse and must always be on our guard." To a change in the English conception of French constancy the Prince, alike as heir-apparent and as king, made conspicuous contribution.

1855
—
Ætat. 13

CHAPTER IV

THE HORIZON WIDENS UNDER NEW RESTRAINTS

I

1855

Ætat. 13

THE glowing experience of Paris and the Imperial Court scarcely reconciled the Prince of Wales to the rigorous tutelage which darkened his life at home. There followed on the return from France many complaints by the boy's father and mother of his slow progress in his studies, and there came protesting bursts of ill-temper from the boy. Prince Albert sadly compared what he termed the Prince's listlessness and indolence with the rapidly developing intelligence of his eldest daughter, who found a literary curriculum thoroughly congenial. In her youthful diaries and essays the father detected a mental promise of which he could find small trace in his son's diaries and essays, which he condemned as bald, ungrammatical, and badly penned.

Orderliness in all directions was enjoined on the youth with new insistence. Both parents now lost no opportunity of inculcating a wise philosophy of dress which should allow a restricted indulgence of personal taste. At fifteen he was given a small allowance for the purchase of hats and ties, for which he carefully accounted to his mother. A year later, when he was advanced to the privilege of choosing his own clothes, the Queen sent him an exhaustive minute on the place which dress should fill in his scheme of life. Its importance might easily be exaggerated, she pointed out, but neatness and taste were essential in persons of high rank. Her son should follow "his own tastes and fancies," but should "never wear anything *extravagant or slang*." He must not identify himself with "the *foolish and worthless* persons" who dress "loudly." The good counsel had the sound authority of Polonius.

The Prince took the advice to heart : to decorum in dress he thenceforth attached an importance which seemed to some exces- sive. Slovenliness he came to abhor, and he insisted on a strict conformity to current fashion in those about him. The Queen's teaching helped to fix his attention on the details of uniforms and on the formalities of official costume, which he came to enforce with all the rigour of his grandfather, the Duke of Kent.

1855
Ætat. 13

II

In the autumn of 1856, when the Prince was approaching his fifteenth birthday, the father, at the suggestion of Tutor Gibbs, wisely tried the effect of a few weeks' release from the parental leading-strings. A walking tour in Dorset, where the Queen remembered to have spent a pleasant holiday in girlhood, was arranged to take the place of the usual migration with the family to Balmoral. The boy was to travel incognito as Baron of Renfrew ; was to be accompanied by Gibbs and Colonel Caven- dish, a groom-in-waiting to Prince Albert ; and was to put up with his companions at inns on the road. A good start was made from Wimborne, and a route was followed through Swanage, Wareham, Dorchester, Bridport, and Charnock. But the secret of the Prince's identity leaked out. Public curiosity led to inconvenient demonstrations of loyalty, and within a week the tour was brought to an abrupt close at Honiton. The experiment was too short to be serviceable.

1856
Ætat. 14

At the end of the year Prince Albert confessed his obstinate misgivings of his son's progress to Lord Granville, the President of the Council in Lord Palmerston's Government. With Lord Granville—a man of wit and common sense—he and the Queen were on confidential terms. Lord Granville frankly canvassed the main principles of the Prince Consort's educational code— especially the withdrawal of the Prince from the society of boys of his own age and the effort to concentrate his attention mainly on books. The critic recommended that the Dorset experiment of sending the boy away from home should be tried again on a larger scale and with more suitable companions. Travel, he suggested, was more likely than anything else to develop the best features of the boy's temperament.

1856
Ætat. 14

"I strongly recommended," wrote Lord Granville when describing his interview with Prince Albert to his friend Lord Canning, then Governor-General of India, "his being mixed up with others of his own age away from home. The visits of Eton boys to the Castle for a couple of hours can be of no use. I questioned the Prince closely about Gibbs. He thinks very highly of Gibbs. He sent for him, and made him give me his views on the education of the Prince. This Gibbs did in a very clear and sensible way. He talked of the advantages and disadvantages of being Prince of Wales in a very uncourtier-like manner. I believe that a journey will be organised for him, and several boys of his own age invited to accompany him. It is intended to send him for a short time to Oxford and Cambridge, and then on a voyage to all the principal British possessions. You will possibly have to receive him in India." [1]

1857
Ætat. 15

Although Prince Albert's faith in the virtues of his system was unshaken, he made some concessions at Lord Granville's persuasion. Without prejudice to the bookish instruction and stern regulation of conduct Prince Albert consented to admit to his code three new and salutary articles: firstly, indulgence in travel at home and abroad; secondly, occasional withdrawals from the parental roof and eye; and, thirdly, increased opportunities of intercourse with young men.

The first fruit of Lord Granville's counsel was a second tour in England—this time in the Lake district. As on the visit to Dorset, Colonel Cavendish and Gibbs were in control, but with them now went four of the Eton boys who had occasionally visited the Prince at Windsor, viz. Charles Wood, William Henry Gladstone, George Cadogan, and Frederick Stanley.[2] Starting from the city of Lancaster, the Prince and his companions visited Bowness and Grasmere, and then climbed Helvellyn. The Prince's spirits ran high in the congenial society. Near Windermere the Prince and Cadogan chased a flock of sheep into the water and were threatened with merited chastisement by the woman who owned them. The Prince sketched the scene in water colours, and the drawing hung in Lord Cadogan's study at Culford for more than half a century.

[1] Fitzmaurice's *Life of Granville*, i. 224–5.
[2] The parental solicitude added a medical attendant in the person of Dr. Alexander Armstrong, then the medical officer on the royal yacht, who had enjoyed some experience of Arctic exploration.

III

But Prince Albert, or Prince Consort, as he was now re-christened for the rest of his life,[1] was discontented with the Prince's tour of the Lakes. His son's diary pained him by its jejuneness. But he was prepared to give the new method of travel further trial, and a foreign expedition farther afield and of longer duration, filled the succeeding summer and autumn. The fresh tour aimed at educational as well as recreative purposes. The Prince was to apply himself to reading as well as to sight-seeing and exercise. Very modest was the amount of reading which was achieved, but the young Prince came into bracing contact with new scenes and persons of historic note.

The first destination was Königswinter, near Bonn, on the Rhine, where the Prince was to concentrate on the study of the German language and literature, subjects which his father thought him to have unduly neglected. A visit to the Swiss mountains was to follow. His companions, as on the tour of the Lakes, included the four Eton boys—Wood, Stanley, Gladstone, and Cadogan—and Tutor Gibbs, but to these were added the instructor Tarver, while Prince Albert sent out two confidential and responsible members of his household—his private secretary, General Charles Grey,[2] and his equerry, Colonel Henry Ponsonby. At a later stage the party was joined by the Prince's young kinsman, Prince Ernest of Leiningen (son of his mother's step-brother), now a naval lieutenant who had seen service in the recent war.

The journey out took a week. Visits to Liége, Namur, and Aix-la-Chapelle preceded the trip down the Rhine. At Königs-winter, where a full month was spent, the Prince, while chafing against the programme of study, welcomed opportunities of meeting some historic notabilities. He renewed acquaintance with the ill-fated Archduke Maximilian of Austria, whom he had already met at Windsor, and with the Archduke's bride, King

---

[1] On 25th June 1857, the Queen had conferred on her husband by Royal Letters Patent the title of Prince Consort. "It was always a source of weakness for the Crown," the Prince wrote at the time, "that the Queen always appears before the people with a *foreign* husband."

[2] In the course of the expedition General Grey was replaced by General Sir William Codrington, who had distinguished himself in the Crimean War.

1857
Ætat. 15

Leopold's daughter, Princess Charlotte of Belgium,[1] who in childhood had at times been his playmate. But the most imposing
figure which now came within the youth's social orbit was that
of Prince Metternich, the veteran Austrian statesman and apostle
of autocracy, now in his eighty-fourth year, whose word, up
to the year of revolution, 1848, had been law in Central Europe
for more than thirty years. On the subsidence of the democratic storm of 1848, during which Prince Metternich sought
an asylum in England, he had returned to his former haunts
although not to his former office. While the Prince of Wales
was at Königswinter, he, according to his wont, was spending
the summer in the neighbouring castle of Johannisberg, and
was still preaching privately to his admirers with unruffled
serenity the political philosophy which was embodied in his
motto, "La force dans le droit" ("Might is right"). At
Johannisberg he received the young heir-apparent of England.
In reporting the meeting to a French correspondent, M. Guizot,
the old statesman amiably wrote: "Le jeune prince plaisait à
tout le monde." But a fit of shyness overcame the youth in
the presence of such aged eminence, and Prince Metternich
added: "Il avait l'air embarrassé et très triste."[2] It was an
ironic scene when the octogenarian evangelist of the losing
cause of despotism blandly pronounced his benediction on the
bashful young heir of triumphant constitutionalism.

The Prince and his party left Königswinter at the beginning
of September for Switzerland. From Martigny they went by
the Tête Noir to Chamounix. There they were met by Albert
Smith, to whose illustrated lecture on the ascent of Mont Blanc
—long one of London's popular entertainments—the Prince and
his brothers and sisters had already listened at Osborne (August
24, 1854). Albert Smith guided the Prince over the Glacier
des Boissons at the foot of the great mountain. No serious
climbing was attempted. Afterwards the Prince walked over
the Grosse Scheidegg Pass. At the moment, Roundell Palmer,

[1] They were on their honeymoon, their marriage having taken place at
Brussels on 29th July 1857.
[2] Reid, *Life of Lord Houghton*. Prince Metternich died at his palace in
Vienna two years later at the age of eighty-six (June 11, 1859). Subsequently
the Prince of Wales came into frequent touch in the diplomatic society of Paris
with Prince Metternich's son Richard and his wife (and niece) Pauline, a
vivacious figure at the Court of Napoleon III. Cf. Metternich's *Memoirs;*
Princess Paul Metternich's *The Days that are no more*, London, 1921.

afterwards Earl Selborne and Lord Chancellor, was traversing the   1857
same road and he described the Prince in his diary as a "slender,   Ætat. 15
fair boy" with a "frank, open countenance."[1]

On the 24th October 1857 the Prince landed at Dover after an
absence from England and from his family of nearly four months.
It was as yet the longest period that he had been free from his
father's surveillance.   News of current political events had been
forwarded regularly.   A tragic episode in imperial history took
place while he was away.   Letters from home kept him well
informed of the harrowing course of the Indian Mutiny which
reached its cruel height while he was at Königswinter, and was
crushed during his stay in Switzerland.   The Prince was later
to extend his travels to the scenes of the Indian tragedy.

IV

The normal routine of study which the Prince resumed under
his father's eye on his return from Switzerland was alleviated
by a domestic episode which profoundly affected the future of
the Prince and of his family.   It brought them into new personal
relations with Prussia and her rulers.

Some two years before, in 1855, while on a visit to Balmoral,   1855
Prince Frederick William of Prussia (afterwards the German   Ætat. 13
Emperor, Frederick III.) had proposed marriage to the Prince
of Wales's eldest sister, the Princess Royal.   He was nephew
of the Prince of Wales's Prussian godfather, King Frederick
William IV., and eldest son of that monarch's brother, the
Prince of Prussia, who was heir to the Prussian Crown.   The
girl was not quite fifteen and the Prussian Prince was nine years
her senior, but there were signs of a mutual affection.   Queen
Victoria and Prince Albert welcomed a Prussian matrimonial
alliance, and the Prince of Wales, while he dreaded separation
from his sister, the constant companion of his youth, found
much to attract him in her simple-hearted lover.   The public
announcement of the engagement was postponed until 29th
April 1857, just after the Princess's confirmation.   The marriage
took place amid brilliant festivities in the Chapel Royal at
St. James's Palace on the 25th January 1858.   The Prince of
Wales, in Highland costume, supported his sister at the altar,

---

[1] Selborne, *Memorials*, ii. 327.

and signed the register next after his grandmother, the Duchess of Kent.

After a few days' honeymoon the Prince joined his sister and her husband in a triumphal procession from Buckingham Palace through the City of London to Gravesend, where the pair embarked on the royal yacht *Victoria and Albert* for Antwerp on their way to Berlin. The Prince of Wales felt the parting acutely. Thenceforth his sister wrote to him once a week and he was nearly as assiduous in reply.

Frequent visits to his sister in her German home created a new link between him and the Prussian dynasty and Prussian society. But clouds gathered from the first on his Prussian horizon. Circumstances attending his sister's settlement in her husband's country, which she reported fully to her brother, bred in him an aversion for the militarist and autocratic traditions of Prussia's ruling class. The Prince's brother-in-law, although by training and profession a soldier, was by disposition a lover of peace, and he cherished numerous social and intellectual interests outside the army. His well-trained wife rapidly gained a dominant influence over him, and at her instance the Prussian Prince challenged the sentiments of his kinsfolk by outspoken sympathy with political Liberalism. There followed differences with his family circle, which his wife encouraged. The English Princess never, indeed, reconciled herself to her German environment, and in her brother's fellow-feeling she found an enduring solace amid the friction at Berlin which came of her English views and temperament.

V

The Prince of Wales was now well advanced in his seventeenth year, and his parents solemnly acknowledged the increased responsibility which the near approach of manhood laid upon them. From the first, care was bestowed on the Prince's religious training. The importance of religious worship was inculcated early: and under his mother's guidance he transcribed at a tender age simple prayers for his own use. His mother, who explained to him in childhood how closely identified he was with the Established Church, at the same time inspired him with her own sentiment of tolerance for religious creeds other than her own. The Prince to the end of his days freely breathed that bracing air and scorned religious bigotry. Yet the Prince Consort taught his son that his religious observances were under as strict a parental control as everything else. When, in July 1858, Tutor Gibbs reported to the Prince Consort that his son intended taking the sacrament at an early service with Mr. Tarver and his newly appointed equerry (Major Lindsay), the father wrote at length pointing out that Queen Victoria and himself had made it their practice to take Holy Communion only twice a year—Christmas and Easter—and that it would be difficult for the Prince to justify divergence from that practice.[1]

The Prince's confirmation on the 1st April 1858 was, in his parents' eyes, an event of profound moment. Preparation for the ordeal was long and thorough. The day before the ceremony, Gerald Wellesley, Dean of Windsor, who enjoyed the complete confidence of the royal family, subjected the Prince, in the presence of his parents and of Archbishop Sumner of Canterbury, to a full hour's oral examination. "The examination," wrote the Queen to her uncle, King Leopold, "was long and difficult, but Bertie answered extremely well."[2] Next day the substantive ceremony took place in the Chapel at Windsor. The Archbishop was supported by Bishop Wilberforce of Oxford, and in addition to the royal family and members of the household there attended the leaders of all political parties, including not only Lord Derby, who had recently become Prime Minister, but also his Liberal predecessor, Lord Palmerston, and Lord John Russell, the late Foreign Minister. To her son's "whole manner and Gemüthsstimmung" (frame of mind) the Queen applied the epithets, "gentle, good, and proper." Such epithets well apply to the Prince's religious attitude through life. The Prince Consort wrote to Stockmar: "The Confirmation went off with great solemnity, and I hope, with an abiding impression on his mind."[3]

The Prince was rewarded for his exemplary behaviour by yet another holiday tour. After Easter he spent a fortnight with his tutor in the south of Ireland, refreshing his acquaintance

---

[1] Prince Consort to his son, 14th July 1858, cited by Lord Esher, in *The Influence of King Edward*, 1915, pp. 32–4.
[2] *Letters of Queen Victoria*, iii. 353.
[3] Martin, *Prince Consort*, iv. 24; *Letters of Queen Victoria*, iii. 353.

with the beauties of Killarney and exploring tourist-wise the quaint little towns of Bandon, Bantry, and Skibbereen.

VI

Meanwhile, the Prince was cherishing hopes of a military career. The Duke of Cambridge's profession seemed to offer him a way of escape from books. His father, while he approved his eldest son's formal association with the army, was grimly loyal to his scheme of literary training, and would sanction no step likely to clash with it. But he gave way to the extent of acknowledging the Prince of Wales's approaching seventeenth birthday to be an appropriate date for his nominal admission to the army. He stipulated that a qualifying examination must first be passed, and he agreed that the preceding months might well be devoted away from home to preparing for that ordeal. Accordingly the Prince Consort made what he regarded as the bold experiment of removing his son from the distractions of the Court and of setting him up temporarily in an independent household. The residence known as White Lodge, in Richmond Park, was chosen for the purpose. The house was the official residence of the Duke of Cambridge, as Ranger of the Park, but was unoccupied. The tutors Gibbs and Tarver were, naturally, to be in general charge of the Prince, but of chief importance in the sight of the Prince Consort was the appointment of three equerries who, serving in a monthly rotation, might encourage the youth in military and other studies, might polish his manners, and share in his recreations.

Little increase of personal liberty was promised the Prince when his father provided him experimentally with a separate establishment. A rigorous code of disciplinary rules was furnished the equerries by the Prince Consort "for the benefit of the Prince of Wales." Their charge, the father pointed out, had reached a critical period of life, and his future depended on his association with "what is commonly called a good set." Only with those in official attendance upon him was it desirable for the Prince to maintain any personal relation. Their influence must fit him to hold the position of "the first gentleman in the country." One section of the exemplary code dealt with the youth's "appearance, deportment, and dress," a second with his "manners and conduct towards others," and a third with the "power to acquit himself creditably in conversation or whatever may be the occupation of society." Good example was to prevent "lounging ways, such as lolling in armchairs or sofas" or "a slouching gait with hands in the pockets." His clothes were to be "of the best quality . . . well made and suitable to his rank and position." He was to be taught the "frivolity and foolish vanity of dandyism." "The most scrupulous civility" should characterise his "manner and conduct towards others." Every mark of respect was to be acknowledged "with an appearance of goodwill and cordiality." A Prince should never say a harsh or rude word to anybody, nor indulge in "satirical or bantering expressions." "*A practical joke* should never be permitted." In conversation the Prince should be trained to "take the lead and should be able to find something to say beyond mere questions as to health and the weather." The Prince Consort's dominant idiosyncrasy comes strongly into relief in the final injunction that under the influence of "persevering example" the Prince should "devote some of his leisure time to music, to the fine arts, either drawing, or looking over drawings, engravings, etc., and should hear poetry, amusing books, or good plays read aloud." In short, "anything that whilst it amuses may gently exercise the mind" was to be sedulously encouraged. Discretion was to be used in pressing such pursuits on the Prince, but the equerries' line of conduct "*on all occasions*" was to harmonise with the demure "principles" which were thus minutely defined.[1]

No exception could be taken to the Prince Consort's choice of his son's earliest equerries, of whose capacity to satisfy his exacting requirements he carefully assured himself. Lord Valletort, eldest son of the Earl of Mount Edgcumbe, was accomplished in drawing and music. The other two were distinguished military officers, both winners of the Victoria Cross in the Crimean War. Major Christopher Charles Teesdale of the Artillery had fought at Kars, while Major Robert James Lindsay, of the Scots Fusilier Guards (afterwards Lord Wantage) had showed courage at Alma and Inkermann, and had the additional qualification of familiarity with French and Italian. From the guidance of such men the Prince Consort sanguinely wrote to Stockmar on the 2nd April 1858, "I anticipate no small benefit to Bertie."

[1] Cited by Lord Esher in *The Influence of King Edward*, 1915, pp. 16–22.

1858

Ætat. 16
At White Lodge, the Prince of Wales's pursuit of study was tempered by occasional rowing on the river or riding with his equerries, by visits from members of his family, and by calls on his great-aunt, the Duchess of Cambridge, at Cambridge Cottage, Kew, where he attended his first private dinner-party away from home. By his father's special direction, intercourse with serious persons of distinction and mature age living in the neighbourhood was also encouraged. Lord John Russell, then out of office, was residing hard by at Pembroke Lodge, a Crown residence which the Queen had bestowed upon him. Another man of eminence, Richard Owen the naturalist, occupied another Crown residence, Sheen Lodge. Both Lord John and Owen were often the Prince's guests at dinner. One of these occasions Owen describes thus:

There was much agreeable conversation, the form of waiting for a remark or question from the royal host not being observed. I told the Prince of the latest news of Dr. and Mrs. Livingstone and of Mme. Pfeiffer, just returned from Madagascar. The history of Richmond Park coming up, General Bowater [another guest] remarked that Charles I.'s enlargement of it was one of the causes of his unpopularity. "Why should that have made him unpopular?" asked His Royal Highness. "Because," replied Mr. Gibbs, "he took other people's land arbitrarily, or not quite according to law." I noted the use of such an opportunity of imparting constitutional principles.[1]

At the last party which Owen attended at White Lodge (November 5) there was, he writes, "a most pleasant, varied chat all dinner time, no sort of formality."[1] But no youths of the Prince's own years were suffered to join the elderly company.

VII

The sojourn at White Lodge was interrupted in August by a rather exciting excursion. His parents summoned their son to accompany them on a second visit (of two days) to the Emperor and Empress of the French at Cherbourg. The Duke of Cambridge conducted him to Osborne on the 4th August. The *Victoria and Albert*, which carried the royal party, was escorted by a squadron of the Fleet, and at Cherbourg was thunderously

---

[1] *Life of Richard Owen*, ii. 74–76.

welcomed by nine French battleships. In the exchange of hospitalities, the Prince of Wales, again in Highland costume, played as prominent a part as at Paris four years before. He dined with the Emperor and Empress on board the royal yacht on the evening of his arrival, joined next morning in the procession to the *préfecture maritime*, where the Emperor and Empress entertained their English guests at luncheon, and afterwards with the rest of the party ascended on foot the great fort La Roule. At the banquet in the evening which the Emperor gave on board the battleship *Bretagne* the Prince of Wales sat on one side of the Empress while his father sat on the other. He listened to the exchange of friendly eloquence between the Emperor and the Prince Consort, and later witnessed the fireworks and illuminations of the two fleets.[1] To his sister in Germany he wrote of the expedition with youthful gusto.

Apparently the Prince of Wales was for a second time taking part in a demonstration of Anglo-French goodwill. But a storm was brewing. The Cherbourg fortifications were ironical pledges of international friendship. The Emperor's embarrassed mood encouraged a growing suspicion that he was meditating anew foreign aggression in the spirit of his great uncle. Despite the exchange of affectionate greetings between the ruling families, the *entente* was in danger.

VIII

On the 9th November 1858 the Prince of Wales entered on his eighteenth year, on the completion of which, as heir-apparent, he came of age and was thenceforth qualified, when the reigning sovereign died, to exercise the royal power. The Prince's mother had become Queen within fourteen weeks of her eighteenth birthday. His solicitous parents treated the opening of the Prince's eighteenth year as a fresh epoch in his career, and they greeted it with characteristic solemnity. The period of childhood was closed and that of manhood begun.

On the morning of the day there was delivered to the Prince a document signed by both parents abounding in sage counsel and rather delusive promises of personal liberty. Some of the salient passages ran :

[1] Cf. Lord Malmesbury, *Memoirs of an Ex-Minister* (1884).

1858
Ætat. 16

1858
Ætat. 17

Life is composed of duties, and in the due, punctual and cheerful performance of them the true Christian, true soldier, and true gentleman is recognised.

You will in future have rooms allotted to your sole use, in order to give you an opportunity of learning how to occupy yourself unaided by others and to utilise your time in the best manner, viz.: such time as may not be otherwise occupied by lessons, by the different tasks which will be given to you by your director of studies, or reserved for exercise and recreation. A new sphere of life will open for you, in which you will have to be taught what to do and what not to do, a subject requiring study more important than any in which you have hitherto been engaged. For it is a subject of *study* and the most difficult one of your life, how to become a good man and a thorough gentleman. . . .

Your personal allowance will be increased; but it is expected that you will carefully order your expenditure so as to remain strictly within the bounds of the sum allowed to you, which will be amply sufficient for your general requirements. . . .

You will try to emancipate yourself as much as possible from the thraldom of abject dependence for your daily wants of life on your servants. The more you can do for yourself and the less you need their help, the greater will be your independence and real comfort.

The Church Catechism has enumerated the duties which you owe to God and your neighbour—let your rule of conduct be always in strict conformity with these precepts, and remember that the first and principal one of all, given us by our Lord and Saviour Himself is this: "that you should love your neighbour as yourself, and do unto men as you would they should do unto you." [1]

The moving words brought "floods of tears" to the boy's eyes as he read them. [2]

In honour of the historic day there were brilliant festivities at Windsor, and rich gifts abounded. The bestowal of the Knighthood of the Garter was announced, although the installation was postponed. But in the youth's eyes the most welcome of the birthday celebrations was his formal enrolment in the army as a Colonel unattached. At once donning a Colonel's uniform, he reported himself at the Horse Guards to "Uncle George," the Commander-in-Chief. The Duke of Cambridge wrote that "he looked very well and seemed very happy."

---

[1] Printed in full by Lord Esher in his *Influence of King Edward*, 1915, pp. 14–15.   [2] *Greville Memoirs, 1852–60*, ii. 213.

There was little latitude in his parents' interpretation of the 1858 personal independence of which they had held out expecta- Ætat. 17 tions. At their request, the tutor Gibbs retired with the reward of the Commandership of the Bath. Despite his tutor's sternness the Prince parted with him in sorrow, and maintained friendly relations with him until his death nearly forty years later. But Gibbs's post was not abolished when he ceased to be tutor. He was replaced by a new officer, invested with far larger powers of control, who received the more dignified and more ominous title of "Governor."

IX

For the new office of governor of his son, the Prince Consort chose a military officer of noble family, Colonel Robert Bruce, next brother of the eighth Earl of Elgin, to whom, when Governor-General of Canada, Colonel Bruce had acted as military secretary. Forty-five years old, he was now colonel of a battalion of the Grenadier Guards.   His sister, Lady Augusta Bruce, the favourite lady-in-waiting of the Duchess of Kent, was a lifelong friend of Queen Victoria, and the Prince Consort wrote of the colonel : "He has all the amiability of his sister, with great mildness of expression and is full of ability."   There was much that was dour in Bruce's Scottish temperament.   He was a disciplinarian, as he himself admitted, to the point of pedantry.   But he possessed a wide range of general culture ; he had lived much in Paris, the home of his widowed mother ; he was liked in society and was reasonably fond of sport and recreation.

On the day when Colonel Bruce assumed the post of governor of the Prince of Wales (November 9, 1858) the Queen signed and handed to him an elaborate paper of instructions.[1]   He was to stand towards the Prince *in loco parentis*, and "his momentous trust" required him unceasingly to impress the Prince with "an adequate sense" of the responsibilities of his station.   He was "to regulate all the Prince's movements, the distribution and employment of his time, and the occupation and details of his daily life."   He was to instil in his charge "habits of reflection

[1] The notes and correspondence of Colonel (afterwards General) Bruce throughout the period of his governorship have been kindly placed at the writer's disposal by their present owner, Colonel Bruce's great-grandnephew, the tenth Earl of Elgin.

1858
Ætat. 17
and self-denial, the strictest truthfulness and honour, above all, the conscientious discharge of his duty towards God and man." There were also to be inculcated the virtue of courtesy to servants, and the need of observing fixed hours for daily study.

Colonel Bruce for the next four years fulfilled his functions with punctilious loyalty to the spirit in which they were entrusted to him. Throughout his term of service he sent to the Queen and the Prince Consort an almost endless series of analytical reports on the Prince of Wales's character and conduct, and he promptly adopted the numerous suggestions which reached him in return from the Prince's parents. From the first Bruce enjoyed the complete confidence of the Queen and her husband. "He seems," the Queen wrote to him a few weeks after he assumed office, 4th December, "to judge his charge's character so truly and to do always the right things. All this is a great comfort to us."

At the outset Bruce frankly complained that his charge had little or no respect for learning; that he tended to exaggerate the importance of dress and etiquette; that he possessed small powers of reflection and was "prone to listlessness and frivolous disputes." But the punctilious governor never ignored the Prince's charm of manner, on which more distant observers were at the time laying a growing stress. His "uncle," the Duke of Cambridge, had recently described the youth as "really a charming and unaffected lad," while the subtler-minded Disraeli, who met him at a private dinner just after his seventeenth birthday, wrote of him that he was "intelligent, informed, and with a singularly sweet manner." [1]

Happily before long the colonel was reporting to the Prince's father a diminution of faults and an increase of merits. There were fewer ebullitions of temper and egotism, less love of domineering and contradiction, a decline in the idle and frivolous tendencies.

"With a considerable share of wilfulness and constitutional irritability," the governor was soon frankly writing, " the Prince combines a fund of natural good sense and feeling. . . . The Prince is really anxious, I think, to improve himself, although the progress is but slow and uncertain."

To the credit of both master and pupil, it should be added

[1] Buckle, *Life of Disraeli*, iv. 189.

that the Prince of Wales, while he chafed against his governor's ever active curb, acquired a regard for him which deepened into affection. His letters to the colonel, whenever they were separated, show perfect friendliness and confidential frankness. In Colonel Bruce's wife, a daughter of Sir Michael Shaw-Stewart, who shared in her husband's surveillance, the Prince recognised from the first a kindliness and breadth of sympathy which always endeared her to him.

X

Shortly after Colonel Bruce's reign opened, the Prince gratified a cherished wish of visiting his married sister in her new home, her husband's palace at Potsdam. Colonel Bruce and Major Teesdale bore him company. The Prince chiefly desired to spend his sister's birthday, the 21st November, with her, but his stay lasted three weeks, and gave him much opportunity of making a first acquaintance with the Berlin Court and society.

The Prince's erratic godfather, King Frederick William IV., had in the previous year shown symptoms of lunacy and was now in retirement. The King's brother, William, the father-in-law of the Princess Royal, had become Prince Regent. More practically minded than his brother and somewhat less affable in social life, the Prince Regent was for the most part a typical Prussian soldier, stolidly devoted to his profession. The coming control of the statesman Bismarck was needed to give him his place in history as the first German Emperor.

The Prince Consort was anxious that no political significance should attach to his son's visit, and that the Prince's studies should proceed without interruption. "It will not be a State but purely a family visit," he had written to the Prince Regent, "and we therefore beg you only to show him such slender courtesies as are suitable to a member, and a very young one, of the family." Governor Bruce was enjoined to keep the young man occupied several hours daily "with serious study," and his sister, in whose society the Prince passed many hours, found time, in loyalty to her father's injunction, to read aloud to him improving books. He was permitted to visit the British Legation at Berlin—it was not an Embassy till 1861—but other Embassies or Legations were to be shunned.

The Prince Regent and his family in consultation with the
British Minister, Lord Bloomfield and his wife, devised a brilliant
programme of hospitality. The Prince Regent ceremonially
promoted the Prince to a higher rank in the Order of the Black
Eagle, subsidiary insignia of which had been conferred upon him
at his baptism. The Prince Consort wrote that he hoped his
son "would at all times prove himself not unworthy" of the
distinction. Lord and Lady Bloomfield entertained the Prince
at a ball which was attended by the whole of the Prussian royal
family. There the Prince danced with much zest his first cotillion.

On all his hosts and hostesses the Prince made an excellent
impression. The Prussian ruler informed the Prince Consort
that his "tact and unaffected courtesy" fascinated the Berlin
Court. On the eve of his son's visit the Prince Consort had
written to the Prince Regent urging on him the wisdom of a
frank acceptance of liberal principles of government. When
the Prince of Wales left Berlin his Prussian host sent by his
hand a letter to his father promising to follow the enlightened
counsel. Happy would it have been for the future of Prussia
and England, and indeed of the world, if the reassuring message
which the Prussian ruler confided to the care of his young
guest had fructified instead of proving barren.

CHAPTER V

THREE MONTHS IN ROME

I

THE Prince still yearned for an active career in the army, and now put in a plea for a course of military training at Aldershot. But his father's former objections were reinforced by Colonel Bruce's emphatically expressed fears of "the temptation and unprofitable companionship of military life." Colonel Bruce declared a conviction that without more moral and mental ballast the Prince could not with profit or safety "be launched into English society." Oxford would provide a profitable regimen later on. At present a foreign tour "for the acquisition of knowledge and information" met the Prince's educational needs. The best intellectual tonic was, in the judgement both of his father and his governor, a course of art and archæology and a study of international politics, to be pursued during a prolonged sojourn in Rome, where interests of the past mingled with those of the present. The Prince's dream of professional soldiering seemed to melt into thin air.

The choice of Rome—Papal Rome, unchanged for centuries—as the next stage in the Prince's special training was well justified by precedent in foreign royal circles. The Prince's brother-in-law, Prince Frederick William of Prussia, had studied there for many months five years earlier, and in the summer of 1855 the boy King of Portugal, Pedro V., and his brother Luis—Saxe-Coburg cousins of Queen Victoria and of her husband—had followed in the Prussian Prince's footsteps.

A systematic course of sight-seeing and reading in archæology and art was to be supplemented by a duly safe-guarded intercourse with persons of interest and importance

57

who might be in Rome at the time, and by regulated observation of the urgent political issues which were agitating Italy
and neighbouring countries. If the political situation allowed,
a four or five months' stay at Rome would be followed by visits
to Florence, Perugia, and other cities of Northern Italy. After
a tour of the Italian lakes, rigorous study might be resumed
at Geneva. A minute programme, punctuated with abundant
cautions, was drafted by the Prince Consort and communicated
to Colonel Bruce. The Prince's governor carried out his instructions with scrupulous fidelity.

There were clear signs, on the eve of the visit to Rome, of
coming political disturbance in Italy. Under the leadership of
King Victor Emmanuel, King of Piedmont and Sardinia, and
of his minister Cavour, the Italian struggle for national unity
was in full cry. The degenerate King of Naples and other
independent rulers were under notice to quit their thrones.
The Pope's temporal sovereignty of the Papal States and Austria's
hold on Lombardy and Venetia were both in danger. The

Prince of Wales's recent host, Emperor Napoleon III., was
rehearsing for the rôle of redeemer of Italy from foreign domination and was meditating war on Austria. At the moment of
the Prince's departure the political ferment was nearing boiling-
point. "The Prince of Wales," his father wrote to Stockmar
on the 15th January 1859, "will have opportunities of seeing
and coming across much that is interesting. In this view we
have thought it better not to change his tour on account of the
crisis in politics." [1]

On the 10th January 1859 the Prince set out for Italy,
spending a leisurely month on the road.[2] Crossing from Dover
to Ostend, he called on King Leopold at his palace of Laeken,
near Brussels, and subsequently went sight-seeing in many
German cities—Frankfort, Innsbruck, Trent, Nuremberg, and
Munich among the rest. At length he entered Italy by the
Brenner Pass, and made at Verona his first stay in an
Italian city.

It was the earnest wish of King Victor Emmanuel, the fore-

---

[1] Martin's *Life of the Prince Consort*, iv. p. 65.
[2] In addition to Colonel and Mrs. Bruce, he was accompanied by his classical
tutor, Tarver, and his wife; by Captain Charles Grey, who now joined him as
equerry; by the Rev. T. K. Chambers as chaplain and archæological tutor, and
by Dr. Chalmers as medical attendant.

most figure in current Italian politics, to offer the earliest welcome on Italian soil to the English heir-apparent. Through his minister, Cavour, he sent the Prince an urgent invitation to make his entry by way of the Sardinian capital of Turin. The King had just opened his Parliament there, and had announced his determination to rescue Italy from her oppressors. On political and social grounds, to the King and Cavour's disappointment, the Prince's parents refused the proffered welcome. The Prince might study Italian politics only at a safe distance from the fires of controversy. Queen Victoria, moreover, regarded the King as an undesirable host for her son. "Il re galantuomo" had visited Windsor some time before (December 1855), and had won the Prince's esteem by the boast that "he could cut off an ox's head with one stroke of the sword." But he had shocked his hostess by his rough speech and manners, and she now feared that her son's innocence would be in peril if he met the unrefined monarch at his own fireside. Cavour remarked with enigmatic irony on this pronouncement that if the Prince brought "cette qualité précieuse," *i.e.* innocence, with him to Turin, he would not lose it there.[1]

At length, on 4th February, the Prince and his party reached Rome, and took up their quarters at the Hôtel d'Angleterre.

II

Study, according to plan, filled from the first the chief place in the Prince's daily routine. A time-table, against whose rigours the Prince at times rebelled, was put straightway into operation. "He learns by heart," Bruce wrote to his father on the 7th February, three days after his arrival, "in the morning before breakfast, and prepares for his Italian master who comes from 10 to 11 A.M. He reads with Mr. Tarver from 11 to 12, and translates French from 5 to 6 P.M., and has the next hour in the evening for private reading or music. He has a piano in his room." The afternoon was devoted to the inspection, under expert guidance, of ancient monuments and ancient and modern works of art.

The Prince Consort attached immense importance to his son's archæological and artistic studies. He had consulted the

---

[1] Nicomède Bianchi, *La Politique du Comte du Cavour*, Turin, 1885, p. 302.

President of the Royal Academy, Sir Charles Eastlake, and the authorities of the British Museum as to the best ciceroni. Joseph Barclay Pentland, the erudite author of Murray's handbook to Rome, who was residing in the city, was chosen to act as archæological guide, while the Prince's inspection of sculpture and painting was directed by the veteran English sculptor, John Gibson, R.A., who had spent a large part of his life in Rome. The Prince's chaplain, Mr. Chambers, also supplemented Pentland's and Gibson's guidance. Before leaving England Chambers applied to Ruskin, the Victorian critic of art, for advice how best to imbue the Prince with artistic sentiment. Ruskin, in an oracular reply, recommended that the Prince should be encouraged to think for himself, should be warned against regarding art "as a mere means of luxury and pride," and should be taught that "one of the main duties of Princes was to provide for the preservation of perishing frescoes and monuments." [1]

Under Mr. Pentland's auspices the Prince assiduously explored the Forum (still unexcavated), the Capitol, the Pantheon, the Coliseum (overgrown with weeds and wild flowers), the Appian Way, St. Peter's, and the Vatican. To the last two buildings he was a constant visitor. Minor churches, museums, and colleges also fell within his itinerary.

At the numerous studios to which Gibson introduced him the Prince made acquaintance with many painters and sculptors, English and foreign. The sociable American sculptors, Harriet Hosmer and W. W. Story, attracted him. Among English painters he was fascinated by Frederick Leighton, a subsequent President of the Royal Academy, now (in the Prince's words) a "young painter of great merit," under thirty. [2]

Much miscellaneous knowledge about the buildings, monuments, and artistic treasures of the city was gradually acquired, but the Prince's information was scarcely full or exact enough to satisfy the standards of his father, to whom Colonel Bruce was continually reporting the Prince's defects in "learning and mental qualities," as well as his ebullitions of temper.

[1] Ruskin's *Works*, ed. Cook and Wedderburn, vol. xxxvi. 297-300.
[2] On his first visit to Leighton's studio (February 24, 1859) the Prince wrote: "I admired three beautiful portraits of a Roman woman each representing the same person in a different attitude." Before he left Rome the Prince purchased a picture by Leighton called "Nanna," which is still in the royal collection.

Yet, towards the end of the sojourn at Rome, the Prince had
learned enough to enable him to act as cicerone to some who
freshly joined the party.   He took pride in conducting over
the Vatican and St. Peter's both Major Teesdale, who replaced
Captain Grey as his equerry, and Prince Victor of Hohenlohe,
the art-loving younger son of his mother's step-brother (better
known as Count Gleichen) who was his guest at Rome near
the end of the stay.

III

The Prince faithfully obeyed the paternal injunction of
keeping a diary at Rome.   Though the style is bald and there
are many echoes of guide-book phraseology, the record is coloured
by some refreshing touches of youthful *naïveté*.   The associations of England with Rome invariably caught the diarist's
attention.   "The Protestant cemetery," he writes, "contains the
tombs of the poets Shelley and Keats, and of Wyatt the sculptor.
Captain Grey discovered the tomb of an uncle of his who died
young, and I noticed that of Lady Hastings, who died in Rome
last year."   When he saw in St. Peter's the tombs of the exiled
Stuarts, James (the first Pretender) and his sons, Charles Edward,
the second Pretender, and Henry, Cardinal York, the Prince notes :
"I was very much interested by the inscriptions over the tombs,
in which succession to the throne of England is claimed by
the last of the Stuarts as James II., Charles III., and Henry
IX."   The experiments in chemistry and electricity which he
witnessed at the University of Rome reminded him of Faraday's
lectures.   Some entries lay characteristic stress on incidents which
made more human than historic appeal.   On the 21st April he
was present in the Sistine Chapel when the Pope washed the
feet of thirteen pilgrims.   His comment in his diary runs :

This I thought very ridiculous, as the Pope did not even
wet the feet of the pilgrims who were all seated in front of him,
but only touched them with a towel, and then gave each of the
pilgrims a medal.

Next day, Good Friday, he was better satisfied with a similar
performance elsewhere :

After dinner, at about 9 o'clock, we went to the Church of
St. Trinita de Monti, and saw some Cardinals wash the feet of a

great many beggars and afterwards wait at table; they really washed the feet of a great many very dirty beggars, and did not pretend only to do so as the Pope did.

The authorised amusements included occasional afternoon rides with Bruce and Grey in the Campagna and two visits a week to the opera.[1] Quite congenial, too, were the eleven days' festivities of the Carnival (February 24 to March 7), which he was allowed to watch at close quarters, either from a hired balcony overlooking the Corso or on drives up and down the thoroughfare. On the 1st March he writes of a drive through the Corso: "We were pelted continually with bouquets and confetti; and we pelted our assailants with a good will in our turn. We all entered into the fun of it with great spirit." At the close of the Carnival he penned the reflections:

The good temper of the people was very observable. For in spite of the pushing and the roughness of the play perfect good humour prevailed, and one could not help thinking how much violence and quarrelling would ensue if such amusement were attempted in Regent Street.

IV

The Prince's programme included a provision for a carefully regulated hospitality resembling that of which trial had been made at White Lodge. Twice a week the youth entertained at his hotel men of promise or of proved distinction in politics, arts, or letters, who were among Rome's numerous winter visitors. The guests were chosen by the Prince's governor who, with his wife, presided over the banquets. For the most part the visitors were the Prince's seniors, but a few were in early manhood, and three of these became fast friends. Most valuable to the Prince of these more youthful acquaintances was Mr. Odo Russell, an English diplomat of high promise in his thirtieth year, who was residing at Rome as intermediary between the English Government and the Vatican, although his formal position was that of Secretary of Legation at Florence to the Grand Duke of Tuscany. Odo Russell was soon in almost daily intercourse with the Prince and thus laid the foundation of a twenty-five years' uninterrupted "intimacy and

[1] Among the operas which he best appreciated were Bellini's *Norma*, which he heard twice, and Verdi's *Un Ballo in Maschera*.

friendship." Of Frederick Leighton the artist, who often joined the Prince's dinner-parties at Rome, the Prince recalled nearly forty years later, on the occasion of the artist's death, the advantage he enjoyed "of knowing him . . . ever since I was a boy (at Rome)." A third guest, the Prince's senior by only a year, who became a close associate, was the tenth Duke of St. Albans, a young man of weak character, who was in Rome with his mother.

But at the Prince's dinner-table ripe leaders in various walks of life predominated, and were encouraged by their young host's governor to give him the benefit of their experience. One chair was frequently filled by the veteran Lord Stratford de Redcliffe, "the Great Elchi," who was residing in Rome after resigning the British Embassy at Constantinople, where for a generation he had valiantly maintained the Sultan's power. Men of letters were well represented by Robert Browning, the poet who, when he accepted an invitation, was warned by Bruce "to eschew compliments and keep to Italian politics";[1] by Jean Jacques Ampère, the distinguished French writer; and by John Lothrop Motley, the American historian, who was writing his history of the United Netherlands and was vainly seeking access to the Vatican archives.[2]

The conversation often soared at the Prince's table above his head and he remained a silent listener. Colonel Bruce nervously feared that he was hardly appreciative of his guests' eminence. "His thoughts," he bewailed to his father, "are centred on matters of ceremony, on physical qualities, manners, social standing, and dress, and these are the distinctions which command his esteem." Yet the Prince's "engaging disposition and manners" gave his guests a favourable impression. Robert Browning declared him to be "a gentle refined boy" who listened attentively if he talked little, while the detailed and perhaps over-indulgent description of the Prince's appearance and demeanour which Motley the American penned after their first meeting at one of the Prince's dinner-parties may be worth quoting by way of a counterweight to the governor's strictures.

"The Prince's profile (Motley wrote) is extremely like that of the Queen. The complexion is pure, fresh, and healthy, like that

[1] *Letters of Robert and Elizabeth Barrett Browning*, ii. 309–12.
[2] *Correspondence of William I. and Bismarck*, i. 61.

of most English boys, his hair light brown, cut short, and curly. His eyes are bluish-grey, rather large, and very frank in his expression; his smile is very ready and genuine; his manners are extremely good. I have not had much to do with royal person- ages, but of those I have known I know none whose address is more winning, and with whom one feels more at one's ease. . . . At dinner he sat on one side of Mrs. Bruce and I on the other, and we talked upon the common topics, the table not being too large for general conversation. After dinner he asked me to take the chair next him and we conversed for half an hour together. He talked about German literature, Goethe and Schiller, and objects of art in Rome. Altogether the dinner was a very pleasant one, and it is very agreeable to me to have made the acquaintance of the future sovereign of the magnificent British Empire in such a simple and unceremonious manner." [1]

Every person of prominence in Rome sought the Prince's notice and usually offered him hospitality. Many would-be acquaintances were deemed by his watchful guardian unfit company for the Prince either on political, on religious, or on moral grounds. In any case Colonel Bruce was enjoined to be present whenever the Prince talked to any "foreigner or stranger," and tactfully to warn off undesirables. It was "indispensable," wrote the Queen, fearful of her son's boyish frankness, "that His Royal Highness should receive no foreigner or stranger alone, so that no report of pretended conversations with such persons could be circulated without immediate refutation" by Bruce.[2] The Prime Minister, Palmerston, according to the Queen, shared this view. Mr. Odo Russell's aid was enlisted in "keeping at arm's length all obnoxious persons and influences with which the Prince was confronted." Invitations to balls and receptions from political quarters were, with few exceptions, firmly refused. But escape from association with controversial elements of society was not always possible, and counsels of common sense showed the nervously anticipated risks of contamination to be negligible.

There was greater embarrassment in declining than in accept- ing the reception offered the Prince by the French Minister at the Vatican, the Duc de Grammont. In that brilliant scene the Prince was the central figure. All the prominent foreigners in Rome were there, and the hostess severally introduced her many

---

[1] Motley, *Correspondence*, ed. G. W. Curtis, 1889, i. 320.
[2] *Letters of Queen Victoria*, iii. 391.

guests to the Prince, who displayed his social self-possession to
advantage under the ordeal.   The importunities of Christina, the
dissolute ex-Queen of Spain, who had lately yielded her throne to
her equally disreputable daughter, Isabella, caused Colonel Bruce
especial perplexity.   The Prince, who met her at the French
reception, satisfied, however, her claims upon him by paying her
one brief formal visit.   The lady's third husband was with her
when the Prince called, and the Prince ingenuously mentioned in
his diary that he was "not of royal blood."   Another sovereign
in retirement at Rome was the Prince's godfather, Frederick
William IV. of Prussia, whose mind had given way.   It was
requisite for the Prince to call on him, but his wife, the Queen of
Prussia, alone received her husband's godson.

The Prince's attitude to the Irish Catholics who laid claim
to some of his attention did credit to all concerned.   Dr. (subsequently Cardinal) Paul Cullen, the Archbishop of Dublin, was staying at the Irish College of which he was rector.   Politically, the
Archbishop was well disposed to the British Crown, but as an ultra-
montane he was bitterly disliked by English Protestants.   The
Prince and his advisers wisely ignored Protestant prejudice, and
showed Irish Catholics in Rome every conciliatory courtesy.   On
St. Patrick's Day (March 17, 1859) the Prince visited both the
Irish Convent of St. Isidore and the Irish College.   Archbishop
Cullen welcomed him effusively to the College, and the Prince
accepted from a priest a sprig of shamrock, which he wore in his
hat for the rest of the day.

V

But above all other puzzles of procedure there towered the
questions raised by the pretensions of the rival potentates Pope
Pius IX. and King Victor Emmanuel—both astute statesmen—to
pay the Prince while on Italian soil personal honour.   Here again
wise courses were followed.

The sovereign Pontiff was at the time temporal as well as
spiritual ruler of Rome.   Mr. Odo Russell, in conformity with
precedent, had informed him of the Prince's coming to Rome.   In
a special audience the Pope had expressed to Russell his gratification that the Prince should prosecute his studies there, and had
directed his Secretary of State, the far-famed Cardinal Antonelli,
to do what he could to make the Prince's visit "useful and

pleasant." He was anxious, he added, that the Prince should carry away agreeable recollections. As soon as the Prince reached Rome the Papal Secretary opened negotiations with Col. Bruce and Mr. Russell for the Prince's early personal intro- duction to the Pope at the Vatican. The Prince's parents and the English Government approved the step, provided the reception were shorn of pomp, and that Col. Bruce was present at the interview. Protestant feeling had recently been stirred in England by the Pope's revival of Episcopal titles for the Catholic clergy in the United Kingdom, and by his defiance of the Ecclesi- astical Titles' Act, whereby the English Government had sought to suppress the titular dignities. The Prince's presence at the Vatican seemed certain to fan in England the anti-Roman flame.

But Queen Victoria was out of sympathy with the "No Popery" cry. She approved her son's visit to the Pope as a conventional act of courtesy on his part to a sovereign whose dominions he was visiting. There was a recent precedent, too, in the case of her son-in-law, Prince Frederick William of Prussia, who, when studying at Rome in 1854, had paid the Pontiff his respects in person. Colonel Bruce cherished some misgivings. None the less, on 10th February, the Prince, accompanied by his governor, Mr. Russell, and Captain Grey, drove to the Vatican in a closed carriage. By a special concession on the Pope's part Bruce was admitted with the Prince to the audience (February 10, 1859). The conversation was carried on in French, and the Pope talked with a friendliness and freedom which put his young visitor at his ease. He hoped the Prince was enjoying the sights of Rome. He remembered with pleasure the visit of the Prince's brother-in-law, Prince Frederick William of Prussia. The Papal power, he lamented, was very limited compared with what it was formerly. He expressed his satisfaction with the Queen's speech of a week before (February 3) in which the cause of peace and the sanctity of treaties had been powerfully urged. Peace was the Pope's earnest desire. Then, turning to a more controversial topic, he startled the Prince's nervous governor by remarking that in seeking to revive the Roman Catholic hierarchy in England he had no intention of manifesting any hostility to that country. In his view the time had come when bishops should replace vicars-apostolic, so as to make the Roman hierarchy complete.

At this point Bruce's patience gave way, and, contravening the 1859
calls of etiquette and to the subsequent resentment of the curia, Ætat. 17
he contrived to bring the interview to a hurried close.

Bruce justified himself to the Prince Consort on the ground
that the Pope was treading on very delicate ground. Another
breach with etiquette, to which his caution impelled him, was
less easy to defend. At the conclusion of the audience tradition
required the Prince to call on the Secretary of State, Cardinal
Antonelli. Mr. Odo Russell and Lord Stratford de Redcliffe
had, beforehand, strongly urged this procedure on the Prince,
but Bruce objected. He and the Prince now left the Vatican
without observing this common formula of courtesy. The
omission was, however, subsequently repaired, and the Prince
cherished kindly memories of the Cardinal's amiability.

The Prince's interview with the Pope, despite Bruce's stub-
bornness, fully satisfied Queen Victoria. To her uncle, Leopold,
she wrote on 15th February: "Bertie's interview with the Pope
went off extremely well. He was extremely kind and gracious,
and Col. Bruce was present; it would never have done to have
let Bertie go alone, as they might hereafter have pretended, God
knows! what Bertie had said." [1]

In spite of the Prince's refusal of King Victor Emmanuel's
early invitation to Turin the King soon renewed his advances,
and it was deemed essential by the British Government that the
English heir-apparent should show as large a measure of courtesy
to the King of Sardinia as to the Pope, the King's determined
foe. The Prince, therefore, accepted, without demur, Victor
Emmanuel's offer to confer on him in Rome the order of the
Annunciation and to entrust the investiture to Massimo,
Marquis d'Azeglio, the Sardinian Commissioner in the Romagna.
The fame of the King's envoy lent distinction to the episode.
The Marquis d'Azeglio ranks with Cavour and Garibaldi among
workers for Italian redemption. His name stood almost as
high in art and literature, as in politics, war, and diplomacy.
His versatile accomplishments deservedly moved the Prince's
astonishment.[2]

---

[1] *Letters of Queen Victoria*, iii. 411.

[2] The Marquis's nephew Emmanuel, Marquis d'Azeglio, was Sardinian
minister in London from 1851 to 1861, and after 1861 the first diplomatic
representative at the Court of St. James's of the newly united Kingdom of Italy.
The Prince frequently met him in London society in the latter capacity.

D' Azeglio reached the Prince's hotel in Rome on the 5th March, accompanied by Antonio Balbo, another distinguished Sardinian statesman. The Prince received the envoy in military uniform, and after D' Azeglio delivered to him a letter from his royal master, the investiture proceeded with much solemnity. In the evening the Prince entertained the Marquis at dinner, and speeches vowing mutual goodwill were exchanged. The Prince, although he scarcely knew or intended it, was voicing the ardent devotion of the mass of his fellow-countrymen to the cause of Italian unity.

The following is the Prince's record of the day's significant events :

Saturday, March 5.—At 11 o'clock the Marquis d' Azeglio, the celebrated Sardinian Statesman and Soldier, came to invest me with the Order of the Annunciation, in the name of the King of Sardinia, who has done me the honour of conferring it on me. The Marquis made a short speech in French before presenting the Order, which I answered in the same language, and begged him to thank the King in my name for it, expressing also my pleasure at receiving it at the hands of so distinguished a personage as himself.

When one considers that in addition to being a Statesman and most able diplomatist, he is a novelist, and an artist of such merit as to be able to support himself (as Mr. Russell told me he does) by the sale of his pictures, one cannot but admire the rich and varied powers of a mind so carefully cultivated. . . .

In the evening there was a dinner-party in honour of the Marquis d' Azeglio; it consisted of Lord and Lady Stratford de Redcliffe, Lady William and Mr. Russell, Mrs. Bruce, the Marquis d' Azeglio and M. Balbo, Count Minerva, the Sardinian Minister in Rome, and his attaché, and Colonel Percy.

After dinner I proposed the health of the King of Sardinia, to which the Marquis replied by proposing the health of my parents, and the Royal Family of England, finishing by saying that he called on the company to drink it—"d'autant plus que nous avons reçu aujourd'hui même, les nouvelles du baptême du fils de la Princesse Frederick Guillaume de Prusse."

The Prince had learnt from home, while travelling through Germany on his way to Italy, of the birth at Berlin on the 27th January 1859 of his first nephew, the future Kaiser William II. of Germany, whose adult career was to introduce elements of storm and stress into the life of the Prince and into the fortunes

of Europe and the world. From the lips of his versatile Italian
guest the Prince first received the news of his nephew's baptism.

VI

At the end of April, when the time for leaving Rome was
approaching, the threat of war which long overhung Italy was
suddenly fulfilled. The Austrian Emperor, aware of Napoleon
III.'s intention of joining King Victor Emmanuel in an attack
on the Austrian rule of North Italy, grasped the nettle and
declared war on the King of Sardinia. Thereupon the Prince's
plans were hastily revised. There was a summary abandonment of the proposed tour of the northern Italian cities and
lakes, and of the subsequent stay at Geneva for purposes of
study. The declaration of war plunged Rome and the neighbourhood into turmoil. The Prince Consort telegraphed to Bruce
to leave Rome at once for Gibraltar, and the Admiralty ordered
H.M.S. *Scourge* to embark the party at Civita Vecchia. On the
29th April the Prince took leave of Cardinal Antonelli, who
"was very civil and showed me his beautiful collection of
marbles." "I left Rome," he writes in his diary three days
later, "with very great regret, as I had spent three months
most agreeably there, and I think most instructively."

There was no wish on the part of his parents for the Prince
to hurry home. He was to seek compensation for his exclusion
from Italy in visits to scenes of historic interest farther west.

H.M.S. *Scourge* rapidly brought the Prince and his party
to Gibraltar, and he had his first view of the Rock. At Gibraltar
the Prince was met by the royal yacht *Osborne*, and in that vessel
he coasted round the neighbouring coast of Spain. He landed
at Malaga, and thence made an inland excursion to Granada,
where he inspected the Moorish palace of the Alhambra and
received from the British residents a rousing welcome. A
few days' walking tour through the romantic scenery of the
Andalusian Mountains brought him to Seville and Xeres, and
so to the sea at Cadiz. Crossing to Tangier on the Morocco coast
—the centre of ample political controversy in future years—
he thence, by his father's orders, turned north to inspect Cape
Trafalgar and Cape St. Vincent—scenes of heroic achievement
in English naval history.

An ironic significance seemed to attach to the Prince's landing at San Lucar, midway between the two capes, in order to visit the Duc and Duchesse de Montpensier (June 6, 1859). The Duc was a younger son of King Louis Philippe, and his marriage to the sister of Queen Isabella of Spain, some thirteen years before, had given such grave offence to Queen Victoria and her Ministers as to shatter the budding hopes of a first *entente cordiale*. Much had happened since that offending union. Its contriver, King Louis Philippe, had died in exile, and his misfortunes had dissolved Queen Victoria's and Prince Albert's resentment. The Prince's visit to the Duc and Duchesse de Montpensier was an act of reconciliation in his parents' name. The Prince made the acquaintance of his host's and hostess's young daughter, Mercédes, who afterwards married, as his first wife, Alfonso XII., King of Spain, but death cut short that marriage after a few months, and thus finally dismissed King Louis Philippe's ill-omened dream of a line of Orléanists on the Spanish throne.

There followed a stay in another part of the Peninsula which had for the Prince a different set of associations. On the 8th June the Prince reached Lisbon to enjoy the hospitality of Dom Pedro V., the young King of Portugal, whom ties of kinship and affection closely linked with the Prince's parents. King Pedro, whom before his accession the Prince had met at Windsor, was the son of that Queen Maria da Gloria who, after being brought up in England as Queen Victoria's playmate, had married Prince Ferdinand of Saxe-Coburg—a first cousin of both Queen Victoria and her husband. Queen Victoria's interest in Dom Pedro had lately been stimulated by his marriage into a younger branch of the Prussian royal family, for members of which she and her husband cherished an especially warm feeling, the bride being Stephanie, eldest daughter of Prince Charles Anthony of Hohenzollern-Sigmaringen.

The Portuguese King and Queen welcomed the Prince with a cordiality which left an indelible impression. Henceforth, the Prince loyally befriended successive wearers of the Portuguese Crown, on whom black shadows were to fall. The tragic ill-luck of Portuguese royalty was indeed ominously adumbrated soon after the Prince's departure from King Pedro's roof. Within a month Queen Stephanie died suddenly of diphtheria. Queen

Victoria, who on receipt of the sad news burst into paroxysms
of grief, was greatly consoled by a letter from her eldest son,
which she deemed to be unusually well expressed and to be a
welcome proof of his developing sympathies. "It is not a month
since I left Lisbon," the Prince wrote; "she was then looking
well and hearty. I never would have supposed that when I
took leave of her that it was the last time I should see her again.
It is a lesson to us how uncertain our life is and how one ought
to value one's friends and relatives when one has them near one."

VII

The Prince reached home at the end of June 1859, after six
months' absence. His return was celebrated by his installation
with full ceremony, at the public expense, as Knight of the
Garter. But his father was in a critical mood. He looked
anxiously for those signs of intellectual improvement in his son
which he had confidently anticipated from the long tour. He
discovered fewer than he hoped for. His son's diary seemed to
him to be meagre and to show little reflective power or marks
of archæological or historical acumen. He admitted that the
youth had exhibited a "turn" for social functions, but external
graces counted for little with the Prince Consort compared
with solid mental acquirements.

On the 26th June, Prince von Hohenlohe, a cousin of Queen
Victoria and a future Chancellor of the German Empire, dined
at Buckingham Palace while on a visit to England. The German
guest learnt from the Prince of Wales "a great deal about Rome
and his sea trip to Gibraltar." The young man gave Prince
von Hohenlohe an impression of good breeding, but the visitor
deplored the Prince's short stature, and was dismayed by signs
of his nervous awe of his father. Prince von Hohenlohe feared
that the Prince Consort was irredeemably a doctrinaire.[1]

[1] Prince Chlodwig of Hohenlohe-Schillingfurst, *Memoirs*, 1906, vol. i. 88.

CHAPTER VI

AT EDINBURGH AND OXFORD

1859

Ætat. 17

ALTHOUGH the Prince of Wales continued to clamour for Aldershot, Oxford, according to his father's comprehensive plan of training, was already appointed to be the next substantive rung in his son's educational ladder. At Oxford the unhappy youth was to specialise in history, in law, and in the practical applications of natural science.

I

To the place of applied science in his son's curriculum the Prince Consort sagaciously attached an especial importance. The development of scientific knowledge and scientific mechanism was a commanding feature of the age and justly deserved in the Prince Consort's view a larger measure of educational recognition than it was receiving. Dr. Lyon Playfair, Professor of Chemistry in the University of Edinburgh, had rendered the Prince Consort important aid in organising the Great Exhibition of 1851 and in developing technical instruction through the country. On Playfair's advice, the Prince Consort decided that his son should spend the summer and autumn, before the Oxford academic year reopened, at Edinburgh, in order to pursue, under Playfair's direction, a preliminary course in applied science. Scientific principles might be studied theoretically and experimentally in the Professor's laboratory, and the Prince might visit with him the iron works and cotton mills of Glasgow and the textile factories and gas works of Edinburgh in order to familiarise himself with industrial processes. A practical knowledge of the staple industries of the country was, Playfair argued, "of great importance to a Prince destined to fill an important position."

72

Opportunities might also be found at Edinburgh for continuing the youth's study of ancient history, Italian, French, and German.

Accordingly, in July, the Prince took up his residence in Holyrood Palace with Colonel Bruce and Mr. Tarver, with a view to a three months' preparation for Oxford. A senior student of Christ Church, now a London barrister, Mr. Herbert Fisher, was summoned to prepare the Prince for the studies in law and modern history to which it was intended that he should apply himself at Oxford.

The Prince Consort also enlisted the aid of the Rector of the High School at Edinburgh, Dr. Leonard Schmitz, whom he sympathetically described as "a German," in instructing his son, for one hour each day, in Greek and Roman history.

The Edinburgh plans of study were punctually carried out, and the results, despite the severity of the discipline, were promising. Playfair interested the Prince in his laboratory experiments. On one occasion the Professor tested his pupil's courage with triumphant result. The Prince and Playfair were standing near a cauldron containing lead which was boiling at white heat. "Has your Highness any faith in science?" asked the Professor. "Certainly," replied the Prince. Playfair thereupon washed the Prince's hand thoroughly with ammonia, and then invited him to place it "in this boiling metal and ladle out a portion of it." The Prince asked, "Do you tell me to do this?" and on Playfair replying "I do," the Prince instantly put his hand into the cauldron and ladled out some of the boiling metal. He suffered no injury in the process, but the experiment required a stout nerve.[1] Dr. Leonard Schmitz also found the Prince a satisfactory pupil. He had been specially warned by a friend at Court, Sir James Clark, the Queen's physician, who had caught the prevailing tone of depreciatory criticism of the Prince, that he would "find the Prince very backward for his age" and that it would be difficult "to keep up his attention even for a short time." But the German scholar, an efficient and experienced teacher, soon reported that "the Prince's powers of application" were underrated and that both his "disposition and capacity" promised well.[2]

1859
Ætat. 17

---

[1] Reid's *Memoirs of Lyon Playfair*, 201.
[2] Three letters from Sir James Clark to Dr. Schmitz in July 1859 discussing

A modest provision was made for recreation. There were excursions to the Trossachs and the Scottish lakes. Thrice a week the Prince exercised with the 16th Hussars, who were stationed in the city. Dinner-parties were arranged at Holyrood on the serious lines which had been followed at White Lodge and at Rome. The Lord Advocate (Lord Melville), the Provost of Edinburgh, the Sheriff of Midlothian, together with Playfair, Dr. Schmitz, and other instructors, made up the solemn company. Any more exhilarating society was proscribed. Invitations to shoot with the Duke of Atholl at Blair Castle, and with other noblemen on neighbouring estates, were declined.

In September the Prince Consort came over to Edinburgh from Balmoral to hold, as he wrote to his friend Stockmar, "an educational conference with all the persons who are taking part in the education of the Prince of Wales." There were present, besides Colonel Bruce and Tarver, Playfair, the other Edinburgh teachers, and Mr. Fisher of Oxford. "All," the Prince Consort admitted, "speak highly of him, and he seems to have shown zeal and good-will." The Oxford curriculum was discussed and drafted and a supplementary course of study at Cambridge was suggested.

Public opinion was somewhat exercised by what was known of the colossal educational regimen to which the Prince Consort was submitting his eldest son. There was a widespread feeling that the training was unduly severe and prolonged, and when rumours of the Edinburgh conference spread abroad, *Punch*, on 20th September, voiced the public doubt in some verses entitled "A Prince at High Pressure." Playful protest was made against the discursive methods of "cramming" which, begun by Gibbs and continued by Tarver, were now being pursued at Edinburgh. *Punch* foretold that after being "whipped to the Isis" the "poor lad" was "to be plunged in less orthodox Cam."

> Where next the boy may go to swell the farrago,
> We haven't yet heard, but the Palace they're plotting in;
> To Berlin, Jena, Bonn, he'll no doubt be passed on,
> And drop in for a finishing touch, p'raps at Gottingen.

Dr. Schmitz's impressions of the Prince's intellectual capacity are in the Advocates' Library, Edinburgh (MS. 20.5.12). They have been kindly communicated by the Librarian to the Advocates' Library, Dr. W. K. Dickson.

Although his father regretted the abbreviation of his stay at
Edinburgh, the Prince arrived at Balmoral on a well-earned
vacation towards the close of September. At Balmoral the
Prince enlarged his experience of sport. He engaged in deer-
stalking, besides making some strenuous expeditions on foot.
He walked with his father up and down Ben Muich Dhui, the
second highest hill in Great Britain (4927 feet high), and the
exploit won the admiration of Queen Victoria.[1] Colonel Bruce
was absent, and the Prince wrote to him of his holiday in
confiding terms, which show that he bore his stern governor no
ill-will. In one letter to Bruce the Prince of Wales (October 2)
reported, exultingly :

Last Friday I was fortunate enough to kill two Royal Stags
which I am very proud of, one weighed 17 stone 2 lbs., and the
other 16 stone 3 lbs. . . . Yesterday the Prince (Consort) killed
a good stag, but he was not as heavy as my two.

II

The Prince's education entered its next appointed stage in
October 1859, when he became an undergraduate of the University
of Oxford. He remained in residence with few interruptions
through the academic year, and returned for the last weeks of the
succeeding Michaelmas term.

For fully a year before, the Prince Consort had been in consultation with Dr. Liddell, the Dean of Christ Church, as to the
conditions of life appropriate at Oxford to the heir-apparent.[2]
The Prince Consort, who was unacquainted with Oxford customs,
at first demurred to his son's association with a "particular
college." His son, he argued, "belongs to the whole university."
He "will always belong to the whole nation, and not to the
Peerage, the Army, etc. etc., although he may form part of them.
He can and ought never to belong to party or faction or coterie
or closed society, etc." But Dean Liddell held out no hope that
the University would allow the Prince to join it on such abstract
terms. The Prince Consort finally agreed to his son's admission
to Christ Church on the understanding that he should reside,

[1] *Journal of our Life in the Highlands*, pp. 184–8.
[2] Dr. Liddell had, as long ago as 1846, succeeded Dr. Samuel Wilberforce
as domestic chaplain to the Prince Consort, and had steadily grown in the
royal confidence.

1859
Ætat. 17

not in the College, but in "an entirely separate establishment," where he might be under the supervision of his governor, Colonel Bruce. Frewin Hall, off Cornmarket Street, was consequently hired for the young man's accommodation, with Colonel Bruce in full control and Colonel Teesdale in residence as the Prince's equerry.

On the 17th October 1859 the Prince arrived in Oxford and formally joined Christ Church in the now obsolete grade of "nobleman," which entitled him to wear a gold-tasselled cap. As soon as Dean Liddell, the head of the College, had entered his name in the College Register,[1] he conducted him to Pembroke College, where the Prince was duly matriculated by Dr. Francis Jeune, the Master, who was at the time Vice-Chancellor of the University.[2] It was the first recorded occasion on which a Prince of Wales had become an Oxford undergraduate. Tradition alone vouches for the matriculation in 1398 of Prince Henry, afterwards Henry V. —Prince Hal—with whom the new royal undergraduate was often to be linked by the satirists hereafter.

The Prince Consort's son, living in more or less seclusion at Frewin Hall, was excluded from many ordinary experiences of an undergraduate. He regularly attended College chapel and occasionally dined in hall at the noblemen's table. But his father deprecated any free association with young men of his own age or any unfettered choice of friends. "The more I think of it," the Prince Consort had written early to the Dean of Christ Church (October 21, 1858), "the more I see the difficulties of the Prince being thrown together with other young men and having to make his selection of acquaintances when so thrown together with them." "The only use of Oxford is that it is a place for *study*," wrote the Prince Consort with rather narrow vision on the 27th October 1859, "a refuge from the world and its claims."[3]

[1] The entry in the College Register is on a page by itself, and is in Dean Liddell's handwriting. The words run: "Celsissimus Princeps Albertus Edwardus, Princeps de Guallia, Admissus XVIImo die Octobris MDCCCLIX." (kindly communicated by Dr. White, Dean of Christ Church).
[2] The matriculation entry in the University Register runs thus:
"Term Mich. Oxoniæ, Die Oct. 17 Anno Domini 1859. Quo die comparuit coram me Albertus Edwardus Walliæ Princeps e Coll. ex Æde Christi, Reg. Angl. Fil. Nat. Max. et admonitus est de observandis statutis hujus Universitatis, et in Matriculum Universitatis relatus est.—Franciscus Jeune, *Vice-Can.*"
[3] Esher, *The Influence of King Edward*, 1915, p. 28.

Distinguished professors undertook, at the Prince Consort's 1859
request, the direction of the Prince's studies. Instruction was Ætat. 17
to be given for the most part privately, but his boy friends,
Charles Wood and William Henry Gladstone, now undergraduates of Christ Church, with four other carefully chosen
members of the College, were suffered to join the Prince at his
special courses. Sir Benjamin Brodie, Professor of Chemistry,
gave the Prince two hours' private instruction weekly in science,
and the young man was also allowed to attend two of Sir
Benjamin's weekly public lectures. The Prince Consort attached
particular importance to his son's religious teaching. This was
entrusted to Arthur Penrhyn Stanley, Professor of Ecclesiastical
History and Canon of Christ Church, who could be relied on to
guard his pupil against extreme views of either the High Church
or the Low Church parties.[1] The youth's study of German
and German literature was guided by Friedrich Max Müller,
Taylorian Professor of Modern European Languages, who
had been first brought from Germany to England by Baron
von Bunsen, the former Prussian Minister. Thrice a week
Goldwin Smith, Regius Professor of Modern History, lectured
informally on English History to the Prince and his select
companions in the dining-room of New Inn Hall, which
adjoined Frewin Hall. It was unfortunate that the professor
should have made his text-book the dry *Annals of England*,
by W. E. Flaherty (1855). His lectures took the form of
epigrammatic comments on the *Annals* as he hurriedly turned
over the pages. Goldwin Smith's effort to stimulate the Prince's
historical interests by turning his attention to Sir Walter Scott's
novels was scarcely successful. The professor found his royal
pupil impatient of steady reading, even in the form of fiction.

Mr. Herbert Fisher of Christ Church, who had already
begun work with the Prince at Holyrood, acted as the Prince's
College Tutor and gave him private instruction in law. At the
end of each term, Dr. Liddell promised the Prince Consort to
arrange for the Prince's examination in each of his subjects
of study, and the Prince Consort frequently visited Oxford
in order to assure himself of his son's good conduct, diligence,
and health, which was looked after by Dr. (afterwards Sir) Henry
Acland, Regius Professor of Medicine.

[1] Prothero and Bradley, *Life of Stanley*, ii. 64.

Whatever boredom the Prince experienced in the Oxford lecture rooms, he was impressed by his teachers' attainments, and with well-nigh all of them he formed the pleasantest relations for life. On his academic guides he made from the first a good impression as far as character and manner went, although they differed about his intellectual capacities. Dean Liddell described him during the first days of his college life as "the nicest fellow possible, so simple, naïf, ingenuous, and modest, and moreover with extremely good wits; possessing also the royal faculty of never forgetting a face."[1] The Prince greatly enjoyed the private hospitalities of the Dean and his family, and remained in friendly correspondence with Mrs. Liddell till her death. After a lapse of forty years he reminded her of the "many charming hours" which he spent at the deanery. Goldwin Smith, in spite of his democratic zeal and his doubts of the Prince's mental vigour, acknowledged his pupil's charm, and the Prince watched with sympathetic curiosity the later fortunes of the professor, who abruptly left Oxford in 1867. "Goldwin Smith," the Prince wrote to Dr. Acland at the time of Goldwin Smith's retirement from the University, with intelligent appreciation of his former tutor's idiosyncrasies, "must be a great loss to Oxford, but the place was too conservative for him. I wonder if he will try to get into Parliament?"[2] The ex-professor soon settled in America, and at the close of half a century the Prince recalled in a kindly message to the voluntary exile their old Oxford association. Dr. Acland and Dr. Stanley, afterwards Dean of Westminster, were the Oxford professors who excited the Prince's warmest admiration. Both frequently entertained him at Oxford and both were his travelling companions in coming tours abroad. With Acland a fifty years' affectionate correspondence survives. When he and Max Müller, also one of the Prince's friends from his Oxford days, died within a few months of one another in 1898, the Prince, writing to Mrs. Liddell (November 15) breathed doubts as to whether men of equal calibre were at hand to "follow in their footsteps."

By way of supplement to the strictly educational routine

[1] Thompson, *Memoir of Liddell*, p. 178.
[2] Prince to Acland, 14th November 1867.

at Oxford Colonel Bruce, by the Prince Consort's direction,
arranged for dinner-parties at Frewin Hall of the accepted
pattern. "Your convivial meetings at dinner," the Prince
Consort wrote to Bruce, "will give the best means for" social
intercourse between the Prince and "the most distinguished
men of the place." Young men, who might be included in the
company to "give variety and interest to the conversation,"
would, the Prince Consort anticipated, enjoy the advantage
of meeting "familiarly those from whom they expect to derive
the benefit of education, and between whom and themselves
the habit and circumstances have placed unnecessary and
hurtful barriers." The talk at the Prince's Oxford dinner-
table was mainly literary and academic, but the Prince followed
it very tolerantly. One of the young men who were among the
guests, Lionel Tollemache, records how, when the merits of
George Eliot's novels—at the time enjoying a great vogue—
came up for discussion, the Prince surprised the company by
speaking admiringly of *Adam Bede*, a work which Goldwin
Smith, the chief guest of the evening, sourly depreciated.[1]

An authorised relaxation from the restraints of Frewin Hall
was occasional attendance at the debates at the Union, of which
the Prince was elected an honorary member on 1st November
1859. He freely criticised the undergraduates' dialectics, although
he was warned against taking sides in current controversies.
The first debate to which he listened (on November 3) concerned
the vexed question of the Abolition of Church Rates. A few
weeks later, 15th December, he heard a fellow-undergraduate
of Christ Church, Sidney Edward Bouverie Pusey, a nephew of
the ecclesiastical professor, propose the motion: "That this
house considers the usual view of Henry VIII. to be the correct
one, as opposed to Mr. Froude's." [2] In a letter to his friend
Cadogan, written the same night, the Prince describes the
debate as "a complete failure. Pusey made a very bad, short,
stupid speech and they had great difficulty to get any one to
answer him."

Although the Queen and the Prince Consort wished their
son at Oxford to confine his athletic attentions to "tennis and

---

[1] Tollemache, *Nuts and Chestnuts*, 1911, p. 19.
[2] Notes from the Union Minute Books, kindly supplied by the Senior
Treasurer, the Rev. Dr. A. J. Carlyle.

1859
Ætat. 17

racquets" and deprecated hunting as an encroachment on study, his governor suffered him occasionally to ride to hounds. With the South Oxfordshire pack, of which Lord Macclesfield was master, the Prince saw his first fox killed on the 27th February 1860, when he was presented with the brush. The hunting field brought him into touch with some young Christ Church men of sporting rather than studious tastes, to two of whom, Mr. Henry Chaplin, afterwards Viscount Chaplin, and Sir Frederick Johnstone, he formed a lifelong attachment. Under their influences the Prince found means of breaking away at times from gubernatorial leading-strings. Smoking was strictly prohibited by his guardian, but he succeeded in making surreptitious experiment in the company of fellow-undergraduates, and he thus formed the lifelong habit of a free indulgence in tobacco.

III

1860
Ætat. 18

Invitations from the great houses around Oxford were as a rule refused by the Prince owing to his father's disapproval of his quitting Oxford during term-time. An exeat was allowed only on rare occasions. As an exceptional concession he was permitted, in his first term, to dine at Nuneham with the Harcourts to meet the Duc and Duchesse d'Aumale, the exiled Orléanists of France, to whom his parents were always wishful that he should pay attention, and he visited the Bishop of Oxford, Samuel Wilberforce, at Cuddesdon.

An important incident in his career withdrew him to Windsor for a day or two in November. There he celebrated his eighteenth birthday—his virtual coming of age (November 9, 1859). The historic importance of the celebration was acknowledged by the leading newspaper, *The Times*, whose editor, Delane, was a sympathetic but frank critic of royalty. In the chief leading-article of the day the writer called attention to the renewed popularity of the monarchy owing to Queen Victoria's "eminent personal qualities," to the conduct of her domestic life, and to her fidelity to the Constitution. The Prince was naturally advised to follow in his parents' footsteps, but there was perhaps a spice of irony in the concluding reflection: "It is the happiness of a King of England that we expect of him no brilliant military

achievements, no extraordinary diplomatic legerdemain, no
startling effects, no scenic pomps, no histrionic dexterity. He
may be great without the possession of extraordinary talents
and famous without dazzling exploits." Delane, who inspired
the article, was in close touch with the Court and echoed the
disappointing conviction cherished there that the heir-apparent,
now come of age, showed no signs of commanding ability.

IV

The Easter vacation (April 6–24, 1860) was once again spent
abroad. He visited his father's kinsfolk in their homes at
Coburg and Gotha. All along the route—at Brussels, Cologne,
and Magdeburg—relatives flocked to offer him warm greetings on
this filial journey of homage to the scenes amid which his father
was born and bred. At Brussels he dined in state at the Palace
with the King. At Magdeburg, at 4 A.M., he met, on the way
to his hotel, "Fritz" (his brother-in-law) hurrying to Potsdam
for a military inspection. Later in the morning he breakfasted with his sister, the Crown Princess, and afterwards improved the occasion by going with her over the Cathedral,
which he described as "very fine." At Gotha the Prince's
uncle, Ernest, the reigning Duke of Saxe-Coburg-Gotha, proved
an untiring host. At the theatre he caused to be acted in his
nephew's honour an opera *Santa Chiarra*, which he had himself
just composed. At Coburg, under his uncle's assiduous guidance,
the Prince closely inspected the places associated with his father's
youth, spending much time at the Natural History Museum, which
his father and uncle had formed in boyhood. There was a hurried
excursion to the centre of old German culture, Weimar, where
"the Grand Duke and Duchess were very civil and the Grand
Duke gave me his order just before I left." Before leaving
Coburg he duly performed, on his mother's behalf, a mission
which excited in him somewhat mixed feelings. Baron Stockmar,
who had finally left England in 1857, was spending in the town
his last years in failing health. The Prince delivered letters
from the Queen to the pedantic contriver of his severe upbringing.
"I visited the Baron after breakfast," the Prince wrote to her,
"and found him looking very well, wonderfully so as he has not
left his rooms for 5 months. He seemed pleased to see me

and to receive your letters." The meeting left on the Baron a favourable impression which was of good augury. On the 24th of April the Prince was back in London. Next day Queen Victoria wrote to her uncle, Leopold :

> Bertie returned last night delighted with his tour and with our beloved old Coburg in *spite* of *snow*. . . . He made a very favourable impression there. He gives a good account of dear Stockmar too.[1]

The Prince brought his father a long letter from the veteran Stockmar congratulating the Prince Consort on the many signs of improvement which he saw "in the young gentle- man." The intimation, the father replied, "is a great joy and comfort to us; for parents who watch their son with anxiety and set their hopes for him high are in some measure incapable of forming a clear estimate and are at the same time apt to be impatient if their wishes are not fulfilled."[2] There was much in this observation to atone for some harsh judgements which the father had already passed on his eldest son.

V

The summer term of 1860 was spent at Oxford on the prescribed lines. The Prince took part in the festivities of Commemoration, and his knowledge of representative men of the passing generation was increased by an introduction to Lord Brougham, who, at the age of eighty-two, received at the Encænia the honorary degree of D.C.L. The veteran law-reformer and educational pioneer well rounded off the list of eminent early Victorian patriarchs with whom the Prince came into contact in his nonage. Some five years later he was interested to meet the same eminent octogenarian again—at a banquet of the Fishmongers' Company in the city of London, and he wrote of the old man to his mother : "Lord Brougham was there and made a very long speech, and at his great age he possesses all his faculties and wonderful memory."

---

[1] *Letters of Queen Victoria*, iii. 504.
[2] Martin, *Life of Prince Consort*, vol. v. 15.

CHAPTER VII

A MISSION TO THE NEW WORLD

I

BEFORE many weeks of the Long Vacation of 1860 had passed the Prince was to tread a larger stage than any before. There was to be a striking expansion of recent schemes of foreign travel. For the first time in history, the heir to the English throne was to cross the Atlantic, and to visit not only the oldest of England's overseas settlements, but also the American Republic.

The Imperialist sentiment was, in the Prince's prime, to link the mother-country and her widely scattered overseas dominions and dependencies in staunch bonds of affection and respect. But in 1860 that sentiment was a sensitive plant of precarious life. Neither of the two great political parties yet fully identified themselves with the principle of Imperial solidarity. Leading politicians in both camps prophesied complacently that, with increase of population and wealth, the British colonies were certain to break away from England, and that, while the holding of India might be necessary to British prestige, small advantage came from England's relations with the rest of her dependencies. Lord Palmerston, who had become Prime Minister in 1859, concentrated too much attention on foreign affairs to consider with any thoroughness colonial problems. The Duke of Newcastle, Lord Palmerston's colleague at the Colonial Office, alone among Cabinet Ministers of the day identified himself with the nascent view that it was the home Government's duty to strengthen Imperial "bonds of mutual sympathy and of mutual obligation." To Queen Victoria and the Prince Consort that enlightened conception of Empire made a steadily growing appeal.

As for the relations of England with the American Republic,

there was, among the wiser heads of both countries, a strong wish
for harmony, but a genuine or permanent cordiality between the
peoples was commonly reckoned a counsel of perfection.   The
sentiment that blood is thicker than water seemed to harbour
small practical virtue.   Memories of the warfare of 1776 and 1812,
though dying, were not yet dead in either country.   Hostilities
might easily revive.   The United States was generally credited
in England with the resolve to annex Canada.   The English
prejudice, too, against the Republican form of government still
lingered, while the recent immigration into America (after the
famine years) of thousands of Anglophobe Irishmen and Irishwomen gave the old Anglo-American rancours a new stimulus.
On the pending anti-slavery agitation, which was soon to issue in
civil war between the Northern and Southern States, English
opinion was sharply divided, and the controversy threatened
fresh causes of estrangement between the two nations.

The bold venture of sending the English heir-apparent on a
mission of friendship to both Canada and the United States was
in many quarters held to be over-rash.   Within the Colonial
Office itself there were reactionary mutterings to the effect that
the Prince of Wales was put forward to draw closer "ties that
might better be slackened."[1] The Prince Consort challenged
such short-sighted vision alike in public and private by declaring
his conviction that it was the duty of English Princes to work for
the consolidation of the Empire.[2] *The Times* in its traditional
tone of independence rejoiced in so signal a breach of the veteran
"tradition of . . . the immobility of royalty."   The journal
assigned much of "the narrowness" of Queen Victoria's
Hanoverian predecessors to their remaining "habitually within a
certain radius of" London.   "For the first time since the discovery

[1] Lyall's *Dufferin*, 1905, vol. i. 285.

[2] At the same time as the Prince of Wales was to make his Atlantic voyage,
it was settled that his next brother, Alfred, should sail to the Cape of Good Hope
and lay the foundation-stone of the great breakwater in Cape Town harbour.
Referring to these two engagements of his sons, the Prince Consort wrote to
Stockmar (April 27, 1860): "What a cheering picture is here of the progress
and expansion of the British race and of the useful co-operation of the royal
family in the civilisation which England has developed and advanced" (Martin,
vol. v. 15-16). A little later the Prince claimed in a speech at a Trinity House
dinner that his two sons might fitly play a beneficent part "in the development
of those distant and rising countries who recognise in the British Crown and
their allegiance to it their supreme bond of union with the mother-country and
with each other" (*ibid.*).

of America an heir-apparent to the British Crown is to cross the
Atlantic and in his character as a future ruler of this Empire to
receive the respects of one of its most flourishing provinces." A
visit to the United States would at the same time "tend to draw
closer the bonds which unite the two countries." The event
confirmed the optimistic argument and refuted all the presages
of evil.

1860
Ætat. 18

II

The circumstances out of which the project of the Prince's
visit to the new world arose are of historic interest.

During the Crimean War the Canadian Government testified
a devotion to the mother-country, which few English politicians
reciprocated, by levying and equipping a regiment of infantry for
service in the field. Subsequently a deputation from Canada
invited Queen Victoria to visit the Colony. She replied that the
risks and fatigues of the voyage were prohibitive. Thereupon
the Canadian Government asked her to send out one of her sons
to serve as Governor-General. The Queen pointed out that her
sons were too young, but in the end she showed her sympathy with
the Canadian Imperial sentiment by promising that the Prince of
Wales, as soon as he was old enough, should pay Canada a visit.
It was this promise that was fulfilled in the autumn of 1860.

The Prince had not yet completed his nineteenth year, but
he had already come to close quarters with Canadian loyalty to
England. On leaving England for his sojourn at Rome some
eighteen months earlier he had paused at Shorncliffe Camp to
present new colours to a regiment (100th Foot) which had
won renown in Canada during the American War of 1812, and
had consequently been christened the Royal Canadians. The
presentation of the new colours to the regiment was the first
military ceremonial which the Prince had conducted, and the
event was commemorated by the expansion of the regiment's
title into "The Prince of Wales's Canadian Regiment." Thus
early he associated himself with the colonial sense of Empire.

The autumn of 1860 presented a peculiarly appropriate season
for the Prince's personal introduction to Canadian territory owing
to the fact that two structures in Canada of imposing significance
were about to be dedicated to public uses: the notable railway
bridge across the St. Lawrence at Montreal was on the point of

1860
Ætat. 18

completion, and the Parliament House at Ottawa, the new capital of the United Canadas, was just rising from its foundations. It seemed to be of happy augury for the heir-apparent to perform in behalf of the sovereign the public ceremonies of opening the bridge and of laying the foundation of the Parliament House. The bridge, on the one hand, was for the time the high-water mark of the world's engineering ingenuity as well as the mighty link between widely divided territories; on the other hand, the projected Parliament House symbolised the fusion of the French and English colonial elements, long deemed incapable of coalescence, into an organic whole.

As soon as the Canadian tour was announced, instincts of hospitality and curiosity were stirred in the United States. James Buchanan, the President, wrote to Queen Victoria inviting the Prince to spend a few days with him at the White House. President Buchanan, now nearing the end of his term of office, was the last Democrat in the Presidential chair to be identified with the cause of slavery, and was soon to give place to Abraham Lincoln, the Republican champion of the slave. President Buchanan had been American Minister to Great Britain for the three years preceding his election to the White House in 1856, and he had helped to smooth irritating difficulties between his Government and England over an alleged infringement of the Monroe Doctrine in British Honduras, where the boundaries were in course of revision. He had been entertained by the Queen at Windsor, as he thought at the time rather coldly. He now prophesied with fervour that the Prince of Wales's visit to Washington would improve the relations between the two countries. At the same time the American Minister in London, Mr. Dallas, offered through the Foreign Secretary, Lord John Russell, an independent invitation to the Prince from the municipality of New York.

Lord Lyons, the British Minister at Washington, who was consulted, was favourable to an acceptance of both American invitations. Compliance, he wrote to Lord John, would be regarded "as a great compliment to the nation." There was not likely (he thought) to be much trouble from the Irish-Americans, but American crowds were apt to be exacting and intrusive, and American railways were not very safe. Queen Victoria followed Lord Lyons's counsel with certain qualifications.

Apart from political circumstance there was a domestic
consideration which justified in the Queen's mind the inclusion
of America as well as Canada in her son's tour. She had often
heard of her father's travel over the same ground, which, though
it happened long before she was born, was a living tradition alike
in the family circle of her youth and across the Atlantic. At
the end of the eighteenth and the beginning of the nineteenth
century, her father, at first as Prince Edward, afterwards as
the Duke of Kent, had discharged military duties in British North
America, and his holiday tours in the United States, during one
of which he attended Mrs. Washington's New Year reception at
the White House, had not yet faded from American memory.
But the Queen's willingness for her son to follow in her father's
American footsteps was guarded by some imperative provisos
of her devising.[1] His status in Canada must be carefully
distinguished from that in America. In Canada the Prince might
act as the sovereign's deputy. But in the United States he was
to figure only "in the character of a student"; was to adopt the
incognito title of Baron of Renfrew; was to study American life;
and, save at Washington, where he might enjoy the President's
hospitality, was to lodge in hotels and not in private houses.
The Prince was all obedience, and readily assured his mother that
he realised "the great importance of the mission" with which she
was entrusting him. "I will do my best," he wrote to her, "to
fulfil it according to your wishes."

The suite in attendance on the Prince was carefully chosen.
The inclusion of the Duke of Newcastle, Secretary of State for
the Colonies in Lord Palmerston's Ministry, lent great weight to
the mission from an imperial point of view.[2] Along with the
Duke went the Earl of St. Germans, Lord Steward of the Royal
Household, who specially represented the Queen. General Bruce,
the Prince's governor (he had been promoted Major-General
on 7th December 1859); Major Teesdale and Captain Grey,
his equerries; Dr. Henry Acland of Oxford, as his physician,

---

[1] Cf. *Greville's Journals; Annual Register*, 1877, p. 67. While the Prince
of Wales was at Boston in September 1860, the American statesman, Charles
Sumner, described in the *Boston Transcript* the visit to the city of the Prince's
grandfather in 1792.

[2] Mr. (afterwards Sir) John Gardner Dillman Englehart, the latest survivor
of the party, went out as the Duke of Newcastle's private secretary. He died
in London on the 10th April 1923, having celebrated his 100th birthday on the
previous 2nd February.

completed the company. Goldwin Smith, who was invited to join, declined.[1]

On 9th July the party embarked at Southampton on H.M.S. *Hero* (91 guns), with H.M.S. *Ariadne* (26 guns) and *The Flying Fish* (6 guns) as escort. The Prince Consort took leave of his son on board. The first fourteen days of the outward voyage were mainly spent by the Prince, under Bruce's guidance, in the study of maps and books dealing with the places to be visited, while the Duke of Newcastle explained to him pertinent political issues. But the Duke's time was chiefly occupied by the preparation of the Prince's replies to forthcoming addresses. Although the Prince Consort had tendered the Duke much advice on this head, the statesman was soon bewailing to the Queen the severe strain on "his powers of originality." All the Prince's companions were at the outset of an elder generation, but he took kindly to them, and received instructions from them so cheerfully that Bruce wrote quite hopefully to the Prince Consort. If the Prince's descriptions of his experiences (in numerous letters to his parents) proved bare and formal, they were relieved by some naïve comments on the persons whom he met, by comparisons of scenes which were new to him with familiar places at home, and by occasional notes on surviving memories of his grandfather. It was the concrete fact which caught his attention, to the exclusion of sentiment.

III

The first four weeks of the Prince's tour of the North American continent were spent in the outlying settlements of Newfound-

---

[1] Two journalists accompanied the party, Nicholas Augustus Woods, representing *The Times*, and G. H. Andrews, R.W.S., an artist, the *Illustrated London News*. The materials for the history of the tour are voluminous. Unpublished letters of the Prince of Wales and the Duke of Newcastle to the Queen, and Lord Lyons's letters to Lord John Russell, give very full particulars. A collection of cuttings from American newspapers of the time, which was procured for the present writer by the late Mr. Charles Francis Adams, has proved serviceable. The English published sources of information are: *The Prince of Wales in Canada and the United States*, by A. N. Woods, correspondent of *The Times* (1861); Bunbury Gough's *Boyish Reminiscences of the King's Visit to Canada in 1860* (1910); J. B. Atlay's *Life of Sir Henry Acland* (1903); John Martineau's *Life of the Duke of Newcastle* (1908); Lord Newton's *Lord Lyons: a Record of British Diplomacy* (1913); *Memoirs of Edward, Earl of Sandwich, 1839–1916* (edited by Mrs. Steuart Erskine), (1919); and the *Illustrated London News* for the period.

land, Nova Scotia, New Brunswick, and Prince Edward Island,
which formed stepping-stones on his road to Canada. St.
John's, the capital of Newfoundland, where the scenery reminded
the Prince of Scotland, was his first landing-place in the New
World. The port was reached on the 23rd July—two days
before the scheduled time. The enthusiastic welcome auspi-
ciously adumbrated what was to come. Three-quarters of the
population of the island crowded into the town. Wearing his
colonel's uniform decorated with the ribbon of the Garter, the
Prince enjoyed his first taste of that monotonous routine of
addresses, processions, levees, and official banquets which marked
every stage of his progress. The balls which the chief towns
on the Prince's route included in their programmes of welcome
provided the main alleviation of the burdens of formality. At
St. John's, too, the Prince held his initial inspection of freshly
enlisted Volunteers. The Duke of Cambridge had impressed
upon him the importance of encouraging this new scheme of
military defence which, lately inaugurated in England, was
in its first stages of adoption by the Colonies.

From Government House, Newfoundland, where he was the
guest of the Governor, Sir Alexander Bannerman, the Prince
wrote to his mother on the day of arrival :

I had to receive fourteen addresses, rather a large number
for the first time. I answered two of the most important ones
singly and the rest were answered altogether, or else it would
have been very difficult to vary the answers. . . . The Governor
who is rather an odd man and about 75 received me very kindly,
and the Government House is very comfortable. St. John's is
a very picturesque seaport town, and its cod fisheries are its
staple produce. The Harbour is remarkably pretty and the
entrance to it is said to resemble Balaclava very much. . . .

On the same day the Duke of Newcastle wrote to the Queen :

His Royal Highness read the answers remarkably clearly and
without apparent nervousness, and altogether performed his part
with no greater amount of diffidence than was perfectly becoming
and proper. His manners with the people were frank and
friendly without any mixture of assumed study to gain popularity
by over-civility.

General Bruce's testimony ran :

H.R.H. acquitted himself admirably, and seems pleased with everything, himself included.

At the Prince's own wish, he paused at Sydney Harbour, Cape Breton Island, on his way from Newfoundland to Halifax, Nova Scotia, the next scheduled place of call (July 26). He desired to inspect at Sydney Harbour more volunteers and to see for the first time an Indian camp.

"The Duke" (of Cambridge), he explained to his mother, "is always very anxious that I should see the Volunteers on every occasion so as to give them as much encouragement as possible, because he says that it is important that the inhabitants of the Colonies should understand that they must have some troops for their own defence which hitherto they have been very slow in comprehending. . . ." Of the Indian encampment he wrote: "They received us very civilly, and they wore more modified Indian costumes than those that are generally represented in pictures."

At Halifax (the capital of Nova Scotia), at Fredericton (the capital of New Brunswick), and at Charlottetown (the modest timber-built capital of Prince Edward Island), the popular enthusiasm grew, and although the accommodation was often rough, the Prince's zest was unabated. The Duke of Newcastle and General Bruce continued to report that he fully entered into "the spirit of the thing." He discovered a resemblance between the river St. John, on which Fredericton lies, and the Thames. In Nova Scotia and New Brunswick, where his grandfather, the Duke of Kent, had spent much time nearly seventy years before, the Prince sought to gratify his mother by reporting to her traces of her father's former residence. Near Halifax harbour, in Nova Scotia, he discovered ruins of a house called the Duke of Kent's Lodge, once in the Duke's occupation. "There is nothing remaining of it," wrote the Prince to his mother, "except a rotunda in which the band used to play. I send you a piece of sweet briar from there which I thought you might like to have."

Prince Edward Island again had an especial domestic claim to the Prince's notice, for it was in honour of his grandfather, who was known as Prince Edward before he assumed the title of Duke of Kent, that its present name had replaced in 1799 its original name of St. John's. At the same time as he assimilated the past interests which attached to the new scenes

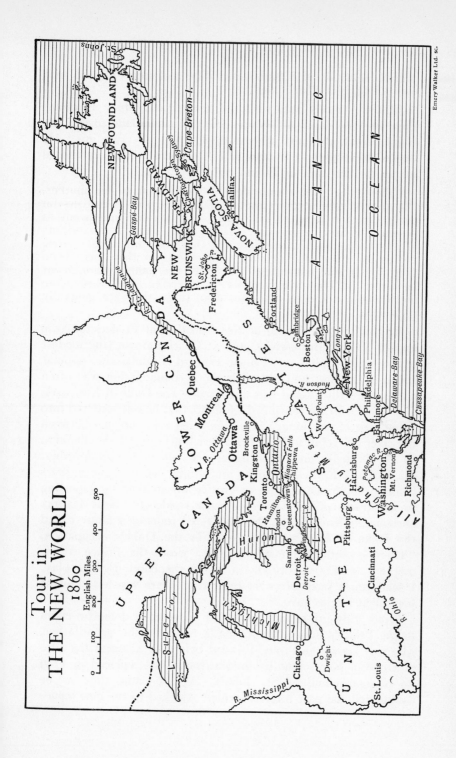

Tour in
THE NEW WORLD
1860
English Miles
0   100   200   300   400   500

UPPER CANADA

LOWER CANADA

St. Johns

NEWFOUNDLAND

PRINCE EDWARD I.

Cape-Breton-I.

Sydney

Charlottetown

NOVA SCOTIA

Halifax

NEW BRUNSWICK

Gaspé-Bay

R. St. Lawrence

St. John R.

Fredericton

Portland

Cambridge

Boston

UNITED STATES

Quebec

Montreal

R. Ottawa

Ottawa

Brockville

Kingston

Toronto

Hamilton

London

Queenstown

Niagara Falls

Chippewa

Windsor

Detroit

Detroit R.

Sarnia

L. Erie

L. Huron

L. Superior

L. Michigan

Chicago

Dwight

R. Mississippi

St. Louis

Cincinnati

R. Ohio

Pittsburg

Harrisburg

Potomac R.

Washington

Mt. Vernon

Richmond

Baltimore

West-Point

Hudson R.

New-York

Long I.

Philadelphia

Delaware-Bay

Chesapeake-Bay

ATLANTIC

OCEAN

Emery Walker Ltd. sc.

of his travel, the Prince kept in close touch with events 1860
at home. At Fredericton a telegram reached him from his Ætat. 18
mother announcing the birth, on 24th July, of his first niece,
his elder sister's first daughter and second child, Charlotte,
afterwards Grand Duchess of Saxe-Meiningen. "Your telegram
reached me," he informed his mother on 5th August, "in seven
days, which is the quickest time ever known."[1]

IV

It was not until Canada was reached that the tour acquired
its full significance. On 11th August the *Hero* anchored for the
night in Gaspé Bay, at the mouth of the great St. Lawrence
river. In the morning a Quebec steamer arrived with the
Governor-General of the Canadas, Sir Edmund Head, and the
leading members of the Canadian Ministry on board. All
spent the day on the Prince's ship. Among the Canadian
Ministers whose acquaintance the Prince now made, were three
men of notable achievement in imperial history. There was
the Premier, (Sir) George Etienne Cartier, an enlightened representative of the French Catholics in Lower Canada, with two
colleagues of memorable ardour in the cause of the Empire;
(Sir) John Alexander Macdonald, joint-Premier and representative
of the Protestants of Upper Canada, and (Sir) John Rose, Commissioner of Public Works. To Rose was entrusted the superintendence of the Prince's Canadian programme, and with him
the Prince was to form a lasting intimacy.

On the 18th August the *Hero* anchored off Quebec, the capital
of French (or Lower) Canada, and the Prince parted company
with the man-of-war until he finally left the North American
continent over two months later. With his state entry on
21st August into Quebec, the imperial import of the Prince's
mission was made manifest. The old Parliament House there
was fitted up for the Prince's residence, and a guard of honour
of one hundred men thenceforth formed his escort in the
Colony.

[1] The first submarine cable between England and America was completed
in the summer of 1858, and Queen Victoria and President Buchanan exchanged
telegraphic messages of congratulation on 5th August, but the cable soon ceased
to work satisfactorily and was not again in good order till 1861; nor was it
permanently in operation till 1866.

The perennial jealousies between French and English seemed for the moment to be exorcised by the Prince's presence. The Duke of Newcastle was somewhat perturbed by the hoisting of the Union Jack and the French tricolour side by side on the towers of the Roman Catholic cathedral in Quebec, but the Roman Catholic Archbishop, on the Duke's representation, readily substituted for the national French flag that of St. George's Cross. There was a warm greeting when the Prince visited the French Catholic university at Laval. Writing to Lord Palmerston, the Duke declared that the only perceptible rivalries in Lower Canada were in displays of "attachment to the Queen and the Prince as her representative."[1]

During his five days in Quebec the Prince exercised for the first time the sovereign's function of conferring the honour of knighthood. The Speakers of the two chambers of the provincial legislature each received that distinction from his hand. He also found time for a visit to the Heights of Abraham and to the spot where General Wolfe fell, while he gave proof of his youthful exuberance by engaging in every one of the twenty-two dances at the Mayor's ball.

From Quebec the Prince went by a small steamer up the St. Lawrence to Montreal, there to perform the first of the two specially prescribed functions of his mission. Amid imposing formalities, he drove the last rivet into the centre of the Victoria Bridge which, two miles long, spanned the St. Lawrence. Thereby he associated himself with one of the mightiest engineering feats in the two hemispheres. The strenuous Montreal programme included the opening of an Industrial Exhibition; attendance at a concert where the Prince first heard Mlle. Patti, the great prima-donna; and a passage on a raft down the rapids of the great river.

There were, too, at Montreal fresh personal introductions which proved congenial. The Prince was the guest of his official guide, (Sir) John Rose, at his home in the city and he enjoyed the society of the family. His eager interest in the Crimean War was stimulated by meeting Sir Fenwick Fenwick-Williams, the hero of Kars, who was now Commander-in-Chief of the Canadian forces. Furthermore, his suite was increased by three men who gave it a new attraction. Lord Lyons, the easy-mannered

[1] Martineau's *Life of Newcastle*, p. 294.

British Minister at Washington, joined the party in readiness
for the visit to America, while two youths of the Prince's own
age, who had just come out from England—Lord Hinchingbrooke,
one of the Eton company at Windsor, and Charles George Eliot,
youngest son of the Earl of St. Germans—became, to the Prince's
satisfaction, additional travelling companions, and qualified the
middle-aged tone of the party.

From Montreal the Prince proceeded to Ottawa to fulfil the
second specific purpose of his journey—the laying of the corner-
stone of the projected Parliament House of the two provinces
of the united colony.   Ottawa, then an embryonic hamlet, had
been improvised in 1858 to form the capital city of the two
Canadas, Lower and Upper.   A building for the new Legislature
had been planned on an elaborate Gothic design, and the Prince
laid the corner-stone on 1st September 1860.   Thereby colonial
unity was symbolically consummated.[1]

V

The Prince's prescribed route on leaving Ottawa lay by
river, lake, rail, and roughly-laid road through the cities and
regions of Upper Canada.   There the strength of Orange and
anti-Catholic feeling furnished, for a time, a disturbing element.
A peaceful entry into the province proved somewhat delusive.
Passing up the St. Lawrence river into Lake Ontario, the
Prince was dazzled, on the night of 3rd–4th September, by the
brilliant illumination of the first town of Upper Canada to be
visited—Brockville on the left bank of the river.   But before
the Prince reached the next and more important town on the
Lake-shore, Kingston, the sectarian storm broke.   Orangemen,
whose chief Canadian centres were Kingston and Toronto, had
bitterly resented the enthusiastic reception of the Prince by
their traditional rivals, the French Catholics of Lower Canada.
While in that province the Prince had been careful to treat both

[1] The fabric of the completed building, save the library and Senate House,
was destroyed by fire on 3rd February 1916.   In the following September the
Duke of Connaught, King Edward's brother, then Governor-General of Canada,
laid the foundation stone of a new building—the corner-stone which King
Edward had laid in 1860 being used again.   In 1919 the Prince of Wales,
King Edward's grandson, laid the foundation stone of a new tower for the
reconstructed Parliament House.

parties with scrupulous impartiality. At St. John's, Newfoundland, he had visited the Roman Catholic Chapel immediately after the Protestant Cathedral, and in all parts of Lower Canada he had shown equal consideration for each of the rival creeds. But such correctness of attitude made no appeal to the fanatical Orangemen of Kingston, who resolved to welcome the Prince as the heir of King William III., their patron saint, and to flaunt their sectarian flags and emblems in his face. The Orange lodges had erected in the Prince's honour triumphal arches which were lavishly decorated with orange colours and portraits of King William III., and bands of men wearing orange badges thronged the streets. The Duke of Newcastle, on learning of the situation, promptly announced that the Prince could countenance no sectarian demonstration. But the Kingston Orangemen scorned the Duke's remonstrance, and the Duke thereupon directed the Prince's steamer to pass the town without landing. As the vessel went by, the bands of the impenitent sectarians played, in the Prince's hearing, on the quayside such provocative airs as "Boyne Water" and "Croppies lie down." Vain protests against Orange obduracy came from the more tolerant inhabitants. The embarrassment was the greater owing to the fact that the Canadian Minister, Mr. J. A. Macdonald, who was accompanying the Prince, represented Kingston in the Canadian Parliament. But the Duke turned a deaf ear to Mr. Macdonald's appeal to restore Kingston to the Prince's itinerary, and some bitter words fell from the lips of Mr. Macdonald and his personal supporters.[1]

Wiser counsels happily prevailed at Toronto, the capital city of Upper Canada, where the Prince spent a successful week at Government House. The Orangemen's threatened displays of factious zeal were dropped at the Duke of Newcastle's entreaty—at least while the Prince was in the city. The concordat was only imperilled at one point. A transparency of King William III.'s passage of the Boyne was suffered to decorate a triumphal arch in spite of a previous promise to substitute for it a portrait of the Prince. The Duke of Newcastle marked his disapproval of the breach of faith by cancelling the invitation of the Mayor and Corporation to the Prince's Levee. An apology from the Mayor happily restored the harmony, which was completely re-established

[1] Life of Newcastle, p. 294; Pope's Correspondence of J. A. Macdonald, p. 8.

by the arrival in Toronto of a deputation from Kingston, to ask
and to receive pardon for what had happened there.

The official part of the Prince's Canadian tour was reckoned
to end at Toronto (on September 12). It was in conditions of
greater freedom that he saw something more of Canadian scenery
and of urban life, before he passed into the United States. But
nowhere in Canada was there any slackening of public interest
in his movement, nor was he suffered to escape the burden of
public functions.

The Canadian Grand Trunk Railway, whose starting-point
was Quebec, carried the Prince from Toronto westwards to the
rising town of London, and thence to the farthest point which the
railway had yet reached—Sarnia, a hamlet of the backwoods on
the banks of another of the great Canadian lakes, Lake Huron.
Retracing his steps, he next lodged for three days in a cottage
which the owner lent him in the village of Chippewa near Niagara
Falls. There he sought to explore, free from ceremony, the
impressive scene. But privacy was even there denied him. The
Falls were illuminated in his honour, and a striking if irrelevant
acrobatic performance was provided to enhance their impres-
siveness. A few days before, Blondin, the daring French
acrobat, startled the world by crossing the Falls from the Canadian
to the American shore on a tight-rope with a man on his back.
By way of celebrating the Prince's visit, Blondin repeated his
exploit in his presence, now wheeling a barrow across the rapids
and returning on stilts. The Prince, who witnessed Blondin's
performance from the suspension bridge, found it somewhat
nerve-racking. But on the safe completion of his feat, the
acrobat approached the Prince with an offer to wheel him in the
barrow across the rope into American territory. The Prince was
sportively inclined to accept the proposal, but his companions
intervened with a stern prohibition.[1]

Near the Falls, on the heights of Queenstown, was the battlefield where the British fought and defeated the Americans in the
war of 1812. There the Prince performed a last public ceremony
of historic interest on Canadian soil. He laid the crowning stone
on the great monument erected on the Heights to the memory of

[1] Cf. Lord Suffield's *My Memories*, p. 87; Lord Sandwich's *Memoirs*, p. 44.
Blondin arrived in England soon afterwards, and startled the English public by
his performances on the tight-rope at the Crystal Palace on the 12th June 1861.
His exploits were often repeated at the same place in later years.

1860
Ætat. 18

Major-General Sir Isaac Brock, the British commander who had fallen in the conflict. Brock's memory was still venerated in Upper Canada,[1] and the attendance at the ceremony of a few survivors of his army stimulated patriotic sentiment.

Throughout the tour, alike in Canada and in the adjoining settlements, the Prince's boyish curiosity had been deeply stirred by the native Indians, who crowded about him whenever they had the opportunity. As in the early days of his tour at Cape Breton, Halifax, and Fredericton, so at Montreal, Toronto, in the rough country at Sarnia, and at Niagara, representatives of the chief tribes offered him greeting and invited him to their encampments. His geniality easily won the Indians' goodwill. At Sarnia, Indian chiefs who welcomed the Prince belonged to the famous tribe of the Chippewas, and he distributed among them silver medals which had been originally cast some sixty years before to reward the military services of the Indians in the American War of Independence. The Prince's kindly reception of one of his Indian admirers had an interesting sequel. At Toronto a young chief of the Mohawk tribe, "with a large ring in his nose and painted," pressed himself on his notice and reintroduced himself later at Niagara. He said his name was Oron-hya-tekha, which he translated into English as "Burning Cloud." "Burning Cloud" and the Prince made an excellent impression on one another. Three years afterwards the Indian came uninvited to Oxford, clad in moccasins and deerhide, and, calling upon Dr. Acland, whom he had met with the Prince in Canada, offered to become a student in the University. Dr. Acland was sympathetic, and sent the news to the Prince, who, greatly amused, followed "Burning Cloud's" Oxford fortunes with eager curiosity. "I have no doubt," the Prince wrote on hearing of his arrival in Oxford (March 27, 1862), "that you will see to his education being properly attended to during his stay in the University, and that he will get a 'Second Class' and end by being made a D.C.L." Subsequently the Prince learned that "Burning Cloud" had "not turned out well." . . . "I am not surprised to hear it," he added. However, the Indian's Oxford career came to a better end than the Prince anticipated.[2]

[1] An earlier monument had been blown up by an American Irishman in 1840.

[2] Acland raised funds on "Burning Cloud's" behalf and secured him admission as a student to St. Edmund Hall. Though he left Oxford without

It was at the town of Hamilton, whither the Prince travelled 1860 from Niagara, that the Prince bade farewell to the Canadian Ætat. 18 people. Thousands of farmers were assembled there at the annual Agricultural Exhibition of Upper Canada, and in reply to the Agricultural Association's address the Prince read the last of that long series of speeches from the Duke of Newcastle's pen, in which throughout the tour he had iterated congratulations on the colonists' devotion to the mother-country despite differences of race and religion, and his personal intention of reporting to his mother the displays which he had witnessed of loyalty to the Throne.

From Hamilton, the Prince passed to the small town of Windsor on the Canadian frontier of the United States. There he was met by the Governor-General, Sir Edmund Head, and the members of the Canadian Government, including Sir George Cartier, the Prime Minister, and (Sir) John Macdonald, who bade him God-speed on his departure from the Colony.

VI

On the afternoon of 20th September the Prince crossed from Windsor the Detroit River and first set foot on the soil of the American Republic in the flourishing town of Detroit. The Duke of Newcastle, General Bruce, and the rest of the Canadian suite continued with the Prince to the end of the tour. But Lord Lyons, British Minister at Washington, who had joined the party at Montreal, took, at Detroit, control of the Prince's movements, and became his inseparable companion until he left for home. In the United States the Prince nominally travelled in a private capacity; yet the spontaneous enthusiasm of the American people rendered the Prince's journey through America as triumphal a progress as through Canada. Some American newspapers warned their readers that in a republic only flunkeys paid honours to royalty, but such remonstrance had no effect on the

---

a degree, he prepared a grammar of the Mohawk tongue for Professor Max Müller. On his return to Canada he obtained a qualification for the practice of medicine, and became medical attendant in the Indian Reserves and head of the Order of Canadian Foresters. On the business of the Foresters he several times revisited England, on one occasion bringing with him his wife and daughter, whom he took to Oxford to introduce to Dr. Acland. Cf. Atlay's *Sir H. W. Acland*, p. 285 note, and a letter from Acland to the Prince, 16th June 1862.

show of popular feeling. The curiosity about royalty which democracy proverbially cherishes undoubtedly swelled the immense crowds which gathered wherever it was known that the Prince could be seen. Certainly there was no note of obsequiousness or of sycophancy in the popular greetings which occasionally disconcerted the Prince's suite by their colloquial familiarity. But pessimists at home who had foretold coolness or insult were confuted, and the few Irish-Americans who murmured protests never raised their voices loud enough to disturb the general harmony. The Prince's ease and charm of demeanour contributed largely to the favourable result. His geniality touched the subconscious sense of filial attachment to the mother-country which, despite all political rancours and dissensions, is rooted somewhere in the hearts of the majority of Americans of British descent. A critical electoral campaign, which resulted in the return of Abraham Lincoln as President, was in progress at the time. The electoral excitement stimulated the Prince's political instincts without reducing the popular interest in him or in his wanderings. Senator Charles Sumner, who watched the tour with observant eyes while he was immersed in electoral activities, declared that "it seemed as if a young heir long absent was returning to take possession."[1] "The whole land," wrote Fanny Kemble, the actress, who was residing in America, "was alive with excitement and interest."[2]

From Detroit the Prince's path lay through the rising cities of the Middle West. Thence he passed to the older and more settled communities of the east coast. He travelled in a director's car on special trains, and at every station, whether or no his train stopped, crowds collected. At Chicago, a new town of 50,000 inhabitants—the first stopping-place after Detroit—the Mayor, John Wentworth, manfully kept in check obtrusive curiosity while he conducted the Prince about the thronged city. On leaving Chicago, two days were spent in the country at the village of Dwight in the state of Illinois, where the Prince had two days' prairie shooting, the game being prairie chicken, quail, and crane. Thence he proceeded to St. Louis—his farthest western point. The annual fair had brought to the town tens of thousands from

[1] MS. letter at Windsor from Charles Sumner to John Evelyn Denison, Speaker of the House of Commons (Boston, 23rd October 1860).
[2] Fanny Kemble, *Further Records*, ii. 227.

the neighbouring country.[1] At the fair the Prince spent three and a half hours at a stretch watching trotting matches.

The long journeys across the plains were often wearisome. From Cincinnati the Prince reached Pittsburg after what he described as "a long and fatiguing railway journey devoid of any interest." But the intense warmth of the reception at Pittsburg proved a compensation. Next day the party crossed the Alleghany Mountains to Harrisburg, the capital of the state of Pennsylvania —a place of greater historic interest than any yet visited. The Governor of the state conducted the Prince over the public buildings and "finished by asking him to sit in the chair in which Hancock had signed the Declaration of Independence." The Prince readily complied, and the Governor acknowledged the visitor's complaisance with a few words in praise of England.

The chief episode of the American tour immediately followed. By way of Baltimore, where Washington's monument recalled to the Prince's mind the Duke of York's column in London, he arrived at the capital city of Washington (October 3). Together with the Duke of Newcastle, Lord St. Germans, and Dr. Acland, he was President Buchanan's private guest at the White House. The rest of the party was entertained by Lord Lyons at the British Legation. Of his first two days at Washington the Prince wrote to his mother, with a somewhat critical glance at certain conditions at home :

The President and (his niece) Miss Lane received us very kindly on arriving, and I did not fail to give the messages which you desired. There was a large dinner at 6.30 at which all the Ministers and their wives, and some others were invited. The President was looking very well, but has grown much stouter. I thought Miss Lane a particularly nice person, and very pretty. The President's house is a very nice one, and the rooms are really very fine, and comfortably furnished. Washington is a fine looking town and contains some striking buildings. The finest is the Capitol, in which the Congress sits, and we visited it the day after our arrival. I shall bring home some drawings of it which will give you a much better idea of it than if I explained

---

[1] Mr. Winston Churchill, the American novelist, in *The Crisis* (1901), a tale of the American Civil War, gives a spirited description of the Prince's visit to the St. Louis Fair in chapter xi. ("How a Prince came"). "There is one Fair," the novelist writes, "which old Louisans still delight to recall—that of the autumn of 1860 . . . when His Royal Highness came to St. Louis and beheld 100,000 people at the Fair."

it now. We visited also the same day the Patent Office which is the same thing very nearly as the United Service Museum in London, and contains models of different inventions. All the Public Offices are in the same building, and we might easily take some hints for our own buildings which are so very bad.

Friday 5th October, the third day of the Prince's visit to the White House, was devoted to a ceremony of historic significance. The Prince, with President Buchanan and Miss Lane, went in an American Revenue cutter down the river Potomac to Mount Vernon, the former residence of Washington while first President of the United States. The excursion proved both memorable and picturesque. After thoroughly exploring the house, which struck him as unworthily dilapidated, the Prince visited the hero's tomb hard by. Near the tomb, at the President's request, he planted a chestnut tree. Very impressive was the scene in which the tall and venerable President (of sixty-nine) and the youthful, short, slender Prince (of nineteen) played, bareheaded, the chief parts.

The Prince described his experiences at Mount Vernon with his wonted simplicity in a letter to the Queen :

Mount Vernon is a much revered spot by the Americans, as the House in which General Washington lived and also died stands there. The visit therefore was a very interesting one ; the house itself is unfortunately in very bad repair, and is rapidly falling into decay ; we saw all the different rooms and the one in which Washington died. We also visited his grave, which is a short distance from the house, and by the wish of the President I planted a Chestnut near it.

More exuberant descriptions of the episode came from other pens. "The visit of the Prince," wrote the President the day after (October 6) to Queen Victoria, "to the tomb of Washington, and the simple but solemn ceremonies at this consecrated spot will become a historical event and cannot fail to exert a happy influence on the kindred peoples of the two countries." The Queen promptly took up the parable. "The interesting and touching scene," she replied, "at the grave of General Washington may be fitly taken as the type of our present feelings and I trust of our future relations." When the news spread on the American continent, this tribute of the grandson of George III.

to Washington's memory was greeted with a loud outburst of applause, which found an echo in England.[1]

The three days' stay at the White House passed off without a hitch. The Prince regretted the puritanic rules of house-keeping which forbade dancing at the White House "even on the carpet." But the President adapted his somewhat conventional habits, as far as his temperament allowed, to making the Prince at home, and he expressed himself to General Bruce as "quite delighted with the result." "In our domestic circle he won all hearts," wrote the President to the Queen; "his free and ingenuous intercourse with myself evinced both a kind heart and a good understanding." In bidding farewell to his host and hostess of the White House the Prince gave them portraits of his parents, which Miss Lane treated as her personal property until President Lincoln, her uncle's successor, claimed them as official heirlooms.

VII

From Washington the Prince went south to Richmond, Virginia, a main bulwark of slavery, where he noted that "every fourth person one meets is black." Thence he passed north to Philadelphia, which struck him as "the prettiest town I have seen in the United States." At Philadelphia he came to close quarters with the pending electoral campaign in which the prolonged controversy over slavery was coming to a head. The result of the election of a Governor of the State of Pennsylvania was declared on the night of his arrival. The election was a critical one in current political history. The triumphal return, by a 32,000 majority, of the Republican anti-slavery candidate, Andrew Curtin, removed well-nigh the last remaining doubts as to the outcome of Abraham Lincoln's contest for the Presidency.[2] The Prince walked about the streets of Philadelphia on the eventful night, and watched bonfires and torchlight processions which made the night "very lively."

[1] "The Prince of Wales at the Tomb of Washington" was the subject set for the English poem at Cambridge University next year. The prize was won by Frederic W. H. Myers, afterwards well known as poet and critic. The poem, although omitted "by request of the author" from the collection (1894) of English prize poems at Cambridge (1859–93), was included in the writer's *Collected Poems*, edited by his widow (1921).

[2] J. F. Rhodes, *History of the United States*, ii. 497–8.

Charles Sumner wrote how he rejoiced that the Prince should see "something of the movement caused by Demos."

Of his further doings at Philadelphia the Prince wrote in his usual vein to his mother:

"We visited the Penitentiary, which is one of the largest prisons in America, that contains about 800 prisoners.[1] We went all over it and I went into one of the cells and visited an unfortunate judge, who for forgery is condemned to prison for twenty years, and only eighteen months of his imprisonment have as yet elapsed; the system of solitary confinement is carried on there, and has been found very efficient. After having visited a lunatic asylum, where we only remained a very short time, we drove a short distance outside the town to see some horse races in the afternoon." The Prince found the racing "not particularly good, the course instead of being of turf was covered with sand or gravel, otherwise it resembled an English racecourse very much."

At Philadelphia Opera House, which he likened to the familiar Princess's Theatre in London, he saw the opera *Martha*, and for a second time in his tour heard Mlle. Patti, who was now first introduced to him. "Mademoiselle Patti," he wrote to his mother, in tones which sound rather subdued in view of her subsequent triumphs and his coming admiration of her powers, "was the prima donna, and she performed her part very well. Her voice, though not strong, is a very pretty one."

There succeeded a thrilling three days in New York, where the popular acclamation reached its climax. Travelling partly by rail and partly by boat, he landed at the Emigrants' Wharf, and was immersed in public activities before going to his hotel.

"We were received," he wrote, "by the Mayor (Mr. Fernando Wood) on landing, and then went into a house and put on our uniforms for a review (of the militia)." 6000 men, infantry, cavalry, and artillery, were drawn up "near the Emigrants' Wharf in a very small space. General Sandford commanded the troops, and after we had ridden down the different lines we got into our carriages and drove at a foot's pace to the City Hall where we got out and the troops marched past before us. I thought that they were a very fine body, and the 7th Regiment looked as well as our Guards."

[1] The civic authorities of Philadelphia took pride in recent reforms of the city prison.

As the Prince's procession slowly passed to his hotel, he was astonished by the density of the crowds.

The people cheered and waved flags, etc., most enthusiastically. I think it is by far the finest reception we have had, and shows that the feeling between the two countries could not be better. I never dreamt that we should be received as we were. During the latter part of the procession it became dark, which was a great pity. I believe that there were 300,000 people in the streets, which was wonderful. After arriving at our Hotel we were very glad to get our dinner and go to bed, as we had had a very tiring day.

The Duke of Newcastle in a letter to Queen Victoria corroborated in more emphatic language the Prince's testimony:

He certainly [the Duke wrote in the third person] never ventured to hope for anything approaching such a scene as probably was never witnessed before—the enthusiasm of much more than half a million of people worked up almost to madness and yet self-restrained within the bounds of the most perfect courtesy, by the passage through their streets of a foreign Prince not coming to celebrate a new-born Alliance or to share in the glories of a joint campaign, but solely as a private visitor and as exhibiting indirectly only the friendly feelings of the country to which he belongs.

Before the Prince left New York, a popular man of letters, writing under the name of " John Downing," humorously declared: "He may consider himself a lucky lad if he escape a nomination for President before he reaches his homeward-bound Fleet."

The public entertainment at New York, which was longer remembered in America than any other of the civic functions arranged in the Prince's honour, was a great ball in the Academy of Music on East Fourteenth Street on 12th October. It admittedly served its purpose as a "national demonstration of regard and affection," but it was not, as the Duke of Newcastle put it, "well managed." "The Prince" (according to the Duke) "was somewhat persecuted by attentions not in strict accordance with good breeding." The Prince's own description to the Queen of the entertainment ran quaintly thus:

The great ball took place, but it was not successful. 3000 people were invited and 5000 came, which of course was not an improvement, the ball-room being the Academy of Music, which did not hold even 3000 people comfortably. We arrived at 10 o'clock, and before the dancing had begun a great part of the floor gave way and it took two hours to set it right, so that dancing did not begin until 12 o'clock, and the crowd was so great that it was very difficult to move, but in spite of these disasters I must say it was a very pretty sight.[1]

Next day the Prince went out to West Point Academy, "the Sandhurst of the United States," with General Scott, the veteran commander-in-chief of the United States. The old General, who told Lord Lyons that he was "enchanted" with the royal visitor, brought home to the Prince the change in Anglo-American relations, to which he and the General were both making contribution. The American General had been taken prisoner by the British in the war of 1812 at that very battle of Queenstown, where there fell the British General, Brock, to whose memory the Prince had unveiled a monument before leaving Canada. Of a torchlight procession of the same evening the Prince wrote to his mother that it "was a beautiful sight, and the firemen who held the torches were 6000 in number." On Sunday morning the crowds on Broadway somewhat incommoded him on his way to Trinity Church where, for the first time since 1776, a prayer was offered for the English royal family. In the warmth of New York's welcome, the Duke of Newcastle saw (he informed Lord Palmerston) conclusive proof that the era of coldness had ended in the relations of the United States with England.

The American tour closed with a visit to Boston, where the Prince stayed at the Revere Hotel. All the luminaries of the place joined in paying him honour. Charles Sumner, despite the calls of the presidential campaign, was assiduous in personal attentions. The writers, Ralph Waldo Emerson and Oliver Wendell Holmes, showed no smaller zeal, while the poet Longfellow, who wrote that the Prince "looked remarkably well on horseback," accompanied him to the customary ball.[2] Years

[1] Memories of the ball are still cherished in New York. When the present Prince of Wales visited that city in November 1919, the proprietor of the Academy of Music gave a reception there to the Prince, at which were present all survivors of the company which had assembled in the same place, nearly sixty years before, in honour of the Prince's grandfather. The hall of the Academy was decorated in precisely the same way as on the earlier occasion (The Times, December 2, 1919).

[2] Mr. E. L. Pierce's Memorials and Letters of Charles Sumner, iii. 620;

afterwards, in 1878, the Prince marked his appreciation of Long-fellow's share in the Boston welcome by acting as Chairman of the Committee which placed a memorial to the poet's memory in Westminster Abbey.

With Charles Sumner and others the Prince drove from Boston to the neighbouring town of Cambridge and attended a reception at Harvard University. Another day was spent at Bunker's Hill, the scene of the Pyrrhic victory of the British troops in 1775.

VIII

The American tour was now at its end. A rapid journey from Boston brought the Prince to Portland, Maine, where H.M.S. *Hero* was in readiness for the homeward voyage (October 20). Charles Sumner and several of the Prince's companions in Boston travelled with him to the Portland Pier, and Sumner described him at their leave-taking as "in good health and unwearied by all the processions and hospitalities." Members of the Canadian Government arrived before the vessel sailed and offered their final benediction on shipboard. The Governor of the State of Maine (in which Portland is situated) was present with them, and the Prince good-humouredly bantered him on the rigorous virtue of his State, which long anticipated the rest of the United States in prohibiting the consumption of alcohol. When taking leave of the Governor on the deck of the *Hero*, the Prince laughingly thought to pose him with the query : "Will you take a little wine, or is the Maine law in force here?" The Governor, equal to the occasion, replied, "I am out of my jurisdiction and will take the consequences."

The *Hero's* voyage home was long and tedious, and was not without its perils. Contrary winds and fog caused wearisome delay, and as many as twenty-six days passed before the *Hero* sighted Plymouth on the 15th November 1860. Amid a boister-ous gale the Prince's nineteenth birthday (November 9) was celebrated in mid-Atlantic. The absence of news caused the

Samuel Longfellow's *Life of H. W. Longfellow*, 1886, ii. 357. At dinner at Charles Norton's (October 18) Longfellow met General Bruce and Dr. Acland. He found them "very pleasant gentlemen both—Dr. Acland with a rather pensive, melancholy face and an agreeable smile, the General with his grey moustache, very urbane, and full of conversation." The Duke of Newcastle, whom the poet also met, he describes as "very hearty and cordial."

Queen and her people much anxiety, and the enthusiasm of the crowds which welcomed the Prince's debarkation at Plymouth bore witness to the public relief at the safe termination of the expedition. The Prince lost no time in rejoining his parents at Windsor, after a separation of more than four months.

IX

"The tremendous tour," as King Leopold called it, must be regarded alike as a notable landmark in the Prince's career and an episode of influence both on his character and on current history. The Prince had responded to the calls of public life with an alacrity surprising in one so young. His genial accessibility everywhere created the most favourable impression. The young visitor's "kind and gentle demeanour," wrote (Sir) John Rose, the Canadian Minister, to General Bruce, taught "the mass of the people" no longer to regard royalty as "the stern and unapproachable thing they were accustomed to consider it." "He has passed," wrote President Buchanan to the Queen (October 6, 1860), "through a trying ordeal for a person of his years, and his conduct throughout has been such as becomes his age and station. Dignified, frank, and affable, he has conciliated, wherever he has been, the kindness and respect of a sensitive and discriminating people."[1]

The Prince's character conspicuously benefited by the experience, which prefigured much that was to follow in his career. Both the Duke of Newcastle and General Bruce acknowledged "the development of mind and habit of thought." The Prince's governor was, as usual, unsparing of criticism in his detailed reports to the Prince Consort. General Bruce regretted that his charge did not shine in conversation, and that a growing sense of his own importance was stimulating a longing for independence of control. But the governor admitted that the Prince "always succeeded in representation and while in movement." At any rate there could be no question of the quickening effect of the

[1] Lord Lyons, in a letter to Lord John Russell (October 26, 1860), on the American part of the tour, bore similar, but perhaps more conventional, testimony to "the patience and good-humour with which His Royal Highness bore what was fatiguing and irksome; and to the judgement and (if I may use the expression) tact with which he maintained his dignity without giving offence to a susceptible people unacquainted with the forms of respect observed towards royal personages."

1860
Ætat. 18

four months' journey on the Prince's sense of camaraderie. Well-nigh all his travelling companions stirred in him personal affection, and as death in the coming years thinned the little band, the Prince, in his private correspondence, noted in pathetic language each shrinkage of the circle whose every member embodied pleasant memories. Nor was he scant in sympathy with the officers of the *Hero*, the ship on which he crossed and recrossed the Atlantic. Several of these he many times recommended subsequently to the Admiralty for promotion. The frequent failures of such efforts he sorrowfully assigned to incurable "red-tapeism."

In estimating the political influence of the tour one has to make allowance for the habitual tendency of contemporary opinion to exaggerate the importance of the public migrations of royalty. At the same time, one should be cautious in adopting the Whig doctrine which, deprecating all prominent association of royalty with political affairs, invariably discountenances the view that a sovereign or his heir may be an effective political missionary. The foreign secretary, Lord John Russell, spoke for the Whigs alone when he estimated the political value of the Prince's tour in these grudging terms:

The tours of great personages seldom have more than a transient effect; they form no real and solid relation of friendship between nations, though if undertaken at a fortunate moment they serve to bring out and demonstrate a friendship already existing. The visit of the Prince of Wales was thus fortunately well timed.[1]

There is abundant evidence which materially qualifies Lord John's disparaging verdict. The inadequacy, at any rate in the Prince's case, of the accepted Whig outlook on royal missions, is amply confirmed by many of his later tours abroad, which bear affinity to his travel through Canada and America.

There was much more than conventional phraseology in the private estimates of the political effects of the Prince's expedition which the Duke of Newcastle sent home during the tour to the Queen and to Lord Palmerston, or in the public declarations which, on the Prince's return, issued from the lips of both Queen Victoria and President Buchanan.

The Duke, in a report to the Queen on the Prince's

---

[1] Newton, *Life of Lord Lyons*, i. 117.

departure from Canada, credited the visit with such political
benefits as these :

> The attachment to the Crown of England has been greatly
> cemented, and other Nations will have learnt how useless it will
> be in case of war either to tamper with the allegiance of the
> North American Provinces or to invade their shores.   A higher
> tone amongst the Public Men of all these Colonies is a great want,
> but there is much in the Population of all Classes to admire and
> for a good Government to work upon, and the very knowledge
> that the acts of all will henceforth be more watched in England,
> because more attention has been drawn to the Country, will do
> great good.

In writing to Lord Palmerston the Duke laid equal stress on
the awakening in the United States of a fellow-feeling with
England with which he knew nothing to compare since the
Republic came into being.

When the Prince was safe at home again, President Buchanan
introduced into his next message to Congress (December 3, 1860)
a forecast, which went uncriticised, of the "consequences" of the
Prince's visit. "The recent visit," said the President, "of the Prince
of Wales in a private character to the people of this country, has
proved to be a most auspicious event.   In its consequences, it
cannot fail to increase the kindred and kindly feelings which, I
trust, may ever actuate the Government and people of both
countries in their political and social intercourse with each other."
The Queen, in her Speech at the Opening of a new session of
Parliament on 5th February 1861, spoke no less confidently on
both the American and the Canadian issues :

> The interest (she said) which I take in the well-being of the
> people of the United States cannot but be increased by the kind
> and cordial reception given by them to the Prince of Wales
> during his recent visit to the continent of America.
>
> I am glad to take this opportunity of expressing my warm
> appreciation of the loyalty and attachment to my person and
> throne manifested by my Canadian and other North American
> subjects on the occasion of the residence of the Prince of Wales
> among them.

The full force of the impetus which the growth of imperial
sentiment received was perhaps only exemplified at a subsequent
period of the Queen's reign.   But the beneficial influence of the

Prince's visit to the United States on Anglo-American relations received practical illustration very soon after the event.

Within five months of the Prince's departure from American shores there broke out the Civil War between the North and the South, which created between the governments of Washington and London a new and critical tension. English feeling in influential quarters inclined towards the South. Fears were soon entertained by the Federal Government (of the North) that Great Britain, with other European powers, designed active support for the Confederate forces (of the South). When war with the North looked inevitable, vivid memories of the Prince's visit evoked efficient guarantees of peace.

Three incidents may be recalled. In the first place, the American historian and diplomatist, Motley, whom the Prince had met at Rome, was directed by the Federal Government to spend the autumn of 1861 in England on his way to Vienna, where he had been appointed American Minister. His instructions were to observe and report on the tendencies of English public opinion, and if possible to give it a direction favourable to the North. In September 1861 Motley visited the Foreign Secretary, Lord John (lately become Earl) Russell, who was staying near Balmoral as Minister in attendance on the Queen. The Prince Consort invited him to an audience with the Queen.[1] Gratitude to the North for the attentions recently bestowed on the son swayed the political judgement of the parents. The Queen, while indicating to Motley her personal sympathy with the Federal cause, expressed her appreciation of the Northern States' hospitable reception of the Prince of Wales. Motley acknowledged that the Prince's welcome by the United States was a factor in the determination of England's attitude to the internecine struggle proceeding in his country.

Secondly, the influence of the Prince's visit was perceptible in the notable and successful effort which his parents, and chiefly the Prince Consort, made, two months after the meeting with Motley, to avert an imminent risk of hostilities between England and the Federals. In November the captain of a Federal ship of war, Captain Wilkes, seized off Havana on board an English mail-packet the *Trent*, two envoys of the South, named Mason

---

[1] Motley described what passed in a long letter to Seward, President Lincoln's Secretary of State.

and Slidell, who were coming to Europe to appeal for intervention on behalf of the Confederates. The Federal captain's
attack on an English ship roused in England a loud cry for
the sternest retaliation. Lord Palmerston, the Prime Minister,
was on the point of yielding to the popular clamour when
the Prince Consort and the Queen, confessing that the Prince
of Wales's American tour was still an efficient motive-force
on their minds, urged with success on the Prime Minister a
moderation which in the result ensured a peaceful settlement.
The Federal Government and the people of the North freely
admitted the service which the Sovereign of England had rendered
the cause of peace, and the friendly spirit which the Prince of
Wales's visit had called into being between America and the royal
family was acknowledged by the Federals to be a solvent of the
international rancour.

Thirdly, there is at hand, at a little later date, a very practical
illustration of the faith in the good effects of the Prince's tour
which lived in influential American circles. In August 1863,
when the Civil War was still raging and public sentiment in
England was still wavering between the combatants, Seward,
the well-known Secretary of State in President Lincoln's Federal
Government, suggested to the British Government, through Lord
Lyons, the British Minister at Washington, that he, or another
prominent supporter of the Northern cause, should visit England
in the same conditions as the Prince of Wales had visited America.
Seward confidently anticipated that a demonstration of the kind
would give the Federal Government an advantage in England
comparable with the benefit which the Prince's visit to the
United States had exerted on American opinion of Great Britain.
Lord Russell lent the suggestion no favour, pleading his wonted
lack of faith in the efficacy of foreign missions, either of royalty or
of other great personages. Lord Russell's opinion has in this
instance to be weighed against that of a shrewd American
statesman.

As the curtain falls on this attractive episode of the Prince's
early manhood, the note of Whiggish disparagement of such
royal activity as the Prince had displayed under General Bruce's
cautious guidance, was echoed, a little obliquely perhaps, by
the Prime Minister, Lord Palmerston himself. There was some

disagreement between the Queen and Lord Palmerston over the
award of honours to such of the Prince's associates on the tour
as had chiefly contributed to its success.   There was unanimity
as to the right of the Duke of Newcastle, who had borne the
burden of the day, to the distinction of K.G., and of both Lord
Lyons and Sir Edmund Head to that of K.C.B.   But the Prime
Minister demurred to the Queen's proposal also to confer the
honour of K.C.B. on General Bruce, to whose control of the
Prince she largely assigned her son's personal triumphs.   Bruce's
services, Lord Palmerston bluntly pointed out, "were of a
private character which it would be inappropriate to recognise
with a public distinction."   The Queen retorted that the Order
of the Bath was instituted to reward "services to the Crown."
"The watching over and training the youth of a future sovereign
is," she asserted, "in the Queen's opinion, one of the greatest
public services which can be rendered in a monarchy."   The
writer thought to clinch her argument by an example : "Look,"
she said, "at the sufferings of Naples, which are traced by all
parties to the faulty education of the young sovereign" (November
26, 1860).   There is just a smack of irony in the Prime Minister's
prompt rejoinder (November 27) :

1860

Ætat. 19

The difference between the Prince of Wales's lot and that of
the Prince of Naples lies far deeper than what depends on a good
governor.   The Prince of Wales has had the good fortune to
inherit admirable qualities from his parents, and to draw from
his earliest years salutary lessons from their precept and example,
while, on the contrary, the unfortunate King of Naples has
derived from similar sources nothing but fatal causes of degrada-
tion and ruin.

On the main point the Prime Minister declined to budge.   At
best he offered to reconsider the question of Bruce's decoration
when his term of office as governor of the Prince should end.
In the result, death prematurely intervened to forbid the
bestowal on the Prince's governor of any honour for those
services in America or elsewhere which the Prime Minister
declined to value at the parental rate.

CHAPTER VIII

LAST STAGES OF UNDERGRADUATE LIFE

I

1860

Ætat. 19

THERE was some incongruity in the Prince's resumption of undergraduate life at Oxford, in the old conditions of restraint, on his return from the American expedition in which he had played a part of the first rank. Even General Bruce pointed out to the Prince Consort that the light of publicity in which the Prince had lately lived could not be suddenly extinguished and that the continuance of the schoolboy discipline was out of keeping with the growth of circumstance.[1]

Nevertheless, the Prince docilely went back to Oxford at his father's bidding within a few days of his landing at Plymouth, and he was once again for a few weeks the pupil of Professor Goldwin Smith and Sir Benjamin Brodie. "I have been attending all my lectures very regularly this week," he dutifully wrote to his mother (November 29, 1860), adding : "To-morrow, if the weather is fine, I hope to go out hunting." His Canadian experience had whetted his interest in the new Volunteer movement, and he rejoiced in the progress of the university corps, although after an inspection which he made of the Oxford Volunteers he wrote with precocious archness : "A great deal of allowance had to be made for them because they were such young troops." Other new phases of undergraduate life moved his interest. He attended the first meeting of the united colleges in a University athletic competition, an event which proved the starting-point of a vast development of amateur athleticism through the country. "On Tuesday," he wrote on the 6th December 1860, "we had

[1] General Bruce to Prince Consort, 14th August 1860.

some athletic sports at which the whole of the University took part; they are going to be annual, so that they will have ample time to prepare for them. The races and the long steeplechases were the most successful, but the ground was in a most dreadful state."

The Prince's hospitalities at Frewin Hall continued. Sir Edmund and Lady Head, the Governor-General of Canada, his recent hosts in the Colony, came on a visit to Oxford and dined with the Prince, along with the Vice-Chancellor, Dr. Stanley, Dr. Jacobson, and Mr. Goldwin Smith. "Sir Edmund," the Prince told his mother, "had been at Oxford with most of the present professors, so that it was very interesting to him to meet them again."

With the end of the term the Prince's Oxford career closed. In spite of its restraints he wrote to Dr. Acland of his regret at leaving: "I have enjoyed my stay very much and I hope I have derived some benefit from it."

II

Meanwhile the Prince Consort, far from dropping any part of his long academic programme, was arranging for the Prince's transfer to the sister university of Cambridge. As at Oxford, it was finally decided that while the Prince should join a college, Trinity, he should live in controlled seclusion outside its walls. Dr. Whewell, the Master of Trinity, insisted, however, on allotting him rooms for occasional use in Trinity Lodge. The Prince Consort selected for his son's Cambridge residence an old and spacious country mansion, Madingley Hall, with large grounds and "capital stables," which, whatever its merits as a quiet retreat, had the disadvantage of being four miles away from the town. General and Mrs. Bruce took domestic charge, and the General was warned not to relax the strict supervision which he had exercised at Oxford. Study remained the first aim. The Prince arrived with General and Mrs. Bruce and Captain Grey at Madingley on the 18th January 1861, and Mr. Herbert Fisher, his Oxford tutor, soon joined the company of control. On 19th January the Master, Dr. Whewell, introduced him at Trinity Lodge to the Vice-Chancellor, the Master of Magdalene College, "the Hon. Mr. Neville" (in the Prince's words) "who is a brother of Lord Braybrooke and seems to be a very nice person," and to the heads of the other colleges. "Then," he wrote to his mother the same evening, "I signed my name in the College Book as belonging to Trinity College. After this ceremony was completed we drove to the Vice-Chancellor's house with Dr. Whewell, where I was matriculated and had to sign my name again. We then returned to the College, and Dr. Whewell showed me the Hall and the various Courts, not Quads as they are called at Oxford. After that I lunched with Dr. Whewell and Lady Affleck (his second wife), who is a pleasing person. After luncheon we visited the Chapel, and then I had a game at tennis with Capt. Grey. . . . On Monday I hope to begin my studies regularly, and I shall work as hard as I can so as to make the most of the short time before me."

Although the Prince wrote to Dr. Acland at Oxford of his admiration of King's College Chapel, he judged the Cambridge colleges to be as a whole "not so fine as at Oxford," but he deprecated comparison between the Universities. "I am glad to say I like Cambridge," he wrote to his Oxford friend (March 24). The Prince saw much of Dr. Whewell, of whom Sidney Smith used to say "science was his forte and omniscience his foible," occasionally dining with him privately, but his relations with him were less intimate than those with Dr. Liddell at Christ Church. He frequently attended College Chapel, and often dined in Hall at the high table, going afterwards for dessert to the Combination room. His college tutor was the theologian, Joseph Barber Lightfoot, afterwards Bishop of Durham, who completely won his regard.

The Prince's curriculum covered a wide range. The Prince Consort urged practice in French and German composition, the languages in which "the young man will have chiefly to correspond." He attended lectures on chemistry, and saw much of Professor Robert Willis, Jacksonian Professor of Applied Mechanics and an authority on architecture. The Prince wrote with some excitement of a visit to the Observatory "to see the comet" which was not visible. "We saw, however, Jupiter and Saturn very well through the large telescope which the Duke of Northumberland presented to the University." But while natural science was not neglected, law and history were the leading studies. The importance of legal studies grew

1861

Ætat. 19

steadily on the Prince Consort, and he told General Bruce to take counsel in the matter with Lord Lyndhurst—a very aged legal oracle. Two hours each week William Lloyd Birkbeck, Downing Professor of Laws, gave him legal instruction which was supplemented by Mr. Fisher.

The Prince's most attractive experience at Cambridge was his association with the Professor of Modern History, Charles Kingsley, the popular novelist and broad-minded social reformer who had long since attracted the Prince Consort's favourable notice. Kingsley had few scholarly qualifications for his professorial chair, but he was full of enthusiasm for his subject and was a vivacious lecturer. The Prince rode over from Madingley thrice a week to the professor's house at Cambridge. On two of the days eleven undergraduates joined him in listening to the professor's eloquence. Each Saturday Kingsley recapitulated the week's work with the Prince alone. The course covered English history up to the close of the reign of George IV., and dealt freely with all aspects of the theme—the growth of the Constitution and of the Empire and the causes of the French Revolution. The historical smatterings which Goldwin Smith conveyed to the Prince's mind at Oxford acquired some consistency under Kingsley's spirited tuition. At the end of each term the Prince was examined by Kingsley in history, while other teachers tested his progress in other subjects. The last of the examinations to which Kingsley subjected the Prince (December 12, 1861) concerned the late eighteenth and early nineteenth century, and the Prince's answer to a question on the causes of the French Revolution shows a quaintly expressed effort to face the problem :

The causes of the French Revolution were the luxury and profligacy of the noblesse and clergy and the national bankruptcy. The poor king, who was surrounded by the noblesse and clergy, had to bear all their blame on his shoulders, and as soon as the tide turned against him they all deserted him. But the Revolution came to an end because the people had shed too much blood and they found that they could not govern themselves and were too happy when the Directorate came to an end and Napoleon became First Consul.

In another answer, the royal examinee deplored the tyranny of Napoleon over Europe and descanted on "the need of crushing him." A strong mutual affection developed between Kingsley

and his pupil. When Kingsley died, in January 1875, his eldest
daughter wrote to the Prince: "Next to his own children I
can truly say there was no human being my father loved as
he did you."

As at Frewin Hall, Oxford, there were private dinner-parties
at Madingley to which General Bruce invited, on the Prince's
behalf, leading members of the University and a few undergraduates. One of the earliest guests was George Otto
Trevelyan, Lord Macaulay's nephew, a promising Trinity man
whose acquaintance the Prince cultivated in London later.
Another of the Trinity College undergraduates who frequently
dined at Madingley was the Duke of St. Albans, whom the Prince
had met at Rome. Although the Prince Consort characteristically deprecated the Prince's acceptance of invitations from the
neighbouring great houses, the Prince was no infrequent visitor
at Wimpole, then the seat of the Earl of Hardwicke, a prominent
sportsman and lord-lieutenant of the county.

The Prince continued to hunt and to play tennis, but remained
a spectator only of the more customary sports of the University.
He maintained the interest which he had begun at Oxford in the
University Volunteers, joining the Cambridge corps, and becoming
Honorary Colonel of the two battalions of the Universities'
Volunteer Rifles. University celebrations attracted him. Writ-
ing to his friend Cadogan of the Commemoration season which
closed the summer term (May 22), he says:

We have been having great doings these last few days. On
Saturday the great Volunteer display took place and the procession of boats, as at Oxford. Monday there was a concert and
two very good cricket matches. Yesterday Lord Elgin [his
governor's brother], Lord Stratford de Redcliffe [his friend of
Rome], Sir Roderick Murchison, General Sabine, Mr. Grote, and
some others had honorary degrees conferred upon them.

One phase of undergraduate recreation which he especially
favoured was the Amateur Dramatic Club, which had existed on
sufferance since 1855. At the Club's premises behind the Hoop
Hotel in Jesus Lane the Prince was an appreciative spectator of
the farces and extravaganzas to which the Club's programmes
were confined, and his favour secured for the Club a fuller academic
recognition than it enjoyed before. With the founder of the Club,
Francis Burnand, he had much pleasant intercourse, which he

continued after leaving Cambridge, and he before long accepted
the office of Honorary President. In later life he revisited the
Club from time to time, presiding at the dinner at Cambridge
which celebrated in 1880 the Club's twenty-fifth birthday.[1]

Yet the Prince often chafed while at Cambridge against the
fetters on his freedom which his father was indisposed to slacken,
and the Prince Consort paid Madingley many visits in order to
give his son disciplinary counsel and to remind General Bruce of
the need of enforcing the old restraints.

III

The year 1861 was of tragic import for the Prince and all the
royal family. At the end of that year the Prince's father
prematurely and unexpectedly died, but the year which closed in
blackest gloom was darkened near its opening by a lesser domestic
grief. On 16th March the Prince's grandmother, the Duchess of
Kent, who had always loomed prominently in his boyish environment, passed away at Frogmore. With his mother's grief he
showed the tenderest sympathy. In the first days of her bereavement he was constantly with her.

"I am glad to say," he wrote to Bruce on the 21st from
Windsor Castle, "that the Queen is better, not quite so depressed
as she was at first. We go every morning to Frogmore (the
Duchess's burial-place), which seems to do her a great deal of
good." To his friend, Acland, he wrote three days later: "We
have all felt the death of the poor Duchess very deeply, but
especially the Queen, who has lost in her, her nearest and dearest
relation and friend. We must, however, be thankful that
Providence granted the Duchess so long and useful a life, and
though she had been in great suffering for some years past, her
death was calm and free from pain."

The Duchess's death was the youth's first experience of death
at close quarters.

When the Long Vacation set him free from Cambridge the
Prince had his first taste of the Court ceremonial of a Drawing-
Room (June 19). The function was held in the sombre conditions
of official mourning, which the Queen prolonged beyond the
customary period. A wholly joyful experience, however, befell

[1] F. C. Burnand, *The A.D.C.* (1880), pp. 212 *seq.*; A. Shipley, *Life of J. W.
Clark*.

him later in the summer. His long-cherished desire for military training was at length gratified. Bruce had changed his view as to the evil influences of military society, and had reached the conclusion that camp life was "a good field for social instruction." The Prince's original choice of Aldershot was still frowned upon, but the Prince Consort and Bruce agreed that some weeks in the summer might profitably be spent at Curragh Camp in Ireland. The Prince arrived at Kingstown on 29th June on his fourth visit to Ireland, with General Bruce and Colonel Henry Keppel in attendance. For the moment he became the guest of the Lord-Lieutenant, the eighth Earl of Carlisle, at Dublin Castle. The people of Dublin received him with acclamation and the Corporation presented him with an address of welcome at the Castle.

At the Curragh Camp he remained some ten weeks, being attached to the 2nd battalion of the Grenadier Guards, which was brigaded with the 36th regiment under Col. Percy. At his wish he was joined by Frederick Stanley, Lord Derby's son, a friend from boyhood, now a subaltern in the Grenadiers. Sir George Brown, who had seen service in the Crimea, was at the time Commander-in-Chief in Ireland, and his Headquarters' hut was made over to the Prince for his accommodation. Colonel Percy saw that the Prince was kept hard at work, but he found opportunities for relaxations free from the supervision of his middle-aged guardians. At the Headquarters' hut he exercised private hospitality. Under the influence of comrades in camp near his own age his outlook on life widened, and he was introduced to dissipations which were new to him. He learned for the first time something of the meaning of unimpeded liberty. At the same time, the significance of discipline was brought home to him by his subjection to punishment for a slight breach of it.

Criticism of his conduct was not wanting. The Duke of Cambridge came to the Curragh to review the troops (August 12 to 14), and deemed the Prince somewhat lacking in energy. On the 22nd Prince Albert and Queen Victoria arrived at the Vice-regal Lodge to see for themselves how their son was faring. On the 24th August there was a review in the Queen's honour. The Queen wrote rather half-heartedly to her uncle Leopold (August 26): "Bertie marched past with his company and did not look at all so very small." She lunched with her son in the Headquarters' hut. The Prince Consort, in conversation with his host, the Lord-Lieutenant, betrayed doubts as to whether his son was taking a sufficiently earnest view of soldiership. The father waxed eloquent over "the idle tendencies of English youth," and lamented that officers of the Army avoided professional topics on the ground that they were "shop."

There was a two days' interruption of the Prince's regimental duties when he accompanied his parents on a tour of Killarney. But the visit to the Curragh lasted till September 10. He then presented colours to the 36th Regiment, and "got through the ceremony nicely," wrote the Lord-Lieutenant. Popular interest in his presence remained active to the last. On 11th September, the day before he sailed for England, he attended a ball in his honour at the Mansion House in Dublin.[1] On the Prince the general effect of the Curragh visit was to stimulate a reactionary impatience of the many restrictions which had hitherto hindered his personal freedom.

IV

The Prince left Ireland in order to revisit his sister at Berlin. He went on a twofold errand. One purpose was to carry his military education a further step forward. He was to be the companion of his brother-in-law at the autumn manœuvres of the German Army about Coblenz. But the Prince's parents and eldest sister had an object other than fresh military experience in arranging for the visit to Germany. On dynastic and general grounds the Prince's relatives and guardians were anxious that he should marry without much delay. Though the Prince was as yet barely twenty, King Leopold and his confidant, Stockmar, had already, with their wonted prevision, brought their minds to bear on this important subject, and the King of the Belgians had prepared a list of eligible brides. In agreement with the current tradition of English royalty, it was from the Continent, and preferably from Germany, that it was proposed to draw the Prince's partner. As early as 20th July 1858 no less than seven young ladies of German princely houses were reported by *The Times* newspaper to be under consideration at Brussels and

---

[1] There are many references to the Prince's experience of the Curragh camp in the privately printed *Extracts from Journals (1843–64)*, by George Howard, Earl of Carlisle (Lord-Lieutenant of Ireland), pp. 327 *seq.*

Windsor. When news of the project first reached the Prince's ears he professed a boyish unconcern. The Queen wrote to him on the subject while he was at the Curragh, and she complained to General Bruce that he replied to her (August 16) " in a confused way."

Fifth on King Leopold's list was Princess Alexandra,[1] eldest daughter of Prince Christian of Schleswig-Holstein-Sonderburg-Glucksburg. Her father was the next heir, through his wife, to the throne of Denmark, which he ascended later (on 15th November 1863) as King Christian IX. Her mother, Louise of Hesse-Cassel, was sole heiress of the old Danish royal family, and the Princess Alexandra, who was barely seventeen, nearly three years the Prince's junior, was born and brought up at Copenhagen. Though her kinship was with Germany, her life was identified with Denmark, while through the old Duchess of Cambridge, who was aunt alike of her father and (by marriage) of Queen Victoria, she was already distantly linked with the English royal family.

The Princess Royal had flung herself with energy into the quest of a bride for her brother, and she learned from her lady-in-waiting, Walburga, Countess von Hohenthal, who was engaged to marry Augustus Paget, the British Minister at the Danish Court, of Princess Alexandra's beauty and grace. At Strelitz, in the palace of a kinswoman on both sides, the Grand Duchess of Mecklenburg-Strelitz,[2] an informal meeting followed between the Danish Princess and the Prince's sister. The Princess Royal declared herself to be "quite enchanted." She had met, she said, "the most fascinating creature in the world."[3] In a letter to her mother she expressed the conviction that Princess Alexandra was bound to succeed in the competition for her brother's hand.

The Prince's parents acknowledged a right on his part to freedom of choice. At their request, the Princess Royal, while her brother was in Germany in the summer of 1861, arranged an initial meeting between him and Princess Alexandra. Princess Alexandra was staying near Coblenz, at the castle of Rumpenheim, with her maternal grandfather, the Landgrave of Hesse-Cassel. Opportunity was given to the Prince of seeing her and of speaking

[1] Alexandra Caroline Maria Charlotte Louise Julia.
[2] The Grand Duchess was the old Duchess of Cambridge's elder daughter, and second cousin to both Princess Alexandra and the Princess Royal.
[3] Walburga Lady Paget, *Embassies of Other Days*, 1923, i. 138 *seq.*; *Empress Frederick: a Memoir*, 1913, pp. 109–10.

to her for the first time in the cathedral of the neighbouring town of Speier on the 24th September. Next day they met again at Heidelberg. Each made a favourable impression on the other. On 4th October Prince Albert wrote: "We hear nothing but excellent accounts of the Princess Alexandra; the young people seem to have taken a warm liking to one another." Again, when the Prince of Wales returned to England a few days later, his father wrote to Stockmar: "He has come back greatly pleased with his interview with the Princess at Speier." The romantic train was well laid, although Time was leisurely in applying the match.

1861

Ætat. 19

CHAPTER IX

THE DEATH OF THE PRINCE CONSORT

I

THE Prince Consort was spinning a fresh educational web. On 13th October 1861 his son resumed residence at Cambridge for a last academic term. In its course the calls of public life from time to time summoned him elsewhere. He came to London on 31st October, when, in accord with royal precedent, he was admitted to the Bar at the Middle Temple and was elected a Bencher; he also opened the Inn's new library. On the 5th November he attended at Windsor Castle the first investiture by the Queen of the newly established order of the Star of India. He and his father both received the decoration. Meanwhile General Bruce was pressing the obligations of the prescribed curriculum and discipline at the University, and the Prince was finding them increasingly irksome. The Prince Consort concluded that the approaching close of his son's Cambridge career should best be followed by another educational tour abroad— this time in the Near East by way of counterpoise to the visit to the West. The Holy Land was to be the goal, with some pauses on the road in Greece, Turkey, and Egypt, and the possibility of an extension to India.

Through the late autumn of 1861 the Prince Consort busily worked out the details of the journey. He consulted expert advisers, notably Arthur Penrhyn Stanley, who had toured the Holy Land in 1852, and had described his experiences in his book *Sinai and Palestine* (1855). On 25th November the Prince Consort arrived at Madingley to discuss the expedition with his son and with his son's governor, and at the same time to calm the impatience which the continued restraint was

provoking. The Prince Consort was suffering from a chill, and
stayed the night. On his return to Windsor the symptoms
developed into what unhappily proved a fatal malady. At
first recovery was anticipated in a few days, but on 7th December
the medical attendants pronounced the Prince Consort's condition to be serious, although by no means alarming. Five days
later, while the Prince was taking his terminal examinations in
history and chemistry at Cambridge, his sister, Princess Alice,
wrote from the sick-room that the Queen was proposing to give
her son, as a Christmas present, "something useful for his coming
journey." She added that her father "is very ill, but continues
to improve." In the middle of the night of 13th December a
wire reached the Prince at Madingley, announcing an unfavourable turn. He at once obeyed the summons to Windsor. Arriving at 3 A.M. next morning, he found his father dying and unable
to recognise him. The son remained at the bedside most of
the day, and at 10.45 P.M. the Prince Consort passed away in
the presence of his wife, his eldest son, and the other children,
save the eldest daughter, who was in Berlin, and the second
son Alfred, who was serving at sea. A career in which the
enjoyment of domestic happiness had been checked by too
exacting a sense of public duty closed prematurely at the age
of forty-two.

The Prince met the tragic blow with admirable feeling. To
his mother he showed all possible tenderness. "When all was
over he threw himself into her arms and said his whole life
should be devoted to endeavouring to comfort her and diminish
the anguish of her bereavement." [1]

The Queen placed for the moment an unprecedented confidence in the Prince of Wales, and entrusted him with the task
of replying to some early letters of condolence. The Prime
Minister, Lord Palmerston, was one of the first to write to her
of her loss, and to him the Prince sent, by her direction, the
following acknowledgement in his own hand :

WINDSOR CASTLE,
December 16th, 1861.

DEAR LORD PALMERSTON—I cannot tell you how touched
my mother was by your kind and sympathising letter.

[1] Maxwell, *Life of Lord Clarendon*, vol. ii. p. 253.

You know the loss which we have sustained, and how irreparable it is to her, to us, and to the country for whom he lived.

My mother wished me to tell you that her life would now be but a life of duty, which she would perform to the best of her abilities, but that her worldly career was closed for ever.

She bears this fearful calamity with a courage which is touching to witness, and you can I feel sure feel for us, who have lost one of the best of fathers who can never be replaced.

You will I hope excuse these hurried lines, but at such a time the words are wanting to express what one feels.—Believe me, dear Lord Palmerston, yours very sincerely,

ALBERT EDWARD.

Two days later the Prince wrote to Lord Russell, the Foreign Secretary, on his mother's behalf, in a similar strain :

She wished me to say that her future happiness was blighted for ever, but that she would now live solely for her duties and try in every way to do that which she thought her departed husband would have wished. My mother hopes that her children will be an assistance to her, and that they will show themselves worthy in every way of such a father.

On the 19th December Queen Victoria, by her uncle Leopold's advice, removed to Osborne, the Prince accompanying her to Gosport. Four days later the Prince Consort's remains were solemnly laid to rest in St. George's Chapel, Windsor. The Prince represented his mother as chief mourner, and showed a distress which pained all onlookers. The same afternoon he joined the Queen in the Isle of Wight. At the Queen's request he at once wrote a letter for publication, identifying himself with her overwhelming desire that her husband's memory should receive all public honour. On the 28th December he offered to place at his own expense, in the gardens of the Royal Horticultural Society, a statue of his father instead of one of the Queen which had already been cast for erection there by way of memorial of the Great Exhibition of 1851.

The condolences of personal friends the Prince acknowledged with simply worded avowals of his affection for "one of the kindest and best of fathers," of his solicitude for the Queen, and of his sense of the misfortune which had befallen him in being deprived of paternal advice and counsel just at the time when he stood most in need of them. To his Oxford friend, Dr. Acland, he graphically described his sense of the "terrible blow," and the comfort which he derived from the general sympathy.

The chaos which *now* exists, and which *will* exist for a long time to come, is too dreadful to think of, as *you* know full well *what* a father he was to us all. Thank God the Queen bears up most wonderfully, and her health has not suffered, but what it has been to *her* is untold; God only knows *how* fearful this blow has been to her; but you may be quite sure that we shall do everything in our power to assist and console her.

It is gratifying to see how thoroughly the whole nation mourns and sympathises with us, and that they feel what a loss *he* is to the whole country, and *how* grateful they ought to be for what he has done for them.

II

The shock of grief faded slowly from the young man's mind. His father's austere habit of reproof had inspired him with a reverential awe without impairing his filial affection. Despite the restraints on boyish liberty and the educational discipline in which the paternal wisdom chiefly made itself visible to the son, the boyish faith in his dead father's exalted and disinterested motive lived on. In later life he often recalled happy memories of their familiar intercourse with one another. "It makes me so sad," he wrote to his mother on 16th August 1863, when she was visiting the scenes of her late husband's youth, "to think that I never went to Germany with dear Papa. I should have liked so much to have visited his home with him and heard and seen him point out those spots of which he used to tell us so much when we were children, but I know them well, and will ever be pleased to go to Coburg and Gotha, which ought always to be so dear to us." So, too, when Queen Victoria, near the end of her career, was celebrating her Diamond Jubilee, thirty-six years after her husband's death, the Prince of Wales, in thanking her for appointing him to the office of Grand Master of the Order of the Bath, which had lapsed on his father's death, gladdened his mother's heart by the words: "I feel it as a very high honour, having succeeded dear Papa after an interval of so many years."

The complete understanding between his mother and father excited, too, his unstinted admiration. Fervently had he joined in the annual celebrations of their wedding-day (February 9), and great was his concern that circumstances compelled his absence on two of these occasions—in 1859, when he was in Rome, and on the latest recurrence in 1861, when detained by his governor at Cambridge, he wrote to his mother: "I hope that you and dear Papa may live to see many more anniversaries of the day"—a hope which he now saw frustrated.

For his mother the Prince's affection was more instinctive than for his father. It was never materially diminished by upbraidings which often echoed her husband's groans over their son's want of application, his frivolous tendencies, and his too "free and easy" talk. His mother's sudden bereavement inspired him with a wish to assuage his mother's sorrows, not only by the personal attentions which affection prompted, but by some helpful participation in those public responsibilities which his dead father had shared with the Queen. From the sense of dependence which his father's training had bred in him, he now reasonably looked—and many encouraged him to look—for a partial emancipation. Recent associates outside his family circle recognised in him the promise of fitness for public life, and they expected the widowed Queen to give her heir the opportunities of putting his qualifications for public responsibility to the test without delay. "The Prince," wrote Lord Torrington, a lord-in-waiting of shrewd common sense, to his confidential friend, Delane, editor of *The Times*, four days after the Prince Consort's death, "is singularly honest and truthful, and wherever he has had a chance, as was the case in Canada, has done his work well. He deserves a little of *her* confidence, and the pretence to consult him would have a great effect on his mind." [1] *The Times* newspaper, immediately after his father's death, drew public attention to his hereditary place in the State and took for granted that public duties would now fall on his shoulders whereby he might "earn the confidence of the country." Lord Palmerston, the Prime Minister, while warning him against "the allurements of fortune, position, and social temptation," reminded him that

[1] Lord Torrington sent to Delane almost daily at this period, frankly written descriptions of Court affairs, often signing himself "Your Windsor official." Selections from Torrington's letters, which cover a wide range of matters affecting the Prince of Wales and other members of the royal family, are printed in Mr. Dasent's *Life of Delane* (1908).

the duties and responsibilities of his station would soon teach
him "how greatly the welfare of this great nation may be influenced by the course which you may pursue." Even General
Bruce was sanguine that he would show himself entitled to
"the affection and confidence of a grateful people" by virtue
of his fidelity to duty.

But all anticipations of the Prince's admission on his father's
death to substantive public responsibilities were defeated by the
action of the Queen, whose will, always strong, now acquired the
force of iron. The welcome which in the first hours of her
bereavement she had given her son's proffers of help was a
surrender to an impulse which she promptly checked. Her sense
of loyalty to her husband's memory convinced her that it was her
first and last duty to perform without assistance from any one, in
his precise way, every iota of his labours, whether in the political
or in the domestic sphere. Hitherto Queen Victoria had viewed
the supervision of her eldest son's life and conduct as his father's
main concern. It was for her, while the Prince Consort lived,
only to endorse the stern and studious discipline to which he
subjected the youth. Now that her husband was dead she
deemed herself under a solemn obligation to enforce on their
son all his father's restraints. She determined to exercise,
without relaxation, the paternal control to which his father had
accustomed him. All the carefully laid plans which the Prince
Consort had formed in his lifetime for her heir's career and
conduct she in her widowhood would execute to the letter.
She reckoned it of advantage that General Bruce was at hand
to help in the rigorous fulfilment of her purpose.

An earlier resolve to prevent any encroachment of her son's
hereditary status on her husband's dignity would have seemed
to colour her present sentiment and action. Before the Prince
Consort's death she had nursed an uneasy fear that the Prince
might in time fill in affairs of State the first place after herself—
a place to which she regarded her husband alone entitled. When
the Prince of Wales had just passed his sixteenth birthday,
she earnestly appealed to Lord Palmerston to introduce into
Parliament a bill giving her husband legal precedence over her
eldest son. She had long meditated such a step in spite of
Stockmar's cautious warnings. Now, in 1857, when the Queen
"was much excited about this matter," Lord Granville, one

of Lord Palmerston's colleagues, appealed to Stockmar to use his influence with the Queen to induce her to drop the proposal. In the result no more was heard of it, but the motive which prompted it was not dispelled.[1] On her husband's death her anxiety to keep the Prince in a subordinate position revived in all its intensity.

Writing to her uncle, King Leopold, on 24th December 1861, she plainly defined her feelings and her intentions ten days after her loss.

"*No human power*," she wrote, "will make me swerve from *what he* decided and wished. . . . I apply this particularly as regards our children—Bertie, etc.—for whose future he had traced everything *so* carefully. I am *also determined* that *no one* person, may *he* be ever so good, ever so devoted, among my servants—is to lead or guide or dictate *to me*."[2]

In a like spirit she explained to General Bruce on the 5th January 1862, that she alone would decide, in conformity with her husband's counsels, to which none but herself had been admitted, the future of the Prince of Wales and her other children.

"About the children," she wrote, "she has had many conversations with her beloved angel and she feels that *she* knows exactly what he wished. This being the case the Queen must decide what she thinks the best and the least likely to injure them permanently. She is ready to take the responsibility of this decision upon herself as she feels *sure* she is acting as he would wish."

In the despondency of her first months of widowhood the Queen often foretold her early death and her son's early accession to her throne. On such grounds she at times admitted that the Prince ought to become "more and more acquainted with affairs and the way in which they are conducted." Yet, with a feminine lack of logic, the admission had no practical effect on her treatment of her eldest son as one *in statu pupillari*, who was permanently incapable of adult responsibilities or confidences.

The Queen's expectations of early death were unfulfilled, and through great part of the remaining forty years of her reign she deemed it her duty rigorously to limit her son's activities

[1] Fitzmaurice, *Life of Lord Granville*, i. 225.
[2] *Letters of Queen Victoria*, iii. 606.

alike in public and in private matters. She convinced herself   1861
that she owed him for life that magisterial guidance in all   Ætat. 19
relations which his father would have given him had he lived.
Successive ministers of State, who differed greatly in temperament and political opinion, were at one in questioning the justice
of her principle of restraint. Their recurring remonstrances
and her questionings of their argument fill a large place in the
Prince's history. The passage of time proved that she over-
estimated her powers of control. The exuberant vitality of
her son's manhood sought all manner of outlets and immersed
him, in spite of the Queen's admonitions and discouragements,
in all the great streams of affairs. From any share in her constitutional functions of rule, she to the last rigidly excluded
him; but when at length her years lay heavy on her and
her son was well advanced in middle life she invited at times
his counsel and co-operation in political, social, and domestic
matters which lay outside the constitutional range. Even then
she found difficulty in divesting herself of her old conviction
that he stood in need of her advice and help rather than that
she stood in need of his.

CHAPTER X

TOURING THE NEAR EAST—SETTING UP AS HOUSEHOLDER
AND COUNTRY GENTLEMAN

I

1862
Ætat. 20

SCARCELY had the first shock of bereavement passed away before Queen Victoria set herself to carry out with scrupulous fidelity the two plans which her husband had devised before his death for his eldest son's welfare—firstly, the tour in the East under the control of General Bruce, and, secondly, his marriage. With all her husband's punctilious precision she spent a great part of the month of January 1862, in drafting the Prince's Eastern itinerary and in determining the conditions of travel which were appropriate to "his present very deep mourning." The detailed plans were penned in her own hand. He was to keep the "very strictest incognito." He might visit sovereigns "in strict privacy"; but could accept no other invitations. No social intercourse was to be permitted save with members of the suite or with persons "of royal or high official or personal rank or those whose superior character and attainments may render their society interesting and improving." Provision was made for reading serious books and for hearing them read aloud.

The proposed route raised some political issues. The Prime Minister, Lord Palmerston, offered objection to a main feature of the Prince Consort's plan—the visit to Syria. There had been outbreaks of disorder in Syria which English and French troops had repressed with difficulty. Lord Granville felt certain that the visit would be "much disapproved by the public, but," he added (in writing to a friend), "the Queen and Prince both wish it so much that it is perhaps better that he should go" (January 16, 1862). The revolt in Greece against King Otho compelled

the omission of that country from the outward route as the
Prince Consort had intended. The Queen thought the projected
extension to India might follow in the autumn and discussed the
point with General Bruce's brother, the newly appointed Viceroy,
the Earl of Elgin, but ultimately the Prince's visit to India was
eliminated. In all other respects the Prince Consort's original
design was unchanged.

At the Queen's invitation Arthur Penrhyn Stanley visited her
at Osborne, to supplement the advice which he had already
given her late husband, and she persuaded him, somewhat against
his will, to act as the Prince's chief guide through the Holy
Land. It was a happy choice. As Jowett, Stanley's friend,
wrote, "there is no one equally fit, no one who could amuse and
influence the Prince in the same way."

The Queen's nervous fears of early death which might place
the Prince of Wales on her throne led her to hasten his departure.
Nothing must interfere, she said, with the execution of a programme on which the Prince Consort had set his heart. Before
the expedition started she prepared instructions for the Prince
in case of his early accession. General Bruce, who was accompanying the Prince in his rôle of Governor,[1] was ordered to sober
his charge's thought by keeping this possibility before his mind.
Bruce assured the Queen that he would do everything to
"inoculate" the Prince "with a taste for useful pursuits."
Furthermore, he undertook to encourage "the contemplated
marriage" with Princess Alexandra, which the Prince Consort
had favoured (January 7, 1862).

II

The five months' tour was marked by a variety of new and
exhilarating experiences, in presence of which the haunting
memories of his father's death faded and his youthful buoyancy
reasserted itself. There was a stimulating expansion of the
youth's acquaintance, alike with historic places and with persons
who played leading parts in the current political drama.

[1] Besides General Bruce, the Prince's companions were the equerries,
Major Teesdale, V.C., and Colonel Frederick Charles Keppel, the Hon. Robert
Meade of the Foreign Office who had accompanied Lord Dufferin on a mission
to Syria in 1860, and the physician, Dr. Minter. Dr. Stanley went out to Egypt
independently.

The start was made on 5th of February, after the Prince had taken leave of the Queen at Osborne. His outward path lay through Germany and Austria to the Austrian port of Trieste, where he was to embark for Egypt. Along the route there were offered him official hospitalities such as the Queen's injunctions vetoed, but they were not always easy to evade.

In his passage through Germany he stopped at Darmstadt to greet young Prince Louis of Hesse, heir to the Duchy, who was recently betrothed to his second sister, Alice. On the 13th February he reached Vienna on what was to prove the first of many visits. Contrary to the Queen's wish, Lord Bloomfield, the English Ambassador, had notified the Austrian Government of his coming. The Kaiser, Francis Joseph, was with difficulty restrained from paying the Prince some prohibited ceremonial attentions—a guard of honour, a State dinner, and a military parade. The Prince lodged privately at an hotel, but the Kaiser, who promptly visited him there, acted as his guide through the chief public buildings; and the Prince always remembered pleasantly his first experience of the Austrian Emperor's smiling but taciturn courtliness. Among those to whom the English Ambassador, Lord Bloomfield, privately introduced him, the most fascinating was the traveller and man of letters, Laurence Oliphant, who had once served as secretary to Lord Elgin.[1] To Oliphant the Adriatic coast of the Mediterranean was familiar country, and he agreed to act as the Prince's cicerone as far as Corfu. At Trieste the royal yacht *Osborne* awaited the party (February 15). Almost furtively they crossed to Venice, where popular hatred of the doomed Austrian rule was rampant. Lord Russell, the Foreign Secretary, peremptorily warned the English agent in Venice that any demonstration of the Venetians in the Prince's honour might offend Austria.[2] It was "in strictest incognito" that the Prince came under the city's enchantment. At Corfu—the chief of the seven Ionian islands which still reluctantly acknowledged the British protectorate—caution was again needed to avoid wounding local sensibilities. The Prince benefited by the expert guidance of Oliphant, who took leave of him at Corfu after "a most pleasant ten days" together. Oliphant's vivacity gave the Prince unqualified enjoyment.

[1] Mrs. Oliphant's *Life of Laurence Oliphant*, i. 269.
[2] *Layard Papers in British Museum*, MS. addit. 39102, ff. 271, 363.

Years later, when he was entertaining him at Abergeldie, he took him over to Balmoral to dine with Queen Victoria, who shared her son's liking for Oliphant's exhilarating talk.

At length, on the 28th February—after a visit to Zante, another Ionian island—the Prince disembarked at Alexandria to make a first acquaintance with Egypt. Dr. Stanley awaited him there, and for the tour in Egypt, Palestine, and Syria was the Prince's inseparable companion and counsellor.[1]

The enlightened and genial Viceroy of Egypt, Said Pasha, son of the famous Mehemet, insisted on showing the Prince a lavish hospitality, in spite of Queen Victoria's demurs. "Everything," wrote Bruce (March 3, 1862), "is found for us"; the Prince reckoned the cost of the entertainment at £8000. A special train was provided for the journey from Alexandria to Cairo, and the palace of Kasr-en-Nil was appointed for the Prince's residence. The Prince was in high spirits, and rather disconcerted an elderly pasha who was told off by the Viceroy to attend on him, by insisting on a donkey ride through the streets on his arrival in Cairo. The example of the sedate French royalist, Comte de Chambord, who on a recent visit had resisted such temptation, was cited in vain. "I remember the donkeys well in Egypt," the Prince wrote some two years later to his friend Earl Spencer, "and the white ones (a specimen of which he accepted from Colquhoun, the English Consul-General) are splendid animals." But the Prince's time in Egypt was mainly spent in a twenty days' ascent of the Nile, for which the Viceroy placed two steamers at the party's disposal. Before joining the boats the Prince climbed the summit of the great Pyramid without assistance and with surprising alacrity (March 6). On the river trip he eagerly explored the chief ruins near the banks,—the temple of Carnac at Luxor, the monuments at Thebes and Philæ, and the temple of Dendera, where he discovered in the features of the statue of Queen Cleopatra a resemblance to those of Bishop Wilberforce of Oxford. "Thebes, especially," he wrote to Acland on the 27th March, "is a most interesting place and contains some wonderful antiquities."

The Prince readily obeyed Stanley's directions as to the strict observance of Sunday, and listened with attention to

[1] During the Egyptian visit the party was also joined by Consul-General Colquhoun and by Captain Power of the *Osborne*.

Stanley's weekly sermons. At the Prince's suggestion Stanley held one Sunday's service within the Temple of Carnac. The voyage gave the Prince opportunity of rough shooting. The prey were chiefly geese and crows. He agreed to keep his gun idle on Sundays, with a sole reservation in favour of crocodiles. There was time on board for reading, and the Prince attacked with unusual zest Mrs. Henry Wood's lately published novel of *East Lynne*. Not only did he recommend it to his companions, but he submitted them, after they had taken his advice, to cross-examination on the details of the story.

The boats did not get beyond the First Cataract. Cairo was reached on the return journey on 23rd March. On disembarking there, Dr. Stanley learnt of his mother's death in England a fortnight earlier, and the Prince showed the liveliest sympathy. "Poor Dr. Stanley," he wrote to Acland, "has felt the death of his mother terribly, but has behaved with the noblest resignation, which so thoroughly marks his character, and he has made up his mind to continue travelling with us, which I am very glad of, as we should miss him very much."

III

The royal yacht *Osborne* brought the party from Alexandria to Jaffa, the port of Palestine, on 31st March. The following five weeks were devoted under Dr. Stanley's tuition to study of scriptural sites. The party pursued their journey on horseback, with an escort of fifty mounted Turkish spearmen, and until Damascus was reached the Prince and his companions camped in tents. Most week-days were spent on the march. Sunday alone was a day of rest. The expedition recalled a very remote past. Nearly six centuries had elapsed since an English Prince —Prince Edward, afterwards King Edward I.—had set foot in the Holy Land.

Through thickets and over stony ridges the Prince rode from Jaffa to the city of Jerusalem, where he was met by the Turkish Governor, Sûraya Pasha; the English Consul, Mr. Finn; and a mob of Franciscan monks, Greek priests, and Jews. The camp was pitched outside the Damascus Gate.[1] Very thorough was

---

[1] An account of the tour through the Holy Land appears in Bradley's and Prothero's *Life of Stanley*, vol. ii., and in Stanley's *Sermons preached before the Prince of Wales during his Tour in the East in the Spring of 1862, with Notices of some of the Localities visited* (1863).

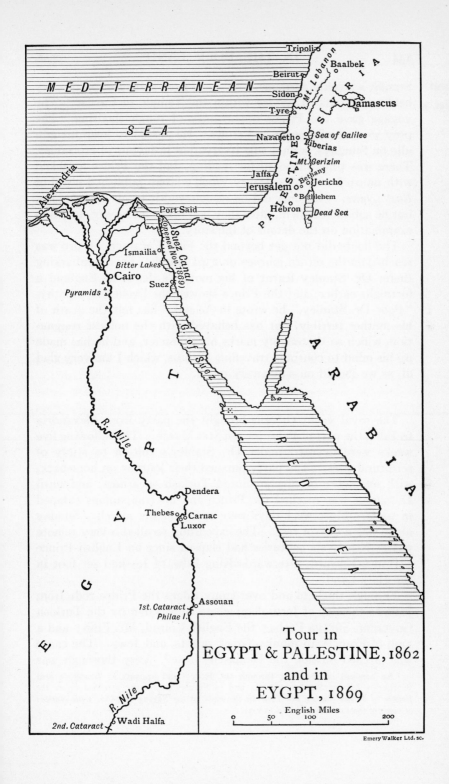

MEDITERRANEAN

SEA

Tripoli

Mt. Lebanon

Baalbek

Beirut

S Y R I A

Sidon

Mt. Lebanon

Damascus

Tyre

Alexandria

Nazareth

Sea of Galilee

Tiberias

PALESTINE

Mt. Gerizim

Jaffa

Bethany

Jerusalem

Jericho

Bethlehem

Port Said

Hebron

Dead Sea

Ismailia

Bitter Lakes

Suez Canal (opened Nov. 1869)

Cairo

Suez

Pyramids

G. of Suez

E G Y P T

A R A B I A

R. Nile

R E D

Dendera

Thebes

Carnac

Luxor

S E A

1st. Cataract

Assouan

Philae I.

Tour in
EGYPT & PALESTINE, 1862
and in
EYGPT, 1869

R. Nile

English Miles

0   50   100   200

2nd. Cataract

Wadi Halfa

Emery Walker Ltd. sc.

the Prince's exploration of Jerusalem and its neighbourhood.
Amid the hills of Judea, the ruined grove of Jericho, on the
shore of the Dead Sea, in Bethlehem, and in Bethany Dr. Stanley
impressed the Prince with the sacredness of the associations.

One experience of sight-seeing was due to an exceptional
concession. The mosque of Hebron, beneath which lies the cave
of Machpelah, the reputed burial-place of the Hebrew patriarchs,
twenty miles south-west of Jerusalem, had been for nearly seven
centuries, since 1187, hermetically sealed to Christian travellers
of every rank. The Turkish Governor gave way with misgivings
to General Bruce's urgent appeal to admit the Prince, who fully
appreciated the privilege, remarking self-complacently: "High
station has, after all, some merits, some advantages." The visit
took place on 4th April, amid much ceremony. The native
populace were kept at a distance, and the Prince passed into the
mosque through an avenue of Turkish soldiers. Dr. Rosen, the
Prussian Consul of Jerusalem, a Palestinian archæologist of
repute, was allowed to join the party.

The Prince's interest was fully sustained on the journey
north towards Damascus. On the 13th April he made the ascent
of Mount Gerizim, near the summit of which he found the small
Samaritan community in tents celebrating the annual passover
with traditional ceremonial. Good Friday (April 17) was spent
at Nazareth, and Easter Sunday at Tiberias, on the shore of the
Lake of Galilee, where the Prince took communion and Stanley
preached. Occasional guests—governors, vice-consuls, and Protestant clergy—were invited to dine on the route in the Prince's
tent, and on Easter Sunday the Prince entertained the Swiss
Lutheran Bishop of Jerusalem, Samuel Gobat, who, as the nominee
of the Prince's godfather, the King of Prussia, was the central
figure in much theological controversy.

Outside Damascus, camp life came to a close. Within the
city the Prince saw the only signs throughout the tour of
Mohammedan disaffection. As he passed through the bazaars
the Muslem traders remained seated, and abstained from offering
salutations. From Damascus the party reached Beirut on the
sea-coast (May 6), inspecting on the road the historic remains
at Baalbek. The reception at Beirut was quite cordial, and none
of the untoward incidents which Lord Palmerston feared broke
the harmony of the Syrian tour. The *Osborne* brought the Prince

1862
Ætat. 20
from Beirut to the sea-ports of Tyre and Sidon, and thence to Syrian Tripoli for a sight of the cedars of Lebanon. From Tripoli sail was set westwards to the Greek Archipelago (May 13), where the first pause was made at the Island of Rhodes. The next landing-place was the rarely visited harbour of Patmos, where Stanley explained the traditional association with St. John the Evangelist. A short stay at Smyrna brought the scriptural tour to an end. Stanley's easy and lively guidance brought out the Prince's best qualities. "It is impossible not to like him," Stanley wrote while they were travelling together; "and to be constantly with him brings out his astonishing memory of names and persons." [1]

IV

The rest of the tour, which belonged to Europe, brought the Prince fresh stores of historic memories, mingled with intimate glimpses of current political movements. At Constantinople, where he was the guest of the British Ambassador, Sir Henry Lytton Bulwer, the Sultan Abdul-Aziz protested against the Queen's veto of a State reception. Lord Palmerston's Government, wishful to conciliate the Porte, acceded to the Sultan's wish to entertain the Prince at a State breakfast (May 20). There the Prince dropped his incognito, and, accepting the honours due to his rank of heir-apparent, he held tactful intercourse with the Sultan, after a little coaching from the British Ambassador. Near the end of the stay, in course of which Sir Henry Bulwer made him acquainted with the picturesque aspects of the Turkish capital, the Prince vainly sought permission to realise a fancy of his boyhood and proceed to Sebastopol, an historic landmark in the Crimean War. "*He is most anxious* to see it," wrote Bruce to the Queen's confidant, Sir Charles Phipps (February 28, 1862), "and I think that as a compliment to the Army his doing so would be well taken." But objection was raised that, if he was to visit the Crimea, he should start elsewhere than at Sebastopol from which British arms had gained small glory. The plan for the time was dropped.

From Constantinople the *Osborne* bore the Prince southwards to Athens. Domestic turmoil rendered his visit hardly opportune. Greece had just expelled her autocratic King Otho

[1] Prothero, *Life and Correspondence of Dean Stanley*, ii. 69.

of Bavaria, and a provisional government was considering how to fill the vacant throne. But a lull in the crisis allowed the Prince to inspect undisturbed the historic scenes and monuments, with the aid of the British Minister, Henry George Elliot, who was seeking to alleviate internal strife. Coming events were casting their shadow before. Fate was about to bring the sovereignty of the restless country within the Prince's domestic orbit, and the fortunes of the Greek throne were to become an active interest of his adult career.

The Prince made his way home through France, sailing direct for Marseilles after a brief landing at yet another Ionian island, Cephalonia. The French Imperial Court offered an elaborate reception, but Queen Victoria would only sanction her son's acceptance of the hospitality due to a private traveller. The Emperor Napoleon III. and the Empress Eugénie obeyed the condition while paying him congenial attentions at their beautiful country palace of Fontainebleau. The lack of official formality inclined to stimulate rather than to check the Prince's appreciation of the frolicsome gaieties of the French Court.

V

On 13th June 1862 the Prince rejoined his mother at Windsor. He was well satisfied with all that he had gone through. Three days later he was writing to Acland: "We arrived here on Saturday last, after having successfully terminated my Eastern tour, which I think can be called in every way a thorough success. I shall always look back to it with great pleasure and interest." The tour would seem to have fully justified his late father's aim. Very varied were the pages of history which his itinerary had revealed to him, and his curiosity concerning prominent actors on the political stage abroad had been whetted by his meeting on even terms with rulers like the Emperor Francis Joseph of Austria; Said Pasha, Khedive of Egypt; and Abdul-Aziz, Sultan of Turkey. More familiar was his intercourse with humbler personages of good judgement and attainments, like Laurence Oliphant, Julian Fane, the accomplished attaché at Vienna, and Sir Henry Bulwer at Constantinople. All, writing confidentially and independently, formed a favourable estimate of the Prince's ease and accessibility and of his alert faculty of observation.

Nor were they blind to defects. Oliphant deemed his chief disadvantage to lie in a "position which never allows him responsibility or forces him into action." Bulwer, while judging it dangerous to submit him to too severe restraints, detected an undue eagerness for amusement. Travel, all agreed, was a better kind of education for him than the study of books. Oliphant sanguinely foretold that "his development will be higher than people anticipate." [1]

It was to a mournful home that the Prince returned. In one of the last letters which General Bruce received on the tour from Queen Victoria, she had bidden him warn her son against indulging in her hearing in "worldly, frivolous, gossiping kind of conversation." The Prince must be prepared to face, in a proper spirit, the cureless melancholy of his poor home. As soon as the Queen greeted her son she summoned Dr. Stanley to her side and begged him to continue an intercourse which might, she believed, give her son's thought a serious turn.

The Prince himself took a lighter-hearted view than his mother of Dr. Stanley's agreeable companionship. "Dr. Stanley," he wrote playfully to Acland, "came back very well, with a formidable black beard which I hope you will see, and got permission from the Queen to preach in it yesterday.[2] . . . Both Keppel and Teesdale have been well, and have also brought hairy appendages to their chins with them." The Prince improved on this example of his seniors. He never used a razor in his life.

At the same time the Prince gave his mother no cause to complain of his levity or resistance to her will. General Bruce had kept the prospect of marriage with Princess Alexandra well before his mind. While in the East the Prince had written to the Queen thanking her for the trouble she and his eldest sister had been taking about his prospects, and expressing the hope that the Queen would be "pleased with the young Princess [Alexandra] when you see her." Once more at home the Prince relieved the Queen of any remaining anxiety about his marriage by showing her "a number of pretty things" which he had

[1] Mrs. Oliphant's *Life of Laurence Oliphant;* letters from Julian Fane in Lady Rose Weigall's *A Memoir* (1923), pp. 96–7; and Sir Henry Bulwer's despatch to Lord Russell in Esher's *Influence of King Edward,* 1915, pp. 34–6.

[2] The sermon preached at Windsor on 15th June was published in the volume of 1863.

bought abroad "for the young lady," and by expressing a wish   1862
for the wedding to take place in the following spring. The   Ætat. 20
gratified mother wrote to her eldest daughter in Berlin soon
after the Prince's arrival at Windsor : "Bertie goes on being
as good, amiable, and sensible as any one of us could wish. . . .
Dear General Bruce's anxious efforts and wishes have not
been in vain." [1]

But General Bruce's term of service was reaching a tragic
close while the Queen was writing to her daughter. In the
marshes of the Upper Jordan he contracted an illness which
gradually developed on the way home. On his return to the
rooms of his sister, Lady Augusta Bruce, in St. James's Palace,
the "low Syrian fever" as the Prince called the ailment,
grew acute, and within less than a fortnight he died there
(June 27). Despite the pathos attaching to General Bruce's
death, it looked at the moment like fate's decree against a
continuance of the tutelage which had hitherto hampered the
Prince's volition.

In presence of the shock the Prince thought only of the
good points in his relationship with his dead Governor. On
the 3rd July the Prince wrote to Acland : "Poor General Bruce's
death has been a terrible blow to me as it has been to everybody
who knew him ; it is really too sad to think that his end was
caused by catching a fever on our tour which we all so thoroughly
enjoyed. . . . I have lost in him a most useful and valuable
friend." By the Queen, General Bruce's death was viewed as
an irreparable misfortune. "He died," she lamented, in her
son's "service," and in the performance of these stern duties
which the late Prince Consort had imposed on him. The
Queen took General Bruce's widow into her household as a
lady-in-waiting, and Mrs. Bruce became one of the Prince's
constant correspondents.

VI

The withdrawal within six months of two such restraining
influences as his father and his Governor gave a promise, which
proved somewhat fallacious, of the Prince's emancipation from
leading-strings. At court, in ministerial circles, and in the
press, there at once circulated suggestions to the effect that the

[1] Walburga, Lady Paget, *Embassies of Other Days*, i. 158.

1862
Ætat. 20

Prince should now be given definite employment with independent responsibilities. The Queen had gloomily admitted that her son "must prepare himself more and more for that position which the Queen cannot help thinking he may not be as far removed from as many may wish to think." There could be no better discipline for early manhood (it was argued) and no better preparation for sovereignty than regular employment. Yet the Queen, despite her satisfaction with her son's attitude to the question of marriage, could not bring herself to break with the rigorous tradition of her late husband's discipline. Major Elphinstone, who was tutor of the Prince's younger brother, Arthur, put the situation in its true light when he remarked: "If given occupation he (*i.e.* the Prince of Wales) will be sure to go right, but I fear the Queen is not disposed to let him interfere in public." [1]

The Times newspaper, utilising hints supplied to the editor, Delane, by Lord Torrington, put forward a considered proposal on the subject of the Prince's occupation. The Queen had publicly announced that she was unequal to the task of entertaining foreign sovereigns or representatives of foreign countries, many of whom were visiting London for the International Exhibition of 1862. In spite of the suspension of court functions the Exhibition, which the Prince Consort had designed and the Duke of Cambridge had opened in May, rendered the season unusually gay, and brought to London throngs of visitors from abroad. The Prince privately inspected the Exhibition immediately on his return, and was "much pleased," he wrote to Acland (June 16), with what he saw, "but it takes a long time to see everything thoroughly." The foreign visitors especially attracted him, and he sought private introductions to several of them. One from France, the buoyant cavalry officer, the Marquis de Galliffet, exerted on him an immediate fascination which led to a lifelong attachment. *The Times*, in view of the Prince's developing social instinct, recommended that the duties of royal host should now officially devolve on the Prince: "We feel sure that His Royal Highness, who has won golden opinions as the guest of foreign sovereigns, will know how to greet the friends of England in his own country."

Yet the Queen ignored all such counsel, turning a deaf ear

[1] Dasent's *Life of J. T. Delane*, 1908, ii. 49–50.

to the spreading cry that "idleness might do her son injury."
Grave offence was indeed caused her by the remark of a former
Foreign Secretary, Lord Clarendon, that even the Prince Consort
would have discovered for his son at full age some kind of
regular work which would keep him "out of harm," whether
as "Regent of Scotland, or a clerk in the Audit Office, or Bailiff
of the Home Farm." [1]

General Bruce's death moved the Queen's thought in quite
a different direction. She set about choosing a new Governor
who might continue General Bruce's control. For this office
the Queen selected General Sir William Knollys, a veteran
soldier, who had instructed the Prince Consort in his military
duties and enjoyed his complete confidence. Sir William was
just completing his sixty-fifth year, and his employment had
been for a generation confined to enforcing military discipline.
In the year of the Prince Consort's death he had accepted the
post of President of the Council of Military Education. The
Prince demurred to his mother's choice, but yielded to her
peremptory persuasion. In the summer of 1862 Sir William
was entrusted with the control of the Prince's affairs. The
appointment proved less oppressive than was anticipated. Sir
William, who remained in the Prince's service for fifteen years,
showed a welcome pliancy in adapting himself to inevitable
changes in the conditions of his office. He won the Prince's
trust by placing the Prince's best interests above everything
else. Soon after he entered upon his duties the Prince wrote
to his mother that Sir William was "a thorough gentleman,
a well-informed man with plenty of tact, and an agreeable
companion."

VII

Although the custom of the Constitution justified the Queen
in denying the heir-apparent any political function, yet hereditary
right assured him on reaching his majority an independent
revenue and the responsibility which went with a private
competence. The heir-apparent's hereditary rank of Duke of
Cornwall gave him, when he came of age, full possession, beyond
parental control, of substantial property. The Duchy of Cornwall, his hereditary appanage, included large estates not only in

[1] Maxwell's *Clarendon*, ii. 284.

1862
Ætat. 20

the county, but in London—in Lambeth and in Kennington. Of the Manor of Kennington the Duke of Cornwall was lord. On the Prince's entry into man's estate the returns of the Duchy were considerable. During the Prince's minority the property was administered by his father in the capacity of Lord Warden of the Stannaries (or tin-mines) and High Steward of the Duchy —offices which he assumed in 1842 and held till his death. The Prince Consort performed his administrative duties with admirable effect. The income rose from £16,000 at the date of the Prince's birth to nearly £60,000 when he came of age. The annual revenue was allowed to accumulate during the eighteen years of the Prince's minority, and in 1860 a capital sum of some £600,000 was at the Prince's disposal. When the Prince Consort's death vacated the offices of superintendence, the Queen conferred them on the Duke of Newcastle. The Prince assumed a personal supervision on the 9th November 1862, when he completed his twenty-first year, and highly satisfactory was the report on the condition of the estates and on the expanding revenues which the Duke of Newcastle then made to the Queen.[1]

Both parents had also recognised early the customary right of the heir-apparent on reaching manhood to a domicile of his own. The Prince Consort, before his death, had busied himself with the provision of both a town and a country residence for the Prince of Wales and the young man spent much time and energy in the autumn and winter of 1862 in supervising the completion of residential arrangements which his father had begun.

Already in 1850 an Act of Parliament had been passed, at Queen Victoria's instance, assigning Marlborough House in Pall Mall for the Prince's use on the completion of his eighteenth year.[2] During the nine intervening years the building was used

[1] The Duke of Newcastle on his death on 18th October 1864 was succeeded as Lord Warden and High Steward by Edward Berkeley Portman, Viscount Portman, who died 19th November 1888.

[2] Marlborough House in Pall Mall was built by Christopher Wren for the great Duke of Marlborough in 1710, and it reverted to the Crown in 1817 on the lapse of the great Duke's long lease. It was thereupon appointed for the residence of Princess Charlotte and Prince Leopold, and Prince Leopold retained possession after the Princess's death. William IV.'s Queen, Adelaide, was allowed to reside there through her widowhood. After Queen Adelaide's death on 2nd December 1849, Lord John Russell, at the instance of Queen Victoria and

as the Government School of Design and the home of the Vernon collection of pictures which had lately been presented to the nation. At the end of 1859 the Prince of Wales, in fulfilment of the Act, took formal possession, the Art School being removed to new buildings at South Kensington and the pictures to the National Gallery in Trafalgar Square. It was not, however, till the summer of 1861, the last year of the Prince Consort's life, that the Government undertook the remodelling of the premises for their new purpose. Up to the moment of his death the Prince Consort showed much interest in the repairs and reconstruction. But the work was not completed till the close of the following year (1862). Then only was the renovated building ready for the Prince's occupation.

The provision of a private and unofficial residence in the country was also set on foot by the Prince Consort. By his direction a large part of the accumulated revenues of the Duchy of Cornwall was invested in a country estate for his son's enjoyment. At an outlay of £220,000 there was purchased from Spencer Cowper, an owner of old county standing although an absentee landlord, the demesne—some 7000 acres in area—at Sandringham in Norfolk, with an estimated rental of some £7000 a year.[1] The house was then little more than a shooting-box, but the estate, despite its long neglect, abounded in varied game. Into the transaction, which was completed in the summer of 1861, the young Prince entered with zest. He looked forward with eagerness to improving the property and managing it himself. The Prince was soon consulting the gardener at Balmoral as to laying out anew the grounds and gardens. A sum of £60,000 was drawn from the accumulated savings of the Duchy of Cornwall for putting the property into good order under the Prince's personal supervision.

Of the sporting capacities of his new country estate the Prince made a first trial at the end of 1862. Public curiosity was now excited, to his frequent inconvenience, by his every

---

the Prince Consort, laid before the House of Commons a Bill, which was duly carried, appropriating the house to the Prince of Wales. The Radical Member, Joseph Hume, deemed the proposal premature and extravagant in view of the fact that Hampton Court and Kensington and St. James's Palaces were already at the disposal of the Crown and were only partially tenanted.

[1] Mrs. Herbert Jones's *Sandringham Past and Present* describes the historical associations of the property.

1862
Ætat. 20
movement, and he resented an attempt to invade the privacy of his shooting-party. One of his earliest letters from Sandringham, which was addressed to Mrs. Bruce, feelingly complains of the enterprise of a local journalist :

Fancy on Saturday last a reporter from Lynn actually joined the beaters while we were shooting, but as I very nearly shot him in the legs as a rabbit was passing, he very soon gave me a wide berth. Gen. Knollys then informed him that his presence was not required, and he "skidaddled," as the Yankees call it. The next day he wrote an apology for his infamous conduct, and I don't think he will trouble us any more.

The conversion of the Sandringham property into a model estate rapidly became one of the Prince's liveliest interests, and in the successful effort he took a lifelong pride. New roads were constructed ; trees were planted ; shooting facilities were largely increased ; gardens, stables, and kennels were perfected, and cottages and farm buildings were refashioned on the best models. Subsequently, an additional 4000 acres were purchased and the house itself was rebuilt on a commodious scale which enabled the Prince to practise there an extensive and a very genial hospitality. "Sandringham improves in appearance every year," he wrote in middle life to his mother (April 23, 1878). In the improvement of his cottage property he was always seeking experienced advice. When inviting his Oxford friend, Dr. Acland, to Sandringham on 14th April 1884, he added the inducement : "We could then look over the cottages together. I have made many improvements which I should like to show you." "Up to the last year of his life he was continually improving his domain, repairing churches, spending money on the place in one way or another." [1]

[1] Lord Suffield's *My Memories, 1830–1913,* p. 91.

CHAPTER XI

BETROTHAL AND MARRIAGE

I

THE Prince's matrimonial plans went steadily forward through the autumn of 1862 and materially increased public interest in his fortunes.

1862

Ætat. 20

The marriage of his second sister, Princess Alice, to Prince Louis of Hesse-Darmstadt, in fulfilment of his late father's wish, took place very quietly at Osborne on the 1st July 1862, and stimulated his own matrimonial resolutions. Since his eldest sister's migration to Berlin, the bride had become his special confidant in the family circle. At her wedding he made a prominent figure, although their uncle, Duke Ernest of Saxe-Coburg, was entrusted by the Queen with the privilege of giving his niece away. The settlement of his second sister as a wife at Darmstadt soon provided the Prince with a second German home at which he was to be a frequent guest, and introduced him to a new German princely circle which had little sympathy with Prussian ambitions.

Queen Victoria lost no time after her second daughter's marriage in bringing to fruition the projected union between her eldest son and Princess Alexandra. A rumour that the Tsar, Alexander II., was meditating an offer of marriage on behalf of the Tsarevitch to one or other of Prince Christian's daughters impelled the Queen to immediate action. In the summer she wrote to Prince Christian, formally soliciting the hand of his daughter, Princess Alexandra, for her eldest son. Assent was at once given. The Queen had resolved to pay tribute to her husband's memory by visiting his early home at Coburg in September. On the journey she paused at Laeken, near Brussels,

her uncle Leopold's palace.   Thither the Queen's host summoned
Princess Alexandra from Ostend, where the Princess was
staying with her father, to make for the first time the acquaintance of her future mother-in-law.   Queen Victoria declared that
her highest hopes of a daughter-in-law were realised.

It was under King Leopold's personal auspices that the
betrothal of the Prince and Princess Alexandra took place.   On
the 7th September the Prince joined her at Ostend.   Two days
later, he and the Princess were King Leopold's guests at his
palace of Laeken, and there they were formally affianced.   Next
day the young couple went together over the battlefield of
Waterloo, and in the evening a Court banquet was given by their
host in their honour.   From Brussels they travelled together to
Cologne, where for the time they took leave of one another.   It
was thus that a new era in the Prince's career definitely opened.

On parting with his betrothed the Prince joined his mother
at Coburg, and the engagement was made public in England on
the 16th September, while the Queen and her son were still
together in the Prince Consort's home.   Queen Victoria herself
drafted the communication to the English Press.   She stated
that the marriage, privately settled at Brussels, was "based
entirely upon mutual affection and the personal merits of the
princess," and was "in no way connected with political considerations."   "The revered Prince Consort," the notification
continued, "whose sole object was the education and welfare of
his children, had been long convinced that this was a most
desirable marriage."   After her return from Germany the Queen
gave her formal consent to the union at a meeting at Windsor
of the Privy Council (November 1, 1862).

Whatever the responsibilities of the Prince's kinsfolk for his
choice of bride, mutual affection gave the betrothal auspicious
sanction.   To Mrs. Bruce the Prince wrote on 19th September
from Reinhardts-brunnen, the ducal castle of Coburg : "I feel
a new interest in everything, and somebody to live for."   "I
indeed now know," he wrote to Acland from the same place
(September 21, 1862), "what it is to be really happy, though I
daresay I have never done anything to deserve it ; but if I can
only continue to make the one to whom I have pledged my hand
and my heart happy, and render her future home a happy one,
I don't think I shall have any reason to complain."

1862
Ætat. 20

The announcement was received in England with unqualified enthusiasm. Lord Granville, in his letter of congratulation, wrote to the Prince: "It is impossible to exaggerate how pleased every one in all classes here is with the good news. All accounts agree as to the beauty, the excellence and charm of the person whom your Royal Highness has secured." Soon after his engagement the Prince wrote with a lover's optimism to his friend Cadogan: "I have received so many kind letters from all my relations and friends, which show that my choice has been approved on all sides."

But it was not solely the youth and beauty of the Princess, nor even the widespread interest in the future of the heir-apparent that accounted for the popular endorsement in England of the betrothal. In spite of the absence of any deliberate political intention, the Princess's identification with Denmark, whose interests were known to be menaced by Prussia, touched a responsive chord in the English people's heart. Abroad Queen Victoria's disclaimer of political significance in the betrothal was openly questioned. For a dozen years or more there had been constant friction between Denmark and Prussia regarding the conflicting claims of the two countries to the Baltic provinces of Schleswig and Holstein, and the long-standing disagreement was shortly to issue in a violent act of aggression on Denmark by the German states under Prussia's leadership. German public opinion speedily sounded an unfriendly note. Throughout Central Europe the project of the Prince's marriage was held to range the royal family of England with the Danes in the further development of the German quarrel. Continental politicians clung obstinately to the view that the foreign policy of England was mainly dictated by royal sentiment and authority, and the Prince Consort, who was held to be responsible for his eldest son's choice of a bride, was freely blamed in Germany for having induced his adopted country to desert the German cause. Queen Victoria's brother-in-law, Duke Ernest of Saxe-Coburg, sharing the common German view, declared that his nephew's betrothal to a Danish princess came on Germany like a clap of thunder. He confessed himself bewildered by the flagrant discrepancy between his nephew's matrimonial contract and the recent marriage of his niece, the Princess Alice, to the heir of the German principality of Hesse-Darmstadt. Nor was public opinion in

Prussia more favourably inclined to the Prince's betrothal when
rumours spread of the part which had been played in its promotion by his eldest sister, now Crown Princess of Prussia.[1] The
Queen was disturbed by German apprehensions. Personally she
cherished no leanings towards the Danish side in the Schleswig-
Holstein controversy, and her son's adoption of a Danish partisanship at the prompting of his bride was an unwelcome prospect.
But she believed her domestic influence equal to repressing any
such tendency.

On parting with Queen Victoria at Coburg at the end of
September 1862 the Prince at her wish remained behind. The
Queen had invited Princess Alexandra to spend some three weeks
as her private guest at Osborne and Windsor in November. It
was contrary to the Queen's sense of fitness that the couple
should see much of one another before their marriage. She
therefore desired her son to spend the autumn months of October
and November out of England—on a Mediterranean cruise.
Objection was taken to the Princess Alexandra's visit to England
in the absence of the Prince by so sympathetic a counsellor as
King Leopold. There was a suspicion in his and other minds
that the Queen designed to exert an undue influence on the
married life of the pair, and was anxious early to obtain a personal control of her daughter-in-law. But the Queen's will was
not to be shaken. She was bent on warning the Princess against
the risks of indulging, on her settlement in England, in too
pronounced a Danish partisanship.

II

On October 6th the Prince, in compliance with his mother's
desire, left Coburg in preparation for a southern tour under
Sir William Knollys' surveillance. But his sense of isolation was
to be lightened by the company of two members of his family.
The Crown Prince and Princess of Prussia, who had been his
fellow-guests at Reinhardts-brunnen, accepted his invitation to
travel with him to the Mediterranean and to Italy.

---

[1] The death, on the 2nd January 1861, of the Prince of Wales's godfather,
King Frederick William IV. of Prussia, transferred his crown to his brother
William, who for two years had been acting as Regent. The new King of
Prussia's eldest son, Prince Frederick William, thereupon became Crown Prince
of Prussia, and his wife, the English Princess Royal, the Crown Princess.

A critical episode in the history of Prussia rendered it congenial to his eldest sister and her husband to accept the Prince's
hospitality. During their sojourn at Coburg a bitter dispute
between the newly crowned King William of Prussia and his
Parliament over his resolve to spend an immense sum of money
on a reform of the army had brought the Government of Prussia
to a deadlock. To extricate himself from his grave embarrassments the King summoned Count von Bismarck from the German
Embassy at Paris to assume supreme power at Berlin (Sept. 19).
That strenuous and relentless champion of autocracy defined
the policy of his life when he inaugurated his long rule at Berlin
with the famous speech to the Budget Committee of the Prussian
Reichstag (September 30, 1862), in which he declared: "It
is not with speeches or with parliamentary resolutions that
the great questions of the day are decided, as was mistakenly
done in 1848 and 1849, but with blood and iron." Through
thirty-eight years of power Bismarck was faithful to this assertion
of force as the principle of government, and a majority of his
fellow-countrymen whole-heartedly accepted his creed. With
the Prussian statesman's challenge of constitutional right the
Prince of Wales's sister and brother-in-law had no sympathy. A
withdrawal from Berlin, such as the Prince of Wales's invitation
offered them, was welcome. The Prince of Wales was thus
identified with a prompt protest against Bismarck's accession to
office. For the first of many times he came into near touch with
a turning-point in Prussian affairs.

From Coburg, the Prince with his sister and brother-in-law
made a leisurely journey through South Germany and Switzerland. On the 22nd October they embarked at Marseilles in
the royal yacht *Osborne*, escorted by the frigate *Doris*. Their
attractive itinerary introduced the Prince to many new scenes,
while it refreshed his memory of some scenes and of some
political issues with which he had already made acquaintance.
He obtained his first knowledge of the Riviera, spending a little
time at Hyères. The next stopping-place was Palermo, in
Sicily, where the Prussian Consul acted as cicerone. Afterwards,
while cruising off the north-western coast of Africa, they landed
at the Goletta fort in the Gulf of Tunis and visited the neighbouring ruins of Carthage. They walked through the bazaar of the
town of Tunis and called on the Bey at his castle of Al-Bar.

From Malta, which the Prince now first inspected, the yacht
brought him, after a rough voyage of fifty-six hours, to Naples.
There a fascinating week was spent and the Prince and his
companions thoroughly explored the city and the country about
the bay.

At Naples the Prince was an eye-witness of the closing
scenes of that triumphant struggle for Italian unity, the initial
stages of which had come under his notice on his previous visit
to Italy. He had shared, while at home, the general excitement
over the fall of the kingdom of Naples before the forces of Garibaldi, the capture of the port of Gaeta, and the flight to Rome
of the Neapolitan King and Queen (February 13, 1861). "What
do you think of the capitulation of Gaeta?" he asked the Queen
on receipt of the news. "The unfortunate King of Naples'
last chance is now gone, and almost all Italy, except the Papal
States and Venice, now belongs to the King of Sardinia. I wonder
how long the Emperor of the French will let him possess it?"
Like most onlookers, the Prince was puzzled by the ambiguous
attitude of the Emperor Napoleon.

Now, when he reached Naples, the twin kingdoms of Naples
and Sicily had disappeared as a separate state and had been
fused with a united Italy under the sway of King Victor
Emmanuel. But the new Neapolitan Government was, in the
sight of Queen Victoria, on probation, and the attentions which
its functionaries pressed on the Prince and his companions
neither the Queen nor the King of Prussia deemed it opportune
for them to accept. But they could not avoid an exchange
of visits with the distinguished Sardinian General, La Marmora,
who was the chief of the new Neapolitan régime. When the
General heard of the royal travellers' intention to ascend Mount
Vesuvius on 6th November, he ordered "several companies" of
Bersaglieri to attend them to the crater. The same evening
General La Marmora dined on board the *Osborne* with the Prince.[1]

It was while still at Naples that the Prince celebrated his
twenty-first birthday (November 9, 1862). It seemed an incongruity to spend the day so far from home, even if family
mourning precluded elaborate festivities. The British men-of-war
in the bay honoured the day by flag-dressing, but the *Osborne*
confined its decorations to crowns of evergreens on the masts.

[1] Bismarck's *Correspondence with William I. and Others*, ii. 98-9.

At dinner in the evening Sir William Knollys proposed the Prince's health, and the British vessels fired rockets and showed blue lights. "I spent my birthday quietly with my sister and brother-in-law at Naples, which is one of the most beautiful places I ever saw," he wrote to Mrs. Bruce on 17th November. To Dr. Acland's congratulations he replied on 23rd November :

The 9th was an important day for me this year, and I am well aware that much is expected of me. . . . You can well imagine that I regretted very much not being at home on that day, but as I could not have taken part in any of the festivities, it was perhaps better that I should be abroad.
I have enjoyed my tour very much, and was very glad to visit Sicily and Naples, which were new to me.

To the Prince, the most gratifying commemoration of his arrival at full legal age was the Queen's announcement that she had conferred on him the military rank of full General. Sir William Knollys had urged that the Prince should receive the inferior rank of Major-General so that he might be qualified to command a brigade on an occasional visit to Aldershot. But the Queen handsomely overruled the advice. A full General might, she retorted, take part in field operations at Aldershot, if the opportunity offered, quite as well as a Major-General.

A ten days' stay in Rome followed the sojourn in Naples. Once again the Prince inspected the chief sights of the city, visiting the sculptor Gibson and other old friends among the British residents. "Mr. Odo Russell," he wrote home, "is in great form, though perhaps rather stouter than when I last saw him." On the 17th November, now accompanied by the Crown Prince and Crown Princess of Prussia, he had a second audience of Pope Pio Nono. No objection was taken by the Queen. The Crown Prince was under orders from Berlin to deliver to the Pope a letter from his father, and Sir William Knollys deemed it essential for the Prince to pay his respects to the Pontiff at the same time. "Under the circumstances," he pointed out to the Queen, "it would have been difficult to explain why the Prince of Wales should not have accompanied his sister and brother-in-law." The interview only allowed of an exchange of compliments. The Prince noted that "the

Pope looks well and very little changed. Cardinal Antonelli looks older, but is as agreeable as ever."

When the stay in Rome closed (November 24) the Crown Prince and Princess took leave of their young host, proceeding to Florence, whence they slowly journeyed back to Berlin. The Prince joined the *Osborne* at Civita Vecchia and sailed for Marseilles.

III

Meanwhile Princess Alexandra's private visit to Queen Victoria had begun and ended. On the 8th November Prince Christian, at the Queen's request, escorted his daughter to Osborne. At the close of ten days the Princess accompanied the Queen to Windsor, where she was introduced to the English Ministers of State. With her future husband's brothers and sisters, notably with Princess Helena, she was soon on familiar terms, and she found sympathetic friends in Princess Mary of Cambridge and in Mrs. Bruce, the General's widow. The Queen took her guest to call on the old Duchess of Cambridge at Kew Cottage, and on the ex-Queen of the French, Marie Amélie, at Claremont. But there were some rifts within the lute. Most of the Princess's time on this first visit to England was spent alone with the Queen, and the atmosphere was still charged with grief. According to the Queen's private secretary, General Grey, the Queen became "daily more fond of her future daughter-in-law," spoke to her openly and unreservedly of her future career, and was gratified by "the manner in which her advice" was received. But the Danish imbroglio was uppermost in the Queen's mind, and her language on the subject could hardly have been quite congenial to her guest. She warned the Princess "particularly of the danger of using her influence to make the Prince a partisan in any political question either at home or abroad. She was right to love her own country, but the consequences of the Prince becoming, through her influence, a partisan in the questions now unhappily in dispute would be to irritate all the Queen's German connections and to create family feuds—destructive of all family comfort and happiness." [1]

The Princess's father fetched his daughter from Windsor

[1] General Grey to Mrs. Paget, Windsor Castle, 27th November 1862; Walburga, Lady Paget, *Embassies of Other Days*, i. 163.

on 28th November. With the Queen's consent the Prince had arranged to meet the Princess at Lille on his way home from the south. Accordingly he hurried from Marseilles to the rendezvous where the Princess awaited him. The following day they spent together at Cologne, and a third day at Hanover. There his kinsfolk, the King and Queen of Hanover, exchanged with the couple warm professions of attachment. On the fourth day the Prince parted with his betrothed at Harburg, not to meet her again until the eve of their wedding, nearly three months later. The Prince reached Windsor on 3rd December. A fifth foreign tour within four years reached its close under happy omens.

1862
Ætat. 21

IV

Despite the satisfaction which her son's approaching marriage gave her, the Queen was deaf to all persuasions of friends and Ministers to relax signs of mourning or to mitigate her seclusion. The Prince spent the first anniversary of his father's death (December 14) in gloomy converse with his mother and his family at Windsor. But the Queen's aversion from public functions led her soon after, at some cost to her pride, to delegate to her son a ceremonial duty of some dignity. On 25th February 1863 a first levee since the Prince Consort's death was held, to the satisfaction of the public, and the Queen's place at St. James's Palace was filled by the Prince of Wales. The ordeal was unusually fatiguing—the presentations exceeding a thousand and the general attendance three thousand. The cordiality of the Prince's demeanour contrasted favourably with the coldness of his late father on such occasions.[1]

A treaty, authorising the marriage of the Prince and Princess Alexandra, had been signed at Copenhagen on behalf of the sovereigns of Great Britain and Denmark on 10th January 1863, and it was at once formally ratified in London by the Queen.[2]

---

[1] The first Drawing-Room of the Queen's widowhood followed five days later at Buckingham Palace. The Queen's place was filled by her eldest daughter, the Crown Princess of Prussia, who had arrived in England to support her mother through the anxieties incidental to her brother's marriage. The Prince stood beside his sister.

[2] Augustus Paget, Minister at Copenhagen, was in constant correspondence with General Grey, Queen Victoria's secretary, regarding these negotiations and the arrangements for the wedding. His assiduity was rewarded by the honour of K.C.B. Cf. Walburga, Lady Paget, *Embassies of Other Days*, i. 167.

The ceremony was fixed for 10th March. The Queen had wished it to take place on her own wedding-day, 10th February, but she assented to the postponement.

The preceding four months were mainly devoted by the Prince to the needful preparations. Under his own supervision his two residences, Marlborough House and Sandringham, were put into final order. The Queen in consultation with the ministers took a leading part in the selection of the personnel of his first household, while Parliament considered the important question of his financial requirements.

Men of character and of diverse qualifications were chosen for the Prince's first household. With most of them the Prince was already well acquainted. General Knollys became head of the new establishment with the title of Comptroller and Treasurer. The Earl of Mount Edgcumbe, who, as Lord Valletort, had been chosen by the Prince Consort to attend the Prince at White Lodge,[1] was made a Lord of the Bedchamber. Robert Henry Meade, the Prince's companion on the Eastern tour, and Charles Wood, afterwards Lord Halifax, the friend of the Prince's boyhood, were appointed Grooms of the Bedchamber. Major Teesdale, Captain Grey, and Lieutenant Colonel Keppel renewed a former association as equerries. Herbert Fisher, the Prince's tutor at Oxford, was recalled from practice at the Bar to act as private secretary.

Two strangers to the Prince's domestic circle gave the new household a political tinge. Earl Spencer, who was ambitious of a political career on the Liberal side, had already served the Prince Consort as Groom of the Stole, and he now accepted the same office under the Prince; while Lord Alfred Hervey, a former M.P. and Lord of the Treasury under both Lord Aberdeen and Lord Palmerston, became second Lord of the Bedchamber. Another Liberal member of the House of Commons, Colonel Robert Nigel Kingscote, who, after seeing service in the Crimea, gained a wide reputation as sportsman, agriculturist, and live-stock breeder on his estate at Kingscote in Gloucestershire, undertook to act as superintendent of the Prince's stables at Sandringham, and was soon appointed an extra equerry. A place was also found in the Prince's new household for an immigrant from Germany—Maurice Holzmann—who was

[1] See p. 49 supra.

appointed librarian; he combined with a Teutonic solidity a sympathy with Liberalism which had been acquired on the Continent; his personal devotion to the Prince and his family grew steadily with his long years of service.

The whole company formed a happy family party, in which changes came slowly and were rarely welcome to the Prince. Sir William Knollys remained in supreme control for nearly fifteen years, and the Prince's regard for him extended to his family. When, in June 1870, Mr. Fisher resigned the post of private secretary on his appointment as Vice-Warden of the Stannaries of the Duchy of Cornwall, Sir William's second son, Francis, took Mr. Fisher's place. In reply to some adverse criticism of his mother, the Prince justified "the appointment of young Knollys"—he was thirty-three—on the grounds that he "has got a very good head and is very hard-working." "Acting conjointly with his father" (then seventy-three years old), the Prince added, "he will be able to take a great deal off the General's hands." Francis Knollys signally fulfilled the Prince's expectations. He broke well-nigh all records by retaining his office for forty years—so long as his master lived. Although he was no linguist and was only on a few occasions the Prince's companion abroad, he carried out the Prince's directions at home with a rare tact and fidelity. He frankly defended the Prince's interests when he thought them to be imperilled in any quarter, boldly resisting in the Prince's name decisions of the Queen or her Ministers which seemed to him to place his master at a disadvantage. The Prince's wife soon shared his own devotion to the Knollys family, and in Francis Knollys' sister, Charlotte, who became Bedchamber Woman to the Princess of Wales (November 4, 1872), the Princess found a lifelong confidant, who effectually promoted her mistress's happiness.

With his equerries the Prince's ties of affection were characteristically strong. One of the most poignant of his early sorrows was the sudden death from pneumonia, at Sandringham, on 10th December 1874, of Major Charles Grey, who had been his equerry since 1859. The Prince attended the funeral at Embleton, in Northumberland, near Howick, the residence of Major Grey's father, the veteran Whig statesman, Sir George Grey. Of his sense of loss on this occasion the Prince wrote from Howick to Dr. Acland (December 16, 1874):

I feel his loss most keenly, as a better, kinder, truer, and more devoted friend to me for sixteen years never existed. During the many years that he was my companion and my friend, we never had an unkind word together—and I cannot now realise that I shall never see his kind and cheery face again.

The Prince had stood godfather to Charles Grey's son, Edward, a boy of eleven at the date of his father's death, who (as Sir Edward and Viscount Grey) was to pursue a distinguished political career. More than thirty years later, when Sir Edward Grey visited Balmoral as a Cabinet Minister, King Edward found satisfaction in showing him places in the neighbourhood which the King still associated with his equerry's companionship.

V

A new session of Parliament, in which the Prince and his affairs were to receive much attention, opened on 5th February 1863. The Queen was absent. Her speech, which was read by the Lord Chancellor, Lord Westbury, announced the coming marriage. The Prince attended the customary ceremony and at its close was admitted a Peer of the Realm as Duke of Cornwall, being introduced by his kinsman, the Duke of Cambridge, and by the Duke of Newcastle. He took his seat on the cross benches and proved his interest in the proceedings by staying until half-past nine at night to hear the debate on the Address. A chief item on the Ministerial programme was the cession to Greece of the Ionian Isles, three of which the Prince had visited the previous year. The Prince listened attentively to the condemnation of the step by Lord Derby, the leader of the Conservative Opposition, and to its defence by Lord Granville, leader of the Liberal Government. But of greater personal satisfaction to the Prince was the favourable comment on his marriage, in which the two political parties combined. In the House of Commons, as soon as Parliament met, the Prime Minister, Lord Palmerston, expressed the general view when he said:

Whereas the common fate of Royal marriages has been that persons are contracted together who have had no previous knowledge of each other, and with whom political considerations are the guiding principle of union, in this case the marriage may, in the fullest sense of the word, be called a "love match," while

the amiable and excellent qualities of both parties give the
fairest promise of permanent and complete happiness.

The Prince's first experience of a debate in the House of
Lords proved pleasurable, and Lord Granville, the leader of the
House, and Lord Palmerston, the Prime Minister, both advised
him to attend regularly. Lord Granville admitted that the
debates were boring, but thought that they might be instructive.
But the Queen demurred to her Ministers' counsel. She deemed
regular attendance in the House of Lords undesirable. Her son
might be there when "anything of interest or importance was
going on if he was in town." Some time consequently elapsed
before the Prince was often seen in the House of Lords. In
later life he was a frequent visitor, not only to the Upper Chamber
but also, on stirring occasions, to the Peers' Gallery in the House
of Commons, where he sat in the centre above the clock.

A few days after the opening of the session a message from
the Queen invited the House of Commons to consider a question
of a kind which commonly raised awkward debate—the making by
the State of pecuniary provision for the bridegroom and the bride
(February 17). But the nation was in no temper to encourage
unfriendly criticism. Lord Palmerston, the Prime Minister,
cautiously examined precedents of the incomes of the former
Hanoverian Princes of Wales. He discovered that George III.'s
heir-apparent had received a net income of £100,000 from the
State, apart from the small revenues (which then amounted to no
more than £13,000) of the Duchy of Cornwall. The State grant
of £100,000 was judged in the present case to be needlessly
generous.[1] The income already at the Prince's private command, according to the unpublished notes of Ministers, was over
£62,000, of which some £50,000 represented the net income of
the Duchy of Cornwall, £5250 the interest on some £163,000,
the balance of the Duchy accumulations,[2] and £7000 the rents
from Sandringham. To this sum the Chancellor of the Exchequer, Mr. Gladstone, after consultation with Lord Palmerston,
proposed to add an annual sum of £40,000 from State funds.
The Government also proposed an annuity of £10,000 for Princess

[1] MS. Memoranda by Lord Palmerston appended to some notes on the
Prince's income which were compiled by Mr. Cardwell—now belonging to
Col. Wilfrid Ashley, M.P.
[2] £100,000 had lately been withdrawn for "outfit."

Alexandra, with a prospective annuity of £30,000 in case of her
widowhood.

When resolutions to these effects came before the House of
Commons, advanced Liberals argued that the revenues of the
Duchy of Cornwall supplied the Prince with all the income that
was necessary.   Complaint was made that public money had been
advanced for the Prince's expenses on his installation as K.G.
and on his American tour.   But Mr. Gladstone, Chancellor of
the Exchequer, a faithful champion of the monarchy, defended
the Government's decision with vigour, and the resolutions
were carried without a division.   A suggestion made by the
Prime Minister that the Prince's expenditure should be controlled by a representative of the Government, who should
not be a member of his household, was withdrawn in view of a
protest from the Queen.   The acquiescence of Parliament and
nation in the grant of public money to a Prince or Princess was
never so complete.   In the case of his two married sisters there
had been far less readiness to provide them, on marriage, with
dowries out of the public purse.   Public impatience was to
increase when the Queen subsequently invited public provision
for her younger children.

The Prince's annual revenues, as fixed on the eve of his
marriage, barely stood the strain of the coming years, but he
was for a generation discouraged by public opinion from appealing
to Parliament for any additional grant.   It was not until twenty-
six years had passed that the government of the day ventured
to propose a further call on the Treasury, and then only in behalf
of the Prince's children on their coming of age and marrying.

VI

The Prince's wedding was now at hand.   Princess Alexandra,
accompanied by her parents, left Copenhagen for her new home
on the 26th February.   On the journey she spent three days
(March 2 to 5) in Brussels as the guest of the King of the Belgians,
who had played a leading part throughout the matrimonial
negotiations.   The royal yacht, the *Victoria and Albert*, on which
the Princess embarked at Flushing, with the British man-of-war,
H.M.S. *Warrior* as escort, passed up the Thames in the early
morning of the 7th March.   The Prince met his bride at Graves-

1863
ÆMtat. 21

end. At the Bricklayer's Arms station, Southwark, which the pair reached by rail, a modest procession was formed of six carriages headed by a detachment of Life Guards. It was thus that the bridal couple drove through the streets of London to Paddington Station, there to take train for Windsor.

The route was lavishly decorated, and triumphal arches of elaborate design spanned the entry to London Bridge and the chief thoroughfares. The boundless elation of the surging masses at the sight of the bride and bridegroom atoned for certain official shortcomings.[1] The meanness of the procession disappointed expectation, while friction between the City of London authorities and the Metropolitan police led to some disorder. The enthusiastic crowds often broke into the roadway, and the consequent delays caused as many as four hours to elapse before the bride and bridegroom arrived at Paddington Station. The fascination which the bride's youth and beauty exerted on the spectators found fitting expression in the verse of the Poet Laureate, Tennyson :

> Sea-kings' daughter as happy as fair,
> Blissful bride of a blissful heir,
> Bride of the heir of the kings of the sea—
> O joy to the people and joy to the throne,
> Come to us, love us and make us your own:
> For Saxon or Dane or Norman we,
> Teuton or Celt, or whatever we be,
> We are each all Dane in our welcome of thee,
>
> Alexandra !

The Queen had chosen St. George's Chapel, Windsor, for the ceremony, pleading her late husband's wish. No royal marriage since that of Henry I. in 1122 had been celebrated there. She ignored the strong body of opinion which urged that St. Paul's Cathedral or Westminster Abbey would be a more appropriate scene. Nor would she yield to the pressure that was exerted on her to give up mourning attire for the day. But she admitted the marriage to be "the only ray of happiness in her life since her husband's death," and raised no objection to its celebration in full pomp.

The wedding accordingly took place on the 10th March 1863 at St. George's Chapel, Windsor, in the presence of some 900

---

[1] Louis Blanc, *Lettres sur l'Angleterre*, 2nd series, p. 13 *et seq.*; Malmesbury's *Memoirs of an ex-Minister*, 1884, ii. 293.

guests, who included representatives of well-nigh all the country's activities. The service was conducted by Archbishop Longley of Canterbury, who had lately succeeded Dr. Sumner, with the assistance of Bishop Tait of London, Bishop Wilberforce of Oxford, Bishop Charles Sumner of Winchester, Bishop Graham of Chester, and Dean Wellesley of Windsor. The greatest singer of the day, Jenny Lind, sang in a chorale by the bridegroom's late father. The Prince, who was supported by his uncle, Duke Ernest, and his brother-in-law, the Crown Prince of Prussia,[1] wore a General's uniform beneath the robes of the Garter. With the Crown Princess was her elder son, Prince William of Prussia, afterwards Kaiser William II.,who, just turned four, wore Highland dress. Queen Victoria, in widow's weeds relieved only by the star and blue ribbon of the Garter, overlooked the proceedings from a gallery above the Chancel. The sadness of her expression moved so unsentimental a spectator as Lord Palmerston, the Prime Minister, to shed tears as he gazed upon her. Yet the ceremony was a brilliant pageant. The Prince bore himself with "serious reverent dignity," wrote his Cambridge professor, Kingsley, who attended as a royal chaplain. "The most moving sight I ever saw," was Bishop Wilberforce's description. "A fine affair, a thing to remember," was the phrase of Disraeli, who was among the guests.

After a wedding breakfast in St. George's Hall the bride and bridegroom left for a week's honeymoon at Osborne. The Eton boys who assembled near the Castle gates bade the pair an uproarious farewell, in which Lord Randolph Churchill, one of the Prince's later friends, then a lad of fourteen, took boisterous part.[2]

Everywhere in the British Isles and the colonies the wedding was celebrated with a barely paralleled ardour. Bonfires on the highest hills and illuminations of all the cities of the United Kingdom (save Dublin) testified to the national goodwill. "I know how much the heart of the people was then touched," wrote Dr. Boyd Carpenter, Bishop of Ripon, to King Edward on the fortieth anniversary of the day (March 10,

---

[1] Six personal friends were present on his special invitation: the Duke of St. Albans, Lord Hamilton (afterwards Marquis of Abercorn), Lord Henniker, Lord Hinchingbrooke (afterwards Earl of Sandwich), Mr. Charles Carrington (afterwards Earl of Carrington and Marquis of Lincolnshire), and Mr. Charles Wood (afterwards Viscount Halifax).

[2] Winston Churchill, *Life of Lord Randolph Churchill*, i. 9.

Mayall & Co. photographers

Emery Walker ph.sc.

The Wedding
10th March 1863

1903), while recalling how "as a Cambridge undergraduate I was nearly crushed to death in the crowd which gathered on Parker's Piece to express their loyalty and their gladness." The throbbing scene which London Bridge, with its throng of people and its dazzling illuminations, presented on the wedding night found record in a painting, which subsequently moved the Prince's lively interest, by the pre-Raphaelite artist, Holman Hunt.[1] The warmth of the City of London's greetings was especially exhilarating to the Prince, and he urged on the Queen that the enthusiastic welcome of him and of his bride should be rewarded by the bestowal of a baronetcy on the Lord Mayor and of knighthoods on the sheriffs. But the Queen vetoed the suggestion, on the ground that such honours were only conferred when the sovereign visited the City.

Abroad, at all the British Embassies and Legations dinner-parties and receptions did honour to the occasion. Even in Germany the misgivings which the announcement of the engagement had aroused seemed for the moment silenced. Only in one quarter in Berlin was there an echo of resentment. When Sir Andrew Buchanan, the British Ambassador, invited the King of Prussia to attend a banquet at the Embassy on the wedding night, Bismarck vehemently urged his master to refuse. For once the Prussian King forbore to follow his Minister's counsel.[2]

[1] The picture is now in the Taylor Buildings at Oxford, to which it was presented by the munificent patron of the painter, Mrs. Combe, widow of the Controller of the Oxford Press. Holman Hunt gives, in his *Pre-Raphaelitism and Pre-Raphaelite Brotherhood*, 1905, ii. 243-4, an interesting account of a visit paid him by the Prince shortly after his marriage, in order to inspect the picture: "H.R.H. . . . asked for the picture of 'London Bridge by Night on the Occasion of the Marriage.' 'Where is the Princess? Where am I?' he inquired in looking on the motley scene. I explained that the picture dealt only with 'London Bridge.' . . . Looking at it from point to point our Royal guest asked many questions about it, but suddenly singling out Mr. Combe's figure which I had introduced into the crowd, with face no larger than a six-pence, the Prince exclaimed: 'I know that man! Wait a minute,' he added. 'I have seen him in the hunting-field with Lord Macclesfield's hounds. He rides a clever pony about fourteen hands high, and his beard blows over his shoulders. He is the head of a house of Oxford and not a college'—as he went on following the trace in his mind—'but I'll tell you—Yes—I remember now—it's the Printing Press, and he rides in a red jacket. Am I right?' 'Your Royal Highness is surprisingly so,' I answered. . . . 'Mr. Combe has often told me that he has seen Your Royal Highness with Lord Macclesfield.' 'Remind me of his name,' said the Prince. Before I had well said it he took me up with 'Yes, I remember, Combe, of course.'" Holman Hunt's record graphically illustrates the Prince's memory for faces.

[2] *Correspondence of William I. and Bismarck*, ii. 12.

VII

1863
Ætat. 21

After a week's honeymoon at Osborne, which was followed by two days at Windsor, the couple took up their residence at Marlborough House (March 19).   Throughout the "season," society made incessant calls on the energies of Prince and Princess.   It was then that they inaugurated an era of social supremacy in Great Britain, which for duration and comprehensive spirit knew no precedent.

On the day after their arrival in town London society opened a prolonged ritual of homage.   To a reception in their honour at St. James's Palace rank and fashion came in crowds.   Until the end of June post-nuptial festivities continued to reflect the national enthusiasm.   Well-nigh all the official bodies in the country presented congratulatory addresses.   Banquets and dances were offered in profusion, both by public institutions and by private hosts and hostesses.   The Prime Minister, Lord Palmerston, and his wife entertained them at dinner (May 13). The Corporation of the City of London conferred the civic freedom on the Prince, and the elaborate ceremonial was followed by a ball at the Guildhall on a scale of unprecedented magnificence (June 7).[1]   The public celebrations in London were brought to a close by a notable ball which the Guards gave in the International Exhibition Building at Kensington (June 26).   Nor were the congratulatory entertainments confined to the capital.   The Prince and Princess visited Oxford for Commemoration, staying with the Dean and Mrs. Liddell at Christ Church.   Very stirring was the applause in the Sheldonian theatre when the Chancellor, Lord Derby, conferred on the Prince the honorary degree of D.C.L. In all the festivities of the Encænia the Prince and Princess joined with spirit, and the Prince confessed the satisfaction which it gave him "to lionise the Princess" in scenes familiar to him.[2]

At the normal social functions of the season the Prince and

[1] The great civic Companies did not lag behind the Corporation in their congratulatory ardours.   As early as 12th February the Fishmongers' Company had admitted the Prince to the livery by patrimony in succession to his father. On the 11th June a second great city Company—the Merchant Taylors—paid him the like compliment.

[2] Next year, at Cambridge, during May week, when he received the Honorary Degree of LL.D., he found equal pleasure in introducing the Princess to his haunts in the sister University.

Princess were also prominent figures. With his attendance at
Epsom, where he witnessed the victory of Mr. R. C. Naylor's
Macaroni in the Derby (May 20), he began that regular attendance at classic race meetings which he never thenceforth interrupted. At the end of the season he and the Princess were the
guests of the Duke of Richmond at Goodwood for the races there,
and from Goodwood they went on to Cowes for the regatta. The
routine of fashion which he now first followed remained a
punctilious concern for the rest of his life.

Meanwhile the bridal couple were prompt in returning the
lavish hospitalities which society was showering upon them.
Cabinet Ministers, foreign diplomatists, kinsfolk, and personal
friends of old as well as of new standing were many times entertained at dinner at Marlborough House, and on 29th June
an evening reception and ball commemorated the completion of
the renovations which had been long in progress there. At
Sandringham, too, the Easter vacation saw the Prince initiating
his long career of country-house host.[1]

Lord Granville, one of the guests at Sandringham, gave the
Queen "great reports" of his stay there. The Queen, in reply,
recalled with a mournful satisfaction those hospitalities of
"right dignity without stiffness" which she and her husband
had practised in happier years. But the Prince's social
activities prompted at the same time the expression of his
mother's fears that social pleasures were claiming an excessive share of his attention. She sought consolation in the
rather delusive hope that a study of serious books "will also
gradually follow." The Queen was mistaking the range of her
son's developing interests and capacities. She was making
insufficient allowance for the virile energy which would long
enable him to combine a strenuous indulgence in social diversions
with an equally strenuous participation in matters and movements of more abiding importance in the country's history. In
spite of his parents' endless exhortations he never acquired the
faculty of reading. A friend credited him in early middle life
with "a singular incapacity to apply his mind to any sort of

---

[1] On Easter Sunday, Dr. Stanley, a Sandringham guest, administered the
sacrament to him and his wife in Sandringham Church; just a year before,
Dr. Stanley and the Prince had joined in the rite on the shores of Lake
Tiberias.

study consecutively for half an hour," but the writer added: "What he hears he never forgets." He had a zest for all kinds of facts, and his agile memory rarely failed him. From conversation with men of varied attainment whom he met socially he was soon gathering a larger mass of information than literary study could easily furnish.

CHAPTER XII

SOCIAL SOVEREIGNTY

I

THE Prince had long to reckon with the Queen's unreadiness to acknowledge his independence in well-nigh any relation of life, as well as with her rooted objection to his participation in public affairs. Yet her persistence in her widowed seclusion promptly had an enfranchising effect on the Prince's position which she failed to foresee, and watched develop with some impatience. London became in her bereavement abhorrent to her, and she rarely visited it, preferring the comparative retirement of Windsor or the isolation of Osborne and Balmoral. An influential section of public opinion was quick to raise objection alike to her secluded mode of life and to the repression of her son. A cry for her abdication in the Prince's favour framed itself on many lips. As early as 4th June 1864 an experienced diplomatist, writing to Lord Clarendon, a member of Lord Palmerston's Ministry, expressed the spreading conviction that she would have done well, in view of "the turn her mind took from the beginning of her widowhood, to abdicate the day her son came of age. She would then have left a great name and a great regret." But it was not too late (the letter continued) to take the momentous step now.[1] The Queen never entertained the contingency of her own political effacement. Her active control of public affairs never slackened, and she viewed all criticism of her withdrawal from the public eye as irresponsible persecution. She deemed herself entitled to her subjects' unconditional forbearance and sympathy.

1864
Ætat. 22

[1] Lord Howden to Lord Clarendon, 4th June 1864, Maxwell's *Life of Clarendon*, ii. 292 (1913).

1864

Ætat. 22

Force of circumstance rendered futile much of the Queen's sturdy resistance to her son's enfranchisement. There could be only one result of the abeyance into which she allowed the Court of the sovereign to fall. After her son's marriage the monarchical principle made it inevitable that the Queen's Court should be largely replaced by that of the Prince and Princess of Wales. The Queen found herself unable to refuse her sanction to the performance by her son of Court functions for which she no longer had heart. The Levees and Drawing-Rooms, which had become repellent to her, were revived under the auspices of the Prince and Princess respectively. With some compunction she suffered her son to play a leading part in the reception of foreign sovereigns whose visits to England national policy favoured. Movements of philanthropy or social welfare which her husband and herself had been wont to promote fell equally with her qualified assent under her son's sway. Against his intervention in political affairs her prohibition was strenuously maintained. To her mind there was a vast interval between the non-political and the political functions of the monarchy. But even in the political direction her purpose of holding the Prince aloof was only partially realised. Her ministers and the diplomatists at the Court of St. James took a view of her son's status and aptitudes which markedly contrasted with her own, and their familiar relations with him largely neutralised the effect of her interdict on his association with affairs. Foreign politics especially became one of his abiding interests, and on certain phases of them he exerted from time to time an historic influence. Nor in domestic politics did he play the cypher's part which the Queen designed for him.

The Prince's incursions into politics, both home and foreign, which are brought to light in this memoir, were unknown to the public of his day. It was as a leading figure in society, in sport, and in the causes of philanthropy and social welfare that before his accession to the throne he acquired a public fame rivalling that of the secluded sovereign.[1] The love of pleasure, with which contemporary scandal made free, fills a large place in a survey of the Prince's character and career; but the commanding features of the picture are the exceptional range and endurance of the

[1] The song, "God bless the Prince of Wales," written in the Prince's honour by a Welsh composer, Brinsley Richards, in 1862, soon came into vogue as a national anthem, complementary to "God save the Queen."

Prince's zest for well-nigh every activity of life, and his alert interest in persons of all degrees of political, social, or other prominence. Few figures in history have had better right to take as their motto the Latin dramatist's familiar tag: "Homo sum: humani nihil a me alienum puto." There are just grounds for describing him as

1864
Ætat. 22

> A man so various that he seemed to be
> Not one but all mankind's epitome.

II

English society, over which the Prince assumed virtual sovereignty near the date of his wedding "season," rapidly acquired a character sensibly differing from that on which his parents had, through the previous generation, set their hall-mark. Queen Victoria and the Prince Consort strictly limited their social circle to their kinsfolk, with a select infusion of officialdom and of the old nobility. Under her husband's influence the Queen came to credit the aristocracy at large with an ingrained frivolity, and confined her social favour to a mere fraction of it which was alone, in her eyes, free from the general taint. The ceremonial reception of foreign sovereigns or of their representatives often varied the routine of the Court during the Queen's married life, and added a note of splendour. But a rigid code of etiquette and a severe principle of eclecticism governed the Queen and her husband's relations with society, and deprived them of breadth or vivacity.

Under the Prince of Wales's ruling auspices London society defied the old and narrow barriers which his parents had carefully guarded. Political, ethical, and economic tendencies were soon deflecting the centre of social gravity and were giving the interests of sport and of wealth and of heterogeneous fame social recognition—a recognition which was ampler than that enjoyed by birth conditioned by virtue or by dignified political office in the days when those qualifications constituted the sole passports to Queen Victoria's social circle. The period of the Prince's marriage witnessed a partial displacement of the blameless hereditary and official oligarchy by other and far more populous social categories. Social enfranchisement was conferred on the nobility and gentry—young and old of both sexes—who made

pleasure and sport their main pursuits; on plutocrats of middle
class or plebeian origin, deriving their fortunes from finance,
commerce, or manufacture; and on ambitious and prosperous
members of the professions—the Civil Service, medicine, law, art,
journalism, and the stage. (Literature was the sole branch of
culture which the new society failed readily to assimilate.)

The Prince, in his position of overlord, was well fitted to give
a decisive impetus to the social transition and transformation.
From boyhood he had given striking proof of sociability, and
amid the rigours of his educational discipline which reactively
stirred a yearning for expansive freedom, he had been taught the
duties of a host. Never, too, had the veteran tradition of the
Grand Tour, with its faculty of broadening the social outlook,
been more practically applied. The New World (Canada and
the United States), Western and Southern Europe (France, Italy,
Germany, Spain, Portugal, Turkey, and Greece), Northern Africa
(Morocco, Tunis, and Egypt) and the Near East of Asia (Palestine
and Syria), had all come within the scope of his foreign itineraries,
while at home he had seen much of Ireland, Scotland, and Wales,
as well as of England. His widely-flung travels served to stimulate his curiosity about persons and about life, and to forbid social
insularity or social aloofness. The taste for travel acquired in
youth became an abiding trait and grew in intensity with the
years. Cosmopolitan habits, interests, and sympathies which
were thereby engendered harmonised with the new social tendencies and encouraged their development.

The Prince was discriminating in his attitude to laws of
etiquette, ignoring many which conflicted with his predilections.
Hired cabs were his frequent means of conveyance about
London. He introduced the practice of smoking immediately
after dinner, and defied all the old social prohibitions against
indulgence in tobacco. Wherever he found himself, he gave a
pleasant impression of sincerity and candour—qualities which
were reckoned rare among princes. One of the best judges of the
traits of royalty during the epoch was the Princess Mathilde,
Emperor Napoleon III.'s first cousin, in whose salon at Paris
scions of all the royal families of Europe foregathered with men
of art and letters. Of the Prince, with whom she often exchanged hospitalities in Paris, the Bonapartist Princess wrote:
"He is open; when he talks he says what he feels; he is not like

other princes, who always give the impression that they have something to hide." [1]

In such conditions the Prince and Princess, at a moment when the Court was well-nigh effaced by the Queen's seclusion, took their place in society as arbiters of fashion, and their wishes and tastes became guides of conduct to a wide social circle. The catholicity of the Prince's social sentiment, by its challenge of class distinctions, associated itself with the new flow of the democratic tide. There was little change in the constitution or in the temper of the society over which the Prince presided, until his accession to the throne. Even during his reign the changes were few and inconspicuous. The doors which were once opened under the sway of his expansive temperament were not again to close.

III

With unswerving loyalty the Prince conformed to the customs and pursuits of society in its broadened reach. At banquets, garden-parties, and balls, at the Italian Opera and at the theatres which were homes of lighter forms of drama, no less than in the hunting field or at shooting-parties, he was in his element. Friends soon introduced him to the turf, in which his interest grew keen: he ultimately owned a breeding stable at Sandringham, and became a prominent owner of race-horses. From the date of his admission (April 3, 1864) to membership of the Jockey Club he was punctilious in attending not only the classic race meetings at Newmarket, Epsom, Doncaster, Ascot, or Goodwood, but also many smaller race-courses, like Sandown, where the regimental races were run. Each August found him yachting at Cowes and each September and October deer-stalking in Scotland. Before long he adopted the growing social habit of spending some three weeks of the early spring on the Riviera and some three weeks of the early autumn at a German watering-place: at first Wiesbaden and subsequently Homburg. At German watering-places and on the Riviera his social range was at its widest; Russian Grand Dukes and Grand Duchesses, Austrian Archdukes and Archduchesses, minor German princes and princesses, the old nobility of France jostled in his environment representatives of his comprehensive English circle. *En garçon* he spent a few days twice or

---

[1] *Journal of the De Goncourts*, 7th March 1888.

even thrice a year in Paris, and there were other foreign trips which were the fruit of family obligations or of love of change or of interest in forms of sport unavailable in England. A visit with the Princess to her relatives in Denmark usually varied the annual routine, and few years passed without his accepting the hospitalities of his married sisters and of his numerous German kinsfolk in Berlin, Darmstadt, Düsseldorf, and elsewhere.

Queen Victoria, who viewed with misgivings the Prince's departure from the social exclusiveness and etiquette of her husband's era, was often moved to somewhat wild reproaches of his devotion to the social calendar of what she called "the upper classes," to whom, apart from a righteous remnant, she continued to deny any aim in life save pleasure-seeking or dissipation. In the heat of her protestations she likened the English aristocracy to the *noblesse* of France on the eve of the French Revolution. In defending from his mother's strictures those with whom he was spending much of his time, the Prince was more argumentative than was his wont. Despite his social liberalism he valued the preservation between the Crown and the proletariat of a class or of classes which, he pointed out to the Queen, merited extinction if her sweeping reproaches were justified.

With regard to what you say concerning the Aristocracy or "upper Ten Thousand" (he wrote to her in 1867), I quite agree that in many instances amusement and self-indulgence, etc. predominate, but it is hard to say that all are so. I know of so many instances where those of the highest rank are excellent country gentlemen—are Chairmen of Quarter Sessions, Magistrates, etc., and the ladies attend to their duties also. In every country a great proportion of the Aristocracy will be idle and fond of amusement and have always been so, but I think in no country more than ours do the Higher Classes occupy themselves, which is certainly not much the case in other countries. We have always been an Aristocratic Country, and I hope we shall always remain so, as they are the mainstay of this country, unless we become so Americanised that they are swept away, and then the state of things will be quite according to Mr. Bright's views, who wishes only for the Sovereign and the People, and no class between.

The men and women who joined the Prince on terms of intimacy in the social throng represented in point of fact well-nigh every social grade between the Crown and the proletariat.

The nucleus was formed of his earliest acquaintances. Middle
life saw a strengthening of the early ties with the companions of
his youth—kinsfolk of his own generation, tutors of his boyhood,
his professors at the Universities, and notably young men of his
own age whom he first came to know when they were Eton boys
and Oxford or Cambridge undergraduates. With these there
mingled sportsmen of all ranks, politicians of all hues and of many
countries, diplomatists, explorers, physicians, actors, and actresses.
Fully did he assimilate the tolerance for wealth with its attendant
luxury which was an integral part of the spirit of the age. Rich
merchants, bankers, financiers, and tradesmen he was soon meeting on an even footing. Foreigners found their nationality no
bar to the Prince's intimacy. His perfect command of the
French and German languages enabled him to cultivate their
society with facility. American visitors to the country could
always count on a ready welcome. Anti-Semitic prejudice was
unknown to him. Abundant was the hospitality which the
Prince offered to the multiform elements of his social world, and
he accepted invitations, both in London and the country, from
hosts and hostesses with a readiness which was unprecedented in
royal circles. The Princess of Wales seconded her husband in
entertaining his comprehensive circle, and she cordially received
the wives and daughters, along with the husbands and fathers,
at Marlborough House and Sandringham, or each autumn, from
1864 onwards, at Abergeldie Castle in Aberdeenshire.

IV

In the Prince's social *milieu* there prevailed the bracing
principle of "non unde es, sed qui sis"—"a man's individuality
counts for more than his origin." High birth, while it was amply
represented, gave in itself no title to admission. Its representatives were judged by the standards which were applicable to
persons of humbler lineage. The Prince loved "good company."
He valued in his companions the easy wit and gaiety of which he
himself had no lack. His ears were never closed to a good story.
He enjoyed on occasion chaff and levity. With asceticism or
prudery he was out of sympathy. Priggishness or snobbish
vanity was intolerable to him. Easy of access, he did not stand
obtrusively on his dignity. Yet he expected from his associates

a certain deference. He set store by good taste in dress, while his insistence on all the regulations of official costume was a conspicuous foible. Undue familiarity or neglect of sartorial convention he could rebuke with a freezing inattention or a biting scorn. Those who could justly reckon themselves his friends well knew how to combine something of his own frank cordiality with a becoming respect for his rank and idiosyncrasies. There were a few incidents in his social experience when men in near personal association with him offended him by infringement of what he regarded as good breeding or good feeling. Such offences drew the Prince's warm resentment, even if he were prepared to entertain a reconciliation on self-respecting terms.

Perhaps the most notable feature of the Prince's social character was his loyalty to his comrades, which no misfortune or even disgrace could diminish. Every man who had enjoyed his confidence could count on his fidelity if he fell into embarrassment. The Prince portrayed himself with veracity, when in a letter addressed to Lord Granville (July 2, 1882) he said :

I may, and have, many faults—no one is more alive to them than I am ; but I have held one great principle in life from which I will never waver, and that is loyalty to one's friends, and defending them if possible when they get into trouble. One often gets into scrapes in consequence, but I consider the risk worth running.

Many times in the Prince's career was this chivalric principle put to convincing tests. With sternness, too, he reprobated slanders of men whether inside or outside his own circle, who were conspicuous for public service.

"I know nothing," he wrote to Lady Dorothy Nevill in April 1889, "of any scandals about Father Damien [who sacrificed his life in the cause of the lepers in the Sandwich Islands], but of one thing I am convinced : he will always go down to posterity as a great man, and as he is no more, I think his character might be left in peace."

The Prince's shrewdness made him on the whole a good judge of character. "He is singularly quick in the knowledge of character, and reads a man like a book," wrote an observant acquaintance in 1872.[1] It was the exception and not the rule

---

[1] (Sir) W. H. Russell to Bigelow, 5th January 1872; John Bigelow's *Retrospections of an Active Life*, v. 5.

for his pleasure-loving tendencies to warp his judgement of the men around him, few of whom, despite Queen Victoria's suspicions, could be justly accused of merely trifling with life. The briefest list of those who were his chief comrades in the opening years of his social reign clears the point of doubt.

Seniors in years who harboured broad if unconventional ideas reflecting the progressive trend of the epoch loomed largest in the company which gathered round him after his marriage. The Duke of Sutherland, whose mother was Queen Victoria's intimate friend, encouraged the Prince in versatile interests scarcely in keeping with the ducal caste. At Stafford House, the Duke's palatial house in London,[1] and at his great country mansions, Trentham in Staffordshire, and Dunrobin Castle in Sutherlandshire, the Prince was a constant guest. When in 1870, Marlborough House was undergoing repairs the Prince and his family took up temporary residence at Stafford House. But the Duke was far more to the Prince than a munificent host. His mechanical proclivities fascinated him. The Prince often watched the Duke drive the steam-engines on the Highland Railway which the Duke had called into being. It was one of the Duke's hobbies, when in London, to aid in the operations of the firemen, and he induced the Prince at times to join him in such exciting ventures. But the Duke cherished far wider prepossessions. He was the untiring champion in England of Garibaldi in his fight for Italian unity, and he enthusiastically supported M. de Lesseps' efforts to build the Suez Canal. Under the Duke's influence Garibaldi and M. de Lesseps long figured in the Prince's gallery of heroes.

Another of the Prince's older friends during his early married life was of a very different type. Richard Monckton Milnes, a Yorkshire magnate, who became Lord Houghton in 1863, combined a mild interest in Liberal politics with literary aptitudes, and a discerning patronage of literary merit. As an assiduous host of celebrities in every sphere, an effective after-dinner speaker, and a man of wit and culture, Lord Houghton exerted his charm on the Prince, whose views again broadened at the persuasion of this great social figure.

The Prince's keen enjoyment of a good story or a humorous anecdote accounted for his intercourse with numerous men of

---

[1] Now the London Museum.

general repute who had a gift that way. Although the Prince was capable of *bon-mots* of his own, he liked to repeat those of others' making. When writing to thank Lord Granville "for a stock of anecdotes" (November 30, 1875), he added with sociable candour: "I shall certainly endeavour to palm them off as my own." Constantly did the Prince entertain at the outset of his social career the brilliant wit, Bernal Osborne, an advanced Liberal politician, whose daughter married the Duke of St. Albans. Another *habitué* of Marlborough House, with similar credentials, but of a different social caste, was "dear old Quin" (Dr. Frederic Hervey Foster Quin), an old-fashioned Irish wag, who belonged to the medical profession, but incurred professional disfavour by his zeal for homeopathy. "Not a Sunday in London that he did not dine with us," the Prince wrote to Lord Granville three days after Quin's death at the advanced age of seventy-nine (November 7, 1878). To Bernal Osborne and Quin there succeeded at the Prince's table in London and at Sandringham a long succession of social jesters of unblemished character drawn from varied social strata.

The chiefs of the racing clique, in whose society the Prince became acclimatised from early days, boasted notable records of sportsmanship, and by no means confined their interests to the turf. It was the Prince's practice to encourage his intimate racing friends to combine with their sporting interests political ambitions, and he freely employed his influence with political leaders to press their claims to office. Henry Chaplin, his sportsman friend from undergraduate days, who married a daughter of the Duke of Sutherland, and Lord Cadogan, a sportsman friend from an earlier epoch, largely owed their political careers to the Prince's counsels and recommendations. The Prince took pride in the great position which a third lifelong sportsman friend, Lord Hartington, a treasury of common sense, made for himself in the sphere of politics. Significant likewise in the early records of the Prince's social career were the intimate terms which he maintained with Lord Spencer, a serious-minded nobleman of great wealth and standing who, while finding recreation in sport, devoted himself unsparingly to public service as a member of many Liberal Ministries. Characteristic, too, were the Prince's relations with a naval officer considerably his senior, Sir Henry Keppel, to whom he gave proofs of attachment through a period of five-and-forty years. "The Little Admiral," as Keppel was called in the Prince's family circle, was an amusing companion, and no mean sportsman. The Prince did all he could to help his professional advancement. As early as 1866 the Prince successfully busied himself to obtain from Sir John Pakington, First Lord of the Admiralty, the command for Keppel of the China and Japan station.[1]

The breadth of the Prince's social instinct was, again, convincingly illustrated by his prolonged personal relations with many men of the sedatest vocations and character. Lyon (afterwards Lord) Playfair, a solemn Scotch professor, who instructed him at Edinburgh, co-operated with him through long years of intimacy in the work of organising exhibitions and technical education. With notable members of the clerical profession, too, the Prince cherished the closest social ties. When Dean Stanley, his companion on his tour in the Holy Land, died in 1881, the Prince expressed regret that of late years he had "not seen as much of him as he should have liked, but," he added, "whenever we met it was as though we had seen one another daily." On the death of Dean Wellesley of Windsor, a broad-minded and shrewd ecclesiastic whom he knew from youth (September 7, 1882), he described him as "one of my oldest and valued friends," and he deemed it his "duty to pay the last mark of respect to his memory" by making a hurried journey from Abergeldie, where he was staying at the time, to Strathfieldsaye, in Hampshire, in order to attend the Dean's funeral.

Nor was there any lack of purpose or ability in the Scotsmen of good family who, among leaders in the world of finance and commerce, were the earliest to join the Prince's circle. His oldest financial acquaintances were Sir Charles Forbes, of Castle Newe,[2] and his brother George, who founded the East India House of Forbes, Forbes & Co. It was these men who introduced the Prince in later life to Horace Farquhar, at one time in their employ. Farquhar joined Scott's Bank in London (afterwards merged in larger concerns) and ultimately became the most intimate of the Prince's coterie of business friends. When Farquhar,

1864
—
Ætat. 22

---

[1] Keppel, *A Sailor's Life under Four Sovereigns*, iii. 113, where is printed a letter from the Prince to Keppel announcing his success in obtaining for Keppel the China command.

[2] Gartley, Aberdeenshire, 4th Baronet.

jointly with his friend the Earl of Fife, rented in 1887 the Norfolk estate of Castle Rising, he joined the Prince's Sandringham circle, with which his associations drew closer after 1895 when he became sole lessee of Castle Rising. The Earl of Fife was another Scot of business aptitudes and ancient family, who had been led by Farquhar to engage in banking with highly successful results. The Earl was long one of the Prince's comrades, and ultimately became his son-in-law.

In his early years the Prince somewhat shocked Queen Victoria and his German kinsfolk by forming a close intimacy with the great Jewish financiers, the heads of the Rothschild family—Sir Anthony, Baron Lionel, and Baron Meyer. Through life he carried on the friendship with the three Rothschild brothers of his own younger generation (Baron Lionel's sons)—Nathaniel, first Lord Rothschild, Mr. Alfred de Rothschild, and Mr. Leopold de Rothschild. He formed, too, as close an attachment to these men's cousins, Baron Ferdinand de Rothschild, at whose beautiful château at Waddesdon, Buckinghamshire, he was no infrequent guest, and Baron Alphonse de Rothschild of Paris, chief of the French branch of the family. The Prince's business instinct enabled him to appreciate the financial acumen of the Rothschild clan, but he was more effectively drawn to its members by their profuse charity, their range of political information, their hospitalities, their patronage of sport and their assiduity in collecting works of art.

The Prince's social liberalism is further attested by his friendly attitude to the club life of London. There were few club houses of the West End with which he was unfamiliar as either member or guest. In the year 1866 he joined the veteran White's Club, and in 1872 the Turf Club which was then only four years old. Especially agreeable to him were the meetings of the Cosmopolitan Club which was established in a house in Charles Street, Berkeley Square, in the middle years of the nineteenth century. The aim was to bring together for informal after-dinner conversation men distinguished in all ranks of life. Scarcely any form of eminence was unrepresented among its members or their guests. Foreign visitors of note were always well received. It was at the Cosmopolitan Club that the Prince met, quite casually, in 1867, the Hungarian traveller Arminius Vambéry, with whom he straightway formed a lasting acquaintance; and he appreciated the compliment which the Club paid him of giving him a special reception on his return from India in 1876.[1] Subsequently he became patron of the Garrick Club, where actors chiefly congregated. Now and then he attended the festivities of the Savage Club, which cultivated more Bohemian traditions. Few opportunities did he neglect of meeting in the convivial atmosphere of clubs men who could be counted on to amuse or interest him.

The Prince bore conspicuous witness to the value which he attached to club life by establishing in 1869 for himself and his personal friends a new institution of the kind, which was christened the Marlborough Club. Premises were acquired at 52 Pall Mall, nearly opposite his London home, Marlborough House. The formation of the Marlborough Club was the Prince's mode of protest against the restrictions on smoking which were imposed on him at White's Club. Greater freedom was a characteristic of the Marlborough, of which the Prince was a *habitué* until his accession to the throne. In the yard behind the house there was at the outset a bowling-alley in which the Prince and his fellow-members constantly played in their shirt-sleeves, until the neighbours raised objection to the annoyance created by the rumbling of the balls. Thereupon a billiard-room was built over the site. The Prince became first president of the club, and his familiar acquaintances to the generous number of 400 were original members. The first list is eloquently comprehensive.[2] Racing was represented by men like George Payne, Henry Petre, and Henry Chaplin; the Prince's household contributed Lord Spencer, Colonel Kingscote, and Mr. Francis Knollys; the

---

[1] Dilke, i. 418; Grant Duff, *Notes from a Diary, passim.*

[2] The first Chairman of the Committee, long known as the Father of the Club, was Viscount Walden, afterwards 9th Marquis of Tweeddale, Lieutenant-Colonel of the Grenadiers, who had seen service in India and the Crimea, and later made a reputation as an ornithologist, becoming a Fellow of the Royal Society. He died in 1878, and was succeeded as chairman of the Committee by Lord Methuen. The subsequent chairmen in the Prince's lifetime were Lord Colville and Lord Redesdale. The original trustees were the Duke of Sutherland, the Earl of Leicester, and Lord Wharncliffe. The original Committee included Count Gleichen (Prince Victor of Hohenlohe), Viscount Royston, M.P. (the Earl of Hardwicke's heir), and the Duke of Manchester. Other original members were the Marquis of Ormonde, the Earl of Rosebery, Lord Carrington, William Howard Russell, Christopher Sykes, Duke of St. Albans, Captain H. Bates van de Weyer, Sir Fenwick Williams, V.C., of Kars, and Sir Charles Lennox Wyke, English Minister at Copenhagen. Among the honorary members was the secretary of the Italian Embassy, Count Maffei.

1869
Ætat. 27
Sandringham coterie, the Earl of Leicester, Lord Suffield, and Mr. Villebois; adventurous travel, Colonel Valentine Baker and Captain Burnaby; the business side of life, Horace Farquhar and a large contingent of Rothschilds. Among the three original honorary members was the Marquis du Lau, a close French associate, from whom the Prince through nearly half a century learned much of the inner workings of French politics. To the end of his life, after he became King, the Prince maintained his active interest in the Club. So long as he lived candidates for election required his endorsement, and he strove to make the membership representative of the whole field of his social ties.

V

1870
Ætat. 28
At Sandringham the Prince and Princess practised a continuous hospitality on a generous scale, especially after the reconstruction of the house in 1870. The familiar ease and charm of country house life was hardly ever better realised. The Prince invariably invited a large party of relatives and other intimates to celebrate there his birthday on 9th November as well as Christmas and Eastertide, but from time to time throughout the year well-nigh all his London friends were entertained, and the varied company embraced all ranks and professions, from dukes and Cabinet Ministers to artists, explorers, and musicians. Foreigners, including many members of the French nobility, were frequent guests. Nearly the whole of East Anglia was also represented in relays at the Sandringham assemblies, and the Prince and Princess welcomed in return the hospitalities of the district. Often did he exchange visits with the Earl of Leicester of Holkham Court, Lord Suffield of Gunton Hall, Lord Hastings of Melton Constable, Sir Somerville Gurney of North Runcton Hall, and Sir William ffolkes of Congham Lodge, the last two very near neighbours.

At Sandringham the Prince and his guests found their chief outdoor recreation in shooting and hunting. Within doors there were ample opportunities for familiar conversation, for cards, and for other ordinary pastimes, which were occasionally diversified by balls. "Pleasant and domesticated, with little state and very simple ways" is the description of the conditions prevailing in the Prince's country home which came from the pen of a clerical

visitor—Bishop Magee of Peterborough, an Irish orator and wit—
in December 1873.

"I arrived," he writes, "just as they were all at tea in the
entrance hall, and had to walk in all seedy and dishevelled from
my day's journey and sit down by the Princess of Wales. . . .
I find the company pleasant and civil, but we are a curious
mixture. Two Jews, Sir Anthony de Rothschild and his daughter
[afterwards Lady Battersea]; an ex-Jew, Disraeli; a Roman
Catholic, Colonel Higgins; an Italian duchess who is an English-
woman, and her daughter, brought up a Roman Catholic and now
turning Protestant; a set of young Lords and a bishop. . . . We
are all to lunch together in a few minutes, the children dining
with us." [1]

The Prince's *bonhomie* as host and his cheerful interest in
his Sandringham guests were well illustrated by his practice of
inviting them on leaving to subject themselves to the test of a
weighing machine, the records of which he kept himself. His
vivid memory enabled him to recall the personal constitution of
his Sandringham parties in distant years. He illustrated his

---

[1] J. C. Macdonnell's *Life of William Connor Magee*, i. 293–4. The Prince
gives typical lists of guests in letters to his friends. On 16th November 1868
he describes a Sandringham men's shooting-party thus: "The Duke of Cambridge, Lord Alfred Paget, Lord de Grey [afterwards Marquis of Ripon], Sir
Frederick Johnstone, Chaplin, General Hall, Captain (Sam) Buckley, Major Grey,
and myself compose the party, and the great Francis [Knollys] arrived on
Saturday, but he is by no means a distinguished shot." To Alfred Montgomery the Prince wrote from Sandringham on 19th January (without year,
? 1880): "We have a largish party staying here this month, including Curzons,
Carringtons, Victor and Lady Agneta Montagu, Lady Dorothy Nevill, H. Stonor,
Sir D. M. Wallace, Tony Macdonell, and some distinguished naval officers.
Weather very fine and mild, but cock pheasants very wild." The Prince's
friend, Lord Sandwich, wrote in his diary of a later typical visit to Sandringham
in November 1883: "On November 5th I went to Sandringham. The guests
were Prince Eddy, the Duke and Duchess of Edinburgh, the Landgrave of
Hesse, Vicomte and Vicomtess de Grefuhle, Comte de St. Priest, Baron von
Holzhausen, Captain von Strahl, C. Vivian, C. E. Sykes, Oscar Dickson, Lady
Emily Kingscote, Francis and Miss Knollys, and A. Ellis in waiting. Tuesday
and Thursday there was partridge-driving; Wednesday, Commodore and
Dersingham Woods; Friday, Woodcock Wood. Friday, the 9th, was the
Prince's birthday, and he received innumerable presents from all sorts and
kinds of people, and there was a ball, which lasted till 4 A.M. In connection
with this party I must give an extraordinary instance of the Prince's memory.
Many years afterwards he was referring to the death of Creppy Vivian, when he
remarked on the number of members of this party who had died, and he really
ran through the names of the people I had met at Sandringham on this occasion.
Considering the number of guests he entertained every year at Sandringham,
I remember telling him with wonder of his marvellous memory" (Erskine's
Earl of Sandwich, pp. 190–1).

passion for punctuality by keeping the clocks at Sandringham half an hour fast.

VI

1865
Ætat. 23

The Prince took delight in the dignity and responsibilities of fatherhood, and he always treated as an uppermost concern the welfare of his five children surviving infancy, his two sons and three daughters, the eldest born in 1864, and the youngest in 1869.[1]

While staying in the winter at Frogmore House, near Windsor, the Princess was somewhat prematurely delivered, on 8th January, of a first child, a son. The Prince showed all a young father's elation. In acknowledging Lord Derby's congratulations, the Prince wrote how he hoped that "the birth of another grandchild may tend to throw a ray of light on the Queen's desolate life, and that her *third* grandson may in future years be a comfort to her."[2] In commemoration of his father's parents (Prince Albert and Queen Victoria), of his grandfather (Edward, Duke of Kent), and of his mother's father (King Christian of Denmark), the boy was named Albert Victor Christian Edward. Among his godparents was the old King of the Belgians, who came over for the christening on his last visit to this country. The ceremony took place at Buckingham Palace on 10th March, the first anniversary of the parents' wedding-day, and the Prince and Princess gave in the evening a reception and concert at Marlborough House in honour of the occasion. The Prince wished that his heir should take one of his own minor titles, but Lord Palmerston, the Prime Minister, vetoed the proposal.

The Prince's second child, again a son (afterwards King George V.), was born on the 3rd June 1865, at Marlborough House. There was a slight difference between the Prince and his mother as to the name which the boy should bear. The Queen criticised the parents' choice of what they described as the English name of "George," after the Duke of Cambridge, who served as one of the sponsors. "George," remarked the Queen, "only came over with the Hanoverian family. However, if

---

[1] The youngest child, a son, Alexander John, born at Sandringham on 6th April 1871, died next day.

[2] Queen Victoria's two earlier-born grandsons were the two sons of her eldest daughter, Prince William (*b.* 1858) and Prince Henry (*b.* 1862) of Prussia.

the dear child grows up good and wise I shall not mind what his name is." [1] The boy was finally named George Frederick Ernest Albert—the last name being added at the Queen's instance.

Three daughters were born later, all at Marlborough House; Princess Louise, on 20th February 1867; Princess Victoria, on 6th July 1868; and Princess Maud, on 26th November 1869.

From their infancy, the elder children accompanied their parents on visits to their grandmother at Windsor or Osborne, to their Danish grandparents at Copenhagen, and to Norfolk neighbours. Throughout the children's youth the Prince joined their mother in ministering to their amusements. A hurried letter to Lord Granville on 21st February 1873, sets him in an engaging parental light; he apologises for leaving the House of Lords late that afternoon before the end of Lord Granville's speech about foreign decorations for English subjects. His excuse is that by way of celebrating the sixth birthday of his "eldest little girl," "the Princess and I are going to take four of the children to the circus at 7.15, and it is now 6.30. I have not a moment left."

VII

In spite of the self-respect of most of the Prince's social allies, temptations attached to some social usages of the upper classes over whom he bore sway, and his varied domestic and other interests and avocations did not always suffer him to withstand the peril. Games of chance appealed to his love of adventure. The vicissitudes of betting whetted the excitement of horse-racing. At times he risked heavy stakes at the card-table on the challenge of highly speculative companions. He openly indulged in the questionable sport of pigeon-shooting at Hurlingham. Late hours were congenial to him. Although he was always businesslike in the distribution of his time, his social life, according to a friendly critic of early days, was a restless rush from one engagement to another—"a perpetual search in the daytime of hours he had lost the night before."

Outbreaks which challenged propriety testified on occasion

[1] The Prince chose as additional sponsors his wife's mother, the Queen of Denmark; his sister, Princess Alice; his grand-aunt, the old Duchess of Cambridge; his brother-in-law, Prince Frederick of Denmark (on whose birthday the baby was born); and Ernest Leiningen, of whom the Prince wrote: "He and I have always been such intimate friends."

to the untamable spirits of himself and his younger friends. When Mr. Disraeli privately dubbed the Prince of Wales "Prince Hal," the statesman had in mind the undignified frolics in which an earlier heir to the throne engaged with an ignoble coterie. Mr. Disraeli's sobriquet, while it ignored dominant aspects and associations of the Prince's life, had a superficial warrant. A few of those who enjoyed the Prince's social recognition were weaklings, who in time came near absorption into the disreputable fringe of the gambling world, or were ruined by wholesale dissipation. "The offending Adam," with which Shakespeare credited his Prince Hal, was not readily exorcised by Queen Victoria's eldest son. Bright society of the opposite sex always attracted him. Throughout his adult life one might apply to him Shakespeare's description of another of his leading characters :

. . . Our courteous Antony,
Whom ne'er the word of " No " woman heard speak.

Of the Prince, no less than of the rest of mankind, does Shakespeare's penetrating deliverance hold true :

The web of our life is of a mingled yarn, good and ill together : our virtues would be proud, if our faults whipped them not ; and our crimes would despair, if they were not cherished by our virtues.

Frank criticism of royalty was a common feature of journalism when the Prince first figured prominently on the social stage. Neither Queen Victoria nor her husband had escaped the thrusts of satire from all grades of the press. The Times was often outspoken in rebuke, and the comic weekly, Punch, habitually indulged in ridicule of the royal family. The Prince was not immune from such attack, either in England or on the continent of Europe, where his habits of travel made him a familiar figure, and excited a widespread curiosity. The Paris boulevards, which he loved to traverse incognito on holiday, soon rang with his name, and French journalists and caricaturists put to his account all manner of apocryphal adventures—sportive and derogatory—echoes of which were heard in the newspapers of London and of other continental capitals. The irresponsible gossip spread a misconception of the Prince as a superman of pleasure, who lacked serious interests. From time to time public opinion was unsettled by the allegation.

Early in 1870 depreciatory rumour seemed in many eyes to

be justified when a member of fashionable society, Sir Charles
Mordaunt, brought an action of divorce against his wife and made
in his petition, solely on his wife's confession, an allegation against
the Prince of Wales. The Prince was not made a party to the
suit, but the cited co-respondents, Viscount Cole, afterwards Earl
of Enniskillen, and Sir Frederick Johnstone were among his social
comrades. Sir Frederick, a well-known sportsman, had been the
Prince's friend since undergraduate days at Oxford. The charge
proved to be the sort of calumny to which persons in the Prince's
position are inevitably exposed. Lady Mordaunt had for some
time been threatened with insanity, and before the hearing of the
case had become hopelessly insane. Apart from her own statement to her husband there was nothing on which to base a
suggestion of misconduct on the part of the Prince save
eleven letters [1] of social gossip which he had written to "My
dear Lady Mordaunt" at various dates, beginning with 13th
January 1867 and ending in December of the following
year. The Lord Chancellor, Lord Hatherley, inspected these
documents and pronounced them to be "unexceptionable
in every way." There were signs of vindictiveness in the
petitioner's conduct of his case. He and his counsel, Serjeant
Ballantyne, subpœnaed the Prince as a witness, and the step
greatly distressed him and his family. After discussing his
course of action with Queen Victoria, with his wife, and with the
Lord Chancellor, he waived any plea of privilege and took his
stand in the witness-box. The trial opened on the 16th February
1870 before Lord Penzance and a special jury, and after a postponement until the 23rd the Prince tendered his evidence that
day. He was examined for seven minutes by Dr. Deane, Lady
Mordaunt's counsel, and calmly denied the accusations against
him. He had good warrant for writing to the Queen: "I
trust that by what I have said to-day the public at large will
be satisfied that the gross imputations which have been so
wantonly cast upon me are now cleared up." The unpleasing
episode ended with congratulations from both Mr. Gladstone, the
Prime Minister, and the Lord Chancellor, on the Prince's "frank
and firm demeanour" in court, which carried a universal
conviction of truthfulness. The editor of *The Times* voiced in a

---

[1] These quite insignificant letters were published in "An Official Report" of
the trial in 1870, pp. 76–8.

1870
Ætat. 28
leading article the sense of relief and joy with which "the whole British nation" read the report of the Prince's evidence.[1] Mr. Gladstone deemed some earnest words of warning appropriate. "The conviction of my mind (he wrote to the Prince) based on no short experience is that, so long as the nation has confidence in the personal character of its sovereign the throne of this Empire may be regarded as secure." Lord Hatherley also pointed out to the Prince that he was bound to set a strict example, his life being "as a city set on a hill."

A section of the public was affronted by the association of the Prince's name with the suit. His next appearance in a London theatre and on the Epsom race-course evoked some cries of disapprobation. The Prince warmly resented the censure, but he bore it in silence, and events soon deprived it of significance. Gossip about the unworthiness of the Prince's comrades or about his own gallantries and gambling excesses was not silenced, and continued to reflect distortingly a negligible segment of the biographic circle. The slanders blindly overlooked alike the Prince's manifold activities in national life and the predominating soundness and sagacity of the Prince's social allies.

VIII

1864
Ætat. 22
The leadership of fashionable life in its varied phases was far from exhausting the Prince's restless energy. Scarcely any form of human activity was excluded from his carefully devised daily programme. There was an inevitable superficiality in some of his incursions into serious affairs, but his memory enabled him to apply pertinently the information with which others furnished him by word of mouth, and his tact and business shrewdness quickly gave value to his impromptu counsels.

From youth he had played with the fancy that the Army was his profession. He had become an unattached Colonel on his seventeenth birthday, and a full General on his twenty-first. The calls of his social sovereignty failed to quench the first hopes of military experience and employment. The Queen, in the opening years of her widowhood, had abandoned, despite her

---

[1] In the result Sir Charles Mordaunt's petition was dismissed on the ground that Lady Mordaunt's mental condition disabled her from being a party to the suit. Much litigation followed, and at the end of five years, on 11th March 1875, Sir Charles Mordaunt was granted a divorce.

tenacious pride in her military prerogative, the visits which she had hitherto been in the habit of paying to the camp at Aldershot. The Prince was bold enough to suggest to her that he might occasionally fill her place there if only to obtain some instruction in the handling of a brigade. The Duke of Cambridge, the Commander-in-Chief, the mentor of his youth, encouraged the Prince's military leanings, and he approved the Prince's suggestion. In July 1864 the Queen gave her assent, with the explicit reservation that her son would exercise nothing of the sovereign's authority or responsibility.

Other opportunities of acquainting himself with a soldier's duties supplemented the Queen's sanction of sojourns at Aldershot. As early as 16th April 1863 he was, to his gratification, gazetted Colonel of the 10th Hussars, a regiment which enjoyed a fine fighting record, having played an active part both on the field of Waterloo and in the Crimea.[1] The Prince of Wales thenceforth came into frequent touch with his regiment. With Valentine Baker, who was the Lieutenant-Colonel from 1860 to 1872, he formed a close friendship, which bore the strain of the officer's chequered fortunes in subsequent years. When the Queen first reappeared at Aldershot on the 9th July 1870, the Prince marched past her at the head of his regiment. In subsidiary developments of the Army, the Prince manifested an equally strong personal concern. In the recent formation of the new Volunteer force he had shown a keen interest during his Oxford and Cambridge days and on his visit to Canada. At his entreaty the Queen permitted him to succeed his father (on August 24, 1863) as Captain-General and Colonel of the Honourable Artillery Company, an ancient Volunteer regiment of the City of London. He prided himself on this appointment, and he rode at the head of the regiment at the great Review which Queen Victoria held in Windsor Park on 7th July 1881, in celebration of the coming of age of the new Volunteer organisation.[2]

[1] The regiment had been nearly identified with the last Prince of Wales (afterwards George IV.), who had been Colonel of the regiment from the 18th July 1796 till his succession to the throne in 1820. As long ago as 1783 the regiment had received the subsidiary title of the Prince of Wales's Own, and had been given permission to wear the Prince of Wales's plume of three ostrich feathers. Cf. Col. R. S. Liddell, *Memoirs of the 10th Royal Hussars, Prince of Wales's Own—Historical and Social*, 1891.

[2] A quarrel among the officers of the Hon. Artillery Company in 1888 led to the Prince's resignation of the Captain-Generalship and Colonelcy. The

1871
Ætat. 29 The Prince's desire to increase his military responsibilities sometimes went beyond what the judgement of the authorities approved. An application in 1870 for the vacant Colonelcy of the Scots Fusilier Guards was rejected, on the ground of insufficient experience. But when in September of the next year the Duke of Cambridge, in emulation of the continental custom, held autumn military manœuvres for the first time in this country, the Prince joined in the experiment along with his brother, Prince Arthur, who was definitely destined for a soldier's career. With the 10th Hussars, the Prince went into camp at Bramshill, Hampshire.[1] Subsequently a brigade of the 2nd Division was placed under his command in his rank of General. The Prince threw himself with ardour into the operations. According to the Duke of Cambridge he performed his duties "with interest and vigour (taking part in the ordinary duties of camp life)."[2] His sister, Princess Alice, who visited him in camp wrote to their mother: "Bertie is full of work and immensely interested in it."[3] Mimic warfare in all its range came his way. On the last day of the manœuvres (21st September) he was taken prisoner while at the head of a detachment of his regiment. The Prince found a first spell of camp life so exhilarating that he engaged in it again next year, when the military manœuvres were repeated on Salisbury Plain. Writing to Lord Granville from Bemerton Lodge, Salisbury, on the 8th August 1872, the Prince remarked, "The Manœuvres are prospering in every respect. The troops have worked very hard, and have done very well. Since I have been here we have been up at six and out at seven, and to bed early, which is a very healthy life."

No further experience of the precise kind was open to the Prince,[4] but his military enthusiasm continued to run high even if future efforts to engage in military service proved unavailing.

---

regiment was disarmed by the War Office on 18th December 1888, but it was reorganised and restored next year, when the Prince resumed his offices.

[1] The Bramshill camp was not far from the village of Eversley, where Charles Kingsley was rector, and the Prince greatly pleased his old Cambridge teacher by riding out to pay him an informal visit before the camp was raised.

[2] Verner, *Military Life of the Duke of Cambridge*, ii. 58.

[3] *Memoirs of Princess Alice*, p. 273.

[4] This second trial of military manœuvres proved the last of the series. The scheme was not revived till the autumn of 1898, when modern manœuvres on a great scale were held for the first time. (See MacDiarmid's *Life of General Grierson*, p. 139.)

On 29th May 1875 he was gratified to receive from the Queen the Birthday Honour of promotion to the supreme rank of Field-Marshal.

IX

Public sentiment was conciliated by the early proofs which the Prince gave of a wish to promote the many public movements of philanthropic, educational, and cultural aim with which his father had identified himself. Although the Queen cherished doubts of the Prince's qualifications to follow in the footsteps of his father, she became reconciled to such displays of filial ambition. In the long run the Prince's prestige was signally enhanced by his association with charitable and other societies and institutions, to the success of which the Prince Consort had personally contributed. Marlborough House added to its reputation by the liberality with which the Prince encouraged meetings there under his chairmanship, to promote causes of public usefulness.

The Prince's participation in work of beneficence and enlightenment began soon after his father's death, and continued without pause as long as he lived. In the summer of 1862 the energetic Society of Arts offered him the post of President in succession to the Prince Consort. At the time the Queen deemed her son too young and too inexperienced for the office, and an octogenarian member of the Society, Mr. William Tooke, the economist, was elected. But on Tooke's death, next year, the Prince was again invited, and he accepted the post.[1] In a letter to the Society the Prince expressed the hope that he might "promote the great and beneficent objects which my father had so much at heart." The Prince was faithful to his charge, remaining in office until his accession to the throne, some thirty-eight years later. Throughout that long period he actively forwarded the Society's interests. One item in the Society's well-filled programmes especially appealed to him. The Society had founded in 1862, in the Prince Consort's memory, the Albert Medal to reward conspicuous service in the arts, manufacture, and commerce. The Prince played a personal part year by year in the choice of recipients, who included men of the highest distinction. When, on his accession to the throne, he exchanged the post of President of the Society of Arts for that of patron,

1864
$\overline{\text{Ætat. 22}}$

[1] Sir H. Trueman Wood's *History of the Royal Society of Arts*, 1913, p. 444.

it was with lively satisfaction that he accepted the Society's award of the Albert Medal to himself. Among more strictly educational institutions in the presidency of which he succeeded his father, was Wellington College, a public school which had been founded in memory of the Duke of Wellington, at the outset, for sons of deceased officers. In 1864 the Prince became President of the Board of Governors, and he never lost touch with its affairs. His election as Life Governor of the Royal Agricultural Society (February 3, 1864) introduced him to a different sphere of public work which especially attracted him as a landowner at Sandringham. The Society greatly benefited the farming industry of the country, and four times the Prince served as its President, for the first time in 1869.

The welfare of hospitals was one of the most active and constant concerns of his adult career. As early as June 1864 he and the Princess inaugurated a lifelong association with the London Hospital in the east end of London, when he accompanied his wife on her laying the foundation stone of a new west wing, which was named after her the "Alexandra Wing." On 20th March 1867 the Prince created a new precedent by accepting the office of President of an older London hospital, St. Bartholomew's Hospital. The Prince came to recognise that the investigation of disease and the cure of suffering were as important as any national causes.[1]

The most distinctive branch of educational enlightenment to which, from early manhood onwards, the Prince devoted his influence and energy, was the development of the many schemes which the Prince Consort designed by way of sequel to the Great Exhibition of 1851. This pursuit gave the Prince of Wales peculiar opportunities of showing his aptitude for organisation. The Royal Commission which had controlled the Great Exhibition was constituted a permanent body, shortly after the Exhibition closed. The object was to apply the profits to the promotion of technology, science, and art. An estate of unoccupied land

---

[1] His philanthropic, cultural, and cognate activities were never confined to London. Their range at this period may be gauged from such typical examples as these: the opening of the British Orphanage at Slough on the 24th June 1863, and of the new Town Hall at Halifax in August 1863; the laying of foundation stones of a new wing of St. Mary's Hospital, Paddington, in May 1865; of the British and Foreign Bible Society on the 11th June 1866; and of new buildings at Glasgow University on the 8th October 1868.

covering 87 acres was purchased at Kensington,[1] and it was the Prince Consort's intention to erect on this estate, with the aid of contributions from the Government and of public munificence, a series of technological, scientific, and art museums which should make Kensington a great cultural "locality." At the date of the Prince Consort's death the only part of this plan which had taken practical shape was a proposal for the erection on the Commissioners' estate of a great Central Hall, where meetings, lectures, concerts, and other improving functions might be held. The Prince of Wales gave prompt proofs of his anxiety for the fulfilment of his father's Kensington plan, and especially for the building of the Central Hall. Lord Derby, an active member from the first of the 1851 Commission who undertook the general supervision after the Prince Consort's death and became President in his place on 16th April 1864, resolved on an appeal to the public for funds wherewith to build the Hall by way of a national memorial to the Prince Consort. On the 11th August 1862 Lord Derby received from the Prince of Wales an offer of general co-operation, and of a handsome contribution to the fund for the Central Hall.[2]

"It will be a great satisfaction to me," the Prince wrote, "to assist in any way towards the success of plans devised by him (*i.e.* the Prince Consort), and calculated in his belief to effect much public good. If I cannot bring to the work his great knowledge and excellent judgement, I can at least bring goodwill and earnestness to the cause. I am most anxious to give proof of this feeling, and concurring in the hope that you express that sufficient funds may be provided for its completion, I shall be glad, when the proper time comes, to contribute £2000 towards the Central Hall, the erection of which you suggest as the commencement of buildings which we may hope to see at no distant

1864
—
Ætat. 22

---

[1] The "main square" of the Commissioners' estate was bounded by Kensington High Street, Exhibition Road, Cromwell Road, and Queen's Gate. The Government, which had instituted in 1853 an embryonic Department of Science and Art, soon dissolved an original partnership with the 1851 Commission and purchased or leased in course of time much of the Commissioners' land, whereon to erect on its own account the South Kensington (afterwards the Victoria and Albert) Museum, the Natural History Museum, the Imperial College of Science and Technology, and other institutions of cognate character. But the 1851 Commission continued independently of the Government to carry out, with modifications, many of the educational plans which the Prince Consort had initiated. (Cf. Eighth Report of the Commissioners for the Exhibition of 1851, 1911, and *The Royal Commission for the Exhibition of 1851*, 1924.)

[2] Maxwell's *Clarendon*, ii. 259.

1864
Ætat. 22

period, dedicated to those educational purposes in which he took so deep an interest."

But the public did not share the Prince's zeal for the projected Hall.[1] Subscriptions came slowly and scantily. The Prince of Wales and his fellow-promoters were unwilling to acknowledge defeat. Mr. (afterwards Sir) Henry Cole, who had actively aided the Prince Consort in his Kensington project, sought the Prince of Wales's ear. At the end of 1864 proposals were drafted for the formation of a private Limited Liability Company which should provide the required funds. The Prince flung himself with ardour into the new plan, and accepted the presidency of a new committee to carry it out. He summoned to Marlborough House a meeting of probable supporters on 6th July 1865. Sir William Knollys expressed doubts of success. But the Prince, encouraged by Lord Derby and by Lord Granville, another prominent Commissioner of 1851, persevered. Preliminary designs for the Hall were prepared by Captain Francis Fowkes, who had already done much architectural work at

1865
Ætat. 23

Kensington for the Commission. Greatly concerned by Fowkes's sudden death at the end of 1865, the Prince intervened in the choice of a successor. He inclined to Sir Gilbert Scott, the architect of the Albert Memorial. Finally, when Major-General Henry Young Darracott Scott was appointed, the Prince induced his Committee to form a supplementary sub-committee of expert architectural and artistic advisers, to which he nominated Sir Charles Eastlake, P.R.A.; Mr. Beresford Hope, F.R.I.B.A.; John Robinson McClean, the President of the Institute of Civil Engineers, together with Sir William Tite, Lord Elcho, and Sir Austen Layard. "Such names," the Prince wrote to Lord Derby (December 11, 1865), "would give the public a greater confidence as to the architectural and general arrangement of the buildings." Thenceforth all went forward satisfactorily. At the Prince's invitation the Queen, on 20th May 1867, laid, with full masonic rites, the foundation stone of the building, which was christened the Royal Albert Hall, and the completed edifice was opened by her in State on the 29th March

[1] An elaborate architectural monument in memory of the Prince's father—the Albert Memorial—which was devised at the same time for a site in Kensington Gardens overlooking the Kensington Road, which runs between the Gardens and the South Kensington estates, seemed to the public at large to satisfy more effectually the memorial needs of the situation.

1871.[1] Whatever the subsequent fortunes of the Royal Albert
Hall, its birth offers substantial evidence of the organising
energy of the Prince in comparatively early years.

On the 18th February 1870 the Prince identified himself
more completely with his father's Kensington project, by joining
the 1851 Commission in the place of President which Lord
Derby's death, some six weeks before, had left vacant. The
Prince retained the presidency until his accession to the throne,
when his son, afterwards King George V., took his place.
Throughout the thirty-one years of his presidential tenure, the
work of the Commission, which the Prince had already carefully
watched from the outside, bore witness to his versatility.

1870
—
Ætat. 28

The first scheme which came to fruition under the Prince's
presidency was a failure. It illustrated, perhaps, too confiding
a filial faith in the principle and practice of exhibitions. A
plan for the erection on a vacant portion of the Commissioners'
Kensington estate of permanent buildings for annual industrial
exhibitions had received his enthusiastic approval in 1868. On
the 15th July in that year he summoned to Marlborough House
another meeting, when there was adopted a proposal to hold ten
annual exhibitions, beginning in 1871, the capital expenditure
to be provided by the Commissioners.[2] In the execution of this
somewhat venturesome enterprise the Prince as President of the
Commission played his part. The annual series started, according to plan, in 1871, and was continued in each of the three
following years; but the scheme failed to attract public favour,
and the Commission lost heavily. Adversity befell the Commission in succeeding years despite the Prince's hopefulness.
Sir Henry Cole, the secretary at the time, proved unequal to the
task of retrieving the financial situation, and on Sir Henry's retirement in 1873 he was succeeded by Major-General Henry Y. D.
Scott, who was no more successful. On Scott's death in 1883 the
Prince saw the need of new blood. He induced his early acquaintance, Dr. Lyon Playfair, who had been an unobtrusive Commissioner since 1869, to undertake the honorary secretaryship
of the Commission in order to restore the financial equilibrium.
The Prince's choice of his old friend was amply justified by the

[1] The Prince's unpublished letters to Lord Granville and Lord Derby;
Sir Henry Cole's *Fifty Years of Public Work*, i. 358–65.
[2] Sir Henry Cole, *Fifty Years of Public Work*, i. 266 *seq.*

1870
Ætat. 28

event. The debt was reduced (from £180,000 to £26,000), and a deficit (of £2000) in the annual income was converted into a surplus revenue (of £5000). A new series of exhibitions retrieved the failure of the series of 1871–74.[1] The Prince welcomed Playfair's suggestion that the surplus income should be devoted to educational uses of more definitive character than before. A scheme was devised for offering scholarships throughout the country to students of science and technology. When Playfair retired in May 1889 the Prince was active in organising a testimonial in recognition of his services. "Nobody but yourself," wrote the Prince to Playfair (May 6, 1889), "could have got us out of the serious pecuniary embarrassments in which we found ourselves placed." The Prince deprecated the cost of the testimonial coming out of the Commission's funds (Prince to Granville, March 28, 1889). The money was furnished privately, and the Prince presented the gift to Playfair at Marlborough House.[2]

The Prince's zeal was not damped by temporary checks, and his faith in the Commission's adaptability to sound purposes was justly confirmed by the new scholarship scheme.

X

1865
Ætat. 23

Another educational venture which engaged the Prince's active attention through the same period was prompted by his love of music and by his view that the wide cultivation and appreciation of music might prove useful solvents alike of class and national jealousies.[3] In an effort to improve the musical education of the people he took a personal part. As early as 1865 the Society of Arts, of which he was President, appointed a committee to inquire into the condition of musical education in the country. The only institution specifically engaged at the time in musical education was the Royal Academy of Music, which had been founded in 1822 under royal patronage. There was a general feeling that the Academy was wanting in efficiency, and on the ground of its imperfections the Great Exhibition (1851) Com-

[1] See pp. 617–18 infra.
[2] Reid, Lyon Playfair, pp. 354–79.
[3] He was not only a regular supporter of the London Opera, but frequently attended musical festivals in provincial centres, notably at Leeds and Norwich. Writing on 15th October 1884, he noted, "To-day we have been to the Norwich festival. Gounod's 'Redemption' was admirably given, and the music was exceptionally fine."

mission had lately declined to provide for it the site of a new
home on their Kensington estates. The Prince was anxious to
protect the interests of the Academy, and while he consented
to act as Chairman of the Society of Arts Committee he made it
a condition that "nothing should be done hostile to the Royal
Academy of Music." The first report of the Prince's committee,
dated June 1866, recommended a reconstitution of the Academy,
and negotiations were opened with that body in order to fit it
for enlarged functions. The Academy, however, disappointed
the Prince by rejecting his Committee's advice. The Prince,
reluctant to come into conflict with the old institution, abstained
for some time from further personal action. He left his brother,
the Duke of Edinburgh—an accomplished violinist who was
also keen in the cause of musical education—to continue the
work which he had begun. The Duke succeeded in founding
at South Kensington, near the Albert Hall, a national training
school for music: the cost of the building being defrayed by a
private benefactor, Mr. C. J. Freake, a building contractor in
a large way of business. The school was formally opened by the
Duke on 17th May 1876. Meanwhile, in his capacity of President
of the Society of Arts, the Prince came forward to supplement
his brother's scheme. He energetically headed a movement to
provide free scholarships for students at the new training school.
On the 17th June 1875 he summoned a large meeting to Marlborough House to organise the scholarship scheme, and by the
time that the training school was ready for work fifty free scholarships were established. The Prince, however, shared a growing
conviction that his brother's training school scarcely met the
needs of the situation. There seemed to him a call for a more
ambitious development. Accordingly, in August 1878, the
Prince again summoned a meeting at Marlborough House, and
there he proposed that a fully equipped College of Music should
supersede the training school. The new proposal was well
received. The Royal Academy had recovered its ground, and
the Prince now felt that no harm would be done it by the creation
of a companion institution with somewhat broader national
aims. The Prince served as Chairman of the new Committee
which summoned the Royal College of Music into existence.
On 28th February 1882, at a representative meeting at St. James's
Palace, he described in full detail the objects of the new venture

and the means of realising them. A year later the premises of
the Duke of Edinburgh's training school were conveyed to him,
and on the 7th May 1883 he formally inaugurated there the
Royal College. In his speech on the occasion he declared:
"Class can no longer stand apart from class. . . . I claim for
music that it produces that union of feeling which I much desire
to promote." He rated highly the services of Mr. Freake, the
donor of the building, and exerted all his persuasive powers on
the Prime Minister, Mr. Gladstone, in order to procure him a
baronetcy. Mr. Freake, he pointed out, was a philanthropist
who was identified with no political party. It took the Prince
a year to convince Mr. Gladstone of Mr. Freake's fitness for the
honour, but the Prime Minister yielded to the Prince's importunity in April 1882, and the baronetcy was announced in next
month's list of birthday honours.[1]

The Prince never lost his interest in the Royal College of
Music. He noted appreciatively the progress which examiners
annually reported to him. On the 8th July 1890 he laid the
foundation stone of additional premises which were provided by
a Leeds engineer, Mr. Samson Fox, and he opened the new
building in full state on the 2nd July 1894.

XI

There was yet another practical field of activity to which the
Prince was drawn. The structural embellishment of London,
which was his birthplace and the main scene of the exercise of
his social sovereignty, was always a personal concern. Whatever
defects may be imputed to his artistic taste he was endowed
with a sense of spacious dignity. That sense was gratified by the
reconstruction which he witnessed of the capital cities of Paris,
Berlin, and Vienna, and he desired to see it embodied in a renovated London. On 11th May 1870 his mother delegated to him
the welcome task of opening so notable a London improvement
as the Thames Embankment, and his mind ran on other cognate

---

[1] The first Director of the College, Sir George Grove, was succeeded in 1894
by Sir Hubert Parry, who on King Edward's death in 1910, delivered an address
to the students on the King as "The Founder of the College." See *College
Addresses* by Sir Hubert Parry, ed. H. C. Collis, 1920, pp. 57-67, and also Sir
Henry Cole's *Fifty Years of Public Work*, vol. i. p. 59 *et seq.*

1884
Ætat. 42

structural reforms of the metropolis. The Prince's interest in London's structural embellishment did not lead to concrete result on any conspicuous scale until he reached the throne. But he contributed in middle life to London's minor amenities. According to Sir Charles Dilke the Prince earnestly interested himself in an abortive plan for the reform of the Government of London in 1882, but it was a wish for London's structural improvement rather than any definite view about its administrative reform that turned his attention to methods of governing London.

His successful solution of a small but urgent town-planning problem in central London illustrated also his adroitness in meeting conservative opposition to structural change. In 1883 the crying need of increasing the accommodation for traffic at Hyde Park Corner was generally acknowledged. The government proposed to widen the thoroughfares in the congested region by sacrificing adjacent portions of Constitution Hill within the railings of the Green Park. But a triumphal arch, surmounted by a colossal statue of the great Duke of Wellington which had been erected at public expense in 1828, stood at the top of Constitution Hill and obstructed the needed extension of the roadway. The statue was an unsightly object, but its demolition clearly offended public sentiment. The Prince undertook to meet the difficulty. Writing to Mr. Gladstone from Sandringham on 8th January 1884 he advised the re-erection of the arch at the entry to the retrenched Constitution Hill, the substitution for the colossal statue of a quadriga on the roof of the displaced arch, and the placing of a new small statue of the Duke on a reserved fragment of the arch's old site, nearly the whole of which was to be thrown into the expanded roadway.

"As regards the old (colossal) statue of the Duke," the Prince added in practical fashion, "I would suggest that it should not be broken up but removed to Aldershot where it would be highly valued by the Army—and would serve as an example to all time. General Reilly informs me that this could be done as a matter of ordinary service by the Royal Artillery without any further cost to the Government than the expense of billeting the men engaged during the days occupied by the transit."

1885
Ætat. 33

Mr. Gladstone wrote next day from Hawarden gratefully accepting the Prince's solution of the difficulty.

The Prince's scheme was duly carried out. His suggestion that the open space encircling the old site of the arch should be called after Parisian precedent "The Wellington Place" was rejected, but the efficient reconstruction of an important centre of London's roadways, with due regard for historic tradition, was a fruit of his practical ingenuity. Of the final step—the transfer to Aldershot of the ugly colossal statue—he wrote to his friend, Alfred Montgomery, on 20th August 1885 :

> We had a very pretty and successful military ceremony at Aldershot yesterday, when I handed over to the General Commanding the troops there [Lieut.-Gen. Anderson] the old statue of the great "Dook."

XII

1863
Ætat. 21

The Prince's success in promoting serious movements in the public interest was greatly aided by the facility which he acquired as a public speaker. His youthful experience in America when replying to addresses stood him in good stead, but the Duke of Newcastle and General Bruce were always at hand there to supply him with his words and to advise on his manner of delivery. When he started on his independent career the desire grew in him to rely as a speaker upon himself. His initial experiment was not wholly promising. During the "wedding season" he made his first of many oratorical efforts at the annual banquet at the Royal Academy of Arts (May 2, 1863). He replied to the toast of his health. With his private secretary's assistance he had prepared beforehand an appropriate reference to his father's interest in the Academy and a few sentences on his appreciation of the national enthusiasm over his marriage. He learnt the whole by heart, and knew it perfectly "in the morning." But in the middle of its delivery at the dinner he broke down "so that everybody thought it was all up with him. But he persisted in thinking till he recovered the thread, and then all went well." [1] To the President of the Academy, Sir Charles Eastlake, he apologised for his "stupidity." His voice struck the audience as "clear and melodious," though the German "r" was noticed. The Prince reached the conclusion that it was a mistake for

---

[1] Lady Eastlake's *Memories*, ii. p. 117.

him to recite a speech learnt by rote, and he resolved to abandon the practice. A more onerous responsibility as a public speaker was thrown upon him when he first presided at a public dinner. On the 18th May 1864 he filled the chair at the annual dinner of the Royal Literary Fund which was held in St. James's Hall, and was attended by a highly distinguished intellectual company. Immense importance was attached in the Prince's family circle to this venture,—one in which many members of the royal family had preceded him.[1] Several speeches were expected of him in the course of the evening. The Prince now committed beforehand nothing to writing beyond the general drift of his utterance. He depended for the rest on the inspiration of the moment.

The plan proved satisfactory. In proposing the chief toast, "Success to the Fund," the Prince made a feeling allusion to the recent death of the novelist Thackeray, who had been an active member of the Committee of the Fund, and he mentioned an institution of like aim recently founded in France with which he suggested co-operation.[2] At the conclusion of the proceedings the Prince created a new precedent by proposing the health of the ladies, whom he described with no particular felicity as "the flowers of society" who ought to be associated with "the flowers of literature." But he well satisfied the calls of the occasion. Eminent auditors made highly favourable reports on his performance to the Queen. "I was sitting next him," wrote Earl Stanhope, the historian, who was President of the Royal Literary Fund, "and I could perceive that, as well became his years, he felt some anxiety and misgiving before he rose, but on 'hearing his own voice' as the phrase is in the House of Commons, that anxiety wore off. He spoke with a modest self-confidence, and had not once occasion to consult his manuscript notes." Lord Russell was no less complimentary:

"Everything the Prince said," the Foreign Secretary wrote to the Queen, "was marked by good feeling and good taste.

[1] The Prince's father made his first speech in public as Chairman of the Royal Literary Fund dinner in 1842. The Prince's grandfather, the Duke of Kent, had presided twice, in 1815 and again in 1816; three of his great-uncles, the Dukes of Sussex, York, and Cambridge, had done the like in later years.

[2] The toast of "Literature," which was proposed by Lord Russell, was acknowledged by another novelist, Anthony Trollope. Subsequently Lord Houghton proposed "The Literature of the World," coupling with it the name of M. van de Weyer, the accomplished Belgian Minister.

His delivery was clear and unpretending, without any attempt to assume the part of an orator and all the more striking from its simplicity. Your Majesty may rest in confidence that on the many occasions upon which the Prince of Wales will be called upon to express his sentiments in public, he will be equal to the onerous duty." (May 19, 1864.)

The Prince himself was well content with the evening.

"Many thanks for your congratulations," he wrote to Mrs. Bruce on 22nd May, "on my first attempt as Chairman of a public dinner. It is a very good thing over, as I was very nervous at first, but felt more at home after the two first speeches. The heat was quite awful, and we were 500 at dinner, and nearly 500 ladies in the galleries."

Pleasant memories of this experience of 1864 led the Prince to preside a second time at the annual banquet of the Royal Literary Fund on 14th May 1890, again in St. James's Hall when the foundation celebrated its hundredth anniversary.

The mode of oratory which the Prince adopted at his first Royal Literary Fund dinner became habitual. Except on occasions when special information and statistics were required and were supplied to him, he mastered beforehand a few general ideas of his own, dispensed with written notes, and left the moment to provide the words. His tact and genial courtesy invariably carried the day. If his speeches lacked original thought or pointed expression he developed a fluent and easy grace, in which few contemporaries were his superiors. Lord Houghton, who was acknowledged to be a past-master in the art of occasional oratory, judged the Prince to be only second to himself.

CHAPTER XIII

THE PRINCE AND POLITICS—HONOURS AND APPOINTMENTS—
ACCESS TO OFFICIAL INFORMATION

I

AMID the multifarious calls of the Prince's busy life the observation, discussion, and criticism of politics knew no interruption at any period of his adult career. If foreign affairs chiefly arrested his attention, he followed home affairs with unceasing zest—especially the changing fortunes of parties and the personal vicissitudes of party leaders. During the four decades that intervened between his twenty-first birthday and his accession to the throne he cultivated intimate relations with successive Prime Ministers, Foreign Secretaries, and many of their leading colleagues. Constantly meeting these men in the society which he swayed, he freely engaged them in political conversation, and questioned them without reserve on pending crises. Nor was he backward in sending them written expressions of his views on those political themes which strongly excited his interest, and in freely offering them recommendations for the distribution of honours and appointments.

Lord Palmerston, who was Prime Minister from 1859 till his death on 18th October 1865 at the ripe age of eighty-one, was the dominant personality in English politics when the Prince's interest in them began, and his political influence long survived his death. The main political opinions to which the Prince was faithful through life reflected Lord Palmerston's creed, of which the chief articles were the maintenance of England's dominant influence on the world, the dissemination through Europe of the principles of constitutional government and of constitutional liberty, the protection of subject races from oppression, confidence

199

in the value of religious toleration, and a suspicion of abrupt change in established institutions at home. In course of time the Prince went farther than the Palmerstonian gospel in his sympathies with social reform, in his antipathy to anything savouring of revolution, and in his dislike of war save as a last resort in settling international disputes. But he never faltered in his faith in a spirited foreign policy, coupled with the main-tenance of a strong navy, or in his conviction that constitutional monarchy was the best of all forms of government. Although he shared the tendency inherent in princes to view royalty of all countries and races as a separate and homogeneous caste, and was always deeply interested in the personal fortunes of all wearers of crowns, he was as distrustful of autocracy as of militant republicanism.[1] Like Queen Victoria, the Prince showed every respect for the memory of the Stuarts, but it was the tragic fall of a royal family from its high estate and not King Charles I.'s method of government that generated his sympathy.[2]

To party programmes he always professed a correct indiffer-ence. Yet in private talk he freely expressed his opinion of measures and policies, inclining now to one side, now to the other. Despite his Whiggish leanings, some Tory elements mingled in his political sentiment. A Conservative leaven was inevitable in the

[1] The Prince was careful strictly to respect the precedence of an acknow-ledged king even of an uncivilised country over an heir-apparent even of one of the great monarchical powers of Europe. On 10th July 1881 he gave a ball at Marlborough House in honour of Kalakaua, King of the Sandwich Islands, and the black monarch danced the opening quadrille with the Princess. The Crown Prince and Princess of Germany were present among the guests, and there was a remonstrance in Germany against the Prince's bestowal on the black king of precedence over the Crown Prince (Tuckwell and Gwynn's *Life of Sir Charles Dilke*, i. 415).

[2] The Prince paid in 1888 a peculiarly fitting and characteristic tribute of respect to the memory of King Charles I. Sir Henry Halford, the favourite physician of George III., had, on 1st April 1813, sacrilegiously opened the vault in St. George's Chapel which contained the coffin of the beheaded King. Open-ing the coffin he removed from the body a portion of the fourth cervical vertebra which the axe had severed, and retained the relic enclosed in an ebony box, which descended to his grandson, Sir Henry St. John Halford. The latter presented the box to the Prince in 1888. In consultation with the Dean of Windsor, Dr. Randall Davidson, afterwards Archbishop of Canterbury, the Prince resolved to replace the box in the royal vault from which the bones had been removed. The ceremony took place on 13th December 1888, when the Prince was accompanied by the Dean of Windsor and Canons Eliot and Dalton. The box, which was placed on the centre of the coffin, was subsequently encased in lead. An account of the episode was entered in the official book of records of St. George's Chapel, and a copy was sent to the Prince.

heir-apparent of an ancient monarchy. "You see what a Con-   1866
servative I am," he wrote to Mr. Disraeli on 26th November 1876,   Ætat. 24
when protesting against the minister's breach with precedent in
recommending a commoner for a place in an order of chivalry
which had hitherto been filled only by peers. His Palmerstonian
faith never completely reconciled him to the full claims of political
democracy. He was slow to recognise that his democratic
tendencies in society might encourage the development of
advanced political ideas. When, in 1865 and 1866, the Radical
demand for an extension of the Franchise evoked violent demonstrations in its favour by democratic leaders, the Prince was
moved in private to harsh criticism which the Queen rebuked.
Somewhat crudely he endeavoured to explain to her his political
position :

> "I did not mean," he wrote, "that the really hard-working
> labouring classes were getting too much power, because they
> indeed deserve to be noticed when they attain a higher sphere
> of existence by their own merits and industry. But I alluded to
> the 'mob,' and what are known as 'roughs,' and they, to a much
> greater extent than people are aware of are getting a greater
> power. They are the people who back up such people as Beales,
> Potter & Co., and who break into Hyde Park and attended the
> meetings at Trafalgar Square, etc., last year."

He was firm in his adherence to law and order, which he thought   1870
to be menaced by the unfettered pretensions of democracy.   Ætat. 28
   Yet in his attitude to some important economic or social
rather than political features of the democratic movement of his
early manhood he soon gave proofs of open-mindedness. His
interest in amelioration of the dwellings of the working classes
and in provision for the needs of the aged poor led him to join
royal commissions of inquiry into both subjects.[1] He came,
too, to acknowledge the wisdom of doing what he could to assuage
the strife between labour and capital. With the general principle
of Trade Unionism he sympathised. During the year 1870 he
boldly made a public pronouncement in the matter. A Workmen's International Exhibition was organised at the Agricultural
Hall in London by way of encouraging industrial progress and
industrial peace. The initiative came from Trade Union
leaders, headed by an influential agitator, George Odger. Of

[1] See pp. 547 seq. and 552 seq. infra.

1870
Ætat. 28

the First International Working Men's Association, which was tentatively formed in London in 1864 to give effect to Karl Marx's economic theory of the iniquity of capital, Odger was the first President. Prominent Liberals, including Mr. Gladstone, the Prime Minister, and the Duke of Argyll, advanced Radicals like Mr. Auberon Herbert, and leaders of the scientific enlightenment of the day, like Mr. Huxley, supported the Trade Unionists' Exhibition. The Queen's favour was enlisted, and the Prince had no hesitation in pronouncing his benediction on the Exhibition—a form of enterprise which was always congenial to him. In his mother's behalf he undertook the task of opening the show on 16th July 1870. In response to an address of welcome which was read by one of the Trade Unionist secretaries (Mr. Probyn) the Prince tactfully pointed out that the Exhibition

cannot fail to meet with cordial approval of all who are interested in the growth and rise of manufactures and wish to connect that growth with a corresponding increase of sympathy and friendly relations between employers and their workmen. . . . Kindly intercourse between countries makes for the peace of the world.

The Prince's remarks had a mixed reception in capitalist circles, but they illustrated his receptivity to developing economic and social ideas, without reference to party cries. With another national social interest which had no political associations he identified himself near the same date. He served on a Select Committee of the House of Lords to inquire into the capacity of the country to supply the present or future demand for horses.[1]

1864
Ætat. 22

There was abroad from his early years a delusive impression that the Prince was personally identified with the Whig or Liberal party. His household, as it was constituted in early days, undoubtedly had a Whig complexion. Colonel Kingscote and Major Grey were acknowledged Whigs; Sir William Knollys and his son inclined to Whig opinions. Some close associates in private life, like Lord Carrington, Lord Spencer, Lord Hartington, and Lord Rosebery, were politicians of the Liberal brand. When near the opening of Mr. Disraeli's second ministry there were signs among the Prince's friends of opposition to phases of the Conservative policy, Queen Victoria impulsively complained of the opposition

[1] The Select Committee was appointed on the motion of Lord Rosebery on 25th February 1873, and reported in the following August. Nothing followed from the recommendations.

tendencies of "the Marlborough House Set." But in point of
fact the Prince's political detachment was never in question.
His personal ties with the Whigs formed only one side of the
shield.   He was, at the opening of his career, in as frequent intercourse with Lord Derby, the leader of the Conservative party, as
with Lord Palmerston, the leader of the Liberals.   Subsequently
he was in as confidential relations with Mr. Disraeli, Lord Derby's
successor, as with Mr. Gladstone, Lord Palmerston's successor.
The Conservative Lord Hamilton (heir of the Marquis of Abercorn), who became a favourite equerry, was as close a friend as
any of Lord Hamilton's Whig comrades at Marlborough House.

Occasional inconsistencies and a touch of opportunism are to
be admitted in the Prince's political views.   His first suspicions
of the wisdom of extending the Franchise did not survive a
Conservative Ministry's adoption of the project with Liberal
support in 1867.   The personal equation had its influence on his
attitude to political causes and events.   He bestowed at times a
greater favour on political opinions which were not in strict
accord with his predilections, because they were held by men
whom he personally liked; while the inverse process was sometimes discernible.   If he were no party politician he was clearly
no political philosopher.   Yet his spontaneous comment on
political affairs bore witness to a native shrewdness, a serviceable
memory, and a penetrating knowledge of many phases of life.
Such credentials for political study ripened with the Prince's
years and came to prove of national value, more especially in the
sphere of foreign policy.   Lord Beaconsfield and, at a later period
Lord Salisbury, often acknowledged that his views on varying
phases of the foreign situation gave them useful suggestion.

II

Although the government's domestic policy through the
decade which opened with his marriage excited no very deep
feeling in the Prince, he closely followed the notable changes in
the personnel.   The protagonists of the Prince's youth, Lord
Palmerston, Lord Derby, and Lord Russell, left the stage.
Death also removed from the political scene, early in the Prince's
adult career, two subordinate actors in whom he placed much
confidence.   The Duke of Newcastle, the Colonial Secretary in

1864
Ætat. 22

1867
Ætat. 25

1865
Ætat. 23

Lord Palmerston's government, who gave the Prince his first instruction in colonial policy, died prematurely on 18th October 1864. "A better man never lived," the Prince wrote to Lord Spencer, another political oracle of his early days. Lord Clarendon, who had filled many posts in Liberal ministries, passed away on the 27th June 1870 while Foreign Secretary in Mr. Gladstone's first ministry. In a letter of condolence the Prince described Lord Clarendon as a "true sincere friend and adviser," and he wrote to the Queen that the dead statesman "could be least spared of all the Ministers." [1] But the disappearance of the prominent figures in the political world of his youth cleared the arena for that golden era in English politics when Mr. Gladstone and Mr. Disraeli—the new chiefs respectively of the two great political armies—engaged in their keenly sustained duel. The heroic combat fostered in the Prince, as in most of his fellow-countrymen, an interest of greater intensity than before in the personal aspect of politics.

The general election of July 1865 gave Lord Palmerston's Government a reduced majority. The incident in the electoral conflict which chiefly interested the Prince was the rejection of Mr. Gladstone by the University of Oxford after eighteen years' tenure of the seat. On Mr. Gladstone's defeat the Prince remarked to Dr. Acland (November 15, 1865): "I quite agree with you in thinking that Oxford made a great mistake in not returning Mr. Gladstone as their member, though I am not surprised at it, as his views were rather too Liberal for the University." Much ministerial reconstruction followed rapidly. On 21st December Lord Palmerston died unexpectedly, and the Prince, who wrote at the time of his "foresight and immense cleverness," attended the funeral in Westminster Abbey. The vacant post of Prime Minister fell inevitably to Earl Russell, the Foreign Secretary, in whom the Prince reposed smaller confidence than in his predecessor. But on personal grounds he saw with satisfaction Mr. Gladstone, who had found a seat at Greenwich, succeed Lord Palmerston as Leader of the House of Commons. Lord Russell's government was short-lived, and its defeat in the House of Commons on an

[1] The early link with Lord Clarendon was long maintained by the Prince's friendly intercourse with his daughter Lady Emily Villiers, who married his early acquaintance in Rome, Odo Russell.

amendment to its Franchise Bill, within fifteen months of its inauguration, placed the Conservatives in office with the Prince's familiar acquaintance, Lord Derby, as Prime Minister, and Mr. Disraeli as Chancellor of the Exchequer and Leader of the House of Commons (February 1867). The Queen gave an unusual proof of friendly confidence in her eldest son by inviting his presence and that of his brother, Alfred, in the small room at Windsor Castle where she received the seals of office from Lord Russell's retiring cabinet and handed them to its Conservative successors.[1]

The Prince's love of speculation was stirred by the efforts of the new Ministry, which was in a minority of the House of Commons, to keep their position, and it was at this period that he formed a lifelong habit of frequenting the Peers' Gallery of the Lower House. To the Conservative Government's handling of the thorny question of the franchise he was soon reconciled. On 25th February 1867 he heard Disraeli introduce his first Reform Bill—a very moderate measure—which was almost immediately withdrawn in favour of a comprehensive scheme of household suffrage. "We have had great political excitement," he wrote to Mrs. Bruce from Marlborough House in April 1867, in the course of Mr. Disraeli's gyrations, "but the Government are, I think, tolerably firm on their legs."

In August 1867 the Conservative Government's Franchise Bill became law, and in the following February Lord Derby's failing health compelled his resignation of the office of Prime Minister in favour of his astute lieutenant, Mr. Disraeli. The Prince, in forwarding his regrets to his old friend, expressed the hope: "Although you have resigned the 'tiller of the vessel' to other hands you will yet be able occasionally to assist in steering the vessel through the inevitable 'shoals and quicksands' which it must encounter" (March 1, 1868).

Despite his personal associations with Mr. Gladstone he deprecated the persistence of his attack on the new Prime Minister. He had little sympathy with the resolutions in favour of the Disestablishment of the Irish Church which Mr. Gladstone carried against the Conservative Government in May 1868; and the ensuing crisis, which involved the question of Mr. Disraeli's retention of office after his defeat, greatly roused the Prince. At a critical interview with the Queen on the 4th May Mr. Disraeli reached

1867
Ætat. 25

1868
Ætat. 26

---

[1] Lang's *Life of Sir Stafford Northcote, first Earl of Iddesleigh*, p. 161.

1868
Ætat. 26

the decision to hold on, and the Queen again showed maternal sympathy with her son's political excitement by directing her secretary, General Grey, to send him an account of the interview. "I was very anxious to hear the result," he wrote to his mother in a letter of thanks. Next day he was again in the House of Commons to hear the Prime Minister's momentous declaration, and he deplored the heat of Mr. Gladstone's reply. "I heard Mr. Disraeli's statement in the House of Commons on Monday," he wrote to the Queen, "and Mr. Gladstone made a very violent and angry speech in return. He, in fact, never loses an opportunity for reproaching and attacking him."

At the end of the year (1868), when Parliament dissolved and the general election drove Disraeli from office and installed Gladstone in his place, the Prince was in Denmark, but he prudently hastened to trim his sails to the oncoming breeze. From Copenhagen in December 1868 he wrote to the new Prime Minister:

I hope you will let me take this opportunity of congratulating you on becoming Prime Minister, and I can assure you that it is with the greatest interest that I have watched the formation of your Government, and I have very much regretted being absent from England during the change of Ministry.

The Prince added a special commendation of Mr. Gladstone's choice of his friend, Lord Spencer, for the office of Lord-Lieutenant of Ireland:

It was with the greatest pleasure that I heard of Lord Spencer's appointment as Lord-Lieutenant of Ireland; he is a great personal friend of mine, and I feel convinced that he will fulfil the arduous duties imposed upon him, with credit to himself, and to the satisfaction of the country at large.

1871
Ætat. 29

The cordiality of the Prince's private relations with Gladstone continued throughout the minister's first tenure of the Premiership. An illustration of the easy intimacy of the two during the period may be cited from Mr. Gladstone's diary of 30th September 1871, when he dined with the Prince at Abergeldie, while he was in attendance on the Queen at Balmoral. The entry in Gladstone's diary runs thus:

Sept. 30.—Last night we dined ten at Abergeldie. The Prince of Wales had his usual pleasant manners. He is far lighter in hand than the Duke of Edinburgh. After dinner he invited me to play whist. I said, "For love, sir?" He said, "Well, shillings and half-a-crown on the rubber," to which I submitted. Ponsonby and I against the Prince and Brasseur, a charming old Frenchman, his tutor in the language. The Prince has apparently an *immense* whist memory, and plays well accordingly.[1]

Meanwhile there was no diminution of the Prince's friendly associations with Mr. Gladstone's rival. He accepted with every sign of pride Disraeli's gift of a copy of his new political romance *Lothair* (May 1, 1870). When in February 1874 Mr. Disraeli, after giving full rein to his gifts of satiric invective, defeated Mr. Gladstone at the polls and was installed as Prime Minister for the second time by a vast majority of votes, the Prince who was far away at the time in St. Petersburg was gratified to receive from the conquering hero an intimation of his victory. The Prince wrote in reply (February 12/24):

I was very much touched by your kindness in writing to tell me of the change of government and of your having been charged by the Queen to form a new one. With the greatest interest I have read . . . the names of the able and distinguished men who are to form part of it.

By way of proving his political neutrality he invited the rival statesmen within a few weeks of Disraeli's assumption of power to dine with him at Marlborough House, where they had "a civil talk" with one another.[2]

Queen Victoria's personal devotion to Mr. Disraeli gave him much influence in the affairs of the royal family, and on the not infrequent occasions when the Queen differed from her son, Mr. Disraeli usually sided with her. The Conservative leader formed a less favourable view of the Prince's aptitudes than Mr. Gladstone, and complained at times of his "chitter-chatter." But Mr. Disraeli reciprocated the Prince's friendly advances by communicating to him much political information and listening to his views with every appearance of attention. "The natural kindness of your disposition," Disraeli wrote to the Prince with perhaps a touch of courtly flattery (December 4, 1876), "and your great tact often lighten my task." The Prince admitted a

---

[1] Morley's *Life of Gladstone*, ii. 378. M. Brasseur lived to a great age in retirement in Paris, where the Prince regularly visited him. (Cf. *The Times*, October 20, 1888.)

[2] Morley's *Life of Gladstone*, ii. 499.

preference, in the social circle, for the epigrammatic sallies of
Disraeli to the more solemn pronouncements which formed the
staple of Gladstone's conversation. There was small ground for
the current gossip that Queen Victoria's private regard for
Disraeli and her steadily maturing impatience with Gladstone
caused in the Prince an inverse attitude to the two men. His
lifelong reverence for Mr. Gladstone was no reaction from his
mother's aversion. Mr. Gladstone played, in the Prince's career,
a more intimate part than any filled by his rival. He had known
the Prince in his cradle, and he outlived Mr. Disraeli by seventeen
years. His handling of both foreign and Irish affairs in later life
was no more congenial to the Prince than to his mother; but
political differences never impaired the affectionate respect with
which Mr. Gladstone inspired him in youth.

III

As early as 1864 the Prince urged the Queen to confer the
place which the Duke of Newcastle's death vacated in the Order
of the Garter on Earl Spencer, his Groom of the Stole. The Earl
hesitated to accept the honour. "I am sure the Queen would
not like your refusing, and I am *quite* certain I should not," the
Prince retorted on 4th November 1864. The honour which
the Prince suggested was duly conferred early next year. The
episode illustrates the Prince's active interest from early manhood in the distribution of the Crown's patronage. It was by
no means only the Queen whom he sought to influence in this
regard throughout his long adult tenure of the heirship to the
Crown. The Prince's familiar relations with Prime Ministers
encouraged him to play unremittingly a part in the exercise of
not the least delicate of their accredited functions—the bestowal
of place and decoration in the sovereign's name. Recommendations for honours and appointments streamed incessantly from
the Prince's pen or lips. His importunities ranged over a wide
field. They concerned not only the most dignified offices of
State and places in the great orders of chivalry, but also posts or
honours of comparative humility. The personnel of the diplomatic corps through all ranks was always a theme which moved
in him fertile suggestion.

When cabinets were in course of formation the Prince from

the first was much excited by the competition which raged among aspirants to office, and gave free expression to his preferences in conversation with his personal friends. In course of time he was bold enough to express to the Queen through her private secretary his view as to the fit person who should be chosen to form a new ministry. He would also make direct to the new Prime Minister suggestions of personal friends for high political posts, and his recommendations were often welcomed.[1]

Although those who had done him any special service, valued members of his household, fellow-workers in philanthropic movements, or in the organisation of exhibitions, figured prominently among his nominees for titles, honours, or place, the Prince showed a sense of responsibility in the choice of his candidates. The calls of gratitude, benevolence, or friendship, to all of which he was responsive, were not allowed to override his judgement of suitable qualifications. Among his recommendations were not infrequently personal strangers, whose achievements in one or other field of distinction had won his admiration. He deemed a baronetcy to be an appropriate reward for expenditure of large sums of money on public or charitable objects. His very human attitude towards the distribution of titular honours may be gauged by his remark to Lord Beaconsfield, whom he was pressing to decorate colonial visitors, fellow-organisers of the Paris Exhibition of 1878: "A Knighthood or a C.M.G. would make them supremely happy, and would be highly appreciated by the Colonies whom they have represented, on their return home" (October 6, 1878). The Prince usually approached the Prime Minister on the theme of preferment by letter. When promotions in the diplomatic service were in question he often took preliminary soundings of the Foreign Secretary, when the Prime Minister did not hold the two posts together. If ministers raised objections to his proposals, he sometimes appealed against them to the Queen. But he did not engage very frequently in his mature years in consultation about honours and appointments with his mother. A first, a second, or even a third rebuff from a minister did not dismay him.

The Prince's pertinacity worked with chequered results. He had to admit some defeats, or at any rate partial victories.

[1] See pp. 513, 525, and 529 *infra*.

1876
Ætat. 34

When in 1868 Sir Robert Napier was made a peer by Mr. Disraeli in recognition of his success in the Abyssinian expedition, the Prince pointed out to the Prime Minister that the services of another general, Sir Hope Grant, leader of the China expedition of 1860, was, by comparison, inadequately rewarded, and the Prince asked that Sir Hope Grant should receive some further honour. Disraeli replied that the•matter could not be reconsidered. At the end of 1876 the Prince pressed with success on Mr. Disraeli the nomination of his friend the Duke of Manchester to a vacancy in the Order of St. Patrick; but his simultaneous recommendation of the Duke of Hamilton for a vacancy in the Order of the Thistle was rejected. The Prince expressed disapproval of the Prime Minister's preference for the vacant Thistle of a commoner, Sir William Stirling Maxwell, who was, Mr. Disraeli pointed out to his disappointed correspondent, "pre-eminent for his abilities, general distinction, and social consideration," and whose works, especially those on Spanish Art, were "classical." [1] "My only fear is," the Prince replied, "that it will make a precedent for a commoner receiving these decorations, which are generally exclusively conferred on Peers." John Rose, whose friendship with the Prince began during the tour in Canada, and was cemented on his settlement in England, was an energetic coadjutor in the Prince's efforts to promote exhibitions. For the aid he rendered the Prince in organising the Paris Exhibition in 1878 he received, on the Prince's earnest appeal to Lord Beaconsfield, the G.C.M.G. But when the Prince asked Mr. Gladstone to recognise Sir John's further service to the India and Colonies Exhibition in London of 1886,

1881
Ætat. 39

by conferring on him a peerage, the suggestion was declined. Twice in 1881 the Prince pressed on Mr. Gladstone the bestowal of baronetcies on Mr. Antony Gibbs ("a strong Liberal"), and Mr. Charles Freake ("no strong politics"). "I only bring them forward," the Prince wrote, "for the philanthropic manner in which they have spent their money." The claim of Mr. Freake, who had generously supported the Prince's scheme of the Royal College of Music, was, after some delay and a third application, alone admitted. No titular recognition came Mr. Gibbs's way. Another failure in an application for a baronetcy concerned Sir Edward Charles Blount, a banker and railway promoter, who

[1] Disraeli to Prince, November 26, 1876.

lived in Paris, and was devoted to the turf. Blount was made K.C.B. by Mr. Disraeli in 1878, but when the Prince pressed his name on both Mr. Gladstone and Lord Granville for a baronetcy in 1884 his claim for the honour was rejected as inadequate.

At another period the Prince was anxious in the public interest for titular recognition of those who had engaged with success in Arctic exploration. In 1876 two Arctic expeditions returned home—that of Captain George Nares and Captain Henry Frederick Stephenson in H.M.S. *Alert*, and that of Commander Allen Young, of the Royal Naval Reserve, in his yacht *Pandora*. The Prince urged Mr. Disraeli to decorate all three men. He proposed Nares for the K.C.B., and the two others for the C.B. Mr. Disraeli complied with a small variation —a knighthood for Allen Young in place of the C.B. It was at the Prince's instance that Lord Salisbury in 1891 recommended Captain Shaw for the K.C.B. on retiring after thirty years' service from the office of Chief Superintendent of the London Fire Brigade.

The manning of the diplomatic service was one of the branches of patronage in which the Prince's interest steadily grew with his years. He was always frank in his judgements of British diplomatists' merits and defects, and often complained of the baleful effects of "red-tapeism" on diplomatic efficiency. Lord Granville, while Foreign Secretary, always showed him the courtesy of consultation in appointments to the Court of the Prince's father-in-law at Copenhagen. When Sir Charles Wyke, minister there for fifteen years, with whom the Prince made great friends, was transferred to Lisbon in 1881, Lord Granville asked the Prince to select a successor, and the Prince's choice fell on Crespigny Vivian. But the Prince had by no means always the last word in the Danish patronage. On Vivian's removal to Brussels three years later, the Prince informed Lord Granville that the Princess desired the vacancy at Copenhagen for Hugh Wyndham, who was then a secretary of legation at Constantinople. "He would," the Prince wrote, "be acceptable to the King and Queen of Denmark." In the event, however, Edmund John (afterwards Sir Edmund) Monson was appointed. Sir Charles Wyke ("such an old personal friend of ours," in the Prince's words) retired from the diplomatic service early in 1884, when the Prince pressed in his behalf for the honour of admission to the

Privy Council. He cited two recent precedents, but Lord Granville was uncompliant. His successor, Lord Salisbury, proved more conciliatory, and Wyke became a Privy Councillor on 6th February 1886.

1884
—
Ætat. 42 The Prince was always specially concerned in the filling of the great embassies, and when one of these high posts fell vacant commonly made uninvited suggestions as to how it might be filled. He kept an eye on the attachés who came under his scrutiny, and formed definite opinions as to their fitness for promotion. The favourable impression which Lord Lytton made on the Prince when he was an attaché at Paris largely accounts for the young diplomat's rise in his profession. Sir Robert Morier, who gained his early diplomatic experience at small German Courts, became one of the Prince's favourite diplomatic protégés. When Berlin became the pivot of European diplomacy from 1880 onwards, the occupancy of the British Embassy there was regarded by the Prince as of very intimate interest. On the occasion of the two vacancies in 1884 and 1895 respectively he reviewed at length in correspondence with the Foreign Secretary the qualifications of numerous candidates, and in the first competition he ran hard but in vain his friend Sir Robert Morier; [1] in the second competition, which was won by Sir Frank Lascelles, the Prince considered many names before coming to a conclusion in favour of Sir Frank.[2]

Ecclesiastical appointments exercised the Prince's mind as much as civil, military, or diplomatic, as an example shows. Early in Mr. Gladstone's second tenure of the office of Prime Minister, which began in 1880, the death of Dean Stanley vacated the Deanery of Westminster (July 16, 1881). The Prince deplored the "irreparable" loss. "He will indeed," he wrote to Acland, 26th July 1881, "be difficult to replace, as the Deanery of Westminster was above all others the very post for which in my opinion he was most qualified. Whoever succeeds him will find it no easy task, however clever or suitable a person he may be." The Prince promptly reached the conclusion that Dean Stanley's best successor would be another of his Oxford friends—Dean Liddell of Christ Church. The Queen and Mr. Gladstone were both favourable to the choice, but the Dean promptly declined on the reasonable ground that he was "five years older than

[1] See p. 482 infra.   [2] See p. 678 infra.

Dean Stanley at his death." The Prince was reluctant to accept
the refusal, and on 9th August 1881 he wrote to Mrs. Liddell
urging her to use her influence with her husband to reconsider
his refusal. "I am sure," he wrote, "he would be the right man
in the right place, and nobody could succeed our dear kind friend
Dean Stanley better than himself. I hope the Dean will pause
to consider before giving his final answer." But Dean Liddell
was immovable, and a close friend of Dean Stanley—Dr. Bradley
—was nominated by Mr. Gladstone, to the Prince's disappointment.

Typical of the kindly energy which the Prince brought from
early days to negotiations touching appointments of a far humbler
kind is a series of letters which he addressed between the years
1866 and 1873 to three Prime Ministers, Lord Russell, Mr. Disraeli,
and Mr. Gladstone, appealing for the preferment of his former
tutor, the Rev. Charles Tarver, who was living in poverty on the
small benefice of St. Peter's, near Margate. At the opening of
this campaign, Lord Russell proved unexpectedly complacent,
and placed at the disposal of the Prince's protégé the Crown
living of Greenwich. But the Prince, after a personal inquiry,
came to the conclusion that the appointment was unsuitable.
There was (he pointed out to Lord Russell on 16th February
1866) "no house, an immense population, and three curates at
least would be required." A less burdensome post was essential.
Two years later the Prince repeated his application to Mr.
Disraeli without avail. On 17th February 1869 he sought the
assistance of Mr. Gladstone, pointing out that Tarver "was
very hardly worked, and his pecuniary means do not allow him
to keep a curate." The third Prime Minister to whom the
Prince addressed himself on Tarver's behalf promised his aid,
although he advised patience for the present. In the result the
Prince, in 1871, with the Queen's concurrence induced Archbishop
Tait of Canterbury to prefer his impoverished client to the fairly
remunerative rectory of Stisted, to which Mr. Gladstone added
in 1873, on a further appeal from the Prince, a Canonry of
Chester.

A similar instance of the Prince's pertinacity in the less
important spheres of honours concerned a Sandringham neighbour, Lewis Whincop Jarvis, a solicitor and banker of King's
Lynn, who had acted for a time as agent for the Prince, and had

been six times Mayor of King's Lynn. Twice did the Prince solicit Mr. Disraeli for a knighthood for Mr. Jarvis, only to receive refusal. But a third appeal dated 23rd December 1877 achieved the desired result.

IV

1864
Ætat. 22

From early days the Prince was bent on supplementing the political information coming fitfully from his political acquaintances by direct and regular access to official papers and despatches. Owing to the Prince's exclusion from any official position in affairs of State, it was only the goodwill of the Queen which could effectually accomplish his desire. The Queen hesitated to recognise the expedience of satisfying the Prince's yearnings, and her attitude provoked a controversy which waged till near her death. At the outset she ascribed to her son a want of discretion which would make confidential intelligence unsafe in his hands. The Prince combated his mother's disparagements. Ministers of state sympathised with his ambition and they on their own responsibility went some way towards meeting his demands. They ignored the Queen's reminders that the constitution debarred them or their secretaries from sending the Prince directly any official papers. On occasion the Queen herself consented to select pieces of confidential information for her secretary to communicate to the Prince. But not until her reign was nearing its close did she, in deference to ministerial counsels, assent formally and substantially to her son's request.

The controversy opened early in 1864 when the armies of Prussia and Austria were invading Denmark and the long-threatened Danish war began. Lord Russell, then Foreign Secretary, supported the Prince's appeal to the Queen to receive copies of the official despatches in the same way as they were forwarded from the Foreign Office to her and to members of the cabinet. The Queen demurred. She would send a précis of such papers as she might choose. The restriction dissatisfied the Prince, and the matter for the time dropped. By the Queen's direction General Charles Grey, her private secretary, at times forwarded to the Prince and Princess scraps of official news regarding the progress of the campaign in Schleswig-Holstein. But the Prince had to look to newspapers, to unofficial correspondence, and to conversation with ministers, diplomatists, and private friends for the bulk of his information regarding the war and the complex peace negotiations which followed.

During the succeeding fifteen years there was no material change in the situation. Mr. Gladstone, during his first ministry, was always ready to explain, by word of mouth, at the Prince's request, points of importance in the government's policy, and when Lord Granville became Foreign Secretary in 1870, the Prince privately learnt much from him of current affairs abroad. Mr. Disraeli during his second ministry was more generous than his predecessor in correspondence with the Prince on public questions. But the supply of first-hand political intelligence remained fitful and dependent on ministers' leisure and goodwill. The Queen upheld her veto on the regular transmission of official news. During Mr. Gladstone's second ministry (1880–85) the Prince had little to complain of the private communicativeness of two of its members—of Lord Granville, the Foreign Secretary, and of Sir Charles Dilke, whose friendship he sedulously cultivated. But the Prince twice lodged with the Queen and the Prime Minister impassioned protests against the limitations which were officially maintained. In 1882 he pointed out to his mother that he was less trusted with official information than the private secretaries of ministers, each of whom possessed a key to open the official boxes of despatches which were daily delivered to them in behalf of their chiefs. In 1885, when Mr. Gladstone was about to retire from office, the Prince again complained that the general information which he was now receiving on sufferance from ministers was below the scale of Lord Beaconsfield's day. He added a new issue when he pointed out that no official intelligence regarding the proceedings of the cabinet had ever been placed at his disposal.

In 1885 Mr. Gladstone acknowledged unequivocally the reality of the Prince's grievance on both heads, the denial of access to cabinet memoranda as well as to the foreign despatches. The Prime Minister deliberately sought a remedy for the withholding from the Prince of all information about cabinet deliberations. He promised to invite the Queen's sanction to his sending to the Prince "anything of importance that takes place in the Cabinet." The Queen at first merely reiterated her old disparaging plea that "secrets" should not be divulged to one

1880
—
Ætat. 38

1885
—
Ætat. 43

who talked too much. To Mr. Gladstone's questioning of the validity of her objection she replied that it would be "quite irregular and improper" for the Prince to receive copies of the cabinet reports with which she alone was furnished, according to precedent, by the Prime Minister.[1] She was not, however, wholly impervious to the Prime Minister's persuasions. She went the length of admitting the Prince's right to receive notice of "great decisions or changes of policy before they became known." But this admission seemed to the Prince a futility. When the Queen further claimed to make her own selection of the cabinet reports, the Prince grew impatient and pointed out that her conditions deprived the concession of the crucial virtue of promptitude, especially while she was at Balmoral. Mr. Francis Knollys, the Prince's private secretary, and Sir Edward Hamilton, Mr. Gladstone's private secretary, took up the cudgels in the Prince's behalf, and both urged on Sir Henry Ponsonby, Queen Victoria's private secretary, the need of some modification of her attitude. At least she might allow the Prime Minister to choose the confidential intelligence for the Prince's eye. The Queen answered that the Prime Minister "can only report to the sovereign, and it would not be desirable that W. G[ladstone] and H.R.H. should have discussions which she knew nothing about. Whereas, on the other hand, it would be natural and constitutional that she should communicate with her son and take counsel with him on questions of public interest." This was as far as the Queen would go. Mr. Gladstone's government resigned office a few weeks later, and for the time the dispute dropped once more.

The struggle, however, was not ended, and in the final rounds the Prince won an almost complete, if belated, victory. Both foreign despatches and cabinet reports were communicated to him. When his personal friend, Lord Rosebery, became Foreign Secretary for a short term of five months in Mr. Gladstone's third ministry of 1886, he, without the Queen's specific authority, caused the foreign despatches to be forwarded from the Foreign Office direct to the Prince in the red leather boxes which habitually circulated among ministers. The boxes were of two kinds, graded

---

[1] The Prime Minister's autograph reports to the sovereign of the proceedings of Cabinet Councils at the close of each meeting were long the sole records of the cabinet's deliberations. Not until 1916 was a secretary appointed to take and preserve minutes.

according to the confidential nature of their contents. The most secret documents were enclosed with others in boxes, keys to which were alone in the hands of the sovereign, the Prime Minister, and the heads of the Foreign Office. The second class of box had another kind of key, known as "the Cabinet key," which was in possession of all ministers and their private secretaries. Lord Rosebery accorded the Prince the most exclusive right by making over to him the special gold key (of the first class) which had belonged to the Prince Consort and was now discovered to be lying forgotten in the Foreign Office. Lord Rosebery also handed to the Prince a "Cabinet key" which opened the second class of boxes. The Queen was disinclined to continue the strife, and although she protested against the Foreign Secretary's concession of the Prince Consort's key, the privilege of access to the foreign despatches was not withdrawn.

Lord Salisbury, when he became Foreign Secretary, qualified the situation by sending boxes of the second class only, and the Prince complained to him (April 9, 1889) that they could only be opened by his "Cabinet key." Finally, all restrictions on the Prince's access to foreign official papers were authoritatively removed, although he had occasion now and then to complain of accidental miscarriages or delays. Nor was the Prince's long-continued effort to obtain regular access to the proceedings of the cabinet finally unrewarded, though the Queen insisted to the last on restrictions. Mr. Gladstone, after he formed his last ministry in 1892, arranged with the Queen's assent that his chief private secretary, Sir Algernon West, should regularly send to the Prince copies of the reports of cabinet meetings which custom obliged him to transmit to the sovereign. Attached to the Queen's assent was the proviso that Sir Algernon's transcripts should be punctually returned to him as soon as the Prince had read them. The Prince kept loyally to his part of the bargain, and all Sir Algernon's records of cabinet business, of which the first was dated 21st November 1892, were sent back by the Prince with the words "Seen, A. E." penned on the margin in the Prince's autograph. This practice was substantially continued, until the Prince ascended the throne, by the private secretaries of Mr. Gladstone's successors, Lord Rosebery and Lord Salisbury.

1886
Ætat. 44

1889
Ætat. 47

1892
Ætat. 50

1892
Ætat. 50

It was thus late in the day—after nearly thirty years of suppli-cation—that the Prince's long-cherished aspiration was realised. Only during the last eight years of his career of heir to the Crown did he come into authorised touch with the full range of the confidential deliberations and decisions of the ministry on both home and foreign affairs. Not before was he made familiar with the whole gamut of the government's operations.

CHAPTER XIV

YEARNINGS FOR POLITICAL EMPLOYMENT—IRELAND, 1865–1901

I

THERE was another and more practical way in which the Prince
yearned to identify himself with the political work of the country.
His social activities and his contributions to varied forms of
philanthropy did not quench a longing for regular political
employment—"to be (in his own phrase) of use" to the government of the country. From the date of the Prince Consort's
death Lord Clarendon had encouraged such an ambition in the
Prince by way of a guarantee against undue indulgence in pleasure.
Lord Clarendon's ministerial colleagues and successors shared
his view, and were invariably ready to help the Prince to this
goal. But the Queen, pleading her wonted scruples in regard
to her son's steadiness of purpose, deprecated every project
which was submitted to her. She sanctioned her son's reception
on her behalf of foreign sovereigns who visited the country on
more or less political missions, and she repeatedly delegated to
the Prince the ceremonial function of opening public improvements or institutions, even surrendering to him the formal
inauguration of so notable a London amenity as the Victoria
Embankment (July 13, 1870). But she succeeded in defeating
every proposal for his employment which involved sustained
and continuous responsibility.

Ireland was the field for the Prince's employment which he
and the ministers first entertained, and continued to urge for a
generation. Both political parties were long agreed that
Ireland's chronic discontent might be assuaged by the Prince's
permanent and intimate association with the country. But in
deference to the Queen's irremovable objections to the Irish

1870
——
Ætat. 28

219

scheme, alternative plans for the Prince's employment were
mooted—also abortively—from time to time.

In 1872 the Prince sketched a plan whereby he should be
attached in succession to various government offices "so that
he might be taught the business of the different departments." [1]
The Queen gave small encouragement.   Mr. Gladstone thought
that, failing Ireland, the Prince might best join the Indian
Council.   The Queen doubted whether the duties of the Indian
Council were onerous enough to keep him genuinely occupied.
Mr. Stansfeld, President of the Local Government Board, proposed that the Prince should be employed in his office.   The
Queen deemed the suggestion barely worthy of notice.   When,
bowing to the Queen's will, the Prince temporarily renounced
the Irish plan (October 27, 1872), he begged the Queen to permit
"an opportunity of discussing with Mr. Gladstone the subject
of some useful employment which I could undertake as your
eldest son, and which I am as anxious as ever to obtain."   But
the Queen's discouragement was unrelaxed.   Save rarely and
temporarily, the Prince had to rest content with official unemploy-
ment.   The Queen allowed him to pay Ireland four short visits
on a semi-official errand.   On some of his tours abroad he undertook missions of a political complexion, but these were usually
self-imposed, and although encouraged by ministers were looked
at askance by the sovereign.   To the end the Queen, to the best
of her powers, denied her heir-apparent any share in her
constitutional duties.

II

A single and somewhat belated exception proves the rule.
When the Queen had nearly completed her sixty-first year of rule
there fell to the Prince, by a sort of accident, a first and last
experience of performing for the sovereign a constitutional
function of State.

In accordance with precedent the Prince had been admitted
a member of the Privy Council on the 8th December 1863.
Occasionally, when the Prince was his mother's guest at Windsor
or Osborne, he, as a Privy Councillor, attended one of the Council's
meetings, over which it was the rule for the Queen to preside.

[1] Col. Ponsonby to Queen Victoria, March 7, 1872.

But her eldest son's presence was invited rarely. A variation in
the formal regulations touching the sovereign's place at the Council
became necessary when the Queen inaugurated in 1868 her habit
of spending a vacation of some four weeks well-nigh each year out
of her dominions. An annual Commission was privately drafted
on the eve of her departure empowering a member of her family,
who was not specified by name, to preside on her behalf at any
special meeting of the Privy Council which should be required on
an emergency during her absence. It was not until 1880 that it
became the practice to introduce into such Commissions the name
of the Prince of Wales as the person who was to fill at need the
place of the Queen. Year after year no meeting of the Privy
Council in the specified conditions was required ; nothing, therefore, came of the entry of the Prince's name. The fact of the
entry was very tardily communicated to him, and then in a somewhat back-handed fashion. In the course of the first year of
Lord Salisbury's third ministry, in the spring of 1896, when both
the Queen and the Prince were leaving England for the South
of France at the same season, Lord Salisbury intimated to the
Prince that the name of his brother, the Duke of Connaught, had
been inserted in the customary annual commission with authority
to preside in the Queen's place at any special meeting of the
Council which might need summoning, while both the Queen and
her eldest son were absent. It was at a little later date, in April
1898, that there arose for the first time a situation which set the
Prince in his mother's place at the Privy Council table. The outbreak of war between Spain and the United States of America
rendered it incumbent on the government to issue a proclamation
of neutrality in the name of the sovereign in Council. The Queen
was out of the country and the Prince was called upon to preside
at that meeting of the Council which could alone give the proclamation legality. It was thus at the mature age of fifty-seven
that he enjoyed his sole experience of serving in an affair of State
as the sovereign's legally appointed deputy.

1868
Ætat. 26

III

It was round Ireland that the controversy regarding the
Prince's official employment waged longest, and with chief energy.
A royal residence in Ireland, which should be occupied for part of

each year by the Prince of Wales, was the earliest form of the
project, but to that proposal there was soon attached the more
important recommendation that the political Lord-Lieutenancy
should be abolished, and that a newly created office of supreme
Governor of Ireland, freed of all political partisan associations,
should be bestowed on the Queen's eldest son. A long succession
of Queen Victoria's ministers believed that, despite a steady
growth of Irish disaffection, the adoption of one or other of these
two designs, and better still, of both, would invigorate the spirit
of Irish loyalty which was justly credited with a promising
sensitiveness to personal contact with royalty. The Prince at
the outset strongly favoured both wings of the scheme, but the
Queen's opposition doomed them to failure, and had the effect
at times of damping her son's enthusiasm for them.

The first chapter in the story bears the date of March 1868
when Mr. Disraeli, immediately on assuming the office of Prime
Minister, pointed out to the Queen that a suitable residence for
the Prince in an Irish hunting county would "combine the fulfilment of public duties with pastime, a combination which befits a
princely life." The Queen replied that such a notion was "not
to be thought of"; it was "quite out of the question" and could
"never be conceded"; other parts of her dominions, Wales and
the Colonies, would claim similar attention. Early in 1871 Mr.
Gladstone, at the instance of his Irish Lord-Lieutenant, Lord
Spencer, and of his Irish Chief Secretary, Lord Hartington, both
intimate associates of the Prince, announced to the Queen that
the twin design of a residence for the Prince and the transference
of the Lord-Lieutenancy to him in reformed and non-political
conditions was coming before Parliament. Again the Queen gave
voice to her impatience. Ireland, she told the Liberal Prime
Minister, was not on the same plane as Scotland as far as a royal
residence was concerned; she doubted the Prince's fitness for
high functions of State, though she would be glad if he were
withdrawn from London during the season; her second son,
Prince Arthur (created Duke of Connaught on 24th May 1874),
had superior qualifications for the Irish Viceroyalty; she added,
her fears that the Prince's equerry and friend, Lord Hamilton,
was infecting him with Orangeism—a factious sentiment which
was a disqualification for any Irish responsibilities. It was in
vain for the Prince to plead with his mother that "a permanent

royal residence in Ireland would do more good than any political measure."

Despite the Queen's rebuffs Lord Spencer held tenaciously by the scheme, and his personal knowledge of the Prince lent weight to his opinion of the Prince's fitness for Irish office. In October 1872, however, the Prince, fearing further friction with the Queen, renounced, although only for the time, his own support of the design. When Lord Spencer was holding the Irish Vice-royalty for a second term (1883–85) he sought a fresh opportunity, with the Prince's approval, of overcoming the Queen's objection. In a personal interview with her at Windsor on 6th May 1885, Lord Spencer solemnly re-invited her assent to the appointment of the Prince (or failing him, of one of his brothers) to a non-political viceroyalty with a fixed residence. The Queen showed illusive signs of yielding; she saw advantage in the abolition of the political Lord-Lieutenancy and approved the conversion of the Viceregal Lodge into a royal palace. Lord Spencer demurred to a royal residence "in the close neighbourhood of Dublin," and thought "that as a trial it would be better to hire a place" in the country with "attractions either of scenery or sport." But the Queen's complacence vanished quickly. To Lord Spencer's dismay she, after a few days' re-consideration, resumed her old attitude; she saw no reason for identifying her eldest son with Ireland, nor any genuine need for a royal residence in that country. "She greatly fears a place will be a great *trouble* and *tie*, which may become inconvenient," she wrote (May 12, 1885). The Queen's renewed hostility to his pet plan almost drove Lord Spencer to despair. "I feel inclined," he wrote to her secretary (May 11, 1885), "to throw up the sponge and retire to my plough in Northamptonshire."

1884
Ætat. 42

The Prince's zeal, too, showed signs for a second time of flagging. A difference arose in June between Lord Spencer and the Prince on an important point of current Irish policy. On learning that Lord Spencer was recommending the dropping of the Coercion Act, which the Prince wished the government to re-enact, he informed the Lord-Lieutenant that he could no longer support his view on other Irish matters. None the less, the Prince remained true to the spirit of his original conviction.

Near the end of his mother's reign, the long-cherished Irish plan was revived, albeit in modified form. In view of Queen

Victoria's advanced age, the suggestion was made that the
Irish Viceroyalty should be conferred on a son of the Prince,
not on the Prince himself, and that the young man should
permanently reside in Ireland. In January 1892, shortly
before the premature death of the Prince's elder son, the
Duke of Clarence, the Prince entertained a vague proposal to
identify the Duke with Ireland by making him Viceroy.[1]
Some six years later a like scheme was more fully discussed
at the urgent instance of the Prince's lifelong friend, Lord
Cadogan, who was at the time Lord-Lieutenant. Lord
Cadogan pressed on the Prince a proposal that his surviving
son, the Duke of York, should make Ireland his chief home.
The Prince's interest in the question returned in full vigour.
But he made his support of a royal residence conditional on the
acceptance by the Queen and the government of the com-
plementary provision of the abolition of the political Lord-
Lieutenancy and the bestowal of a non-political Viceroyalty on
his son. The permanent presence in Ireland of both a Lord-
Lieutenant and a member of the royal family would mean (the
Prince pointed out to Lord Cadogan, November 18, 1897)
"two kings in Brentford." Neither he nor Lord Cadogan
saw any difficulty in getting rid of the Lord-Lieutenancy.
The cabinet, while strongly favouring a royal residence, did
not, however, see its way to legislate immediately in the
second direction. A cabinet minute to that effect was
forwarded to the Prince on 15th November 1897. The Queen
remained of her old mind, and Lord Cadogan's proposal proved
as fruitless as its forerunners. Yet the veteran scheme still
lingered in the Prince's thoughts. Just before he ascended the
throne he spoke of making, as soon as he became King, his son
and heir, the Duke of York, his deputy in Ireland. Lord Cadogan
declared himself eager to retire in the Duke's favour. The press
of other business on King Edward's accession compelled postponement of the question, and it escaped further consideration
during his short reign.

It is an interesting theme of speculation for the political
student whether or no the adoption of the ministerial plan for
the Prince's residence and employment in Ireland in the practical
shape which it first assumed in 1871 would have altered in any

[1] Maurice and Arthur, *Life of Lord Wolseley*, 1924, p. 258.

material way the subsequent course of Irish history. The 1865
sanguine anticipations of the Prince, Mr. Gladstone, and Lord Ætat. 23
Spencer that the Prince's official and permanent contact with
Ireland would have blunted the edge of Irish disaffection, at
any rate deserves the political student's attention.

IV

Although the long-discussed scheme of the permanent
association of the Prince with Ireland came to nothing, all the
Viceroys who held office through the Prince's adult career,
whatever the differences in their policies, were at one in their
endeavours to give the Irish people detached opportunities of
acquainting themselves at close quarters with the Prince's genial
temperament. Queen Victoria had thrice visited Ireland with
her husband and son, to the popular satisfaction. When the
Queen's seclusion seemed to forbid her return, the hope spread
that the Prince and the Princess would come in her stead. Four
times—in 1865, in 1868, in 1871, and in 1885—the Queen, on
the initiative of Irish Viceroys, reluctantly sanctioned, without
prejudice to any larger issues, short sojourns of her son in Ireland.
At the dates of the last three of these visits menacing notes were
deepening in the political temper of the country, but the
authorities were always sanguine of the soothing effect of the
Prince's transient presence.

Early in 1865, when political disaffection was just renewing
its activity after a quiet interval, Lord Palmerston's Lord-
Lieutenant, Viscount Wodehouse, who was to be created Earl
of Kimberley next year, was anxious to make the opening of
an International Exhibition of art and industry, which was to
be held in Dublin in the summer, a demonstration of political
harmony. The invitation to open the Exhibition reached the
Prince in February 1865. An industrial effort of the kind always
proved for him a tempting bait. His only hesitation arose from
the Princess's inability, owing to her approaching confinement,
to accompany him.

"Although," he wrote to Lord Wodehouse, "I am quite
ready to go by myself, which I should consider as a duty, I fear
the visit will be considered rather flat if the Princess does not
accompany me. . . . I think it is of great importance that some

one should go over, as a great deal depends on the popularity of the Crown there, if they are humoured a little and taken notice of. The Exhibition is a great national undertaking, which ought certainly to be encouraged and supported, and it will I hear be a very fine one."

Lord Palmerston favoured the visit even in the absence of the Princess. The Queen gave a halting assent, which did not grow more cordial when Lord Palmerston described the expedition as "a journey for a political purpose in place of Her Majesty." He added that "it was politic and useful for the Prince to hold a levee in Dublin Castle." The Queen argued that the Lord-Lieutenant was her lawful representative, and should not be superseded even temporarily. Mr. Gladstone, Chancellor of the Exchequer, inclining apparently to the Queen's view, declined to defray the expenses out of public funds. The Prince urged that his income was scarcely able to meet what amounted to uncovenanted official expenditure.

A four days' visit to Ireland followed in May. On the 8th the Prince arrived at the Viceregal Lodge in Phœnix Park, accompanied by the Duke of Cambridge, with Lord Spencer in attendance. Next day he opened the Exhibition on behalf of the Queen. Greatly to his satisfaction a company of his own regiment, the 10th Hussars, who were billeted at the Curragh Camp, escorted him through the streets. In the evening the Lord Mayor of Dublin, Sir George Brown, entertained him at a ball at the Mansion House. There followed a military review in Phœnix Park, when the Prince wore his regimental uniform. He held a levee at the Castle, despite his mother's misgivings, and before leaving Kingstown, on the 12th, he offered hospitality on board the royal yacht the *Victoria and Albert* to a company which included both the Lord Mayor of Dublin and the Lord-Lieutenant. The purpose of challenging an expression of Irish loyalty, was, in contemporary judgement, satisfactorily fulfilled by the earliest visit, which the Prince paid Ireland semi-officially.

Early in 1867 the Marquis (afterwards Duke) of Abercorn, father of Lord Hamilton, the Prince's confidential equerry, was installed as Lord-Lieutenant by Lord Derby's Conservative ministry. In the autumn the Marquis sounded the Prince as to his willingness to re-visit Ireland. The Prince heartily assented. At the time serious disorder threatened the country.

The American-Irish Fenian brotherhood were planning terrorist outrages with the object of completely severing Ireland from England, and of establishing an Irish republic. The Prince was not deterred by the menace, but a postponement was deemed prudent when some Fenian conspirators startled the English public by attempting, in the truly Hibernian spirit of paradox, to blow up Clerkenwell Prison where two of their comrades were awaiting trial. The Prince showed his concern at this barbarous outrage by promptly examining the damage wrought by the explosion, and by twice visiting the wounded in St. Bartholomew's Hospital, of which he was President. On 10th January 1868 he wrote to 1868
the Queen of the "sad impression" which the sight of the victims Ætat. 26
made on him : "It is fearful to think that so many people should in one moment be reduced to the fearful misery they are now in."

In spite of the general alarm Mr. Disraeli, on becoming Prime Minister in February 1868, pressed for the Queen's assent to the projected visit of the Prince to the Lord-Lieutenant. To her annoyance the Queen had not been previously notified of the design. She now complained that the government intended to use the Prince for "political purposes." On the ground that the Prince was too fond of race-courses, she took exception to Lord Abercorn's proposal to include in the programme visits to Punchestown races. But the Prime Minister persisted. No political capital, Disraeli wrote to her on 6th March 1868, was sought, only the tranquilisation of the disturbed country, "the most important subject with which Your Majesty's government has at present to deal." The Queen slowly gave way. She was mollified by the Prime Minister's suggestion that the Prince ought to be installed as Knight of St. Patrick. On her last birthday she had bestowed on her son the chief Scottish order, that of the Thistle—a decoration which the Prince wrote to her he had "long wished to have on account of my love for Scotland and bearing five different Scottish titles." [1] The chief Irish order seemed to the Queen an equitable complement. The Prime Minister's plea "that during two centuries the sovereign has only passed twenty-one days in Ireland" also had its effect.

---

[1] After King Edward's death, a fine bronze statue of him in the robes of the Order of the Thistle was erected in the courtyard of Holyrood Palace as the principal feature of Scotland's national memorial. The statue, which was the work of Mr. S. Gamley, R.S.A., was unveiled by King George V. on 10th October 1922.

In the event the Queen informed the Prime Minister of her anxiety "to do everything in her power to mark her sense, in spite of the disaffection so widely spread in certain classes, of the general loyalty and good disposition of her Irish subjects by allowing the Prince of Wales to go now, and by permitting similar visits from time to time from other members of her family." The Queen enhanced the fair promise of her concession by expressing her willingness that the Princess, who had just recovered from serious illness, should accompany her son. In thanking his mother for her assent, the Prince prided himself on the thought that he "could in any small way strengthen the Crown and Government with regard to the Irish question." He regarded the visit not as an amusement but "as a duty." His presence at Punchestown races was, he urged, justified by the fact that "such a large concourse of people would be gathered together from all parts of the country who look upon those races as a kind of annual national festival that they would have a better opportunity of seeing me there than at Dublin. It would give them an occasion to display their loyalty to you and our family if (as it is to be hoped) such a feeling exists."

The obvious political aims of the visit, despite the Prime Minister's disclaimer, excited some public criticism. "It cannot be concealed," *The Times* wrote, "that this visit at a time of great political commotion has something the look of a studied, and therefore awkward, arrangement." The visit took place in April, and lasted nine days (15th to 24th April). In order to bring into prominence its pacific intent Fenian prisoners were, in advance, released from Irish gaols. From the moment that the Prince and Princess landed at Kingstown there was no ground for questioning the warmth of the welcome, which exceeded the most sanguine expectations. "There were," the Prince wrote to his mother after his arrival at Dublin Castle, "an enormous quantity of people in the streets who cheered very lustily, and with the exception of a very few and slight hisses, the people seemed determined to give us a thoroughly cordial reception." On each of the next two days the Prince attended the Punchestown races; the numbers in attendance on the first day were reckoned above a hundred thousand.

The chief event of the visit, the installation of the Prince as a Knight of St. Patrick, took place with gorgeous ceremony

in the renovated St. Patrick's Cathedral on the 18th. "All 1868
the streets were lined with troops," the Prince wrote to the Ætat. 26
Queen of the State procession from the Castle to the Cathedral.
"Thousands of people gave us such a reception that we shall
not easily forget it. . . . The ceremony was, I think, very
imposing and the Cathedral looked very well." In the evening
at a State dinner at the Castle, in honour of the new Knight,
the Prince's speech, which was entirely of his own composition,
struck to admiration the right notes of sympathy and goodwill.
"Although he had thought beforehand of what he would say,"
wrote Sir William Knollys, "he made no notes, and it was the
mere result of the feeling of the moment." On the 21st he unveiled, outside Trinity College, a statue of Edmund Burke, whom
he described as "one of Ireland's most distinguished statesmen,"
and he received from Dublin University the degree of LL.D.[1]

Everything passed off triumphantly. Before he left Dublin
the Prince wrote to his mother: "I only wish, dear Mama,
that you could have been here instead of us, as I feel sure that
you would have been astounded by the expressions of loyalty
you would have received, and the people, though excited, were
so good-humoured and orderly." The Lord-Lieutenant wrote
to the Queen on the departure of his guests in an even more
confident strain (April 25, 1868): "I was hardly prepared for
the progressive increase of welcome, amounting to real
enthusiasm." Even "persons who had been known to be
active sympathisers with Fenian propensities cheered with real
cordiality." The Duke of Cambridge, who had accompanied the
Prince and Princess, writing from Dublin to the Queen on the 20th
April, also discovered a new development of loyalty in "a very
impressionable people." He urged the Queen to "come over
to convince and satisfy yourself of the force of the affectionate
feeling," which, if it were adequately encouraged, he ingenuously
believed, would be capable of putting an end to Fenianism. But
the Queen declined to follow in her son's footsteps. If the
acclamations of the Dublin crowds meant no dispersal of Irish
discontent, a faith in the Prince's sympathetic attitude spread
among the Irish people.

---

[1] Other episodes were a ball at the Mansion House, which the Prince
described as "very full and very hot," and a review of the troops in Phœnix
Park, where the onlookers were estimated to number 150,000.

V

1870
Ætat. 28

The new Liberal Government which Mr. Gladstone formed at the end of the year (December 1868) was pledged to remedy Irish grievances. The appointment by Mr. Gladstone of the Prince's friend, Lord Spencer, to the office of Lord-Lieutenant whetted the Prince's interest in Irish affairs.

"You will have," he wrote to Lord Spencer on 14th October 1868, "by no means an easy task before you, and the Irish Church will yet be a nightmare for Mr. Gladstone. I will not now give you my views whether the Established Church in Ireland ought to be abolished or not, but I sincerely hope that the present government will look on that important question not as a Party question but as one that ought to be most carefully considered, and that the great object in view is that it should be solved in such a manner so as to give contentment to the Irish people. . . .

"I hope that our visits to the Emerald Isle may not be 'few and far between,' and we have now an additional inducement to cross the Irish Channel."

During his first session Mr. Gladstone carried an act for the disestablishment of the Irish Church. For the measure, as it was ultimately shaped, the Prince showed qualified enthusiasm, but the second session (of 1870) was devoted to a reform of the Irish Land Law in the interest of the tenant, and on that thorny question the Prince sympathetically sought instruction. On 21st January 1870 he wrote to ask the Prime Minister to see him before the meeting of Parliament so as "to hear from you the views of the government on the Irish Land question." Some fortnight later (February 7, 1870), when Mr. Gladstone had finally decided on the form of his Bill, he spent an hour with the Prince explaining its provisions to him. "He has certainly," Gladstone noted in his diary, "much natural intelligence." [1]

1871
Ætat. 29

The government's conciliatory policy found small favour with Fenian agitators. Although their violence had been checked, many parts of the country were still disturbed. Lord Spencer, however, urged the Prince to spend the first week of August with him in Dublin to test again the strength of Irish loyalty. The Queen put no obstacle in the way of the venture, although she manifested for it little sympathy. The Prince reached Dublin once more for a five days' sojourn on 3rd August,

[1] Morley's *Life of Gladstone*, ii. 294.

when the annual Horse Show filled the Irish capital to overflowing. 1871
His younger brother, Arthur, who was now much in his society, Ætat. 29
and whose names pertinently included that of Patrick, accompanied him, and he was also joined by his newly married sister, Louise, and her husband, the Marquis of Lorne.[1] "The cheering in the streets mingled," he wrote to the Queen on his arrival, "with some hissing, chiefly in those quarters where Fenianism is said to exist." But a friendly feeling predominated. His brother Arthur, he added, was "always hailed as Prince Patrick or Pathrick *tout court*. . . . They quite look upon him as their especial Prince."

The Prince was unsparing and catholic in his activities, and everywhere showed an exceptional tact. Of the dinner of the Royal Agricultural Society at which the Prince presided—the main item of his programme—the Prince wrote to his mother that he "felt far more nervous than usual, since he had to take great care not to say anything which might be taken up in any way." According to Lord Spencer, he "not only avoided every topic on which he might have been misunderstood (not a very easy task in Ireland), but touched some chords which made the influential audience see that he wished to give a practical and good example to landlords and others." His popularity steadily grew. At the review in Phœnix Park in the Prince's honour, all records of Dublin crowds, Lord Spencer estimated, were broken. He was assiduous in attendance at balls and dinners; visited the Horse Show and National Schools; and was shown over the Mater Misericordiæ Hospital by Cardinal Cullen, whom he had met years before in Rome.

But the sailing was not in all directions quite smooth. The Fenian murmurs burst into angry shouts before the stay ended and disturbed the equanimity of the Prince and his hosts. For the penultimate day of his visit—Sunday, 7th August, when he was resting at the Viceregal Lodge in Phœnix Park—the Fenians announced a "monster meeting" in the Park to demand "the release of the political Fenian prisoners still confined in English dungeons." "It is only the duty of the people," declared the Fenian newspaper, "to demonstrate that patriots are dearer to their hearts than princes." The authorities forbade the meeting; the leaders ignored the prohibition, and the police dispersed

[1] They had been married on the 21st March 1871.

1871
Ætat. 29
the mob by force. The disturbance took place within sight of the Prince.[1] When he and his companions left, as already arranged, for Kingstown next day, the cheering in the Dublin streets (wrote Lord Spencer to the Queen), was not great, but there was no breach of order.

On the Prince's mind the outbreak of the 7th August left an unfavourable impression, but Lord Spencer's faith in his soothing influence was unshaken. In spite of signs of reviving Fenian agitation, he early next year sanguinely appealed to the Queen to follow her son's example. He requested her "to take part in the inauguration" of a statue of the Prince Consort on Leinster Lawn facing Merrion Square. Her presence would reinforce, he assured her, the effect of the recent visit of the Prince by showing "how empty and shallow are the disloyal professions so loudly proclaimed in the extreme press and adopted by only the low rabble of the towns and cities." The Queen peremptorily declined the suggestion. The sequel was not reassuring. The statue was duly unveiled by Lord Spencer on 14th March, and two months later, to the Queen's mortification, an attempt was made by the Fenians to blow it up.

Meanwhile the Prince reached the conclusion that short stays with the Lord-Lieutenant gave too little scope for the exercise of his personal influence to warrant their continuance. A permanent Irish residence and office seemed to him alone worth trying. In the result, he accepted Irish hospitality before his accession on only one further occasion and that after an interval of fourteen years. It was in 1885 that, yielding for a fourth and last time while heir-apparent to the sanguine promptings of political hope, he revisited Ireland.

VI

1876
Ætat. 34
Three Lord-Lieutenants came and went in that fourteen years' interval. At the opening of Mr. Disraeli's ministry of 1874 the Duke of Abercorn temporarily resumed the office. When he retired in the summer of 1876, the Prince, with his mind still drawn towards Ireland, informed the Prime Minister of his active

[1] Reports of the riot were greatly exaggerated, but there were many casualties, and some damage was done to property. In the House of Commons the repressive action of the Irish government was harshly criticised, and an official inquiry was promised.

interest in the choice of a successor.   The Prime Minister seized
the opportunity of indicating the needful qualifications of an
office for which the Prince had himself already been suggested.
The Prince strongly recommended his friend, the Earl of Hardwicke, an active sportsman, who was at the time Master of the
Buckhounds.   Disraeli promptly dissented, and explained to the
Prince that it was essential to find a man who united in himself
"rank, character, some degree of popular talent, particularly the
gift of speech, considerable wealth, and freedom from strong
religious partisanship."   Mr. Disraeli confidentially added an
annotated list of those whom he had already considered.   "Lord
Brownlow has been sounded but not successfully."   The Duke of
Marlborough refused the post on the formation of the government,
but might accept it now.   Lord Waterford, though "rich and
Irish," lacked the indispensable "popular qualities" (July 22,
1876).   The Prince was not silenced.   "I must confess," he
replied, "that I see drawbacks to all those whose names you have
mentioned.   I am still strongly of opinion that if his private income is sufficient Hardwicke would be successful in such a post."
The Prime Minister finally selected the Duke of Marlborough.
In spite of the Prince's friendly relations with the new Viceroy, he
resisted his persuasions to retread Irish soil under his auspices.

On the accession of Mr. Gladstone to the Premiership in April
1880, when Lord Cowper, an old-fashioned Whig, became Viceroy,
Ireland again dominated the political arena.   The Prince had
thrown out the suggestion, without result, that his brother-in-law,
the Marquis of Lorne, then Governor-General of Canada, might
be moved to Ireland.   His sister, Princess Louise, Marchioness
of Lorne, he thought, might, as mistress of Dublin Castle, put
to the test the effect on Irish sentiment of royalty installed there.
But the omens in Ireland hardly favoured such an experiment.
In the later years of the Conservative administration, Irish
agitators had been organising under the sway of a new leader,
Mr. Parnell, a fresh conflict with England.   When Mr. Gladstone
assumed office, the struggle came to a head both in Ireland and in
the House of Commons.   Mr. Gladstone met the agitation with
the double weapon of conciliation and coercion.   The Prince
studied the situation with earnest attention.   He was at first
sanguine that concessions to the Irish Nationalists' agrarian
demands might effect a pacification.   An Irish Land Act, which

1881
Ætat. 39

gave the Irish tenant well-nigh all that he claimed, was passed into law in August 1881. The Prince was hopeful of the result. "I must write to you" he wrote to Gladstone from Cowes on 18th August 1881, "a few lines to congratulate you on the passing of the Land Bill, and my earnest hope that the measure will greatly benefit Ireland." To Lord Granville he expressed, the same day, his trust that the Land Bill "will above all make the Irish people contented and quiet." But Mr. Parnell and his supporters refused the olive branch and did all in their power to render the new Act inoperative. The government replied by imprisoning Mr. Parnell and other agitators.

1882
Ætat. 40

The Prince watched the fresh turn of events none too sanguinely. In acknowledging Mr. Gladstone's congratulations on his fortieth birthday, on 10th November 1881, he wrote: "You have been obliged to take some very forcible measures regarding Ireland, but I sincerely hope that they will have good results, and that at any rate the Land Act may have a chance of being properly carried out." The situation remained unchanged at the close of the year, and on New Year's Day, 1882, the Prince expressed to the Prime Minister his sincere hope "that the dark clouds that have been hanging over Ireland in 1881 may be dispersed in 1882."

The Prince's hope was not realised. Mr. Gladstone's alternating policy led him in the spring to release Mr. Parnell and his fellow-prisoners on an understanding, which the Prince regarded as mystifying, that they should aid the Government in a further attempt to redress agrarian grievances. Lord Cowper, the Lord-Lieutenant, and Mr. Forster, the Chief Secretary, declined to be parties to the compromise, and resigned office, to be succeeded respectively by the Prince's intimate friend, Lord Spencer and by Lord Frederick Cavendish, brother of Lord Hartington, another close associate. These changes, which for the Prince had a personal concern, had scarcely been announced than all prospects of an accommodation were gravely prejudiced. The new Irish Secretary, Lord Frederick Cavendish, and Mr. Burke, the permanent Under Secretary at Dublin Castle, were brutally assassinated in Phœnix Park (May 6, 1882) by extremists among the Irish agitators whom Parnell was unable to control. As soon as the startling news reached London (May 7) the Prince, in a letter to Mr. Gladstone, gave voice to the prevailing sense of shock.

Although I begged Lord Granville to give you a message from me, I cannot resist writing you a few lines to express my great horror and indignation at the terrible tragedy which has just been enacted at Dublin.

1882
—
Ætat. 40

Putting on one side the great merits of poor Frederick Cavendish and the loss he will be to you as a member of your government I feel that as a devoted friend and near relation you will deplore his loss even still more.[1]

On Monday, 8th May, the Prince and Princess paid Lady Frederick a visit of condolence, and three days later the Prince attended Lord Frederick's funeral at Chatsworth.

The choice of Lord Frederick's successor in such ominous circumstances profoundly exercised the Prince's mind. He inclined to Sir Charles Dilke, then Under Secretary for Foreign Affairs, with whom at this period he was in intimate relations, and from whom he was deriving much political information. The Prince advised Dilke to accept the Irish Secretaryship only on the condition that he was admitted to the cabinet, but Mr. Gladstone rejected Dilke on these terms, and Sir George Trevelyan, the Prince's Cambridge acquaintance, who had won for himself a prominent place in the Liberal ranks, became Chief Secretary without a seat in the cabinet. The Prince showed a shrewd insight into the situation when he wrote in commendation of Dilke's attitude:

If you had accepted the post without a seat in the cabinet your position, especially at the present moment, would be a very unsatisfactory one. If the policy, whatever it is, prove a success, I doubt whether *you* would have obtained much credit for it; and if it turned out a failure, you may be quite sure that a great deal of the blame would fall upon you without your having been responsible for the initiation of the steps that were adopted.[2]

VII

The brunt of the continuing Irish fight lay on the shoulders of the Prince's old ally, Lord Spencer, who remained Lord-Lieutenant after the murders. His strenuous endeavours to enforce law and order brought upon him reckless denunciations of tyranny and threats of vengeance. A campaign of terrorism

1884
—
Ætat. 42

[1] Lord Frederick's wife was a niece of Mrs. Gladstone.
[2] Gwynn and Tuckwell's *Life of Sir Charles Dilke*, i. p. 444.

was waged by Irish-Americans in London and other parts of
England, where attempts were made to blow up public buildings
by dynamite.

When Lord Spencer's struggle with the Irish-American
disorder was at its height he sought once more the countenance
of the Prince. He clung to his old belief that, despite all signs
to the contrary, loyalty was still alive among the mass of Irishmen, and that its display was hindered by the failure of the
royal family to give practical proof of interest in the country.
Lord Spencer found the Prince a willing ally. The Prince agreed
to suppress his misgivings of 1871 and revisit Ireland with a view
to identifying himself with Lord Spencer's difficult rôle. But
the Queen's pleasure had to be taken.

When Lord Spencer was on a visit to Balmoral in the autumn
of 1884 he urged the Queen to sanction a tour of the Prince
through both the "disloyal" South and the loyal North of
Ireland. The Queen was not encouraging, but Lord Spencer
was persistent. During the following January much correspondence passed between the two. The Queen argued that
the step would be regarded "as an attempt at conciliation in
reply to the recent (dynamite) explosions in London." At any
rate a postponement was desirable, seeing that the Prince might
be exposed to outrage, and it would be difficult to take adequate
precautions for his safety. To Lord Spencer's further proposal
that the Prince should hold a levee in behalf of the Queen at
Dublin Castle, the Queen raised her old objection that the
Viceroy's authority might thereby be impaired. There was also,
the Queen pointed out, the question of expense.

Ultimately Lord Spencer succeeded in overcoming the
Queen's scruples. The English government was ready to defray
the cost. Lord Spencer would personally take upon himself
the expenses of hospitality in Dublin. He questioned (he wrote
to the Queen) the

right to deviate from any action which is right or likely to lead
to improvement in the country in consequence of the dastardly
outrages in London. . . . The dynamiters have the sympathy
of no Irishman whose loyalty we wish to secure. We cannot
conciliate those who sympathise with them, but we may discourage them by showing that considerable numbers of Irishmen are loyal. A royal visit brings these loyalists to the front.

The special permission to hold a levee, which the Queen
granted to the Prince, might "be regarded as an exception."

An independent suggestion was made at the same date that
the Prince should visit Ireland in a capacity quite different from
that of the sovereign's son. The Royal Commission on the
Housing of the Working Classes, of which the Prince was a
member, was proposing to inspect the poor districts of Dublin,
and it was suggested that the Prince should accompany his
colleagues. The question was referred to the cabinet, which
answered it in the negative, while fully endorsing Lord Spencer's
plan of an extended tour. The Prince expressed his readiness
to fall in with Lord Spencer's scheme (February 3). Mr. Gladstone wrote to him "in succinct but unequivocal terms" of his
"very lively satisfaction" at his consenting to undertake the
tour. Mr. Gladstone's language implied that the Prince's visit
was his own "desire." The expression evoked a protest from
the Queen, who reminded her son that the visit was made at
"the expense and responsibility of the government."

The Prince's Irish visit in 1885 involved him more directly
than before in pending political controversy. Mr. Campbell-
Bannerman, who had become Chief Secretary in the previous
October, in succession to Sir George Trevelyan, scarcely shared
Lord Spencer's confidence in the wisdom of the project. At any
rate he deprecated the endeavour to identify the Prince with
any political move in the conflict. There were moderate politicians of both parties, who urged that the Prince's visit should
be made the occasion of some official pronouncement of a fresh
departure on the government's part in the effort to conciliate
Irish discontent. More drastic land legislation might be foreshadowed, along with an extension of local government, the
abolition of the separate administration of Ireland and some
regular scheme of royal visits.[1] But the notion of associating
the Prince with a political manifesto was wisely dropped.

Meanwhile the announcement of the visit set loose floods
alike of imprecations and of benedictions on the Prince. The
curses came from the Irish Nationalists on both sides of the
Atlantic, and the blessings from the Irish loyalists and the more
moderate Home-rulers. The irreconcilable Fenians in America
denounced the Prince as a representative of "British tyranny,"

[1] Spender's *Life of Sir Henry Campbell-Bannerman*, i. 71 *seq*.

and the United Irishmen there offered in February 1885 $10,000
for his body—alive or dead.   The Queen anxiously inquired of the
Home Secretary Sir William Harcourt: "Is no notice to be taken
of the open, monstrous threat in a newspaper published in America
by the Irish to kill the Prince of Wales?"[1]   But the "open,
monstrous threat" was justly scorned by the minister.   In Ireland
the Nationalists were scarcely less restrained in their invectives,
but no murderous intention could be imputed to them.   A manifesto of the party stated that the Prince was coming to Ireland
as the champion of an "alien faction," and that the visit was
designed "to strengthen the policy of coercion, to embarrass our
national cause, and to bring comfort and aid to Ireland's arch-
oppressor."   The City Council of Dublin resolved on the 16th March
by 41 votes to 17 to take no official part in the Prince's reception.
The Nationalist journal *United Ireland* brought out a special
supplement containing adverse comments on the proposed visit
from the Archbishop of Cashel and the most influential of the
Nationalist champions.   The loyalists, in spite of some resentment at the recent neglect of Ireland by the royal family, were
stirred by Nationalist bitterness to boundless enthusiasm.

The Prince surveyed the party skirmishes on the eve of his
departure from England with an engaging coolness, but he
welcomed some evidence that the Nationalists were not altogether
united against him.   At a sitting of the Royal Commission on
Housing the Prince genially remarked to a fellow-member,
Mr. Dwyer Gray, a Nationalist M.P., formerly Lord Mayor of
Dublin: "I hope you think the visit is a good thing," and
Mr. Gray reassuringly replied: "I am delighted at it, and I hope
you will be satisfied with your reception."   The more moderate
Nationalists believed that the Prince's charm of manner might
serviceably qualify extreme and irrational anti-English feeling.

VIII

On the 7th April, accompanied by the Princess and their
elder son, the Prince arrived at Kingstown in the royal yacht
Osborne, which was escorted by the Channel Squadron,—on this
fourth and most important of his semi-political appearances,
as heir-apparent, in Ireland.   The reception in Dublin belied

[1] Gardiner's *Life of Sir William Harcourt*, i. 418.

prophecies of evil. The royal party drove in the afternoon
from Dublin Castle through crowded streets to Ballsbridge,
where they attended an agricultural show. The next day the
Prince wrote from the Castle to his friend, Alfred Montgomery,
at Cannes: "You will, I am sure, be glad to hear that we met
with a very enthusiastic reception here to-day, and I confess
I was surprised at the enthusiasm displayed after all that I had
heard. We are most comfortably lodged here, and nothing
could exceed the Spencers' kindness." On the 9th Lord Spencer
reported to the Queen that the Dublin reception "was most
genuine and hearty from all classes of the community." An
immense impetus, he said, was given to trade. The Nationalists
at any rate made no untoward sign. At no stage of the well-
filled programme in the Irish capital was there anything to
disturb the royal visitors' equanimity. The Prince, in the
name of the Queen, held at the Castle the controverted levee,
while the Princess presided at a Drawing-Room. The honorary
degree of Doctor of Laws was conferred by the newly founded
Royal University of Ireland on the Prince and that of Doctor of
Music on the Princess. One morning the Prince, with Prince
Albert Victor, anticipated the arrival of the Housing Commission
from London by inspecting artisan dwellings in the poorest districts of Dublin. He drove from the Castle without an escort,
and the populace welcomed him with open arms.

But the risk of hostile demonstration was not past. The
Nationalists were taunted with self-effacement in the capital,
and resolved on retaliation in the provinces. After leaving
Dublin on 13th April for the south, where visits were paid to
Lord Listowel's seat near Ballyhooly, and to the Marquis of
Waterford's residence of Curraghmore, the royal party encountered much ugly feeling. At Mallow railway station a
disaffected mob, under the leadership of three Nationalist M.P.'s,
Mr. William O'Brien, Mr. John Redmond, and Mr. John O'Connor,
was with difficulty restrained by the police from grossly insulting
both the Prince and the Princess. Along the railway line black
flags were derisively waved, with skulls and crossbones painted
upon them. The Queen learned with horror of these marks of
hostility and wired to Lord Spencer to change the route. But the
appointed itinerary was followed without alteration. When the
Prince and Princess drove through the streets of "rebel Cork"

1885
Ætat. 43 displays of Nationalist rancour, though highly offensive, were balanced by more conspicuous demonstrations of respect. Two days were spent peacefully on the Lakes of Killarney, but on the return journey to Dublin by way of Tralee and Limerick, the disagreeable incidents were renewed. Although the Prince was displeased, his composure was outwardly undisturbed. Through the rest of the tour all went well. In Dublin, which was reached on the 20th on the return journey, the Viceroy received the royal party at the Viceregal Lodge, whence the Prince attended Punchestown Races, as well as a Citizens' Ball at the Agricultural Hall of the Royal Dublin Society at Ballsbridge. In the North, where four subsequent days (23rd to 26th) were spent, the incessant cheering of the Loyalists helped to atone for the Nationalist incivilities of the South. Belfast and Londonderry accorded the Prince brilliant receptions, and the tour wound up most pleasantly with a night at Baronscourt, the residence of the Duke and Duchess of Abercorn. On the 27th April the Prince arrived in London. Congratulations abounded on the coolness with which he and the Princess had faced the Nationalist affronts. Nationalist disappointment over the prevalent warmth of the Irish greeting found a passing echo in the House of Commons, where some Nationalist members spoke with approbation of the insulting episodes. Their language was well calculated to try the Prince's patience, and he deemed it deserving of official rebuke, but the Irish Secretary, Mr. Campbell-Bannerman, satisfied him that it was futile to make heroes of the offenders. "The general effect of the Irish visit was unmistakable," the Irish Secretary added, "and the feeling in the House of Commons is one of admiration and gratitude for a great public service" (April 21, 1885).[1]

The Prince had reason to be content with the impression which the expedition made on the public mind. A letter from Mr. Gladstone which awaited the Prince's arrival in London dwelt on "the great service which your Royal Highness and the Princess have rendered to the Queen and to the country," in spite of the rifts in "the perfect harmony and brilliancy of the reception . . . at one or two points of the Royal progress." The Prime Minister acknowledged "the sound judgement, the admirable tact and feeling with which your Royal Highness

[1] Spender's *Life of Campbell-Bannerman*, i.

turned the occasion to account and sowed a seed of which I
hope the fruit may yet be seen in years to come." "Things,"
he hoped, "may take such a course as to offer no discouragement
at a suitable time to the renewal of this patriotic effort."

The Prince wrote in reply :

Candidly I am inclined to think that our visit has been a
success much more so than I honestly expected. Though there
were occasions when the Nationalists tried to mark their disapproval of our presence in given places, still the enthusiasm
displayed by the loyalists was so great, that it made amends for
the discordant sounds we heard.

If the visit of the Princess and myself has been the means
of stimulating the feelings of loyalty to Crown and Constitution
in Ireland we shall be amply repaid by our efforts, and shall be
ready to pay another visit to Ireland, and I hope at a not distant
date.

In diplomatic circles the Irish visit was regarded as a deliberate
and successful effort on the part of the English government
to employ the Prince's tact in easing the threatening Irish
difficulties.[1]

IX

No further visit was paid Ireland by the Prince while the
Queen lived. Lord Spencer's satisfaction with the general result
of the Prince's recent presence in Ireland led him to make a last
appeal to the Queen to associate the Prince or one of his brothers
in permanence with the government of Ireland. The Queen's
final rejection in very positive terms of the project chilled the
Prince's desire for an early repetition of his recent experience.

There were other deterrents. Lord Spencer's faith in the
efficacy of coercion was, to the Prince's dismay, declining, and he
was meditating reliance on the ordinary law. As the year closed,
Mr. Gladstone, moreover, gave clear indications that he was
seeking a solution of the Irish problem on the lines of Home Rule.

The Prince was convinced that the grant of Home Rule to
Ireland was incompatible with the maintenance of the integrity
of the Empire, and that coercion of the disaffected Irish was an
essential safeguard of the Union. Lord Hartington, Mr. Goschen,
and other prominent Whigs promptly declared that they would

[1] Russian Embassy Archives, 3/15th March 1885 (M. de Staal to M. de Giers);
Mme. Waddington, *Letters of a Diplomatist's Wife*, p. 310.

be no parties to any measure which should loosen the bonds connecting Ireland with the English Parliament. With that declaration the Prince was in agreement. He was therefore disquieted, when he heard how Mr. Gladstone, on assuming the office of Prime Minister for the third time in February 1886, told the Queen somewhat nebulously that he was seeking "some means, if the Irish members are reasonable, of meeting the wishes of the people of that country and of preserving the integrity of the United Kingdom under the paramount rule of the Queen and the Imperial Government." "That sounds like an Irish bull," the Prince retorted to his informant, Colonel Ponsonby, Queen Victoria's secretary, "either Mr. Gladstone's government must go in for Home Rule, or for coercion. I see no alternative. If the former, which means 'meeting the wishes of the people,' the integrity of the United Kingdom cannot be maintained; if the latter, then only can it exist."

Though Lord Spencer gave Mr. Gladstone's new Irish policy full support, other of the Prince's Liberal friends, Lord Harting-ton, Sir Henry James, and Mr. Goschen, led a secession from the party, calling themselves Liberal-Unionists and resisting with tenacity Mr. Gladstone's measure. Queen Victoria also was from the first strenuous in opposition. Mr. Gladstone's policy of Home Rule rapidly matured, and on 8th April he introduced his first Home Rule Bill in the House of Commons. The Prince, from his accustomed place in the gallery, listened attentively to the statesman's impassioned oratory, but he was unconvinced. The cause of Irish loyalty seemed to him to be lost.

On the eve of the second reading debate the Queen made a despairing effort for its postponement. She recommended Mr. Gladstone to make "further inquiry and study of the complex problem" (May 9), and pointed to the grave doubts and appre-hensions which were gathering strength. Gladstone impenitently assured her that experienced statesmen like Lords Granville, Spencer, and Carnarvon, as well as the mass of the English and Irish peoples, were with him. The Queen forwarded the corre-spondence to the Prince, who acknowledged it instantly.

"I am deeply touched," he wrote, "by your great kindness in sending me a copy of your letter to Mr. Gladstone and his answer—as you know the deep interest I take in this unfortunate Irish measure.

"It was I think most desirable that you should clearly give Mr. Gladstone your views on the subject so that he might have no misapprehension concerning them. If you will allow me to say so I think your letter an admirable one, but I confess that I do not share the same views concerning the answer.

"His is no direct answer, and the allusions to Lords Granville, Spencer, and Carnarvon are not happy ones. I cannot think that the Bill will pass the second reading, and should the cabinet make considerable alterations and concessions they will never be accepted by the 86 Irish members."

The Prince's forecast of the Bill's failure in the House of Commons was realised. After a debate lasting sixteen parliamentary days, the second reading of Mr. Gladstone's Home Rule Bill was on 7th June defeated by 343 to 313, 93 Liberals voting in the majority. The session was promptly brought to a close, and Mr. Gladstone impetuously dissolved Parliament in spite of the Queen's warnings.

Mr. Gladstone was left in a minority at the polls and Lord Salisbury became the head of a new Conservative administration which lasted six years. At the Prince's instance, his friend Lord Londonderry accepted the office of Lord-Lieutenant. As soon as Lord Salisbury began his task of cabinet-making the Prince spoke to him "about bringing Lord Londonderry into the ministry." The Prince made no mention of Ireland, but Lord Salisbury promptly chose Lord Londonderry for the Irish Viceroyalty, and requested the Prince to exert his influence with his friend to induce him to accept the office (July 27, 1886).

His acceptance would be of the greatest service, I may say, of the greatest importance to us at the present time, and I venture to invoke your Royal Highness's powerful assistance and advocacy with Lord Londonderry to induce him to accept it. It is important to have an Irishman, and few are wealthy enough. . . . Lord Londonderry, by his private character and known opinions, as well as his family connections, unites the necessary qualifications in a singular degree. I hope your Royal Highness will forgive me for entreating you to assist us.

The Prince, ever ready "to do anything to help in forming a government," applied his influence to overcoming Lord Londonderry's scruples, and was warmly thanked by Lord Salisbury for the success of his efforts. The Prince's protégé at Dublin Castle filled the office with social credit till September 1889, although for most of his term he was politically overshadowed

1886
—
Ætat. 44

1887
—
Ætat. 45

by the more forcible Chief Secretary for Ireland, Mr. A. J. Balfour
(afterwards Earl of Balfour).

The new Viceroy urged the Prince, early in 1887, to come over
and encourage the Irish Loyalists.   But Lord Salisbury had meanwhile revived the policy of coercion and the House of Commons
was busy at the moment with coercive legislation.   In a letter
of 5th March 1887 the Queen pointed out to Lord Londonderry :
"The present moment would not be a good one for the Prince of
Wales to visit Ireland.   She thinks it should be delayed till at
any rate the Coercion Bill has passed."   Lord Londonderry
replied that the postponement would be "a great disappointment
to the loyal inhabitants of Ireland."   The Prince agreed with
his mother in judging a visit at the moment to be inopportune.

Meanwhile Mr. Gladstone pursued his Home Rule propaganda
with unflagging spirit, and the angry passions which burnt fiercely
on both sides of St. George's Channel, slackened the Prince's Irish
sympathy.   He viewed with especial repugnance the obstructive
tactics to which the Nationalist party resorted in the House of
Commons in order to defeat coercive measures.   "It is high time
Parliament was up," the Prince wrote towards the close of the
session (Sept. 15, 1887), "as the House of Commons has become
quite a *disgrace* to a civilised country."   Nor was the Prince
reassured after Mr. Gladstone's return to office in 1892, by his
introduction into the House of Commons of a second Home Rule
Bill on 13th February 1893.   The Prince made a show of impartiality by entertaining the Prime Minister at Marlborough House
on the eve of his renewal of his Home Rule plea in the House
of Commons, and he patiently listened to the long speech in which
the aged minister introduced his fresh measure.   But the Prince's
doubts of Mr. Gladstone's prudence persisted, and it was with no
repining that he saw the new Home Rule Bill, after its safe passage
through the House of Commons with a majority of 44, decisively
rejected by the House of Lords by a majority of 378.

Although the Prince personally held aloof from Ireland
throughout the prolonged Home Rule agitation, he suffered his
two sons to take part on the Queen's and on his own behalf in the
Dublin celebrations of the Queen's Jubilee in June 1887, and ten
years later, on the occasion of the Queen's Diamond Jubilee, the
Prince's son and daughter-in-law, the Duke and Duchess of York,
travelled, as representatives of the Queen and the Prince, over

much the same Irish ground as the Prince and Princess had
traversed in 1885. Lord Cadogan, who became to the Prince's
satisfaction Lord-Lieutenant in 1895, yielded to none of his predecessors in his anxiety to enlist royal co-operation in the Sisy-
phæan task of pacifying Ireland. But the Prince, while he encouraged the visits of his son the Duke of York, and was gratified
by the warmth of the Duke's reception, still refrained from crossing the Irish Channel himself.[1] The Queen contended that the
Nationalists' political agitation must subside before members of
her family could make a practice of visiting the country. Better
than her word, however, she herself, after an interval of nearly
forty years, added, within a few months of her death, a fourth
visit to the three visits which she had paid Ireland in the early
years of her reign. She stayed at the Viceregal Lodge in Phœnix
Park from the 4th to the 25th April 1900. His mother's heroic
exertion in extreme old age, moved the Prince's warmest admiration. "We are indeed delighted," he wrote to Lord Spencer on
13th April 1900, "at the success of the Queen's visit to Ireland, and
the enthusiasm displayed is most gratifying. She writes quite
delighted with everything." But the Prince did not exaggerate
the political influence of his mother's last and belated greeting
of her Irish subjects in their own land.

Among Lord-Lieutenants of differing political creeds and
among many dispassionate Englishmen and Irishmen his own
fitful association with Ireland had raised high hopes of his power
to lead Ireland into paths of peace. Some blame, when all is
said, may attach to his refusal, before he became King, to return
to the country after the visit of 1885. Yet the Queen's unwillingness to give his peacemaking tendencies a fair trial and the vacillations in the Irish policy of successive English governments must
be held mainly responsible for the disappointment of those who
expected much from an assured enlistment of the Prince's
personal magnetism in the service of Ireland.

[1] Queen Victoria wrote characteristically to Lord Cadogan on 3rd September
1897: "It is very satisfactory and gratifying that the Duke and Duchess of
York's visit went off so well in every part of Ireland. It was the same on the
occasion of our three visits there, but, alas, it did not produce a lasting effect,
and the Queen feels this may still be the case. . . . Various intended visits
had to be given up on account of the bad state of the country caused by agitators
kept for party purposes. The Queen hopes this will not happen again."

CHAPTER XV

FOREIGN AFFAIRS, 1863–1866—THE DANISH AND THE SEVEN WEEKS' WARS

I

1863
Ætat. 21

THE Prince on his youthful travels had caught generous glimpses of the dominant features of the European political landscape. The later stages of the realisation of Italian unity came well within his horizon. He discovered something at first hand of the causes of the distrust which attached outside France to the Emperor Napoleon III.'s policy, although his innate French sympathies were scarcely affected by the discovery. He had learnt from his sister, the Crown Princess, much of Prince Bismarck's ominous designs. It required no profound political insight to foresee explosions in Central Europe which might easily involve English interests. If the Prince from an early period intuitively studied the course of continental politics in the light of his personal associations with the protagonists, the larger issues did not escape him. It was the critical fortunes of his wife's Danish kinsfolk in the second year of his married life which drew him towards the brink of the continental whirlpool. The experience impaired for life his faith in the honesty of Prussia, and stimulated his leanings towards Prussia's rival, France.

One inherited personal tie with Germany was fortunately unloosed soon after the Prince's marriage. His father died heir of his elder brother Ernest, the reigning Duke of Saxe-Coburg-Gotha, who was childless and likely to remain so. The Prince Consort's title to the Saxe-Coburg succession passed on his death to his eldest son, the Prince of Wales. Neither in Germany nor in England was the prospect welcomed of uniting in a single person British and German sovereignty, as had happened in the

case of Hanover. The thought of the possibility of the English   1863
heir-apparent doubling the rôle of ruler of a German Principality   Ætat. 21
easily developed in Berlin the fear that Queen Victoria and her
family meditated interference in German affairs. But the
threats of embarrassment were largely removed by the Prince's
renunciation in October 1863 of his heritage in the Saxe-Coburg
duchy in favour of his next brother, Prince Alfred. This settlement took effect amid some Prussian growls thirty years later.
In 1893, on Duke Ernest's death, Prince Alfred, then Duke of
Edinburgh, succeeded to his uncle's ducal throne. The Prince
was thus early relieved of a personal German entanglement which
was calculated to hamper the freedom of his foreign outlook.

The social intimacy which the Prince, as soon as he set up   1864
his household, cultivated with foreign diplomatists at the Court   Ætat. 22
of St. James's materially supplemented the intelligence which
he gleaned from English Ministers' conversation. The French
Ambassador, Prince de La Tour d'Auvergne, who, like his imperial
master, attached to the Prince's expressions of opinion an
authority scarcely allowed them at home, at once joined the
Prince's inner circle of friends. Count Apponyi, the Austrian
Ambassador, and Count Brunnow, the Russian Ambassador,
were also communicative hosts or guests. Only with the surly
Prussian Ambassador, Count Bernstorff, among the envoys of the
Great Powers, did the Prince find it difficult to maintain amenity
of intercourse.

The ardour with which at this period he sought personal
access to leading actors on the political stage of Europe
ignored all conventional barriers. Early in 1864 the Prince's
adventurous friend, the Duke of Sutherland, entertained at his
mansion in London, Stafford House, Garibaldi, the picturesque
if self-willed hero of the Italian war of emancipation, who,
at the head of an improvised army of a thousand Italian
patriots, had rid Italy of the last of its petty tyrants and had
brought Italian unity to fruition. The rapturous welcome which
the London populace offered the visitor, clad in his red shirt
and blue-grey cloak, was currently likened to the enthusiasm
attending Princess Alexandra's entry two years before. But
official eyes even in Italy looked askance on many of Garibaldi's
headstrong exploits, and in England orthodox political and
religious sentiment was inclined to view him as a rebel. The

Roman Catholics denounced his reception as "seditious tom-foolery," and Queen Victoria spoke with disdain of the popular honours paid to a subverter of thrones. The Prince at the moment was at Sandringham. Caught in the tide of the popular excitement, he hurried to London to pay his respects to Garibaldi. Queen Victoria, who said she felt "half-ashamed of being the head of a nation capable of such follies," joined the old Duchess of Cambridge in warm expressions of disapproval. She warned her son against continuing his friendship with the Duke of Sutherland. "What do you think," wrote Disraeli to his friend Lady Dorothy Nevill (April 21, 1864), "of the Prince of Wales and Garibaldi? For a quasi-crowned head to call on a subject is strange, and that subject a rebel!"[1] The Prince's visit was striking evidence of the irresistible fascination which a maker of history exerted on him.

II

The Prince cherished an affectionate interest in his wife's family. Very soon after his marriage he personally introduced to Dean and Mrs. Liddell, at Christ Church, her elder brother Frederick, the Crown Prince of Denmark (afterwards King Frederick VIII. of Denmark), who, under the Prince's auspices, became an Oxford undergraduate.[2] With keen sympathy the Prince followed the chequered fortunes of the Princess's second brother, William, who, under the altered name of George, was elected King of Greece on 5th June 1863. The kingdom of Greece thenceforth became a pivotal point in the Prince's lifelong survey of European complications. But, meanwhile, the career of the Princess's father chiefly riveted the Prince's attention. He flung himself with impulsive warmth on his father-in-law's side into the controversy over the conflicting claims to the Schleswig-Holstein duchies which issued in war between Germany and Denmark.

The Princess of Wales's father succeeded to the throne of Denmark as King Christian IX. on 15th November 1863. King Christian's predecessor, Frederick VII., just before his death proclaimed the incorporation in the Danish kingdom of the

[1] Lady D. Nevill's *Reminiscences*, p. 243.
[2] The Prince of Wales corresponded copiously with the Liddells about Prince Frederick's career at the University, which was cut short by the outbreak of war between Denmark and Germany.

duchy of Schleswig, which had long been an independent state 1864
under the Danish king's personal rule, but had, by the decision Ætat. 22
of an European conference, meeting in London in 1852, been
declared incapable of incorporation with Denmark. King
Christian ratified King Frederick's action three days after his
accession, and Bismarck saw in King Christian's policy the
opportunity which he had long sought of forcibly depriving
Denmark of its hold on Schleswig and of annexing to the Kingdom
of Prussia that duchy as well as the duchy of Holstein, a member
of the German Confederation of which the King of Denmark
claimed to be hereditary Duke. Prussia's cherished ambition of
securing an extended seaboard on the Baltic could be realised only
at Denmark's expense. To both the duchies there was a third
claimant, in addition to the Kings of Denmark and Prussia, in
the person of Duke Frederick of Schleswig-Holstein-Sonderburg-Augustenburg.[1] Duke Frederick's claim was a peculiar rock
of stumbling for the English royal family. His partisans included
the Crown Prince and Princess—the Prince's brother-in-law
and sister—the King of Hanover, Queen Victoria's first cousin,
and many other prominent Germans who had no love for Bismarck.
The Prussian statesman scorned Duke Frederick's pretensions, and
having, by unscrupulous diplomacy, gained the support of Austria,
saw the road clear to the successful expulsion of Denmark from
the duchies. With characteristic promptitude he issued an ultimatum to the King of Denmark on the 16th January 1864,
bidding him abandon Schleswig within forty-eight hours. On
the failure of King Christian to obey the summons, Prussian and
Austrian troops invaded the disputed territory, with disastrous
consequences for Denmark. The Danes put up a stout but
hopeless resistance.

The conflict caused in England immense excitement. Lord
Palmerston, the Prime Minister, and Lord Russell, the Foreign
Secretary, accurately reflecting public opinion, denounced the
brutal attack on a small and weak Power like Denmark by
Prussia and by Austria, Prussia's ally for the occasion. The cry
for England's active intervention on Denmark's behalf grew loud.
But Lord Palmerston's government stopped short at threats,
and critics charged them with a pusillanimous betrayal of

[1] Duke Frederick declined to recognise the renunciation of his rights to
the duchies to which his father had assented at the London Conference of 1852.

Denmark. Meanwhile the Queen vehemently directed her influence to the maintenance of England's neutrality, on the ground, it was generally alleged, of her German prepossessions. She declared that the Prince Consort, who never favoured the Danish pretensions, would have at all hazards avoided a British conflict with Prussia.

The Prince from the first professed profound sympathy with his wife's country and with his wife, who acutely felt her father's peril. The Queen was embarrassed by the warmth of his feeling, and family harmony was disturbed. The Prince's relations were strained, not only with his mother, but also with his brother-in-law and sister, the Crown Prince and Princess of Prussia, who regarded Duke Frederick as the rightful claimant to the duchies, although they were bound to identify themselves with Prussian policy. In December 1863, when the outcome of the crisis was in suspense, the Prince and Princess were fellow-guests at Windsor with the Crown Prince and Princess, and the Queen forbade the subject of Schleswig-Holstein to be mentioned. Early in 1864 the Crown Prince joined the Prussian army for active service against Denmark—to the Prince's unconcealed impatience.

The Prince attended the House of Lords at the opening of the session (February 5, 1864), and heard the Lord Chancellor read the Queen's Speech in which his mother had substituted for her minister's threats to Prussia a pious promise to do all she could to bring about a reconciliation between that country and Denmark. The Prince, according to an onlooker, "looked well and dignified. He kept his hat on all the while and seemed very attentive." [1] But he was ill content with the government's irresolution. In a letter to Mrs. Bruce (February 17, 1864), the Prince freely confessed his feelings :

This horrible war will be a stain for ever on Prussian history, and I think it is *very* wrong of our government not to have interfered before now. As to Lord Russell's everlasting Notes nobody cares twopence about them on the continent, and the Foreign Ministers to whom they are addressed probably only light their cigars with them.

The Prince adhered to the conviction that decisive action at the outset on the part of the English ministry would have prevented the conflict, to the advantage of England's prestige.

[1] Lady Bloomfield's *Reminiscences*, ii. 166.

"I always say," the Prince wrote to Lord Spencer on 5th May, "that if we had sent our fleet to the Baltic at the beginning, all this bloodshed might possibly have been avoided, and we should cut a much better figure in Europe than we do at present."

The Prince and Princess were kept supplied by the Queen's special favour with the latest reports from the theatre of war, but her remark that it was no disgrace for the Danish troops to retreat before superior forces gave them cold comfort. The Prince was soon eagerly looking to the English government to contrive diplomatic means of suspending active operations in which Denmark could hope for no genuine success. "I rejoice to hear," he wrote to Lord Russell on 24th February 1864, "that there is a chance of a Congress taking place, and I see by the papers that Austria and Prussia are willing to accept our proposal—though at the same time hostilities will continue, which is very much to be deplored."

Count Bernstorff, the ungenial Prussian Ambassador, complained of the Prince's frank avowals of Danish partisanship. The Queen, who was voluble in rebuke of her son's freedom of speech, entreated Sir William Knollys to urge on the Prince greater reticence. In the spring of 1864 the old King of the Belgians came on a last visit to the Queen, and reinforced her appeal. The Prince was not uninfluenced by these warnings, but found self-restraint difficult. In March he heard that the Emperor Napoleon was about to intervene in a manner that seemed unlikely to be of advantage to Denmark. During the celebrations at Marlborough House which attended the christening of his first-born son, he promptly challenged the French Ambassador, Prince de La Tour d'Auvergne, who was one of his guests, as to the truth of the report. The Prince with some heat reminded the Ambassador that the Danes were a brave people, who were ready to meet death rather than any kind of humiliation. The Ambassador, in reporting the conversation to his government, noticed the Prince's indifference to strict rules of etiquette, at the same time as he pointed out the significance attaching to the views of one in the Prince's position.

Under pressure of the Queen, and of the march of events in Denmark, the Prince subsequently showed greater caution. The French Ambassador was again a guest at Marlborough House on

the 22nd March—this time at a dinner-party—and found his
host in a less pugnacious mood. The Prince remarked that
Denmark would be wise in assenting to a pacification, and that
her future safety would best be assured by a union of the
Scandinavian countries. The Ambassador treated the suggestion
respectfully.[1]

On the 25th April a Conference of the interested parties,
at the suggestion of the English government, met in London,
but it was soon apparent that there was little chance of Denmark
benefiting by the negotiations. Inconclusive proposals for an
armistice were long under discussion. In the meantime, the
fighting went on with increasing injury to the Danes. The
Prussian capture by assault of the fortress of Dybböl on the
18th of April was a staggering blow.

"You can imagine how distressed," the Prince wrote to Lord
Russell on 21st April, "we were on hearing of the fall of Dybböl,
as we had so much hoped that the Danes might have still held
it when the Conference commenced, but the Prussians seemed
to have been equally anxious to take Dybböl before an armistice
was discussed. I sincerely hope that Denmark will agree now
to an armistice, as she can now have nothing more to gain by
fighting. I should be much obliged to you if you could let me
know from time to time how the proceedings at the Conference
are going on, and I sincerely hope that Denmark may be enabled
to make good terms for herself."

The Danish losses at Dybböl, which he characterised as
"tremendous," depressed him. His main wish, he told the
Foreign Secretary, was that "the deliberations may prove
successful in terminating this dreadful war." In May the Prince
rejoiced in a report of the Danes' delusive success in an encounter
with Austrian ships. "Everybody seems delighted with the
news," he wrote to his informant—the Secretary for War, Lord
de Grey (afterwards Lord Ripon)—"and it will be some encourag-
ment to the poor Danes."[2] But the peril of Denmark was
undiminished. "This dreadful war in Denmark," the Prince
wrote to Lord Spencer on 5th May, "causes both the Princess
and myself great anxiety, and the conduct of the Prussians and
the Austrians is really quite scandalous."

On 9th May the Conference at length arranged a month's

---

[1] *Les Origines diplomatiques de la guerre de 1870-71*, Paris, 1910, tome ii.
pp. 109 *et seq.*   [2] Wolf's *Life of Ripon*, i. 206.

truce to take effect three days later. The Prince doubted Prussia's loyalty to the terms, and the suspension of arms proved only temporary. The Conference dissolved on the 22nd June without reaching a settlement, and hostilities were resumed on the 26th June. But the Danes were in no condition to continue the struggle, and quickly sued for peace. On the 12th July the Prince wrote to Lord Russell: "The news is indeed more cheering, and I only hope that a permanent cessation of hostilities may be come to, as a continuance of hostilities must be ruinous to the Danes. The terms which they will get from Austria and Prussia will, I fear, not be very good ones, but still anything is better than a continuance of this dreadful war." A fresh armistice which followed on 18th July was soon followed by a peace which secured Prussia and Austria in the joint occupation of the two duchies.

III

The Prince was now tutoring himself to control the open manifestation of his Danish ardours. The Princess was anxious to visit her parents in Copenhagen in September, and the Prince wished to accompany her: Denmark was for him new ground which he was desirous of exploring, and he knew the Queen would not sanction the step unless he convinced her of his self-command. In a conversation in July with two members of Lord Palmerston's ministry, Lord Granville and Mr. Gladstone, both of whom had resisted any active support of Denmark, he showed, according to the latter, only "a little Danism."[1] In August there was a large gathering of the royal family in Scotland, when the Queen unveiled a statue of the Prince Consort at Perth. The Prince's uncle, Ernest, was a guest at Balmoral, and the Prince and he went deer-stalking together. The Prince gave his uncle in private to understand that he now loyally accepted the neutral policy of the British government.[2] The Queen deemed the time inopportune for foreign travel, but Lord Palmerston was in a more conciliatory mood, and the Queen waived her objections to the Danish visit provided that the Prince and Princess travelled quite privately, eschewed political discussion, and, by including Germany in their itinerary, avoided any show

[1] Morley's *Gladstone*, ii. 120.
[2] Duke Ernest's *Memoirs* (English translation), iv. 167, 197.

1864
Ætat. 22 of preference for Denmark over Prussia. The Prince played with the fancy of extending the tour to the northern capitals of St. Petersburg and Stockholm, and even to Paris and Vienna. Lord Palmerston demurred to both Berlin and Vienna, and warned the Prince off Russia on the ground that, had that Power joined with England, the war on Denmark might have been averted. At any rate the Prince was grateful to Lord Palmerston for removing all obstacles to the visit to Copenhagen, and on 1st September he wrote to him from Abergeldie:

I have to thank you for your letter of the 23rd, and feel much obliged to you for having told the Queen that you thought the expression of my feelings and opinions on the late sad events in Denmark would be tempered with due discretion.

I sincerely trust that nothing I may say during our visit to Copenhagen would give annoyance to the Queen or H.M. Government.

In the result, although Berlin was excluded, brief visits were paid to other parts of Germany; the Prince's introduction to Scandinavia extended beyond Denmark to Sweden, and his new acquaintances among foreign royalty included members of his own generation in the family of the Tsar. Loyal to his word, he made no obtrusive parade of his political opinions, but the varied society which he encountered brought home to him with novel force the complexities and mutations of international policies.

On the 7th September 1864 the Prince and Princess, with their infant son, arrived at Elsinore in the yacht *Osborne* from Dundee.[1] Thence they passed to the castle of Fredensborg to join the Danish royal family. The popular reception was enthusiastic. The Prince was enchanted with his first view of Copenhagen, and the impression was amply confirmed by subsequent experience. "It is a most interesting and picturesque town," he wrote, "and there is much to be seen." He always admired "the Tivoli gardens in the evening," and he watched appreciatively the growth of the city, with its "very fine new buildings" and "the old ones of historic interest well preserved."[2]

---

[1] Sir William Knollys, Lord and Lady Spencer (at the Prince's earnest entreaty), and Drs. Sieveking and Minter as medical attendants, were also of the party.

[2] Letters to Alfred Montgomery, 15th July 1885 and to Lord Spencer, 13th April 1900.

At the end of September the Prince and Princess interrupted their Danish sojourn to pay a ten days' visit to Stockholm, the capital of Sweden. The Queen found fault with her son for accepting on arrival there a public reception and for staying at the Palace. The cultured King of Sweden, Charles XV., a grandson of Napoleon I.'s General, Bernadotte, proved a congenial host, and his son, Prince Oscar, the Crown Prince, had, in the Prince's sight, much of his father's charm. The King of Sweden's racial affinities were wholly with France, and he reciprocated his English guests' suspicions of Prussia. His Swedish host's hospitable programme included a day's elk-shooting—a new experience for the Prince.

On his return to the castle of Fredensborg, the arrival of a fresh foreign guest, the Grand Duke Nicholas of Russia, the Tsar Alexander II.'s eldest son and heir, gave for the time a new turn to the Prince's political thought. The Grand Duke was bent on matrimony, and a betrothal followed between him and Princess Alexandra's youngest sister, Marie Dagmar. The Prince deemed the match "in every way a good one" in spite of religious differences, and he expressed a wish to pay a first visit to Russia in order to attend the projected marriage next year. But fate frustrated such a plan. To the distress of the Prince and Princess, the Grand Duke fell ill and died before the marriage (April 1865). But Princess Dagmar soon transferred her hand to the Tsar's next son, Alexander. To him the Prince made friendly advances, and he saw in the new domestic relationship between the heir to the Russian Crown and himself a ground for reconsidering the old sentiments of political hostility long persisting between the two peoples. The mood of political benevolence proved transient, but in the coming years the notion of an Anglo-Russian *entente* was to gather strength in the Prince's mind.

The visit to Denmark ended on the 12th October, when the infant prince was sent back to Scotland. Proceeding to Germany, the Prince and Princess revisited the King of Hanover—who was soon, at Prussian hands, to suffer expulsion from his throne—and at Darmstadt they greeted his sister, Princess Alice of Hesse, while at Cologne the Prince had a brief meeting with the Crown Princess and her husband. The family differences over the Danish war, although they were soon to subside, were for a moment reinvigorated in the Prince's thought by his encounter with the Crown Prince, fresh from victory on the battlefields of Schleswig. "I can assure you," he wrote to Lord Spencer on 7th November, "it was not pleasant to see him and his A.D.C. always in Prussian uniform flaunting before our eyes a most objectionable ribbon which he received for his *deeds of valour ? ? ?* against the unhappy Danes." The Prince's hope of spending a day on the way home at Compiègne privately with the Emperor Napoleon III. was frustrated by the fiat of Lord Cowley, the British Ambassador in Paris, who held that the Emperor would disapprove of a visit incognito.

The Prince reached London on the 6th November after pausing at Brussels to listen for the last time to the political counsels of the old King of the Belgians. The King's occasional reproofs, which had a steadying effect, never weakened the Prince's regard for him, and the King, on his part, always cherished deep affection for his grand-nephew. Before the end of the coming year, on 10th December 1865, within six days of his seventy-fifth birthday, the King died. In acknowledging the Prince's latest birthday congratulations, the King had signed himself : "From the earliest days of your existence, Your true and faithful friend" (December 19, 1864). To Lord Derby, on the day after the King's death, the Prince wrote : "I shall ever mourn him as the kindest relation and friend I ever possessed, and he will be mourned throughout Europe and in this country as an excellent sovereign, great statesman, and good man." With his brother Arthur, the Prince hastened to Brussels to attend the funeral, and to congratulate the late King's eldest son on his accession as Leopold II. A link with the past was broken. There was no survivor to whose counsels the Prince paid the same deference. With the new King of the Belgians, an associate from boyhood, the Prince engaged in much private and political correspondence. The new King's faculty as a raconteur amused the Prince. But he regarded himself as better qualified to advise King Leopold II. than to be advised by him. Leopold II.'s reign of forty-four years closed within a few months of King Edward's own death, but the amiability of their early relations ceased long before the end. After the death of King Leopold I. the royal palaces at Brussels and Laeken were no longer for the Prince shrines of political wisdom.

IV

The Danish war was only a rung in Prussia's tall ladder of aggrandisement. Her alliance with Austria had for the time served its turn and was an obstacle to her further advance. The two Powers together had driven Denmark out of the disputed duchies which remained in their joint occupation. But it was Bismarck's intention to incorporate them with Prussia. To effect this purpose it was essential to shake off the Austrian alliance. At the conclusion of the Danish war he entered on an intricate and deceptive course of diplomacy which issued in war between the rival states. In June 1866 Bismarck challenged Austria and many of the German minor states which supported that power, to defend in the field Austria's claim to share in the government of the duchies. There followed the Seven Weeks' War, which ended by giving Prussia the hegemony of Central Europe.

Prussia's course of action, after her brutal usage of Denmark, exasperated the Prince. Prussia to his mind was steering for a general European war as soon as she could force the independent German states to unite under her banner. A few years before, Queen Victoria had described it to be "a sacred duty" to strengthen Prussia's prestige. But now she shared her son's dismay. A war between Prussia and Austria meant civil war within her own and her son's family circle. The Queen's son-in-law of Darmstadt, her cousin of Hanover, her brother-in-law of Saxe-Coburg and many others of her German kinsfolk were ranging themselves on Austria's side. Her Prussian son-in-law was bound, whatever his private sympathies, to fight at the head of a Prussian army against his wife's German relatives.

Meanwhile Bismarck was in no temper to conciliate Queen Victoria and her children. He was incensed by the sanction which the Queen had given somewhat obtrusively in the autumn of 1865 to the betrothal of her daughter Helena to Prince Christian of Schleswig-Holstein-Sonderburg-Augustenburg. Prince Christian, who was to become the Prince of Wales's third foreign brother-in-law, was younger brother of that Duke Frederick whose claim to the duchies of Schleswig and Holstein had been supported by the smaller German states, as well as by the Crown Prince and Princess, and had been contemptuously

1866
Ætat. 24
dismissed by Bismarck. After the Danish war Bismarck had deprived Duke Frederick and his family of their property and standing, and Prince Christian of his commission in the Prussian army. Prince Christian's betrothal took place at Coburg, whither the Queen had summoned the Prince of Wales and the rest of her family to witness her unveil a statue of her late husband (August 26, 1865). Altogether twenty-four of the Queen's near kinsfolk—the majority of them German—attended the ceremony, with the Prince and the Crown Princess at their head. For the Queen to publish in such circumstances her assent to an engagement which profoundly offended Prussian susceptibilities, was interpreted by Bismarck as a demonstration of defiance on the part of herself, her eldest son, and her eldest daughter.

Through the events leading up to the Seven Weeks' War, and indeed through its progress and sequel, there was small difference in the resentful moods of both the Prince and his mother. On the 10th May 1866 he wrote to his mother: "I fear the news from Germany is still very bad, and everything looks very black from that quarter. Count Apponyi [the Austrian Ambassador in London] says that he sees now no possible chance of avoiding war, and, once begun, God only knows where it will end."

Yet there was one point in the Prince's outlook which the Queen was scarcely prepared to adopt. The Prince acknowledged only one way whereby to defeat Prussian aspirations. It was England's duty to form a firm alliance with France. At dinner in London on 6th June 1866, some ten days before the outbreak of the Austro-Prussian war, the Prince lucidly stated his views to the French Ambassador. The threatened war, he said, disquieted him. Although his eldest sister and her husband were Prussians, his sympathies were wholly on the side of Austria. The Ambassador suggested that the Prince meant that he was on the side of peace. The Prince agreed, but claimed that Austria stood for right and justice, and that he felt bound to avow his adherence to her cause. The Ambassador pointed out that Austria was the traditional enemy of Italy, and that Italy with whom England had fostered a close friendship would be certain, in the event of war between Prussia and Austria, to attack Austria. The Prince urged that Italy was not concerned in the quarrel, and that it was the duty of France to restrain her from

interfering. It was not to the interest of France to take any
other part in the struggle. The Ambassador replied that no
human power could prevent Italy from joining in the strife. It
was France's intention to remain neutral provided Austria
followed moderate counsels. The Prince brought the discussion
to a close with the significant remark that, while neither England,
nor France could be indifferent to the lot of Italy: "Complications could best be avoided and the general interests of Europe
could best be served by an *entente* between England and France."
The Ambassador in his full official report to the French Foreign
Office of the whole conversation added the comment that the
entente cordiale which the Prince had suggested would, he believed,
be approved by English opinion.[1] Both the Prince and the
Ambassador were in advance of their time.

The ease and rapidity with which Prussian strategy, as devised
by the Chief of the Staff, Count von Moltke, brought Austria
and the minor states which fought with her to their knees,
redoubled the anxieties of the Prince. Italy's attack on Austria,
although partially beaten off, deepened her misfortunes. The
decisive defeat of the Austrians by the Prussians at the battle of
Königgrätz or Sadowa, in Bohemia, on 3rd July, practically
brought the war to an end in favour of Prussia and Italy. Lord
Stanley, the Foreign Secretary, sent the Prince a full report of
the battle by an English officer. In acknowledgement the Prince
wrote, on the 20th July:

There is no doubt that the Prussian needle-gun caused the
Prussians to be victorious, or else so fine an army as the Austrian
could not have been so utterly beaten. I only trust that our
army will be equipped with the same weapon, though I trust
we shall have no occasion to use it.

An unprecedented circumstance gave the Prince, in spite of
the Queen's continuing veto on his access to State papers,
opportunities of following at close quarters the negotiations
which led to peace. To the Prince's satisfaction, Napoleon III.
not only offered his mediation between the belligerents but also
wrote directly to him (July 11) requesting him to use his influence
with Lord Derby's government so as to induce them to support
the imperial offer. The Emperor's diplomacy readily brought
Austria and Prussia to a parley. The French Ambassador

---

[1] *Les Origines diplomatiques de la guerre de 1870–71*, tome x., Paris, 1915.

1866
Ætat. 24 granted, without hesitation, the Prince's request to receive copies of the various despatches dealing with the French intervention, which the French Foreign Office sent to its representative in London. At this critical juncture the French Ambassador kept the Prince as well informed as the English Foreign Secretary of what was going on at the Quai d'Orsay.[1] Under Napoleon III.'s auspices a settlement between Prussia and Austria was rapidly reached. A truce was arranged near the end of July; a preliminary treaty was signed at Nickolsburg on the 26th July; and the definitive treaty at Prague on the 22nd August. Italy absorbed Venetia, and Prussia obtained substantially all that she had sought. Her boundaries were greatly extended. The Kingdom of Hanover was incorporated with Prussia. Hesse-Cassel, the domain of the Landgrave, the Princess of Wales's maternal uncle, became a Prussian province, and part of the landed possessions of the Duke of Hesse-Darmstadt, whose heir was the Prince of Wales's brother-in-law, passed into Prussian hands. But of greater advantage to Prussia was the hegemony which she gained of the reconstructed German Confederation from which Austria was expelled. Hardly less important was Prussia's acquisition of the port of Kiel with the neighbouring coast of Holstein which enabled her to satisfy her cravings for a powerful navy—with momentous effect on her own destinies and those of the world.

The Prince was acutely distressed by the Treaty of Prague which aggrandised Prussia and degraded many of his German kinsfolk. The exiled King of Hanover excited his profound pity. With intense anxiety he followed the long controversy between Bismarck and the ex-king over the latter's right to the Hanoverian "family funds"—the Welf-Fond—which Prussia for the time confiscated. Painful also to the Prince and his wife was the punishment meted out to the Landgrave of Hesse-Cassel, whose sovereignty was sequestrated, although his property was left untouched. Prussia's hand fell heavily on the relatives of the Prince and his wife.

In one clause of the Treaty of Prague the Prince found a new hope for Denmark's recovery from her recent humiliation. The Prince's friend, Napoleon III., had caused a cheering proviso in

[1] *Les Origines diplomatiques de la guerre de 1870–71*, tome xi., 11 juillet-6 août 1866, Paris, 1922, pp. 24, 146.

Denmark's favour to be inserted into the fifth clause.   The clause   1866
in question provided that Schleswig should be ceded to Prussia   Ætat. 24
only on the condition "that the people of the northern district of
Schleswig, if by free vote they express a wish to be united to Denmark, shall be ceded to Denmark."   Much significance attaches
to the strenuous but vain fight which the Prince waged for the en-
forcement of the proposed concession to Danish national pride.   To
the Prince's irritation Prussia took no steps to carry out the stipu-
lation.   Bismarck ignored the impressive appeals for a plebiscite
which the inhabitants of North Schleswig made to him, both in
1869 and 1877.   The Prince continued to plead strenuously for
Schleswig's treaty-right of self-determination.   When there were
fears that embittered Denmark might rashly join France in the
Franco-German war and attack Prussia, the Prince wrote to the
Queen (August 4, 1870): "If only Prussia would give them
North Schleswig as they promised in the Treaty of Prague that
might alter matters."   In 1878, after the Congress of Berlin,
Bismarck resolved to get rid of the offending proviso and made,
on 11th October 1878, a secret treaty with Austria annulling it.
In exchange Bismarck supported Austria's pretensions to Bosnia
and Herzgovina.   When this injustice to Schleswig and to Den-
mark was revealed in the press (February 1879), the Prince
addressed a heated protest to Lord Salisbury, then Foreign
Secretary.   From Sandringham on the 4th February 1879 he
wrote of the press reports of Austria's renunciation of Clause V.
of the Treaty of Prague: "As it is a matter which concerns
Denmark so closely I ask if it is true.   If so the conduct of
Austria is simply disgraceful, and only shows how little faith we
can place in her with regard to the observation of treaties."
Lord Salisbury forwarded such explanation as he had received
from the Austrian Ambassador, Count Karolyi.   The Prince's
comment on the behaviour of the Austrian government, of which
Count Andrassy was the head, ran thus (February 11, 1879):

Austria may soon regret to have altered a Treaty of such
importance, and it remains to be seen how soon the German
Chancellor, of whom Count Andrassy has such a wholesome dread,
will compel her to alter the Treaty of Berlin; as long as Prince
Bismarck terrorises to the extent he does now over the governments of other countries, they will be forced to agree to anything
he wishes—a very pleasant state of things for the maintenance
of Peace in Europe.

The Prince's complaint of the English government's passive indifference proved ineffectual. But he was not silenced. When his brother-in-law the Crown Prince of Germany ascended his father's throne in the grip of death in March 1888, the Prince who had faith in the dying man's ingrained sense of justice, startled the Berlin Court by a frank avowal of his expectation that Germany would then by the restoration of North Schleswig make atonement to Denmark. It was, however, only after a delay of another thirty-one years, when the Prince himself had lain more than nine years in his grave, that his strongly held wish bore fruit. Article 109 of the Treaty of Versailles of 1919 revived, with decisive effect, Clause V. of the Treaty of 1866. Early in 1920 a plebiscite was held in Northern Schleswig, with the result that in May of that year all but a single zone of the province was restored to Denmark, and the wrong which had moved King Edward's fiery indignation was tardily repaired.

CHAPTER XVI

THE AFFAIRS OF GREECE, 1863–1876—HOPES AND FEARS
OF RUSSIA, 1866–1875

THE family sentiment which was bred of the Prince's union with
a Danish princess rendered the current political history not of
Denmark only, but also of Greece, an intimate concern. The
Prince's domestic relations with Greece indeed became in course
of years a larger factor in his foreign political outlook than his
domestic relations with Denmark. His views of foreign policy
were also influenced by the personal association into which his
wife's Danish kinship brought him with the ruling family of
Russia. If political sentiment often estranged him from
Russia, domestic sentiment often drew him towards her. In
the conflict between the two the political sentiment at many
critical junctures got the better of the domestic, and the Prince's
hostility to Russia and to Russian royalty was for a period
pronounced. Yet in the later years of his life the Prince's
political and domestic feelings were at one in seeking a good
Anglo-Russian understanding.

I

On returning from his tour of the Holy Land in 1862 he had
visited Greece at the time when a provisional government was
tentatively considering how to fill the throne after the expulsion
of King Otho of Bavaria. At the close of that year England's
treaty obligations turned the attention of Queen Victoria and her
ministers to the filling of the vacancy. The Prince manifested
a lively interest in the issue. Greece showed at first a strong
inclination for a ruler who should be nearly associated with
England. The Greek National Assembly canvassed the claims

of three candidates who satisfied the condition of English ties—
the Prince's next brother, Prince Alfred; his uncle, Duke
Ernest; and the Earl of Derby's eldest son, Lord Stanley, with
whom and with whose family the Prince was well acquainted.
But none of these names satisfied the English government or
the European Powers with whom it was co-operating. Ultimately the choice fell on the Prince's brother-in-law, Princess
Alexandra's younger brother—William of Denmark—a youth of
barely more than seventeen, "a slight, graceful, and elegant
boy," as he was described at the time. He had visited England
for his sister's marriage, and had won the regard of his brother-
in-law. Less than two months later, on 6th June 1863, the
young Danish Prince was elected King of the Hellenes under
the name of George I. He was crowned, and took the oath to
the constitution at Athens on 31st October.

From his accession until his death at an assassin's hand on
5th March 1913, the new King of the Hellenes faced formidable
embarrassments at the hands of his restless subjects, and his
chequered fortunes were for the Prince and Princess a source of
unceasing anxiety.[1] The final cession by England of the Ionian
Islands to Greece, which took place in the early months of
King George's reign, seemed to promise him personal popularity.
But the promise was delusive. The strife of political parties
over his rights and revenue combined with the spread of
brigandage and other disturbance through the country to rouse
in him a sense of insecurity. Some sign of alleviation of the
King's troubles was visible in course of the second year of his
reign. On 29th March 1865 the Prince wrote to Lord Russell,
the Foreign Secretary:

You can well imagine how happy the Princess is to hear
better news, as all the last accounts have caused her great anxiety
about her brother, who she was so anxious should never have
accepted his present position. I am very glad to hear that you
will keep two English ships at the Piraeus at present—it will at
any rate have a good effect.

The efforts of the island of Crete to throw off the yoke of
Turkey and unite itself with the kingdom of Greece soon after-

[1] In July 1864, when the Prince was dining with the Prime Minister, Lord
Palmerston, he summoned to his side a fellow-guest, Sir Horace Rumbold, then
secretary of the British Legation at Athens, to discuss King George's difficulties
(Rumbold's *Recollections of a Diplomatist*, 1902, ii. 175).

wards involved the Prince's brother-in-law in a new and pro-   1866
tracted ordeal. Greece fanned the Cretan agitation, which   Ætat. 24
Turkey and the treaty Powers treated as rash rebellion. King
George sought the Prince of Wales's intervention. He begged
his support for a compromise whereby the turbulent island
might be placed under the protection of England or another of
the interested Powers. "How would not your name," King
George wrote to the Prince (October 4, 1866), "be blessed could
they (the Cretans) know that you take some interest in their
destiny." The Prince consulted Lord Stanley, newly become
Foreign Secretary, who deemed King George's proposal worthy
of consideration. But nothing was done, and enthusiasm for   1868
the Cretan cause seemed to be driving Greece into war with   Ætat. 26
Turkey. To Queen Victoria's consternation, the Prince defended
the King of Greece's challenge of the Porte. A conference of
the Powers was summoned to Paris to bring Greece to a more
reasonable frame of mind. Lord Clarendon, who succeeded
Lord Stanley at the Foreign Office in 1868, urged the Greek ruler
to offer the Porte the guarantees of the *status quo* which it
was demanding, and the Queen called the Prince's attention to
Lord Clarendon's "excellent" advice. She pointed out to him
"that all governments except that of Russia agree that there
is nothing but what the Porte had the right to ask, and have
urged the Greek government to comply" (December 28, 1868).
The Prince yielded to his mother's remonstrance, and successfully
counselled his brother-in-law to comply with the Powers'
demands. Yet the Cretan controversy, although for the moment
stayed, remained for half a century an open sore in Turco-Greek
relations.

II

Meanwhile the young King of the Hellenes had sought to   1867
strengthen the political position of Greece by a matrimonial   Ætat. 25
union with the royal family of Russia. On October 15/27, near
the close of his twenty-second year, the King married at St.
Petersburg the Grand Duchess Olga (Constantinovna), niece of
the Tsar Alexander II., a girl of sixteen. The Prince was justified
in his doubts as to whether Russian policy would allow Greece
to reap much substantial political benefit from the matrimonial
alliance.

In the spring of 1869 the recent rancours between Greece and Turkey were sufficiently appeased to allow the Prince and Princess to pay the King of Greece a first visit in his adopted country (20th April–1st May 1869). The King received them at the Piraeus with youthful buoyancy. At Athens he conducted them over the Acropolis and the other historic memorials of the city. Thence he passed with his guests to Corfu, where his wife and two infant sons—Constantine and George—were in rural retreat. A pleasant week was spent by the party without formality—mainly in country excursions. The King forgot his troubles amid the genial domestic environment.

The lull in the King's political storms was transitory. Within a year a fresh crop of troubles in Greece renewed the Prince's solicitude for the welfare of his wife's brother. The spring of 1870 saw British feeling very deeply moved by a brutal outrage on the part of Greek brigands, who captured a band of English travellers and held them to ransom. The Prince shared the English public's anxiety. A brother-in-law of the Prince's friend, Lord de Grey (afterwards Marquis of Ripon), was among the captives. To Lord de Grey the Prince wrote from Sandringham
(April 22, 1870): "I feel much anxiety for your brother-in-law Fred Vyner's safety. The demands of the brigands are quite outrageous, but I trust that Vyner will soon be liberated." [1] On the day that the Prince was writing, Mr. Vyner and three other of the English travellers (Mr. Lloyd, Mr. Herbert, and the Count de Boyl) were murdered by their captors. In many letters to the Prince, the King of the Hellenes poignantly described his distress at the outrage, his alarm at the denunciations of Greece by the English press, and the incessant friction between himself and Greek political leaders. The Prince forwarded to Mr. Gladstone, the Prime Minister, one of the longest of the King's letters, with a covering note (May 5, 1870) which feelingly described his brother-in-law's depression:

He is quite prostrated with grief at what has occurred, and what he feels still more keenly is—that he was utterly powerless to prevent the catastrophe. His position in his adopted country is also such a painful and difficult one, as he does his utmost to ameliorate the country, and is thwarted on all sides either by the opposition, or by the constitution which keeps his hands tied.

[1] Wolf, *Life of Lord Ripon*, i. 289.

Unless he has some absolute power given him, I feel convinced   1870
that his life is wasted in Greece.   ———
                                                                 Ætat. 28

Mr. Gladstone replied (May 6, 1870) sympathetically, if with
turgid vagueness :

I am sure, Sir, that your R.H. may safely assure the King
that though for the moment something of haste and of the injustice it is certain to entail may be observable in the tone of the
English press, the lapse of a short time will restore the balance
of the public mind, and the cause of Greece and its Government
will be appreciated with equity.

III

It was beyond the Prince's power now or hereafter materially   1875
to lighten King George's burden, the weight of which never   ———
diminished. In the coming years, at his brother-in-law's   Ætat. 33
promptings, the Prince lost no opportunity of bringing to
the notice of successive English governments the territorial
ambitions which the King voiced in the name of his people.
But the most substantial service which the Prince rendered him
lay in his transmission to him of the moderating counsels of
English ministers, and in his recurrent appeals to English
governments to protect King George and his subjects from the
consequences of reckless violence in asserting what they deemed
to be their rights.

The upheaval in the Near East which started in 1875, revived
in full intensity the national aspirations of Greece, and the
Prince's desire to help his brother-in-law at times embarrassed
his relations with Mr. Disraeli's government, whose policy
scarcely favoured Greek aggrandisement. At intervals, through
this critical period, the Prince and the King had renewed opportunity of meeting, and of supplementing their correspondence
by confidential talk. On his way out to India in 1875 the Prince
spent a day with his brother-in-law at his country house of
Tatoi ; and from a tower in the grounds the Prince saw (he
wrote) "the haunts of the notorious gang [of brigands] into
whose hands Lord Muncaster,[1] Mr. Vyner, and Mr. Herbert fell
a few years ago."

In July of the following year, while nationalist excitement

---

[1] Lord Muncaster was released to obtain a ransom.

1875
Ætat. 33
in Greece ran dangerously high, the King and Queen of Greece were the Prince's guests at Marlborough House. The Prince arranged interviews between the King and Mr. Disraeli and his colleagues, and the Prince warmly welcomed the Queen's consoling complacence in bestowing the Garter on the distracted monarch. Both Prince and Princess listened attentively to the King's account of his difficulty in restraining his excitable subjects from invading not only Crete, but also Thessaly and Epirus—all parts of the Turkish dominions. "I grieve to think," the Princess, who was greatly oppressed by her brother's trials, had recently written (March 17, 1876), "what a hard task my poor brother has before him, and all that he has gone through these twelve years past." It was a satisfaction to her to spend the next spring with him at Athens, the Prince escorting her as far as Naples. While brother and sister were together, the Prime Minister bade the Prince (May 20, 1877) impress on the Greek King "the urgent desirableness at the present moment" of refraining from joining Russia and the Balkan peoples in the hue-and-cry against Turkey. The Prince duly telegraphed this advice to the King, and watched with alert anxiety the effects of the warning through the critical years that followed.

IV

1866
Ætat. 24
With the closing of the Seven Weeks' War there befell the Prince a new foreign experience to which there attached a diplomatic significance more specious than real. The Prince fulfilled an old-standing wish of visiting Russia. His wife's family was desirous that he should attend the wedding at St. Petersburg of his wife's sister, the Princess (Marie) Dagmar, with the Tsarevitch Alexander, afterwards Tsar Alexander III. The Russian royal family seconded the proposal. At first the Queen deemed it sufficient for the Prince to be represented by "one of his gentlemen," but her son pressed for permission to go in person. "It would interest me beyond anything to see Russia," he wrote to his mother on 14th October, and although she held that some other occasion than a wedding would offer a better opportunity, she gave her consent.

The Queen sagaciously regarded as illusory the political

grounds which led Lord Derby's government to favour the visit. Russia's relations with England seemed on the surface to be taking a new turn.   Russia, under the sway of the newly appointed Chancellor, Count Gortschakoff, was showing more cordiality towards England than at any time since the Crimean War, and the English ministers were tentatively exploring the possibility of a friendly understanding.   The Prince had fully assimilated Lord Palmerston's suspicions of Russian designs on India, and their grip on him was still strong.   But the growing difficulties, in which his brother-in-law, the King of Greece, was involved with Turkey, had somewhat shaken his faith in the advantages of England's traditional friendship with the Sultan, and he played with the fancy that a friendly gesture to Russia, which would alarm the Porte, might slacken the tension between Turkey and Greece.   The Prince gave voice at times to such "strong anti-Turkish opinions" in Greek interests that Lord Stanley, the Foreign Secretary, feared that he might give the Tsar's Court a wrong impression of England's present attitude to Turkey.[1]   But the Prince promised caution.   "Any act of courtesy," he pointed out to the Queen, "would be highly appreciated by the imperial family."   He was confident that he might discreetly help to allay Russia's and England's mutual animosities.   To the Prime Minister he wrote on 13th October : "I should only be too happy to be the means in any way of promoting the *entente cordiale* between Russia and our own country. . . . I am a very good traveller, so that I should not at all mind the length of the journey."   The outcome was indecisive.   The Prince's first visit to Russia illustrated the common experience that advances in private cordiality between the royal families of different countries gives small guarantee of improved political relations between governments and peoples.

At the end of October 1866 the Prince set out with his equerry, Major Teesdale, who was well acquainted with Russia, for his Russian destination.   On the way he met the lately crowned King Leopold II. in Brussels, and he also spent three days with his sister at Potsdam.   The Crown Prince had already started for Russia on the same errand as himself.   At the Queen's and his sister's wish, he made an effort to restore at Potsdam that private cordiality with the Prussian royal family which the recent wars

[1] Newton's *Life of Lord Lyons*, i. 162.

had prejudiced. He called upon the King of Prussia at Schloss Babelsberg, and the King returned the courtesy by attending a dinner-party which the Crown Princess gave in her brother's honour at the Neues Palais.

In Russia all went smoothly. On 6th November the Prince reached St. Petersburg, where the Tsar and all the male members of his family met him at the railway station. The Tsar personally conducted him to his apartments in the palace of the Hermitage next to the Winter Palace. Next morning he spent a couple of hours in formal visits to the Grand Dukes and Duchesses. The bridegroom, whose stolidity was very rarely relieved, showed an unusual affability. The marriage took place at the Winter Palace on the 9th, the Prince's twenty-fifth birthday. The Prince prolonged his stay till near the end of the month. He attended parades of the troops, which the Emperor held on the Champ de Mars, and in the great Riding School; he joined a hunt on the 14th at Gatchina, where seven wolves were killed, and spent the next two days at Moscow, where the welcome (he wrote) "was most cordial, and every *moujik* in the street seemed as anxious to show some signs of goodwill as the officials." The Governor of Moscow, Prince Dolgorouky, entertained him at a ceremonial banquet and fête, and he diligently saw the sights of the town. On his return to St. Petersburg on the 17th the English Ambassador, Sir Andrew Buchanan, gave a ball, at which the whole of the imperial family were present; out of compliment to Sir Andrew the Prince wore Highland dress.

The visit was judged for the moment to be of political service. The Prince with sanguine impetuosity reported somewhat prematurely that the last traces of the Crimean animosities had disappeared. Major Teesdale informed the Queen (November 27) that the Prince left Russia "carrying with him the goodwill and affection of every one with whom he had been thrown in contact." Lord Augustus Loftus, the rather short-sighted British Ambassador at Berlin, whom the elated Prince met on his way through Germany on the homeward journey, minuted the favourable promise of his "ingratiating manners" on England's international relations.[1] Lord Stanley gave proof of his appreciation of the Prince's effort by contributing public moneys to the expenses of the tour. Sir William Knollys, in a

[1] Lord Augustus Loftus, *Diplomatic Reminiscences*, second ser., i. 149.

letter of thanks on the part of the Prince, assured the Foreign Secretary that "the Prince trusts that the result of his visit will be as beneficial to the interests of the country as the hospitality and attention which he received made it in every respect gratifying to himself" (December 27, 1866).

1866
Ætat. 25

V

There were too many adverse influences to justify the Prince's sanguine expectations of any sudden reversal of Anglo-Russian feeling. The main conditions of Russian polity which his visit could not affect were hardly favourable to a new departure. The footing was treacherous. The amiability and cloudy humanitarianism or idealism of the Prince's host, the Tsar Alexander II., thinly veneered his absolutist and chauvinist predilections, which affronted dominant English sentiment. If, in a unique flash of enlightenment, the Tsar by autocratic decree had emancipated the serfs in 1861, he yielded easily to the persuasions of the bureaucrats about him that political discontent could best be allayed by persecution, a pernicious doctrine which ultimately cost him his life. Russia's aggressive external ambitions, both in Europe and Asia, knew no arrest, and fostered English suspicion. Still at heart a Palmerstonian, the Prince was not restrained by his nascent friendship with the Russian royal family from protest against the threats by the Tsar's government of English interests. Prussian diplomacy, which the Prince always suspected, had also to be reckoned with. Prince Bismarck was known to be experimenting with the Machiavellian plan of stimulating Russian bluster by way of putting spokes in the wheel of an Anglo-Russian *rapprochement*. Hardly, too, had the Prince returned home from St. Petersburg than he perceived that, however the hopes of his brother-in-law of Greece might be disappointed, it was unsafe for England definitely to alienate the Porte, whose goodwill must serve as a counterpoise to Russia's aggressiveness.

1867
Ætat. 25

The Emperor Napoleon III., who throughout this period was rather wildly seeking supreme control of Europe—if not of the world—caused England some embarrassment by the splendid hospitality which he pressed with pride on European rulers on the occasion of the Paris International Exhibition of 1867.

1867
Ætat. 25
He succeeded in drawing to his Court as his guests well-nigh all the sovereigns of Europe, including the rulers both of Russia (Tsar Alexander II.), and of Turkey (Sultan Abdul-Aziz). The British Government deemed it a point of policy not to fall behind the Emperor of the French, whose attitude to England was ambiguous, in personal courtesies to the two sovereigns, with both of whom they deemed it prudent at the moment to keep in friendly touch. Of the two, Lord Derby, the Prime Minister, inclined to pay the Sultan chief attention, but he was unwilling to take any course which might give umbrage to the Tsar. The Queen's persistence in her seclusion raised a difficulty, the solution of which increased the Prince's prominence in national affairs. The profuse entertainment which he had lately enjoyed on his visits abroad was held seriously to reflect on the Queen's obstinate refusal to offer foreign royalty any fitting hospitality. *The Times* of 2nd December 1864, on the Prince's return from his first visits to the courts of Denmark and Sweden, laid vehement stress on the humiliating contrast between his reception abroad and the widowed Queen's practice of suffering royal visitors to England to board in hotels. All the omens, the newspaper urged, pointed to the Prince as the destined official host in behalf of the nation.

The Prime Minister in 1867 sought, as far as the Tsar was concerned, to respect the Queen's scruples. Lord Derby contented himself with proposing to forward to the Tsar, Alexander II., while he was in Paris, the insignia of the Order of the Garter. The Queen gave a reluctant assent. But when the minister offered to add an expression of regret that the Tsar was not coming to England to receive the honour in person, the Queen took the exception that in her widowhood she had "never invited sovereigns to come," and any expression of regret at the Tsar's absence would look "something like an indication" that she was about to resume her earlier habit of entertaining foreign royalties. She was determined to restrict her hospitality to foreign rulers' wives who were her special friends, such as the Queen of Prussia and the Empress Eugénie, each of whom at her invitation was, during this period, her private guest.

The question of the visit of the Sultan, Abdul-Aziz, who had already lavishly entertained the Prince at Constantinople in 1862, stood, in the Prime Minister's view, on a different footing. After accepting the French Emperor's invitation to

Paris he had informed Lord Lyons, the British Ambassador in
Constantinople (May 1867), that he wished to extend his journey
to this country. Lord Derby regarded it as essential to English
interests, even at the risk of incurring the Queen's displeasure,
not merely to favour the potentate's wish, but also to make
him the guest of the State. The Queen gave way unwillingly.
She minuted the Sultan's letter of acceptance, which was
addressed to Lord Lyons, with the words: "*No* invitation but
acquiescence in a proposal of his to come here." At the Prime
Minister's request, the Prince, who retained agreeable memories
of his meeting with the Sultan five years before, took on himself
the duty of devising a reception for the Sultan which should
not prove inferior in pomp and splendour to the welcome in
Paris of which the Prince was himself a witness. But the Queen,
while she showed no enthusiasm for the Prince's efforts, made it
plain to him that she would countenance national hospitality to
no other of the Emperor Napoleon's guests. When the Khedive
Ismail of Egypt, nephew of Said Pasha, the Prince's host at Cairo
in earlier days, arrived in London from Paris on his own
initiative, the Queen paid no heed to her son's remonstrance
that the new ruler of Egypt, to whom he had lately been introduced at Paris, was lodging like an ordinary tourist at Claridge's
Hotel.

The Prince and the Prime Minister needed all their powers of
persuasion to induce the Queen to receive the Sultan in person.
Writing to Lord Derby on 2nd July 1867 the Prince pointed out:

He is really *most* anxious about it, and I must say candidly,
having some slight experience with these Oriental Potentates,
that it would *everywhere* have a very bad effect if the Queen did
not consent. . . . I am sure we are all anxious to receive him
with courtesy and respect, and his visit is really of a great public
character. . . . I think it would indeed be bad policy on our
part if we affronted him in any way, and these Orientals are *very*
sensitive.

The Queen, yielding to her son's earnest representations, invited
the Sultan to lunch with her on the second day of his visit.

Another point which provoked controversy was the sort of
decoration which the Queen should bestow on the nation's
Turkish guest. The Prince urged that only the highest orders
were deserving of consideration. "His predecessor," he wrote

to Lord Derby on the 12th of July, the day of the Sultan's arrival, "had the Garter, and the Viceroy of Egypt and Bey of Tunis have the Order of the Bath, so I think it would hardly do for him to leave without receiving either one or other of the two first Orders. If my views coincide with yours I wish you could write to the Queen on the subject as soon as possible, as there is no time to be lost." Lord Derby inclined to the G.C.S.I., but the Sultan let it be known that only the K.G. would satisfy him. The Queen raised the objection that it was unfitting, in spite of precedent, to bestow a Christian order on a Mussulman. Again, she surrendered with grave misgiving to the Prince's and the Prime Minister's importunity. There is a touch of irony in the circumstance that, after a long passage of years, the Prince himself, when on his mother's throne, was to reiterate her scruples as to conferring the Order of the Garter on a non-Christian sovereign.

On the 12th July the Prince met the Sultan at Dover on his way from Boulogne and conducted him with imposing ceremonial to Buckingham Palace. Next day the Prince escorted him to the Queen's luncheon at Windsor. For more than a week and a half, until the guest re-embarked at Dover for Calais on the royal yacht *Osborne* (on the 23rd), the Prince rarely left his side. The political importance which the government attached to the Sultan's visit was illustrated by a special reception at the India Office, at the expense of the Indian Exchequer. The function was a testimony to the bond uniting the Sultan, as Caliph of Islam, to the Mohammedans of the Queen's Indian dominions. But the most spectacular item of the long programme of hospitality was an imposing review of the Fleet which the Queen herself, after much searching of heart, conducted at Spithead on the 17th. On board the royal yacht *Victoria and Albert*, the Queen, the Prince, and her guest moved down the lines of the formidable array of ships of war. The weather was bad, and it was amid a howling storm that the Queen, on the yacht's deck, bestowed on the Sultan in the Prince's presence, the coveted Knighthood of the Garter.

The habitually impassive Oriental was moved almost to tears by the Prince's attentions. Although he spoke only Turkish, conversation was made possible through the fluent French of the Grand Vizier, Fuad Pasha. When the Sultan reached Calais from

Dover on his departure he telegraphed to the Prince exuberant expressions of gratitude.

VI

With the words of the Sultan ringing in his ear and the renewed conviction of the prudence of conciliating the Porte, the Prince harboured for the time doubts of the policy of Mr. Gladstone and his government which, assuming office in 1868, showed Russia a benevolence calculated to move Turkey's resentment. Events soon arose which reinforced the Prince's doubts.

Late in 1870, when France was crippled by the disasters of the Franco-German War, Russia without warning took a step which, profoundly moving the Prince, fanned the flame of his Palmerstonian faith, and confirmed his suspicions not of Russia alone, but of Prussia as well.

On the 31st October 1870 the Russian Chancellor, Prince Gortschakoff, suddenly announced Russia's repudiation of the clauses of the Treaty of Paris of 1856, which, at the close of the Crimean War, had neutralised the Black Sea and excluded Russian and all other ships of war from its shores and surface. On the 21st November the Prince wrote to Lord Granville, the Foreign Secretary, of his alarm "at the serious complications that may arise at the outrageous conduct of Russia at the present moment." He begged for precise information, seeing in Russia's cynical contempt for the sanctity of a ratified treaty the promptings of Prussian diplomacy. "I very much fear," the Prince added, "that Prussia stands in with her." "If Austria, Turkey, and Italy," he proceeded, "would act offensively with us, we might, I think, still 'hold our own.'" The British government, taken by surprise, shared, for the moment, the Prince's indignation. Gladstone denounced Russia's action as "a blunder and a crime"; the Queen nervously foresaw a new Crimean War; but the Liberal Government shirked decisive action, and to the Prince's dismay contented itself with what he called "strong, though not too strong language." Mr. Odo Russell, the Prince's friend of Roman days, had recently been recalled from Italy to serve as Under-Secretary at the Foreign Office in London, and when, on the 12th November, he was sent to Versailles to negotiate personally with Bismarck on the Russian imbroglio the Prince hoped against hope for some favourable

turn. The Prussian statesman, although he cherished no kind-
ness for England, advised her to act with Austria and his own
country. Lord Granville acknowledged that the Powers of
Europe were indisposed to join England in resistance to
Russia, and the English government, finding itself without an
ally, agreed to Bismarck's proposal of a European conference.
The German statesman suggested the place of meeting should be
St. Petersburg, but yielded to Lord Granville's wish to substitute
London. The London Conference took place in March 1871. The
outcome justified the Prince's fears. Although Russia agreed
to abide by the verdict of the Powers, Prussia induced the
Conference to leave the Black Sea at Russia's disposal. England's
diplomatic defeat was complete. Her protest against Russia's
action served no purpose save that of embittering Anglo-Russian
relations and of strengthening the ties that bound Russia to
Germany.

VII

The Prince's mood was variable and sensitive to circumstance.
The propitiatory policy which Mr. Gladstone's government continued to pursue towards Russia led before long to a recrudescence of the Prince's hope that good domestic relations with
the Tsar and his family might help to ease the political strain.
Many opportunities were offered him of meeting Russian royalty.
The Tsarevitch, now his wife's brother-in-law, was to become, with
himself, a regular frequenter of the family circle at Copenhagen.
An earlier domestic link with the Tsar also promised to gather
strength. Prince Louis of Darmstadt, the husband of the Prince's
sister, Alice, was nephew of Tsar Alexander II.'s wife (formerly
Princess Marie of Hesse), and it became the habit of the Russian
sovereign and the Tsaritza, after taking the waters of a summer
at Ems, to enjoy for some weeks the hospitality of the reigning
family at Jugenheim, the ducal château of Hesse-Darmstadt.
There, in August 1871, in spite of political clouds, the Prince and
Princess with the Prince's brother, the Duke of Edinburgh, were
fellow-guests with the Tsar, his wife, and children. Controversial
themes were avoided. The Tsar professed himself charmed anew
with the Prince's geniality, and pressed on him a second visit,
this time with the Princess, to St. Petersburg during the coming
winter. The Prince's illness defeated that plan.

Two years later events were conspicuously to illustrate the vanity of seeking, at this period at any rate, an antidote to Anglo-Russian political rivalry in a strengthening of domestic ties between the two royal families. Bismarck's formation of the Drei-Kaiser Bund between the Emperors of Germany, Austria, and Russia suggested the futility of England's pursuit of political intimacy with Russia. Yet the Prince was reluctant to relinquish the politico-domestic quest, even if his confidence in the issue wavered. His clearer-sighted mother cherished fewer illusions than he in the matter.

The Prince was of two minds regarding the earliest and most notable episode which the year 1873 presented in the domestic associations of Anglo-Russian royalty. The introduction, in the haven of Jugenheim, of the Prince's next brother, Alfred, Duke of Edinburgh, to the Grand Duchess Marie, only daughter of the Tsar Alexander II., and the Tsarevitch's only sister, bore fruit in their betrothal in April 1873. Writing on the 24th to Lord Granville from Darmstadt, where the Prince proffered his congratulations to the newly affianced couple, he expressed a guarded hope that his brother's future might be "as bright as he supposes." The public announcement of the engagement on 12th May caused some bewilderment in England. Mr. Gladstone, in the House of Commons, sought to satisfy public doubt by declaring the engagement to be free of political intention, although he welcomed it as a possible step towards that better understanding with Russia which was part of the Liberal programme. The Prince remained less sanguine, but was quite ready to turn the situation to any good account that seemed possible. In June 1873 he invited the Russian heir-apparent, brother of the bride-elect, with his wife, the Princess of Wales's sister, and their two young sons Nicholas and George, to spend some weeks at Marlborough House. The Prince designed for his guests a more impressive reception than his cautious mother quite approved, but, on her son's impetuous representations, she sanctioned an escort of the 2nd Dragoon Guards when the Prince and Princess conducted their visitors through the streets from Woolwich, the place of debarkation, to Marlborough House. The stay gave the Prince every opportunity of exercising his talent for hospitality. Time was to lend a peculiar touch of pathos to this genial episode.

The youngest member but one of the party, the Grand Duke Nicholas, afterwards Tsar Nicholas II., the last of the Romanoff rulers of Russia, always cherished among the pleasantest memories of his ill-starred career, this first introduction, at the age of five, to England and to his "Uncle Bertie."

A public engagement which it fell to the Prince's lot to fulfil while the Russian heir and his family were under his roof illustrates the difficulty of keeping domestic amenities apart from ruffling political issues. The Asiatic interests of both England and Russia made of Persia an apple of discord. Both parties throughout the Prince's career sought control of this semi-civilised country, rich in potential produce. Early in 1873 the Shah, Nasr-ed-Din, created a new precedent by setting out on a tour of Europe, with St. Petersburg as his first halt. By way of proving his wish to hold the balance even between the pretensions of England and Russia he included London among the capitals which he designed to visit. The English government, in spite of its pacific leanings towards Russia, acknowledged the obligation of fostering the Shah's goodwill. It was desirable that the display of England's friendly disposition toward Persia should countervail any development of Russian ambitions. The English government, following the precedent of the Sultan's case in 1867, at once constituted the Shah a guest of the State, and, in deference to the Queen's unwillingness to take a prominent part in functions of public hospitality, again laid on the Prince's shoulders the main burden of the entertainment. The Shah arrived at Buckingham Palace on 18th June, while the Tsarevitch was still at Marlborough House. Next day the Prince gave there an elaborate banquet in the Shah's honour, to which the presence of the Tsarevitch lent piquancy. The Prince did not allow any political suspicions on the part of his wife's Russian brother-in-law to impair the energy with which he sustained his rôle of national host of the Shah. The Persian monarch's visit enthralled the London populace, and the Prince pleased public sentiment by the attentions which he paid the visitor. He introduced him to the Queen at Windsor on the day after the banquet at Marlborough House, and witnessed with satisfaction the reluctant bestowal by his mother of the Order of the Garter on a second Oriental sovereign. Under the Prince's general supervision the programme, as on the visit of the Sultan,

included a naval review, together with a military review in
Windsor Park, receptions at the Albert Hall and the Crystal
Palace, and a ball at the Guildhall. The Prince found the companionship of the distinguished traveller something of a trial.
Private visits to English magnates were arranged, and the Prince
was on occasion the Shah's fellow-guest. Together they paid a
visit to the Prince's friend, the Duke of Sutherland, at the ducal
seat of Trentham. There the Shah, with native simplicity and
embarrassing curiosity, inquired of the Prince whether, when he
came to the throne, he would not behead their ducal hosts. The
Prince, with ready adaptability, replied that great nobles were
too numerous in England for him to undertake a clearance of
them.[1]

The Shah's visit, to the success of which the Prince materially
contributed, was reckoned in Russia no very friendly bid against
Russia's claims on Persia. The Prince showed clearly that
his hospitality to the Tsar's kinsfolk was not weakening his
zeal for England's interest when they came into rivalry with
those of Russia. It was soon equally apparent that his brother's
approaching marriage with the Tsar's daughter, which he
described soon after the Shah's departure as giving an illusion
of *couleur de rose*, was in no way slackening his watchful scrutiny
of Russia's dubious movements in Asia. Private information,
which caused him uneasiness respecting Russia's advance towards
the Indian frontier, reached him at the end of the year in which
he had entertained both the Tsarevitch and the Shah.

During the summer the Prince's friend, Colonel Valentine
Baker, of the 10th Hussars, made an adventurous journey in the
track of the Russian expedition which had reached Khiva (on
June 10). On his return to England at the end of the year
Colonel Baker was the Prince's guest at Sandringham, and he
disquieted his host by his graphic description of the Russian
operations, which the Prince eagerly followed on a map of
Baker's devising. The Prince promptly wrote to Lord Granville
(January 9, 1874): "Unless we are firm on the Central Asia
question, we may have much trouble in store for us in the
future. . . . They (*i.e.* the Russians), may soon come un-
pleasantly near Afghanistan, unless by real firm language we
give them to understand that if they go beyond Bokhara our

[1] Lord Ronald Gower, *Reminiscences*, p. 306.

policy with regard to India will not allow it." Lord Granville was indisposed to make any "real firm" protest.

VIII

Meanwhile the Tsar made every effort to rekindle the sympathies of the Prince, whose brother was marrying his daughter. The Prince and Princess accepted his pressing invitation to attend the wedding at St. Petersburg, which was fixed for January 11/23, 1874. The Tsar also offered the Prince a special compliment which made a direct appeal to the Prince's idiosyncrasy, and was calculated to promote personal harmony. Through the Duke of Edinburgh the Prince learned of the Tsar's wish to confer on him during the wedding festivities the colonelcy of a Russian regiment. Queen Victoria, whose sanction was needful, remained circumspect, and hesitated acquiescence. "The Emperor," the Prince urgently wrote to his mother, "has always been so very kind and gracious to me that this fresh proof cannot but be very flattering to me, and I feel convinced that you would not wish me to do anything which might look like a rebuff on my part, by refusing it" (December 20, 1873). The Queen was unmoved by the argument. She had no wish to consult the Tsar's feelings. "I should never offer," she replied (December 23, 1873), "one of my regiments to a foreign prince or sovereign. Our customs are totally different, and I think we are more independent without all these foreign honours." [1]

In no quarter at home did the Prince find much encouragement. Lord Granville and Mr. Gladstone, as well as the Duke of Cambridge, supported the Queen's view. "We are insular," wrote Lord Granville, "and there are many advantages in remaining so." The Liberal ministers' plea of the sacredness of precedent moved the Prince's scorn. "I certainly cannot coincide in their [the ministers'] views," he

---

[1] The Prince Consort, the Queen added, had been offered a like distinction by the Emperor of Austria, and the government had then vetoed its acceptance. The Queen questioned the pertinence of precedents which were cited in the cases of George IV. and the Duke of Wellington; the former had become a colonel of an Austrian regiment, and the latter of a Russian. George IV., the Queen pointed out, received the honour at the end of the Napoleonic War, and the great Duke of Wellington had Russian troops in the field under his command.

wrote to the Queen on 31st December 1873. "The reason of 1874
not changing an old-established precedent which they seem Ætat. 32
to lay such stress on seems rather unnecessary on their part
considering how many precedents they break down to suit their
own purposes." "Times change, and precedents also," he
wrote in a like strain to Lord Granville, "and this I should
think H.M.'s Government know better than any one. The
acceptance of the regiment would have given great pleasure to
the Emperor, and its refusal has placed me in a very awkward
position." The Tsar declined to treat as final the Duke of
Edinburgh's intimation of the Queen's disapproval of the
intended courtesy. As soon as the Prince arrived in St. Petersburg (January 6/18, 1874), he telegraphed to the Queen again
requesting her sanction. The Queen resented the revival of
the matter, and wired her regret at "being compelled to decline
your friendly offer of giving the Prince a regiment which he
could not accept, as it is contrary to the custom of this country."
Thus the little controversy ended, but the point at issue was
revived before long, and the Prince had the satisfaction of seeing
his mother adopt the view for which he had pleaded. The
Queen herself, some years later, received from a foreign sovereign
the kind of honour which she vehemently deprecated when the
Tsar proposed to bestow it on her son. Military and even naval
honours were indeed to be exchanged by the sovereign of England
with many foreign rulers.

At St. Petersburg the Prince and Princess were lodged in the
Anitchkoff Palace. The bridegroom's family was also represented by his next brother, Arthur, who came with the Prince
and Princess, by the Crown Prince and Princess of Prussia, and
by his uncle, Duke Ernest of Saxe-Coburg-Gotha. All attended
the two marriage ceremonies, one according to the rites of the
Greek Orthodox Church, which took place at the Winter Palace,
and the other according to the Anglican rites, which was performed by Dean Stanley (January 23, 1874). The Prince and
Princess figured prominently in the protracted and varied
festivities.[1]

But all was not quite plain sailing. The Queen, despite
the new domestic tie, cherished old-standing suspicion of

---

[1] In a boar-hunt near St. Petersburg, in which the Prince engaged, as many
as eighty boars were killed, and an excursion to Moscow followed.

Russia's political designs. She could not easily reconcile herself to her government's friendly approaches to Russia, on which her son seemed to bestow confusing alternations of assent and dissent. A breach on a minor issue threatened on the eve of the wedding, and the Queen inclined to inflame rather than to heal it. One Mitchell, an attaché at the British Embassy at St. Petersburg, who was attached for the marriage ceremonies to the suite of the Prince and the Duke of Edinburgh, was reported at the Russian Foreign Office to have expressed doubts as to the possibility of permanent harmony between the two countries. In consequence, the Tsar and his Chancellor requested Mitchell to leave Russia. The Queen, on learning of the affront to a British subject, wrote indignantly to the Foreign Secretary, Lord Granville (January 7, 1874): "The Queen feels very strongly that in consequence of the marriage, the Russian government intend to be more than usually *haughty and exigent*, and mean to *try* to order us about as they formerly did other Courts related to them." The flattery which the Russian Court was lavishing on her two sons "was throwing dust in our eyes." Lord Granville clung to the view that good Anglo-Russian relations promised peace to Europe. He regarded Mitchell's language as indiscreet, and he contented himself with a mild protest to Prince Gortschakoff, the Russian Chancellor, against his expulsion. To the Queen he explained that a concession was worth making, in view of the essential need of keeping on amicable terms with Russia. "Russia," he earnestly added, "is the country which could the most easily assist in preventing a European war." Finally he adjured the Queen not merely to abandon her anti-Russian prepossessions, but to write to the Tsar, or to the Crown Prince of Prussia, in a conciliatory way "on this terribly important question" of an Anglo-Russian entente.

An uncovenanted and inauspicious incident preceded the dispersal of the wedding-party. A fresh guest of arresting prominence arrived in the person of the Austrian Kaiser Francis Joseph. His presence recalled the Prince's thoughts to the ambiguities of the Tsar's foreign policy. The newcomer and his host formed with the German Emperor that triple Bund which sought to keep England in isolation outside it. At a State banquet in the newcomer's honour the Prince listened to the Tsar's laudations of the Drei-Kaiser Bund, praises which he qualified in view of the Prince's presence and of the new matrimonial alliance of his daughter with the Prince's brother, by an interpolated mention of his friendship with Queen Victoria. In a not very convincing context, he cited his amicable relations with the British sovereign as a guarantee of the world's peace. The speech which sounded hollow throughout, was in one respect obviously maladroit. The omission of any mention of France provoked the French Ambassador, who was present, to exclaim ironically: "When will our turn come?"[1]

Officially the Prince's visit was described as going without a hitch. Lord Augustus Loftus, the British Ambassador recently transferred from Berlin, who was in no great favour with the Prince, credited him and the Princess with gaining "during their stay fresh laurels of popularity."[2] To Mr. Disraeli, who became Prime Minister in the Prince's absence from England, the Prince wrote while still in Russia: "Our visit here has been one of great satisfaction and pleasure to ourselves, and nothing could exceed the kindness of every one." There was an unconscious ring of irony about the innocent words. The statesman whom the Prince addressed was about to bring Russia and England to the verge of war. Political differences and political rivalries between the two countries lay indeed very near the surface, even when the Prince and Princess reached London on their return from St. Petersburg on 5th March. The day of reckoning was not just yet. Lord Granville had set his heart on preventing, or at least postponing, a breach, and the Queen, yielding to his counsels, had consented, in the last days of the Liberal Government, to take a step which might possibly avert it. Before her son left the Russian capital she went the length, at Lord Granville's prompting, of inviting the Tsar to pay England a visit in May.[3]

Once more, the Prince undertook to relieve the Queen of the labour incident to the entertainment of a foreign sovereign, and he threw himself with his usual vigour into the organisation of

1874
Ætat. 32

[1] Eduard von Wertheimer, *Graf Julius Andrássy, Sein Leben und Seine Zeit* (1913), vol. ii.

[2] Lord Augustus Loftus, *Diplomatic Reminiscences*, ser. 2, ii. 81–95.

[3] As many as thirty years had elapsed since a Tsar of Russia had visited England. In 1844 Tsar Alexander II.'s father, Nicholas I., had been Queen Victoria's guest.

1874
Ætat. 32

the Russian Emperor's welcome. The Tsar arrived at Dover on the 14th May with a large suite of fifty-one persons, and was conducted by the Prince to Windsor Castle. Two days later he removed to Buckingham Palace, and during the rest of the visit the Prince took personal charge of the hospitality. On the night of the 15th there was an elaborate dinner at Marlborough House which, the Queen was assured by her equerry in attendance on the Tsar, "was exceedingly well done." Both Mr. Disraeli and Mr. Gladstone were present. Next evening the Prince and Princess, with the Duke and Duchess of Edinburgh, attended a brilliant fête in the Tsar's honour at the Crystal Palace. The Tsar's health suffered under the strain of the hospitable attentions. But he was well enough to receive at the Guildhall a flattering address, to which he replied with a declaration of Russia's friendship for his daughter's adopted country (May 18). A review at Aldershot and a ball at Buckingham Palace preceded the Tsar's departure from Gravesend on 21st May. He seemed to reciprocate the Prince's energetic cordiality, and the mutual friendliness appeared at the moment to promise a clear political sky. The genial atmosphere prompted the Queen in an unusually optimistic telegram of farewell to assure the Tsar that "our countries will remain on friendly, nay cordial, terms." But affable greetings of royalty could not check the tide of political rivalry between the two countries. The glowing mirage was delusive. It vanished in the twinkling of an eye.

CHAPTER XVII

VISITS TO FRANCE, 1867–1869—A SEVEN MONTHS' FOREIGN TOUR, 1868–1869

I

HOWEVER much the Prince's mind was occupied and perplexed by the domestic and political aspects of the affairs of Greece and Russia, he recognised from the first that a more critical interest for England and for Europe attached to political movements in continental countries nearer at hand—in France and Prussia.

1867
—
Ætat. 25

The fascination which French life and society exerted on the Prince at all stages of his career brought French politics equally within his range. He was flattered by the social attentions which the soft-voiced Emperor Napoleon III. paid him unceasingly, and by the weight which the Emperor seemed to attach to his political opinion. With intense gratification he received in London in March 1865 a special envoy, Baron Gros, who was charged by the Emperor to invest him with the insignia of the Grand Cordon of the Légion d'Honneur. In the closing years of the imperial régime the Prince availed himself of every opportunity to visit Paris, and to bask in the brilliance of the imperial Court, which was destined for a premature grave. He became a familiar and a popular figure in fashionable Parisian circles. But all the time he watched with a nervously alert eye the ominous turns of French imperial policy. In spite of the personal attraction that the French Emperor had for him he shared Queen Victoria's dismay at the patent discrepancy between his motto, "L'Empire, c'est la paix," and his aggressive demeanour in the councils of Europe.

In 1867 Paris of the Second Empire was the scene, for a second time, of an International Exhibition. The Prince became an

active member of the British Royal Commission which helped
to organise the British section. In that work he was nearly
associated with his fellow-commissioner, Lord Granville.[1] The
Emperor of the French sought by this tribute to the world's
industry to parade a questionable zeal for universal peace. By
way of emphasising his professed aspiration he offered princely
hospitality to the rulers of the world. Every sovereign of
Europe, save the Pope, accepted the imperial invitation. The
highest peak in the Emperor's overweening career was scaled.
The sovereigns of Europe, who crowded his palaces, at length
treated him as one of themselves. His experience of 1867
graphically illustrates in the retrospect the fickleness of royal
or imperial fortune.

The Prince joined early the distinguished throng of visitors.
The Exhibition was opened by the Emperor on the 1st April
without formal ceremony, before, indeed, the preparations were
complete. In May the Prince paid the Exhibition a first visit
of inspection which lasted nine days. He left London on the 10th,
immediately after the christening at Marlborough House of his
first daughter, and third child (Louise Victoria Alexandra
Dagmar), afterwards Duchess of Fife and Princess Royal of
England. The Princess of Wales was unable to join her husband,
and his brother, the Duke of Edinburgh, was his companion.
They stayed at the British Embassy with the Ambassador, Lord
Cowley, who was postponing his retirement in order to act as
host. A memorable ball which Lord Cowley gave in their
honour was attended by the Emperor and Empress, and by their
guests, the new King and Queen of the Belgians.

But Emperor Napoleon designed to make the 1st July, the
day of the distribution of the prizes to the exhibitors, the supreme
occasion. By that date the leading personages of Europe had
assembled in Paris at his hospitable bidding. The Tsar,
Alexander II., was there with his powerful minister, Prince
Gortschakoff; so, too, was the King of Prussia, attended by
Count Bismarck, whose "glacial politeness" was justly reckoned
ominous; so, too, were the Sultan of Turkey and Khedive Ismail
of Egypt. The Emperor of Austria accepted an invitation, and
was hourly expected. The Prince of Wales and the Duke
of Cambridge, now a favourite travelling companion, put up

[1] Sir Henry Cole, *Fifty Years of Public Work*, i. 258 *seq.*

on 29th June at the Hôtel Bristol,—thenceforth the Prince's regular stopping-place.

Scarcely had this sojourn of the Prince in Paris begun than the shadows lengthened on the imperial horizon. On the eve of the great ceremony of 1st July there arrived in Paris private news of a grievous disaster, which was to cloud the splendours of the day for the Prince and for many others. The Emperor of the French, in his yearning for domination, had sought to extend his influence to the American continent. He had aimed at French control of Mexico. His armies had occupied the country, had suppressed the native republic there, and had set up an Empire, the throne of which the French Emperor chose Maximilian, the brother of the Emperor of Austria, to fill. It was a reckless adventure, doomed to failure. The Mexicans soon rose in revolt against Napoleon's appointed ruler. The French troops were recalled, the Emperor Maximilian declined to leave with them, and on the 19th June, twelve days before the prize-giving at Paris, he was shot at Queretaro. The Emperor Maximilian had married a kinswoman of the Prince, Princess Charlotte of Belgium, the daughter of the late King Leopold I. and sister of the present King. Many months before her husband's assassination, when his fortunes in Mexico were falling, she had vainly sought in Europe assistance from his and from her kindred. Her distresses unseated her reason, and before the final catastrophe came she was a hopeless imbecile. She had been a playmate of the Prince of Wales's boyhood, and he had often met her with her husband in later years.

It was while reports of the Mexican tragedy were unofficially percolating through the Emperor's distinguished audience—the news was officially withheld—that the prize-giving ceremony took place. There was no departure from the elaborations of the pre-arranged programme. The Emperor outwardly pre-served his serenity. But the Emperor of Austria, who was starting for Paris when the tragic news reached him, kept away. "The ceremony of the distribution of prizes at the old exhibition building yesterday," wrote the Prince to Lord Derby, the Prime Minister, on 2nd July 1867, "was a very fine sight, and the Emperor's speech well worth hearing." But the rumours of the Mexican catastrophe obsessed him: "Everybody here is in great dismay at the news from Mexico. I have just seen

M. Moustier, who fears that it is only too true that the unfortunate Emperor Maximilian has fallen a victim to that bloodthirsty villain Juarez. If true it is really too horrible." Great was the Prince's perturbation when "all the sad details of poor Max's death" were fully revealed.[1] The revelations cast a profound gloom over the company at the imperial Court. Emperor Napoleon could not resist the prevailing depression, and he curtailed his scheduled entertainment, although he induced his guests, the Prince among them, to stay on. The Prince made much of the opportunities of discussing foreign affairs with many who were moulding them. But he returned home disquieted. "Future troubles," he wrote to Mrs. Bruce on 10th August, "are brewing between France and Prussia; in fact things don't look very pleasant or quiet."

II

Emperor Napoleon's courtesies were uninterrupted. Early next year he offered the Prince and Princess a house in Algiers on hearing a rumour of the Princess's intention of visiting that country for her health, and when he subsequently learned that the Prince and his wife were bent on a long foreign tour he invited them to accept his hospitality at its beginning and end. At the close of November the Prince and Princess joined him and the Empress for two days at their country seat of Compiègne. The Prince and Princess's presence there was reckoned of political value in dispelling a sense of soreness which a recent manifestation of Queen Victoria's aloofness had aroused in French public opinion.[2] At Compiègne the Prince met an attractive company. Besides many diplomatists accredited to the imperial Court, his fellow-guests included Count von Moltke, the great Prussian strategist, who was soon to overthrow his host on the field of battle; Marshal Bazaine, whose military career was about to end in sensational disaster; and the Marquis of Lansdowne whose maternal grandfather, Comte de Flahault, was

---

[1] Subsequently the Prince sent his equerry, Lord Hamilton, to Vienna to attend on his behalf the Mexican ruler's funeral.

[2] Newton's *Life of Lord Lyons*, i. 199. The French press had taken some offence at an apparent slight to the imperial family on the part of Queen Victoria, who, in the summer of 1868, passed through Paris on her way to and from Lucerne, where she was seeking change for the first time on the continent. The Empress Eugénie paid the Queen a visit on her passing through Paris on her way out, but the Queen failed to return the call on the homeward journey.

one of the Emperor's staunchest adherents, and who was just 1868
embarking on a distinguished political career in England. The Ætat. 27
Prince engaged in varied sport with the Emperor and the rest
of the company. A stag-hunt—"la chasse à courre"—which was
conducted with the spectacular effects usual on the continent,
"was," the Prince wrote, "very interesting to see, but compared
to our own hunting it is very tame." In the course of the day he
was thrown from his horse, which "was anything but pleasant,"
although he suffered no injury. While in the French capital the
Prince also saw much of the new British Ambassador, Lord Lyons,
his old friend of Washington, who had now moved to Paris,
and of many leaders of French society whose personal charm
never failed in his eyes. With the Princess he now first visited
the salon of the Emperor's cousin, the Princess Mathilde, the
rendezvous of all who were eminent in French letters and art,
as well as the Paris studio of Queen Victoria's favourite German
portrait-painter Winterhalter.

Seven months later, in May 1869, the Emperor and Empress 1869
welcomed the Prince and Princess to the profuse splendours of Ætat. 27
the Tuileries, and the Prince had his last glimpse of the radiant
imperial Court. To the chiefs of the army, who were soon to
tempt fate in the field, and to the diplomatic corps he was, as
always, especially drawn. He enjoyed familiar intercourse with
the chivalric soldier but ineffectual politician, Marshal MacMahon,
with the brilliantly versatile Colonel Galliffet and his beautiful
wife, with Prince and Princess Paul Metternich. Prince Paul
the Austrian Ambassador was son of the old oracle of reaction,
and his wife was a leader at the imperial Court in all its madcap
revels. Little more than a year was to pass before his host and
hostess were to fall from their high estate into the abyss of foreign
exile. Hereafter the Prince was to meet his friends of the
imperial régime in wholly changed surroundings. It was a
fateful parting with the imperial family and its circle which the
Prince and Princess took on leaving Paris on 12th May 1869.

III

The zest for foreign travel, the Princess's health, the pressure
of social burdens and the irritation caused by whispered scandal,
were the primary causes of the Prince's resolve to spend the long

1868

Ætat. 27

winter and spring of 1868–69 abroad with his wife. There were supplementary inducements in the Princess's desire to pass Christmas with her parents at Copenhagen and subsequently to visit her brother at Athens, as well as in the Prince's inclination to repay at Constantinople the Sultan's recent visit to England and to inspect the engineering feat of the Suez Canal, now approaching completion, of which he had heard much from the Duke of Sutherland. The Prince had visited Turkey, Greece, and Egypt before, but he was well pleased to introduce his wife to foreign scenes with which he was already familiar.

When, in the autumn of 1868, the Prince brought his project to the notice of the Queen (October 22), she pointed out that the itinerary must be settled in consultation with herself, "as every movement of yours abroad or indeed anywhere is of political importance." She assented to the proposal only on conditions which recalled earlier days: that a strict incognito should be preserved, that a rigorous eye should be kept on the expenses, that invitations should only be accepted from the Courts of near relatives, and that Sundays were to be devoted to rest and not to amusement. A programme, which was calculated to cover some seven months and to observe these provisos, was rapidly devised. It gave ample scope for both sight-seeing and political observation.

The party left London on the 17th November on the eve of the general election which was to give Mr. Gladstone his first term of office as Prime Minister. With the Prince and Princess there went as far as Copenhagen their three eldest children—Prince Albert Victor, Prince George, and Princess Louise.[1] After eight days in Paris the Prince and Princess travelled slowly through Germany to Lubeck there to embark for Denmark. They paused at Cologne to "see the Cathedral, which is now (the Prince wrote to his mother) progressing very well and is really quite magnificent." A short visit was paid at Düsseldorf to the Hohenzollern-Sigmaringen family, a circle in which he always

---

[1] Throughout the journey the Prince and Princess's suite consisted of the Hon. Mrs. William Grey, Colonel Teesdale, Captain Arthur Ellis, Lord Carrington, Oliver Montagu, and Dr. Minter as medical attendant. Mrs. Grey, who was a favourite bedchamber-woman of the Princess, was a Swede who "spoke English with a pretty little accent" (Lady Battersea's *Memoirs*, p. 342). She published her diary of the tour. Lady Carmarthen, Sir William Knollys, and Colonel Keppel accompanied the party only as far as Copenhagen.

felt at home.   Shortly after his arrival in Copenhagen the Prince
renewed (December 16–22) his pleasant memory of Stockholm,
spending there six days, as the guest, for a second time, of King
Charles XV. of Sweden.   At Stockholm a new path of social
philanthropy was opened to the Prince.   King Charles introduced him to a new philanthropic interest by initiating him
into the Order of Freemasons.   The Prince remained through
life an adherent of the craft.   On returning to England he
received the rank of Past Grand Master of England at a meeting
of the Grand Lodge on the 1st September 1869.   His zeal for
Freemasonry steadily grew.   Before long he was promoted
Grand Master of the Order in England (September 2, 1874) in
succession to Lord Ripon, and by virtue of that office became
chief of the Royal Arch Masonry.[1]

1868
Ætat. 27

The cheerful Christmas hospitalities which the King and
Queen of Denmark offered their daughter, son-in-law, and grandchildren at the Castle of Fredensborg lasted the best part of six
weeks.   On the 16th of January 1869 the Prince and his wife
bade farewell to their children, who were taken back to England,
and they themselves left Copenhagen to be the central figures
in a series of imposing demonstrations of honour elsewhere.   In
Berlin and Vienna they received, in rapid succession, welcomes
from sovereigns who had lately faced one another on the field
of battle.   The Prince and Princess seemed to be embarked on
a mission of peace.

1869
Ætat. 27

At Berlin the Prince and Princess stayed with the Crown
Prince and Princess of Prussia (Jan. 18–20).   On the 19th the
King of Prussia convened, in the Old Schloss of the German
capital, a special chapter of the Order of the Black Eagle at which
to invest the Prince with the collar and the mantle.   The Prince
had been appointed, in his cradle, a Knight of the order by his
godfather, the former King of Prussia, but the full investiture
required his attendance at a formal chapter.   Much interest
attached to the ceremony.   The collar with which the Prince
was invested had belonged to the Prince Consort.   Among the
Knights Grand Cross who were present, in addition to the
Crown Prince, were Count von Moltke and Bismarck—pillars of
Prussia's newly acquired prestige.   At a State banquet in the new
knight's honour in the evening the Prince had opportunities of

[1] See p. 568 *infra*.

conversing with the chief contrivers of Prussian aggrandisement. His love of intercourse with notable figures in current history overcame, for the occasion, his distrust of Prussian ambitions. The veteran Field-Marshal von Wrangel, who had often led Prussian troops to victory, engaged the Prince in animated talk. For the first time he found himself speaking familiarly with Bismarck, who showed every outward courtesy. With a somewhat ironic complaisance the Prussian statesman had obeyed the command of his master to wear the Danish Order of the Dannebrog by way of compliment to the Princess of Wales.[1]

From Berlin the travellers passed to Vienna, where, in spite of the Queen's prohibition, the Emperor Francis Joseph brooked no refusal of a full royal reception. The party were housed at the Burg (January 20–26). "Friday (the 21st), was spent in paying visits to the imperial family, and as there are twenty-seven archdukes now at Vienna it was hard work to get through the list. In the evening there was a *familien tafel* at the Burg, after which their Royal Highnesses went to the ballet." [2] A record frost somewhat hampered the fulfilment of the elaborate programme. Mourning, too, for the Comte de Brabant, only son and heir of King Leopold II. of Belgium, whose wife was an Austrian archduchess, forbade dancing. But there was a brilliant succession of State dinners, of concerts, and of visits to the Opera. The rigid etiquette of the Austrian Court proved rather oppressive to the visitors, and their ease of manner contrasted with the prevailing stiffness. But the Prince found compensation in the companionship of the Austrian minister, Count von Beust, with whom the Prince was to grow intimate during his coming tenure of the Austrian embassy in London, and of a Saxe-Coburg cousin who resided in Austria, Prince Augustus, whose wife, Clementine, was eldest daughter of King Louis Philippe. There was a reminder for the Prince and Princess of Prussia's highhandedness, in the condition of the King and Queen of Hanover, who, fallen on evil days, were living near Vienna in retirement at Hietzing. The English travellers found a melancholy satisfaction in visiting their distressed kinsfolk, victims of Bismarck's ruthlessness.

[1] Lord Augustus Loftus, *Diplomatic Reminiscences*, series 2, I. 244.
[2] Lord Bloomfield to Lord Clarendon, 27th January 1869; Lady Bloomfield to Queen Victoria, 26th January 1869, Vienna.

IV

At Trieste the Prince and Princess embarked (January 27) for
Egypt on H.M.S. *Ariadne*, which was fitted up as a yacht.   Cairo
was reached from Alexandria on 3rd February, and there the
most attractive part of the tour opened.[1]   A long stretch of the
river Nile and the whole length of the Suez Canal were to be
explored.   Khedive Ismail, with the aid of his son and heir,
Tewfik Pasha, sought to outdo the brilliant hospitality, which
his late uncle and predecessor, Said Pasha, had lavished on
the Prince seven years before.   The Esbekieh Palace was placed
at the disposal of the royal party, and a flotilla of varied
river craft was provided for the expedition up the Nile.   At
Cairo the Prince's party was joined, for the river trip, by a notable
company of English tourists.   The Prince's friend, the Duke of
Sutherland, had brought out to Egypt three men of high repute
to watch the last stages in [the construction of the Suez Canal.
The Duke's travelling companions were Richard Owen, the
naturalist, whom the Prince had known in boyhood as a friend
of his father ; William Howard Russell, the Crimean war correspondent of *The Times;* and John Fowler, eminent as an engineer.
Sir Samuel Baker, a brother of the Prince's friend, Colonel
Valentine Baker, had also just reached Cairo after an heroic
exploration of Central Africa, in course of which he had discovered the source of the Nile in the lake Albert Nyanza.   The
Prince eagerly enlisted the aid of the Duke's party and of Sir
Samuel in providing both amusement and instruction on the
voyage up the Nile.[2]   Baker, an expert big-game hunter, undertook to arrange the sport ; Owen was to lecture on the zoology
of the Nile region and on the geology of the Suez Canal, while
Fowler was to describe the engineering triumphs of the Suez
venture before the Prince came to close quarters with them.

On the 6th February the start was made from Cairo for a
six weeks' trip.   Throughout, the Prince was in the gayest

1869
Ætat. 27

---

[1] The tour in Egypt and the Crimea of 1869 is fully described in *A Diary
in the East,* by W. H. Russell (1869).   See also *Journal of a Visit to Egypt, etc.,
in the Suite of the Prince and Princess of Wales,* by the Hon. Mrs. William Grey
(1869), and Murray and White's *Sir Samuel Baker: a Memoir,* 1895, pp. 132-3.

[2] Other fresh guests who joined the Prince at Cairo for the river trip, apart
from the Duke of Sutherland's party and Sir Samuel Baker, were Prince Louis
of Battenberg (afterwards Marquis of Milford Haven), Colonel Stanton, Consul-
General of Cairo, Sir Henry Pelly, and two of the Duke of Sutherland's sons.

humour, showing a lively interest in everything, putting all his
guests at complete ease, and engaging at times in harmless jokes
at their expense. The party disembarked, as on the Prince's
former Nile voyage, to explore the ruined monuments near the
banks, or to shoot in the neighbouring country. At Assouan
Sir Samuel Baker and the Prince engaged in a crocodile hunt.
From the First Cataract, which was reached on 21st February,[1]
the expedition proceeded in dahabeahs over what was a new
route for the Prince, to the Second Cataract. They arrived at
Wadi Halfa on 2nd March and there turned back. On the return
journey the party paused to climb the Pyramids. The river trip
had covered a distance of a thousand miles. On 16th March
the Prince and his friends were again in Cairo, receiving new
proofs of the Khedive's hospitality.

Under the personal guidance of the Khedive, who was
the chief shareholder in the undertaking, the Prince and his
companions proceeded to inspect the Suez Canal (on March 24).
Much dredging and excavation had yet to be done before the
new waterway was ready for navigation. But the main processes of construction were completed, and within eight months
the canal was formally opened for traffic (November 17, 1869).
From Suez the Prince passed to the Khedive's chalet at Ismailia,
midway down the water-way. There the Prince opened the
sluice of a completed dam, allowing the Mediterranean to flow
into an empty basin connecting with the Bitter Lakes. But the
Prince's most interesting experience at Ismailia was his meeting
with M. de Lesseps, the engineer of the great design. Lesseps
proved a perfect guide. His gracious manner and clear
explanations captivated the Prince.

In conversation with Lesseps and the Khedive, the Prince
discussed many important issues. He had already formed a
decided opinion as to the importance of the canal to English
interests. He now acknowledged a poignant sense of regret that
the English government had allowed French enterprise to accomplish a work of such critical value to communication between
Europe and India. Lord Palmerston, he said, had been guilty

----

[1] Next day the Prince, with wonted courtesy, paid a visit to Lady Duff
Gordon, an English lady of literary repute who had made the Nile her home,
and was living in a dahabeah moored off Assouan. Her recently published
Letters from Egypt had stirred in the English public a wide interest in Egyptian
life.

of a lamentable lapse of foresight in declining to back up the 1875
project when it was first suggested. Ætat. 33

This sound view gathered strength in the Prince's mind with
the passage of time. Six years later, when on his way to India,
he passed through the completed canal. Then he wrote to Lord
Granville (October 29, 1875) : "The Suez Canal is certainly an
astounding work, and it is an everlasting pity that it was not
made by an English company and kept in our hands, because, as
it is our highway to India, we should be obliged to take it—and
by force of arms if necessary." To his delighted surprise, he
heard, scarcely a month later, that the neglect of opportunity
which moved his impatience was largely repaired by an astute
stroke of Mr. Disraeli, the Conservative Prime Minister. On
25th November 1875 Mr. Disraeli's government purchased for
£4,000,000 the 177,000 shares which the Khedive held in the
Suez Canal Company. The Prince, who was at the time touri
India, burst into almost dithyrambic praise of the Pri ie
Minister's masterly step.

"In the eyes of the whole world," the Prince at once wrote to
Disraeli from Government House, Lucknow, "it is a step which has
met with the highest approval, and one which must bring the highest
credit and honour to the First Minister of the Crown (if you will
allow me to say so). On all sides I hear what an excellent effect
it has had on the continent, showing that England still intends
keeping up her old position as one of the great powers. In India
this great work is naturally looked upon as one of the greatest
importance, and I only hope that the day is not far distant when
all the shares will be in our hands."

Nor did he conceal his elation from his Liberal friend, Lord
Granville, to whom he wrote to the same effect (March 21, 1876).[1]

[1] The Prince's eldest sister echoed his exultation. On the 3rd December
1875 the Queen sent Disraeli an extract from the Crown Princess's letter to
her which "she thinks will gratify him." The Crown Princess's letter, dated
30th November 1875, ran as follows: "I must congratulate you on the newest
deed of your government, the buying of half the shares of the Suez Canal;
it sent a thrill of pleasure and pride, almost of exultation through me! It
is a delightful thing to see the *right thing* done at the *right moment*. Everybody
is pleased here, and wishes it may bring England good; even that great man
[Bismarck] expressed himself to Fritz in this sense yesterday evening!"
The writer's elder son, a boy of sixteen, afterwards Kaiser William II., joined
in the general jubilation. "Willy," his mother added, "writes from Cassel:
'Dear Mama, I must write you a line, because I know you will be so delighted
that England has bought the Suez Canal. How jolly!'" (Buckle, *Life of
Disraeli*, v. 452).

But the Prince's sturdy conviction of England's urgent need of the control of the canal only served to enhance his estimation of M. de Lesseps' engineering achievement. Shortly after the canal was opened he induced the Society of Arts, of which he was President, to bestow on Lesseps its highest distinction—the Albert Medal—"for services rendered to arts, manufactures, and commerce by the realisation of the Suez Canal." The Prince reserved to himself the duty of handing the medal in person to M. de Lesseps, who arrived in London to receive it early in July 1870. The presentation took place on 4th July. In well-turned phrases the Prince greeted Lesseps as his personal friend whose companionship at Ismailia he had highly valued. "England," the Prince assured Lesseps, "will never forget that to you was due the success of that great enterprise, which is so much calculated to develop the commercial interests subsisting between herself and her Eastern Empire." In reply Lesseps congratulated himself on his good fortune in travelling with the Prince in the desert "where a man, however highly he may be placed, shows himself as he is."

It was not only of the canal that the Prince talked with the Khedive in his chalet at Ismailia. The anarchic condition of the Sudan, which was not yet under Egyptian control, was another theme. The Khedive expressed a wish to suppress the slave trade and to establish good order in the region. He spoke of his intention to invite Sir Samuel Baker to undertake the great task. The Prince warmly approved the Khedive's choice, and made practical suggestions as to the terms on which Baker might render the Khedive the needful service.[1] It was an important departure. Baker, the first Englishman to assume high office under the Egyptian government, sought, with wavering success, during the next four years in the capacity of Governor-General of the equatorial Nile basin, to bring under an orderly sway the vast stretch of African territory. The Prince was in later years to encourage many other strenuous efforts to bring the Sudan under English control.

V

While on the Nile news had reached the Prince that Greece and Turkey had for the time composed their differences, and that

[1] W. H. Russell, *A Diary in the East*, p. 384.

it was open to the royal party to fulfil an intention of visiting
Constantinople and Athens.   On the evening of 30th March the
Ariadne, escorted by the British cruisers *Psyche* and *Caradoc*, and
by the Sultan's yacht *Pertif Piali*, entered the Dardanelles.   They
anchored off the port of Gallipoli on the north-east coast of that
Gallipoli peninsula which was to acquire, over half a century
later, a tragic fame in the annals of the British Empire.   The
region already enshrined mournful memories of the Crimean War
which always appealed to the Prince.   He at once landed, and
walked through the narrow streets of the town to visit the
neglected cemeteries of French and British soldiers who had died
in the camp formed there at the opening of the Crimean War.

On 1st April Constantinople was in sight and, transferring to
the Sultan's yacht, the Prince and his party passed the entrance
to the Golden Horn and landed beside the Saleh Palace which the
Sultan had placed at the Prince's disposal.   The Prince, attended
by the British Ambassador, Sir Henry George Elliot, at once
called on the Sultan, who strained every nerve to prove his
appreciation of the personal honour and the political expectations
excited by the Prince's visit.   For the first time he sacrificed
many traditional usages.   Ladies, and those Christian ladies,
were included amongst his guests at an imposing banquet which
he gave the royal visitors at his palace of Dolmabakshi.   On no
former occasion had the Sultan invited to his table any guest
save his Grand Vizier.   Now his guests numbered twenty-four,
of whom twelve alone were Turks.   The other twelve included,
besides the Prince and Princess, the British and Russian Ambassadors with their wives, the French Ambassador and the Austrian
Nuncio.   Though the dishes were alternately Turkish and
French, the dinner was served *à l'Européenne*.   The Sultan led
in the Princess of Wales, and the Prince the wife of the Russian
Ambassador, M. Ignatiev, an expert explorer of Central Asia.
The company greatly interested the Prince, and he lost no time
in speaking to M. Ignatiev of his adventures in a region where
England had no desire for an extension of Russian travel.   The
Sultan looked pleased, but spoke little, lamenting through his
interpreter that he could speak no language but his own.   The
innovation in procedure was a bold breach of Mohammedan
custom and it offended pious co-religionists, but it evinced
the host's burning anxiety to make a good impression on his

visitors. A few days later the Sultan further illustrated his breadth of mind by attending, with a great train of officers of state, a state ball at the British Embassy in honour of the Prince and Princess. He had attended such a function in London. Now he expressed to his royal visitors his regrets that his religion did not allow him personally to offer them a like entertainment. The Prince and Princess found opportunities during their time at Constantinople for much informal recreation. They visited the bazaars like ordinary tourists, taking for the occasion the names of Mr. and Mrs. Williams. "Mr. Williams," an eye-witness reported, "enjoyed a pipe, and Mrs. Williams fascinated the hardest bargainer in all Stamboul." On the 10th April the visit came to an end with a farewell déjeuner by the Sultan, again at the palace of Dolmabakshi.

The Sultan and the Prince were to meet only once again, and that a few days later, when the Prince left Turkish waters after a visit to the Crimea. Much tribulation was to fall on the Prince's Turkish host soon after the final parting. Despite his courteous bearing to his guests and his challenge in their honour of the social customs of his religion, he clung with fatal obstinacy to degenerate methods of government which ultimately exasperated beyond endurance not only the public sense of Europe, but a formidable section of his own subjects. He was one of the many occupants of his throne who were to be deposed and, after deposition, to be assassinated.

VI

The Prince's vivid interest in the Crimean War led him to spend a Sunday afternoon while at Constantinople in the British cemetery at Scutari where lay buried many of the military victims of the war. On leaving the city he gratified a long-cherished wish of inspecting the Crimean battlefields and cemeteries. M. Ignatiev, the Russian Ambassador, encouraged the project, and the Tsar, in conciliatory mood, directed the Russian authorities to render assistance. The *Ariadne* carried the Prince and his companions through the Bosphorus and the Black Sea to the Crimea, and on 12th April the ship anchored in the harbour of Sebastopol, where Sir Andrew Buchanan, the British Ambassador, joined the party from St. Petersburg.

William Howard Russell, with whom the Prince had parted at

Cairo, also arrived to guide him over ground with which he was 1869 thoroughly familiar. A three days' tour was made by carriage Ætat. 27 under the general direction of Aide-de-Camp General de Kotzebue, Governor of New Russia and Bessarabia and the Commander of the Forces of the military district of Odessa. From Sebastopol the party drove to Balaclava and the Alma. The ruins of the war were still unrepaired, and it was with much emotion that the Prince inspected scenes like the Redan ; the Valley of the Shadow of Death, where the Light Brigade had met disaster ; the Malakoff Tower, in the ditch of which 4000 Frenchmen were interred ; and the room at the English headquarters where Lord Raglan died. The night of the 14th was spent, on the Tsar's invitation, at the Imperial Palace at Livadia, which the Prince and Princess were to revisit on a more mournful errand a quarter of a century later. On the 15th they re-embarked on the *Ariadne*, after exchanging complimentary telegrams with the Tsar and with his chief minister, Prince Gortschakoff. Off the Bosphorus, on the 16th, the Sultan, still hopeful of good relations through the Prince with the British government, came aboard to take his final leave.

Sail was set for Greece, where a pleasant eleven days (April 20–May 1) were spent at Athens and Corfu with King George and his family. At Brindisi the Prince and Princess took train for Paris by way of the Mont Cenis tunnel, and a six days' sojourn at Paris brought them to London on the 12th May, after a total absence of seven months. The first-hand knowledge which the Prince had gathered through eye and ear in many lands lent a fresh alertness alike to his political hopes and to his political fears in the years at hand.

CHAPTER XVIII

THE FRANCO-GERMAN WAR, 1870–1871

I

1870 Ætat. 28 THE Prince was about to suffer greater anxiety and perplexity than any which international affairs had yet cost him. France and Germany, the two continental countries whose fortunes absorbed for life his closest attention, put, in July 1870, their traditional rivalry once more to the arbitrament of the sword.

It was the domestic difficulties of Spain, which the Prince had long watched with concern,[1] that formed the ostensible cause of the outbreak of the Franco-German War. Throughout 1867 the discontent in the Peninsula with the corrupt rule of Queen Isabella was driving her subjects into revolt. Next year a military rising succeeded in driving the Queen from her throne, and at the end of September 1868 she was a refugee in France. Her flight was followed by fierce internal dissensions over the form which the new government of Spain should assume. There was a powerful republican party, while the supporters of a monarchy were hopelessly divided as to the choice of a successor to the deposed sovereign. On 4th October 1868 the Prince wrote to his mother :

> The Spanish Revolution is as you say a sad thing, but I think for the last two years every one could have foretold it sooner or later. I am only surprised they allowed the Queen to remain in Spain as long as she did, as besides being one of the worst sovereigns in Europe, her character is, I fear, very indifferent. The whole country, too, is in a state of poverty, disaffection, is priest-ridden and, to use a common expression, "rotten to the core."

[1] See p. 65 *supra*.

The Prince had his own notion, which recalled past controversy, as to how the vacant throne should be filled. "I shall be very curious to hear if the Duke of Montpensier [King Louis Philippe's younger son and ex-Queen Isabella's brother-in-law] will be asked to become king." The Prince had visited Montpensier on his tour in Spain in 1859. At the same time the Prince confessed a preference for Montpensier's brother, the Duc d'Aumale, whom he knew well in his English exile. "What an excellent thing," he wrote, "the Duc d'Aumale's election would be, but the Emperor N. would never stand it, I should think."

Spain proved wholly unable to settle her domestic dissensions, and the persistent commotion throughout the country impelled France, her neighbour, to announce early in 1870, an intention to intervene. To the dismay of the French Government, Prussia retorted with an intimation that she proposed to place on the Spanish throne a candidate of her own choosing. At Bismarck's bidding the King of Prussia offered the Spanish crown to Prince Leopold of Hohenzollern-Sigmaringen, heir of the younger branch of the Prussian royal house. Prince Leopold's younger brother, Charles had, through the machinations of Prussia and to the disgust of Europe, been elected King of Rumania on May 12, 1866. It was clearly Bismarck's intention to make his brother Leopold also serve the turn of Prussian aggrandisement. On the 4th July 1870 Prince Leopold accepted the Prussian nomination.

Prussia's high-handed action had a strong personal interest for the Prince. With Prince Leopold, whose wife Antonia was sister of the Prince's acquaintance and distant kinsman, King Luis of Portugal, he was on terms of intimacy, and on his journeys through Germany he frequently paused at Düsseldorf to enjoy the congenial hospitality of Prince Leopold, his father and family.[1] But despite his affection for Prince Leopold the Prince scented mischief in Bismarck's designs and deplored his friend's surrender to the Prussian minister's blandishments. Prince Leopold's sister Marie was wife of the Comte de Flandres,

---

[1] The marriages of the children of Prince Karl Anton, the reigning Prince of Hohenzollern-Sigmaringen, created special ties between this German family and the Prince of Wales. Another daughter, Stephanie, was the short-lived wife of Dom Pedro V. of Portugal, brother of King Luis (see p. 70 *supra*), while the Comte de Flandres, second surviving son of old King Leopold I. of Belgium, married Prince Karl Anton's daughter, Marie (on April 25, 1867).

King Leopold II.'s brother. Queen Victoria appealed to the Comte de Flandres (July 6, 1870) to dissuade Prince Leopold from the perilous course on which he was entering.

At the moment there took place in the control of the British Foreign Office a change which extended the Prince's opportunities of first-hand knowledge of foreign affairs. The Foreign Secretary, Lord Clarendon, had just died and his place was at once filled by Lord Granville. The Prince had been on familiar and confidential terms with Lord Granville from childhood, and he could discuss politics with him more volubly and frankly than with any of his predecessors. On assuming office, Lord Granville made the notorious declaration that no cloud obscured the peace of Europe. The first business with which he was called upon to deal was Prince Leopold's candidature for the Spanish Crown, and he was fortunately able to write to the Prince of Wales on the 10th July that the provocative nomination had been withdrawn by Prussia. Very promptly the Prince sent Lord Granville "hearty congratulations to you and the country on the excellent news you have been kind enough to send me. Let us trust that the clouds that have overshadowed Europe may be dispersed without their bursting over our heads."

The danger was far from dispelled. Napoleon III. accepted Prince Leopold's withdrawal with reservations. He asked for a guarantee against a repetition of the offence. Bismarck resented the demand and assumed a defiant attitude. France resorted to the desperate expedient of declaring war on 15th July. There was a dinner-party at Marlborough House that night. Delane, the editor of *The Times*, was one of the Prince's guests. The startling news was forwarded to Delane from *The Times* office while the dinner was in progress, and he communicated it at once to his host.[1] The Prince was profoundly disturbed.

Mr. Gladstone's government, after an eleventh-hour offer to mediate which neither party took seriously, at once proclaimed England's neutrality. A few days later Mr. Gladstone announced that if the armies of either France or Prussia violated the neutrality of Belgium, Great Britain would co-operate with the other for its defence, without taking part in the general operations of the war.

[1] Lady Wester-Wemyss's *Memoirs and Letters of Sir Robert Morier* (1911), vol. ii.

II

The proclamation of war abroad and of neutrality at home 1870 excited in the Prince conflicting emotions. He had come into Ætat. 28 close personal contact with both belligerents. His private friendships were warm with the leading combatants on either side. He had lately accepted marked attentions, not only from the Emperor Napoleon, but also from King William of Prussia. His friend and brother-in-law, the Crown Prince of Prussia, was destined for high command in the German army of assault. Yet his sympathy with the life and sentiment of France and his dislike of Prussian ambitions were both already parts of his nature.

Disagreements in the Prince's family circle were inevitable. His eldest sister, the Crown Princess, whatever her doubts of Bismarck's policy, now fervently identified herself with the Prussian cause. His mother, in her private intercourse and correspondence, did not conceal her German leanings. Before the fighting began, the Queen and her eldest daughter acknowledged a nervous apprehension that Germany would be defeated. The Prince expressed his confidence that Germany would be well "able to hold her own," but he showed the bitterness of his heart when he added that the Crown Princess's fears of a French victory would the better enable her to realise "what the feelings of little Denmark must have been when they heard that the armies of Prussia and Austria were against them" (Prince to Queen, July 20 and 21, 1870).

Queen Victoria was firm in the belief that France was the aggressor and that Germany was the injured party to the quarrel. She averred that Germany was forced by French insolence into a war of liberation, which was as righteous an obligation for Germany now as it had been in 1813. While she pointed out to the King of Prussia that she was bound by the declared neutrality of her government, she felt the sting of his reproaches for her country's refusal of aid. Personally she regretted that Prussians and Englishmen were not, as at Waterloo, resisting the French side by side. Germany stood, in her eyes, for "civilisation, liberty, order, and unity," while France stood for "despotism, corruption, immorality, and aggression." The Prince Consort had foreseen "the necessity that this vainglorious and immoral

people should be put down." When the fortunes of war inclined
against France the Queen saw the finger of God in French humiliation, and declared that France was earning a just retribution.
Carlyle denounced the sins of France and lauded the virtues of
Germany with scarcely less vehemence.

To the Prince such opinions were highly uncongenial. He
acknowledged some force in Gladstone's verdict: "The two
moving spirits on the respective sides, Napoleon and Bismarck,
are nearly on a par." But despite his effort to respect with outward correctness the calls of official neutrality, his private feelings
inclined too ardently towards France to spare him public and
private embarrassment. Prussia showed a sensitiveness to his
opinion which could not fail to provoke misunderstanding. The
Prince appreciated the force of the Crown Princess's remark that
it was "a most trying time for those who are both German and
English."

Within three days of the declaration of war the Court and
government circles at Berlin were, on rather flimsy grounds,
declaiming against the Prince's French partiality. The Prince
fell under the suspicion of the Prussian Ambassador in London,
Count von Bernstorff, between whom and himself no love had
been lost in their previous intercourse. Some irresponsible
gossip, testifying to the Prince's French leanings, was embodied
in a despatch to Berlin. The Prince had dined (Bernstorff's
story ran) at the French Ambassador's in London immediately
after the outbreak of war, and had there expressed his hopes of
Prussia's defeat. He had spoken in the same sense to a fellow-
guest, the Austrian Ambassador in London, Count Apponyi,
who had vaguely enlisted the Prince's sympathy with a proposal
for an alliance of Austria with France. Bernstorff's tale flamed
through the Prussian Court, and greatly moved the Crown
Princess, who reported her brother's alleged indiscretion to her
mother. As soon as the matter came to the Prince's notice he
flatly denied the truth of the story, in the form at any rate in
which Bernstorff had promulgated it.

To Mr. Gladstone, the Prime Minister, he wrote:

I think it right to inform you that the Prussian Ambassador
has thought fit to inform my sister, the Crown Princess, of
statements supposed to have been made by me at a dinner
lately given by the French Ambassador very derogatory of

Prussia. I beg to assure you that these statements are without any foundation (July 21).

Mr. Gladstone thought that "the authority on which Bernstorff's statements are made should be investigated." Count Apponyi was emphatic in denial that at the dinner-party in question he had discussed politics with the Prince.

The Queen desired Lord Granville to send to Berlin a contradiction of a "story which may be productive of many bad consequences and much ill-feeling if allowed to pass uncontradicted." Lord Granville preferred that the Prince should send a contradiction to his sister, who declared that her brother's words were "quoted everywhere" in Germany. Mr. Francis Knollys, the Prince's secretary, called on Bernstorff, and in his master's behalf disclaimed any word implying "satisfaction at the idea that the Prussians would be unsuccessful in the approaching war." The close family connection which the Prince "enjoyed with Prussia" would not allow of such a view. The ambassador equivocated, but professed to accept the Prince's assurances.

As the controversy proceeded the Queen took her son's part. "Bernstorff," she wrote to Lord Granville, "always tries to calumniate the Court and our family whenever he can." To the Crown Princess the Queen wrote of Bernstorff as "a shocking mischief-maker. He ought in the interests of both countries to be removed." But the German critics were unsatisfied, and Bismarck, within a few weeks, bluntly asserted that Prussian aspirations had a foe in the heir to the British Crown.

A domestic incident in the Prince's affairs was also reckoned by the Queen and the government to add fresh trouble. A week before the declaration of war the Princess of Wales had arrived in Denmark on what was intended to be a long stay with her parents. There was much uncertainty as to the intentions of Denmark in the coming conflict. France was persuading her to avenge her wrongs by joining in an attack on Prussia. On the declaration of war the Queen and Mr. Gladstone insisted that the Princess's visit to Denmark should be brought to a summary close, and that the Prince should at once leave for Denmark to escort her home. In a personal interview Mr. Gladstone warned the Prince that "his stay at Copenhagen at this moment might be the subject of comment and suspicion," and bade him maintain "an extreme reserve in regard to the expression of opinion on the causes of this miserable war, or the merits of the respective parties to the quarrel."

The Prince made a hurried journey to Copenhagen at the end of July, and was back in England with the Princess by 3rd August. He at once reported orally to Gladstone and Granville on the Danish situation. Despite his prepossessions, he had become firmly convinced that Denmark's safety required her to keep out of the war. Writing to the Queen he pointed out:

The position of Denmark is just now a very critical one. She has proclaimed her neutrality, and is most anxious to adhere strictly to it. At least the King and government are, but they don't know how long that neutrality may last unless the great neutral powers use a strong pressure on France to observe that neutrality, as the French are doing their utmost to drag Denmark into the war, and if they are found to go with France, then later I feel sure Germany will "swallow them up." . . . The people are very strong for a French alliance, and the government may not be able to resist.

A week later the Prince reached Abergeldie Castle for the autumn vacation, but his thought was concentrated on the battlefields of France. Before the end of the first month of war the successes of the German armies in the field foretold the ultimate result. A decisive German victory was won as early as 6th August at Wörth by the army commanded by the Prince's brother-in-law, the Crown Prince, who defeated the French army of the Rhine under Marshal MacMahon. "This defeat," wrote the Prince to Granville, "will be a terrible blow to the Emperor, and the feeling at Paris is easier imagined than described." The weeks that followed brought torturing anxiety to all English friends of France. Some six days after Wörth, Marshal Bazaine collected the greater part of the French army outside Metz, and after a series of sanguinary engagements was almost completely surrounded by the foe. Meanwhile the Emperor managed to join other French forces under the command of Marshal MacMahon at Châlons. It was at once seen to be doubtful whether they could hold their own.

III

The avalanche of French disasters and the heavy losses of life on both sides caused the Prince throughout this month of August acute distress. During the middle week his mother forwarded to him a descriptive letter from Lord Lyons in Paris, and in reply he lamented the "sad state of things there." "There will, I suppose," he proceeded, "be a battle near Châlons, and if the French are again beaten, which seems inevitable, the war must come to an end. The army having been beaten now so often, the wretched Garde Mobile will become easy victims, and the battle more like a 'battue,' and it is really too dreadful to think of."

The desperate situation of France roused to fever-heat the Prince's innate passion in great crises "to be of use." His thoughts ran on a personal effort to abate the terrors of the struggle. On 21st August he implored the Queen, not merely herself to intervene in the cause of peace, but to authorise him to get into personal touch with the leaders on either side, with both the Emperor Napoleon and King William of Prussia in order to bring about a pacification. Writing from Abergeldie Castle he exclaimed (August 21):

If only something could be done to stop this terrible war. Could not England, backed up by the other neutral powers, now step in, to try and induce the belligerents to come to terms, as it might yet save the lives of some thousands of fellows? I cannot bear sitting here and doing nothing, whilst all this bloodshed is going on. How I wish you could send me with letters to the Emperor and King of Prussia, with friendly advice, even if it ultimately failed. I would gladly go any distance, as I cannot help feeling restless when so many one knows and likes are exposed to such dangers.

The Queen and her advisers deemed the Prince's "anxiety to be of use" to be highly creditable to him, but to be impossible of practical application. Neither party would consider mediation at this stage. The Queen added that she feared the Prince of Wales's position "would make it impossible, even if he were personally fitted for such a very difficult task, to undertake such a mission." Even the Prince Consort could have done nothing at this juncture, although preliminary advice from him might possibly have prevented much which had happened during the

1870
Ætat. 28

1870
Ætat. 28

past eight years, and have saved the world great misery. Reluctantly the Prince accepted Lord Granville's conclusion, "that the moment has not yet arrived for us to offer our services as peacemakers."

"I quite understand," the Prince wrote to the Queen (August 27, 1870), "it is hardly yet the moment for us to undertake the task of mediator, although I hope that before long we may be of use. I only hope, dear Mama, you will not forget my offer if I can be of any use. These times are of such momentous interest that my greatest ambition would be to play however small a part especially if good would come out of it. . . . Let us only hope that this bloody campaign may be now rapidly drawing to a close, although what may yet happen we cannot tell."

On 1st September there came for France the crowning tragedy of Sedan, where the Emperor Napoleon and MacMahon's army of 100,000 men surrendered to the enemy. The Emperor was carried prisoner to Wilhelmshöhe in Cassel. In Paris the news brought about a revolution, which declared the imperial régime at an end, and set a Republic in its place. The Empress Eugénie, the friend and hostess of the Prince, had acted as Regent since her husband's departure for the front, and was now in imminent personal danger. In disguise she escaped to the coast at Deauville, where she succeeded in persuading an Englishman, Sir John Burgoyne, whose yacht happened to be lying in the harbour, to bring her to the Isle of Wight (September 9). Her son, the Prince Imperial, managed with his tutor to reach England a few days later through Belgium. The Empress's arrival in England was privately communicated by Lord Granville to both the Queen and the Prince, but for the next few weeks little was known of her movements. At first she contemplated staying in England only a few days, but before long a sympathiser offered her a permanent residence, Campden Place, at Chislehurst.

The turn of fortune which had overwhelmed the Emperor and Empress touched the Prince to the quick. Ignorant of the Empress's plans, he impulsively offered to provide her with a home. Late in September he was staying with his intimate friends, the Duke and Duchess of Sutherland, at Dunrobin Castle, in Sutherlandshire, and he sent to the Empress, by the hands of his equerry, Lieutenant-Colonel Keppel, the following letter :

DUNROBIN CASTLE,
SUTHERLAND, *2nd October* 1870.

MADAME—J'ai remis jusqu'à present d'écrire à Votre Majesté
craignant de Vous importuner au premier moment de Votre
arrivée en Angleterre avec une lettre, ayant aussi appris que
Votre Majesté n'y resterait que quelques jours; mais comme
j'entends que Votre M. s'est décidée à faire un plus long séjour
dans mon pays je ne puis remettre plus longtemps d'exprimer
à V. M. ma plus vive sympathie aux grandes épreuves et toutes
les affreuses inquiétudes par lesquelles V. M. ainsi que l'Empereur
a du passer.

J'espère que V. M. ne doutera jamais des sentimens de reconnaissance dont je suis rempli et que je garderai toujours en
rappelant toutes les preuves de bonté et d'amitié que Vous
avez bien voulu me témoigner depuis 1855. Croyez-moi, Madame,
j'en suis bien sensible, et je ne serais que trop heureux si jamais
l'occasion se présenterait que je pourrais d'aucune manière être
utile à V. M.

La Princesse et moi ayant pensé qu'une résidence près de
Londres Vous serait agréable, j'ose offrir à V. M. notre Maison
de campagne "*Chiswick*" qui serait entièrement à la disposition
de V. M. et nous serions bien heureux si Vous l'accepteriez.[1]

J'ai prié mon aide de camp, le Colonel Keppel, qui est chargé
de cette lettre à V. M., de prendre Vos ordres.

J'espère que V. M. a des bonnes nouvelles de l'Empereur, et
en Vous priant de me rappeler au bon souvenir du Prince Impérial,
je suis, Madame, de V. M. le bon frère et cousin,

ALBERT EDWARD.

1870
—
Ætat. 28

Unfriendly views were taken of the Prince's step. The
Prince forwarded to Lord Granville a copy of his letter to the
Empress. The Foreign Secretary expressed admiration of its
tone and style, but doubted its prudence. He was unmoved by
the Prince's plea that "though the Queen might find some
difficulty in offering a house there surely could be no objection
to *our* doing so." From all sides indeed came protests. Lord
Hatherley, the Lord Chancellor, wrote to the Prince that in view
of England's coming recognition of the new Republican Government his offer might well be misunderstood. When the Prince
informed Queen Victoria of his action she took exception to what

---

[1] Chiswick House, which belonged to the Duke of Devonshire, had been
lent to the Prince. The gardens were the scene, during the past and the succeeding seasons, of many largely attended garden parties, under the auspices of
the Prince and Princess.

1870

Ætat. 28

she regarded as a presumptuous indiscretion. The moment of the Prince's intervention was rendered peculiarly inopportune, the Queen pointed out, by a mysterious visit which had just been paid to the Empress in England by one of her husband's generals, Bourbaki. General Bourbaki had escaped in disguise from the siege of Metz with the connivance of Marshal Bazaine (and, it was suspected, of Bismarck), in order, it was alleged, to enlist the Empress's assistance in a French plot for a restoration of the Empire.[1] The Empress protested to the Queen her innocence of any political conspiracy; she assured her that Bourbaki's visit was one of Bismarck's tricks, and that she alone looked for a restoration of peace to the counsels of the neutral powers. The Empress, however, relieved the strain of the situation by promptly declining the Prince's offer of Chiswick House, on the grounds that she had already taken Campden Place, where she sought "tranquillity and calm."

IV

The Prince and Princess quickly paid the desolate Empress at Chislehurst a visit of sympathy and condolence. Nor was the Queen backward, in spite of her recent reservations, in showing pity for the fallen sovereign. On 30th November she followed the example of her son and daughter-in-law, and sought in person to console the refugee.

Meanwhile, early in September 1870, Queen Victoria, regarding further resistance on France's part as hopeless, deemed it opportune to ask the King of Prussia to offer France reasonable terms. With Queen Augusta of Prussia Queen Victoria was always in confidential relations. From her the Queen now first learned (Sept. 17, 1870) that Germany regarded the cession by France of Alsace and Lorraine to be an essential condition of peace, a decision which was to bear evil fruit.[2]

The German armies were now rapidly moving on Paris. On the 19th September 1870 the city was completely surrounded. An abortive meeting between Bismarck and Jules Favre, the head

[1] Du Barail, *Mes Souvenirs, 1820–70*, iii. 211 *seq.*

[2] On the 13th September M. Thiers, as the representative of the French provisional Republican Government, arrived in London with a view to soliciting the English government's mediation, but nothing resulted from his efforts in London or from subsequent visits to Vienna and St. Petersburg.

of the new French government, for the discussion of an armistice followed next day. Bismarck insisted on the cession of the two provinces, and the Frenchman replied that France would cede no inch of her territory nor a stone of any of her fortresses. The city of Paris at once organised a determined defence. The Prince was kept informed of the negotiations, and accepted his mother's view that France in her desperate position was unwise to reject unconditionally Prussia's proposals. Queen Victoria complained of France's bombastic attitude, and impatiently disclaimed any intention of further interference. She warned her son anew against doing anything which might alienate Germany, "who resents our neutrality." "A powerful Germany," she wrote on the 9th September, "can never be dangerous to England, but the very reverse, and our great object should therefore be to have her friendly and cordial towards us."

The part which the Prince played at this period in a subsidiary episode of the warfare effectively illustrates his fidelity in friendship. The Marquis de Galliffet—an efficient soldier, a shrewd judge of affairs, and an expert in the social diversions, riding, dancing, card-playing—had already won the Prince's admiration both in London and at the imperial Court. In the early stages of the Franco-German War the marquis greatly distinguished himself. In command of the second brigade of General Margueritte's division of light cavalry, he made at Sedan an adventurous charge which was one of the redeeming features of that unlucky engagement. The close of the battle saw Galliffet a prisoner in German hands, and he was confined in the castle of Coblenz. Galliffet yearned to resume his place in his country's fighting line, and his thoughts turned for rescue to his friends in England, chief among whom he reckoned the Prince of Wales. An appeal from Galliffet to the Prince to procure his exchange was forwarded by the Governor of Coblenz through the Duchess of Manchester, who belonged to the Prince's circle of friends. It reached the Prince's hands while he was staying at Dunrobin Castle. Galliffet's epistle ran thus:

Coblenz,
27th September 1870.

Monseigneur—Je prie instamment et avec respect Votre Altesse Royale de s'intéresser pour quelques minutes à un pauvre prisonnier, qui rougit de vivre dans un coin, pendant que ses compatriotes se font tuer pour la défense du sol français. Je demande en vain, à tous les échos la réponse d'une demande d'échange que j'ai adressée il y a trois semaines.

Il peut se faire qu'un général de Brigade ou Colonel, ou tout autre officier de l'Armée Prussienne, soit fait prisonnier. Dans ce cas il serait facile à Votre Altesse Royale d'obtenir la faveur qu'un échange ait lieu entre lui et moi. Si Votre Altesse Royale recommandait cette demande à S.A.R. le Prince Royal de Prusse, j'aurai une vraie chance de réussir.

Je serai d'autant plus reconnaissant à V.A.R. que si je reste ici jusqu'à la fin de la guerre il ne me paraîtra pas permi de rentrer avec une telle honte dans mon pays. Je crois à la durée de la guerre ; les conditions de paix imposées par un ogre le Cte. Bismark sont inacceptables.

Je prie Votre Altesse Royale de vouloir bien me pardonner cette demande et de me croire son très respectueux et dès aujourd'hui reconnaissant serviteur,

GALLIFFET.
Prisonnier de guerre,
COBLENZ.

The Prince promptly replied :

DUNROBIN CASTLE,
SUTHERLAND, *October* 9/70.

MON CHER GALLIFFET—Je viens de recevoir votre lettre, que la Dsse. de Manchester m'a fait parvenir et je vous en remercie mille fois. Je puis très bien comprendre avec quelle empressement vous désirez obtenir un échange—et vous pouvez être certain que je ferai tout mon possible de plaider votre cause.

J'expédie cette lettre à Lord Loftus notre ambassadeur à Berlin, en lui priant en même temps de faire toutes les démarches possibles pour votre échange. Mais quant à y réussir je crains que cela ne soit une question assez douteuse.

J'entends de tous côtés combien vous vous êtes distingué à la guerre et que la charge de Cavalerie que vous avez commandé a été superbe.

Adieu, mon cher Galliffet. Je vous souhaite mes meilleurs vœux et je vous prie de me croire votre bien sincère ami,
A. E.

The Prince left no stone unturned to procure the French officer's exchange. He at once took counsel with Lord Granville : "Should I write to Bernstorff and ask him to communicate with the Crown Prince of Prussia on the subject or will you kindly speak to that amiable individual yourself ?" Apart from some anxiety about his wife and children, of which Galliffet had written

to the Duchess of Manchester, the Prince was of opinion that
"Galliffet's only wish was" to "mourir pour sa patrie." Lord
Granville readily offered to solicit Bernstorff's courtesy in forwarding to the Prussian royal family any appeal in Galliffet's
behalf which the Prince cared to send. The Prince promptly
framed a letter to the King of Prussia, but the surly ambassador
objected that the Prince's intervention was irregular and declined
to transmit the epistle to his sovereign. The Prince confessed
himself baulked, but he let Galliffet know that he had done what
he could. To criticism of his action in his own circle he made the
characteristic retort: "When one's friends are down in their luck
one would wish to help them if one can." Galliffet's gratitude was
not impaired by the Prince's failure, nor was his native cheerfulness
altogether overcast by similar defeats at the hands of M. Gambetta,
of the German headquarters staff at Versailles, and of highly
placed personages in Vienna, to all of whom he pleaded for freedom. To the Prince of Wales he continued to write from captivity
long letters of sprightly reflection which supplied the Prince
with valuable conversational ammunition.[1] He well knew that
he was pouring his confidences into a sympathetic ear. His
imprisonment lasted until the preliminaries of peace were signed
by Thiers and Bismarck on the 1st March 1871. Then Galliffet
returned to his own country and placed his sword at the disposal
of the new Republic, prominently aiding in the overthrow of
the anarchist Commune which devastated Paris from the end
of March to the end of May 1871. There was no cessation in

1870
Ætat. 28

[1] Writing to the Prince on 31st October from Ems, where he was sent from
Coblenz for change of air, Galliffet expressed the hope that in years to come
he might still fight as a simple soldier with his fellow-countrymen. He defended the course which Marshal MacMahon had taken at Sedan; the Marshal
had tried loyally to carry out the impossible orders of the civil authorities.
For MacMahon he remarked to the Prince, "nous conservons les mêmes
sentiments." Galliffet reported a visit to the Emperor Napoleon III. at
Wilhelmshöhe, whose depression of spirit had not affected his health. He
justified the capitulation of Metz, while he deeply regretted it. He hoped for
an early peace, but had no belief in the generosity of Prussia, and was confident
that if Alsace and Lorraine had to be abandoned to Germany, France would
in due time "seek to reverse the defeat and the annexation." He wrote
ironically of the new Republic, and of British neutrality. He believed that
Russia might take advantage of the war to pay a visit to Constantinople, and
made touching reference to the perils of his wife, who was at Paris between
the claws of the revolutionary Parisians and those of the Prussians, and he
addressed his prayers to St. Bombard, St. Krupp, and company that M. von
Moltke might spare her innocent head. The General separated from his wife
in later years, but the Prince continued on the best of terms with both.

the intimate intercourse between the Prince and his gallant French friend till the latter's death a year before his own.

In another negotiation of mercy in which the Prince of Wales engaged with his customary zeal during the Franco-German War, he met with better success than in his efforts on Galliffet's behalf. After the German investment of Paris, M. Rosencrantz, a secretary of the Danish legation there, fell fatally ill. The sick man's wife sought permission to pass through the German lines, in order to reach her husband's deathbed. General von Moltke, the German commander-in-chief, promptly refused her permission. The Prince's influence was solicited on the lady's behalf; at his urgent entreaty his old friend, Mr. Odo Russell, who was at Versailles at the German headquarters on a special mission from the English Foreign Office, was instructed to protest to Bismarck against Moltke's decision. Contrary to expectation Bismarck lent a favourable ear to the Prince's appeal, and the Prince had the satisfaction of learning that owing to his intervention the Danish diplomatist's last moments were soothed by his wife's presence.

V

At the end of October 1870 the Prince's attention was partially diverted from the progress of the war in France to Russia's high-handed action in regard to the Black Sea.[1] While the Russian negotiation was running its unsatisfactory course, the French defeat became complete. The sufferings of France at the ruthless hands of the German conqueror at length moved in the Queen something of her son's pity. The protracted siege of Paris awoke his mother's sympathy with the French people. As early as 25th October she telegraphed to Queen Augusta that she was doing her utmost to arrange an armistice, in the hope of abridging the siege which had then lasted some six weeks. When, two months later, the Germans threatened to bombard the city unless it surrendered at once, Queen Victoria appealed to Queen Augusta and the Crown Princess to use their influence with Bismarck to spare the French capital this crowning ignominy. The feminine influence succeeded in postponing the evil day for two weeks; but Bismarck, who chafed against "petticoat interference," had his way early in January, when Paris was subjected

[1] See p. 275 *supra*.

to the final torture. The proclamation, with imposing ceremony,
on 18th January in the palace at Versailles of the King of Prussia
as German Emperor brought home to the Queen and the Prince
the effect of the war on the realisation of the Prussian dream of
ascendancy in Europe. Paris capitulated ten days later, and
France was in no position to refuse the onerous terms which
Bismarck soon dictated at Frankfort-on-the-Main.

Queen Victoria's sympathy with the sufferings of France
failed to reconcile her to her subjects' growing animosity against
Germany, and she warned her eldest son against his frankly
expressed displays of anxiety to give France material assistance
in her sore need. On the 2nd January the Prince thought to
aid a fund "for sending corn to French farmers for relief of the
peasantry." He invited Lord Granville's opinion, and the
Foreign Secretary peremptorily bade him avoid such action.
Prussian susceptibility in regard to his French proclivities was
now more acute than ever. The Prussians had lately raided the
Château of Cerçay near Versailles, belonging to M. Rouher, who
was Napoleon III.'s Minister of State from 1863 until the fall
of the Empire. Lord Granville was informed that Rouher's
papers contained compromising reports of the Prince's conversations with Prince de La Tour d'Auvergne, the French Ambassador
in London, throughout which the Prince was represented as
expressing bitter hostility to Prussia. "Prussia," Lord Granville
remarked, "is likely to misinterpret anything which the Prince
does." [1]

Throughout the war the Prince was kept well supplied with

---

[1] M. Rouher, fearful of a popular rising in Paris, had carried off to his
château at Cerçay a large collection of State papers belonging, not only to the
Foreign Office, but also to the cabinet of the Emperor. All the papers, including M. Rouher's private correspondence, were, after his château was raided
by Prussian troops, sent by Prince Bismarck's direction to the Foreign Office
at Berlin, and they remained there till the close of the war 1914-18. By
article 245 of the Treaty of Versailles of 1919 the Cerçay collection was restored
by Germany to the French Foreign Office. An "inventaire" is printed in
Les Origines diplomatiques de la guerre de 1870-71, tome xii. (Paris, 1921),
pp. 408-446. The papers have not yet been exhaustively examined. While
the collection was in Berlin some fragments, mainly dealing with the secret
efforts of the Emperor Napoleon to annex Belgium and to detach the southern
German states from Prussia, were published by the German government in
1871 and the following years. In 1911 Professor Ruville, of Halle University,
based on the Cerçay documents his *La Restauration de l'Empire Allemand:
Le Rôle de la Bavière* (French translation: with an introduction by Joseph
Reinach).

first-hand information, especially that reaching England from
German headquarters.   The Queen gave him access to many
of the communications which were sent her by the Crown
Princess and other German kinsfolk.   Her son-in-law, the
Crown Prince, regularly forwarded to her his private journal,
and she lent it to her son.   The Prince described it as "naturally
and plainly written.   I only wish all his countrymen had as
pleasant a 'gemüth' (disposition) as he has."   The Prince
had also a specially efficient informant in his friend W. H.
Russell, who was correspondent of *The Times* at the Crown
Prince's headquarters, and who regularly visited the Prince
whenever he was on leave in London.

There was a disposition among some ardent English friends
of France to attribute to all members of the royal family, including the Prince, the Queen's Teutonic sentiments, and a
strange ambiguity developed in the public mind at the end of
the war as to the Prince's precise attitude to suffering France.
Late in February 1871, while peace was in process of negotiation, the whisper ran in England that the English royal family
were sending to the Crown Prince congratulatory messages on
the humiliation of France.   The newspapers in London made
play with the rumour, and the *Pall Mall Gazette* (February 23,
1871), of which Frederick Greenwood, an enthusiastic votary
of France, was editor, comprehensively indicted the Queen and
her family of a breach of neutrality in private correspondence
with the King of Prussia, the Crown Prince, and other chiefs of
the victorious German army.   Sir Henry Hoare, a member of
Parliament for Norwich, who, with Sir Charles Dilke and a few
other colleagues, lost no opportunity of manifesting their pity for
France in her distress, brought the alleged German predilections of the Queen and her family to the notice of the House of
Commons (February 24).   Sir Henry reported that Captain Henry
M. Hozier, a Queen's messenger attached to the Foreign Office, had
"been charged with messages to the Crown Prince of Germany
from Her Majesty, the Prince of Wales, and the Duke of Cambridge, of congratulation upon the successes won by his army."[1]

Mr. Gladstone sought to allay the storm by a stream of
dialectical subtleties.   He pointed out that the English royal
family was naturally solicitous about the health of their Prussian

[1] *Hansard*, third series, vol. 204, cols. 866–8.

friends and kindred at the close of a strenuous campaign which 1871
had strained their physical and nervous powers. The Foreign Ætat. 29
Office in London was in constant communication with its
representative, Mr. Odo Russell, at Versailles, and the Queen
and some of her children and relatives had availed themselves
of Mr. Russell's presence to send by the hand of a Foreign Office
messenger inoffensive personal greetings such as kinsfolk were
in the habit of exchanging.

The Prince of Wales was irritated by the popular agitation,
which did him signal injustice. For the private information
of the Foreign Minister, Lord Granville, he penned in his own
hand a full statement of his position in the affair. Captain
Hozier, a Foreign Office messenger, had called on him without
notice to tell him that he was taking despatches to Versailles.

" He asked me," wrote the Prince, " whether he could be
the bearer of any letters to the Crown Prince or others. I said
I had none, but I wished to be affectionately remembered to
the Crown Prince, the Duke of [Saxe] Coburg, the Landgrave
of Hesse, and Prince Adolphus of Mecklenburg-Strelitz, and
my best regards to Odo Russell and Dr. [W. H.] Russell [the
war-correspondent] of *The Times*, but to no one else."

The four specified German princes were kinsmen in more or less
near degree. The Crown Prince was the Prince's brother-in-law,
the Duke of Saxe-Coburg was his father's brother, and the other
two German princes were cousins. Apart from the Crown Prince,
none had taken responsible part in the war. The Prince had
furthermore pointed out to Hozier that "all the great military
people at Versailles report that I was entirely French in my
feelings." But he wished the Crown Prince to know that he had
respected the call of neutrality which his own country imposed
on him. At the same time the Crown Prince ought to be informed
"that my sympathy was great with the French since all the
disasters that had fallen upon them," and "that I hoped the
Germans would not exact such conditions of peace as would
utterly cripple France." The Prince added some conventional
compliments on the German conduct of the campaign "in a
military point of view," and he trusted "that the bad feeling
which the Germans entertained towards England would soon
cease." Captain Hozier expressed the view "that in three years
or less Germany would make war on us." The Prince canvassed

the justice of the prophecy. "To the best of my recollection," the Prince's statement concluded, "this is all that passed between Hozier and myself."

There was of course no question that the vague report of the Prince's solicitude for the German High Command, completely misrepresented his dominant bias throughout the recent conflict. Captain Hozier, in a report of his own to Lord Granville, independently corroborated the Prince's statement. But he admitted that the messages were welcomed at Versailles as at any rate a partial refutation of the rumours of the Prince's irreconcilable attitude to Germany. "The messages were well received because of the idea, at German headquarters, that there was great animosity towards Germany on the part of both the Prince of Wales and the Duke of Cambridge. This idea was removed by the fact of a message being sent to all."

At the conclusion of the peace of Frankfort, in March 1871, Queen Victoria was anxious to restore harmony between the Prince of Wales and his brother-in-law and sister, the Crown Prince and Princess. The Crown Prince had shown himself less disturbed by the Prince's French leanings than his wife, who had gone to the length of suggesting that her brother's views were coloured by envy of "Fritz" who "has such a trying but such a useful life." Still the affection of sister and brother proved equal to the strain, and when the Crown Prince and his wife and family arrived in London in July at the Queen's earnest request, the Prince showed them his old cordiality. At the outset, the Crown Prince and Princess stayed (from July 3 to 13) at the German Embassy, where the Prince and Princess often visited them. The Prince found that his brother-in-law and he were in agreement on many points, notably in their joint "horror" of Bismarck, whose unprincipled "driving power" was, the Crown Prince deplored, "omnipotent." [1] After the Crown Prince returned to Germany his wife remained to spend the summer and early autumn with the Queen at Osborne or Balmoral. At both places she had many opportunities of sealing her reconciliation with her brother. Bismarck detected in his kindly courtesy towards his sister and brother-in-law signs of a diminishing love for France, and laid much stress on the fact that the Prince and "his

[1] Extract from Queen Victoria's diary, cited in article "Queen Victoria and France," by R. S. Rait in *Quarterly Review*, July 1919, pp. 10, 11.

Danish Consort . . . even put in an appearance at the German
Legation." [1]   But there was no ground for any deduction which
implied a change in the Prince's outlook on foreign affairs or in
his suspicions of Prussia's barely veiled purpose of bringing all
Europe under her domination.

[1] Busch's *Bismarck*, ii. 116.

CHAPTER XIX

THE PRINCE'S ILLNESS AND THE REPUBLICAN WAVE

I

1871
Ætat. 30

AT the close of the year 1871 the Prince's life was to be menaced by serious illness, and the English people, with the inhabitants of the Empire and of well-nigh all foreign countries, were to give emphatic testimony to their concern for his welfare.

In the autumn there had been some interesting variations in the Prince's annual routine. August was exceptionally well filled. On his return from his visit to Ireland he was the guest of his sister, Princess Alice, and her husband's family at Jugenheim near Darmstadt, where members of the Russian royal family were his fellow-guests. There followed a tour of the battlefields around Sedan and Metz, under the guidance of a Belgian acquaintance, the Prince de Ligne. The Prince travelled over the historic ground incognito, as Baron Renfrew. On August 16th he eagerly inspected the "Weaver's Cottage" at Domchéry, near Sedan, where Emperor Napoleon, after his surrender, had a memorable conversation with Bismarck. Passing through Alsace under its new rulers he joined the Princess at Kissingen, where she was taking the cure. When their stay there ended they witnessed, in strict privacy—without even reserving places—the performance, at the village of Ober-Ammergau in Upper Bavaria, of the decennial Passion Play. That experience made a serious impression on the Prince, who talked with the peasant who played the part of Christ, and declared that he "had never been so struck with any one in his life." [1]

A great part of September was devoted to the military manœuvres in Hampshire. At the end of October, on his way

[1] Lady Rose Weigall, *A Memoir*, 1923, p. 165.

back to Sandringham from his ordinary sojourn in Scotland, he stayed with his friends, the Earl and Countess of Londesborough, at Londesborough Lodge near Scarborough. Soon after his arrival at Sandringham, where he celebrated his thirtieth birthday (on November 9), the Prince fell ill, and his illness was diagnosed as typhoid or enteric fever. A public announcement to that effect was made on 23rd November.

The disease had clearly been contracted at Londesborough Lodge. Two of the Prince's companions there, the eighth Earl of Chesterfield, and the Prince's groom, Blegge, were also attacked, as it proved, fatally. The Earl died on the 1st December and the groom thirteen days later. Meanwhile the Prince's condition rapidly became critical. On the 29th of November, when Queen Victoria arrived for a day, there seemed some improvement, but on the 6th December a relapse set in, and during the next week the Prince's life hung by a thread. On the 8th of December Lord Granville wrote to Queen Victoria "that there hardly seems to be hope left." Queen Victoria returned to Sandringham the same afternoon and remained for eleven days. Sunday, 10th December, was appointed for a special form of intercession in the churches throughout the country. Next morning (December 11) *The Times'* leading article opened with the words : "The Prince still lives, and we may still therefore hope ; but the strength of the patient is terribly diminished, and all who watch his bedside, as, indeed, all England watches it—must acknowledge that their minds are heavy with apprehension." Five alarming bulletins were issued from the sick chamber later in the day. The anxiety was rendered the more poignant by the circumstance that, just ten years before, the illness of the Prince Consort, which was of the like kind, had passed through the same phase before its fatal termination on the 14th December 1861. Princess Alice, the Prince's second sister, who had helped to nurse her father, had come with her husband, Prince Louis of Hesse, on a visit to Sandringham for the Prince's birthday. She joined the Princess of Wales in ministrations in the sick chamber.

As if by miracle, early on the morning of the 14th, the anniversary of the royal family's great bereavement ten years before, when all seemed lost, the physicians perceived an amelioration in the Prince's condition. At 8 A.M. the bulletin announced "some abatement of the gravity of the symptoms," and at noon it was notified that the morning's gain was maintained. Thenceforth there was steady progress to recovery. On the 15th the cabinet met, and the Prime Minister added to his customary report for the sovereign's eye :

All here are rejoiced to think that yesterday, which was so deeply marked in your Majesty's thoughts with the recollections of irreparable calamity, should have been in the midst of this new trial a day of hope and comfort. The series of telegrams which have reported gradual improvement has now grown rather a long one, and it is impossible to repress the cheerful feeling which they inspire.[1]

A bulletin on the 21st December announced that the danger was past. A mighty outburst of joy succeeded the many weeks of sorrow. On no occasion in the country's history had the public manifested so personal an anxiety in the peril of a royal personage. In Ireland, as Lord Spencer wrote to the Queen (December 27), all parties echoed the British nation's distress during the season of crises, and its relief at the happy issue.[2] The same feeling was evinced in India and Canada. The ex-Emperor of the French, in his gloomy retreat at Chislehurst, when reading of the fortunate turn of events, remarked that fate had told him that the Prince's

---

[1] Mr. Gladstone's "cheerful feeling" was well justified. Convalescence was somewhat retarded, but was not interrupted, by an affection of the left hip. The date, 14th December 1871, was long thankfully remembered. The Princess of Wales presented to Sandringham Church a brass eagle lectern inscribed with the words: "A thanksgiving for His mercy, 14th December 1871." "That time is as indelibly fixed on my memory as that of 1861, when the witnessing of your grief rent my heart so deeply," wrote Princess Alice to Queen Victoria a year later. "The 14th will now be a day of mixed recollections and feelings to us—a day hallowed in our family, which took away one 'great spirit,' and left another of the family to fulfil his duty and mission" (Letters of Princess Alice, p. 288).

[2] "It is very agreeable to Lord Spencer to be able to inform your Majesty," Lord Spencer wrote to the Queen, "that Ireland has very widely shown this feeling; in Dublin the bulletins were expected with the deepest anxiety, and crowds collected round the newsvendors' stalls to read them. It was remarkable to notice how the tone of the most Fenian and extreme papers, the Irishman and the Flag of Ireland, was changed. When the Prince first became seriously ill these papers had articles stating that whatever the English and Scotch felt, the Irish were indifferent as to the recovery of the Prince; but this evidently did not accord with the sentiments of the people who like these low papers, for the following week they altered the spirit of their enmity, and expressed sympathy for your Majesty and the Princess of Wales. The Home Rule Association adjourned on account of the illness; the Cardinal postponed a great meeting which had been convened in Dublin to discuss denominational education, and the Londonderry anniversaries would have been neglected had not improvement taken place in the Prince's health."

life would be spared. On 26th December the Queen, for the first 1871
time in her career, published a letter to her people thanking them Ætat. 30
for their sympathy.

"The Queen is very anxious," the message ran, "to express
her deep sense of the touching sympathy of the whole nation on
the occasion of the alarming illness of her dear son, the Prince of
Wales. The universal feeling shown by her people during those
painful terrible days, and the sympathy evinced by them with
herself and her beloved daughter, the Princess of Wales, as well
as the general joy at the improvement in the Prince of Wales's
state, have made a deep and lasting impression on her heart
which can never be effaced. It was indeed nothing new to her,
for the Queen had met with the same sympathy when just ten
years ago a similar illness removed from her side the mainstay
of her life, the best, wisest, and kindest of husbands."

II

As early as 18th December Queen Victoria was in correspondence with the Prime Minister respecting some form of
public thanksgiving. Mr. Gladstone, after examining precedents,
recommended a procession of the Queen and her son through
London to St. Paul's Cathedral, where a special service should
be held. The Queen demurred to "this public show" on the
ground of "the dreadful fatigue" for the Prince and of the
incongruity of making religion "a vehicle" for a demonstration
of popular feeling. But the Princess of Wales, writing for her
husband as well as for herself, took a juster view of the situation.

"I quite understand your feelings," the Princess wrote to
the Queen, "about the public thanksgiving. I do not either
like it myself, for it seems to me also to be making too much an
outward show of the most sacred and solemn feelings of one's
heart, and I quite agree that a simpler and more private service
would be more in accordance with one's own wishes. But then,
on the other hand, the whole nation has taken such a public
share in our sorrow, it has been so entirely one with us in our
grief, that it may perhaps feel it has a kind of claim to join with
us now in a public and universal thanksgiving."

It was with some reluctance, due in part to uncertain health,
that the Queen assented to a great public ceremony. The
government regarded the step as politic and in the interests of
the monarchy. Mr. Gladstone introduced into the draft of the

Queen's speech for the opening of Parliament on 6th February
not merely a renewed expression of thanks on the Queen's part
for the "profound and universal sympathy" of her people, but
an announcement that, "conformably to the good and becoming
usage of former days," the thanksgiving ceremony would take
place in St. Paul's Cathedral on Tuesday the 27th inst., and that
it was the Queen's "desire and intention to be present." The
Queen criticised Mr. Gladstone's draft, urging the omission on the
ground of tameness of the Prime Minister's qualifying clause,
"conformably to the good and becoming usage of former days"
and the substitution of the word "hope" for "intention" in the
Prime Minister's statement of her "desire and intention to be
present," with the addition of the words "if my health permit."
Mr. Gladstone accepted the Queen's emendation of "hope" for
"intention," but made no other change.

On the 27th February the Queen, forgoing her scruples,
joined her son in the thanksgiving ceremony at St. Paul's Cathedral amid an enthusiastic demonstration of public sympathy.
"Hearty," "sincere," "sublime" were epithets applied by level-
headed witnesses to the demeanour of the vast crowds which
greeted the royal procession as it drove to and from St. Paul's
Cathedral.[1] The Prince was greatly moved. "I cannot tell
you," he wrote to his mother on his return to Marlborough House,
"how gratified and touched I was by the feeling that was displayed in those crowded streets to-day towards you and also to
myself." Next day Mr. Gladstone congratulated the Queen
"very sincerely on the extraordinary manifestation of loyalty
and affection in the celebration of yesterday"; he described the
celebration as "perhaps more solemn and more satisfactory"
than any that the City of London had yet witnessed. Mr. W. E.
Forster, a member of the cabinet, ventured on the suggestion that
the Queen should write "a short letter expressing her feelings
with regard to the reception." "A few of your Majesty's own
kindly words might give an almost perfect ending to this event
so auspicious and memorable, and in all its circumstances unprecedented." The suggestion was taken, and on 29th February
there was published a letter of appreciation from the Queen to
Mr. Gladstone. "Words are too weak," the Queen wrote, "for
the Queen to say how very deeply touched and gratified she has

[1] Lady Jebb's *Life and Letters of Sir R. C. Jebb*, pp. 126-8.

been by the immense enthusiasm and affection exhibited towards her dear son and herself, from the highest down to the lowest in the long progress through the capital." Tennyson, the Poet Laureate, in his epilogue to the *Idylls of the King*, which he inscribed "To the Queen," bore impressive witness to the fervour of London, with its reverberations in the remotest corners of the Empire:

> Bear witness that rememberable day,
> When, pale as yet, and fever-worn, the Prince,
> Who scarce had plucked his flickering life again
> From halfway down the shadow of the grave,
> Past with thee thro' thy people and their love,
> And London rolled one tide of joy through all
> Her trebled millions, and loud leagues of man
> And welcome! Witness, too, the silent cry,
> The prayer of many a race and creed, and clime—
> Thunderless lightnings striking under sea
> From sunset and sunrise of all thy realm.

III

The Prince completed his convalescence on a tour in France and Italy, which opened and closed in Paris, and included some yachting in the Mediterranean. Leaving London on the 9th March 1872 the Prince and Princess were absent from England until 1st June. They travelled incognito as the Earl and Countess of Chester.

Restored health kindled anew the Prince's zest for European politics and society. In the French capital he visited M. Thiers, the first President of the French Republic, and refreshed his intimacies with leading figures of the old régime. In Italy, where political again mingled with social interests, his experiences were especially stirring. The political situation at Rome had lately undergone drastic changes. The withdrawal during the Franco-Prussian War of the French garrison which had safeguarded the Pope's temporal rule, had converted the city into the capital of the kingdom of Italy, with King Victor Emmanuel installed at the Quirinal. The Pope, deprived of the last shreds of his temporal power, had become the voluntary and protesting prisoner of the Vatican, and he viewed his supplanter, the King of Italy, with no friendly eye. The Prince promptly exchanged visits with King Victor Emmanuel and with his heir, Prince

1872
Ætat. 30 Humbert; while the kindly attentions which were paid the Prince and Princess during their stay in Italy—in Milan as well as in Rome—by Princess Margherita, Prince Humbert's wife, made her a friend for years to come. The Prince's attitude to his old acquaintance, the dispossessed Pope Pio Nono, provoked embarrassment, but all parties—the Prince, King Victor Emmanuel, and Mr. Gladstone, the Prime Minister—deemed it conformable with policy and good feeling to pay the Pontiff a visit, as (in Mr. Gladstone's words) "a personal act of compliment, courtesy, and respect." Little passed at the interview save the Pope's congratulatory words on the Prince's restoration to health, with some expression of papal satisfaction at Queen Victoria's good feeling towards Roman Catholics and of admiration of the religious spirit of the English people. A rumour, reported by *The Times*, that the Prince with indiscreet sympathy invited the Pope's views on so delicate a question as the recent crisis in papal affairs was summarily denied by the Prime Minister in the House of Commons.[1]

The social pleasures of the Prince and Princess's sojourn in Rome were enhanced by the presence of the King and Queen of Denmark, with their youngest son Waldemar and their daughter Thyra, together with the no less welcome figure of ex-King of Hanover's heir, Duke of Cumberland. This family meeting subsequently bore auspicious fruit in the betrothal of the Duke with the Princess of Wales's sister Thyra.

The Italian tour, which wound up at Cadenabbia on Lake Como, completed the Prince's cure,[2] and he resumed in June with fresh energy his sovereignty of London society. His "breakfasts," or afternoon garden parties at Chiswick House, which the Duke of Devonshire lent him through several seasons, improved on all precedent in the range of guests. The entertainments at Marlborough House assumed an increased brilliance.

1874
Ætat. 32 There the Prince brought to a close the season of 1874 with a fancy-dress ball (July 21) on a scale of splendour greater than any social function that he had yet attempted.

"It was very picturesque," wrote one of the guests, Lord Ronald Gower, "and some of the dresses (the Duke of Buccleuch's

---

[1] Cf. *Times*, 2nd March 1872; Hansard, 5th April 1872.
[2] The Italian itinerary included Florence, Milan, Venice, besides Cadenabbia on Lake Como, whence Paris was reached by way of Genoa.

for example) quite superb.   Billy Russell looked well in a black
cavalier costume, wearing a Shakespearean tuft on his chin.
The Duke of Wellington, as a Spanish hidalgo, wore his father's
Order of the Golden Fleece.   Poor old Quin appeared in a
Charles II. dress.   The Prince looked well, and gained in height
in a cavalier's dress [a Van Dyck costume with doublet and cloak
of light maroon satin embroidered in gold], and, as usual, the
Princess was the most beautiful and graceful woman in the place;
she wore a Marie Stuart dress." [1]

1874
—
Ætat. 32

The ball opened with a Venetian quadrille—the Princess's partner
being the Marquis of Hartington and the Prince's the Duchess of
Sutherland.   The only guests who were excused fancy dress were
the Duke of Cambridge and Disraeli.   The Prince's social
exploits could always count on imitation.   Two days later the
Duke of Wellington offered the Prince a like festivity of equal
radiance at Apsley House, where the Prince wore the same Van
Dyck dress.

IV

A main effect of the outburst of popular sympathy which the
Prince's illness evoked was vastly to strengthen throughout the
country the monarchical sentiment.   "Incontestably this crisis"
(*i.e.* the Prince's illness), wrote Baron Brunnow, the Russian
Ambassador in London, to Prince Gortschakoff, the Chancellor
of the Russian Empire, "has produced in England a happy
reaction in favour of the monarchical institutions which govern
this great land" (December 15/27, 1871).[2]

1870
—
Ætat. 28

The reinforcement of monarchical feeling in the country was
peculiarly opportune.   During the year preceding the Prince's
illness a challenge had been thrown down to the British
monarchy.   The overthrow of the French Empire and the substitution for it of the Third French Republic had powerfully
reacted on advanced political opinion in England.   A cry was
raised for a similar form of government in this country in
many quarters—by Radical politicians, under the leadership
of Sir Charles Dilke, by intellectual theorisers, and by trade-
unionist leaders.[3]   The poet Swinburne, then coming into

---

[1] Lord Ronald Gower, *My Reminiscences*, p. 318.
[2] Russian Archives.
[3] On the proclamation of the French Republic (September 4, 1870),
Bradlaugh, the leading republican agitator, joined George Odger, the trade-
unionist leader, Sir Henry Hoare, M.P. for Norwich, and the Positivist philo-

general if somewhat equivocal fame, stirred the imagination of
an impressionable section of the English public by his eloquent
congratulatory *Ode on the Proclamation of the French Republic*, and by his defiant *Songs before Sunrise* (1871).   Throughout the year 1871 the agitation held its ground, despite the
shock to general feeling of the atrocities of the Paris commune
after the Franco-German War ended.   Republican clubs sprang
up in London, Birmingham, Plymouth, Norwich, Aberdeen,
Cardiff, and other large towns.   On 16th April 1871 the government permitted a republican demonstration in Hyde Park.

Serious onlookers regarded the situation as ugly.   In the
autumn of 1871 a thoughtful writer in a London newspaper,
the *Pall Mall Gazette*, spoke of "republicanism of a very revolutionary form flooding in" (September 29).   In letters to both
the Queen and to her heir, Mr. Gladstone, the Prime Minister, a
staunch champion of the monarchy, made no concealment of his
apprehensions, and the equanimity of the Prince and his family
was disturbed.   One of Mr. Gladstone's colleagues, Lord Selborne,
who succeeded Lord Hatherley as Lord Chancellor in 1872, was
bold enough, when he was the Queen's guest at Windsor, to warn
her that if the French Republic held its ground England was
likely to seek the same goal.

The republican advocates laid chief stress on the pecuniary
burden of royalty and on the Queen's prolonged retirement, to
which Mr. Gladstone had never succeeded in reconciling himself ;
but current gossip which the Mordaunt case had stimulated about
the Prince's life sensibly fanned the flame of the agitation.
Charles Bradlaugh, an active spokesman on republican platforms,
freely associated the Prince's name with that of King George IV.
in a widely circulated pamphlet entitled *An Impeachment of the
House of Brunswick*.   The popular suspicion of the Prince's
excessive devotion to pleasure was also reflected in the vast
circulation which was enjoyed at the end of 1870 by *The Coming
K——*, a skilful parody of Tennyson's then popular *Idylls of the*

---

sophers, Dr. Congreve and Professor Beesly, in urging an immediate recognition
of the Republic.   M. Gambetta, the moving spirit of the new French Republic,
addressed a letter of thanks to Bradlaugh for his support, and Bradlaugh,
following the precedent set by Tom Paine in the French Revolution of 1789,
offered himself as a candidate for Paris at the elections of the National Assembly
in February 1871.   The British government recognized the French Republic
on 12th February 1871.

King. The brochure purported boldly to draw the veil from the private life of the Prince and of his comrades, and to suggest his unfitness for the succession to the throne.[1]

The Prince's illness and the popular sense of loyalty which it intensified beyond recent precedent dealt the republican agitation a blow from which it never recovered.   During his convalescence the republicans were preparing a fresh advance.   A conference on the national organisation of the republican movement was summoned to meet at Birmingham in January 1872.   But the Duke of Cambridge, with unaccustomed shrewdness, estimated the situation aright when he wrote to his mother, the old Duchess: "The republicans say their chances are up—thank God for this! Heaven has sent this dispensation [of the Prince's illness] to save us." [2]   It was in vain that Sir Charles Dilke moved in the House of Commons on the 19th March 1872, in the republican interest, for a full inquiry into Queen Victoria's expenditure.   The chief effect of the motion, which was seconded by Auberon Herbert and ignominiously defeated, was to draw from Mr. Gladstone, the Prime Minister, amid the tumultuous applause of the House, an impressive confession of his firm faith in the monarchy. Lord Henry Lennox, a leading member of the Conservative party, wrote significantly to Disraeli: "What a sell for Dilke this illness has been."

The sentimental excesses of the loyal emotion provoked inevitable reactions in stalwartly independent minds.   Mr. Fawcett, the blind Radical M.P. and professor of political economy in the University of Cambridge, questioned if the Prince's recovery would prove of real benefit to the throne.[3]   But the general view

1872
—
Ætat. 30

---

[1] Through each of the next four years effusions of like temper, but of diminishing pungency, pursued at Christmas time the attack on the Prince, and on the society which he ruled. *The Coming K——*, which was anonymous, was from the pen of Mr. A. A. Dowty, of the Paymaster-General's Office, who was subsequently a contributor to the weekly paper *Truth* (*Truth*, January 3, 1917). The second item of this series of satires was *The Siliad* (1872); the third, *The Fijiad* (1873); the fourth, *Faust and Phisto* (1874); and the fifth, *Jon Duan* (1875). The concluding issue was the more genial *Edward VII.: A Play on the past and present Times with a View to the Future.* In the sequels there are signs of Dowty's hand, but much of the work was done by Mr. S. O. Beeton, an industrious compiler, who was associated with the publishing firm of Ward, Lock & Co. The brochures were issued under the general title of *Beeton's Christmas Annual.* Beeton died in 1876.

[2] Sheppard's *Duke of Cambridge*, i. 310.

[3] Lady Jebb's *Life and Letters of Sir R. C. Jebb*, 1907, p. 113; Cf. *Letters of J. R. Green*, ed. Leslie Stephen, 1901. John Richard Green, the Radical

1872
Ætat. 30
held by men of sagacity was reflected by the remark of R. C. Jebb, another professor in the University of Cambridge, that Providence had given the Prince "the chance, if he knows how to use it, of becoming the most popular man in England. . . . The prolongation of his life means the indefinite prolongation of the life of the monarchy." [1] A wise friend of the Prince, William Howard Russell, echoed sound strains of thought in a letter to an American publicist: "When all seemed hopeless," Russell wrote of the illness, "my great grief was that the country would never know in general what a good fellow, to use the best phrase about him, he was." Russell believed that the ordeal through which the Prince had passed would prove a benefit to himself as well as to the country. He felt confident that the Prince, in restored health, would respond to "the manifestations of affectionate loyalty" by justifying in the way of public service "the good opinion of his friends." [2]

V

1874
Ætat. 32
The efforts of the Prince, with the concurrence of Mr. Gladstone and other ministers, to obtain on the recovery of his health regular official employment, were defeated by Queen Victoria's unabated opposition. A handful of Radical politicians continued to stir the dying embers of the republican movement by murmuring against the cost of the monarchy; and from time to time their grievance gave fresh life to imputations, which became stock themes of the world's scandal-mongering press, against the alleged idle life of the Prince, of his financial extravagance and a consequent heavy indebtedness.

Early in the summer of 1874 journalists spread reports that the Prince owed £600,000, that Mr. Gladstone had been requested and had declined to ask Parliament for an increase of the Prince's statutory income, that the appeal was to be repeated to Mr. Disraeli who had just become Prime Minister, and that, failing

---

parson and historian remarked: "I am sorry when any young fellow dies at thirty, and am far more sorry when any mother suffers; but the sentiment of newspapers and town councils over 'telegrams from the sick-bed' is simply ludicrous. However, one remembers that all France went mad with anxiety when Lewis the Well-beloved fell sick in his earlier days, and yet somehow or other '89 came never the later."

[1] Lady Jebb's *Life and Letters of Sir R. C. Jebb*, 1907, pp. 111-12.
[2] John Bigelow's *Retrospections*, v. 5-6 (letter from W. H. Russell).

Parliamentary help, the Queen had undertaken to liquidate the Prince's debts. The Queen deemed a public refutation of the misstatement essential. Her confidential friend, Sir Arthur Helps, contributed to *The Daily Telegraph* on 17th September 1874 an anonymous paragraph denying on authority that there was "a single word of truth" in the rumours. A little later the editor of *The Times*, Mr. Delane, was taken into council, and on 1st October 1874 the first leading article of his newspaper supplied an official disclosure, somewhat rhetorically phrased, of the Prince's financial position. It was pointed out that the Prince's income and expenditure were carefully audited, and that the periodical balance-sheets relieved the Prince of the charges which ignorance or malevolence had invented. Owing to the Queen's seclusion the Prince was performing social duties of hospitality, especially in the reception of royal visitors from abroad, which were not anticipated when the Parliamentary grant was originally made him. He had "represented the Royal House of England in visits to the chief Courts of Europe. . . . In Paris and Vienna, on the banks of the Suez Canal, or amid the splendours of the Russian capital, the heir to the British Throne has been more than an ordinary Prince, and could not, without what would seem unworthy parsimony, avoid incurring great expenses. A large retinue, long journeys, and a hundred minor but necessary outlays would strain a far larger income than the Prince has ever received." The Prince's revenue of £100,000 a year was less than that enjoyed by "many private Peers." Rarely were contributions to the expenses of the foreign tours made from the public purse. Yet in spite of all his financial responsibilities the excess of the Prince's expenditure over income ranged from no more than £10,000 to £20,000 a year. That deficit had hitherto been defrayed from the capital sum accumulated during his minority out of the receipts of the Duchy of Cornwall. It was perilous to draw on one's capital, but there was no cause for disquiet.

Criticism was not wholly silenced by Mr. Delane's pronouncement, which travelled far and wide. The Russian Ambassador, Count Schouvaloff, when forwarding *The Times* statement to the Russian Foreign Office, suggested that the revelations were incomplete. In Radical circles *The Times* was blamed for omitting to mention that the rent and maintenance of Marlborough House

1874
Ætat. 32
and the upkeep of the royal yachts came out of public funds. There was a renewal of earlier complaints that the Queen in her retirement was hoarding money, some part of which she ought to share with the Prince as her social representative.

The Prince's attitude to the question at issue was free from ambiguity. His expenses were undoubtedly growing, and he deemed himself entitled to a larger income than he was receiving from the State. He had no hesitation in pressing for special grants to defray the cost of foreign travel or ceremonial business at home which touched public interests, and his appeals met with varying success. Personal friends urged Mr. Disraeli, the Prime Minister, to invite Parliament to provide him with ampler means, but neither the Queen nor the Prime Minister deemed the step to be prudent in view of certain phases of public feeling. In the result the Prince was left for many years to face as best he could such pecuniary embarrassments as he incurred. No further endeavour was made officially to challenge the fable of his debts with which journalistic and social gossip long made free all the world over. Careful administration enabled the Prince to keep the deficit in his accounts within moderate bounds. It was not until 1889, when his sons and daughters were reaching adult years and were making new calls on his purse, that the leaders of the two great parties jointly induced Parliament permanently to improve the Prince's financial position out of public funds.[1]

1872
Ætat. 30
The Prince, while he resented public criticism of his private affairs, was politic enough to seek to propitiate Radical criticism which still savoured of a theoretic leaning to republicanism, by inviting social intercourse with representative Radicals. His personal charm rarely failed in its effect. When he met Mr. Frank Hill, the editor of the chief Radical journal, the *Daily News*, at dinner at Lord Granville's, he wrote to his host next day (July 7, 1872) for Mr. Hill's address, with a view to offering him hospitality. He enjoyed putting his personal fascination to the test by giving those from whom he differed proofs of his *bonhomie* and shrewdness.

In 1874 the Prince made an especially bold experiment in this direction. He proposed to pay with the Princess a first visit to the city of Birmingham—a stronghold of advanced Radicalism. The Mayor, Mr. Joseph Chamberlain, a friend of Sir Charles

[1] See p. 602 *infra*.

Dilke, was acquiring a general reputation as an advocate of
extreme political opinions, and had in some recent articles in the
Fortnightly Review betrayed republican sympathies. The visit
was duly arranged, and the programme included a procession of
the Prince and Princess through the streets of the city, the reception of an address in the town hall, an entertainment at lunch by
the Mayor, and visits to leading manufactories (November 3,
1874). Constraint or unpleasantness between the Prince and
the Mayor was generally anticipated, but the anticipation was
signally belied. Mr. Chamberlain was well qualified fitly to face
the situation. He proposed his guest's health in the tactful
words: "Here in England the throne is recognised and respected
as the symbol of all constituted authority and settled government." The Prince was as discreet in reply (November 3). A
cartoon by (Sir) John Tenniel in *Punch* (November 14, 1874),
entitled "A Brummagem Lion," showed Mr. Chamberlain as a
lion gently kneeling before the Prince and Princess, and the
accompanying verses congratulated him on concealing his "red
republican claws and teeth," and on comporting himself as "a
gentleman" in the glare of the princely sun. In later years the
Prince and he were to come, both in public and private, into less
ambiguous relations. An amiable light is shed on the characters
of the two men by the conditions attaching to their first introduction to one another.

The Prince's readiness to meet socially critics of monarchy and
of himself was not always at first blush encouraged, but the
Prince's tact and grace usually won the day. His first invitation
of the Radical stalwart, Mr. Fawcett, to a garden party, was
refused; but Mr. Fawcett subsequently accepted the Prince's
hospitalities, and Mr. Chamberlain, silencing any early scruples,
became the Prince's frequent guest. Of greater significance was
the fact that Mr. Chamberlain's friend, Sir Charles Dilke, the
Radical champion of the anti-monarchical movement, soon joined
the Prince's intimate social circle. The Prince carefully watched
the steadily rising influence of these two allies in the House of
Commons during Mr. Disraeli's last ministry, and made social
advances to both betimes. On 4th March 1879 the Prince's
friend, Lord Fife, invited Dilke, to his surprise, to meet the Prince
at dinner. "The Prince laid himself out," Dilke wrote, "to be
pleasant and talked to me nearly all the evening, chiefly about

French politics and the Greek question." [1] Next month Mr.
Chamberlain, the former Mayor of Birmingham, in spite of some
perplexities, accepted an invitation to dine at Marlborough House.
The republican wave had spent itself, and there was to be no
personal strife between the Prince and the forces of Radicalism.

[1] Gwynn and Tuckwell's *Life of Sir Charles Dilke*, i. 302.

CHAPTER XX

THE RESURRECTION OF FRANCE, 1871–1880

I

THE internal affairs of France after the war proved for the Prince
a fascinating study, even if they roused in him divided feelings.
He never lacked sympathy with the French national hope—
proof against all internal dissensions—that France would ultimately wipe off the stain on her national honour left by the severance of Alsace and Lorraine.   He long clung to the illusory belief
that his brother-in-law the Crown Prince, in whose sense of
justice he trusted, would, when he came to the German throne,
effect the desired reparation.   At the same time he recognised
from 1871 onwards that peace abroad was France's urgent
interest.   He was prepared to use his influence in warding off
the surprise blows which Germany was suspected of designing,
before France's recovery was complete.   His avowals of pro-
French enthusiasm were bound to provoke afresh Prince
Bismarck's irritation.   The continued interchange of visits with
his brother-in-law and sister, the Crown Prince and Princess of
Germany, taught him that they shared in all essentials his own
political outlook and predilections.   Such intercourse increased
his distrust of the German Chancellor's domineering policy.

Nevertheless, it was with difficulty that the Prince reconciled
himself to republican institutions, at any rate in Europe.   Innate
as was his affinity with the French temperament, and desirous
as he was of seeing England and France linked in firm bonds of
amity, it was after a severe inward struggle that he acquiesced
in French republicanism.   Through the early years of the Third
French Republic he put to his soul the flattering unction that
the republican régime was only a temporary expedient, and that

335

1871
Ætat. 29

some form of monarchy would be soon reinstated. The formidable opposition in France to the Republic justified this frame of mind. It was not until 1878 that he reached the conclusion that the French people was preponderantly committed to the Republic, whereupon he waived his personal prejudices and did homage to the accomplished fact. Subsequently, spasmodic royalist agitation shook his confidence anew in the stability of the new form of government, but he ultimately, if tardily, came to realise that no other had in France a chance of endurance.

The British government officially recognised the Third French Republic on the 12th February 1871, as soon, indeed, as a national assembly had been elected to endorse the action of the provisional republican government of 4th September 1870. The mission of the Assembly was also to devise a lasting form of constitution, and round that theme there was to wage a prolonged and perilously heated controversy between monarchy and republicanism. M. Thiers, a leading member of the provisional government, was chosen first President on the 31st August 1871, and he held that office precariously for two years.

1872
Ætat. 30

The Prince's monarchical predilections failed to withdraw him long from "the pleasant land of France," even under republican rule, and the requirements of international comity brought him early into some personal touch there with the Republican Government. On his visit to Paris after his illness (his first after the war) he was requested by the Foreign Secretary, Lord Granville, to pay President Thiers a formal call. He assented reluctantly to a step which, as he pointed out, "went very much against the grain." But the Prince's social tact proved equal to the occasion which, despite his prejudices, stirred his curiosity. Accompanied by the British Ambassador, Lord Lyons, the Prince, soon after his arrival in Paris, proceeded to Versailles, where the President was in official residence, and he responded cordially to M. and Mme. Thiers' effusive warmth (March 11, 1872). No other person of royal rank had yet shown the Republic a similar attention, and like most continental politicians M. Thiers believed implicitly in the Prince's political influence. The Prince confirmed the favourable impression by going from the presidential audience to a sitting of the National Assembly. Next day President Thiers returned in Paris the Prince's visit.

At Berlin, where the Prince's activities continued to be narrowly watched, the Prince's deference to diplomatic usage soon gave rise to uneasiness. When cruising, in the following autumn, off the north coast of France with his friend the Duke of St. Albans in the Duke's yacht *Xantha*, the Prince made a short landing at Trouville, and there accidentally met M. Thiers for a second time. The Prince and the President had a long conversation. Confiding to his visitor a suspicion that the German government was spoiling for a further trial of strength with France, M. Thiers begged the Prince to find an opportunity of impressing on the German Emperor and his counsellors the desire and indeed the resolve of the French government to maintain peace.[1] The meeting was observed by a German spy, and was reported to Berlin. Prince Bismarck affected serious disquietude. He detected in the Prince's wholly unpremeditated interview unwelcome signs of a coming understanding between England and France.[2]

1872
Ætat. 30

II

The change in the form of French government in no way slackened the Prince's social ties with the rival heirs either of Bonapartism or of Legitimism and with their bands of supporters. He greeted with equal cordiality imperialist and royalist princes. His impartially distributed and openly displayed intimacies with the mutually warring claimants to the French throne aroused frequent misgivings on the part of British ministers, who feared that the Prince might give the republican leaders erroneous impressions of British sympathy with the Republic's French competitors.

The Bourbon and Orléanist princes, whom the Empire had kept in exile, were allowed by the Republican Government to return to France. The Prince's personal relations with them remained what they were when the princes were refugees in England. After their readmission to France they still passed much time in England. The Prince not only continued to exchange hospitalities with them there, but from 1872 until

[1] Newton's *Life of Lord Lyons*, ii. 29.
[2] Knollys to Granville, 23rd August 1872. Gontaut-Biron, *Mon Ambassade à Berlin, 1872–73*, Paris, i. 80.

1872
Ætat. 30

his death he also welcomed to his table in Paris all the repatriated Orléanists whom he met there.   The Comte de Paris, the head of the royal house of France ; the Comte's brother, the Duc de Chartres (the Prince's senior precisely by a year, for whom he cherished a special tenderness) ; the Comte's uncles, the Duc de Nemours, the Prince de Joinville, and the Duc d'Aumale were repeatedly, with their wives, the Prince's guests or hosts during his Parisian sojourns.   The Duc d'Aumale's beautiful château at Chantilly became a highly favoured resort, and the Prince watched with interest the embellishments which the Duc was constantly making in his buildings and art collections.   The marriage in 1885 of the Princess of Wales's youngest brother Waldemar to the Duc de Chartres' elder daughter Marie formed a subsequent link between the Prince's kindred and the Orléanists. After 1880 there was in France a recrudescence of republican suspicion of royalist pretensions, and the cry was raised for a second banishment of the royalist chieftains.   The Prince censured in private the rash threats which the Comte de Paris levelled against the French Republic, thereby helping to keep alive the hostile agitation against the French princes.   But the Prince disliked the republican attack on the monarchists, and his social relations with its victims showed no signs of cooling, whatever their political indiscretions.   When the threatened blow fell and the Comte de Paris reached England for a second and

1886
Ætat. 44

lifelong exile on 24th June 1886,[1] the Prince was unfailing in the marks of respect which he paid the refugee, if at the same time he deplored his want of political tact.   The Comte remained in England, first at Sheen House and then at Stowe House until his death, eight years later.   The children of the Prince and of the Comte de Paris emulated the later intimacy of their fathers, and at one time there seemed a likelihood that a marriage in the younger generation might result.   In June 1889 the Prince and Princess, with their sons and daughters, joined all the members of the Orléans family at a *fête-champêtre* at Sheen House in

[1] On the 14th May 1886 the Comte de Paris gave a reception to all his kinsfolk at the house where he was staying in Paris, in honour of the marriage of his daughter Amélie to Dom Carlos, the heir to the throne of Portugal. The wide publicity which was given to the incident seriously ruffled republican susceptibilities, and M. de Freycinet, the Prime Minister, rapidly passed into law a bill for the expulsion of the Orléanist princes.   Cf. De Freycinet, *Souvenirs, 1878-93*, Paris, 1913, pp. 338 *seq.*

celebration of the Comte and Comtesse's silver wedding.[1] When
the Comte died at Stowe House on 8th September 1894 the Prince
promptly paid a visit of condolence to the widow and to her eldest
son, the Duc d'Orléans, although the latter's pompous bearing
tried the Prince.   In sympathetic terms he reported the widow's
grief to his mother at Balmoral.   Next year (June 25, 1895) he
attended at Kingston the wedding of the late Comte's second
daughter, Heléne, to the Duke of Aosta, nephew of King Humbert
of Italy, for which "nearly all French society came over," as
he wrote to Lady Londonderry.

The Comte's uncle, the Duc d'Aumale, against whom the
decree of banishment of 1886 was also aimed, soon qualified
republican hostility by announcing his intention of bequeathing his château of Chantilly with its treasures of art to the
Institut de France.   The decree for his expulsion was consequently revoked on 12th March 1889.   As of old he thenceforth divided his time between England and France.   Until the
Duc's death in 1897 there was no interruption of his familiar
intercourse with the Prince, whether in France or in England.

The only member of the Orléans family with whom the Prince
fell at any time out of sympathy was the Comte de Paris's un-
grateful heir, the Duc d'Orléans, who acquired in the coming
years marked Anglophobic tendencies.[2]   The Duc d'Orléans'
unmannerliness dispelled at the end of the nineteenth century
the Prince's last lingering regret, as he looked backward, that
the crown of France had been withheld from the head of the
Duc's father or grandfather.

III

The Bonapartist princes fared in their effacement as sympathetically as the royalist at the Prince's hands.   To the
fallen Emperor, Napoleon III., to the ex-Empress Eugénie, and
to their son, the Prince Imperial, to all of whom he had grown
attached on his visits at the Tuileries or at Compiègne, he showed
every personal consideration in their retreat at Chislehurst.   In
the early days of the Republic he felt a bewildering uncertainty
as to which of the rival claimants to the French throne would

---

[1] Russian Archives, 23rd May/4th June 1889.
[2] See p. 781 *infra.*

1872
Ætat. 30
prevail—whether the royalists would carry their candidate or the Prince Imperial would become Emperor Napoleon IV. The catholicity of his sympathy was ingenuously illustrated in the summer of 1872. To a garden party at Chiswick House he proposed to invite not only the ex-Emperor Napoleon, the ex-Empress Eugénie, and the Prince Imperial, but also all the members of the Orléans family. He asked beforehand Lord Granville's opinion as to whether guests of such opposed interests were likely to coalesce. Lord Granville expressed grave doubt, and the plan was dropped.

1873
Ætat. 31
When the ex-Emperor died somewhat unexpectedly at Chislehurst on the 9th January 1873, the Prince claimed on the grounds of friendship the right to play a prominent part in the funeral ceremonies. The Queen suggested that the Prince's brother, Prince Alfred, and his brother-in-law, Prince Christian, would be more appropriate representatives of herself and her family. But the Prince, who urged "one cannot be wrong in showing respect to fallen greatness," argued that if he were absent no other representative of the Queen ought to be present. The Queen gave way. Within two days of Napoleon III.'s death the Prince was at Chislehurst to offer the widowed ex-Empress his personal sympathy. Her health did not allow her to receive him until three days later, when he was again at Chislehurst to attend the lying-in-state. At the funeral on the 15th, which brought from France to England numerous supporters of the Empire, the Prince warmly greeted all living members of the Bonaparte family, including the Princesse Mathilde—one of his regular Parisian hostesses. A delegation of Bonapartist artisans who came over, believing the Prince to be the friend of their cause, embarrassed him by offering him an address. He declined a personal presentation, and when the address was forwarded to him he prudently contented himself with a formal acknowledgement. To the widowed ex-Empress and her son, the Prince Imperial, the Prince remained assiduous in tender courtesies. The Bonapartist heir won his warm affection, and he emphatically approved Queen Victoria's sanction of the youth's admission to the Royal Military Academy at Woolwich in order to be trained as an artillery officer.

The engaging disposition of the heir of Bonapartism and his sincere devotion to England often inclined the Prince, while the form of supreme power in France still hung in the balance, to favour a restoration of the Empire as a settlement of best promise.

"I had always," he wrote later of his young friend, "entertained towards him feelings of the greatest friendship and affection, and always looked towards the day when he might be called upon to rule the destinies of that great friendly power France" (July 16, 1879).

"If it had been the will of Providence" he remarked in a public speech near the same date "that he should have been called to succeed his father as the sovereign of that great country our neighbour, I believe he would have proved an admirable sovereign and that he, like his father, would have been a true and great ally of this country."

The ghastly tragedy of the Prince Imperial's death in South Africa destroyed all Bonapartist hopes, and caused the Prince acute personal sorrow.

IV

By way of showing his gratitude to England for providing him and his family with an asylum, the Prince Imperial offered in the spring of 1878 to take part in the war which England was waging in South Africa with the native Zulus. The offer involved some delicate political considerations, and the British government hesitated to accept it from a reluctance to ruffle French republican susceptibilities. Queen Victoria, however, persuaded Lord Beaconsfield, against his better judgement, to grant the young Napoleon's request on the condition that he went out as a spectator and not as a combatant. The Prince of Wales applauded the young man's courage, and he and other friends were lavish in entertainment on the eve of his departure. In France criticism came mainly from the Bonapartists. When in the summer of 1878 the Prince of Wales met, in Paris, the Bonapartist officers, Marshal Canrobert and General Fleury, they complained to him of the rashness of the adventure, and confessed their anxiety respecting its outcome. The Prince Imperial left England on the 27th February, and on 19th June he was suffered to take part in a reckless reconnaissance in the enemy's territory, in course of which he was killed by a party of Zulus. The circumstances of his death provoked heated recriminations as well as infinite sorrow.

The Prince of Wales shared the shock which the news caused
alike in France and England.   At first he freely blamed Lord
Chelmsford, the English commander-in-chief, and Captain Carey,
who was specially detailed to protect the French prince.   "I look
upon his loss as a national one to his country and party," he
wrote to the Duke of Cambridge on 21st June 1879.   "Of the
poor Empress," he added, "all she had left to live for was her
son, and now he is gone."   To his mother, who was overwhelmed
with grief, he wrote next day :

I cannot get the poor little Prince Imperial out of my thoughts,
and look upon his untimely and horrible death as a most dreadful
catastrophe.   When I first heard of it I was quite dumbfounded,
and were it not for the too graphic details would have only too
gladly discredited the accuracy of the news.   He has, I fear,
utterly thrown his life away for want of the most ordinary precautions.   The poor, poor Empress, what has she to live for now ?
Nothing.   Her last hopes, her last interest in life is at an end.   It
is really too dreadful, too awful.   My heart bleeds for her,
especially as one feels that one can offer her no consolation.
There is no ray of hope, nothing but the bare ghastly fact.

To Sir Bartle Frere, the High Commissioner in South Africa,
the Prince wrote strongly of the neglect of the British authorities.
"His life was wantonly sacrificed ; he was deserted in the hour
of danger."   The "horrible and untimely death" of the young
Prince was "a blot on our army in South Africa."   On the
afternoon of Thursday 26th June, the Prince and Princess went
to Chislehurst to offer their condolences to the Empress, and
in the evening, when the Prince presided at Willis's rooms at
a dinner in aid of the funds of the West London Hospital, he
spoke touchingly of the Prince Imperial's untimely death and
his own regard for the young man.

The Empress Eugénie decided that her son's body should be
brought back to Chislehurst for burial beside his father, and the
question of the ceremonial honours which the British Government should offer provoked a difference of view between the
Prince and the Prime Minister.   With poignant feeling and at
the risk of public criticism he urged the payment by the
country of the highest funeral honours to the young Frenchman
who lost his life while serving against an enemy of England.
The Prince thought also to offer a tribute of benevolence to a
lost political cause, which, no longer capable of either good

or evil, had for him very human associations.[1] The Prince's
personal feeling scouted the minister's warning that marks of
respect should be curtailed from regard for the feelings of
Republican France. The Queen was in sympathy with her son.
Largely at his persuasion she directed a man-of-war to bring
the coffin back to England.

1879
Ætat. 37

"It gives me such pleasure," he wrote to his mother (June 28,
1879), "to hear that no political considerations will prevent you
from showing all proper respect to the remains of one who was
our guest and son of our greatest ally. I think a man-of-war of
good steaming powers will be best, where proper arrangements
for a mortuary chamber could be made."

On arrival at Spithead, on board H.M.S. *Orontes*, on 11th July,
the coffin was transhipped to the *Enchantress* for conveyance
to Woolwich. The Prince of Wales insisted that no official
attention should be withheld, and that all the military honours
due to an officer of the Royal Artillery should be paid. At his
suggestion twenty-three minute guns, one for each year of the
Prince's short life, were fired off Spithead, and the same number
on the landing of the body at Woolwich.[2] In the funeral, which
took place at Chislehurst on 12th July, the Prince acted as pall-
bearer, while Queen Victoria remained with the Empress during
the ceremony. Writing to his mother on 14th July, the Prince
said :

You were, I am sure, as much impressed as we all were at
the sad ceremony of Saturday. One has, at any rate, the satisfaction of feeling that everything that could be done to pay all
honour and respect to the poor young Prince . . . was done.[3]

[1] The Prince Imperial devised by will his pretensions to the imperial crown
of France, to Prince Victor Napoleon, elder son of a first cousin of the Emperor
Napoleon III., Prince Jerome Napoleon, known as "Plon-Plon." Prince
Jerome had hitherto regarded himself as the next heir of the French empire
after the Prince Imperial. He declined to yield his claims to his son, with the
result that the dwindling Bonapartist party in France was divided into opposing
factions known respectively as "Jeromistes" and "Victoriens" until Prince
Jerome's death in 1891 left once again only one Bonapartist Pretender in the
field. But the Bonapartist pretension to the sovereignty of France, for practical
purposes, ended with the Prince Imperial's death, although both Prince Jerome
and Prince Victor were expelled from France with all members of former
reigning families in 1886.

[2] Prince to Queen, July 5th.

[3] The coffin of the Prince Imperial was placed in a mortuary chapel within
St. Mary's Chapel, Chislehurst, beside that of the Emperor Napoleon III.
When Empress Eugénie removed from Chislehurst to Farnborough, she built
there a mausoleum, to which both coffins were transferred on 9th January 1888.

Lord Beaconsfield wrote, somewhat cynically (July 12, 1879), of the Queen's and the Prince's satisfaction : "I hope the French government will be as joyful. In my mind, nothing could be more injudicious than the whole affair."[1]

The Prince's proofs of devotion to the Prince Imperial's memory did not end with his funeral. When the young man's sorrowing mother, the ex-Empress Eugénie, decided in the spring of 1880 to visit the scene of her son's death in South Africa, the Prince wrote commending her to the special care of his friend, the High Commissioner, Sir Bartle Frere, and Frere kept the Prince fully informed of the ex-Empress's progress through the colony. The proposal to erect in England a public monument in the French prince's honour was welcomed by the Prince, but it raised further controversial issues. Immediately after the tragedy the Prince joined a committee, which the editor of the *Morning Post* formed, for the purpose of erecting a statue to his memory in London. To the suggestion that the statue should be placed in one of the parks the Prince raised objection.[2] Meanwhile he warmly approved the Queen's subsequent offer of a monument in Westminster Abbey. A vote of the House of Commons condemned this proposal (July 12, 1880), and the Queen appointed another site for her monument—in St. George's Chapel, Windsor. The *Morning Post's* original scheme matured slowly, but it at length took effect in a statue of the Prince Imperial, which was executed by the Prince's cousin, Count Gleichen. On the 13th January 1883 the Prince unveiled this memorial in the grounds of the Royal Military Academy, Woolwich.

Through all the later years of the Prince of Wales's life the ex-Empress, who survived him by a decade, remained an object of his solicitude. Any political hopes which she cherished were buried in her son's grave. The tragic fate to which Bonapartism succumbed in 1879 impressed the Prince as deeply as any of the vicissitudes of eminent fortune which he encountered in the course of his career.

V

With the fashionable dwellers in the Faubourg St. Germain who had frequented either King Louis Philippe's or the Emperor

1 Buckle, *Life of Disraeli*, vi. 437-9.   2 Knollys to Ponsonby, 30th June 1879.

Napoleon's Court, the Prince's good relations continued un- 1871
broken after the Franco-German War. Most of these men and Ætat. 29
women cherished for the Republic a frank aversion, and avoided
association with republican partisans, ridiculing their manners
as well as condemning their opinions. The Prince was always a
popular figure in the aristocratic and anti-republican preserves
of the French Jockey Club, which he joined in the days of the
Empire and of which he remained a member to the end. At
the same time many soldiers and diplomatists of aristocratic
lineage entered, on the fall of the Empire, the service of the
Republic in the confident belief that that government would
soon yield to a royalist restoration, and the Prince assiduously
cultivated the society of these seekers after a working compromise.

London as well as Paris gave him opportunity of keeping
in touch with French aristocrats, who, serving the Republic
with far-reaching reservations, were well disposed towards
England. In the early years of the Republic a rapid succession
of diplomatic representatives of France in London came from the
royalist ranks of the French nobility. The Prince was always
seeking congenial spirits in the diplomatic corps. Desirous, too,
of good political relations with France under whatever form of
government, he showered his social graces on the earliest line of
republican envoys—most of whom he had met already in French
salons, and all of whom were distinguished by their birth, bearing,
and goodwill for England.

The first of the republican envoys to the Court of St. James
was the cultured Duc de Broglie (February 24, 1871), who was
succeeded (June 7, 1872) by the Comte Bernard d'Harcourt; and
on Count Bernard's retirement in the autumn of 1873 the post
was filled for two months by a more notable figure, the Duc
Decazes, who was recalled to Paris to undertake for four eventful
years the ministry of foreign affairs. "Very clever and pleasant"
was the description the Prince gave of the Duc Decazes, with
whose long-continued endeavours to promote an Anglo-French
entente he was in complete accord.

The three French ambassadors in London who owed their
nomination to the Duc Decazes strongly recommended themselves to the Prince's notice by reason alike of their rank and
their international outlook. Warmly did he welcome to London
in November 1873, as Duc Decazes' successor, the Duc de la

1873
Ætat. 31

Rochefoucauld-Bisaccia, who represented France in almost royal pomp until the following September. The Duc and his (second) wife, Princess Marie de Ligne, entertained the Prince and London society on a princely scale. To the Prince's satisfaction the aristocratic Duc made on Duc Decazes' behalf a tentative suggestion of an Anglo-French understanding which recalled the advances of Napoleon III. some eighteen years before. The ambassador's soundings of the Queen's government drew from her some ominous warnings, which fell lightly on her son's ears.

"A new intimate alliance with France" (her secretary, Colonel Ponsonby, wrote on 17th August 1874 to Lord Derby, who had newly entered on the office of Foreign Secretary), "especially with Republican France, the Queen would strongly deprecate. Germany, Austria, and even Russia are far more useful, natural, and good allies for England; but we should always try to be on good and friendly terms with France. The Duke of Wellington used to say, when that great intimacy in the time of King Louis Philippe existed, 'Plenty of friendship, but no love,' and this is quite true. The extreme intimacy with the Empire during and directly after the Crimean War was also a bad thing for this country."

The Prince held a different view, and when the Duc was succeeded, two months later, by the Comte de Jarnac, he encouraged him to pursue the friendly discussion. The Comte de Jarnac, for whom the Queen had little kindness, was well fitted by his early training for the pacificatory rôle. He had been attached to the London Embassy in King Louis Philippe's day, when he incurred the Queen's dislike, and he was credited with the invention of the phrase *entente cordiale* while discussing, in the Prince's infancy, Anglo-French relations with Lord Aberdeen, the Foreign Secretary. But Jarnac's efforts were cut short by his premature death within four months of his arrival—on 22nd March 1875. At the very moment, the Prince and Princess, unvarying in their courtesies to him, happened to be calling at the Embassy.

The project of the *entente* made some further progress at the hands of Jarnac's successor, the Marquis d'Harcourt, yet another aristocrat of pronounced social gifts who arrived in London in June 1875 and proved a companion after the Prince's heart. At once on reaching England the Marquis joined one of the Prince's Chiswick parties, which Queen Victoria happened to be honouring with her rare presence. At the request of Madame d'Harcourt,

a niece of Marshal MacMahon, the Prince found a means of paying   1875
her, before the party opened, the unusual compliment of making   Ætat. 33
a formal presentation of her to his mother. The Marquis was
the first French Ambassador of the republican era to remain
at the Court of St. James for a substantial period. His term
of office lasted nearly four years, and throughout he played a
leading part in the Prince's social circle. The Marquis went
further than his two predecessors in seeking the Prince's countenance for an understanding between the two countries. The
Duc Decazes, his chief at the Quai d'Orsay, instructed him carefully to distinguish between an alliance and an *entente*, but to
press for the latter. The Prince on a visit to Paris in 1877
endeavoured to persuade his French friends—Baron Alphonse de
Rothschild among them—to work to such an end. But little
positive success was scored diplomatically. Many Frenchmen
were reluctant to second England in putting pressure on Russia
during the Balkan crisis of 1877–78. A rumour spread that
France and Russia were meditating an alliance.[1] But the Prince
made personally, while in Paris during 1878, heroic efforts to
counter-check the adverse tendencies.

VI

The range of the Prince's French interests spread far beyond   1874
the confines of aristocratic society, but his openly displayed   Ætat. 32
intercourse with the French nobility fostered certain anxieties
among politicians on both sides of the English Channel. In
the late autumn of 1874 he bore bold witness to his sympathy with the French aristocracy in a way that stimulated the
uneasy feelings. The Duc de la Rochefoucauld-Bisaccia was
recalled from the French Embassy in London in the summer of
1874 on the sufficient ground that while in Paris in June he had
vainly proposed in the National Assembly a motion for the
restoration of the Legitimist monarchy. On bidding farewell
to the Prince and to London, the Duc pressed the Prince to visit
him in October at his ancestral château on the Loire. The
Prince readily accepted the invitation. The Duc's beautiful
renaissance château of Esclimont, near Rambouillet, was the
centre of a district resplendent with palaces of the old noblesse.

[1] Hanotaux, *Contemporary France*, iv. 310.

1874
Ætat. 32 The Duc's neighbours urged that the Prince should include their residences in his itinerary. The Prince was complacent and the rumour ran in the French republican press that a royal progress through the aristocratic region was contemplated by the heir to the British Crown. Queen Victoria intervened with a strong warning of the impolicy of the Prince's procedure. She asked Disraeli, newly become Prime Minister, to dissuade her son from his purpose. Disraeli professed reluctance to interfere, but he wrote to the Prince that "a visit to France at all at this moment" was of doubtful prudence. In any case he warned the Prince that whether or no his intended route lay through Paris, it was essential that he should pay "some act of marked respect to the Chief of the French State." The French government, Disraeli assured the Prince, was very sensitive on this point (Disraeli to Prince, October 3, 1874). The strife of parties in France over the constitutional issue was acquiring a fresh fury. M. Thiers had recently been succeeded in the Presidency of the Republic by the Prince's old friend, Marshal MacMahon, whose royalist leanings were anything but a bar to their meeting.

The Prince, who was at the moment staying with his wife's family in Denmark (October 7, 1874) replied to Mr. Disraeli that he proposed "to pass through Paris next week incognito under the name of Earl of Chester," and should "make a point of asking to see Marshal MacMahon if he should be either in Paris or Versailles." He "adopted the same course two years ago with M. Thiers." His subsequent visits "to personal friends at their country seats" would, "of course, be of a purely private character."

The Prince was faithful to his original plan. His hosts and hostesses included many noble monarchists in addition to the Duc de la Rochefoucauld at Esclimont. The most famous of the French noblesse vied with one another in sumptuous hospitality. There were sport, music, and dancing in lavish measure. The Duchesse de Luynes, de la Rochefoucauld's widowed daughter, entertained the visitor at the Château de Dompierre; the Duc and Duchesse de la Tremoïlle at the Château de Serrant; the Prince and Princesse de Sagan at the Château de Mello; and the Duc and Duchesse de Mouchy at Mouchy-le-Chatel (Oise).[1]

---

[1] The beautiful Duchesse de Mouchy, grand-daughter of Napoleon I.'s brother-in-law, Joachim Murat, once King of Naples, was the confidante of the ex-Empress Eugénie in the later years of the Empire.

The Prince punctually fulfilled his promise to the Prime   1874
Minister of a visit to the head of the state in Paris. Accom-   Ætat. 32
panied by Lord Lytton, poet and *attaché* at the British Embassy,
whose vivacity he appreciated, the Prince paid a ceremonial call
on Marshal MacMahon, and accepted the Marshal's invitation to
join in a stag hunt at Marly.[1] The conversation with the President avoided the constitutional controversy pending in France;
it turned mainly on the menacing attitude of Germany. Before
the Prince returned home he spent a pleasant day with the
Duc d'Aumale, the Duc de Chartres, and other members of the
Orléans family who were assembled at Chantilly.

Public criticism of the expedition was frank, and it went some
way to justify the misgivings of the Queen and the Prime Minister;
but the Prince quickly turned the tables on his critics by the
completely reassuring evidence (which he soon offered) alike of
the genuineness of his love for France and of his sympathy with
the national aspirations of Frenchmen and Frenchwomen without
distinction of rank or party.

VII

The resilience of the French temperament was never seen to   1875
better advantage than in the promptitude with which France   Ætat. 33
set about healing the wounds of war. Before the end of 1873
she had paid off the indemnity of £200,000,000, which Bismarck
had imposed on her under the Treaty of Frankfort. German
troops had evacuated her territory, and she was on the road to
recovery from her military humiliation. Bismarck watched the
French rebound with dismay. He hinted not obscurely that
German security required the armies of Germany to teach her
neighbour another lesson. It was of the German threat that both
President Thiers and President MacMahon had talked with the
Prince, and they found in him a sympathetic listener.

The threatening crisis in Franco-German relations culminated
for the time in the summer of 1875. Germany professed to be
shocked by a proposal of President MacMahon early in that year
to increase the French army. Rumours that France was im-
porting horses from Germany on a huge scale led to a German
decree prohibiting their exportation. In point of fact Bismarck,
in order to meet what he represented as a projected surprise on the

[1] *Letters of Robert, First Earl of Lytton*, i. 315, *seq.*, 1906.

part of France, was planning to be first in the field.   The Prince
identified himself completely with the French view of the situation.

In 1873 Count Bernstorff, the curmudgeonly German Ambassador in London, with whom the Prince's relations had always
been strained, died at his post, and he was succeeded by Count
Münster, a member of a Hanoverian family, whose social
temperament left nothing to be desired.   With Count Münster
the Prince could indulge in frank conversation which was
impossible with his predecessor.   To the Count he now confided
his abhorrence of Bismarck's ominous attitude.   On 13th April
1875 Count Münster reported to the German Chancellor a conversation with the Prince, who called the Count's attention to the
grave anxiety which the alleged policy of Bismarck was causing
Paris.   The Prince related how Marshal MacMahon, in conversation with him during November, denied the German allegation
about the importation of horses from Germany, and the Prince
justified French resentment at the recent German prohibition.
Count Münster sought to calm his interlocutor's mind by a comprehensive denial of warlike intention, and warned him against
prejudiced statements from French sources.[1]   But the Prince
put little faith in Count Münster's assurances, and eagerly
welcomed Queen Victoria's endeavour to checkmate Bismarck's
move.   Both the Queen and her daughter, the Crown Princess,
fully shared the Prince's present impatience with Bismarck's
bluster.   The Queen appealed in an autograph letter to Bismarck's
master, the Kaiser Wilhelm I., against fomenting another war
with France, and she appealed to the Tsar Alexander II., the
Kaiser's uncle, who was in Germany at the time, to employ his
influence at Berlin in the same direction.   Bismarck, who in
private used bitter language about the English royal family,
bade the Kaiser reply to the Queen that she was misinformed,—
that she was misled by an imaginary scare.   In the result
peace was unbroken.[2]   After the immediate danger had passed,
the Queen echoed the Prince's habitual note when she wrote to
the Crown Princess on the 8th June 1875:

---

[1] *Die Grosse Politik der Europäischen Kabinette*, i. pp. 259–60.
[2] The evidence which is now at the public disposal clearly proves that the
Queen and the Prince's suspicions were justified.   It was mainly owing to the
Tsar's opposition to Bismarck's policy that the Prussian statesman's plan of
1875 was foiled, but the postponement of the evil day may be assigned, in part
at least, to the resolute stand taken by the Queen and her son.

Bismarck is a terrible man, and he makes Germany greatly   1875
disliked—indeed *no one* will stand the overbearing insolent way   Ætat. 33
in which he acts and treats other nations—Belgium for instance.
You know that the Prussians are not popular unfortunately,
and *no one* will tolerate any Power wishing to dictate to all
Europe.   This country, with the greatest wish to go hand in hand
with Germany, *cannot* and *will not stand it.*[1]

There was another feature of Bismarck's policy which added
fuel to the Prince's wrath.   Bismarck's Kultur-Kampf, or warfare
on the independence of the Roman Catholic Church in Prussia,
had brought him, in 1873, into collision with the Roman Catholic
bishops of both France and Belgium, who denounced his persecution of their Prussian co-religionists.   Bismarck called on the
Governments of both France and Belgium to disavow sympathy
with the episcopal attitude and to prohibit further manifestations
of episcopal fury.   In the case of France the Prince deemed it
politic for the French Government to yield to Bismarck's representations, and in agreement with his view the French Prime
Minister, the Duc de Broglie, and the Foreign Minister, the
Duc Decazes, deemed it prudent in January 1874 to make
the reparation which the German Chancellor demanded.
But the Belgian Government was less complaisant, and the
Prince regarded Bismarck's increasingly peremptory demands
on Belgium as intolerable.   He interpreted them as a menace
of Belgian independence.   In July 1874 Count Schouvaloff, the
Russian Ambassador, who had recently replaced the veteran
Baron Brunnow at the Court of St. James and was in the early
years of his London stay in confidential communication with
the Prince, reported to St. Petersburg on 1/15th May 1875 how
the Prince spoke to him of Bismarck's harrying of Belgium
"with visible irritation."   The English, the Prince told Count
Schouvaloff, took Prince Bismarck's menaces "so much to
heart that, if need be, this country (*i.e.* England) would be
ready to take up arms for the defence of Belgium's rights."[2]

The Belgian dispute was ultimately adjusted, but it sharpened
the Prince's eye for fresh signals of Bismarck's intimidatory
mood.   Two years later, in 1877, the action of the German
general staff gave cause for renewed French alarm, of which the

---

[1] Cited in "Queen Victoria and France," art. in *Quarterly Review*, July
1919.
[2] Archives of the Russian Embassy, London.

1877
Ætat. 35

Prince learned on a visit to Paris. Immediately on his return to Marlborough House he wrote to Lord Beaconsfield, then Prime Minister (May 7, 1877): "I arrived here this morning from Paris in eight hours and a quarter! Everybody there was in great agitation about the attitude of Germany and Moltke's speeches." A fellow-feeling with France rendered him sensitive to every whisper of the German menace of aggression.

VIII

1873
Ætat. 31

The Prince's friend, the Marquis de Galliffet, more far-seeing than his monarchical associates in the civil or military service of the Republic, came to recognise, while the Republic was yet young, that it was destined to endure. It was mainly Galliffet's persuasive tongue that moderated the Prince's anti-republican prejudice and prepared the way for his full acceptance of the republican form of government. An inseparable companion of Galliffet, the Marquis du Lau d'Allemans, shared his frank intimacy with the Prince, and facilitated the process of the Prince's conversion. The Marquis du Lau's rank of Lieutenant of Dragoons was scarcely commensurate with his social prominence. From the days of the Empire he was (in the Prince's words) "a great personal friend." In spite of his legitimist convictions, du Lau followed with detachment all the moves on the French political chessboard after the Republic was installed, and he diagnosed with singular accuracy the various turns of the political wheel. From du Lau, who came to incline towards moderate republicanism, the Prince derived much sound information as to the course of events, and learned most of the inner workings of the triangular duel which long waged in France among the Royalist, Bonapartist, and Republican forces. The talk of Galliffet and du Lau whetted the Prince's curiosity regarding the leading spirits of French republicanism, and he was soon seeking the acquaintance of the republican apostle, M. Gambetta. The Prince's tact and geniality quickly made him as thoroughly at home with staunch supporters of the Republic as with the royalist and imperialist aristocracy, with whom his social relations remained undisturbed.

While the Prince overcame his mistrust of republicanism of the sane and moderate type, which men like M. Gambetta or

General Galliffet espoused, the Prince never failed to reprobate revolutionary aims which he imputed to M. Clémenceau and other leaders of the extreme left wing of the republican party. The day of French royalist and aristocratic diplomats at the Court of St. James's had ended with the retirement of the Marquis d'Harcourt in 1879. The Prince made a pronounced avowal of his animus against the republican "tail," when in June 1880, M. Challemel-Lacour, a reputed Communist, was nominated by M. de Freycinet, the French Prime Minister, to the French Embassy in London. The Prince's Legitimist friends in Paris reported to him that M. Lacour had, as Communist préfet of the Rhone in 1871, been guilty of brutal outrages at Lyons, and had on that ground been refused as ambassador by four foreign governments. He viewed with dismay the succession of a Frenchman of such antecedents to the French aristocrats with whom he had cultivated so close a social intimacy in the Republic's earlier years. He appealed to Queen Victoria to veto M. Lacour's appointment, but Lord Granville, the Foreign Secretary, pointed out to her that the charges against M. Lacour of aggressive Communism were unsubstantiated, and that he was the close friend of both M. Waddington and M. Gambetta. The Queen declined to act on her son's suggestion.[1] Sir Charles Dilke, then Under-Secretary for Foreign Affairs, ultimately conquered the Prince's scruples by assuring him that the French Ambassador-designate was "not of the Clémenceau type," was a man of varied culture, and was misrepresented by the Paris *Figaro* which the Prince was in the habit of reading. With his usual adaptability the Prince accepted the situation, and received M. Lacour on his arrival in London with every courtesy, acknowledging the charm of his manner and conversation.[2] But despite

1880
Ætat. 38

[1] Queen Victoria had just vetoed the proposed appointment to the London Embassy of the Marquis de Noailles on a personal moral ground. The Marquis was an experienced diplomatist and an efficient historian who had already seen service in Washington and Rome and was to pursue his career at Constantinople. The Prince took no exception to the Marquis de Noailles. It was only after the Queen's rejection of the Marquis that the French Prime Minister, M. de Freycinet, at his wits' end to find an occupant of the London Embassy, nominated M. Lacour. In the House of Commons the choice of M. Lacour was warmly denounced by an Irish Catholic member, Mr. F. H. O'Donnell, on the ground of his anti-clerical and free-thinking tendencies.

[2] M. Challemel-Lacour's tenure of office only lasted till February 1882, when he was recalled at his own request. He soon became Foreign Minister in M. Jules Ferry's second government (Feb. 21, 1883), and was succeeded in London by M. Tissot.

the steady growth of his sympathy with moderate Republicanism, the Prince continued to keep his distance from French politicians who were reputed to favour the social revolution—among whom he long included M. Clémenceau.

IX

1873
Ætat. 31

The resolve of the French government to make manifest to the world its rapid recovery from the effects of the war by organising an international exhibition for the year 1878, offered the Prince an opportunity of identifying himself more conspicuously than before with French aspirations, and justified his right, despite monarchical sensitiveness, to the title of friend of France *sans phrase*.

The Prince had recently illustrated his confidence in international exhibitions as magnets of peace by taking a prominent part in the organisation of an important effort of the kind at Vienna in the spring of 1873. A Royal Commission had been appointed in the previous year to organise a British section at Vienna, and the Prince accepted, for the first time, the post of President of such a body, over which he now exercised a very practical control. At the end of April he, with the Princess, and his brother Arthur (whom he looked after on the trip with fatherly care), and one of his favourite half-cousins, Prince Leiningen, set out at the Emperor Francis Joseph's invitation for Vienna to attend the formal opening on 1st May. Vienna was reached on 28th April, and the Prince and Princess were lodged in Prince Eugene's Palace (better known as the Finanz Ministerium).

The royal company at Vienna, in which the Prince and Princess were included, seemed to obliterate the wounds of past strife and to suggest a fresh guarantee of the peaceful settlement of Europe. There were present the German Emperor William I., and his heir, the Crown Prince, together with King Victor Emmanuel. The Triple Alliance (of Germany, Austria, and Italy) was in the making. Emperor Francis Joseph had not met his former arch-foe of Italy on so promising a footing since the war of 1866. The two monarchs were, within a lustrum, to form with their formidable German fellow-guest that Alliance

which long claimed, somewhat ambiguously, to counter-check   1873
or render innocuous all European rivalries.   Ætat. 31

On a personal ground the Prince was scarcely reassured as
to the place that England was intended by Prussia, the main-
spring of the diplomatic machine at Vienna, to fill in the coming
regrouping of nations. Apart from the ceremony of inaugurat-
ing the imposing buildings of the Exhibition in the Prater on
1st May, there was a long programme of official banquets and
receptions. The Prince was disquieted by learning the Emperor
Francis Joseph's decision that the Crown Prince of Germany should
precede him at all functions of State. The Prince suspected something other than a personal affront; the incident suggested to
him that Austria was committed to serve as Prussia's catspaw.
The Prince's equanimity was hardly restored by the Emperor's
assurance that all the Powers were equal at his Court, and that he
only recognised the alphabetical order of their sequence.

In all other respects the visit to Vienna passed off pleasantly
enough. The Prince was impressed by the structural improvements of the city since his last visit in 1869. "During the four
years since I was here" (he wrote) "Vienna has increased very
much in size and most splendid houses are being built everywhere,
and the streets widened, which is very necessary, as the old ones
are so narrow." The personal friendliness of the Prince's intercourse with his sister and brother-in-law was unimpaired by the
difficulty of precedence, and he greeted genially their elder son
"Willy," the future ex-Kaiser, who accompanied them. With
a sort of dramatic irony, in view of the future relations of uncle
and nephew, the Prince in a letter to his mother, 2nd May 1873,
described his nephew as "much grown and such a nice boy."
The Prince was also attracted by the Austrian Emperor's heir,
"the young Crown Prince Rudolph, a very nice boy," whose fate
was to prove more personally calamitous than even that of the
Prince's Prussian nephew.

After twelve days in Vienna the Prince, with the Princess and
his brother Arthur, passed on to Buda-Pesth, which was new
ground for the Prince as well as for his companions. There the
Archduke Joseph, the commander-in-chief, was their host.
The Hungarian people welcomed the Prince with an impressive
heartiness and gave the visit, which was private in form, a public
significance which was perhaps exaggerated.

"This demonstration of national sympathy for the Princes of the Royal House of Great Britain," wrote Edmund Monson, British Consul-General at Buda-Pesth, rather cumbrously to Lord Granville (May 14, 1873), "has been so unequivocally genuine and spontaneous, so universal and so persistent as to convince every Englishman and Foreigner who witnessed it of the sincerity of the oft-repeated declaration that while on the one hand the Hungarians know that of all the European nations there is none that can vie with England in interest in their constitutional life and progress and in their efforts to maintain and develop their national freedom, so there is on the other hand no country to which they themselves are more attracted by similarity of character and habits, by identity of policy and interests, and especially by admiration of our Sovereign and of all the members of the Royal Family."

The Prince was gratified by the Hungarian welcome, and with many of the Hungarian noblemen whom he now met for the first time he formed associations which led him later to return to their country to enjoy sport and hospitality. Under the guidance of such experts as Count Longay, lately Prime Minister and President of the Hungarian Academy, and of Professor Vambéry, the Asiatic explorer whose acquaintance he had already made in London, he inspected the places and objects of interest.

X

The visit to Vienna in 1873, although it embraced much other interest and activity, was mainly identified with the success of the International Exhibition, in the organisation of which the Prince had borne part. It was the first time that he had engaged in the active organisation of an exhibition on a great scale, whether at home or abroad. The experience which he thus gleaned he placed at France's disposal five years later.

In April 1876, while the Prince was on his way home from his visit to India, Lord Lyons, the British Ambassador in Paris, intimated to the British Foreign Office that the French government desired the Prince to be President of the British section of the approaching Paris International Exhibition, which was appointed to open in the spring of 1878. The Prince was gratified by the invitation, and the Queen readily assented to his acceptance. In the autumn, when the formal appointment of a Royal

Commission to organise the British exhibit was under the government's consideration, the Duke of Richmond, President of the
Council, claimed, *ex officio*, the presidential office.   But the Prince
cited the precedent of Vienna, and in fulfilment of his request to
be invested with the fullest powers, he was formally appointed
President with unrestricted authority and with power to nominate
his fellow-commissioners.   The Prince ruled that India and the
Colonies should be represented by the British Commission, and
should not be in separate communication with the French
government.

The Prince flung himself with all his energy into the congenial
work of organisation, and he spared no time or trouble to make
the British share in the French enterprise an outstanding success.
He invited direct intercourse with English manufacturers, whom
he impressed with his business aptitude.   In connection with the
projected gallery of British Art in the Exhibition he signed with
his own hand letters inviting co-operation from owners of pictures
of the English school, and did what he could to overcome the reluctance of lenders.   As soon as the English pavilion in the
Champs Elysée and the other buildings of the British section were
in being, he supervised on the spot the final arrangements in
minute detail.   " I find I shall have a great deal to do with the
Exhibition," he wrote to the Queen from the Hôtel Bristol,
Paris, on 1st March 1878.   Until the following October he was
repeatedly in Paris, and both there and in London was rarely
free from the pressing business of the Exhibition.

Although the Prince valued the Exhibition as a demonstration
of the progress of industry and art, he saw in it an outward and
visible sign of France's renewed vigour and prosperity, as well as
of her leadership in the arts of peace.   Nor did he conceal from
himself the aim of its foremost promoters to make of it a victorious
rally of the republican forces—a celebration of the republicans'
triumph over monarchist rivalries.   Few royalists or imperialists
accorded the Exhibition much countenance.   Marshal MacMahon
was nominally at the head of the great enterprise, being still
President of the Republic, but he was nearing the end of his
political tether, and his monarchical leanings were losing their
significance.   The Prince's faith in the Marshal's political
sagacity was declining.   After an interview with him on 1st
March 1878 he wrote to Lord Beaconsfield : "I saw the Marshal

to-day, but he can hardly be considered a far-seeing statesman."
The Prince had made up his mind publicly to salute the Republic
as the expression of the national will, and incidentally to take
precedence of the royalty of Europe in payment of homage to
the republican form of the French government.

On the 26th April the Prince arrived anew in Paris—on this
occasion with the Princess—to stay at the Hôtel Bristol for near
three weeks, in order to attend the inaugural ceremonies and to
perform the multifarious duties of President of the British section.
On 29th April, two days before the opening, he gave a *déjeuner*
at the Café de la Paix to all members of the British Commission,
to whom, as well as to the British exhibitors, he was always
accessible throughout the time that the Exhibition was in being.
On 3rd May 1878 the Prince wrote to the Queen how his
"hard work" had been

amply rewarded by the great success of the British section, which
is almost entirely complete, and no other country, not even
France, can say the same. I think I have seen everything we
have to show and talked almost with every exhibitor. . . . The
Exhibition as a whole, that is, as far as I can judge, is very fine
and quite immense, and endless what one has to see, but certainly
not so fine a building as the Vienna one. The money that has
been spent is something incredible, and shows what a rich country
this is.

The Queen was so impressed by her son's enthusiasm that she
contemplated inspecting the Exhibition for herself in the summer,
and in corrrespondence with Lord Lyons canvassed the conditions
in which she might pay Paris a visit, but after much deliberation
she abandoned the intention, mainly on the grounds of the heat
and fatigue. The Prince regretted her decision. He took especial
pleasure in acting as guide to relatives and friends who were
visiting the Exhibition. His sister, the Princess Louise, and her
husband, the Marquis of Lorne, made a tour of the buildings under
his direction. The success of the British section was universally
assigned to the Prince's energy. "The Prince has done much
to put our people on their mettle, and to show what England can
do," wrote the Liberal politician, Hugh Childers, on 21st June, on
an early visit to the Exhibition.[1]

Although the Prince valued the praise that was bestowed on

---

[1] Spencer Childers, *Life of Childers* (1901), i. 254.

him as the main organiser of the British section, it was not exclusively in that rôle that he wished for recognition. He sought to fill a larger part on the stage of France, if not of Europe which was watching events from afar. At the formal opening by the President of the Republic in the palace of the Trocadero on 1st May the Prince was almost as prominent a figure as the two men with whom he walked in the main procession— the Marshal and the Duc d'Audriffet-Pasquier, President of the Senate. Although all the countries of Europe, save Germany, were represented by their ambassadors, there were notable gaps in the company of royal personages who supported the Prince. The great governing houses of Europe were disinclined to pay personal court to the Republic. At the Prince's side were no more than five of royal rank, and those not in the highest category. The Prince's brother-in-law, the Crown Prince of Denmark, was there, with the Italian Prince, the Duke of Aosta (the deposed King Amadeo of Spain), Prince Henry of the Netherlands, the Prince of Orange, and, finally, Don Francisco d'Assisi, consort of the dethroned Queen Isabella of Spain, who only by courtesy could be reckoned of royal status at all. The Prince enjoyed his comparative isolation. He was in the happiest mood, and when some deputies roguishly cried "Vive la Republique" as he and his royal companions passed them, the Prince laughingly acknow- ledged the greeting. In the evening Marshal MacMahon enter- tained the foreign visitors at the Elysée at a dinner and at a reception, of which the Prince wrote, "the heat and crowd I shall not easily forget."

Two days later he made a public declaration of his potent faith in the *entente cordiale*, and of his cheerful acquiescence at the same time in the victory of the Republic. Much historic interest attaches to the occasion. The British exhibitors, under Lord Granville's chairmanship, entertained him on 3rd May at a banquet at the Hôtel du Louvre. There was a notable gathering of Frenchmen as well as Englishmen. Among the latter were the Prince's intimates, the Dukes of Manchester and Sutherland, with Lord Northbrook and Mr. Lyon Playfair. After the chairman had given the toast of the Queen, the Prince proposed the health of the President of the French Republic. It was the first time that he had publicly honoured the head of the Republican Government. Subsequently he delivered a striking speech on the relations between the countries. The first part was delivered in English, and was in reply to the chairman's toast of his own health.

"I am glad to think," ran a notable passage, "we should have met here this evening in a country and a city which have always received Englishmen with hospitality, and that though, not many years ago, there was a time when we were not so friendly as we are now, still that time is past and forgotten. The jealousy which was the cause of the animosity has now, I feel sure, ceased for ever, and I am convinced that the *entente cordiale* which exists between this country and our own is one not likely to change."

The Prince devoted the rest of the speech to toasting in French "The French Executive" (of the Exhibition), and great applause welcomed his concluding sentences, which ran :

C'est avec un grand plaisir que je viens remercier la nation Française tant en mon nom qu'au nom de la Commission Royale Britannique de tout ce qu'elle a fait ; et j'ai l'honneur de vous demander d'accepter mes remercîments comme un témoignage public de la manière gracieuse et courtoise avec laquelle vous nous avez prêté votre concours. Vous voudrez donc bien m'accorder la faveur d'accepter ici cette expression de mon opinion personelle ; L'Exposition Universelle de 1878 est sans contredit un grand succès. Aussi permettez moi de vous dire et de dire à La France entière que la prospérité de ce pays et celle de la Grande Bretagne ont un intérêt essentiellement réciproque. La participation cordiale apportée au triomphe des arts dans cette lutte pacifique est de la plus haute importance pour nos deux nations et pour le monde entier. L'Exposition Internationale dans laquelle nous avons tenu à prendre une large part est le meilleur moyen de sympathie que nous puissons donner au peuple Français au quel nous devons tant.

The speeches were fully reported in the press on both sides of the Channel. Beyond all misconception had the Prince nailed his French colours to the mast. In French official and social circles he was at once hailed as the "accredited representative of courageous and high-spirited Young England which was about to supplant decrepit and hesitating Old England." The checks of the British Constitution could scarcely, it was confidently argued, withstand the influence of the Prince's enlightened ideas.[1] Such phrases tended to overestimate the Prince's

---

[1] Hanotaux, *Contemporary France*, iv. 310, citing the *Mémorial Diplomatique* for March 16, 1878, p. 184.

political position at home. Nor was the Prince's present effort
to knit France and England together politically destined for
more than temporary effect. Yet for the time the promise
looked great. Even so cautious a diplomatist as Lord Lyons
wrote to Lord Salisbury, the Foreign Secretary, on 11th May:
"England is very popular here at this moment, and the Prince
of Wales's visit has been the principal cause of this."[1] Two
months later the sky grew overcast, and though the Prince
heroically succeeded then in scattering the clouds, they gathered
subsequently in a density greater than that which it was in the
Prince's power to disperse—at any rate until some two or more
decades had passed over his head. But even now, by virtue of
his personality, he was preparing the ground for the far-off event
of a durable Anglo-French *entente*.

XI

There was in Paris much social festivity in which the Prince
figured prominently through the season of the Exhibition. He
made it clear that his social ties with Imperialists or Royalists
were unaffected by the new links, social as well as political, which
he was fashioning with the Republicans. The most imposing
of the entertainments in May was a ball (on the 14th) in honour
of the Prince and Princess at the British Embassy, where there
assembled the President of the Republic, representatives of
all political parties, and the foreign diplomatists. The Prince
opened the dancing with Mme. Waddington, the Foreign Minister's
wife, an American lady whose social charm appealed to him;
while the Princess's partner was the Duc d'Alençon, grandson of
the Duc de Nemours, the second son of Louis Philippe. Royalists
still stood high in the Prince's social favour. In the same month
he was the chief guest at a *déjeuner* given by the Duc de Chartres,
and he spent a Sunday at Chantilly. To the Bonapartists the
Prince showed himself equally accessible. At a *déjeuner* at
the Princess Mathilde's he renewed acquaintance with her
brother of ambiguous reputation—Prince (Jerome) Napoleon,
nicknamed "Plon-Plon." The Prince found him "aged a good
deal, but very interesting in conversation." Always eager to
extend his knowledge of persons of note he readily consented to

---

[1] Newton's *Life of Lord Lyons*, ii. 139.

be introduced at an evening party in the Faubourg St. Germain
to the Spanish royalist pretender, Don Carlos, and his wife, the
Duchess of Madrid. "He is a handsome man," the Prince
wrote, with customary ingenuousness, "but has not a pleasant
expression. She is very amiable, but plain."

But of far greater moment was an acquaintanceship soon
to ripen into friendship which the Prince first formed, within a
few days of the opening of the Exhibition, with the greatest of
the republican leaders. At a dinner-party at the Quai d'Orsay
on 6th May, over which the Foreign Minister, M. Waddington,
presided, Lord Lyons presented to him M. Gambetta, with whom
he enjoyed a long conversation. "The experience," the Prince
wrote, "interested me very much." The republican leader had
been, since the fall of the Empire, the most notable man in France.
Throughout the Franco-German war he had by his energy
and eloquence, saved his country from despair, and though he
was unable to retrieve the military defeat, he kept alive his
fellow-countrymen's hopes of the future. After the peace of
Frankfort he devoted his genius to maintaining the cause of the
Republic against the assaults of Imperialists, Monarchists, and
Communists alike. Although factious dissensions long excluded
him from ministerial office, he was the dominant figure of the
Chamber of Deputies. To him more than to any other, France
owed that triumph of the Third Republic, the permanent confirmation of which synchronised with the Exhibition. Un-
distinguished in appearance, of squat figure and small stature,
and with an Italian cast of countenance rendered unattractive
by the loss in youth of an eye, Gambetta commanded all the arts
of conversation, and charmed every one with whom he came into
social intercourse. The Prince had already heard Gambetta
speak in the Chamber of Deputies, and had been fascinated by
his eloquence. Now at their first meeting at M. Waddington's
table, the Prince fell completely under M. Gambetta's spell.

Gambetta was in an amiable mood. After thanking the Prince
for the sympathetic words on France which he had spoken at
Lord Granville's dinner, he assured the Prince that friendship
with England was the desire of himself and his political friends.
The Prince replied that at every period of his life he had
been the friend of France. The Prince frankly spoke of the
dangers with which party polemics threatened the country's

internal tranquillity, and Gambetta answered that the example of ordered political progress in England was exercising on France a healthy influence. Both were in agreement as to their distrust of Bismarck's policy, and in their "strong dislike of the doctrine that, nations having large armies at their command, might upset all treaties in defiance of protests from those concerned and contrary to public law." [1] The talk lasted three-quarters of an hour, and at its close the Prince introduced Gambetta to the Crown Prince of Denmark, his wife's brother. The friendly conversation came to a close with a pressing invitation from the Prince to Gambetta to visit him in England.

Though the Prince's hope of entertaining Gambetta in London or Sandringham was not fulfilled, the Prince found many later opportunities of improving his relations with the statesman in Paris, and of exchanging with him political confidences to the advantage of the two countries' political ties. Gambetta's familiar dictum, "Le Prussianisme voilà l'ennemi," embodied a sentiment which came home to the Prince. In their subsequent interviews the first impressions of political sagacity and knowledge which the Prince left on Gambetta were amply confirmed. It was a profound calamity that so promising an intercourse should have been abruptly ended by Gambetta's premature and tragic death on 21st December 1882, four and a half years after the two men first met.

XII

In June 1878, when the Prince was again in Paris on the business of the Exhibition, he publicly presented himself to the people of Paris, by an accidental coincidence of melancholy tenor, in the guise of a frank sympathiser with a victim of Prince Bismarck's ruthless policy. On the 12th June there died in exile in Paris the blind ex-King of Hanover, George V., Queen Victoria's first cousin. The ex-King, who had paid his last visit to England as the guest of the Queen in the summer of 1876 had, since his expulsion from his throne and country, moved the Prince's profoundest pity. Under the patronage of the French government a funeral procession through Paris was now organised by the dead man's friends. Attended by a French military escort the cortège passed, on 16th June, from the ex-

[1] Buckle, *Life of Disraeli*, vi. 291.

1878
Ætat. 36

King's residence in the Rue Pressbourg through the Champs d'Elysée to the Lutheran Church in the Rue Chauchat. At the head of the procession the Prince walked with the chief mourner, the ex-King's son and heir, Ernest Augustus, Duke of Cumberland. Sympathetic onlookers lined the streets, among them the Shah of Persia, the Prince's guest of 1873, who had come on a second visit to Europe to inspect the Paris Exhibition,[1] although, not altogether to the Prince's regret, he omitted England from his present itinerary. The Lutheran church, where a religious service was held over the ex-King of Hanover's remains, was filled to overflowing with the Prince's French friends of Bonapartist and Royalist leanings. The Princesse Mathilde was there with Princess Paul Metternich and the Duc de la Rochefoucauld-Bisaccia.[2] It was inevitable that Berlin should raise protests against the Prince's apparent leadership of an anti-Prussian demonstration in the French capital.[3]

Prussia suspected some ulterior meaning in the Prince's open display in the French capital of friendship for his Hanoverian kinsfolk. To the satisfaction of his French friends, the Prince showed himself in no mood to assuage Prussian suspicion. The Duke of Cumberland, claimant to his father's throne, was betrothed to the Princess Thyra, youngest sister of the Princess of Wales, and the Prince made no concealment of his strong interest in the young man's future. The domestic associations of the Prince and the Duke served to intensify Prussian heartburnings when the Duke, with the Prince's approval, renewed his dead father's protest against Prussia's suppression of his hereditary throne and against the seizure of his family's fortune. Prussian feeling was further exasperated by the arrival in Denmark of a great concourse of the bridegroom's German adherents to attend his marriage with Princess Thyra at Copenhagen at the close of the year (December 21). The Prussian government imputed the most inimical intentions to the gathering, which naturally cherished no love of Prussia, and the German minister was by way of threatening protest withdrawn from the Danish capital. The Prince was unable to attend the wedding

---

[1] Diary of the Shah, 1878, p. 186.
[2] Jules Hansen, Les Coulisses de la Diplomatie, 1880, pp. 363–4.
[3] After the religious service the ex-King's coffin was removed to Windsor for interment by Queen Victoria's order in St. George's Chapel.

owing to the death of his sister, Princess Alice of Hesse-Darmstadt   1879
but he was moved to fierce indignation by this affront to Denmark.   Ætat. 37

"The German government," he wrote, "are no doubt capable of any amount of bullying, but they cannot have the 'brass' to pick a quarrel [with Denmark] because some old friends and adherents of the Duke of Cumberland were at his wedding" (Prince of Wales to Ponsonby, January 26, 1879).[1]

The Prince's many manifestoes, the first of which he openly launched in Paris, of fraternal regard for the Duke of Cumberland, came to be interpreted in Berlin as part of the Prince's deliberate scheme to thwart Prussian policy. When the Prince visited his sister, the Crown Princess, at Potsdam in November 1880, he formed the impression that Prince Bismarck and the Prussian Court looked upon him as a French spy.[2] The persistence with which he inveighed against Prussia's meanness in withholding from the Duke of Cumberland his family property gave rise to one of the Prince's early differences with his German nephew William, on the young man's accession to the throne as Kaiser William II. On the other hand, his French friends of all political creeds rejoiced in the strength of the Prince's Hanoverian sympathies, to which he had testified in the streets of Paris, while his speech of 3rd May still echoed in Parisian ears.

XIII

The dominant political question which engaged the attention   1878
of Mr. Disraeli's second ministry, 1874–80, was the struggle   Ætat. 36
between Russia and Turkey for the control of the Balkan States, and for the hegemony of Eastern Europe. All Europe was interested in the dispute, and the nations approached its consideration from different points of view. While the Prince was occupied with the Paris Exhibition, the momentous controversy was in its most critical stage. The various European Powers agreed to remit the settlement of the controversy to a

[1] The Prince's tender feeling for his Hanoverian cousins failed to reconcile him to the marriage, which Queen Victoria favoured, of the Duke of Cumberland's only sister, Princess Frederica of Hanover, with her father's former equerry Baron Pawell-Ramingen. The Prince shared a general view that the union was a *mésalliance*, and he absented himself from the wedding on 24th April 1880, which the Queen arranged to take place in the private chapel at Windsor.

[2] Gwynn and Tuckwell, *Life of Sir Charles Dilke*, i. 341.

congress which met at Berlin from 30th June to 30th July. Political parties in France were by no means at one in their views of the Eastern Question.

England was protecting Turkey against Russia, and the Prince discovered in Paris signs of sympathy with Russia of which, he wrote to his mother on 11th May, it would be well for the English government to take account. M. Gambetta and those who followed him differed from a host of their countrymen in the favour which they bestowed on the main lines of Lord Beaconsfield's anti-Russian policy. During his first conversation with the Prince on 6th May, Gambetta, according to his interlocutor, "expressed his hearty approval of every step taken by Lord Beaconsfield in connection with the Eastern Question."

But the development of an Anglo-French *entente* which M. Gambetta and the Prince desired, was hampered by the doubts of Lord Beaconsfield's foreign policy which had taken root in many French minds. A formidable section of French political opinion was profoundly disturbed by the announcement on 8th July of a convention into which England and Turkey had secretly entered a month before—on the eve of the Berlin Congress— whereby Turkey ceded to England the island of Cyprus and England undertook to defend Turkey against Russian encroachment on her Asiatic territory. Furious cries were raised in France that England was threatening French influence in the Mediterranean as well as in Egypt. The Prince was proposing to revisit Paris in mid-July on the business of the Exhibition. Lord Lyons, writing on 12th July, urged him to stay at home. There were mutterings on the boulevards that he had misled France as to English policy.[1]

The Prince was not so easily daunted. He not only adhered to his plan of revisiting Paris, but he resolved to employ himself in an endeavour to allay French political excitement. On the 18th July he arrived in the French capital. He discovered that M. Waddington, the French Foreign Minister, who had just returned from Berlin after representing France at the Congress, was not unfavourable to the Anglo-Turkish convention. But the French government's nerve was somewhat shaken by the threat of a hostile motion in the Chamber. Uncertainty prevailed as to the intentions of M. Gambetta, who, in spite of his general

[1] Newton's *Life of Lord Lyons*, ii. 154.

sympathy with English policy in the Near East, was not well disposed to the ministry in power under M. Dufaure, and confessed to
being taken by surprise in the matter of the cession of Cyprus.
The Prince decided to discuss the points at issue with M. Gambetta.   On the ground of their common interest in the Exhibition,
he invited the great Frenchman to lunch with him at the Café
des Anglais.   The invitation was readily accepted.   The British
Ambassador, Lord Lyons, was not asked to join the party ; a
junior secretary was bidden to represent him.   At the luncheon
Gambetta and the Prince thoroughly discussed the crisis, and
M. Gambetta accepted the Prince's assurances that the Anglo-
Turkish Convention, with the transfer of Cyprus, in no way
affected French interests.   The Prince told Lord Lyons that

"Gambetta spoke strongly in favour of an alliance between
France and England—declared himself more or less reconciled
to the Convention of 4th June—and spoke in the most disparaging
terms, not so much of the Foreign Policy of Russia, as of the
institutions, the government, and the administration of that
country."   "I hear from other quarters," Lord Lyons reported
to Salisbury, "that Gambetta was extremely pleased with the
interview.   I am assured also that the Prince of Wales acquitted
himself with great skill." [1]

Two days later the Prince pursued his self-imposed mission
of mediation.   He met M. Waddington at luncheon at the British
Embassy, and relieved him of anxiety by communicating to him
Gambetta's latest view, which meant that M. Dufaure's government, in which M. Waddington was Foreign Minister, was in no
immediate danger.   The reconciliation of Gambetta to Lord
Beaconsfield's action deprived the French agitation against it
for the time of most of its strength.

The Prince arrived in London on the 22nd July, and two days
later he was gratified by receiving from Lord Salisbury, the
English Foreign Secretary, a generous acknowledgement of the
success of his intervention :

I trust your Royal Highness will not think I am guilty of an
intrusion if I venture, on the score of my official position, to
thank your Royal Highness very earnestly for what you have
done in Paris.   The crisis has been one of no little delicacy : and
if the leaders of French opinion had definitively turned against

---

[1] Newton's *Life of Lord Lyons*, ii. 152.

us, a disagreeable and even hazardous condition of estrangement between the two countries might have grown up, which would have been very much to be regretted. Your Royal Highness's influence over Monsieur Gambetta, and the skill with which that influence has been exerted, have averted a danger, which was not inconsiderable. It has been necessarily my duty to watch anxiously the movement of feeling in France at this moment.

The Prince replied the same day :

If I have in any way by the personal interview I had with M. Gambetta tended to allay the irritation which was manifest in France by our taking Cyprus I am beyond measure pleased, as nobody would have deplored more than I would that any estrangement between the two countries should occur. M. Gambetta told me that after the paragraphs of the Treaty of Berlin had been read and digested the feelings of his countrymen greatly subsided.

Any immediate danger of friction between France and England was thus removed by the Prince's sagacity.

Other troubles between the two countries were brewing which proved less easy of accommodation. The control of Egypt was becoming a bone of bitter contention. But when the Exhibition closed on 21st October the pacific atmosphere which the Prince had helped to foster in its opening days seemed rich in promise. The Prince, accompanied by the Princess, attended the concluding ceremony, when the President distributed the awards to the exhibitors and declared the Exhibition closed. The Prince sat on the dais at the President's left hand, while Don Francisco d'Assisi was on the President's right. It was the last occasion on which Marshal MacMahon spoke in public. Three months later the republic's stability was to be finally assured by the Marshal's resignation of his office to a convinced republican, M. Jules Grévy (January 30, 1879) ; and by the accession of the Prince's new friend, M. Gambetta, to the responsible position of President of the Chamber of Deputies. Until his death on the 17th October 1893, at the advanced age of eighty-five, the Marshal during his retirement from public life maintained friendly relations with the Prince. In his last year the Marshal wrote in his own hand to him (April 29, 1892) of the approaching marriage of his second son, Emmanuel, a notification which the Prince cordially acknowledged. But the Prince's faith in the Marshal's political capacity had long since evaporated, and he viewed his disappearance from the public stage as a benefit to France.

The day after the Exhibition closed, 22nd October, Earl Granville presented to the Prince on behalf of all who had taken part in organising the British section, an address of thanks for his manifold labours. The Prince's last exertion was to urge the Prime Minister to bestow titular honours on his most active collaborators. He was particularly desirous that his Colonial helpers should be decorated. "I am sure you will agree with me," he wrote to Lord Beaconsfield (October 6, 1878), "that the present is not an unimportant moment for our paying the Colonies a compliment; they have come forward most liberally, and really have had most creditable exhibits." [1]

The Paris Exhibition of 1878 had given the Prince more extended opportunities than he had yet enjoyed of "being of use." If the harvest which he anticipated from the Anglo-French *entente* for which he pleaded throughout his association with the Exhibition was to be tardily reaped, French and English politicians and peoples must divide between them responsibility for the unpropitious delay.

[1] The Prince pressed with success on Lord Beaconsfield's notice his old host in Canada, Sir John Rose, for the G.C.M.G. (October 29); Philip Cunliffe Owen, for K.C.M.G. (October 29); and Sir Richard Wallace, whose previous services to the Vienna Exhibition of 1873 the Prince eulogised, for the K.C.B. (November 14).

CHAPTER XXI

THE INDIAN TOUR, 1875–1876

I

1868
Ætat. 26 THE Prince's visit to India in the winter season of 1875–76 was an impressive and a fruitful experience. New vistas of life were opened to him, and he was brought into touch with the most difficult of all imperial problems—the problem of how to harmonise Western methods of rule with the sentiments and ancient civilisations of the East. When no more than nineteen the Prince had, as the sovereign's heir, toured the northern American colonies, and his boyish presence there had stimulated the personal loyalty to the Crown of Great Britain's oldest settlements overseas. The political, ethical, and ethnical relations of the varied peoples of India with Great Britain differed widely from those of the inhabitants of Canada, whether of French or of English origin. The coming of the heir-apparent of England in his mature years into personal contact with the vast and populous Indian dependency was a bolder experiment than the North American expedition of his youth. It conformed with the outlook of British imperialists and raised their hopes high. Experienced Anglo-Indians were confident that thus might be forged a new link of untold promise between the British Crown and native India.

A visit of the Prince to India had been vaguely contemplated by his father as a part of his educational curriculum as long ago as 1856, and the opinion of Lord Canning, the Viceroy of the day, was then invited. Just before his death in 1861 the Prince Consort planned an Indian supplement to the Prince's tour in the Holy Land, and Queen Victoria, in the first days of her widowhood, consulted Lord Elgin, Lord Canning's successor in

the Indian Viceroyalty, as to the possibilities of carrying out
the suggestion.   Nothing came of these schemes, but the notion,
which appealed to the Prince, simmered in his mind, and when
the Indian visit came to fruition in 1875 the Queen described it
as "an old wish of his."

The Prince had occasion for considering afresh the favoured
design in the summer of 1868.   His sailor brother, the Duke of
Edinburgh, then captain of H.M.S. *Galatea*, was bent on including
India in a professional cruise which he was making round the
world.   The Duke had lately returned from Australia and was
preparing to extend his voyage to the Far East, in the course of
which he proposed to travel across India.   The Prince urged on
the Queen's attention the profound difference between the visit
of a son of hers to Australia and his visit to India.   Australia,
"a country colonised by the English," and India, "a great
Eastern country conquered by the English," had, from the
imperial point of view, he reminded his mother, little in common.
His brother, the Prince added, must visit India not as a naval
commander but as "the Prince and son of the sovereign, and as
no son of any sovereign had been in India before, he will have
to travel in great pomp, or it may not have a beneficial effect
on India."

The Prince's advice was not neglected.   The Duke of Edinburgh made a three months' "progress through India" (December 22, 1869, to March 12, 1870) as the guest of the Viceroy,
Lord Mayo, and of some of the ruling princes.[1]   A dignified
reception was accorded him.   The Indian populace flocked to
welcome him as his mother's son, and gave voice to their
hopes that he would on his return home speak to her of them.
But neither the Indian nor the British government credited the
Duke with a political status.   He was officially regarded as the
Queen's son who, being a naval captain, came to India in the
normal course of his professional career.

Even in its limited conditions the Duke's Indian visit appealed

1868

Ætat. 26

1870

Ætat. 28

---

[1] The Duke landed at Calcutta on the 22nd December 1869.   There were
ceremonial receptions at Calcutta, Bombay, Madras, and many smaller cities,
and ruling princes who were the Duke's hosts in the Upper Provinces provided
for him big-game shooting on a munificent scale.   A few days after his arrival
in Calcutta he was invested by Lord Mayo, the Viceroy, amid the pageantry
of a special Durbar, with the insignia of a Knight Grand Cross of the Star of
India.

sufficiently to Indian sentiment to encourage the Prince's hope that he might follow with effect in his brother's footsteps in the full dignity of heir-apparent and future ruler of the Empire. The pleasurable features of the adventure were not ignored, but he felt confident that it might stimulate in India personal loyalty to the Crown.

Since the reconstitution of the government of India after the Mutiny in 1858, when the East India Company was abolished and its controlling power was transferred to the Crown, Queen Victoria figured in the visions of Indian princes and peoples as their guardian and protector. But native India could never be pronounced wholly free from unrest. There had been since 1870 some sporadic if indecisive evidence of disaffection. No political significance was assignable to the terrible tragedy of the assassination by a madman of the Viceroy, Lord Mayo, while visiting a convict settlement on the Andaman Islands on 18th February 1872.[1] But suspicions were still entertained of a few of the ruling princes, notably of the Holkar of Indore, whose attitude during the Mutiny had been ambiguous; and the attempt in 1874 of the Gaekwar of Baroda to poison the English Resident, Sir Robert Phayre, tended to disturb the sense of security.[2] Mr. Gladstone attested his conviction that the Prince's association with India would be of political service by recommending his appointment to the Indian Council in London—a suggestion which the Queen had vetoed. Sir Bartle Frere's ripe Indian experience, which was gained as Chief Commissioner of Scinde, as Governor of Bombay, and, since 1867, as member of the Indian Council at Whitehall, lent much weight to his view that a visit from the Prince might beneficially bring home to the native princes and troops the human signification of the sovereignty of the Crown, which was for most of them an abstract rather than a substantive

[1] The outrage had especially shocked the Prince who had seen much of Lord Mayo on his visits to Ireland, when Lord Mayo was Chief Secretary.

[2] A mixed Commission consisting of three Englishmen—Sir Richard Couch, Sir Richard Meade, and Mr. P. S. Melvill, and of three Indians—the Maharajah Sindhia of Gwalior, the Maharajah of Jaipur, and Sir Dinkhar Rao, of the Viceroy's Council, with an English President, Sir Lewis Pelly, tried the Gaekwar on the charge at Calcutta. The trial opened on 23rd February 1875 and closed on the 30th March with a verdict of "Not Proven" by the three Indian members against the three Englishmen's verdict of "Guilty." The Gaekwar was thereupon acquitted, but he was deposed by the Viceroy for misgovernment on the 23rd April, and was succeeded by a boy of eleven, who was the adopted son of the widow of the deposed ruler's brother and predecessor.

conception. Anglo-Indian opinion generally agreed that the
Prince's genial bearing was well calculated to allay passing
winds of native discontent without exposing him to personal risk.
Mr. Disraeli's government, which took office in 1874, eagerly
availed itself of the Prince's readiness to put these notions to a
practical test.

1875

Ætat. 33

Accordingly Lord Salisbury, the Secretary of State for India,
announced on 17th March 1875, to both the Queen and the
Prince, the Indian Council's adoption of the project. To the
Queen Lord Salisbury wrote of the visit : "The Council think it
will have a highly beneficial influence upon the minds of Your
Majesty's subjects in that country generally and on the feudatory
princes of Your Majesty's Empire in particular." To the Prince
Lord Salisbury sent an assurance of the Council's "great gratification at hearing of a determination so advantageous to India,
and their cordial willingness to make the requisite financial
arrangements." Lord Northbrook, the Viceroy, who had been
appointed by Mr. Gladstone's ministry to succeed Lord Mayo,
was directed, despite the Queen's warning against any premature announcement, to give public notice of the tour at an
approaching Durbar. The Viceroy took no exception to the
general design, although he reserved his opinion on details, and
informed Lord Salisbury (from Simla, April 29, 1875) of his
desire "not only that the visit shall be agreeable to H.R.H., but
also that it may produce political advantage." On 3rd May
Lord Salisbury wrote to the Queen that the visit was "looked
forward to in all parts of India with great enthusiasm."

II

Many difficult corners had to be rounded before the procedure of the Prince's Indian tour was finally determined. The
Queen showed no enthusiasm for the project, which she described to her daughter, the Crown Princess, as "quite against my
desire" (June 8, 1875). She admitted the likelihood of political
advantage, but deemed the estimate to be exaggerated. There
was no special crisis in Indian affairs to call for any unusual
step on the part of her government. "We are not alarmed
about India," she remarked to the Crown Princess. Her chief
cause for hesitation was a fear of the strain which the tour

would entail on her son's bodily strength, of which, in her view, he was none too careful. She deplored his prolonged withdrawal from her society and from that of his family. With maternal solicitude she repeatedly urged on him before he started, care in diet, due observance of Sundays, and the desirability of going to bed at ten o'clock each evening.

The Queen claimed the right to supervise beforehand every detail of the programme in consultation with the Prime Minister, Mr. Disraeli, and Lord Salisbury, the Indian Secretary. In the embarrassing negotiations which ensued, the Prince had often reason to complain that he was overlooked, and that ministers were unwilling to comply with his wishes. The Queen's attitude often tried his temper. When the tangle was in course of final unravelment the Prime Minister, who tried to satisfy both mother and son, wrote to the Prince (August 10, 1875):

I deeply regret that the relations between your Royal Highness and Her Majesty's Government with respect to your Royal Highness's Indian visit have been unfortunate. I will not stop now to speculate on the cause. There have been too many cross-purposes.

The main theme of controversy touched the relations in which the Prince should stand to the Viceroy. The Queen insisted that the status of the Viceroy as the Queen's sole official deputy must in no way be prejudiced by her son's presence. She was quite content for the Prince to be merely the Viceroy's private guest. The Prince and his friends urged, on the other hand, that he should fill in India the sovereign's place, and that his mission, which was of political significance, should not be hampered by disparaging official limitations. The issue somewhat resembled that which had arisen on the Prince's visits to Ireland, with this crucial qualification. The Indian Viceroy, Lord Northbrook, unlike the Irish Viceroys, stood firmly by the Queen's view that it would be injurious to his prestige for the Prince to come out as the Queen's official representative. He pleaded that the Prince's rank of "first subject of the realm" should be recognised only so far as it respected his own precedence. Lord Salisbury supported the Prince's attitude and thereby added fuel to the flames of controversy. At the time the relations between the Liberal Viceroy, Lord Northbrook, and the Conservative Secretary of State, Lord

Salisbury,[1] were strained on wide grounds of general policy, and early in 1875 Lord Northbrook had privately intimated his intention of retiring. He had consented to postpone his departure from India until the close of the Prince's visit—a circumstance which was withheld for the time from the Prince's knowledge. The somewhat comprehensive breach between Lord Northbrook and Lord Salisbury aggravated the conflict respecting the Prince's status. Writing to the Queen's private secretary on 3rd July 1875, Lord Salisbury summed up, a little allusively, his conception of the danger lurking in the Viceroy's claim to precedence over the heir-apparent :

> For nearly a century the Governor-General was nominally responsible not to the Queen, but to a Company of Merchants. The natives of India learnt during that time to think that his was the highest personal authority with which they had to deal : and the lesson is one which they have been slow to unlearn. There is therefore some real danger that if the Queen's own Son is put in a position of obvious inferiority, the true relation of the Viceroy to the Queen will be misunderstood or ignored. I fear that in such a case the prestige of H.M.'s Dynasty will be lowered.

Happily a compromise on a crucial phase of the controversy was reached at the suggestion of Lord Northbrook's private secretary, Captain Evelyn Baring, afterwards famous as Lord Cromer. Lord Northbrook was willing for the Prince to hold levees when he was not present, but he took the strongest objection to the proposal of a great and spectacular Durbar which he and native princes should attend under the Prince's and not under his own presidency. Such a surrender of his prerogative would in native eyes mean (he argued) his subordination to the Prince and the suspension of his authority throughout the tour. Captain Baring suggested that the proposed Durbar should take the form of a special Chapter of the Star of India, and that the Viceroy, as Grand Master of the Order, should, at the opening of the proceedings, read a special commission from the Queen deputing the Prince to preside on so exceptional an occasion.

---

[1] Lord Northbrook resented the active control of the government in India by the India Office at home. He disapproved of Lord Salisbury's alarmist attitude to the Afghan problem and, in spite of his free-trade convictions, was opposed to the Lancashire cry which the home government supported for the remission of Indian import duties on Lancashire cotton.

Thereupon the Viceroy would "cede first place to the Prince, and all the rest of the proceedings would be conducted in his (H.R.H.'s) name." A settlement was reached on these terms, the Queen yielding her misgivings beneath the pressure of her ministers. On 19th August 1875 Lord Salisbury assured the Viceroy that there would be no derogation from his supreme power. The Prince would receive "all the honours due to his exalted rank," but his political mission, apart from the special investiture, would be to "convey to the chiefs and princes who rule in India under the paramount protection of the Queen of England the assurance of those gracious sentiments which have ever been entertained towards them by his Royal House." The Viceroy accepted the situation. He promised to make the Prince's tour as pleasurable as possible and, so as to avoid any constitutional misunderstanding, would be in personal attendance only at certain stages of the Prince's journey.

The cost of the tour raised an embarrassing issue of a rather different kind. The Prime Minister undertook that the Prince's expenses should be defrayed out of public funds. A prominent section of the Liberal party viewed with dislike all additional grants to royalty, and was furthermore unwilling to sanction any call on the Indian exchequer for expenses requisitioned by the English government. On 8th July Mr. Disraeli proposed to the House of Commons that the Admiralty should be empowered to spend £52,000 on the transport of the Prince to and from India, and that £60,000 should be allowed by the Treasury for the Prince's personal expenditure, including presents to native rulers. No conditions were imposed on the distribution of the second sum; it was essential, Disraeli wrote, that the Prince's gifts "should have the appearance of arising from the spontaneous liberality of the illustrious traveller." The Indian government would be required to make a special grant to the Viceroy of £30,000 in order to enable him to provide for the Prince appropriate entertainment. Disraeli explained that there was no intention of investing the tour with the costly pomp which would be essential if the Prince travelled as the formal representative of the sovereign.

The proposed sums were deemed in many quarters inadequate. *The Times* pointed out on 10th July: "The Prince must exercise extraordinary powers of management if Mr. Disraeli has not to ask for a supplementary grant next year." At the same time the editor, Delane, privately warned the Queen's secretary (July 9, 1875) that "care should be taken that the sum granted should not be exceeded, as, if it were, and if a supplementary vote were asked for next year after the visit was over, it would produce the very worst effect." Sir Bartle Frere complained that £60,000 would hardly meet the calls on the Prince's generosity in view of the extravagant gifts which the Indian Princes intended to offer the visitor. The young Rajah of Kolapore was building in honour of the visit a hospital costing £20,000. The Prince's friend, Lord Hartington, the leader of the Liberal party, also deemed a more generous sum desirable. But the government stood by their figures. When the resolution for the appropriation of the money came before the House in Committee of Supply, Mr. Fawcett moved an amendment "that it was inexpedient that any part of the expenses of the general entertainment of the Prince of Wales should be charged on the revenues of India," but the amendment was defeated by 379 votes to 67. Mr. Gladstone and Mr. Bright supported the government's proposals, which were finally carried with insignificant dissent. Happily the Prince's expenses were kept well within the amount of the Parliamentary grant, and the audited accounts showed a small credit balance. The lavish gifts made by the Rajahs to the Prince far exceeded the value of those which he made to them, but no invidious comparisons were drawn.

A further embarrassment arose from the fact that Ceylon was included in the itinerary, and that the arrangements there were in charge of the Colonial Office and not of the India Council. Lord Carnarvon, the Colonial Secretary, was therefore called into council and some of his proposals were combated by the Queen. It was with difficulty that Lord Carnarvon, who quoted the precedents of 1860 when the Prince in Canada knighted the Speakers of the two Houses of Legislature, persuaded the Queen to allow him to confer the K.C.M.G. on Mr. William Henry Gregory, the Governor of Ceylon.

III

A last theme of conflict concerned the choice of the Prince's suite. The Prince claimed permission to select whom he would,

1875
Ætat. 33 but Lord Salisbury pointed out to him (June 5, 1875) that the cabinet had decided to treat all arrangements for the visit as official questions and that they regarded the "number and composition of the suite as a matter of public importance." There was no difference of opinion as to the fitness of Sir Bartle Frere to take general control. Dr. Joseph Fayrer's expert knowledge of the Indian climate and of the sickness incidental to it obviously fitted him for medical adviser.[1] But the Queen, while nominating Lord Alfred Paget, her clerk-marshal, to go as her representative, scrutinised dubiously the large personal following on which the Prince had set his heart. Yet there was small ground for complaint when the list was finally settled. The Prince's equerry since 1872, Colonel Dighton Probyn, was peculiarly well-qualified to accompany him. He had seen distinguished service in India as a cavalry officer, and had won the V.C. there for his gallantry. Probyn had, moreover, attended the Duke of Edinburgh through India in 1870, like two other of the company, Dr. Fayrer, and the breezy Irishman, naval Lieutenant Lord Charles Beresford, who went out as an aide-de-camp.[2]

The Prince, who was anxious to placate any political opposition to the project of the tour, suggested an addition to his suite by way of dispelling some apprehension which was reported from Russia. He proposed to invite the Tsar to nominate a Russian officer. The Prime Minister pointed out that other countries might expect a similar concession, and that it was undesirable to expand unduly the number of the Prince's companions. Before

[1] Fayrer had been Professor of Surgery at the Medical College, Calcutta, and was now President of the Medical Board at the India Office.

[2] Other officers of the Prince's household who toured India with him were his equerries, Colonel Arthur Ellis, Lord Suffield, and Mr. Francis Knollys, his private secretary. Colonel Owen Williams served as an aide-de-camp, and Lieut. (Sir) Augustus Fitz-George, the Duke of Cambridge's son, was an extra A.D.C. The Rev. Robinson Duckworth, a clergyman popular at Court, was chaplain. William (afterwards Sir William) Howard Russell, the special correspondent of *The Times*, was given the brevet rank of honorary private secretary. Mr. Sydney P. Hall, the artist, was commissioned to make sketches. Mr. Clarence Bartlett, assistant-superintendent of the Zoological Gardens, was appointed taxidermist. Sir Bartle Frere took as his private secretary, Mr. Albert (afterwards Earl) Grey. Three private friends of the Prince—the Duke of Sutherland, the Earl of Aylesford, and Lord Carrington—were personal guests. Prince Louis of Battenberg, naval Lieutenant on board H.M.S. *Serapis* (afterwards Admiral and Marquis of Milford-Haven), joined the Prince through great part of the tour.

leaving London the Prince informed Count Schouvaloff, the
Russian Ambassador, of the suggestion and of its fate. He
wished the Tsar to be informed that though the plan had proved
impracticable it "had been approved in principle." [1]

IV

On the evening of Monday, 11th October 1875, the Prince,
with Lord Charles Beresford, the Duke of Sutherland, and other
intimates of his party, set out from London on an overland
journey to Brindisi. In a sermon preached at Westminster
Abbey the day before Dean Stanley dwelt on the profound interest
attaching to the first occasion on which an heir to the English
throne had "ever visited those distant regions which the greatest
of his ancestors, Alfred the Great, one thousand years ago so
ardently longed to explore." The Princess accompanied her
husband as far as Calais. "I left with a heavy heart," the
Prince wrote to Lord Granville (October 29), "and was so
depressed in spirits on reaching Paris that I felt seriously inclined
to return home instead of going on." But his spirits soon revived
in the French capital where he lunched with Marshal MacMahon
at the Élysée on the 13th; had an interview with the Foreign
Minister, the Duc Decazes, and called on the Duc d'Aumale.

Brindisi was reached on the 16th.

"Our journey through Italy," the Prince noted, "was on
the whole rapid but somewhat monotonous; Charlie Beresford
kept up our spirits when they flagged. Augustus Paget [British
Ambassador at Rome] met us at Turin, where we stayed a night.
The King [of Italy] was there but did not show, though he kindly
sent an A.D.C. to meet me."

At Brindisi he was met by Count Andrea Maffei, who while
attached to the Italian embassy in London was a popular
member of the Prince's circle. "The Count told us he was
farming, but we could not gather what special branch of
agriculture he was studying." The Duke of Sutherland was
greeted by the crowd as "l'amico di Garibaldi."

H.M.S. Serapis, which had been elaborately fitted up by the
Admiralty for the voyage, was waiting at Brindisi to embark
the party. The ship paused on the 18th at Athens, to enable

[1] Archives of the Russian Embassy.

the Prince to spend a day with the King and Queen of Greece. On the 20th the Suez Canal was entered. The passage through the canal brought home to the Prince its supreme importance as the highway to India, and he sent home renewed expressions of regret that England had refused to co-operate in its construction. To his relief he was to learn on reaching India that the situation had from his point of view been saved by Mr. Disraeli's *coup* in purchasing the Khedive's shares.[1]

At Ismailia the Prince left the canal for Cairo, where he enjoyed once more the profuse hospitality of Khedive Ismail. "The Khedive, as usual," the Prince wrote to Lord Granville on the 29th October, "was most hospitable, and kindness itself—and lodged us in a most splendid palace—called Ghezireh—about 20 minutes' drive from Cairo." He noticed changes in the city since he was last there:

Cairo has changed a good deal since my last visit six years ago—many old houses have been thrown down and fine large ones built in their place, and streets widened and new gardens and even squares are in course of construction. Fortunately most of the old Bazaars remain intact and it would be a great pity for the sake of the picturesque to destroy them. The town is quite assuming the aspect of a French-Oriental one. There is a very pretty Opera House—and we saw a very well acted French play and a fair ballet.

After his wont the Prince renewed many old acquaintance-ships at Cairo. General Stanton, the Consul-General, "seems," he wrote to Lord Granville, "as popular as ever, and had great weight with the Khedive. So I hope it will be long before he is replaced. A good many of our diplomats abroad would do well to take a leaf out of his book." He sought out, too, with character-istic kindliness, an old French friend, the widow of M. Persigny, a confidant of Napoleon III. who, as French ambassador in London and Minister of the Interior at Paris, had been known to the Prince from boyhood:

Hearing that Mme. de Persigny (now Mme. le Moine) was at Cairo, I went to see her, and although it is many years since I saw her last—and she had certainly grown older and stouter—she has still *des beaux restes*, but has grown very deaf, and con-versation became rather tiring in the hot weather.

[1] See pp. 294–5 *supra*.

There was much in the political and financial condition of
Egypt to give the Prince earnest of coming change.   The critical
state of the Khedive's finances was, after much international
wrangling, soon to bring Egypt under England's sway.   The
Prince's companion, Sir Bartle Frere, reported to him the talk
about the Khedive's financial embarrassments which Sir Bartle
and General Stanton had with the spendthrift Khedive and with
his chief minister, Nubar Pasha, who was bent on financial
reform.   The Prince put little faith in the plausible assurances
in which the Khedive was lavish, and he recognised that his host
was on the verge of bankruptcy.   The Prince performed with zest,
however, the congenial duty with which the home government had
entrusted him of knitting closer in a public ceremony England's
personal tie with the Khedive's son and heir—Tewfik.   On the
25th October he invested the young man with the Order of the
Star of India.   An elaborate ritual was followed.   The Prince
wore his new uniform of Field-Marshal—the high military rank
which, to his gratification, the Queen had conferred on him on her
last birthday.   "The investiture," the Prince wrote home,
"gave great pleasure, and we made the ceremony as formal as
we could.   The recipient is a very intelligent young man but it
is a great pity he had not been in Europe as his three younger
brothers have."   Sir Bartle Frere reported to the Queen the
graceful terms in which the Prince, addressing the Egyptian heir,
expressed his hopes of friendly relations between the English and
Egyptian governments.

The Prince re-embarked at Suez in the *Serapis* on 26th
October.   Writing to Lord Granville while passing through the
Red Sea he described his experience and the harmony prevailing
aboard :

We left Suez in the evening of the 26th, and since 10 yesterday
morning have been in the Red Sea, which might well be named the
Red *hot* Sea.   Though in our cabins with all the ports and doors
open the temperature has not exceeded 84°, there is a close damp
heat, like being in a hot house, which is rather trying—however
we are *unberufen* all well.   It was 109° in the sun yesterday, and
I went down to the engine-room just before dinner where it was
118° and in the stokehole 129°!   So you can easily imagine I
was not sorry to leave those lower regions.   Stafford [*i.e.* the
Duke of Sutherland] is in great force—and so is Alfred Paget,
who has been surnamed by the younger members of the party

"Beetroot." We are all charmed with Sir Bartle Frere—who is quite charming, and so full of information on every subject. I think all the party "pull together" as well as possible.

Reports which reached the Queen of the merry mood of the Prince and his companions through the voyage, roused her fears that they were indulging in more practical joking than was dignified, but Sir Bartle Frere assured her that there was no breach of decorum.

At Aden the Prince landed (November 1) and held a levee— the first of a long series—which Arab chiefs attended in great numbers. An address from Parsee merchants gave him the first taste of the exuberance of oriental adulation.

V

A week later, on 8th November, the *Serapis* reached the harbour of Bombay.[1] The Prince suffered no injury from the heat of the voyage, and the vigorous health in which he arrived at Bombay was fully maintained during the tour through all alternations of climate. At Bombay Lord Northbrook, the Viceroy, came on board, followed by Sir Philip Wodehouse, Governor of Bombay, and two military officers who joined the Prince's suite for special purposes. Major-General Sir Sam Browne, V.C., undertook control of transport and Major Edward Bradford looked after the Prince's personal safety. At the landing the Viceroy introduced leading Anglo-Indian officers and some seventy princes or chiefs who, in glittering costume, accompanied by their dewans and sirdars, awaited the disembarkation. The Viceroy avoided any problems of precedence by parting with the royal visitor after the presentations, to rejoin him at Calcutta later. The reception impressed the Prince.

"I was very much struck," he wrote to the Queen (November 14), "by the attitude of the natives in my landing at Bombay. As a rule the Easterns are not given to be demonstrative, but I

[1] Full first-hand details of the tour are recorded in letters to Queen Victoria from the Prince, Lord Northbrook, Sir Bartle Frere, and Lord Lytton, and in the Prince's detailed correspondence while in India with Lord Granville and Mr. Disraeli. Very little of this material has been published. The main printed sources are W. H. Russell's *Diary* (1877); Sir Joseph Fayrer's *Recollections of my Life* (1900) and *Notes of the Visits to India of the Prince of Wales and the Duke of Edinburgh, 1870-76* (printed privately, 1879); and (Sir) Bernard Mallet's *Memoir of Thomas George, Earl of Northbrook* (1908).

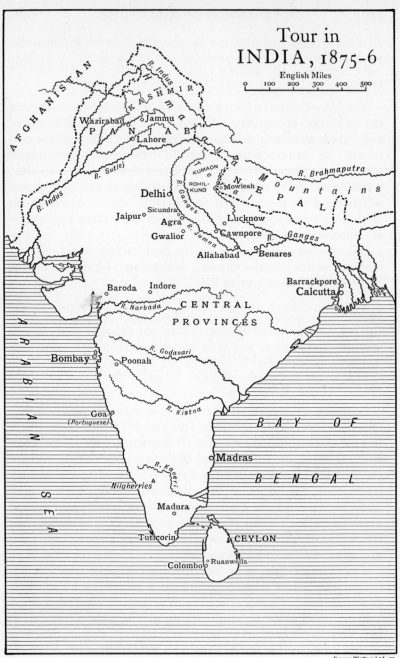

Tour in
INDIA, 1875-6

English Miles

0   100   200   300   400   500

AFGHANISTAN

R. Indus

KASHMIR

Himalaya

Wazirabad   Jammu
PANJAB
Lahore

R. Sutlej

R. Indus

KUMAON   Mountains

ROHIL-   Mowleah   R. Brahmaputra
KUND

Delhi   R. Ganges   NEPAL

Jaipur   Sicundra   Lucknow
Agra   Cawnpore
Gwalior   R. Jumna   R.   Ganges

Allahabad   Benares

Baroda   Indore   Barrackpore
Calcutta

R. Narbada   CENTRAL

PROVINCES

R. Godavari

Bombay   Poonah

R. Kistna

Goa
(Portuguese)   BAY   OF

BENGAL

Madras

R. Kaveri

Nilgherries

Madura

Tuticorin   CEYLON

Colombo   Ruanwella

ARABIAN   SEA

Emery Walker Ltd. sc.

received a perfect ovation (on the six mile drive) from the dock-yard at Bombay to Government House at Parell, where we have been staying. The Parsee community, which is by far the largest, took the lead, and are most demonstrative."

The Prince's thirty-fourth birthday was fervently celebrated the day after his arrival. At night the town was illuminated and "there were among the loyal devices which the natives contrived" (so Lord Northbrook reported to the Queen), some quaint mottoes; one ran: "How is your Royal Mother?" and another, "Tell Mama we're happy." Among the many public functions which the Prince performed in Bombay, the most serviceable to the city's prosperity was the laying of the foundation stone of the Elphinstone Dock.

The new environment of native peoples and rulers was the chief attraction for the Prince. He declared himself fascinated by "the novelties of Indian life."

"A drive though the streets of Bombay," he wrote to the Queen (November 14) "is most interesting, and you see mixed together natives of all classes, creeds and origin. Their houses are very picturesque, and they are all painted different colours. The lowest classes and children hardly wear any garments at all. The vegetation is very plentiful and the cocoanut palm trees are excessively fine."

At levees and receptions he showed the native princes and their ministers every genial courtesy, and with his usual promptitude formed shrewd judgements of their character. Sir Bartle Frere wrote to the Queen of the astonishment with which he watched the emotion caused among the natives by the Prince's presence (November 14, 1875). Frere discerned useful results almost immediately. All the chiefs looked pleased and happy beyond his expectation. "This is of great importance," he added, "for the feeling of the upper classes towards our government is not now always what could be wished."

Sir Bartle yielding, as he said, to a sudden inspiration, resolved to put the Prince's soothing influence on native feeling to a practical test. During the Prince's stay at Bombay, short sojourns were made in neighbouring places. The Prince spent his first week-end, November 13–15, at Poonah. For a second excursion Sir Bartle chose the state of Baroda, where the excitement arising from the recent deposition of the Gaekwar, although subsiding, left the future in some doubt. Sir Bartle deemed the Prince to be capable of calming the still troubled waters. A three days' stay at Baroda (November 19–22) was hurriedly arranged. The Prince's host and hostess at Baroda were the new Gaekwar, a boy of the humblest origin, and the Ranee—a former Gaekwar's widow and the present Gaekwar's foster-mother. They and their advisers responded eagerly to the Prince's advances and provided picturesque entertainment. There was a lavish display of "barbaric pearl and gold," while opportunities for sport were offered the Prince for the first time on the tour. He hunted cheetahs and hogs, and shot quails. The visit, which immensely interested him, answered well-nigh all Sir Bartle's expectations. The Prince's presence (he reported to the Queen, November 27) "had the most marked and powerful effect in reconciling all classes to a complete change of rulers, and to a transition from a regime of frightful tyranny and corruption to an orderly and well-regulated native administration." Frere appreciated the Prince's "kindly and discriminating notice of all classes of natives, from the Ranee and her little adopted son down to the old native officers of the regiments present, who went away delighted with having been presented to and spoken to by H.R.H." The twelve-year-old ruler, who was "quite over-loaded with jewels," greatly attracted the Prince. "The little Gaekwar of Baroda," the Prince wrote to Granville on 30th November 1875, "who is as old as our oldest boy [Prince Albert Victor was ten months younger] seems really a very intelligent youth, though only six months ago he was running about the streets adorned with the most limited wardrobe." The Ranee and the boy Gaekwar warmly reciprocated the Prince's friendly sentiments. After he had taken leave of them, both, speaking in Marathi, begged Sir Bartle to explain to him their feelings.

The Ranee (Sir Bartle noted), who is a very sagacious sensible woman, well schooled in severe adversity, doubtless felt that the Prince's recognition gave stability to her position and to the new order of things, but the young Gaekwar's emotion was the simple feeling of a boy. There was no minister nor any one else near to prompt him as he said to me, "Do tell the Prince how much we all feel his kindness. Beg him not to forget to tell the Queen how thankful we are to her for letting him come."

VI

The Prince, in his own words, was "not letting the grass grow under his feet." "He certainly outworks any one on his staff," Sir Bartle Frere was soon writing to the Queen (February 10, 1876) "and shows less susceptibility to heat and exposure to the sun than any of us." The Queen, who was in constant receipt of letters not only from the Prince, but from the Viceroy, Sir Bartle Frere, Mr. Duckworth, Dr. Fayrer, Francis Knollys, and other members of the Prince's suite, was often disquieted by the accounts of his activities, and kept the wires busy with maternal counsels. She begged Dr. Fayrer to use her name freely in remonstrance against "over-exertions." But he and his companions were happily able to quiet the Queen with assurances that the Prince's health was never better.

An early change in the itinerary was rendered needful by an outbreak of cholera in the Madras Presidency. The direct journey from Bombay to Madras became impossible. It was determined to go south to Ceylon, and thence after visiting the south-eastern corner of the Indian peninsula, to reach Madras by sea.

On his voyage from Bombay to Ceylon the Prince landed (November 27) at the old Portuguese settlement of Goa, "where," Sir Bartle Frere wrote, "the Governor-General of all the Portuguese Indies, including Timore on the coast of New Guinea and Mozambique in East Africa (Tavares de Almeida), received His Royal Highness in a quaint old Palace of the Viceroys with portraits of all his predecessors from Vasco da Gama and Albuquerque."

Colombo was reached on 1st December, and three days later the Prince duly conferred the K.C.M.G. on Mr. Gregory, the Governor of Ceylon. Big-game shooting was provided on an elaborate scale. A camp was formed at Ruanwella, not far from the city. There the Prince for the first time hunted elephants, and the sport involved him in some danger, owing to a sudden rush of the maddened animals. On the 7th he telegraphed to the Queen: "Shot one elephant and wounded severely two others." Crossing to the mainland, near Tuticorin, on 9th December, he passed by train through the mountainous scenery of the Nilgherries and inspected the temples and palaces of the ancient

1875
Ætat. 34 kingdom of Madura. Madras was reached on the 13th. The Duke of Buckingham and Chandos, who had just arrived as Governor, was the Prince's host, and the rajahs of the neighbourhood came as at Bombay in brilliant array to greet him. A review of troops was one of the impressive episodes of the full six days' programme, and the Prince was enchanted with the illumination of the surf, "than which," wrote his companion, W. H. Russell, "man never saw any spectacle more strange, nay, awful."

Calcutta was reached by sea on the 23rd Dec., and the Viceroy resumed his rôle of host. "Calcutta people are not used to cheer," he wrote to the Queen of her son's reception (Dec. 24) "so that there was not so much noise as at Bombay, but there was much more cheering and clapping of hands than Lord Northbrook ever noticed before at Calcutta."

The native Princes, whom the Prince received at the Government House on the 24th, included all the influential rulers of Northern India—the Maharajahs of Kashmir, Indore, Gwalior, Jaipur, Jodhpur, Rewah, and Patiala. Through all that night the city was illuminated; but the Prince after dinner sought a reminder of home by going with the Viceroy to the theatre to witness the popular farce of *My Awful Dad*, rendered by one of the Prince's favourite London comedians, Charles Mathews, who was on tour in the city. Next day the Prince drove to Barackpore, the Viceroy's suburban residence, to spend Christmas.

1876
Ætat. 34 On New Year's Day, 1876, a chief ceremony of the tour took place at a great encampment on the Maidan, near Calcutta, when 12,000 spectators assembled amid dazzling pageantry. The Prince presided at that special Chapter of the Star of India, the design of which had caused in earlier months so much heartburning. A special warrant from the Queen was read at the opening of the proceedings, and the Prince ceremoniously admitted to the Order two Maharajahs (of Jodhpur and Jheend) as G.C.S.I. and seven chiefs as K.C.S.I., together with General Henry Ramsay, the benevolent English Commissioner (or "King" as he was popularly called) of Kumaon in the United Provinces.[1]

[1] A brother of the twelfth Earl of Dalhousie, Sir Henry, ruled as a paternal despot the districts of Kumaon and Garhwal for more than a quarter of a century (1856–1884). He had kept the mountainous tract of country quiet throughout the Mutiny, and was thoroughly trusted by the native people, who called him either "King of Kumaon" or "Ramjee Sahib."

"The ceremony," wrote Lord Northbrook on 7th January, "passed off well." [1] On the 4th the Prince bade the Viceroy farewell and left Calcutta to fulfil a long series of engagements farther north.

In Central and North India the Prince passed rapidly from place to place, living in elaborately equipped camps, exchanging visits with native princes, inspecting scenes and buildings of historic or archæological interest, and enjoying abundant opportunities of big-game shooting. Everywhere native rulers, with throngs of their subjects, came to greet him, and the favourable impressions which his levees in Bombay, Madras, and Calcutta had created in the minds of the princes were confirmed.

The Northern tour opened at Benares, the sacred city of the Hindus, near which the Prince's camp was pitched for two days. Sir John Strachey, the Lieutenant-Governor of Bengal, acted as host. At Lucknow, the next stopping-place (Jan. 6) the Prince inspected with painful interest the ruins of the buildings which were associated with the heroic defence of the city against the mutineers of 1857. Under the guidance of Dr. Fayrer, who had himself played a part in the defence, he visited the room where Sir Henry Lawrence had died in the hour of victory, as well as Lawrence's tomb in the churchyard hard by. The Prince laid, too, the foundation stone of a memorial, the gift of Lord Northbrook, to the natives who fell in defence of the Residency, and he expressed satisfaction "in doing honour to the memory of the gallant men who had set such a noble example of fidelity and devotion to duty." "Every survivor" (wrote an eye-witness to the Queen) "whose home was near enough to enable him to come to Lucknow was there," and each was presented to the Prince.

After a short pause at Cawnpore, a great military demonstration awaited the Prince at Delhi, where a large part of the Indian Army was encamped (Jan. 11). It was congenial to the Prince to meet at the head of the assembled troops the Indian Commander-in-Chief, Lord Napier of Magdala, who was just bringing his six years' tenure of the post to a close. An engineer officer of acknowledged efficiency and most courteous bearing, Lord Napier was a soldier after the Prince's heart. He had done good service

---

[1] After the investiture the Prince unveiled a statue to Lord Mayo, the assassinated Viceroy, and on 3rd January he was created D.C.L. by the University of Calcutta.

in the Mutiny, but the exploit which brought him renown was his prompt capture of Magdala, the capital city of Abyssinia, in the spring of 1868. The Prince chanced to be dining early in June of that year with the Duke of Cambridge, when there burst on the company a young officer from Magdala who was charged to deliver to a fellow-guest, Sir Stafford Northcote, then Secretary of State for India, Lord Napier's account of his recent triumph. The messenger was Lieutenant Frederick Roberts, who subsequently became Field-Marshal Lord Roberts of Kandahar. The Prince at once plied the young man, whom he had not met before, with pertinent inquiries, and was moved by the subaltern's recital to warm admiration of Lord Napier's exploit.[1] The Prince had joined in London's great welcome of Lord Napier on his return from Magdala and now greeted him at Delhi with overflowing cordiality.

On the 12th the Prince and Lord Napier reviewed at Delhi 18,000 troops. Next day the Prince watched a well-contested sham fight in which, to his satisfaction, his own regiment, the 10th Hussars, took an effective part. Lord Napier and his colleagues of the Indian army attached a far-reaching sentimental value to the Prince's prominence at Delhi. Native officers and men proved sensitively responsive to their meeting in the flesh with the heir of the far-away suzerain of their dreams.

"H.R.H.'s manner and bearing," wrote Lord Napier in high feather to the Queen, from the great camp (January 28) "have realised their idea of a Prince: they have long been without one of their own race worthy of the name, and during more than a century have been subject to an indefinite authority which they could never understand clearly; now they are prepared to receive with loyalty and affection the Prince whom Your Majesty has sent them."

A personal compliment which the Prince paid at Delhi to two native officers brought further home to the native troops his personal fascination. Two rasaldars of a native regiment, the 11th Bengal Lancers, which he inspected, were invited to join his staff as orderly officers for the remainder of his tour. One, Sirdar Anoop Singh, was a Sikh, and the other, Sirdar Mahomed Afzul Khan, a high-class Afghan. Both had served

[1] Lord Roberts, *Forty-One Years in India*, p. 302.

with distinction in "Probyn's Horse," and their former colonel,
Dighton Probyn, the Prince's equerry, took special charge of
them during the months that followed.[1]   "Fine soldierly fellows,
who look as if they might have been born sword in hand and
cradled in a military saddle" was Lord Lytton's description of
them when he met them later.[2]   By way of keeping alive the
stimulating memory of the Prince's visit to Delhi, the title of
"The Prince of Wales's Own" was conferred on four native
regiments—the 11th Bengal Lancers, to which the Prince's native
orderly officers belonged, the 2nd Gurkhas Regiment, the 4th
Madras Light Cavalry, and the 2nd Bengal Light Infantry.[3]

After Delhi there followed more bouts of sight-seeing, of native
hospitality and sport in the Central Provinces.   From Lahore,
in the Punjab, the capital city of the soldierly Sikhs, where the
weather turned very cold, the Prince made excursions to Wazirabad and to Jammu, where the Maharajah of Kashmir provided
him with sport on a royal scale.   Five days were spent in camp
near Agra (January 25–30) in course of which he visited the
Taj Mahal, the most beautiful tomb in the world, and the
monument of the Emperor Akbar at Sicundra.   On the last day
of the month the Prince was the guest of the Maharajah of
Gwalior, the most influential prince of Central India, who
received him magnificently, and left no doubt on the Prince's
mind of the sincerity of his devotion to the British crown.

The whole of the month of February and the first few days of
March were devoted, under the shadow of the Himalayas, to the
pursuit of big game, chiefly tiger and elephant hunting.   The
sporting expedition was designed by way of a comparative rest
for the Prince, but it was strenuously pursued.[4]   The excursion
gave (Sir Bartle Frere wrote) "people at a distance an impression
of manly vigour and power of endurance which pleased every
one, Europeans and natives alike."   Through the first weeks
the general direction was undertaken by the veteran General

---

[1] So well did the two officers appreciate their association with the Prince
that at their own request they accompanied him to England and they stayed
there some six months.   See pp. 391–2 *infra*.

[2] Lord Lytton to Queen, 26th March 1876.

[3] At the same time four other native regiments—the 2nd Bengal Native
Infantry, the Guide Corps (Punjab Frontier Force), the Madras Sappers and
Miners, and the 3rd Bombay Cavalry—were gazetted "The Queen's Own."

[4] For an account of the sport on the Indian tour, see A. E. T. Watson's
King Edward as a Sportsman, chapter x. pp. 342 *seq*.

Sir Henry Ramsay, "King of Kumaon," whom the Prince had knighted at Calcutta.

The Prince shot his first tiger on 5th February while the party was staying at the Residency at Jaipur, where the Maharajah joined Sir Henry Ramsay in devising and carrying out the Prince's sporting programme. Subsequently the Prince and his companions camped at various stations in the Rohilkund Terai, the wooded belt at the base of the mountains, where all manner of big game abounded. On 20th February, at the urgent invitation of the Maharajah (Dhiraja) of Nepal, the party proceeded to the Nepal Terai. There the veteran Prime Minister, Sir Jung Bahadur—a notable figure in native history—took Sir Henry Ramsay's place as the Prince's guide.[1] On the 25th an exciting hunt of wild elephants took place near the camp at Mowleah. The sporting holiday in the Nepal Terai lasted till 6th March. One of its most notable features was the mutual regard which developed in its course between the Prince and his native companions. On Sir Jung Bahadur and his family, as well as on the Maharajah of Nepal, the Prince left an abiding impression of kindly and cheerful sympathy.

The more formal conditions of the tour were resumed at Allahabad on 7th March—the day after the sporting expedition ended. There Lord Northbrook and Lord Napier of Magdala rejoined the Prince for a final leave-taking, and a second but informal Chapter of the Order of the Star of India was held by special leave of the Queen. It was a drawing-room investiture to which ladies were invited. The recipients of the order of knighthood at the Prince's hand were three companions whose services he desired conspicuously to acknowledge, viz.: Major-General Sir Sam Browne, V.C., Major-General Probyn, and Surgeon-General Fayrer. All were created K.C.S.I.

Fit recognition of the services which his companions were rendering him was always in the Prince's thought. As early as 9th January 1876, while at Lucknow, he had written asking Mr. Disraeli to secure the G.C.B. for Sir Bartle, whose deserts he rightly valued at the highest rate. "If he could be gazetted and receive the intimation before we leave India in March, I would be

[1] Sir Jung Bahadur, whose youthful career was turbulent, caused himself in 1846 to be appointed for life Prime Minister of Nepal. He proved an enlightened ruler and showed much attachment to the English, bringing a troop of Gurkhas to the assistance of the loyalists of Oudh during the Mutiny.

. 1876

Ætat. 34

most grateful.   On my return home it would be a matter for
future consideration whether you consider him worthy to be
raised to the peerage."   The Prime Minister usually took his
time in reaching a decision on this kind of application from the
Prince.   In Frere's case he refused the suggestion of a peerage,
but so far followed the Prince's recommendation as to offer Sir
Bartle on his return home the choice between a baronetcy and
the G.C.B.   Sir Bartle chose the latter honour, but ultimately
the Prince's pressure led to the bestowal of a baronetcy in
addition, by way of acknowledgement of Sir Bartle's companion-
able and instructive guidance.[1]   To every one of his companions
on the tour he was anxious to give proof of his regard.   When
the vicarage of Sandringham fell vacant next year, the Prince
promptly offered it to Mr. Duckworth, who had served him as
chaplain in India.   The offer was declined, but the spirit which
dictated it was characteristic.

VII

The tour was now coming to an end.   On 9th March the Prince
arrived at Indore, where the Holkar, who did not make a favourable impression, awaited him in great state, and he received at the
Residency many minor rajahs.   From Indore the Prince travelled
to Bombay to embark for the West.   Smallpox was raging in the
town, and the departure was made with curtailed ceremony.
H.M.S. *Serapis*, "freshly decked with white paint and regilt,"
steamed out of Bombay harbour at 4 P.M. on Monday, 13th
March, just seventeen weeks after her arrival.   The Prince's
suite had undergone only a few changes.   His personal friends.
the Duke of Sutherland and Lord Aylesford, as well as Albert
Grey, Frere's secretary, went home before the rest of the party,
Mr. Duckworth, who had fallen ill of typhoid fever, was left
behind at Lahore.   But an interesting addition was made to the
original company in the person of the two Indian officers, who
had joined the Prince's suite at Delhi.   They, at their own request,
accompanied the Prince to England (with two native troopers to
attend on them) and Sir Joseph Fayrer taught them English on

[1] On 15th May, four days after the Prince was again in London, Disraeli
wrote to the Prince that a G.C.B. would be conferred in person on Frere by the
Queen, and that Lord Suffield would be made K.C.B., and Francis Knollys C.B.
"Thus," Disraeli wrote, "in the distribution of honours in commemoration of
the great Indian visit every division of the Order of the Bath will be represented."

1876
Ætat. 34

the voyage.[1] The native princes' lavish gifts to the Prince greatly increased both the bulk and value of the *Serapis's* cargo on the homeward trip. Articles of virtu abounded, but many of the gifts were animals alive and dead, wild and tame, together with orchids and other rare plants. Sir Jung Bahadur had given the Prince a small fleet cheetah and a grey Arab horse. Five tigers, seven leopards, four elephants, a Himalayan bear, and three ostriches formed part of the ample menagerie of 65 mammals and 96 birds which lent the *Serapis* something of the aspect of a living Noah's Ark.[2]

[1] On their arrival in England they were generously entertained by the Duke of Sutherland and other friends of the Prince. Sir Dighton Probyn showed them the sights of London. They left for India in the autumn, although they were anxious to remain as Queen Victoria's bodyguard. (Letter from Sir Dighton Probyn, 26th November 1922.) The Queen fully approved their aspiration. At a later date, on March 5th, 1883, she asked Mr. Gladstone to request the Cabinet to provide her with an Indian bodyguard of 20 non-commissioned officers of the native cavalry. The request was refused (Gwynn and Tuckwell's *Life of Dilke*, i. 522). Not until the Prince came to the throne was the scheme adopted of appointing a rota of Indian officers in attendance on the King-Emperor.

[2] Lord Lytton, who inspected the *Serapis* on its passage through the Suez Canal, sent the Queen (March 26, 1876) a lively description of the home-bound ship with its multifarious cargo :

"As Noah's Ark was supposed by the Rabbins to be a type of the whole world, the *Serapis* may really be regarded just now as a sort of picturesque epitome of Your Majesty's Indian Empire, for, uniting the marvels of the East with the luxuries of the West in her decorations and furniture, she also contains just now splendid specimens of what India can produce, in the way of tigers, leopards, and elephants, as well as of what England can produce in the way of soldiers, thinkers, and writers. With the exception of one young tigress, whose mother was shot by His Royal Highness, and whom he is bringing home to England as an interesting orphan, the Prince really seems to have won the hearts not only of the Rajahs and Maharajahs, but also of the wild beasts in India; for the representatives of these latter walk about the deck of the *Serapis* with the most amiable expressions, wagging their tails affably, and apparently disposed to fraternise with every visitor. One little tiger pup, not bigger than a stable cat, and gifted with the most engaging manners, I found especially attractive. The other young tigress, however, appears to have been much embittered by her early domestic griefs, and snarls and growls horribly at all who approach her cage."

Besides the live animals and birds, skins, horns, and heads figured largely among the Prince's collections, and his taxidermist, Mr. Clarence Bartlett, was kept busy. On the Prince's arrival in London, the Indian gifts of virtu were exhibited for the season at the South Kensington Museum and the animals and birds at the Zoological Gardens. To the Zoological Society, the Prince presented two tigers, two leopards, an elephant, two antelopes, and two tragopans, and in acknowledgement of his generosity, the Society presented him with its gold medal (*Zoological Soc. Council's Report*, 1877, pp. 28 *seq.*). Provision was ultimately made for housing at Sandringham both the artistic and zoological collections.

VIII

There was a general consensus of opinion in official circles   1876
both in England and in India that the Prince's tour had produced   Ætat. 34
the favourable results expected of it. Parliament had met on
8th February, 1876, when the main part of the Prince's Indian
programme was completed. *The Times* stated on that day:

If there were any doubts as to the success of his visit these
have been completely dissipated and even those who are least
disposed to attach much importance to Courtly vanities recognise
that in the particular circumstances of India, and having regard
to the character of its Princes and people, the visit of the Heir
of the British Crown is likely to prove a great political event.

In the speech from the throne the Queen introduced the
sentences:

I am deeply thankful for the uninterrupted health which my
dear son, the Prince of Wales, has enjoyed during his voyage
through India. The hearty affection with which he has been
received by my Indian subjects of all classes and races assures
me that they are happy under my rule and loyal to my throne.

In the letters to the Queen from the Prince and Sir Bartle
Frere and in the reports of the English officials of the districts
which the Prince had visited there was ample justification for
the Queen's roseate pronouncement. There was unanimity,
according to Sir Bartle, in the confidential deliverances of native
chiefs, who all declared to him in almost identical phraseology:
"We have seen the reality of that of which before we had only
symbols and representatives. That which was only an abstrac-
tion before is now to us a visible and tangible reality" (Frere
to Queen, February 10, 1876).

"The effect of the Prince on the Chiefs is miraculous," wrote
Sir Henry Daly, Agent in Central India, to the Viceroy, of the
Prince's passage through the vast district under his control.
"There is a sentiment in their feudalism which has been touched.
Nobody could foresee this result, but it has been happy and the
mark will remain. His manner and air to them is perfect. He
listens to tales of service with an air of interest and wins his way.
Englishmen can hardly understand the feelings with which the
Chiefs of ancient Houses regard the Queen's Son with the Royal
Standard."

The Prince was deeply impressed by all that he had seen. Throughout the tour of "this splendid country" (as he called India) his interest never flagged. "My tour through India continues to interest me in the highest possible degree," he wrote to Mr. Disraeli from Lucknow (January 9, 1876). "The work has been hard at times, but the reception from all classes of the Natives has been most gratifying." "Nobody can form any idea from accounts what the country is like till one has seen it," the Prince wrote to Granville (March 21, 1876). "I might have learnt more," he remarked to Frere after their parting (April 8), "but I have learnt much which will be of immense use to me now and hereafter."

IX

The Prince's genial accessibility to Indians left an impression that was very slow to fade. There was far more than courtly compliment in the reports which successive Viceroys made to the Prince through later years of "the very lively and pleasant recollections which the native chiefs everywhere retain of your visit." [1] When in 1878 the Prince's Bombay admirer, Sir Albert Sassoon, presented to the city of Bombay a colossal equestrian statue (by Sir Edgar Boehm) of the Prince in the uniform of the 10th Hussars, he was responding to a widespread sentiment. The value of the precedent which the Prince's Indian tour created was acknowledged by those who were responsible in later years for the government of India. The Prince's sons and grandson, who were in direct succession to the Crown, subsequently followed in the Prince's steps through the great dependency. [2]

The high conception of the Prince's influence which was formed at native courts is graphically illustrated by events in Nepal which

[1] Marquis of Ripon to the Prince Jan. 9, 1882. Lord Dufferin wrote to the Prince, in similar terms, Oct. 11, 1886. In the autumn of 1903 Lord Curzon, a later Viceroy, wrote to King Edward that when on tour in the Himalayas, he was approached by a Gurkha, who showed him a handsome knife with the royal motto on the scabbard in silver. The Gurkha said it had been given to his father, a native officer, by King Edward (when Prince) at the same remote spot twenty-seven years before.

[2] In 1887 the Prince's elder son, Albert Victor, Duke of Clarence, made an Indian tour, and some sixteen years later the Prince's second son, King George V., when Prince of Wales, did the like. Both Princes in their itineraries followed closely their father's footsteps. In 1922 King Edward's eldest grandson, yet another Prince of Wales, pursued again the same path.

happened shortly after his departure. The soil there was hardly
favourable to Western civilisation, and the Prince's name was
invoked with some effect to discourage the continuance of a
barbarous native custom.

A month after the Prince parted with Sir Jung Bahadur,
who had directed the hunting expedition in the Nepal Terai, a
tragedy befell Sir Jung's family.   His son-in-law, a nephew of the
reigning Maharajah, died, and the widow, Sir Jung's daughter, at
once "poured water over her head and cried 'Ram, Ram!'"—
implying according to Brahmanic law a binding vow to commit
suttee, that is, to immolate herself on her dead husband's funeral
pyre.   The practice of *suttee* had been condemned as illegal
throughout India by the British government as early as 1829,
but it was still followed in Nepal, despite the British prohibition.
Sir Jung was personally opposed to the custom, but his efforts
to suppress it had met with limited success.   In the present
instance the Maharajah of Nepal deprecated the suicide of Sir
Jung's daughter, but the priests insisted that no retractation
of the woman's solemn vow was possible.   The Maharajah was
unwilling to defy the priests and her father despaired of saving his
daughter's life.   The Maharajah sent word of the ghastly problem
to the British Resident at his court, Mr. Charles Girdlestone, who
at once sought in aid the Prince's potent reputation.   The
Maharajah, the British Resident pointed out, had enjoyed close
personal intimacy with the Prince on the visit to Nepal, and the
Prince would be placed in an unenviable position if his friend and
host failed to place his veto on a form of suicide which was in
open conflict with the Prince's conception of right.   The argument hit home.   The Maharajah and his Prime Minister confessed
themselves loath to forfeit the Prince's goodwill.   The Maharajah
defied the priests, and Sir Jung's daughter was rescued from her
fatal vow.   The Indian government sent the Maharajah a
message of approval, and Lord Salisbury, in forwarding to the
Prince a full account of the incident (June 25, 1876) remarked:

"I feel sure that your Royal Highness will be interested to
know that your presence in India, besides all the other benefits
it caused, has had the effect of materially checking this horrible
crime in its last retreat.   I think it would be desirable that your
R.H. should express to Sir Jung Bahadur your aversion to *suttee,*
and your hope that it may be entirely suppressed in Nepal.

Such an expression of opinion would probably be far more effective than any pressure which the government of India could bring to bear."

The Prince complied with the request. But faith in *suttee* was too deep-seated in Nepal wholly to disappear at the word of the Prince, and there were other members of Sir Jung's family who sought to reconcile genuine respect for the Prince with persistence in the barbarous practice. A year later, the Prince received from a member of Sir Jung's family a frank although deferential intimation that the horrible custom could still count on willing victims. In the early spring of 1877 the Prince heard to his regret from Lord Lytton, the new Viceroy, that his friend Sir Jung had died on 25th February 1877, in somewhat suspicious circumstances. His death was assigned to "an overdose of opium immediately followed by a dose of castor oil," which pointed to suicide. Despite Sir Jung's disapproval of *suttee* three of his wives at once announced their intention to commit it in his honour. On the day after her husband's death the chief of them (the Bara Maharanee) addressed to the Prince a pathetic letter, describing Sir Jung's fatal illness and his devotion to him and to British rule. It was, she wrote, her husband's lifelong endeavour to maintain Nepal's friendship with the British government, and she hoped that the good relations would continue between England and Sir Jung's posterity. At the same time she informed the Prince with tragic earnestness of her resolve to accompany her late husband on his journey to the next world.[1] The writer duly carried out her threat, and she and Sir Jung's two other wives were cremated alive on the funeral pyre of the Prince's old comrade. The Bara Maharanee's letter brings into strange juxtaposition a strong regard for the Prince and a relentless attachment to a religious observance which was known to repel him.

X

During the Prince's tour his attention had been directed to many political issues affecting India, but it was mainly focussed on the character and conditions of the native princes, their

[1] The letter was forwarded by the Resident, Mr. Hendly, to Lord Lytton, who transmitted it to the Prince.

ministers, and subjects. His judgements invariably illustrated his broad sympathies and often his shrewdness. Of the chief minister of Baroda, Sir Madhava Rao, he wrote to Lord Granville that he was "a wonderfully intelligent and shrewd man, a strict Brahmin, and talks English as well as you do." The Prince was immensely impressed by Sir Salar Jung, the able Prime Minister of Hyderabad, who was one of the earliest Indian politicians to be introduced to him on his arrival at Bombay. Of him the Prince wrote to the same correspondent (November 30) : "The person who struck me most, and who is fit for the most enlightened society in Europe, is Sir Salar Jung. His wonderful ease of manner and conversation, with that wonderful Eastern dignity, made a great impression on me. He is, of course, a strict Mahommedan. He speaks English quite perfectly, although he has never been in England."

In a few instances the Indian princes incurred the Prince's suspicion. After his visit to the Holkar of Indore he expressed the opinion that "the Holkar cannot be trusted but need not be feared, owing to his extreme unpopularity amongst his own people." On the other hand, he was disposed to take a more lenient view than Anglo-Indian officials of the conduct of some of the ruling chiefs. The Prince, for example, deprecated censure of the boy-Nizam of Hyderabad (Sir Salar Jung's sovereign prince), who failed to pay his respects in person on the Prince's arrival in Bombay.

The Nizam (the Prince reasonably pointed out) is only nine years old, very scrofulous and sickly, and the journey from Hyderabad to Bombay would certainly have been fraught with the greatest danger to his life, so that it would have been most imprudent to let him travel. Sir Salar Jung, who is the real ruler of the State, came with an immense retinue, and was a most proper representative of the Nizam.

The Prince had a thorough faith in the virtue of personal intercourse between Englishmen and Indians. After his return from India he encouraged native princes to correspond with him, to send him their portraits and to visit this country. Prominent men of business in India also received from him marks of favour when they arrived in England. With Sir Albert Sassoon, the Jewish Croesus of Bombay, who ultimately settled with his family in this country, the Prince formed a close intimacy, which extended to Sir Albert's brother, Arthur Sassoon, and many other of Sir Albert's kinsfolk.

On occasion his expansive cordiality to Indian visitors was held from a political point of view to be open to misconstruction. Sir Salar Jung, of whom he wrote so eulogistically to Lord Granville from Bombay, arrived in England on a first visit in June 1876— soon after the Prince came home. English society endorsed the high opinion which the Prince had formed of the Indian statesman, and accorded him a brilliant reception in which the Prince and his friends played a foremost part. Oxford bestowed on him the honorary degree of D.C.L., and the Corporation of London gave him the Freedom of the City. But Sir Salar had come on a political rather than a social mission, and the government insinuated that he ought not to be encouraged to put a political value on the friendly attentions shown him by the Prince and other Englishmen. It was the hope and ambition of Sir Salar's career to regain for his state of Hyderabad the district known as Berar, which had been transferred to the British government in 1861 in exchange for other territory and the cancellation of a large debt. The Indian government was disinclined to satisfy Sir Salar's aspiration, and the Secretary of State, Lord Salisbury, laid on the Prince (June 26) the embarrassing task of warning the visitor that the notable demonstrations in his honour were not to be interpreted as any indication of the government's willingness to grant his request.

Hospitality to Indian visitors the Prince reckoned a valuable and an effective solvent of their reserve and distant feeling. When in the course of the Anglo-Russian quarrel in 1878 seven thousand Indian troops were brought to Malta to meet the possibility of a war with Russia, which was happily averted, the Prince urged that some portion of them before their return to India should visit England. On the 26th June 1878 he wrote to Lord Beaconsfield: "The effect of a certain number of the Indian native troops now at Malta coming over here for a short time for the Queen and the Country to see, would have a most beneficial effect on our Indian as well as British Empire."

Perhaps the most notable lesson which the Prince's Indian experience brought home to him was the obligation which lay on Anglo-Indian officials of treating the native subjects of the British Crown with generous consideration and urbanity. His

humane insight led him to condemn the harshness of bearing
towards native princes and peoples which he saw prevail in many
branches of Anglo-Indian government.

His comments on this delicate issue bore fruit of value.
Quite early in the tour he wrote to the Queen from Poona
(November 14, 1875):

What struck me most forcibly was the rude and rough manner
with which the English "political officers" (as they are called,
who are in attendance upon the native chiefs) treat them. It is
indeed much to be deplored, and the system is, I am sure, quite
wrong. Natives of all classes in this country will, I am sure, be
more attached to us if they are treated with kindness and with
firmness at the same time, but not with brutality or contempt.

To the same effect he wrote to Lord Granville while on the
voyage to Ceylon, Nov. 30, adding the significant words:
"Because a man has a black face and a different religion from
our own, there is no reason why he should be treated as a brute."
He declined to qualify his views on this critical matter. Very
emphatic was his language to Lord Salisbury, the Secretary of
State for India, when directing his attention a little later "to
the disgraceful habit of officers in the King's service speaking of
the inhabitants in India, many of them sprung from the great
races, as 'niggers.'"

The Prince's representations drew sympathetic acknowledgements from the Queen, the Prime Minister, and Lord Salisbury.
Lord Salisbury indeed sent stringent instructions to the government in India to check the arrogance which English military
and civilian officers frequently displayed towards the natives.
Mr. Disraeli, acting on the Prince's hints, informed the Queen
on 24th Dec., that the Resident in Hyderabad (Mr. Saunders)
had been "recalled in consequence of his offensive behaviour
to the Princes and people." Lord Lytton's chequered term of
office as viceroy in succession to Lord Northbrook was honourably
distinguished by his endeavours to improve the tone of British
officials towards the native population, and Lord Salisbury, when
commenting ironically in a letter to Lord Lytton on certain
Anglo-Indian resentments, wrote that the Viceroy's benevolent
native policy was attributed to "the malign influence of the
Prince of Wales." [1]

[1] Lady G. Cecil's *Life of Lord Salisbury*, ii. 68. The Queen held equally

The rancour which Anglo-Indian racial scorn excited in the hearts of Indians, especially those of strong religious prepossessions, could not be dispelled by the Prince's personal sympathy or influence. His conviction that Anglo-Indian lack of sympathy with Indian sentiment weakened England's hold on India received indeed confirmation while he was in the country. His visit and its pageantry—notably the military demonstration at Delhi —left on some native minds unpleasing impressions. Sir Alfred Lyall, a distinguished member of the Indian Civil Service, who was with the Prince at Delhi and fully understood native feeling in all its aspects, wrote two striking poetic *Studies at Delhi*, 1876, illustrating the barriers of thought which cut off both "the Hindu ascetic" and the fanatical "Musalmán" from approbation of the ceremonial reception of the Prince. The Hindu saw in him and his escort with the roaring cannon and gleaming bayonets only "phantoms" that "flicker away," while the less civil spoken Mohammedan, as he watched some of the Prince's English companions playing badminton after the great Delhi review

> said, as he counted his beads and smiled,
> " God smite their souls to the depths of hell." [1]

The inevitable native murmurs against English domination rendered all the more valuable the sort of sympathy which the Prince himself displayed and counselled others to assimilate. Sympathy was the only sure palliative of racial antipathy and disaffection.

At the same time the Prince harboured no doubts of the traditional system of Anglo-Indian government, and listened impatiently in later years to pleas of Indians to share with Englishmen the responsible rule of British India. While sharply condemning the arrogant temper of some members of the Anglo-Indian Civil Service he generously admitted the indebtedness of the dependency to "the energy, perseverance, and intelligence" of the majority of Anglo-Indian civilians. He felt some doubt of "the competition system for appointments," and even went so far

---

strong views on the need of treating Indians with scrupulous respect and kindness. Cf. Queen's letter to Duke of Cambridge in Sheppard's *Duke of Cambridge*, ii. 181. In the early months of 1887 the Queen engaged two Indians as personal attendants; one of them, Munshi Abdul Karim, taught her Hindustani.

[1] Poems by Sir A. C. Lyall, in *The Muses' Library*, pp. 88–91.

as to describe it as "a failure judged by its results." But at the end of his Indian tour he laid chief stress on the obligation of trusting "the man on the spot." Above all he deprecated undue interference by the Home government with their representative whom they had invested with supreme authority. "India," he wrote to Lord Granville on 21st March 1876, "is a country which can only be governed on the spot. The power of the Viceroy should not be weakened, but strengthened, and he should not be fettered by instructions from Downing Street." This conviction had been brought home to him when he learnt for the first time at Lucknow that Lord Northbrook's differences with the Home government had led to his resignation some months before, although it was not to take effect until the Prince left India.

"It is with great regret," the Prince wrote to Disraeli (Jan. 9, 1876) "that I heard of the resignation of Lord Northbrook since leaving Calcutta, as from all sides I heard that he had gained the esteem of all classes and was looked upon as a most able administrator."

None the less the Prince's regrets for the withdrawal of Lord Northbrook did not diminish his confidence in Mr. Disraeli's choice of Lord Lytton to succeed him. The Prince had delighted in the society of Lord Lytton when he was an attaché in Paris, and had used his influence in securing Lord Lytton's promotion to be minister at Lisbon, whence he was now to be transferred to India. The Prince sent to the Prime Minister from India warm congratulations on the appointment, in the devout hope that the new Viceroy would be given a free rein.

XI

Two political questions which occupied the Prince's thought while he was in India travelled beyond India's internal administration. In the first place, Queen Victoria and her Conservative Government resolved, after the Prince left England, to add to her titles the new designation of "Empress of India"; thus the sovereign of Great Britain might, it was urged, be graphically associated with the rule of the great dependency. In the second place, the Prince learnt much of the problems affecting the North-West Frontier which involved the relations of the Indian government with Afghanistan and with Russia ; the Tsar's government was judged to be seeking control of the Afghan Amir with the intention of contesting England's hold on India. The first question came suddenly under the Prince's notice and at the moment evoked heated protests which before long he withdrew. The second question made on his mind a more lasting impression, and he pursued its consideration in the light of his Indian experience long after his tour closed.

On 8th February 1876 the Queen in her Speech from the throne at the opening of the new session of Parliament, supplemented her reference to the Prince's Indian tour with the words :

At the time that the direct government of my Indian Empire was transferred to the Crown no formal addition was made to the style and titles of the Sovereign. I have deemed the present a fitting opportunity for supplying that omission and a bill upon the subject will be presented to you.

The proposal to give the British sovereign an Indian title had been first made without result in 1858 when the Crown, after the Indian Mutiny, took over the government of India from the old East India Company. It was now adopted by Mr. Disraeli at the Queen's express desire. A Royal Titles Bill for conferring on the Queen the additional title of Empress of India was introduced into the House of Commons in March. Strong opposition came from the Liberals, who saw in the Bill poisonous fruit of the Prime Minister's magnified Imperialism. Liberal orators charged him in heated philippics with exalting unduly the Crown's prestige, and he described himself as exposed for many weeks to "a fiery furnace." The Bill, however, passed its third reading in the House of Commons on 20th March, and in the House of Lords on 7th April, when it received the royal assent. No notification of these proceedings reached the Prince in India from either the Queen or the Prime Minister. It was solely from the newspapers that the Prince gained his information. The reticence of his mother and Mr. Disraeli ruffled him. He took the view that inasmuch as his future status and appellation were involved in the step which the government was taking his wishes should have been consulted beforehand. Sir Bartle Frere sought to assuage his feelings by arguing that the Imperial title would improve the Queen's relations with the natives and bring home to them her personal supremacy. But the Prince spoke disparagingly of the proposed dignity. Writing to Lord Granville on 21st March he denied that any interest was taken in the matter in India, and suggested that the proceedings were an outcome of the Prime Minister's grandiose conceptions. He reserved a final opinion till he had received fuller intelligence. During April, while slowly travelling towards England, the Prince frankly laid his grievance before Mr. Disraeli :

"As the Queen's eldest son," he wrote on the 22nd April, "I think I have some right to feel annoyed that . . . the announce-ment of the addition to the Queen's title should have been read by me in the newspapers instead of (my) having received some intimation of the subject from the Prime Minister."

Mr. Disraeli in reply soothingly suggested that the Prince as heir-apparent might also receive an addition to his titles. The Prince assumed that there was an intention of giving him the new designation of "Imperial Highness." He promptly retorted with a firm refusal of "his consent to any change in his title," and asked that no such proposal should be made. Mr. Knollys went as far as to point out to Mr. Disraeli in the Prince's name (April 22, 1876) that : "If it leaked out that such a suggestion had been made and refused by the Prince it would, though increasing his popularity, damage that of the Queen and her ministers." In political circles English controversy dragged on after the Royal Titles Bill had received the royal assent. Mr. Disraeli had assured Parliament that the Queen would not use the Imperial title save in her official intercourse with India. A Royal Pro-clamation, which announced the Queen's assumption of the title of Empress of India, seemed to the Liberal leaders inadequately to restrict its employment. Sir Henry James, a prominent member of the Liberal opposition, whose sporting tastes had won him admission to the Prince's social circle, gave notice of a motion of censure.[1] But the Prince was not disposed to press his case to extremities. The Queen's admission that he had been denied fitting consideration—a default for which she took the blame on herself—and Mr. Disraeli's blandishments

---

[1] An unauthentic rumour reached the Queen that several other friends of the Prince, who were in the House of Commons, notably Colonel Nigel Kingscote and the Marquis of Stafford, the Duke of Sutherland's son, intended to vote with Sir Henry, and were forming a "Marlborough House party" to act against the government.

rapidly cured the wound. On the day of the Prince's arrival
in London the government triumphantly defeated Sir Henry
James's motion by a majority of 334 to 226. Disraeli described
the victory as "a crowning mercy." The vehemence of the
opposition's attack on the government in the House of Lords
as well as in the Commons led the Prince to withdraw from
the fray. "Greater nonsense," he wrote to the Queen, "was, I
think, never spoken in both Houses of Parliament." [1] The
Queen, who deplored differences between her son and her trusted
minister, was finally relieved of anxiety by the receipt from the
Prince on the day after his arrival in London from India of the
following letter :

I have not the slightest wish but to receive Mr. Disraeli in
the kindest manner possible, and he wrote me a very kind letter
on my return. I have no doubt that it was an oversight on his
part not letting me know of the Royal Titles Bill, though of course
I looked upon it as a slight to me, and as your eldest son also to
you.

The personal grievance thus received honourable burial. In due
time the Prince assumed the title of Emperor of India without
demur.

XII

While the Prince was in India the friendly relations of the
Amir of Afghanistan with Russia provoked disquiet in Indian
Government circles. The Prince was already convinced that
Russian designs on Afghan independence were a menace to
British influence. Under the sway of Sir Bartle Frere the
Prince's disposition towards decisive action was powerfully
reinforced. He frankly identified himself with the party in favour
of a "forward" policy to which he strenuously adhered when he
was back in England.

During the course of the Prince's tour, the Amir Shere Ali
took the ambiguous course of promising to receive a Russian
mission at Kabul at the same time as he declined the offer of a
British mission. Lord Northbrook was reluctant to protest, but
his successor, Lord Lytton, was scarcely installed in the viceregal
chair before he resolved on active intervention. The Prince
on his return home emphatically declared that, in the light of

[1] Buckle, *Life of Disraeli*, v. 471.

information which he had gathered on the spot, he was in favour of Lord Lytton's resolve :

"I sincerely hope," he wrote to Colonel Ponsonby on 7th Sept. 1876, from Abergeldie, "that the weak policy which Lord Lytton so well describes that we adopted regarding Afghanistan will now change. It is a matter of the greatest importance that we should have a clever and a big man as our representative with the Ameer; should strengthen our garrison at Peshawar (though it is a very unhealthy station) and hasten the railway from Lahore."

A month later he was confiding to his friend Sir Bartle Frere his belief that war with Russia would alone solve the North-West frontier problem.

Lord Lytton was not precipitate. He designed a mission to Kabul in the autumn of 1876, but he postponed its dispatch for some two years—until he had learned of the Amir's actual reception of Russian envoys. Accordingly (in August 1878) Sir Neville Chamberlain, Commander of the Madras army, was sent from Peshawar with an escort of a thousand soldiers, to demand admission to the Afghan capital on the same terms as had been accorded to the Russians. "Afghanistan is what ought to occupy our greatest attention," wrote the Prince to Sir Bartle Frere (September 8, 1878), and he expressed high approval of the mission of the veteran Sir Neville, who had seen service in the British expedition to Afghanistan some thirty-seven years before. "I don't suppose," he added, "that a better man . . . could have been chosen." Lord Beaconsfield, at the Guildhall on 9th November 1878—the Prince's thirty-seventh birthday —declared that the main aim of Sir Neville's expedition was to secure "a scientific frontier." The Amir, however, proved intractable. To an advance guard of Sir Neville's escort there was delivered at Ali Musjid, in the Khyber Pass, the Amir's brusquely-worded refusal of permission to proceed. An ultimatum, which the Indian government thereupon addressed to the Amir, was ignored. War consequently opened on the 21st November.

The Prince followed closely the fortunes of the British expedition which advanced in three columns, commanded respectively by Sir Samuel Browne, the Prince's friend, General Roberts, and General Sir Donald Stewart. Afghan resistance, though obstinate, proved ineffectual, and after the death of the unfriendly Amir Shere Ali on 20th February, negotiations for peace were opened. The Prince strongly resented the fulminations of the leaders of the Liberal party against the Afghan campaign, which they denounced as the fruit of Lord Beaconsfield's and Lord Lytton's high-flying imperialism. His personal view of the needs of the situation passed indeed somewhat beyond what even the "forward" Indian school advocated.

"For the last two months," he wrote from Sandringham on 17th Jan. 1879 to his tutor on North-West Frontier problems, Sir Bartle Frere, then in South Africa, "we have been engrossed here by the Afghan War, and I trust that you approve of what has been done till now. You will have been hardly edified by the speeches of Lds. Grey, Northbrook, and Lawrence in the Afghan debate, and to me it is astounding that statesmen and men who know India should have talked such nonsense and for the sake of party feeling have propounded sentiments regarding our Indian Empire that they would never have dared utter if they had been in office. You will be glad to see how well our friend Sam Browne has done. In fact nothing could have been better than the conduct of the whole army. I must confess I don't yet see how it is all to end. If I had my way I should not be content until we had taken the whole of Afghanistan, and kept it, letting Russia take as much as she likes up to it (leaving Persia of course) as I am quite sure we should be far better friends as close neighbours and trust one another more, and that there would be less chance of intrigue than with a neutral zone between us. I fear, however, that this view of mine is not shared by many."

Through the spring of 1879 the British claims on Afghanistan seemed in course of a settlement which conformed with the Prince's view. On 12th April Lord Beaconsfield wrote to the Prince: "The accounts from Afghanistan are favourable. . . . I shall continue to write as affairs develop." Ultimately Yakoub Khan, son of the dead Amir Shere Ali, was placed by the British envoys on the Afghan throne (May 9, 1879), and a treaty of peace was signed at Gandamak on 26th May. The treaty provided for the establishment of a Resident at Kabul and an annual subsidy of £60,000, to the Amir. But the promise of peace proved delusive. The Afghan crisis was far from ended. The new British Resident, Sir Louis Cavagnari, had scarcely arrived at Kabul when he and his suite were massacred by mutinous Afghan soldiers

(September 3, 1879). The startling crime recalled to the Prince's mind the historic tragedy of 1841, when a British envoy, Sir Alexander Burnes, suffered at Kabul the like fate. Writing to Frere on 26th September he lamented "the loss of so distinguished and valuable a public servant as Cavagnari," and despaired of providing any "safeguard" against such treachery. The assassination led to a prompt renewal of the war in the course of which General Roberts conspicuously maintained the prestige of British arms by his triumphant march from Kabul to the relief of Kandahar. But internal dissensions involving civil war among the Afghans prolonged the conflict. In the autumn of 1881, however, a new Amir, Abdur-Rahman, succeeded, with British help, in bringing all Afghanistan under a single sway, and peace was at length achieved. Amir Abdur-Rahman faithfully kept his engagements to the British government during the twenty years of his reign, which ended with his death on the 3rd October 1901—some eight months after King Edward's accession. The Prince regarded the settlement of the Afghan difficulty as a justification of the policy which he had espoused on his Indian tour and had since supported with steadily increasing zeal. Throughout King Edward's reign Amir Abdur-Rahman's son and successor, Amir Habibullah, followed in his father's footsteps and cherished goodwill for the British rule of India.

1879
Ætat. 37

1881
Ætat. 39

CHAPTER XXII

A LEISURELY HOME-COMING BY WAY OF SPAIN

I

1876
Ætat. 34

THE Prince had travelled back from Bombay at a leisurely pace and did not reach London till 11th May—more than eight weeks after his embarkation. Cautious medical advice recommended delay in facing the asperities of the English spring. Recent incidents at home, too, had caused the Prince some irritation which needed a little time to allay. His companion, Lord Aylesford, had been recalled from India by a matrimonial difficulty which scandalised society, and the Prince incurred some social criticism by his characteristic chivalry in standing by his friend. There was also the disquieting controversy over the Royal Titles Bill. The time which the slow journey consumed was far from wasted. It gave the Prince new opportunities of satisfying his political curiosity and of moulding his political views.

After stopping to coal at Aden, the *Serapis* reached Suez on 25th March. There the Prince had interesting meetings with Lord Lytton, who was on his way out to India to take over the office of Viceroy from Lord Northbrook, as well as with General Stanton, the Consul-General at Cairo, whose views on Egyptian affairs he valued, and with M. de Lesseps. There was much talk with Lord Lytton of the condition of India.[1] The new Viceroy undertook to keep the Prince fully informed of his experiences as supreme governor of the dependency, and there followed throughout Lord Lytton's tenure of office an intimate correspondence between the two. At Cairo, the Prince again enjoyed for a week

[1] In describing the interview to the Queen, Lord Lytton wrote: "If judged by the appearance of the Prince and his Staff, India should be the healthiest country in the world. I never saw His Royal Highness looking so well and strong—not a trace of fatigue about him." (March 28, 1876.)

408

the hospitality of the Khedive at Ghezireh Palace, where the
Prince's party was joined somewhat ironically by the Grand Duke
Alexis of Russia, a younger son of Tsar Alexander II. The week
was divided between archæological study under the direction of
the Egyptologist Marriette Bey, and friendly intercourse with
the Khedive Ismail, whose financial embarrassment had been
little relieved by England's recent purchase of his Suez
Canal shares. The Egyptian government was nervous of the
pressure of French creditors, and sanguinely believed that
the Prince's influence might diminish the Khedive's difficulties
in that quarter. At Alexandria Sir Bartle Frere bade the Prince
farewell, and the *Serapis* went on to Malta. The Prince spent
five pleasant days (April 8–13) at Valetta as the guest of the
Governor-General van Straubenzee. Gibraltar was reached on
17th April, and the Duke of Connaught, then Assistant-Adjutant-
General, joined his brother in the abundant entertainment which
was offered the royal traveller on shore.

Love of adventure and sight-seeing combined with political
curiosity to prolong the Prince's stay in the peninsula. The
Serapis was in need of repairs, and it was resolved to rejoin her
at Lisbon after refitting at Gibraltar. The royal yacht *Osborne*
arrived to take the Prince and his party to Cadiz. Thence they
proceeded on an inland journey of very varied interest. The
first three days were devoted to sight-seeing at Seville (April
21–24) ; the next five days were spent in somewhat singular
circumstances at Madrid, a city to which the Prince now paid
his first and only visit ; the following week saw him for a second
time at the friendly Court of Lisbon.

II

For some eight years Spain had been in a state of almost continuous revolution, the varied phases of which the Prince had
watched with keen attention. When the disreputable Queen
Isabella had consented, while a refugee in Paris, formally to
abdicate the Spanish throne on the 25th June 1870, she had made
the proviso, which for the time was ignored, that her thirteen-
year-old son, Alfonso, should succeed her. The boy found an
asylum in England where both Queen Victoria and the Prince
interested themselves in his welfare, and encouraged his hope that

he might yet wear his country's crown. The Queen sanctioned his admission as a cadet to Sandhurst. Meanwhile the Prince was disturbed by the confusion which prevailed in Spain. He showed no great enthusiasm for the election to the vacant throne of Amadeo, Duke of Aosta, King Victor Emmanuel's second son, after the withdrawal of the candidature of the Prince's friend, Leopold of Hohenzollern-Sigmaringen. King Amadeo found himself in Spain between two fierce fires—between the supporters of older royal lines and the advocates of a republican form of government. In May 1872 Laurence Oliphant, the brilliant but unbalanced writer, whose conversation always charmed the Prince, wrote suggesting that the Prince should visit Spain in order to encourage and counsel King Amadeo in his embarrassments. The Prince declined the suggestion, and his private secretary remarked to Lord Granville: "It is no part of the Prince's business to go about Europe consolidating dynasties." At the end of the year King Amadeo was forced to abdicate and, to the Prince's dismay, a republic was established. In a letter to Lord Granville on receipt of the unwelcome news the Prince admitted that the deposed monarch was "a true-hearted gentleman and a man of honour."

"It is indeed difficult to see," the Prince added despondently, "what the future of that benighted country will be. But there seems little hope for its prosperity, and those men be they able or the reverse who have to govern the country are steeped in every incredible vice and iniquity and have not even that one redeeming quality—patriotism."

In spite of the active hostilities of the two rival monarchical parties—the Carlists and the royalists—and of the communists, the Spanish republic stood its ground till the end of 1874. The assumption by Marshal Serrano of the office of Dictator-President on 3rd January 1874, seemed sufficient evidence of the republic's stability to lead all the great powers except Russia to recognise it. The step was welcomed by neither Queen Victoria nor the Prince, who regarded with favour the claims of their Sandhurst protégé to the lapsed monarchy.

Their hopes were soon fulfilled. On the last day of the year (1874) the army revolted against the republic and declared for a new king in the person of the English refugee—then seventeen years old. From Sandhurst the youth issued, early in January

1875, a manifesto accepting the Spanish crown under the title of Alfonso XII., and on the 14th January he arrived in Madrid. But the turmoil in Spain was not yet ended. The Carlists refused their allegiance, and civil war broke out afresh. A year passed before the Carlist forces were disarmed and King Alfonso's authority confirmed (in February 1876).

Throughout King Alfonso's year of struggle the Queen and the Prince privately gave his cause every mark of sympathy. Early in 1875 the Queen sent him her congratulations, and both she and the Prince protested against the refusal of Lord Derby, the Foreign Secretary, to recognise his régime. They knew that Lord Derby was acting on the advice of Sir Austen Layard, the British Ambassador at Madrid, and the Queen in a strongly worded letter to Disraeli (on February 15), cited the Prince's quip that the Ambassador well deserved his old nickname of "Lie-hard," and his view that Sir Austen should be given leave of absence. The desired recognition did not take place before the autumn. Sir Austen reported (October 15, 1875) how in an interview the king expressed a desire to prove his gratitude for the Queen and the Prince's kindness by governing Spain on the lines of the British constitution.

III

In April 1876, when the Prince, on his way home from India, decided to greet the new Spanish sovereign in his capital, scarcely a month had elapsed since he had made his triumphal entry into Madrid (March 20), after decisively routing his rival Don Carlos. Every branch of government was as yet disorganised. Lord Derby thought the moment for the Prince's visit ill-chosen. While the Prince was at Seville he wired from London a note of warning (April 20):

Our relations with Spain are not wholly satisfactory, and we have many causes of complaint against the Spanish government. It is not advisable that anything should be said or done which would lead the Spaniards to attach less importance to these grievances or mislead them as to the state of feeling here.

The Prince at once replied:

You need be under no apprehension that I shall in any way compromise H.M. government while in Spain.

1876   At Seville, too, the Prince received a characteristic message in
Ætat. 34 cypher from Mr. Disraeli which was sent on 20th April 1876, not
only to Seville but also to the care of the Governor of Gibraltar:
"Pray be careful," the message ran, "your Royal Highness is
not taken prisoner like Cœur de Lion on your return home from
your Crusade." The Prince replied that he was "much amused
by your telegram, but do not apprehend that I shall share the
fate of my distinguished ancestor on returning from the East."

At Madrid the Prince was received on 25th April by the young
king and by his sister, the Princess of the Asturias, who both
offered him affectionate greeting. The new king had occupied
his palace for barely a month, and the domestic equipment was
consequently makeshift. But no hospitable attention that
was practicable was spared. The Prince in his field-marshal's
uniform attended a state dinner and a review of 25,000 Spanish
troops, while excursions were made with the king to Toledo and
the Escurial. On 28th April the British Ambassador entertained
the Prince at a banquet which the King of Spain paid the
royal visitor the unusual honour of attending. It was the
first occasion on which a Spanish king had dined in Madrid
outside his palace.[1]

The Prince's unconventional visit to Spain was far from
causing the new régime or Anglo-Spanish relations the harm
which the ministers at home feared. It gave the boy king new
confidence and prestige. The country remained tranquil, and a
reformed constitution was soon in operation. The Prince continued to manifest a kindly interest in the youth's welfare
throughout the nine years that intervened before his premature
death. Old associations commended to the Prince the young
monarch's marriage on the 23rd January 1878, to his first cousin,
Mercédes, daughter of the Duc de Montpensier. But that union
was abruptly terminated by the Queen's death five months later,

---

[1] An invitation to a bull-fight was pressed on the Prince but was refused,
although he witnessed at a theatre a burlesque of the national sport. At the
Escurial the Prince greatly admired some tapestries designed by Goya, the great
Spanish artist, and the young king at once offered to present copies to the
Prince. By an error of a court official the king's order was neglected. Some
time later the Prince caused an inquiry to be made as to the reason why the
promised copies had not reached him. Thereupon the young king, on learning
for the first time of his official's omission, munificently forwarded to the Prince
the original pieces. These tapestries have long been among the ornaments of
the dining-room at Sandringham.

and King Alfonso married a second wife, the Archduchess   1876
Marie Christina, daughter of the Austrian Arch-Duke Charles   Ætat. 34
Ferdinand, on the 29th November 1879. The promotion of the
Prince's friend, Sir Robert Morier, to the embassy at Madrid in
1881 tended to increase his interest in the Spanish Court and
in Spanish affairs.   In the autumn of 1883 King Alfonso proposed
to visit England, and the Prince urged both his mother and the
Foreign Secretary, Lord Granville, to respond favourably to the
proposal.   The Prince deemed the month of May 1884 the most
convenient time, and he wrote to Lord Granville that he would
"be delighted to look after him, and I know him very well."
The visit failed to mature, but the Prince spent several days in
the young king's company in the autumn of 1884, when both were
attending the German military manœuvres as the Kaiser's guests.
   On the announcement of the king's premature death on
25th November 1885, at the age of 28, the Prince pressed on the
government the need of sending a special representative to the
funeral.   He was perfectly ready, he told the Foreign Secretary,
Lord Salisbury, to undertake the mission.   "I should be only
too glad," he wrote (Nov. 29, 1885) "to personally testify my
respect to the memory of one whom I held in high esteem and for
whom I had a great personal friendship."   Ultimately the Duke
of Wellington represented the Queen at the obsequies at Madrid,
and the Prince was represented independently by his equerry,
Colonel Stanley Clarke.   After the king's death there was born
to his widow his son and heir, King Alfonso XIII. To the
new King of Spain as he grew to manhood the Prince continued
the attentions which he had shown his father, and the young
king's marriage to the Prince's niece, Princess Ena of Battenberg,
in 1906 with his full sanction, crowned the benevolent relations
between the Prince and the royal family of Spain, of which he
gave crucial proof on his way home from India in 1876.

IV

   One more visit to a foreign court was paid by the Prince
before he turned his face homewards from his Indian tour.
From Madrid he passed to Lisbon to visit his kinsman and
old acquaintance, Dom Luis, and to converse with his
favoured comrade of the diplomatic service, Sir Robert Morier,

who had just succeeded Lord Lytton as British minister to
Portugal, where he was to stay for five years before migrating
to Spain. The Portuguese king and his father, Prince Ferdinand
of Saxe-Coburg, Queen Victoria's aged cousin, were assiduous
in their attentions. At the customary state dinner the Prince
and Dom Luis, whose English sympathies had lately showed
themselves in a translation of several plays of Shakespeare,
exchanged the time-honoured vows of traditional friendship
between their two countries. "In the monotonous life of the
Portuguese nation," Sir Robert Morier wrote in somewhat
heightened language on the 8th May 1876, "the visit will long
continue not only an event of great political importance but one
replete with glad and brilliant associations."

After a week at Lisbon, on 7th May, the Prince, with Robert
Morier among his companions, set out at length for England on
board the *Serapis*, which had come on from Gibraltar after
completing her repairs. Four days later, early in the morning
of 11th May, the Princess and the children, who had come out on
the *Enchantress*, joined the Prince in the Solent. The landing
was made at Portsmouth, where a magnificent welcome was
offered him. From Portsmouth the Prince made a triumphal
progress by rail to London through decorated stations and
cheering crowds. The Prime Minister, who was kept away by
public business from the terminus, Victoria Station, gave expression in a letter of apology to the popular sentiment when
he wrote that the country "is justly proud of many things but
at this moment prouder of nothing more than its Prince."

From Victoria Station the Prince drove to Buckingham Palace
to greet the Queen. A long series of congratulatory ceremonies
followed. On Sunday 14th May the Prince attended at Westminster Abbey a thanksgiving service for his safe return. The
public welcome culminated on the 19th in a banquet at the
Guildhall, which was followed by a ball. The Prince, in returning
thanks at the banquet for the toast of his health, spoke feelingly
of the new knowledge that he had acquired in the four months of
his tour, of the need of a far longer period to learn the full lesson
that India had to teach, of his satisfaction with the condition of
the Indian army and navy, and of his gratitude to the princes and
peoples of India for their generous reception. Messages of congratulation which came from all quarters in eulogistic strains

played variations on Lord Granville's theme that the success of   1876
the expedition was due to the Prince's tact and energy.   The   Ætat. 34
general view that his Indian tour was a national service even
softened the tone of the persiflage with which the free lances of
the press still pursued him.   When, at the end of 1876, the series
of annual satires which *The Coming K——* had inaugurated at
Christmas 1870,[1] reached its sixth and last instalment in a
burlesque play in "seven acts" prophetically entitled *King
Edward VII.*, the visit to India, which was good-humouredly
burlesqued, was hailed as a final proof of the Prince's fitness for
the succession to his mother's crown.   The last scene of the piece
showed him ascending the throne with the goodwill of his fellow-
countrymen on the abdication of the Queen in his favour.

[1] See p. 329 *supra*.

CHAPTER XXIII

POLITICAL ESTRANGEMENT FROM RUSSIA, 1876–1878

1876

Ætat. 34

ON the Prince's return from India, Europe was confronted with a storm in the Balkans which threatened the peace of Europe. The course of events revived in full strength the Prince's youthful faith in the Palmerstonian creed which made it England's solemn duty to protect Turkey's integrity from Russian aggression. The Prince's visit to India and his discipleship to Sir Bartle Frere tended to counteract the effects of recent domestic friendship with the Russian royal family, and to deepen the conviction that England's prestige, alike in Asia and in Europe, required her to show Russia a bold front. The Prime Minister, Mr. Disraeli, strenuously sought to protect what he deemed to be British interests against the Russian menace, and he now found in the Prince an ardent supporter.

I

The Prince's intimacy with the Prime Minister steadily grew. Hospitalities in London were constantly exchanged between the two men, and invitations to Sandringham were frequent.[1] With the Prime Minister's private secretary, Mr. Montagu Corry, the Prince also cultivated a close friendship. Mr. Disraeli kept the Prince informed of every turn in the many critical issues which faced him during his remaining years of office. The Prince was unceasingly fertile in comment and suggestion, while the Queen paid an unusual consideration to the Prince's views, which now coincided with her own.[2]

[1] Buckle, *Life of Disraeli*, vi. 116, 169.
[2] Access to the extensive correspondence between the Prince and Lord Beaconsfield has been given to the present writer by Lord Beaconsfield's trustees. Some further interesting letters from Disraeli to the Prince are

The Prime Minister illustrated the value which he set on the 1876
Prince's confidence by privately informing him on the 9th August Ætat. 34
1876 of his intention (not yet publicly divulged) to accept a
peerage. His health, he explained, did not allow him to continue in the House of Commons, but the Queen had counselled
him against resignation and had suggested an alleviation of his
labours by retiring to the House of Lords. "I place," Mr. Disraeli
informed the Prince, "the whole matter before your Royal
Highness in the hope that you may not think unfavourably of
my course." The Prince heartily approved the step which Mr.
Disraeli was taking, and warmly congratulated him on his choice
of the title of Earl of Beaconsfield. The Prince's attendance in
the House of Lords grew frequent in order to hear and observe
the new peer in his new environment.

A visit which the Prince paid to the statesman at his country
home at Hughenden when his tenure of power was nearing its end
attests the constancy of the Prince's sympathy. The Prince
offered himself as Lord Beaconsfield's guest, and in view of the
limited accommodation at Hughenden the compliment somewhat
troubled the aged host. The Prince arrived on Monday 12th
January 1880, and stayed over the next day. There were four
fellow-guests. Lord Salisbury and Sir William Hart Dyke, Chief
Whip of the Conservative party, represented serious politics,
while the social world was represented by Lord Rosslyn and Mr.
Bernal Osborne, in whose witty talk the Prince had long delighted
—"two clowns, and both capital ones," as Lord Beaconsfield 1880
called them. Lord Beaconsfield wrote to the Queen (January 14) : Ætat. 38
"The conversation was grave as well as gay, and H.R.H. maintained his part with felicity—even distinction. . . . Lord Rosslyn
and Mr. Osborne expressed and elicited many a flashing phrase."
The host told his confidential friend, Lady Bradford, that the
Prince

said some good things and told more. We played whist in the
evening—his own choice. I had hoped to have induced him to
play nap, which would have left me alone, for I don't understand
that mystery. But he would not have it, and insisted on playing

---

among King Edward's papers. Sparse fragments only of this correspondence
are cited in Mr. Buckle's *Life of Disraeli*. References are here given to Mr.
Buckle's work in the case of such limited portions of the correspondence
as he quotes.

1880
Ætat. 38

with B. O. against Salisbury and myself at whist. He beat us, which does not displease him.[1]

There was no slackening in the Prince's pursuit of Lord Beaconsfield's society during the remaining fifteen months of the statesman's life.   After Lord Beaconsfield's fall from power in the spring of 1880 the Prince continued to seek his society and to yield himself to the fascination of his flashes of sardonic humour, nor did the statesman interrupt his observant scrutiny of the Prince's activities.   The last dinner-party but one which Lord Beaconsfield attended was at Marlborough House (on Saturday, March 19, 1881).   It was the final meeting between the two men.   Exactly a month later Lord Beaconsfield died.   The Prince, as his mother's representative, attended the funeral at Hughenden on 26th April, and he laid on the coffin a wreath with a card on which he had written the words: "A tribute of friendship and affection." Thus ended an interesting episode of friendship in which the Prince's shrewd wit matched itself not unsympathetically or unsuccessfully with the brilliant intellectual and imaginative endowments of the Conservative chieftain.

II

1876
Ætat. 34

In December 1875, while the Prince was in India, the Porte's Christian subjects in the provinces of Bosnia and Herzgovina —on Turkey's Austrian frontier—broke into rebellion.   The disturbance spread in the following spring to Bulgaria, in the near neighbourhood of Russia.   Turkey embarked on a merciless course of repression.   Public opinion in England was soon greatly excited and greatly divided by the Balkan struggle.   The Prince was under no delusion as to the degeneracy of Turkey, despite his amiable intercourse with Sultan Abdul-Aziz.   At the outset he approved Disraeli's action in protesting with other European powers against Turkish misrule and in urging the Porte to reform its ways.   But the Porte, relying on its old ties of friendship with England, ignored the good counsel.   In May 1876 the suggestion was made that a congress of the great powers should assemble with a view to the pacification of the Balkans and to the regeneration of Turkey.   Mr. Disraeli promptly informed the Prince of the proposal:

[1] Buckle, *Life of Disraeli*, vi. 471–2.

"There is no doubt," he wrote on 29th May 1876, "that France
is strongly urging a Congress, and, I am assured, at the instance
of Russia. . . . My own opinion is that the Congress will be
held. If we are firm, as well as conciliatory, it may not only
secure peace, but increase and establish the influence of England."

The Prince, replying the same day, expressed his agreement, with
a reservation :

Should a Congress be the means of securing peace, you will I
am sure be one of the first to wish England to join the other
Powers, but the question of course remains whether a Congress
will get the Porte out of the serious scrape she has got into.

Startling events were meanwhile happening at Constantinople.
On the same day as the Prime Minister and the Prince exchanged
these letters, a progressive party there, headed by Midhat
Pasha, endeavoured to placate the Powers by deposing the Sultan,
who was soon afterwards assassinated.

Through the summer and autumn of 1876 the confusion
in the Balkans grew apace, despite the change of ruler at Constantinople. The autonomous provinces of Serbia and Monte-
negro declared war on Turkey, their suzerain. The Prince
shared Lord Beaconsfield's belief that Russia was behind the
spreading insurrection. Early in July he admitted to Count
Schouvaloff, the Russian Ambassador in London, that his sister,
Princess Alice of Hesse-Darmstadt, who was on intimate terms
with the Tsar, had assured him of the Tsar's peaceful intentions,
but he feared that the Tsar's agents in the disturbed districts
were otherwise inclined. The Prince, without questioning the
beneficial outcome of the suggested Congress, now advised its
postponement until the pending struggle between Turkey and
Serbia had better disclosed the strength of the combatants. In
the meantime the Prince deprecated intervention on the part of
any individual power. Count Schouvaloff detected in the
Prince's remarks pronounced Russophobe and Turcophil leanings
—an impression which later conversations powerfully confirmed.[1]

Barely two months later, the Prince was requested to make
a personal experiment in peacemaking. Serbia, which had
rashly challenged Turkish vengeance, lay at Turkey's feet. The
country was overrun by Turkish troops. The Prince's former
equerry and close friend, Colonel Loyd Lindsay, afterwards Lord

[1] Schouvaloff to Gortschakoff, June 24/July 6, 1876 (Russian Archives).

1876
Ætat. 34

Wantage, visited the Serbian seat of war in August to ascertain the true facts of the situation. He sent the Prince a full report of the Serbians' plight (Sept. 5), after convincing himself that the Serbian outbreak was the work of Russia, whose officers he found in command of the Serbian army. He urged the Prince to exert "his great influence . . . to bring about a cessation of this useless and disastrous strife" by writing to the Tsar and by bringing home to him "the wickedness of driving a people into rebellion against their will." The Prince consulted the Queen and the Prime Minister. The Queen thought that a direct appeal to the Tsar might be of some avail. The Prime Minister was less sanguine, and the Prince held his hand.

III

In the same autumn Mr. Gladstone, who had for the time nominally withdrawn from the leadership of the Liberal party in favour of the Prince's friend, Lord Hartington, suddenly emerged from his retirement and sought by dint of impassioned oratory to rouse the country against Mr. Disraeli's ministry, on the ground that they had failed to protect the Balkan Christians from the "atrocities" of the Turkish irregular troops—the Bashi-Bazouks. For many months Mr. Gladstone and some able lieutenants led an oratorical crusade against the Porte and against the Prime Minister through the length and breadth of Great Britain. To the Prince the campaign made no appeal. He succinctly condemned as "rubbish" the vehement expressions of sympathy with the Serbians which came from the lips of Mr. Gladstone's ally Mr. John Bright. Despite his private regard for Mr. Gladstone, he impatiently deprecated his present fury. On 14th September he wrote to Mr. Disraeli :

I deeply deplore the present agitation over the so-called Bulgarian atrocities, which is now so prevalent throughout the country. It must, I fear, weaken the hands of the government, who are so anxious to do all in their power to obtain peace.

Next day the Prime Minister, who was profoundly disturbed by his rival's "verbosity," replied that the "short-sighted faction" was prejudicing England's influence in Europe. But to the regret of both the Queen and the Prince, the agitation steadily made headway. Disraeli's withdrawal to the House of

Lords had left vacant the Parliamentary representation of
Buckinghamshire, and the election of a successor took place during Mr. Gladstone's crusade. The Conservative candidate, T. F. Fremantle, faced vehement opposition, and the Prince eagerly followed what he called "the Bulgarian election." Lord Beaconsfield assured the Prince that "a Turk would be returned," yet Mr. Fremantle's election on the 22nd September, by a narrow majority of little more than 200, was not encouraging. On 6th October the Prime Minister pointed out to the Prince that, owing to the "frenzy of a portion of the public," Russia was making on Turkey extravagant territorial demands which England was bound to resist.

Serbia's sufferings were still acute, but when, under English persuasion, Turkey showed a willingness to grant a six months' armistice, the Serbian leaders hesitated to accept the offer. Russian intrigue was generally assumed to be responsible for the Serbians' hesitation, and the Prince's antagonism to Russia redoubled. He came to the conclusion that England would have to engage in active hostilities with Russia before a settlement of their many rivalries could be reached. To Sir Bartle Frere, whose views coincided with his own, he wrote on the 14th October 1876 :

The affairs of the East still look very grave and the six months' armistice granted by the Porte does not seem favourably entertained by Servia. Of course Russia is at the bottom of this. Sooner or later we must come to blows with our Northern friends, and I am inclined to think the sooner the better. The Eastern question and the Indian Frontier question will then be solved for ever.

Lord Beaconsfield warned the Prince (November 30) that, unless England made a resolute stand, a partition of Turkey on the lines of the partition of Poland might be looked for.

The Prince's suspicion of Russian intentions was powerfully confirmed by expert information which reached him from a private source. Valentine Baker, Colonel of his own regiment—the 10th Hussars—had, in the autumn of 1875, been dismissed the service after conviction on a serious charge, but the Prince deemed the punishment unduly severe, and with his customary chivalry maintained his old relations with his friend. On his release from prison Colonel Baker returned to the field of exploration in the

Near East in which he had in earlier years proved his competence. He offered his services to the Porte, which were before long accepted. On 2nd November 1876 he sent the Prince from Constantinople a useful survey of recent military operations together with a report on the military strength of Turkey, suggesting a plan for fortifying the Dardanelles in the neighbourhood of Constantinople in view of a possible Russian attack. The Prince at once forwarded Colonel Baker's information to Lord Beaconsfield (Nov. 28). The Prime Minister replied (on Nov. 30) that Colonel Baker's suggestion had been anticipated, but the Prince held to his view that the Colonel's expert observation ought not to be overlooked. Colonel Baker returned to London for a short period in December. After an interview with him the Prince informed the Prime Minister that he "found him most interesting," and he appealed to Lord Beaconsfield to see Colonel Baker before he left the country to return to Turkey. The Prime Minister did not, however, take the Prince's advice.

IV

The recent suggestion of an international Conference which should reform Turkey's administration of her subject provinces was at length nearing fruition. Russia gave a tardy assent, and it was agreed that the meeting-place should be Constantinople. But the Prince's earlier hope of a useful result had dwindled. His doubts of Russia were crystallising into a firm conviction of her hostility to England. He welcomed, however, the Prime Minister's appointment of Lord Salisbury, the Secretary of State for India, as Great Britain's representative.

"Lord Salisbury's appointment," wrote the Prince to the Prime Minister's private secretary, Montagu Corry, on 8th November 1876, "seems an excellent one, but your chief is always happy in the choice he makes. I own I do not feel very sanguine, however, as to the ultimate results attained by the Conference, as I fear that we shall never agree with the Russian proposals, nor they with ours."

One preliminary step which contravened what the Prince regarded as the "red tapeist" traditions of the Foreign Office he pressed, through the Prime Minister, on Lord Salisbury. The British envoy, he urged, should, on his way out to Constantinople, call at Paris, Berlin, Vienna and Rome, the capitals of the four great powers, and interview personally the rulers and chief statesmen so as to ascertain in advance their views of the situation. Lord Tenterden, the permanent Under-Secretary of the Foreign Office, condemned the suggestion as unusual and superfluous, but the Prince, who invariably believed in personal intercourse as a touchstone of harmony and mistrusted the distant formalities of professional diplomacy, persisted in his counsel, which Lord Beaconsfield cordially adopted. Lord Salisbury on the Prince's initiative was despatched on a "pilgrimage of consultation." Writing to Lord Salisbury on 10th November 1876 the Prime Minister remarked :

I think on these matters H.R.H. is a better counsellor than Lord Tenterden. The Prince of Wales is a thorough man of the world, and knows all these individuals personally. You must remember we suffer from a feeble and formal diplomacy and that there has been little real interchange of thought between the English government and foreign Powers. I agree with the Prince and think it highly desirable that at this moment our communications with the Powers should be lifted out of the slough of despond they have so long grovelled in.[1]

Accordingly Lord Salisbury left England on a tour which proved of great service to him in his coming career as Foreign Secretary. In agreement with the Prince's plan he saw in Paris the Duc Decazes, the French Foreign Minister, and Marshal MacMahon ; in Berlin the Emperor William I., the Crown Prince and Princess and Prince Bismarck; in Vienna Count Andrassy ; and in Rome Prince Humbert and several Italian ministers.

The Conference assembled at Constantinople to discuss preliminaries on 12th December 1876, and was in formal session until 20th January 1877. The Prime Minister fully reported the proceedings to the Prince, who followed them with close attention. The prospects of the Conference were never bright. Russia's attitude was ambiguous, and Turkey's unwillingness to accept an International Commission which should supervise internal reform brought about a collapse. On 9th January 1877 the Prince inquired of the Prime Minister as to the truth of a statement in the *Morning Post* to the effect that "Russia proposed to give up her demands and

1876
Ætat. 34

1877
Ætat. 35

1 Lady Gwendolen Cecil's *Life of Lord Salisbury*, ii. p. 95.

to make a secret treaty with Turkey on condition that Russian men-of-war (and those of no other nation) should be allowed to enter the Bosporus." On the 13th January Lord Beaconsfield wrote confidentially to the Prince :

> The conference meets again to-morrow, but I have no hope of any satisfactory arrangement. Lord Salisbury had an interview with Midhat *yesterday* on which I think all depended. The Grand Vizier absolutely declined any Commission which should contain any foreigners in any form. . . . He refused any territorial extension to Servia or even Montenegro, and, in short, offered nothing but trifles. Lord Salisbury left him quite hopeless.

Next day, while thanking Lord Beaconsfield "for the last news from Constantinople," the Prince added :

> I only wish it were more satisfactory. It is indeed hard on Lord Salisbury after all the hard work which his most delicate and difficult mission has entailed [that it] should have no result. We must still hope that at the last moment Midhat Pasha's obduracy may be overcome.

But the Conference impotently dissolved on the 20th January 1877, and Lord Salisbury reached London early next month.

On 10th February Salisbury saw the Prince and described his experiences. He found that the Prince was far from sharing his own feelings of exasperation with the Turk. The "Turkophil party" at home, Lord Salisbury wrote next day to his wife, found its chief strength in the Prince's "clique," notably in the Prince's friend, the Duke of Sutherland.[1] The Prince's confidence in Lord Salisbury's political insight was somewhat impaired by the interview.

Russia's action immediately after the abortive Conference was puzzling. She professed anxiety to maintain the European concert. In March, General Ignatieff, the Pan-Slavist explorer of Central Asia and Russian Ambassador in Constantinople, who had represented his country at the Conference there, began at Paris a tour of the capitals of Europe in order to explain the Tsar's readiness to continue his co-operation with the other powers. From Paris the Russian general and diplomatist proceeded to London, where he was hospitably received, staying from 14th to 22nd March. The Prince had met him on his visit to the Sultan in 1869, and readily renewed the acquaintance with a view to acquiring all the

[1] Lady G. Cecil's *Life of Lord Salisbury*, ii. 127.

information possible on the pending issue. The General and his wife not only visited Marlborough House (17th March), but when, four days later, Lord Beaconsfield, rather against his will, entertained the Russian envoy and his wife at dinner, the Prince put in an appearance as a self-invited guest, and Mme. Ignatieff was, at his suggestion, his partner at the dinner-table.[1] Nothing that he heard from the General or his wife allayed his suspicions of Russia. Early next month he re-explained his position to Count Schouvaloff, the Russian Ambassador in London, at an accidental meeting. He deprecated the notion of any personal hostility to the Ambassador or to his master, but he insisted that, like the majority of his fellow-countrymen, he was resolved to defend the Ottoman Empire from attack. The Count frankly replied that his views as those of a mere Englishman were negligible, but they had a high importance as those of the future sovereign of England. In reporting the interview to Prince Gortschakoff (Feb. 23/March 7) the Count finally described the Prince as "the most Turkish of all Englishmen," and declared that he was bound to treat him with the utmost caution.[2]

V

Lord Beaconsfield was quite willing to act with the other powers in their endeavours to reform Turkey, provided that both Russia and Turkey agreed to disarm. If that guarantee of peace were forthcoming, England proposed to urge anew on the Porte a joint protocol of domestic reform. The Prince commended the cautious proposal. "I entirely agree with the views the government have taken," he wrote to Lord Beaconsfield's secretary, Montagu Corry, on the 23rd March 1877, "not to sign any protocol till Russia has consented to disarm at the same time as Turkey does, or else Constantinople will become a second Khiva." But all hopes of accommodation on such lines as these were dispelled by Russia's declaration of war on Turkey on April 24, 1877.

In the fierce struggle that followed, the Prince's pro-Turkish sympathies, fanned by Queen Victoria's passionate hostility to Russia, burnt more briskly than ever. His mother did all she could to whet her son's feelings. She asked the Prime Minister

[1] Buckle, *Life of Disraeli*, vi. 128.　　　[2] Russian Archives.

to keep him informed of "the plans and proceedings of Russia and of the extreme danger of being deceived by them" (June 7, 1877).[1] Both the Queen and the Prince were greatly disturbed by the Russians' initial victories. Both, too, found a new anxiety in the lukewarm attitude which the Foreign Secretary, Lord Derby, manifested towards the cause of Turkey. To their dismay, Lord Derby failed to warn Russia that England would not suffer her to occupy Constantinople. The Prince of Wales, she wrote to Lord Beaconsfield (June 27, 1877), was "frantic" at discovering from Lord Derby's recent speeches his passive indifference to Russia's certain triumph in the current campaign.[2] In July, after Bulgaria was occupied and the Balkans were crossed, the progress of the Russian troops was miraculously checked by the heroic resistance of a Turkish army under Osman Pasha, who, for five months, from July until December, stemmed at Plevna the Russian advance southwards. But the check was only temporary. On the fall of Plevna on 10th December the Russians were on the high road to Constantinople, with scarcely a barrier in the way. Thereupon, in spite of Gladstone's impassioned pleas in Russia's behalf to which *The Times* lent support, and in spite of the government's indecision owing to divided counsels, public feeling against Russia rose to fever heat, and the cry for war rang through the country. The Prince appealed to Lord Beaconsfield to make a bold stand. Writing to Lord Beaconsfield's secretary on the 26th December 1877, he pointed out "the fix we shall be in—if Russia annexes Armenia—although that Russian organ, *The Times*, advocates it. I shall be most anxiously expecting to hear what the government intend doing. Depend upon it, words not backed up by deeds now are perfectly useless."

Parliament reassembled on 17th January 1878, and the Queen's speech from the Throne, an early copy of which was forwarded to the Prince, gave him the assurances which he desired. The government promised to come to Turkey's rescue. A credit of £6,000,000 for special war expenditure was proposed. The Army reserves were summoned on active service, and 7000 Indian troops were ordered to Malta. A direction to the British Mediterranean Fleet at Malta to proceed through the Dardanelles to Constantinople and protect the Turkish capital was issued on

[1] Buckle, *Life of Disraeli*, vi. 144.   [2] *Ibid.* vi. 149.

the 23rd January 1878, but was cancelled next day. It was, however, repeated and duly carried out on the 13th February.

Such measures, which seemed to bring the two countries to the brink of war, met with the Prince's full approval. Any apparent weakening in the government's plan of operations against Russia during the next few weeks drew from him impatient protests. When the British fleet on 18th February was ordered to leave Constantinople for a station thirty-five miles to the south of the city, he wrote to his mother from Berlin, where he was on a visit (February 20): "The effect of the fleet having retired is by no means a good one, and the article in the *P.M.G.* (a fanatical Turkophil organ) on Monday, although very strong is also true." But at whatever distance from Constantinople, the presence of British ships of war inside the barrier of the Dardanelles was a challenge which Russia could hardly decline.

VI

The Prince played with the fancy, not for the first or last time, of a high military command in the event of war, and he suggested to Lord Napier of Magdala, who was designated for the post of Commander-in-Chief, that he should join his staff if an expeditionary force were sent out. But Queen Victoria, in spite of her anti-Russian zeal, summarily declared against the Prince's active participation in hostilities.

Meanwhile the Russian Ambassador's relations with the Prince grew painfully strained. Writing to Prince Gortschakoff, (Jan. 29/Feb. 10, 1878), he sadly reported the Prince's manifest elation at the thought of a rupture with Russia. Count Schouvaloff, however, consoled himself with the thought that there was a different drift of opinion in the Prince's own household. The Princess of Wales's sister, Dagmar, was the Tsar's daughter-in-law, and the Prince's brother, the Duke of Edinburgh, was married to the Tsar's daughter. The Duke espoused his father-in-law's cause, and irritated his brother by his frank denial of England's obligation to intervene on the side of Turkey. In April 1878 the Crown Prince of Denmark, who was brother to both the Princess of Wales and the Tsarevitch's wife, was a guest at Marlborough House, and he confided to

Count Schouvaloff's ear that the Princess and all her father's family favoured Russia's pretensions. At the Prince's fireside the friends of Russia predominated. Count Schouvaloff's despatch was grateful reading for the Tsar.[1]

In the event, a second Crimean war was averted. Not all Lord Beaconsfield's colleagues shared the Queen's and the Prince's warlike ardour. Lord Derby, the Foreign Minister, who was out of sympathy with his chief's attitude, resigned office, after much delay, on March 28, 1878. Lord Salisbury accepted the vacant place and entered on his long career of controller of England's foreign policy. Meanwhile hostilities in the Balkans ceased. On the 31st January 1878 the Turks successfully sued for an armistice with a view to peace. Representatives of the two Powers accordingly met at San Stefano. On the 3rd March 1878 the treaty of San Stefano was signed, and it was ratified at St. Petersburg a fortnight later.

The effect of the treaty was to bring Turkey largely under Russian sway, and to transform Bulgaria into an autonomous principality within the sphere of Russian influence; yet the terms proved more moderate on Russia's part than were anticipated. At many points, however, the Treaty of San Stefano was held by the British and other governments to contravene clauses in the Treaty of Paris of 1856, to which all the powers were parties. The English government therefore insisted on a revision of its provisions by the great powers. The grounds for such a course were announced in a masterly circular to foreign courts, which Lord Salisbury drafted almost as soon as he became Foreign Secretary (April 2, 1878). The Prince wrote to the Queen from Paris on May 11: "From all the men of note here and in Society generally there is but one opinion, that England holds a firm position since Lord Salisbury's circular."

Outside Russia there was a general consensus through Europe in favour of the course for which Lord Salisbury pleaded. Russia raised formidable objections, but in view of unanimity among the other European Powers she, after much intricate negotiations, yielded her scruples. Prince Bismarck had offered as early as February to invite collectively the powers to Berlin to consider the Near Eastern situation, and to act as "honest broker"

[1] Russian MS. Archives (Schouvaloff's despatches), Jan. 29/Feb. 10, 1878, and 4/16 April 1878.

among them. That offer, after three months' consideration,
was in May accepted by England and the other Powers of
Europe.

VII

Despite the impetuosity with which the Prince waged his
present feud against Russia, he remained, in the Prime Minister's
phrase, "a man of the world." He knew that a war with Russia
could not be safely waged unless the other great Powers either
lent England a hand or kept the ring. This conviction was in
his mind when he pointed out to the Prime Minister, on 1st March
1878, that "we cannot afford to despise" the opinions "of other
countries." Naturally he scrutinised narrowly the opinion of
Germany, whose relations with Russia were not easily gauged.
The Prince was uncertain whether Germany was Russia's friend
or foe, and he did what he could to clear the point of doubt.

No love was ever lost between the Teuton and the Slav.
It was Bismarck's tortuous purpose to reduce Russia's influence,
by keeping outwardly on good terms with her while deceptively
embroiling her with other countries, especially with England
and Austria. The Drei-Kaiser Bund of 1872 never possessed
elements of endurance. Austria's Balkan ambitions ranged her
with Russia's enemies. The Anglo-Russian quarrel well harmonised
with the German Chancellor's diplomatic scheming. The whispers,
first heard in 1875, both in Russia and France, of a Franco-Russian
alliance rendered more active than before Prince Bismarck's
desire effectively to check Russia's power, even if he continued
to speak to her smoothly. At the same time he sought to
confirm the German hold on Austria, and he played with the fancy
of a possible understanding with England. In the event of his
forming a defensive alliance with Austria, he meditated an
invitation to England to come to some definite agreement with
the two Central Powers. Thus he thought, even if a Franco-
Russian alliance materialised, to render Germany less liable to
attack on both her western and her eastern frontiers, and,
while seeking meanwhile to delude Russia with conciliatory
gestures, safely to take at need in his own time the offensive both
westwards and eastwards.

The Prince's fidelity to France was not open to question, but he agreed with the Prime Minister that the conflict with Russia enjoined on him a prudent restraint of his habitual censures of Prince Bismarck and of his policy, the current involutions of which could at best be no more than surmised.

Domestic calls which involved no immediate political considerations had often summoned him in recent years to Germany. His relations with his sisters at Darmstadt and at Potsdam had known no cloud since the Franco-German War, and he repeatedly exchanged visits with them. The growing intercourse with his brother-in-law, the Crown Prince of Germany, strengthened his hope of a regenerate spirit in German rule and of the coming substitution for Prince Bismarck's "blood and iron" principles of a liberal constitutionalism. When, in July 1874, the Prince was seeing much of the Crown Prince and Princess while they were staying at the German Embassy in London, *The Times* newspaper, echoing the Prince's view, described his brother-in-law as "the consistent friend in Prussia of all mild and liberal administration." With the peace-loving Crown Prince at the head of affairs in Germany the main obstacles to friendship between the two countries would, the Prince anticipated, disappear without prejudice to his French prepossessions. In the growing families of his two sisters in Germany the Prince always took an affectionate interest. In September 1874 he and the Princess attended the confirmation of his nephew, Prince William of Prussia—his sister's elder son. Although the youth was already showing signs of a self-willed temper, none yet foresaw the stormy petrel's part which he was to play in the affairs of his family, his country, and the world. At the boy's confirmation his uncle showed him the tenderest solicitude. On 1st September 1874 he wrote, with simple sincerity, to the Queen from the Neues Palais:

I was much struck with the solemnity and simplicity of the service. Willy went through his examination admirably, and the questions he had to answer must have lasted half an hour. It was a great ordeal for him to go through before the Emperor and Empress and all his family. I was only too glad to take the Sacrament with them, Vicky and Fritz and Willy, after the ceremony, and the service is almost the same as ours. Willy was much pleased with your presents which were laid out in my sitting-room. Your letter to him and the inscription you wrote in the Bible I thought beautiful, and I read them to him. All you said I thought so very true.

Family affairs again called him to Germany in February 1878, while the Anglo-Russian crisis was at its most threatening stage, and the Prince thereupon resolved personally to take the bearings of insidious Prussian policy. In Berlin he diplomatically cultivated the good opinion not only of his royal kinsfolk, but of such influential personages as Prince Bismarck and Field-Marshal von Moltke. As a political observer, he also enjoyed, at Berlin, the advantage of a close friend at the British Embassy. Lord Odo Russell had in 1871 succeeded there Lord Augustus Loftus, whose alleged inefficiency was rewarded by transference to St. Petersburg. Although the Prince took a line of his own, in discussions with Lord Odo, he valued the opportunities of gathering information from him and of coming under his auspices into touch with prominent Germans.

1878
—
Ætat. 36

Domesticities loomed largest in the Prince's Berlin programme of February 1878, and his reception at the German court was thoroughly cordial. The object of the visit was to attend two marriages in the Prussian royal family. The eldest daughter of the Emperor's nephew, Prince Frederick Charles, "the Red Prince," who had distinguished himself in the Franco-German War, was to marry Frederick Augustus, heir to the Grand Duke of Oldenburg. But more interesting to the Prince was the first marriage of a grandchild of Queen Victoria—the union of his niece, Princess Charlotte of Prussia, the eldest child of the Crown Princess, with the Hereditary Prince Bernhard of Saxe-Meiningen. The double wedding was celebrated at Berlin on the 18th February 1878, with an exhausting ceremonial which lasted more than six hours. The Prince's friend, Lord Odo Russell, gave an imposing banquet five days later in honour of the newly married couples, when the German Emperor and Empress showered attentions on the Prince and on the Duke of Connaught who accompanied his brother.

We have been most cordially, and I may say affectionately, received by all the Family, the Prince wrote to his mother, 20th Feb., and it is evident the very great pleasure it has given them all that we came here for the two marriages. The Emperor is looking wonderfully well, and in a few days he will be eighty-two. Vicky and Fritz are most blooming. It is impossible to find two nicer boys than William and Henry, and they are continually with us, as Fritz and Vicky have so much to do.   Dear little Charlotte looked charming at the wedding, like a fresh little rose.[1]

But the Prince was giving as much attention to politics as to domesticities.   "Of politics," he wrote to his mother, "I think it more prudent not to write about by post. . . . I had a long and very interesting conversation with Prince Bismarck on Saturday and with Moltke to-day."

The Prince set a just value on the first political conversation in which he engaged with Prince Bismarck.   He wrote of the experience more explicitly to Lord Beaconsfield (March 1) than to his mother.   The Chancellor's words somewhat mystified his hearer, but his genial tone conquered something of the Prince's mistrust, while Bismarck, on his part, admitted the charm of the Prince's manner.   When Prince Bismarck suggested that it was foolish for England to hold her fleet inactive off Constantinople, the Prince ingenuously invited Bismarck's opinion as to what he would do were he Prime Minister of England.   The Chancellor oracularly replied that he would "take or occupy Egypt and perhaps Crete and withdraw our fleet to these places."   The Prince pointed out that France was likely to raise objection to a British occupation of Egypt, whereupon Prince Bismarck, who was well aware of the Prince's French leanings, ominously retorted "that he would find means to prevent their (i.e. France's) quarrelling with us (i.e. England)."   Both men sympathised with Austria's dread of Russian predominance in the Balkans,[2] but both agreed that Austria's threat of action against Russia ought not to be taken seriously.   Before they parted the Chancellor spoke darkly of Germany's grounds for hostility to Russia, and asked the Prince if Germany could depend on England's support

[1] The genial domestic atmosphere bred of the two marriages led a few months later to yet another matrimonial union between the royal families of England and Germany.   A sister of one of the brides, a younger daughter of the "Red Prince," was betrothed to the Duke of Connaught.   Within little more than a year, on the 18th March 1879, the marriage of the Duke and of Princess Margaret, third daughter of the "Red Prince," was celebrated at St. George's Chapel, Windsor, in the presence of the Queen and the Prince and numerous kinsfolk of the bride as well as of the bridegroom, and with a pomp which recalled the wedding in the same place of the Princess Royal and the heir to the Prussian throne one-and-twenty years before.

[2] The Prince's account of his conversation with Bismarck, in a letter to Lord Beaconsfield dated from the Hôtel Bristol, Paris, on the 1st March 1878, is supplemented by the report received from Berlin by Count Karolyi in Vienna.   The Austrian report of the interview is summarised in Corti's *Alexander von Battenberg*, p. 31 *seq.*

should Russo-German relations come to a rupture. According to
Bismarck's account of the interview the Prince replied in the
affirmative. The Chancellor lost no time in communicating the
Prince's affirmation to Prince Gortschakoff at St. Petersburg.

After the interview the Prince confessed himself almost
persuaded that in view of the Russian conflict it was to England's
advantage "to be on the most friendly terms with Germany."
But the wily part which the Chancellor was playing was not
lost on the Prince. Though he was complimented by the Chancellor's outward marks of confidence, he placed no great faith in
the sincerity of his counsels. His resolute attitude to Russia
was encouraged by the thought that Germany might possibly
co-operate with England against her, but he would prefer England
in a struggle with Russia to have French support if (as seemed
well-nigh certain) it were impracticable to count on the goodwill
of both France and Germany, and if choice had to be made
of one only of the two countries. At any rate, he lost no
time in proving the steadfastness of his devotion to France.
He passed directly from Berlin to Paris, there energetically to
pursue his endeavour to win over French feeling, while he was
busy with the organisation of the French Exhibition.

VIII

While the scheme of the Berlin Congress was taking shape,
the Prince reached the conviction that none but Lord Beaconsfield
ought to represent England at its deliberations. With promptitude he wrote "most confidentially" to the Queen on 28th May:

I had occasion to see Mr. M. Corry to-day on several matters—
and in course of conversation we discussed the chances of a
Congress becoming daily more likely and as to who was going to
represent England. I said of course Lord Beaconsfield was the
only man who could go—as however clever Lord Salisbury
undoubtedly was, still after his fiasco at Constantinople he really
would not do. Then Lord Lyons is not a Cabinet Minister and
if he went it would be almost an affront to Lord Odo Russell—
and then he would have to refer everything home. I understand
that Pr. Bismarck particularly begs that there should be no "ad
referendum." Under these circumstances it strikes me more
forcibly than ever that the Prime Minister is not only *the* right
man to represent us at a Congress, but the *only* man who can go—
as he would show Russia and the other Powers that we were really

in earnest, and that Lord B. was himself going to carry the Policy we had laid down in Parliament and announced to the World at large—into Congress, and stick to it to the last. If a Congress takes place, it must be the *last* one on the Eastern Question—which must be finally settled and I trust for ever. Mr. Corry says that there are some difficulties in Lord B.'s going— and I fear the Cabinet are more in favour of Lord S. than him. Now, do let me implore you to urge Lord B. to go—as it is a matter of such vital importance to our Country and dignity that we come out of the difficulty masters of the situation. It struck me that if you wrote a Mem. which was to be laid before the Cabinet—in which you expressed your positive desire that Ld.B. should go—the matter would then be settled. Of course Ld.B. would take a large Staff who would assist him in tech- nical matters. Of course this letter is only intended for you— and for nobody else's eyes. Excuse my having written on the subject—but it is one in which I take such interest, that I could not help doing so.

The Queen was by no means enamoured of the projected Congress, and while she appreciated the main points of the Prince's argu- ment, hesitated for the time to adopt his suggestion on the score of Lord Beaconsfield's age, health, and duties at home. Her reply to her son, dated from Balmoral 30th May 1878, ran:

I hasten to answer your letter just received. The subject of Lord Beaconsfield attending the Conference has been before me, and if it were to be at Brussels, The Hague, or Paris, I should (and I have done so) urge it, but you know that Lord Beaconsfield is 72 and a half, is far from strong, and that he *is* the firm and wise lead and hand that rules the government, and who is my great support and comfort, for you cannot think how kind he is to me, how attached! His health and life are of *immense value* to me and the country, and should on no account be risked. Berlin is decidedly *too* far and this is what I have said. I wrote to him on the subject, two days ago, and have not had an answer yet. I don't believe that *without fighting*, and giving those detestable Russians a good beating *any* arrangement will be lasting, or that we shall ever be friends! They will always *hate us* and we never can trust them.[1]

Ultimately the Queen gave way to her son's urgency, and Lord Beaconsfield joined Lord Salisbury as England's repre- sentative at the Berlin Congress.

At length on Sunday, 2nd June 1878, under the eye of the

[1] This letter and the one preceding it are partly printed in Buckle, vi. 305 *seq.*

Prince, the German Ambassador in London, Count Münster, handed to the Foreign Secretary, Lord Salisbury, at his house at Hatfield, Prince Bismarck's official invitation to Great Britain to take part in the Berlin Congress.[1] A distinguished party was gathered under the Foreign Secretary's roof. The Prince was there with the Princess, his brother (the Duke of Connaught) and his cousin (the Duke of Cambridge). But the chief guests were the Crown Prince and Princess of Germany, who were returning at Marlborough House the visit which the Prince and Princess of Wales had paid them at Potsdam earlier in the year. The tranquil feeling which was evoked in the minds of Lord Salisbury and his royal guests by Count Münster's hopeful message of peace was rudely disturbed within a few hours by the arrival of news of the attempted assassination in Berlin of the Crown Prince's father, Kaiser William I. The thought flashed through more minds than one at Hatfield that on the eve of the coming Congress an unforeseen guarantee against future war and autocracy was to be vouchsafed Europe by that new dispensation at Berlin to which the Prince was sanguinely looking forward. The Prince hastened with his brother-in-law, in whom the great hope centred, to the station at Hatfield, whence the Crown Prince made a hurried journey to Germany.

The Kaiser proved to be severely though not fatally wounded, yet the Crown Prince, on reaching Berlin, was invested with the Regency of the German Empire to fill the responsible office for six months. It was while the Crown Prince was serving his country as Regent that the Congress of Berlin performed its work. The Crown Prince's liberal aspirations had, however, little opportunity of practical exercise during his short term of power. The potent will of Prince Bismarck, who resolutely clung to office, remained in the ascendant, and there was nothing of that change of spirit in the German government for which Queen Victoria and the Prince of Wales waited in vain. Kaiser William I., restored to health at the end of the year, was to survive another decade, at the close of which the Crown Prince was himself to lie in the grip of death. There was to be no fulfilment of the Prince of Wales's roseate forecast that with the accession of his brother-in-law to the German throne, German policy, both foreign and domestic, would be purged of its evil tendencies.

[1] *Die Grosse Politik*, ii. 323; Lady G. Cecil's *Life of Lord Salisbury*, ii. 275.

1878

Ætat. 36

IX

1878
Ætat. 36

The fateful Congress of the Powers was in session at Berlin from 13th June to 13th July. Heavy work fell on the shoulders of Lord Beaconsfield, England's chief envoy, yet he snatched sufficient time from his scanty leisure to write to the Prince in his flowing hand detailed accounts of the critical course of events. On 22nd June he told the Prince how Bismarck, whom Lord Beaconsfield ironically described as "your friend," had put in the first place on the agenda the thorny question of the future of Bulgaria, on which depended "whether there should be a Turkey in Europe or not." The Russians had fought hard for Turkey's surrender of all rights in Bulgaria, but Beaconsfield firmly resisted Russia's demand.

"Yesterday afternoon, about five o'clock," he told the Prince in triumph, "the Russians surrendered unconditionally. . . . European Turkey is again a fact . . . and Russia is now more hopelessly than ever excluded from that Mediterranean to gain which they embarked on the late war and on others before. . . . The voting was five to two, Germany only, mighty Germany, voting for Russia, but in this affair she is bound hand and foot to her. . . . We have made a book with Austria, and Turkey is in my pocket."

"In the evening," Lord Beaconsfield went on to inform his correspondent, "I dined with Bismarck, and had to smoke a great deal, but if I had not I should not have gained many points."

Four days later the Prince replied from Marlborough House :

The Russians are I hear powerless to do anything. We have only to demand what we want and they must agree "bon gré, mal gré." . . . I rejoice that Austria is so entirely with us, and though "the great man" (B.) is by way of supporting Russia, I feel sure that he sides with us in reality in the Eastern Question. How I should have liked to have seen him and you together.

When the Congress was nearing its close, Lord Beaconsfield found time again to write at length to the Prince on further crucial themes (July 6, 1878). The Prince's brother-in-law, the King of the Hellenes, had urged him to employ his influence with the Prime Minister so as to secure from the Congress recognition of the pretensions of Greece to the Turkish provinces of Epirus and Thessaly. But the Prince, although he expressed sympathy with the Greek claims, was at first reluctant to press them in view of larger issues. "About Greece," he had written to Lord Beaconsfield before the Congress was in being (March 1), "I cannot offer an opinion, as I am egotistical enough to think only of my own country." Subsequently the Prince pleaded the wish of both the Princess and himself that Greece should not be dismissed from the Congress empty-handed. Just before it dissolved, Lord Beaconsfield succeeded in securing the adoption of a rather illusory rectification of the frontiers of Greece at Turkey's expense. From Berlin on 6th July 1878 he wrote in a courtly strain to the Prince:

1878
Ætat. 36

> I did yesterday something for Greece. It was very difficult, but it is by no means to be despised. It was all done for Her Royal Highness's sake. I thought of Marlborough House all the time, and it was not decided after many efforts until the last moment.

In the same letter (of July 6) Lord Beaconsfield first brought to the Prince's notice the secret arrangement between the British government and Turkey which handed over Cyprus to England. "England," the Prime Minister wrote, "enters into a defensive alliance with Turkey as respects all her Asiatic dominions, and with the consent of the Sultan we occupy the island of Cyprus. It is the key of Asia, and is near to Egypt. Malta is too far for a military base for these purposes." This piece of intelligence caused the Prince especial concern. The publication of this Anglo-Turkish Convention—two days after Lord Beaconsfield sent the Prince the news of it—was to disconcert and affront the Prince's political and social allies in France and was to move him to a striking effort in diplomatic strategy which successfully relieved a perilous tension.[1] But the Prince delayed the serviceable mission to Paris which the Near East controversy invited in order to witness on 16th July from the house of his Whig friend, Lord Carrington (afterwards Marquis of Lincolnshire), the triumphal return of Lord Beaconsfield to London from Berlin. From a window of his official residence in Downing Street the veteran statesman told the cheering crowds that he had brought back "Peace with Honour."

The Treaty of Berlin undoubtedly kept peace among the great

[1] See pp. 367-8 *supra*.

Powers for six-and-thirty restless years. England, France, and
Germany professed satisfaction in varying tones of hesitation.
But much in the treaty rankled from the first in the minds of
one or another of the signatories. In Russia, the Pan-Slavists
were profoundly disappointed that the fruits of their country's
military victory over Turkey should have been snatched from
her hands, and Russia's constant efforts to override salient provisions of the Treaty of Berlin kept, to the Prince's dismay,
the old turmoil alive. Austria remained discontented and the
hopes of Greece were belied. The Prince's brother-in-law, the
King of the Hellenes, was soon indeed importuning him to come
to his aid in compelling the fulfilment of the treaty's promises
in regard to Greece. The Prince took rather too sanguine a
view in spite of his tell-tale reservation when he wrote to Sir
Bartle Frere on the 8th September 1878: "We must anyhow
congratulate ourselves on the Treaty of Berlin, though it is not
the finale of the Eastern Question."

CHAPTER XXIV

SIR BARTLE FRERE IN SOUTH AFRICA

I

"THOUGH I think no ministry had so many and so great diffi- 1879
culties to contend against," wrote Lord Beaconsfield to the Prince Ætat. 37
on 12th April 1879, "I should not despair of controlling all of
them were it not for South Africa, which is as it were beyond one's
influence."

A personal factor rendered the Prince's interest in South
African affairs peculiarly acute. Sir Bartle Frere, for whom the
Prince conceived a deep affection on the Indian tour, was nominated, at the end of 1876, Governor of the Cape of Good Hope, and
High Commissioner of South Africa. The Prince writing on
24th November warmly congratulated Sir Bartle on his appointment, and thenceforth was in continuous correspondence with
him regarding his South African experiences. Sir Bartle's main
instructions were to give effect to a carefully drawn scheme for
the confederation of the South African colonies. But on his
arrival in Cape Town early in 1877, the new Governor was confronted with a series of intestine troubles which postponed
indefinitely all hopes of confederation. The annexation of the
Boer republic of the Transvaal and native wars kept South
Africa in unceasing turmoil while Sir Bartle was in control.

Frere was in no way responsible for the subjection of the
Transvaal republic to British rule, which was proclaimed in April
within three months of his arrival,[1] and provoked protracted
controversy. At the same time the Kaffirs suddenly rose in

[1] This action was taken by the Home government on the advice of Sir
Theophilus Shepstone, who had been sent out in 1875 to report on the
condition of the Boer State.

439

1879

Ætat. 37

rebellion. Frere faced the situation with great courage and energy. The Kaffir outbreak was repressed by June, and Frere firmly, and as he thought finally, rejected the appeals of the Boer leaders to regain their independence. The Prince was perturbed by the embarrassments of "good, excellent Sir Bartle," but on 8th September 1878 he wrote to him, "I have watched with the greatest interest the difficulties you have had at the Cape and rejoice to think that they are gradually diminishing."

But a greater difficulty was to make Frere the target of heated political invective at home. His high principle was not in question, but his tact in handling native problems was warmly disputed. Frere found himself unable to compose a long-standing quarrel between the Boers and their Zulu neighbours. The Zulu King, Cetewayo, urged claims to adjoining territory which it was impossible to recognise, and he gave signal proof of his obduracy by a raid into Natal for which he declined to make adequate reparation. An ultimatum which Frere addressed to him in December was left unanswered, and on the 11th January 1879 Frere directed Lord Chelmsford—commanding the British troops in Natal—to invade Zululand. On 17th January 1879 the Prince wrote sympathetically to Frere, "You have, indeed, not got a bed of roses and have had a most anxious and most trying time. Your difficulties also are I fear not over. Lord Chelmsford's account of the Zulu army interested me very much. Please thank him for sending it to me." Five days later the defeat by the Zulus at Isandhlwana of the invading British army provoked consternation in England.

The British government, while sending out reinforcements to retrieve the disaster, publicly blamed Frere for exceeding his instructions "in forcing Cetewayo to face the alternative of amendment or war."[1] The condemnation reached the Cape in the form of a despatch from the Colonial Secretary, Sir Michael Hicks-Beach. Sir Bartle refrained from offering his resignation, nor was he recalled, although that step was contemplated by the cabinet. A fierce controversy raged round both his conduct and his treatment by the government. The Prince made no secret

---

[1] Mr. Basil Worsfold, who prints in *Sir Bartle Frere: A Footnote to the History of the British Empire* (1923), most of the Prince's letters to Frere in South Africa, shows on the later admission to Frere of Sir Michael Hicks-Beach that the government changed their policy abruptly and Frere was unable to adapt his prearranged course of action to the cabinet's sudden change of front.

of his sympathy with his friend. In the rather too sanguine belief that the clouds would soon disperse, he earnestly if injudiciously advised Frere to face the storm and remain at his post. Writing to Lady Frere at the end of March, after the disaster of Isandhlwana, he explained at length his view of the course which, in his opinion, Sir Bartle should pursue :

I have never ceased exonerating Lord Chelmsford from the blame which many here attach to him ; alas, he who fell (Colonel Anthony William Durnford, R.E.) and led that attack was in my mind the only culprit. You will receive by this mail the account of the debate in the House of Lords of the 25th, and you will see the Ministers of the Crown have defended Sir Bartle. I much deplore the censure passed on him by Sir Michael Hicks-Beach in his despatch. But I sincerely and earnestly hope that your husband will not think of resigning. Let me implore you and him not to think of such a step, as his presence and the great ability that he possesses are so much needed in S. Africa. A public man must lay himself open occasionally to censure.

A few days later, on 4th April, he wrote direct to Sir Bartle in the like sense, bidding him abandon all thought of retirement :

You may be assured that my thoughts are continuously with you, and how deeply I feel for you during the difficult and harassing times you are going through. I would almost advise you not to read the accounts of the last debate on the South African question in the House of Commons, as it cannot fail to annoy you ; and at the same time you have been too long in the public service not to know that one cannot please everybody, especially the government. I only earnestly hope that you will stick to your post, and not think of resigning, as in the present critical state of affairs in the Cape Colony it would be most disastrous your leaving.

Meanwhile, to the dismay of the government and the public, military operations were for the time suspended in Zululand.

II

Throughout this time of South African trial Lord Beaconsfield and the Prince were in almost daily communication with one another. On 12th April the Prime Minister complained to the Prince of "a want of energy in that quarter [*i.e.* South Africa] which is most deplorable. . . . A general of genius might," he added, "put all right, but I fear he does not exist, or is locked up at Cyprus." The Prime Minister was vaguely contemplating the despatch of Sir Garnet Wolseley, who was at the time Governor of Cyprus, to take Lord Chelmsford's place. The Prince surprised Lord Beaconsfield by his optimistic confidence in both Chelmsford and Frere. "Both Sir Bartle Frere and Lord Chelmsford will come out of their troubles with flying colours," he wrote on the 13th April 1879. Lord Beaconsfield gloomily replied next day: "We had a telegram last night from Chelmsford. It was in the morning papers; very meagre. The mortifying affairs in South Africa weaken us at every Court." To his friend Lady Bradford the Prime Minister wrote the same day: "Prince Hal is sanguine—nay, sure—that Bartle Frere and Chelmsford will come out triumphant. I wish I shared his convictions." [1] A day later the Prince showed signs of hesitation: "The news from South Africa is certainly very meagre, but we surely must soon hear something decisive." Lord Beaconsfield's growing pessimism began to tell on the Prince, but he urged a more vigorous support of Lord Chelmsford by the authorities at home.

"I confess," he wrote from Sandringham, April 18, 1879, "that the last news from South Africa are not satisfactory and I am always in dread of hearing of great loss of life, as the Zulus seem on all occasions to outnumber us, I don't like to say outmanœuvre us. I much fear we have not even now the sufficient number of troops to thrash the Zulus. As yet we have only been able to act on the defensive, and what will be necessary is to act promptly on the offensive."

In May the ministry decided to send out Sir Garnet Wolseley to untie the intricate South African knot. On the 23rd May he was nominated Commander-in-Chief and High Commissioner of Natal, the Transvaal, and adjacent territories including Zululand. Both Lord Chelmsford and Frere were thus placed in a humiliating position. Lord Chelmsford was to become Wolseley's second-in-command, and Frere, whose authority was to be confined to Cape Colony and adjacent territory, was virtually deprived of the status of High Commissioner of South Africa. The Prince, while mindful of Wolseley's merit, promptly warned Lord Beaconsfield that Frere's position was clearly

[1] Buckle, *Life of Disraeli*, vi. 428.

prejudiced. "I only hope," he wrote to the Prime Minister on
28th May of Lord Wolseley's appointment, "it may not have
the appearance in the eyes of the world that he is sent to supersede
Sir Bartle Frere." As for Wolseley's personal qualities and
prospects, the Prince added genially : -

> Anyhow the gallant general is a worthy man, and if I live long
> enough I shall expect to see him a Duke and K.G., and possibly
> Prime Minister or Commander-in-Chief of the British Army.
> Whether my prophecy will ever come true, I cannot say.

While Wolseley was preparing for his voyage to the Cape
(June 23), the South African situation brightened. Lord
Chelmsford was at length in a position to advance on the Zulu
stronghold of Ulundi with every prospect of success, and a
victorious close of the campaign was in sight. On 4th July the
Zulus were decisively defeated by Lord Chelmsford at Ulundi.

Lord Wolseley had reached the Cape on 23rd June, and five
days later was installed as Governor of Natal. On 15th July
he took over from Lord Chelmsford the office of Commander-in-
Chief, and Lord Chelmsford, declining the position of second-in-
command, sailed for England on the 27th July accompanied by
two fellow-officers—both of them well known to the Prince—
Colonel Evelyn Wood and Major Redvers Buller. The tragedy
of the Prince Imperial's death in the campaign deepened the
gloom in which the South African imbroglio plunged the Prince.
He blamed Lord Chelmsford not only for the early disasters of
the war, but for his failure to safeguard the French Prince.[1] Yet
at the end, when victory, however tardily, crowned the efforts
of the South African Commander-in-Chief, the Prince deemed
him to have been harshly used. Despite the Prime Minister's
frowns, the Prince paid Lord Chelmsford the compliment of
meeting him on his arrival at Plymouth on 19th August.

Lord Chelmsford's resignation drove the Prince to the just
conclusion that Frere's self-respect required him to take the
same step on Wolseley's arrival at the Cape. On September 21,
1879, the Prince wrote to Frere :

> I can well understand and share your feelings, and I am not
> sure whether you can well retain your present important post
> with dignity to yourself. It is of course not for me to suggest

[1] See pp. 340 seq. supra.

anything, but as Sir G. W. has been sent out in reality to supersede everybody it must render your position a most difficult one.
Lord Chelmsford felt this so strongly that he had no other course
left open to him but to come home.

The Prince's advice was sounder than that which he had
tendered in an opposite sense five months before. But Frere,
largely owing to the Queen's persuasion, stayed on at the Cape, to
the injury, as the Prince rightly foresaw, of his reputation. On
30th October Frere pointed out to the Prince that "Ministers
wish me to remain"; he had reaped, he admitted, "nothing
but abuse for my share in the wars which have been forced upon
us, and have averted great dangers"; but he added, "I see
serious dangers looming in the distance which might be increased
by my leaving my post just now."

Frere's long-threatened severance with South Africa was
not long delayed. During the general election of March 1880
his conduct of South African affairs was sternly denounced by
Mr. Gladstone and his followers, and he was half-heartedly
defended by Lord Beaconsfield's party. On Mr. Gladstone's
victory at the polls, Frere's resignation or recall only became a
question of time. For a few months the Queen pressed on Mr.
Gladstone a postponement of the final decision, despite the partisan
outcry. The Prince warmly resented the charges brought in
Parliament against his friend of high-handed incompetence and
of tyrannical usage of native races; and he was perturbed by the
scorn which both parties lavished on him as a scapegoat.[1] The
blow fell on the 2nd August when Frere received his recall. To
the Prince he at once forwarded further explanations of his
failure to follow the Prince's good counsel by resigning earlier.[2]
But the Prince, while he expressed lively sympathy with Frere in
the ungenerous treatment which had been meted out to him,
deemed the dismissal to be a happy release from an incurable
embarrassment.

To the last the Prince manfully stood by his friend. As soon
as Frere and his family arrived in England the Prince telegraphed
an invitation to Sir Bartle to visit him at Abergeldie.

[1] Lord Suffield's *My Memories, 1830–1913*.
[2] Worsfold, *Sir Bartle Frere*, pp. 250–51.

III

The following year saw the undoing, by the Liberal Government, of much of Frere's South African work. The Prince resented such procedure. The vacillations which characterised the new government's attitude to the Transvaal especially irritated him. The Boer problem was no easy one to solve. Sir Bartle held that the annexation of the Transvaal, once effected, must be maintained, and felt confident that time would cure the unrest of the Boers who had been brought unwillingly under the British flag. Their attempt, after Frere's recall, forcibly to shake off British rule created a situation which puzzled all parties. The Liberals faced it with divided purpose. Military forces in Natal proved unequal to the task of meeting the Boer attack. After three minor reverses the Natal army was decisively routed by the Boer burghers at the battle of Majuba Hill on 27th February 1881, when the commander of the British force, Major-General Sir George Pomeroy Colley, was killed. Thereupon something like a panic seized the British government, and General Roberts was hurried out with large reinforcements to retrieve the disaster. The Prince, who was on a visit to Germany at the moment, thought the military position to be less desperate than the home authorities represented. He was of opinion that less heroic measures might meet the case. Sir Leicester Smyth, a Crimean veteran, was on the spot as Commander-in-Chief at the Cape, and the Prince demurred to his supersession by Roberts. Sir Leicester, he thought, should be left to deal with the Boer insurrection. The ultimate outcome caused the Prince and others of his countrymen a painful shock. Before the battle of Majuba Hill was fought Mr. Gladstone had entertained a notion of yielding to the Boers' demands for a restoration of their autonomy. General Roberts on landing in South Africa learned that the home government had allowed the claim of the Boers to independence under British suzerainty. A peace was arranged on these terms. The Prince regarded this episode as a humiliating surrender which ill contrasted with the decisive temper of his friend Sir Bartle.

The repeated encroachments by the Boers in the years that followed, on the terms of settlement of 1881, drove home the conviction that Mr. Gladstone's exercise of magnanimity was a blunder. Its deep-seated effects were ultimately revealed in the protracted Boer war of 1899–1902, which darkened for the Prince and the country the close of the old and the opening of the new century, and cast its shadow over the period coincident with his accession to the throne.

On Frere's death, on 29th May 1884, the Prince hastened to express to his widow his "heartfelt condolence." In acknowledgement Lady Frere wrote how her husband had learned to know and love the Prince on the Indian tour, and had cherished for him since "a deep and loyal affection." She thanked the Prince for having "always so nobly stood by him in life." Nor after Frere had passed away did the Prince fail to pay conspicuous honour to his memory. He was president of a committee for erecting a statue of Frere, and he unveiled it on the Thames Embankment on 5th June 1888, when he described Frere as "a highly esteemed and dear friend." Next year (August 1, 1889), when the Prince presided at the Guildhall over a memorable meeting to celebrate the jubilee of the abolition of slavery in the British colonies, he paid a stirring tribute to the services of his friend Sir Bartle as an enlightened colonial governor. Frere's chequered fortunes in South Africa never indeed wholly passed from the Prince's mind. Years later, when the Prince was King, another South African governor, Lord Milner, became the centre of acute party controversy and the theme of parliamentary censure. Lord Milner's fortunes vividly recalled to King Edward's mind Frere's fate, and he privately taxed Lord Milner's political censors with the same lack of generosity that he had already imputed to Frere's critics. The Prince had never much patience with the rancours of party feeling, but they were intolerable to him when they sought to involve an honourable public servant in disgrace.

CHAPTER XXV

THE ANGLO-FRENCH *ENTENTE* IN PERIL—EGYPT, 1878–1883—
THE DEATH OF GENERAL GORDON

THE Prince's hopes of an Anglo-French *entente* soared high during the Exhibition year of 1878, but they were destined in the course of the next two decades to encounter an ominous series of checks.   The affairs of Egypt nurtured morbid germs of political estrangement.   Subsequent differences in other parts of the world between the two governments and the two peoples widened the breach until it looked to be beyond repair.

1878
—
Ætat. 36

No early recovery of the lost provinces of Alsace and Lorraine seemed possible to sagacious French statesmen, and they designed an imposing overseas empire by way of solacing the nation's wounded *amour propre*.   The efforts to put the ambitious design into operation meant a colonial rivalry between France and Great Britain which strained the relations of the two countries well-nigh to breaking point.   At the opening of the period of stress, the Prince pleaded with both English and French politicians his cherished conviction of the supreme need of safeguarding at every hazard an Anglo-French understanding.   But circumstances tended in course of time to slacken the Prince's confidence in his own prescription.   The strength of his private friendships with Frenchmen of various schools of political thought was unimpaired by his political doubts, and he lost no reasonable opportunity of reasserting his hopes that the future would see political differences reconciled.   But in the heat of the successive crises he un-reservedly acknowledged England's obligation to make stern retort to her neighbour's ungainly manifestations of jealousy or ill-will.

447

I

Egypt proved the first rock of stumbling in the road of the
entente. That country's financial difficulties, for which Khedive
Ismail, the Prince's munificent host of past years, was personally
responsible, affected equally the investing public of France and
England. The traditional claims of France to a predominant
influence over Egypt foreshadowed friction as soon as England's
interests required intervention in Egyptian affairs. In correspondence with Lord Beaconsfield through his last years of power,
the Prince consequently upheld with eagerness the principle of
full co-operation between England and France in the necessary
task of reforming Egyptian finance. In the autumn of 1878 the
Khedive, under the pressure of foreign creditors, authorised his
Prime Minister, Nubar Pasha, to carry out a sound scheme of
finance, and at the same time agreed to confer on an Englishman,
Mr. (afterwards Sir) Charles Rivers Wilson, and on a Frenchman,
M. de Blignières, the portfolios respectively of finance minister
and minister of works in Nubar Pasha's ministry. For a few
months the arrangement worked well, but in February 1879 the
Khedive rebelled against all ministerial restraint, and with the aid
of a Nationalist military party he dismissed Nubar Pasha and his
English and French colleagues and repudiated his financial
obligations. A rapid exchange of views followed between the
Prince and the Prime Minister as to the best means of dealing
with the refractory ruler. On 12th April 1879 Lord Beaconsfield,
while apologising to the Prince for his inability, owing to public
business, to fulfil an engagement to stay at Sandringham, wrote
despairingly of Egyptian affairs and expressed grave misgivings
of the attitude of France.

"The Egyptian question," he said, "is one of life and death,
if not to France, certainly to the French ministry (of M. Waddington). . . . *Entente cordiale* between England and France really
means in the latter country the maintenance of Egyptian credit,
but the figures of the problem render that difficult. Interest of
debt seven millions out of a revenue of eight millions!!! Lord
Lyons is gloomy."

The Prince in reply next day reviewed the situation and pressed
the Prime Minister on no account to alienate France :

"This Egyptian question," he wrote, "is indeed a most

difficult and troublesome one, and I only hope that we shall act
in concert with the French Government, and together bring
matters to a successful issue.

"I cannot help thinking that though Mr. Rivers Wilson is a
man of undoubted ability, and acted from the best of motives,
he has managed to lose instead of gaining the confidence of the
Khedive, and has been in the pocket of Nubar Pasha, who is the
Khedive's sworn foe. Though he (Rivers Wilson) may resist
and his French colleague also—through the support of the two
Govts.—his position must become untenable. Can we depose
the Khedive? If we do, who shall we put in his place? His
son Tewfik or his Uncle Halim? If the newspapers are to be
credited the Sultan seems anxious to support us at the Khedive's
expense. But the back of the latter is up, and if he runs to take
recourse in hostilities, what are we to do? We cannot eat
humble pie!"

France answered the Prince's vaticinations by tentatively
suggesting the deposition of the Khedive. Lord Beaconsfield
hesitated to assent and complained to the Prince of French
vacillation (April 14). On the 15th April the Prince wrote again :

I entirely concur with you that if European Ministers are
again appointed in Egypt, those who have just been dismissed
could not be forced again on the Khedive or his successor. I don't
know whether you have seen Mr. C[respigny] Vivian [then
Consul-General] since his arrival from Egypt, but he has much
of interest to relate and valuable information to give. The
difficulties in Egypt seem to me very great, and I am glad it
does not depend upon me to "cut the Gordian Knot."

The next news from Lord Beaconsfield was more hopeful. It was
now clear to all parties that the Khedive must be removed, but
France deprecated Lord Beaconsfield's suggestion of an appeal
to the Sultan to depose his vassal. On the 17th the Prime
Minister wrote to the Prince :

Though we are working well with France and wish to do so
completely, it is curious how the traditionary jealousy of that
country as to influencing Egypt through the Porte curiously
prevails and must be humoured.

In acknowledgement (April 18) the Prince confessed his anxiety
for a settlement which he admitted was "far from easy" to reach.
"It is a most difficult nut to crack," responded Lord Beaconsfield.
At length the Sultan was persuaded to apply pressure to the

1879
Ætat. 37

Khedive. The latter, however, remained obdurate. Ultimately, with the Sultan's approval, England and France joined in Ismail's dethronement and jointly set up his son Tewfik in his place. Khedive Tewfik was to govern under the supervision of two Controllers representing respectively England and France. France nominated M. de Blignières. England appointed Sir Evelyn Baring. The Prince had known Sir Evelyn when he was Secretary to Lord Northbrook, the Indian Viceroy, and had every faith in his administrative efficiency. The services which Sir Evelyn (afterwards Lord Cromer) was to render Egypt for the space of thirty years moved in the Prince an unfaltering enthusiasm, even if he at times deplored Sir Evelyn's "over-bearing" manner.

II

1881
Ætat. 39

The Prince was somewhat over-sanguine in his view of the Dual Control which was thus set on foot. He regarded it as a practical guarantee of the *entente*. But the Dual Control proved workable for no more than three years, 1879–82. It then dis-solved, with disastrous consequences to Anglo-French harmony.

While the clouds were gathering the Prince's zeal for the Anglo-French *entente* increased. His friendly relations with Sir Charles Dilke, foreign under-secretary in Mr. Gladstone's new ministry of 1880, enabled him to gratify his unceasing ambition personally to engage in the endeavour to smooth the difficulties between the two governments. On his own initiative he played a part in the difficult negotiations in which the two governments engaged during the spring of 1881 over a new commercial treaty. Meeting Dilke at a dinner-party at Lord Spencer's house in London on 19th February 1881, the Prince offered on an approach-ing visit to Paris to interview the French Prime Minister, M. Jules Ferry, and to urge on him the advantage to the two countries of commercial reciprocity. Dilke at once acquiesced, and next morning drafted for the Prince a paper of "instructions." On his arrival in Paris in March 1881, the Prince saw M. Ferry, and persuasively represented to him how a fair treaty, while it need in no way run counter to the French statesman's protectionist principles, would advance the cause of the *entente*. According to M. Gambetta, who was in close intercourse with the French Prime

Minister, the Prince made "some impression." The Prince also discussed the main points at issue with M. Tirard, the Minister of Commerce. Sir Charles Dilke arrived in Paris a few days later to pursue the negotiations in technical detail, and he acknowledged the usefulness of the Prince's intervention. But the result was disappointing. The negotiations continued uneasily for a full year and then broke down. In October 1881, when the Prince was again in Paris, he proposed to Sir Charles Dilke to renew his conversations with the French ministers with a view to oiling the wheels of negotiation, but the situation had become too intricate to warrant the acceptance of the proposal.

With every scheme which might have the effect of drawing England and France closer together the Prince at this time evinced sympathy. He contemplated with approval the proposed construction of a Channel tunnel.[1]

III

The Prince's confidence in the fair prospects of Anglo-French amity was fostered by his continued intercourse with M. Gambetta, the most potent force in France, whose Anglophil sympathies were never in doubt. Since 31st January 1879 M. Gambetta had filled the influential but detached position of President of the Chamber of Deputies. Sir Charles Dilke was the illustrious Frenchman's friend of long standing, and the Prince's intimacy with Sir Charles increased his opportunities of association with M. Gambetta. At many informal meetings between 1879 and 1882 the Prince and M. Gambetta conversed of public affairs.

"The politics of Europe and the world interest him as much as they interest us," Gambetta told his friend and political disciple, Mme. Adam. "It is no waste of time to talk with him even over a merry supper at the Café Anglais. He loves France at once *gaîment et sérieusement*, and his dream of the future is an *entente* with us."

---

[1] In the course of the year (1881) a serious attempt was made to build a Channel tunnel which should unite France and England by an underground railway. Borings were begun near Dover. The Prince favoured the design, and inspected the preliminary workings in March 1882. But the soundness of his views on this matter was questioned by the military authorities. The ministry was divided, and Sir Charles Dilke before long converted the Prince, somewhat against his will, to the opinion that the tunnel might prejudice the defence of this country in case of war.'

Like most prominent French republicans M. Gambetta looked forward to his country's colonial expansion, but he recognised therein no cause for England's suspicions. He induced the Prince to favour the first advance which the Republic was contemplating in the imperial direction—the formation of a protectorate over Tunis. (This step was duly proclaimed on the 12th May 1881.) During 1879 Gambetta was frank in his admission to the Prince that his former mistrust of Russia was giving way to a belief that a thoroughgoing Franco-Russian understanding, which had been vaguely suggested a year or two before, might effectively guarantee France against further German aggression. In letters to a friend M. Gambetta represented that the Prince acknowledged the value to France of Russia's friendship, but the French statesman apparently attached a more immediate significance than was justified to the courteous tone of the Prince's reception of his new point of view. The Prince who at the moment cherished no love of Russia, was solely desirous of stimulating M. Gambetta's leanings towards England.[1] Two decades were to pass before the Prince was fully to reconcile himself to a league between France and Russia.

A special interest attaches to one of the Prince's reunions with M. Gambetta for which the responsibility lay with Sir Charles Dilke. On the eve of M. Gambetta's assumption for a short sixty days of the office of Premier in succession to M. Ferry, Dilke entertained the Prince and Gambetta at a *déjeuner* at the old Moulin Rouge Restaurant in the Chausée d'Antin (October 30, 1881).[2] Political confidences were freely exchanged and the *entente* seemed to be promised a new stability. After they parted the Prince, through Sir Charles Dilke, asked Gambetta to send him a signed photograph. Gambetta complied, inscribing the photograph with the words: "Au plus aimable des princes, un ami de l'Angleterre."[3]

The Prince also maintained at full strength his old friendship with General Galliffet, who now identified himself with Gambetta's political point of view. Sir Charles Dilke had demurred to the

[1] *The Times*, 30th December 1915, reproducing from *Le Matin* extracts from M. Gambetta's letters to M. Ranc, cf. Gwynn and Tuckwell's *Sir Charles Dilke*, ii. 506-7; Madame Adam, *Mes Souvenirs*, vii. 15-17, 33, 146, 167, 187, 314.

[2] Besides the Prince, Gambetta and Dilke, the party consisted of Mr. Austin Lee, commercial attaché of the British Embassy, and Colonel Ellis and Colonel Stanley Clarke in attendance on the Prince.

[3] Gwynn and Tuckwell, *Life of Sir Charles Dilke*, i. 403-4.

1881
Ætat. 39

Prince's suggestion that Galliffet should join the party at the Moulin Rouge. Not long afterwards, however, the Prince contrived to fulfil his wish of bringing together under his auspices as host the two Frenchmen who chiefly commanded his admiration, and who were in his view the most effective guarantors of the *entente*. After Gambetta had agreed to dine with the Prince at the Café Anglais, the Prince met Galliffet by chance, and easily persuaded him to join them.

Galliffet's record of some of the casual conversation, to which he listened on this occasion, preserves graphically the frank tone of the relations which subsisted between the Prince and M. Gambetta.

"A dîner," Galliffet wrote, "causerie à propos d'une et d'autres choses, puis :

"Le Prince : Monsr. Gambetta, permettez-moi de vous demander pourquoi vous et vos amis vous éloignez des affaires l'aristocratie française ?

"Gambetta : Mais, Monseigneur, il n'y a plus 'd'aristocratie' en France. Il n'y a que des ducs qui ne conduisent aucune armée ; des marquis qui ne sont préposés à la défense d'aucune 'marche' du pays ; les comtes, vicomtes et barons n'ont ni terres, ni autorité, ni influence.

"Le Prince : Mettons que j'ai voulu parler de nobles.

"Gambetta : Mais ils n'ont aucune envie d'être employés—ils se savent roulés. Ils boudent : c'est leur emploi définitif ; on ne les rencontre que dans l'armée la marine. Quelquefois dans la diplomatie. Dans ces carrières ils font bonne figure : j'en conviens.

"Le Prince : Mais pourquoi ne feriez-vous pas comme dans mon pays où nous prenons ce qu'il y a de plus distingué dans l'industrie, les sciences, les lettres, le commerce, etc. etc. De ces hommes nous faisons des nobles—et notre noblesse reste une véritable aristocratie.

"Gambetta : Chez vous, c'est possible encore pour quelque temps—chez nous, non. Le duc de La Roche-qui-Mousse ne voudrait pas frayer avec le duc de l'Industrie, le duc de la Science, celui des Beaux Arts, etc. etc. En république nous ne pouvons avoir qu'une aristocratie, celle de la science et du mérite—elle s'affirme sans avoir besoin de titres.

"Le Prince : Vous êtes un vrai républicain, Monsr. Gambetta.

"Gambetta : Permettez-moi de l'avouer, Monseigneur. Je trouve logique que vous, vous soyez royaliste.

"On rit de bonne humeur," Galliffet adds, "et l'on parla d'autre chose."

General Galliffet's notes put both Gambetta and the Prince in an engaging light. The Prince's profession of preference for a titled aristocracy of talent over one of hereditary right is evidence of the kind of enlightenment which free intercourse with all sorts and conditions of men was fostering in him.

Admirable indeed was the temper which characterised M. Gambetta's relations with the Prince so long as the Frenchman lived. On 12th March 1882 Queen Victoria was shot at, happily without effect, by a lunatic named Roderick McLean, at Windsor railway station. M. Gambetta, who had just closed his short term of office as Premier, sent to the Prince a gracefully worded letter of sympathy and congratulation on the Queen's escape. As "un ami sincère de votre maison et de votre noble pays," writing on behalf of "tous les rangs de la France republicaine," he told the Prince of the respect felt for "la grande et gracieuse souveraine par tous les peuples de l'univers quelles que soient leurs formes de gouvernement." It was a grievous loss for the Prince, for France, and for England that the last day of the same year should see the sudden and premature close of M. Gambetta's short eventful life, and the disappearance from the scene of that Frenchman among the Prince's friends whose personal force could alone at this epoch make the Prince's favoured policy of the *entente* prevail.

IV

The development of affairs in Egypt during 1881–82 threatened that cordiality of Anglo-French relations which M. Gambetta was bent on upholding. Egyptian nationalism girded itself to try conclusions with the Dual Control. With the aim of ridding Egypt of foreign rule, Arabi Pasha, a colonel of the Egyptian army, sought in the autumn of 1881 to set up a nationalist dictatorship. At the end of 1881 M. Gambetta, the Prince's friend, who had just become Premier of France, drafted a strongly worded note in which he announced that France and England would at all hazards protect the Khedive's government, which the Dual Control dominated, from nationalist attack, or indeed from any interference whether internal or external. Mr. Gladstone's government signed M. Gambetta's note without apparently realising precisely to what it committed them. M. Gambetta's sudden

fall from power early in 1882 added to the ambiguities of the
situation. M. de Freycinet, M. Gambetta's successor, proved
reluctant to intervene in Egyptian affairs, while the English
government declared that the Suez Canal was their main practical
interest in Egypt, and as the Canal was in no present danger,
there was no call for immediate action. The English and French
governments each deemed it prudent, however, to send to Alexandria a naval squadron to watch events. Arabi's power meanwhile grew, and under nationalist compulsion Khedive Tewfik
constituted him Minister of War. The position of Europeans,
especially of French and English subjects, in Egypt was clearly in
peril.

The storm broke on 11th June 1882, when, in a nationalist
rising at Alexandria, fifty Europeans were killed and many
others wounded. For the moment the challenge seemed to pass
unnoticed by the two controlling Powers. Each remained
quiescent. In England the Conservative party and its press
called loudly for open war on Arabi and his adherents, but
Mr. Gladstone, the Prime Minister, and his Foreign Secretary,
Lord Granville, closed their ears to the outcry.

The Prince was among those who regarded the government's
supineness with dismay, and the indiscreet confidence of a friend
who was clamouring for England's active intervention brought
him into a relation of some delicacy with his old, but irresolute,
friend Lord Granville, who was mainly responsible for the current
policy of drift. Lord Charles Beresford, the Prince's comrade in
India and elsewhere, was with the British squadron off Alexandria
in command of the gunboat *Condor*. An habitual correspondent
of the Prince, Lord Charles communicated to him his conviction,
formed at close quarters, that unless Arabi's movement were
forcibly arrested, England's position in Egypt and her hold on the
Suez Canal were doomed. The Irish sailor further informed the
Prince that he had sent an account of the critical conditions at
Alexandria to the *Morning Post*, the Conservative organ, which was
inflaming public opinion against the government. A Liberal
acquaintance of the Prince, the Earl of Dalhousie, advised him
to forward Lord Charles's letters to Lord Granville.

A commotion followed. The harassed Foreign Secretary
focussed his attention on Lord Charles's admission of an infringement of naval regulations by supplying the press with news.

Lord Granville informed the Prince that he had brought Lord Charles's offence to the notice of his colleagues, and requested his royal correspondent "to let Lord Charles Beresford know of your disapprobation of the thing itself and of his having informed Your Royal Highness of it." The Prince, while he admitted Lord Charles's indiscretion and promptly warned him against a repetition of it, was bitterly annoyed by what he viewed as a breach of confidence on the part of Lord Granville, "an old friend and a man of the world," in communicating the information to his colleagues. The Prince feared the effect on their long friendship. As for Lord Charles's imprudence, he pleaded with Lord Granville (June 29, 1882) to let the matter pass

in justice to the great friendship and regard I feel for Beresford. . . . He is an Irishman, and in consequence hasty and impetuous, but I feel sure that the Queen does not possess a more zealous and loyal officer than he is, and as a rule a more punctilious observer of the regulations of the service.

In the result, the Prince's plea prevailed. Lord Charles escaped rebuke, and the relations of the Prince with Lord Granville resumed their cordiality. Unluckily, the Prince's indulgence tended on more than one future occasion to encourage his Irish friend's native impulse to air in the press his political or professional views and grievances, to the embarrassment of colleagues or superiors.

While this episode was closing, the government, tardily abandoning its hesitation, proceeded to answer Arabi's challenge in what the Prince agreed with Lord Charles to be the only way possible. On 11th July the British squadron, on orders received from home, bombarded Alexandria. To the Prince's gratification, Lord Charles Beresford's skilful and courageous handling of his gunboat *Condor* during the action made him a popular hero and procured him promotion to the rank of captain. But the French squadron declined to take part in the operations, and steamed away before the firing began. France sullenly resolved to leave the resettlement of Egypt in England's unaided hands, with the result that those good relations between the two countries, by which the Prince set store, were jeopardised.

Arabi replied to the bombardment of Alexandria by a declaration of a holy war or Jehad against all foreigners in Egypt, and the English government acknowledged its single-handed

obligation of defending the authority of the Khedive, which   1882
Arabi was defying, by sending out a military expedition. Sir   Ætat. 40
Garnet Wolseley was appointed to the command of the
expeditionary force, and although the Prince was inclined to
deprecate Sir Garnet's rapid promotion, he cordially corresponded with him, alike while the general was making his
preparations for departure and throughout the campaign.

V

The Household Cavalry and a Guards Brigade were ordered
to the front. Many officers of the Guards were among the
Prince's friends, and in his capacity of Colonel-in-Chief of the
Guards Regiments, he reckoned it his duty to accompany them.
Had the Anglo-Russian crisis of 1878 led, as was anticipated, to
war, the Prince had then made up his mind to take the field.
Now, on 26th July, always anxious "to be of use" in a national
emergency, he apprised the Queen and the Duke of Cambridge
of his resolve to go out. But he was not his own master, and he
was in his forty-first year. The Queen, while appreciative of
his motive, deemed it out of the question for him to run the
inevitable risks, and the government backed her veto.[1]

" It is highly creditable," Lord Granville wrote to the Duke
of Cambridge on 30th July 1882, " to the pluck and spirit of the
Prince to run the risks both to health and to life which the campaign offers, but it is clearly undesirable that H.R.H. should go.
This is one of the penalties which attach to his high position." [2]

The Queen sought to soften the blow of her prohibition with
kindly words of appreciation :

"Y.R.H.'s gallant offer of joining the expedition to Egypt
has greatly troubled the Queen," wrote her secretary, Sir H.
Ponsonby, to the Prince (on July 31). " H.M. agreed with
Y.R.H.'s desire to be of use, and warmly appreciated the gallant
wish to see service, *but* the imperative demands of public duty
compelled H.M. to point out the grave difficulties and incon-
veniences of such a proceeding, and having been advised by the
Govt. as well as several leaders of the opposition that it would
be inexpedient and most unwise, considering your R.H.'s
rank and position, to join the expedition as a spectator—and

[1] Gwynn and Tuckwell's *Life of Sir Charles Dilke*, i. 473.
[2] Verner, *Military Life of the Duke of Cambridge*, ii. 235.

impossible for your R.H. to be attached to it on duty, the Queen finally and conclusively decided that it was necessary to ask your R.H. to abandon the idea.   But H.M. was so pleased at the proposal having been made, and so convinced that it would be heartily appreciated by every one, that I think the Queen would be glad if it were made generally known."

The Prince's acquiescence was qualified by the hope that before the campaign ended the Queen's veto might be withdrawn.   He discovered some encouragement of his aspiration in the appointment of his brother, the Duke of Connaught, to the command of the Guards Brigade.

Condemned to remain at home, the Prince offered comment and warning on the equipment of the expedition to all in responsible position.   He vainly urged General Wolseley to allow his sailor friend, Lord Charles Beresford, to join his army in Egypt. He showed his eager anxiety for the suppression of the rebel leader Arabi by informing Lord Granville on 31st July, "on very good authority," that Arabi was in receipt of confidential intelligence and encouragement from England.   The offender, Mr. Wilfred Blunt, the Prince wrote, was not merely sending out secret intelligence, but was about to join Arabi with some £20,000, which he had raised by the sale of his jewels and furniture.   "Can nothing be done," the Prince asked, "to stop this disloyal and eccentric Jesuit?   People are beginning to speak very seriously of his conduct, and no wonder."   On the eve of the departure of the Life Guards and the "Blues," the Prince inspected the regiments in Hyde Park and entertained the officers to dinner at the Marlborough Club.[1]

VI

The Egyptian campaign proved brief.   It practically ended on 13th September with the defeat of Arabi and of his army at Tel-el-Kebir, and with the triumphal entry of Wolseley into Cairo next day.   Arabi's army was completely broken, and he himself was taken prisoner.   Warm were the Prince's congratulations to Wolseley (Sept. 15) on "the taking of Tel-el-Kebir with the loss of so few men."   Though the war was over, the Prince trusted that "an adequate number of troops will still remain for some long time to come to occupy the country and put matters

[1] Sir George Arthur's *Story of the Household Cavalry*, 1909.

1882
Ætat. 40

in order." On England's future relations with Egypt he held strong views. "After this campaign," he added, "we must for ever keep a strong hold over Egypt, as our interests are too great ever to be lost sight of again." The Prince was gratified by the praise bestowed by Wolseley on the Household Cavalry and the Guards. He never looked on the Guards as "carpet knights":

"Your praise," he added, "of the Household Cavalry has gratified me immensely. I felt sure that they would keep up the reputation they acquired at Waterloo, and though the service they have been required to perform is very different from what they have been accustomed to, I am inclined to believe that they have set an example."

Before the end of the month the Khedive's authority was fully restored in Egypt, and while 12,000 British soldiers remained there under Sir Archibald Alison, Sir Garnet Wolseley returned home with the rest of the troops. Many honours, including a peerage, were conferred on the victorious general.

1883
Ætat. 41

The Prince's strong view that England should thenceforth maintain on Egypt the hold which Lord Wolseley's victory promised, divided opinion in England, and while it wounded Turkey which claimed Egypt as a subject province of the Turkish Empire, it disconcerted France. On the continent of Europe the English occupation of Egypt found ostensible favour only with Prince Bismarck, who diplomatically welcomed it as a wedge likely to keep France and England asunder. The Prince visited Berlin early in 1883, and the German Chancellor, although in ill-health, granted the Prince's wish for an interview, and spoke to him with plausible amiability of his hope that English troops would remain in Egypt to guarantee "the safety and stability of Europe." But Turkey and France at once questioned England's title to stay in Egypt, at any rate for an indefinite period. A diplomatic wrangle between France and England continued for the next twenty years over the question of a date when England's occupation should terminate, and the dispute contributed to the alienation of the two countries. But with the lapse of the Dual Control and the defeat of Arabi Pasha, the responsible administration of Egypt, while remaining under the nominal rule of the Khedive, passed into the hands of Englishmen.

1883
Ætat. 41 Sir Evelyn Baring became the chief administrator of the new English control under the modest designation of Consul-General and Diplomatic Agent. The Prince thoroughly approved the investment of Sir Evelyn with supreme responsibility. In manning an important department of the anglicised government of the country the Prince powerfully supported an appointment which did credit to his good feeling. The reorganisation of the local army was one of the most pressing needs of the resettlement of Egypt in the new conditions. The Prince chivalrously directed all his influence towards setting at the head of the reconstituted Egyptian army his old friend Colonel Valentine Baker, who, since his dismissal from the British army, had served first as officer in the Turkish army and then as controller of the Turkish gendarmerie. The project seemed at first to promise well. To the Prince's satisfaction the Khedive, with the approval of Lord Dufferin, British Ambassador at Constantinople, and of Lord Wolseley, nominated Baker to the office of Commander-in-Chief, or Sirdar, of the new Egyptian army, and at the end of the year 1882 Baker left Constantinople for Cairo to assume his new duties. But the Prince's self-congratulations proved premature. To his profound disappointment he soon learnt that the British Cabinet declined to sanction the nomination. Baker's wife pathetically appealed to the Prince to help her husband under this crushing blow, and the Prince fought with energy to obtain a reversal of the government's harsh decision. To Mr. Gladstone and Lord Granville he sent copies of Mrs. Baker's letter, and to both, as well as to Lord Wolseley, he wrote in moving terms on behalf of his friend of tarnished reputation. His appeal to Gladstone (December 3, 1882) ran :

It is not for me to comment on the decision of the Cabinet, but I must confess that I think Baker Pasha has been very hardly and unfairly treated, as he went out to Egypt with the approval of H.M.'s Government and with the entire concurrence of Lords Dufferin and Wolseley. To deprive him now of the important command which the Khedive has conferred upon him is simply ruin to him.

To Lord Wolseley he wrote on the same day :

Can nothing be done for poor Baker Pasha ? . . . Now, with apparently no rhyme or reason, he is ousted, and finds himself naturally in the position of having " fallen between two stools."

The Egyptians, with the keen perception of an Eastern nation, will look upon him as disgraced, and even should he receive a minor command, such as the Gendarmerie—as is, I believe, proposed—he will never more command the respect of his subordinates.   The Government and Mr. Gladstone do not seem to think, or probably even care for this.   Surely Baker has been sufficiently punished in days gone by without being now *utterly* ruined, and especially after having rendered, in a military point of view, most important services in Turkey.   I know the Duke of Cambridge quite shares my views in this matter, but I wish it were possible for you to put in a good word with the Government for Baker, and point out to them that they are simply ruining him for the rest of his life by depriving him of his command.

Lord Granville replied on behalf of the cabinet that the hostile verdict must stand, and the Prince unwillingly reconciled himself to the intimation that the post of chief of the Egyptian gendarmerie or police was the only one that could be placed at Baker's disposal.   General Evelyn Wood accepted the office which was withheld from Baker, who had to content himself with the humbler command of the Egyptian police.

Some seven years later the Prince took occasion to revisit Cairo to study the result of the British control.   He accepted the friendly hospitality at Ghizeh Palace at Cairo of Prince Hussein, the former Khedive Ismail's brother, who was himself to become Sultan of Egypt for a short term at the outbreak of the Great War in 1914.   The Prince was also lavishly entertained by the Khedive Tewfik, the son of his former acquaintance, Ismail. Under the guidance of Sir Evelyn Baring, the English administrator, whom he described at the time as "a very able man with no manners," the Prince had full opportunities of studying the method of British control which had brought the country peace and prosperity.   He went over the battlefield of Tel-el-Kebir, and together with the Khedive he held a review of the garrison of Cairo, when 1700 British soldiers paraded before him with 4000 Egyptians.   The Prince formed the impression that the problem of Egypt had been satisfactorily solved.[1]

VII

England's final supersession of France in Egypt kept alive an ugly ferment in French public opinion.   Colonial enterprise

---

[1] Sir Rennell Rodd's *Diplomatic Memories, 1884-93*, pp. 189-91.

elsewhere served to accentuate the tension with England. In the island of Madagascar, off the east coast of Africa, the French engaged in a long conflict with the native inhabitants, who appealed, without result, to England for protection. French endeavours to possess themselves of Tonkin and Cochin China to the east of India invited a collision with China and seemed to prejudice English interests. National unrest also manifested itself in Paris in attacks on the royalist princes in whose welfare the Prince was deeply interested. Anarchist riots, which were anathema to him, fanned the anti-royalist agitation. The Chamber of Deputies passed on 25th January 1883 a Bill for the expulsion from France of all members of the Bourbon and Bonapartist families. The Senate rejected the Bill, and M. Jules Ferry, on forming a new ministry, decreed by way of compromise the retirement from the army of the three Orléanist princes with whom the Prince was peculiarly intimate, the Duc d'Aumale, the Duc de Chartres, and the Duc d'Alençon. The fickle Parisian populace, who regarded the Prince as the chief representative of England, was disposed to vent some of its spleen on his familiar name. In consequence, on the advice of Lord Lyons, the English Ambassador in Paris, the Prince saw fit to take the unprecedented course of abandoning his customary visit to the French capital in the spring of 1883.[1] But the popular ill-feeling lost something of its intensity next year and the Prince re-visited Paris in May 1884. Calling on President Grévy at the Élysée, he listened attentively to his assurances that the French occupation of Indo-China would furnish the world at large with new openings for trade. The Prince, however, formed an unfavourable impression of the attitude of French commercial circles to England. He inferred that they were in no mood to encourage English trade in the Far Eastern territory which France had occupied. Nor, in spite of his recognition of the political indiscretions of the Comte de Paris, were the Prince's French sympathies conciliated by the rancours which continued to pursue his Orléanist friends and culminated in 1886 in the banishment of them as well as of the Bonapartist pretenders. The varied domestic disquietudes of the country with which he was reluctant to loosen the bonds of a lifelong attachment, caused him perplexity. Doubts of the stability of France crossed his mind at this period, and inclined him to play

[1] Newton's *Life of Lord Lyons*, vol. ii. p. 311.

temporarily with the fancy that Germany, which was cunningly affecting much friendliness for England, might prove in the long run a more trustworthy ally.

VIII

England's occupation of Egypt not only brought in its train the alienation of French goodwill, together with some fateful moves on the diplomatic chessboard of Europe, but it also stirred up tumult in Central Africa which involved England in a military adventure of no advantage to her prestige.

The Khedive's subjects in the spacious southern province of the Sudan refused to acknowledge the authority which England was exercising over Egypt, and, after Arabi's insurrection had been suppressed, the Sudanese broke into rebellion against the Egyptian troops who were trying to hold the country. The leader of the insurgent Sudanese claimed divine inspiration, and was known as the Mahdi or the Prophet. Through the year 1883 his forces gathered strength and threatened the Egyptian garrisons distributed through the disaffected districts, while one of the Mahdi's chief lieutenants, Osman Digna, menaced the shore of the Red Sea and the passage of the Suez Canal. In November an Egyptian detachment under Hicks Pasha made a reckless dash into the Sudanese territory and was annihilated by the Mahdi's followers. Shortly afterwards Colonel Valentine Baker, the Prince's friend, at the head of an ill-equipped force of gendarmerie, was defeated near the Red Sea by Osman Digna in an attempt to relieve the Egyptian garrison of Tokar. The second disaster was partially retrieved by the despatch to Suakin, on the Red Sea, of a brigade of the British army of occupation at Cairo under the command of Sir Gerald Graham. To the Prince's satisfaction Valentine Baker Pasha served with Sir Gerald as intelligence officer. A decisive victory was scored over Osman Digna's army at El Teb near Suakin (February 29, 1884), and the danger in the neighbourhood of the Red Sea was sensibly allayed. But, by order of the Home government, Sir Gerald's success was not followed up, and he returned with his troops to Cairo.

It was with deplorable ineptitude that Mr. Gladstone's government now faced the problem of the revolt, which rapidly reached threatening proportions. Mr. Gladstone disclaimed further intention of resisting the Mahdi's power, and announced that the rescue of the beleaguered Egyptian garrison within Sudanese territory was all that English honour required.

The Queen and Prince were aghast at a decision which seemed to them to be a surrender to rebellion; nor did they brook with composure the delay which, owing to differences within the ministry, postponed action on behalf of the imperilled garrisons. At length, under journalistic pressure, the government took the indefensible step of sending out General Gordon to negotiate single-handed with the Mahdi for the garrisons' relief. General Gordon, who was well acquainted with the Sudan and was credited with a potent personal influence over the natives, arrived at Cairo on 25th January 1884, and accepted from the Khedive, in defiance of instructions from home, the appointment of Governor-General of the Sudan. On 18th February 1884 he reached Khartoum, the chief city of the province. Two months later the news reached England that he was closely besieged in Khartoum by the Mahdi's troops.

The Queen and the Prince, who had questioned the prudence of Gordon's mission, joined in a popular outcry for the despatch of a military expedition of rescue. Mr. Gladstone's government pusillanimously shrank from decisive steps, but the Queen's importunities overcame their hesitation. After much controversy among the military experts as to whether Khartoum could be better reached by way of the Nile or across the desert from the Red Sea, a relieving expedition was organised in August to take the river route. The Prince truthfully prophesied that action was taken too late.

Lord Wolseley's appointment to the command of the Sudan expedition was coolly received by the Prince, who wrote to the Queen (August 28, 1884) : "So Lord Wolseley is going out to Egypt after all. The Government seem to have no confidence in any other general in our army." But the Prince did not permit his doubts of the prudence of the selection to delay an application to join the expedition. The application was seriously considered.[1] "I indeed wish it were possible," Wolseley wrote to the Prince on the 28th August, "that you, Sir, could take part in any expedition that may possibly be sent up the Nile." But the Queen and the government revived their old objection to the

---

[1] Sir George Arthur's *Story of the Household Cavalry*, ii. 672.

Prince undertaking active service. His wish was unfulfilled. Lord Wolseley left England on 1st September without him.

The Prince, who was profoundly impressed by the urgency of the long-neglected situation, was fertile in suggestions which he sent by letter to Lord Wolseley both before and after his departure. Lord Wolseley was in a more submissive mood than the Prince had yet known. Again the Prince urged that Lord Charles Beresford should go out as the Commander-in-Chief's A.D.C., and this time the suggestion was adopted. Lord Charles rendered useful services, reports of which gave the Prince abundant satisfaction. The Prince was gratified to learn of Wolseley's intention to make Valentine Baker head of his Intelligence Department (August 31, 1884). "We must hope," he wrote, "that this may be the means of restoring to him his rank in our army, which I am sure nobody but the most narrow-minded person could object to." Unluckily Baker's appointment for a second time was prohibited by the government. Some other of the Prince's recommendations of officers for special service which Lord Wolseley amiably accepted did not in the result prove quite felicitous.

From the date of Lord Wolseley's arrival at his headquarters at Korti on the winding river Nile, he kept the Prince informed of his movements "on this difficult military expedition," and the Prince promptly sent in return full comments on each step in the campaign. The correspondence reflects with graphic vivacity the anxieties attendant on the hazardous course of events. The passage of the British forces up the Nile to Korti, whence Khartoum was to be reached overland, proved more tedious than was anticipated, and the slowness of the operations depressed all concerned. On 5th December 1884 the Prince wrote to Wolseley :

I can well understand how vexed you must be at the slowness of getting all the force up, but it was unavoidable owing to the lateness, for which H.M.'s Government are alone responsible. However, "slow and sure" is not a bad motto on the present occasion. For the sake of my friends who have not seen active service, I hope that your surmise about accomplishing your mission *without* fighting may not come true, though perhaps I ought not to say so. We get varied, inaccurate reports of what goes on, amongst others that the Mahdi is dead. But the report needs authentic confirmation. I trust that you are satisfied with the Camel Corps, especially with the Light Camel Corps, and that Stanley Clarke does his duty well. He writes with great enthusiasm regarding his duties.

On 28th December 1884 Lord Wolseley wrote hopefully to the Prince of "the last scene of our Nile drama," the risks of which he did not underrate. He expected to reach and relieve Khartoum "within a week of your receiving this letter," and warned the Prince against putting any faith in premature announcements in the sensational Press of "the death and defeat of Lord Wolseley."

From a wire dated 21st January 1885, the Prince was relieved to learn of the victory of Lord Wolseley's chief coadjutor, Sir Herbert Stewart, at Abu Klea. Sir Herbert was in command of an advance column which had crossed the desert from Korti on the way to Metemmeh—a point on the Nile within easy reach of Khartoum. The sequel of Sir Herbert's engagement at Abu Klea was, however, a grievous disaster. The general was seriously wounded in an ambuscade next day, with the result that he died at Korti a month later. On the 22nd January the Prince reviewed at length, in a letter to Wolseley, the situation as far as it was known to him. He congratulated Wolseley "on Stewart's important and decisive action at Abu Klea," and expressed once more the earnest hope that Khartoum would be safely reached, Gordon rescued, and the Sudan reconquered.

"Indeed," he wrote, "you have every reason to be proud of so gallant an officer [as Sir Herbert] and the troops under his command. One regrets the severe losses and especially so many good officers, but campaigns cannot be undertaken without loss of life. The Mahdi's troops are not to be despised, and the Sudanese proved themselves as brave and determined as the Egyptians are the reverse. . . . Your task has indeed been no easy one, and will remain a difficult one to the end. Most sincerely do I trust that you will get safely to Khartoum without any great casualties, and find Gordon safe and sound. But what will you do with him when he is released? and what will you do after occupying Khartoum? That is the question. I sincerely hope that we are not going to hurry away and leave the Sudan in the state you have found it. Not being a member of H.M.'s Govt., I can give no opinion on the subject, and whatever private opinions I may hold I think I had better keep to myself. You may, however, be sure that I, in common with all H.M.'s subjects, shall continue to watch with the greatest interest

and anxiety the successful result of the arduous Expedition under
your command.

"Your skill and knowledge—and may I also say good luck—
will, I am sure, enable you to surmount every difficulty."

But the Prince's sanguine forecast was not realised. Lord
Wolseley's expedition was doomed to tragic failure. Sir Charles
Wilson, who on Sir Herbert Stewart's disablement took command
at Metemmeh (January 19) of the advanced column, delayed
his passage up the Nile towards Khartoum in order to meet
a threatened attack of the enemy. Three precious days were
thereby lost. When Sir Charles arrived within hail of Khartoum
on 28th January, he discovered that it had been stormed by
the Mahdi's troops two days before, and that Gordon had been
killed. Sir Charles Wilson could only retrace his steps and carry
back to Korti the heartbreaking news, which reached London
on the 5th February. On the 15th, Lord Wolseley, writing to
the Prince, deplored the series of misadventures which had
ruined his hopes: "With no one fit to command," he wrote of
Wilson's approach to Khartoum after Sir Herbert Stewart was
incapacitated, "everything went badly . . . it is indeed hard
to bear our disappointment." Without instructions as to what
step to take next, Lord Wolseley despaired of any fresh attack
on the Mahdi before the autumn. In reply on 13th March 1885,
the Prince feelingly wrote :

Well can I understand what a terrible blow it must have been
to you to hear of the fall of Khartoum and death of poor brave
Gordon—just at the moment, too, after such successes with so
severe trials and losses, the relief of the town seemed certain.
Most sincerely do I deplore with you the deaths of Generals Earle
and Stewart. Two such distinguished officers could indeed be
ill spared. So many other brave and valuable officers of all
ranks have fallen, and I cannot say how greatly I admire the
discipline, steadiness, and valour of all officers and men during
those long and fatiguing marches they went through, suffering
every possible discomfort from climate, hunger, and thirst.
You may indeed be proud to command such an army. . . . I am
sorry to think that the troops under your command will have to
remain inactive till the end of October. I fear that the excessive
heat and monotony of their existence will tell greatly upon them.

The Prince had lately watched the departure "of three fine
battalions of Guards on their way out to Suakin." He trusted

that the men "might be instrumental in assisting to smash Osman Digna," who was giving renewed trouble.

The single source of satisfaction which the Prince found in Lord Wolseley's letters was his praise of Lord Charles Beresford, who had accompanied Sir Charles Wilson on the Nile passage to Khartoum, and had taken command of the flotilla. At this critical point in the operations the Commander-in-Chief described Lord Charles as "the only person who really had his wits about him"—commendation which the Prince capped with the comment that he "was the only man for the work you gave him to do." Later in the year the Prince urged Lord Wolseley to recommend Beresford for some mark of the Queen's favour, and when, on 2nd December, the Queen bestowed on Lord Charles the decoration of C.B., the Prince sent him a "miniature C.B." which he described in an accompanying letter "as a token of old friendship and sincere regard." "I trust," the Prince added, "that an opportunity may ere long arise for you to get the K.C.B."

IX

At home weak and vacillating counsels still prevailed, and the government, after some costly experiments with a railway from Suakin across the desert to Berber in order to bring the Sudan within easier range of a fresh expedition, decided to abandon the whole country to the Mahdi. In the long interval which elapsed before an English government tried to retrieve the disaster of 1885, the Prince found a ray of flickering light in an heroic private enterprise which sought to palliate the tragedy of Khartoum. Adventurous travel had always excited the Prince's keen interest, and he now followed with zest the fortunes of a traveller whose gifts seemed capable of mitigating the humiliation which the English name had suffered in the Sudan. The African explorer, Henry Morton Stanley, set out, under the auspices of a private committee of which Sir William Mackinnon was chairman, to rescue Emin Pasha, Gordon's lieutenant at Khartoum, who with the last surviving garrison of Egyptian soldiers, long succeeded in holding out against the Mahdi's hordes at Wadelai on the Nile in the extreme south of the Sudan, near Lake Albert Nyanza. The Prince was in frequent intercourse with Mr. Stanley while he was making his preparations, and he invited him to Sandringham to explain his plans before his departure at the beginning of 1887. Mr. Stanley spent three years in his search for Emin Pasha. Throughout the period he kept the Prince regularly informed of his adventures, which were marked by many tragic incidents, and were brought to a halting close at the end of 1889 by Emin Pasha's refusal to return to Europe with his would-be deliverer. On Stanley's journey homewards through the African continent he discovered a new lake, which he christened Albert Edward Nyanza in the Prince's honour, and thus associated the Prince's name with chequered English enterprise in the Sudan. When Stanley arrived again in London, the Prince welcomed him with warmth, and at a meeting of the Royal Geographical Society held in the Royal Albert Hall on 5th May 1890, after the explorer described his adventures, the Prince moved an appreciative vote of thanks and presented him with the Society's gold medal. But he had to acknowledge that, great as were the geographical fruits of Stanley's courage and endurance, he had failed to dissipate the gloom in which Gordon's death still involved the Sudan.

1889
Ætat. 47

The sacrifice of Gordon and the events which immediately followed it roused the Prince's indignation, and he lost no opportunity of giving public vent to his feelings. On the 26th February 1885, he was in his place in the House of Lords when Lord Salisbury moved a vote of censure on the government for their disastrous vacillations, which was carried next day by a majority of 121.[1] He attended the service in St. Paul's Cathedral on the day of mourning for the hero's death, 13th March, and he played an active part in the various movements for commemorating Gordon's heroism and fate. At the meeting held at the Mansion House on the 14th March 1885 the Prince moved the first resolution, which tentatively proposed the erection of a Gordon Memorial Hospital at Port Said, and he expressed a wish that Sir Herbert Stewart, the victim of Abu Klea, should be commemorated along with Gordon. For this proposal there was soon substituted a scheme for a "Gordon Boys' Home" in England, where poor boys should be trained mainly for the army and navy. This project was successfully accomplished with the Prince's active aid. On the 12th January 1886 he summoned the council of the Home to

1885
Ætat. 43

---

[1] A similar vote of censure was lost in the House of Commons by the small majority of fourteen.

Marlborough House to consider ways of increasing the endowment, and on the 8th May he presided at a festival dinner, when £5000 was collected. Four years later, on the 19th May 1890, he unveiled Mr. Onslow Ford's statue of Gordon, which the corps of Royal Engineers erected in their great comrade's memory at Chatham. There the Prince lamented anew that the army which was sent out to Gordon's relief arrived too late, and that in consequence the great-hearted soldier "earned the martyr's crown."

Eleven years were to pass after Gordon's death before Lord Kitchener by virtue of his genius for organisation succeeded in reconquering the Sudan and in wiping out the stain which Mr. Gladstone's infirmity of purpose left on the British name. France watched with no friendly eye England's fresh raid on those southern territories of which the Mahdi's rebellion had robbed Egypt. After Gordon fell, France's swelling colonial aspirations challenged England on many distant boundaries of the British Empire. But no phase of Anglo-French colonial rivalry roused more bitter feeling than the sensational endeavour of the French explorer, Captain Marchand, in the name of his government, to dispute at Fashoda, on the borders of the Sudan, England's right to enjoy the fruits of Lord Kitchener's Sudanese victory of 1898.

CHAPTER XXVI

RELATIONS WITH GERMANY, 1879–1886

I

WHILE the Berlin Congress was under way Prince Bismarck had 1879
made strategic professions of goodwill towards England. After Ætat. 37
the Congress ended, he explored the possibilities of an alliance.
His motives were not in doubt. By steady pressure on Austria
he was converting her into a catspaw which would well serve
Germany's turn in resistance to Pan-Slavist agitation. But
Russia was a standing danger, and France needed a watchful eye.
With England in diplomatic harmony with Germany and Austria
he thought confidently to face the combination, which was clearly
threatening, of France and Russia. He did not underrate the
obstacles in the way of a friendly understanding between England
and Germany. He was well aware that he had to reckon with the
personal antipathy which his feud with the Crown Princess stirred
in her mother, Queen Victoria. Nor did he overlook the Prince's
French leanings, in which he scented a substantive menace to his
purpose. His cordial relations with Lord Beaconsfield, however,
encouraged him in the autumn of 1879 cautiously to sound the
English government as to the likelihood of reaching an effective
accommodation.

On 26th September Count Münster, the courtly German
Ambassador in London, paid a secret visit to Hughenden, and,
according to his report to Berlin, represented to Lord Beaconsfield
that owing to Austria's strained relations with Russia, Germany
was contemplating an alliance with that neighbour, and that it
might be to England's interest to join the two Central Powers.
There was little doubt, Count Münster suggested, that Russia was
designing an attack on Austria. France, in the view of Count
Münster, was meditating an alliance with Russia, but there was

small likelihood of any disturbance to the peace of Europe if England ranged herself on the German side. He admitted, somewhat paradoxically, that England was likely to prove unwilling to break with France, but he argued that an English understanding with Germany did not necessarily forbid an Anglo-French *entente*.

Count Münster represented that he was especially anxious to ascertain from the Prime Minister the attitude which the Prince of Wales and his mother were likely to assume to his proposals. He credited Lord Beaconsfield with the statement that while the Queen's antipathy to Russia would incline her to an agreement with Germany, the strength of the Prince's sympathies with France would place him on the side of that power if there were war between her and Germany. At the same time, Lord Beaconsfield, according to Count Münster, implied that the dislike of Russia which the Prince shared with his mother might draw him away from France and towards Germany if France combined with Russia.

Doubt is permissible whether Count Münster quite accurately reproduced Lord Beaconsfield's words. In any case they misrepresented the current view of both Queen Victoria and her son, both of whom were at the moment equally desirous of conciliating France. The Queen was as little inclined as the Prince to prejudice Anglo-French friendship by encouraging an alliance with Germany. The Queen's old dislike of Prince Bismarck's internal polity had been lately stimulated afresh by information which had reached her from the Crown Princess. "We must not alienate France," she wrote, on learning from Lord Beaconsfield of Count Münster's mission.[1]

---

[1] Queen Victoria assigned two recent attempts on the life of the Kaiser to the growing influence in Germany of socialism and atheism—forces which were to her mind the inevitable reactions of Bismarckian autocracy, while she was so profoundly impressed by the chauvinism of the Junkers and the domestic distress caused by the severities of military conscription that she had naïvely begged Lord Beaconsfield when in Berlin to "give some wholesome advice on the subject." Lord Beaconsfield, according to Count Münster's memorandum of the conversation at Hughenden in September 1879, was vaguely encouraging, but committed himself to nothing. He referred his visitor to Lord Salisbury, the Foreign Secretary, if Germany wished seriously to pursue negotiation. Count Münster accordingly went over the ground with Lord Salisbury, adding that Germany hoped to assure herself of the neutrality of Italy as well as of France should Russia attack the Central Powers. Lord Salisbury replied sympathetically. He agreed that circumstances might require England to stand by Austria in the event of Russian hostilities (*Die Grosse Politik*, iv. 8, 9; see also Buckle, *Life of Disraeli*, vi. 486 *seq.*).

The Prince doubted the prudence of the discussion. His
intercourse at the time with M. Gambetta rendered it from his
point of view peculiarly inopportune. In the result the German
overture bore no fruit. On 27th October Count Karolyi, the
Austrian Ambassador in London, announced to Lord Salisbury
the formal conclusion of an Austro-German alliance. The news
was regarded by the English Ministry as a salutary check to
Russia. Prince Bismarck still vaguely professed a hope that
England might extend to the arrangement some active benevolence. "The German Empire, in alliance with Austria," he
sanguinely wrote to the King of Bavaria, "would not lack the
support of England." But there was no renewal of Count
Münster's offer. "We are well out of it," was the Queen's final
comment on the German reconnaissance. Nor did she or her son
regard the Austro-German alliance with the complacence of her
Ministers. Both feared that it might "give umbrage to France."
But the Prince's confidence in the policy of France was about to
be shaken with sufficient vigour to induce a reconsideration of
Germany's friendly gestures.

1879
Ætat. 37

II

While the gathering shadows on the Anglo-French horizon
inevitably tended to qualify the Prince's political mistrust of
Germany, current domestic episodes quickened for the time his
affection for his German kindred. His attitude of political
aloofness from Germany underwent modification. The policy
of isolation, to which English politicians long committed England
in Europe, never excited his enthusiasm. France's estrangement
from England and her inclination towards Russia, England's
foe, brought home to him the prudence of conciliating Germany,
though he deemed a "loose rein" and no hard and fast chain to
be the only practicable' mode of attachment between the two
countries. When his thought first moved in this direction,
German professions looked on the surface encouraging. He did
not foresee the formidable factors of dissension lurking in the
coming ambitions of Germany to found a colonial empire and to
build a fleet, both on British patterns, nor in the ill-omened
aspirations of his nephew, Prince William of Prussia, who succeeded in 1888 to the throne of his father and grandfather.

1881
Ætat. 39

In the spring of 1881 the Prince was summoned to Berlin on a domestic errand. The air seemed full of happy auguries, but fate was scowling behind the scenes. The marriage of the Prince's nephew, Prince William of Prussia, was to be celebrated with appropriate festivity in the Berlin Schloss on 27th February.

Throughout the bridegroom's youth the Prince had shown him all the genial tenderness which an uncle could bestow on a nephew. As a boy the young prince seemed to reciprocate his uncle's affectionate interest in his welfare, but the customary military education of the heirs of the Hohenzollerns had an unfavourable influence on his adolescence. His social intimacies were almost wholly confined to Junker officers, and their bluster tended to corrupt his filial sentiment, and to render aggressive war a supreme object of worship. His mother's English leanings and her sway over his father became a personal grievance. A sentiment of devotion to Queen Victoria, his grandmother, which Prince William's visits to her engendered in his youth, remained proof against most, although not against all, of the malignant chauvinist tendencies of his maturing character. But his mother's brother, the Prince of Wales, to whom he assigned a deleterious influence on his parents, soon excited his scorn and impatience.[1] Although he could scarcely refuse the kindly attentions which the Prince continued to show him, the young man's wilfulness of temper led him frequently to resent his uncle's solicitude. Very slowly and reluctantly did the Prince of Wales come to realise that despite his sedulous endeavours to preserve the cordiality of the atmosphere of his German family circle, he had in his self-assertive nephew a malignant and unmannerly critic of himself and of his country.

Prince William's choice of his bride commended itself to the English royal family. He had affianced himself in June 1880 to Princess Augusta Victoria of Schleswig-Holstein-Sonderburg-Augustenburg. The bride's father was that Duke Frederick who some twenty years before had laid claim to the Duchy of

[1] The Prince's friend, Sir Robert Morier, who was in intimate relations with the Crown Princess of Germany and her family, cherished some early fears of the boy William's incipient Anglophobia, and in 1875 encouraged his old tutor at Oxford, Dr. Jowett, Master of Balliol, in a plan for bringing the youth to Oxford for a term or two, so as to give him an opportunity of studying English people and affairs. The plan came to nothing (*Letters of Benjamin Jowett*, 1899, pp. 198 seq.).

1881

Ætat. 39

Holstein, and whose pretensions had been brutally quashed by Prussia at Bismarck's prompting. Queen Victoria and her family saw in Prince William's choice a sign of grace on the part of Prussia towards a persecuted victim of its ambitions. The bride's father was elder brother, too, of the Queen's son-in-law, Prince Christian—the husband of Princess Helena—who had shared the sufferings of his family at Prussia's hand. Prince Christian was reconciled by the match to Prussia and the Hohenzollerns after a long estrangement. In the following autumn Prince William spent a month in England (October 21– November 22) as the guest of Prince Christian, his bride's uncle, at Cumberland Lodge, Windsor.[1]

On the 21st February 1881 the Prince left London for the wedding at Berlin. The Princess did not accompany him. In Berlin he was welcomed with open arms. On his arrival at the railway station (February 22) the whole of the Prussian royal family, excepting the aged Emperor and Empress, assembled to greet him, and amid much military display the band played with vigour "God Save the Queen." The reconciled Prince Christian was on the platform, and the Prince of Wales failed to recognise him in the unaccustomed dress of a Prussian general officer. His gift of memory proved unequal to the occasion. To the amusement of his relatives the Prince asked: "Who is that old German general? I am sure I have seen him before!"

At the wedding ceremony the Prince was in high spirits, and accepted with zest the varied hospitalities. His friend, Lord Odo Russell, the English Ambassador, gave a dinner in his honour on 2nd March. The great ball which followed was attended by the bride and bridegroom, and the bride was the Prince's partner in the opening quadrille.

III

Amid the marriage festivities the Prince found opportunity to canvass the political situation. He saw much of his old friend,

---

[1] On Prince William's arrival in England he visited the Prince of Wales at Marlborough House, and the Prince joined his nephew in a shooting-party in Windsor Forest. Prince William accepted an invitation to take part in the celebration of the Prince's thirty-ninth birthday at Sandringham on 9th November. But although his nephew accompanied the Prince and Princess from London to their country home on 6th November, the young visitor capriciously returned to Cumberland Lodge on the 8th.

Odo Russell, whose diplomatic services were rewarded on the occasion of the wedding by his elevation to the peerage as Lord Ampthill (March 7, 1881).   Lord Ampthill had formed a helpful friendship with the Crown Princess, and the Prince was appreciative of the Ambassador's efforts to assuage her impatience with forbidding elements in her German environment.   The Ambassador's friendly counsels confirmed the Prince in his present disposition to favour the amelioration of Anglo-German relations.

Prince Bismarck readily granted the Prince an interview. As he entered the Chancellor's room, the Prince was gratified by the sight of a portrait of Lord Beaconsfield hanging on the wall. The Chancellor was in a bluffly genial mood, and set his visitor completely at his ease.   The Prince was curious to learn at first hand Prince Bismarck's view of the new French aim of overseas expansion, which France's recent declaration of a protectorate over Tunis initiated.   Though the German Chancellor talked with apparent freedom, he paid no close attention to his inter- locutor's leading questions, and avoided controversial issues. During the two hours that they were together, the Chancellor gave the Prince no opportunity, it was said at the time, of "getting in a word."   He cordially endorsed, however, the Prince's opinion of Sir Charles Dilke's sagacity, and expressed his readiness to receive Sir Charles in Berlin.   The Prince afterwards pressed on Lord Ampthill the advantage that might come of such a meeting, and the Prince's equerry, Colonel Ellis, who was with him in Berlin, communicated the suggestion without delay to Sir Charles—who failed to act on it.   Bismarck and the Prince parted outwardly on the best of terms.   The Chancellor told Lord Ampthill that he was captivated by his visitor's light- hearted talk.   After the interview the Prince sent the Chancellor a photograph of himself.   Bismarck, in conveying his thanks to Lord Ampthill for "the admirable likeness," added: "It will be the finest ornament of that room where the portrait of the Earl of Beaconsfield attracted the attention of the Prince" (March 5, 1881).

But the Prince was as yet loth to surrender any of his hopes of France, and, as in 1878, he went straight from Berlin to Paris to hold conversations with M. Gambetta and to help on the negotiations for a commercial treaty between France and

England with the Prime Minister, M. Ferry, and his Minister of
Commerce, M. Tirard.[1]

IV

Prince Bismarck, still bent on probing the chance of a
rapprochement with England, reckoned it germane to his purpose
to keep the Prince in good humour. In the summer of 1882 he
sent to England his son, Count Herbert Bismarck, on a somewhat indefinite mission. Count Herbert was to get into touch
with persons of prominence and to do what he could to overcome
their misgivings of German policy. The Count remained in this
country, with intervals, for more than two years. With the
Prince's friend, Lord Rosebery, he formed something like a close
intimacy, and throughout the period of his sojourn he was
frequently in the Prince's society. There was little in the Count's
manner, which was distant and harsh, to attract the Prince.
But Prince Bismarck was gratified by the report, which his
son sent him, of the Prince's cordiality and of his readiness
amiably to consider Germany's political proposals. Although Mr.
Gladstone's government gave no certain sign of encouragement,
the Prince of Wales informed his brother-in-law, the Crown
Prince, soon after Count Herbert's arrival in England, that a
strong desire was growing in the English political world, irre-
spective of party, "to establish a more intimate relationship
with Germany."[2] On 4th September the Crown Prince sent
the news to the Chancellor, who ostensibly welcomed it warmly.

During 1883 the Prince's conciliatory attitude to Germany
seemed in German eyes to grow firmer. Twice he revisited the
country and saw much of the German royal family. In February
he attended the silver wedding of the Crown Prince and Princess,
and was a witness of the elaborate pageantry which made the
occasion notable. An honour which he highly valued was
conferred on him by the old Kaiser, who made him on 5th

[1] See p. 450 *supra.* Lord Beaconsfield, now near the end of his life, in his
last letter to his confidential friend, Lady Bradford (March 16, 1881), expressed
admiration of the Prince's opportunities of familiar converse with the two
masters of Europe's destiny: "The P. of W. has seen a great deal in his
fortnight's absence; all the great men and, I suppose, some of the famous
women—Bismarck . . . and Gambetta, with whom he breakfasted, 'quite
private,' alone, and who seems to have been as loquacious as his German rival"
(Buckle, vi. 608).

[2] *Die Grosse Politik,* iv. 31.

February honorary colonel of the 5th Pomeranian ("Blucher") regiment of Hussars in the Prussian army. It was the first honorary military distinction which a foreign sovereign bestowed on the Prince, and the Queen acquiesced in her son's acceptance, despite the strong objection which she had raised in 1874 to his receiving a like mark of recognition from the Tsar of Russia, on the just ground that it was out of keeping with English tradition. The Prince showed his habitual cordiality towards Prince William, his ambitious and critical nephew, by presenting him with a costume of Royal Stewart tartan, with all the accoutrements of the Highland dress, for him to wear at the fancy dress balls which formed brilliant features of the silver wedding programme. Prince William had always delighted in wearing the kilt on his visits to his grandmother at Balmoral in boyhood, and in later life he took a childish pride in recalling the becomingness of the apparel.[1] Now he caused himself to be photographed at full length in the Scottish dress which was his uncle's gift, and he distributed copies among his friends. But there was a dark presage in the English sentence which he inscribed beneath his signature on each print : "I bide my time."[2]

Prince Bismarck, although in ill-health, admitted the Prince once again to a short interview, and to his hearer's satisfaction spoke approvingly of England's occupation of Egypt.[3] The gruff Chancellor repeated his delight in the Prince's alluring manner.

In the autumn of the same year, 1883, the Prince made another appearance in Germany to which greater political significance seemed to attach. On the invitation of the Kaiser he attended the autumn manœuvres of the German army, accompanied by his brothers, the Duke of Edinburgh and the Duke of Connaught. Among his fellow-guests were the young King of Spain, whom the Prince had not met since his visit to Madrid in 1876, King Albert of Saxony, and King Milan of Serbia. The operations took place in the neighbourhood of Frankfort, and the Prince watched them with keen attention for four days. The Kaiser's advisers deemed it politic to impress the Prince with the efficiency of their military preparedness, and the Prince gratified them by

[1] Writing to his uncle on 30th December 1901, Prince (then Kaiser) William recalled how he had last worn the Highland dress in September 1878.
[2] Communication from General Sir Leopold Swaine, British Military Attaché at Berlin, 1884–94.
[3] Fitzmaurice's Life of Earl Granville, ii. 317.

the assurance that he believed the German army to be "the 1884
finite in the world." Ætat. 42

The opening of the next year, 1884, saw the fair promise of
an Anglo-German *rapprochement* overcast. Elements of danger
were diagnosed by English statesmen in a somewhat sudden
change which took place early that year in Prince Bismarck's
attitude towards his fellow-countrymen's cry for a German
colonial empire. The Chancellor had hitherto looked with an
indifferent eye on the nascent hopes of Germany to create a
German empire overseas. So far, a few German traders had
settled on the African coast and in some islands in the Pacific.
But the miniature German colonial settlements had received little
political encouragement at home. Early in 1884 Prince Bismarck
frankly adopted an imperialist colonial policy, and he invited
the English government to recognise the claims of German
plantations in distant places to the status of full-fledged German
colonies. The English government showed unexpected hesitation, and the diplomatic flirtations between the two governments
developed into ugly wrangles.[1]

Prince Bismarck's new colonial aspirations, if they somewhat
perplexed the Prince, seemed to him modest compared with the
French and to be entitled to considerate study. There was
disunion in the cabinet as to the right course to pursue, and the
lack of decisiveness in the ministerial pronouncements provoked

[1] A German explorer had stolen a march on England on the Guinea coast
of Africa, and proclaimed a protectorate over Togoland and the Cameroons
before the English government seemed to be aware of the presence of Germans
in that region. A German expedition into the Sultanate of Zanzibar on the
East African coast also excited English apprehension, and German traders
were setting foot in the Pacific island of Samoa. But for the moment more
perplexing issues were raised by German claims on Angra Pequena, a small
town on the coast of south-west Africa, as well as on the north-eastern portion
of the island of New Guinea to the north of the Australian continent. A very
acrimonious controversy arose between Bismarck and the English ministry in
respect of these two incursions, which were resented by the English colonists
respectively of the Cape and Australia. The English government especially
disliked the contiguity of a German colony in South Africa. There were good
reasons to believe that the Germans would, there if anywhere, prove uncom-
fortable neighbours. President Kruger, of the Transvaal Republic, whose
relations with England were newly strained by his claims to control the border
region of Bechuanaland, had been in suspicious negotiations with German envoys
and immigrants. In the Queen's eyes Lord Derby, the Colonial Secretary,
was "tamely swallowing every insult which the Boers are ready to offer us,"
but there was no wish, either in Downing Street or at the Cape, to see Germany
take a hand in the quarrel of England with the Boers.

1884
Ætat. 42

the Prince's impatience. His friends Sir Charles Dilke and
Mr. Chamberlain, the advanced wing of the government, were
resolute in hostility to Germany's colonial pretensions, while Lord
Granville and Lord Derby, who belonged to the right wing, were
less inimical. But by delaying replies to German communications and by what Prince Bismarck denounced as "unconciliatory
evasions," the English foreign and colonial secretaries kept
Germany in a state of irritation. The Prince took the view that
piecemeal negotiations were futile, and that a full and frank
discussion of the whole colonial question was alone worth while.
The Queen, in her comprehensive distrust of Liberal statesman-
ship, was now pleading with her ministers that Germany would
be England's benevolent friend and ally "if she were not treated
with suspicion and opposition." The Prince avowed some
sympathy with the rebuke which his mother administered to
Lord Granville for objecting (as she alleged) to "*any* country
but *ourselves* having *colonies*."

Count Herbert Bismarck's English mission was coming to a
close, and in the autumn of 1884 he paid farewell visits to the
Queen at Balmoral and to many noblemen at their Scottish
seats. In September he spent a week with the Prince at
Abergeldie. The Count sought the Prince's countenance for
Germany's colonial pretensions. He reported to his father the
Prince's dissatisfaction with both the colonial and the foreign
policies of Mr. Gladstone's government; his host, he told his
father, deplored Lord Derby's ungenial vacillations, but he
looked forward to a friendly settlement. According to Count
Herbert's sanguine representations, the Prince was "striving
for a real and lasting alliance with Germany, which alone could
further England's welfare." [1] Under that impression Count
Herbert took leave of the Prince at Abergeldie at the end of
September, and with unctuous effusiveness thanked him by
letter after his departure for a hospitality which left "beautiful
memories" (September 30).

But the Prince's view of German colonisation had hardly
crystallised in so firm a mould as his guest imagined. The
ultimate acceptance by the English government of the
German proposals in regard to the German settlements on
the African coast and in New Guinea seemed to him politic.

[1] *Die Grosse Politik*, iv. 84-5.

But he was inclined to attribute much of the subsequent German 1885
ill-feeling in regard to colonial problems to Lord Derby's waver- Ætat. 43
ing tones and procrastinations in the first stages of the negotiation; of these delays Prince Bismarck and his German followers made the most. At the same time the Prince shared the
apprehensions which were even then rife in the British Empire
concerning the future scope of German colonial enterprise. He
attached importance to a long letter which Sir Henry Loch, Governor of Victoria, wrote to him from Melbourne (April 29, 1885) reporting Australian suspicions of the German annexation of New
Guinea, and imputing to the German government a resolve to
absorb the Dutch colonies in the Far East.

During the closing years of Kaiser William I.'s long life, however, the Prince maintained his friendly attitude to the German
Court and to the German government. Russia's advance in
Central Asia in the spring of 1885 seemed to threaten a fatal
breach between England and that country, and the Prince acknowledged the especial value of German sympathy. He visited
Berlin in March in order to congratulate the old Kaiser on his
eighty-eighth birthday, and aired in political circles the notion
that it would be an advantage if Prince Bismarck would agree to
consult a member of Mr. Gladstone's government with a view to
common action in the Anglo-Russian imbroglio. In conversation
with Count Herbert Bismarck he suggested that either Sir Charles
Dilke or Lord Rosebery should go to Berlin for the purpose.
Count Herbert favoured the suggestion, and the Prince's friend,
Lord Rosebery, who had just joined Mr. Gladstone's cabinet,
went over to consult the German Chancellor on the general
question of Anglo-German relations. If nothing came of the
English minister's interview with Prince Bismarck, the Prince's
suggestion illustrated his faith in the value of direct personal
intercourse between responsible leaders of opinion.

V

On the eve of the development of Anglo-German rivalry in 1884
colonial fields, there died at Potsdam (August 25, 1884) the British Ætat. 42
Ambassador, Lord Ampthill, the Prince's friend of old standing,
whose tact had long been a favourable ingredient in Anglo-German
relations. The Prince deplored Lord Ampthill's death on both

personal and public grounds. He had found in him a faithful
friend since his boyhood, while his sister, the Crown Princess, had
greatly benefited by his kindly counsel. Writing to the Queen
(August 28) of Lord Ampthill's loss, he recalled the intimacy which
had first begun when they met at Rome in 1859: "His loss to
the country," he continued, "not to speak of his family, is very
great, and at Berlin quite irreparable. Well can I understand
how much dear Vicky must deplore his loss."

The removal of Lord Ampthill turned the Prince's attention
to the choice of his successor—a matter involving delicate issues.
With immense energy the Prince pressed on Queen Victoria and
her government the claims of a diplomatist who enjoyed his warm
regard. Sir Robert Morier had served in early life at a succession
of small German courts, including Darmstadt, the residence of the
Prince's sister, Princess Alice, where the Prince first made his
acquaintance. Subsequently Sir Robert had represented England
at Lisbon and Madrid. The knowledge which he had acquired of
Germany during his long sojourn there was profound. As the
friend of rulers of small principalities he cherished no love for
Prince Bismarck, or for his son, Count Herbert, who indeed treated
him with rancorous bitterness. But he thoroughly believed in
the advantage of good Anglo-German relations. The Prince was
always loud in praise of "his wonderful quickness and cleverness,"
and in Morier's dislike of the Bismarcks he saw no insuperable
bar to his appointment to Berlin. "It seems to me," he now
wrote to his mother on 28th August, "that Sir Robert Morier
is the only one in our diplomacy fit for such an important post
on account of his thorough knowledge of Germany." "Berlin
is," he wrote to Lord Granville, "perhaps the most important
embassy we possess. I know," he added, "that Morier is not
popular with the Foreign Office, and though he has his faults
(and who have not?), still I think that his great abilities pre-
ponderate over them."

The Crown Princess supported her brother's plea, but Lord
Granville somewhat brusquely declined to entertain it on the
reasonable ground that Sir Robert would not be agreeable to
Prince Bismarck, and was too outspoken and impulsive to conciliate dislike. It was slowly and unwillingly that the Prince
acknowledged the force of Lord Granville's argument. In the
generous desire to serve a friend the Prince clearly underrated

Prince Bismarck's antipathy to all—whether Germans or foreigners
—who identified themselves with the fortunes of the petty German
states. But at the back of the Prince's mind was the sanguine
belief that the accession of his brother-in-law, the Crown Prince,
could not, in view of the great age of the present ruler of Germany,
be long delayed, and that Morier's presence at Berlin and his expert knowledge of Germany might somehow encourage the liberal
régime which (the Prince was confident) would soon be inaugurated
by his brother-in-law to the benefit of the world's peace.

Though the Prince's special candidate for Berlin was soon out
of the running, the Prince did not relax his activities in canvassing
the claims of others, all of whom he compared with Morier to their
disadvantage. He deprecated, although he did not wholly dis-
countenance, the candidatures of men who did not already belong
to the diplomatic profession.

"Of course," he wrote to Lord Granville (September 15, 1884),
"Lord Dufferin stands highest among our diplomatists, but then
he does not know Germany, and I always hope he may be Lord
Ripon's successor, and for the sake of India, the sooner the better.
Mr. Goschen might be thought of, but his appointment would be
a hardship to the profession as taking promotion from them."

He disapproved of the Crown Princess's suggestion of Lord Acton
or Lord Arthur Russell on the ground that, like Mr. Goschen,
they were outside the diplomatic ring. Lord Lansdowne, then
Governor-General of Canada, was mentioned, but there was no
reason to think that he would desire a transference to Berlin.
When the Prince learned that Sir Edward Malet, who had been
usefully employed in Egypt and was now British minister at
Brussels, was the final choice of the Foreign Office, he grudgingly
acquiesced in the appointment.

The Prince's interest in Morier did not abate. He continued
a campaign on behalf of his promotion elsewhere. Lord Dufferin
was soon nominated to the Viceroyalty of India and thus the
Embassy at Constantinople fell vacant. The Prince promptly
suggested that his protégé should fill that post. Lord Granville
retorted (September 17, 1884) that Morier had no experience of
Orientals. The Prince complained that to exclude him from
Constantinople as well as from Berlin was to cast "some slur"
upon him. "I may add," the Prince characteristically remarked,
"that this comes entirely from myself and that I have had no

communication with him on the subject." Finally, the Prince's urgency was rewarded by Morier's nomination to St. Petersburg on 1st December 1884.

In Russia Morier remained for the rest of his professional life. The Prince's confidence in him ran high to the last, and the Ambassador's influence on his zealous patron increased rather than declined as their intercourse grew to a close. Under Morier's persuasions there was a renewal of the Prince's early suspicions of Prince Bismarck's Prussianism and of Germany's imperial policy. Yielding former scruples, the Prince owed to Morier's counsels the prospect of a political accommodation with Russia. Therein he came to perceive an untried means, the value of which grew on him in the years that followed, of countering the menace of Germany's developing ambitions.

VI

A proleptic interest attaches to the part which the Prince was playing in the international situation on his visits to Berlin in the years 1884 and 1885. Behind the scenes his nephew, Prince William, under the sway of his militarist and Anglophobic associates, was giving a significant foretaste of his coming attitude to his uncle. The fire-eating Count von Waldersee was indoctrinating the self-confident young man with a reckless passion for war, and was persuading him that the German domination of Europe could alone be assured by an attack on England and by England's decisive defeat, and, after England was out of the way, by a similarly drastic treatment of Russia.[1] Count von Waldersee convinced him that the chief obstacle to these fell purposes lay in the over-cautious and over-crafty diplomacy of Prince Bismarck and in his parents' pacific and Anglophil predilections which the Prince of Wales, his uncle, encouraged. Prince William's tortuous nature rendered it congenial to him to play for the

[1] *New Chapters of Bismarck's Autobiography*, p. 261 *et seq.*, and *Memoirs* of Alfred, Count von Waldersee, English translation, 1924, pp. 117 *seq.* Under date 26th December 1884, Count von Waldersee, who found Prince William from the first an apt pupil, writes in his Diary: "The Prince has taken up an attitude strongly against England, a quite natural reaction for the most part against the efforts of his mother to make Anglo-maniacs of her children." Many entries which follow illustrate the abuse which Prince William, in talk with his confidants, was in the habit of lavishing on his parents and on his uncle before he came to the throne.

present a double game in regard to Russia—to profess devotion to her interests and to whet her enmity against England. Before Germany should overwhelm Russia, that Power should serve Germany's turn in the conflict with England. Prince William foolishly believed that by lavishing personal and political blandishments on Tsar Alexander III. he might win Russia's active help in laying England low—the first step, in his and his comrades' view, on Germany's road to ultimate aggrandisement.

In May 1884 Prince William paid a first visit to St. Petersburg to attend the coming of age on his sixteenth birthday of the Tsarevitch, the future Tsar Nicholas II. He described himself at the time as "a blunt soldier unversed in the arts of diplomacy," but he won the ear of his Imperial host by enthusiastically pledging himself to do all he could to aid Russia in her quarrels with England. With impetuous volubility he set himself the task of poisoning the Tsar's mind against his uncle as Russia's irreconcilable enemy. On his return to Berlin the young man initiated an intimate correspondence with the Tsar in which he reported with irresponsible exaggerations the gossip which reached him from England of England's plan to thwart the Tsar's purposes in both the Balkans and Central Asia.[1] He styled his uncle Russia's most formidable foe, and alleged that the Prince of Wales was seeking through his mother, the Crown Princess, to stir up Germany as well as England against Russia. In June 1884 the Prince of Wales visited Prince William's parents, and the nephew, with a ludicrous display of blind egotism, informed the Tsar of the personal efforts that he was making in order to countermine the alleged conspiracy of which he represented his uncle to be the active centre:

The visit of the Prince of Wales has yielded and is still bringing extraordinary fruit, which will continue to multiply under the hands of my mother and the Queen of England. But these English have accidentally forgotten that *I* exist! And I swear to You, my dear cousin, that anything I can do for You and Your country I will do, and I swear that I will keep my

---

[1] The Kaiser's letters of 1884–85 to Tsar Alexander III. are printed in English, the language in which they were written, in the "Periodical of the Central Archives, Administration of the Russian Soviet Republic." See the *Morning Post*, 16th January 1923. A French version has since been published with a Russian translation, and an English rendering of the French version appeared in the *Westminster Gazette*, 12th September 1924: these French and English versions travel far from the original English text.

word! But only it will take a long time and will have to be
done very slowly.

In the following year, when the Prince of Wales was expected
in Berlin on the occasion of the Kaiser's eighty-eighth birthday,
the Tsar's correspondent seemed to lose all self-control in his
desperate and unprincipled resolve to keep the Tsar and his
uncle—and thereby, as he believed, their respective countries—
at incurable enmity. On 13th March 1885, Prince William wrote
to the Tsar:

> We shall see the Prince of Wales here in a few days. I am
> not at all delighted by this unexpected apparition, because—
> excuse me, he is Your brother-in-law—owing to his false and
> intriguing nature he will undoubtedly attempt in one way or
> another to push the Bulgarian business [against Russian interests]
> —may Allah send them to Hell, as the Turk would say!—or to do
> a little political plotting behind the scenes with the ladies.

With reference to the pending campaign of the English in the
Sudan, the graceless writer added: "May the Mahdi chuck them
all into the Nile."

The Prince's arrival in Berlin in March 1885 prompted his
nephew to send the Tsar further venomous reports of his uncle's
alleged views and intentions. The Penjdeh crisis was a delect-
able morsel for Prince William's acidulated palate.[1] While congratulating the Tsar on what the writer represented as Russia's
triumph over her rival in Central Asia, he announced that the
Prince was unalterably bent on immediate vengeance and had
persuaded the Crown Princess, in spite of her wonted pacifism,
to join him on the warpath. From the lips of gentlemen in
attendance on the Prince in Berlin and from the English military
attaché (Colonel Swaine) there, Prince William professed to have
heard the baleful words: "Sooner or later the two countries (i.e.
Russia and England) will come to blows, as there is no possible
way to avoid it" (May 4, 1885).

The Prince, although he was hardly cognisant of the full range
of his nephew's braggadocios, heard enough from his sister to
regard the young man's future career with anxiety. But he
looked forward to the rapidly approaching day when his brother-
in-law the Crown Prince should succeed to his great inheritance.

[1] See p. 510 *infra.*

and he sanguinely believed that any power for evil which his 1886
Junker nephew possessed would then be effectively checked, Ætat. 44
Fate decreed otherwise. At the end of 1886, to the Prince's
lasting grief, the Crown Prince was smitten by a mortal disease,
and Prince William was elevated prematurely in 1888 to a place
of supreme authority in which his unwholesome spirit had free
vent.

CHAPTER XXVII

THE RESTLESSNESS OF GREECE, 1879–1900—RELATIONS WITH
BULGARIA AND RUSSIA, 1879–1886

1878

Ætat. 36

THE six years which followed the signing of the Treaty of Berlin formed a more disquieting period in the history of Eastern Europe than the Prince had foreseen, and circumstances so developed as to involve him personally in many of the critical issues. The disappointment of Greece over the Treaty's restricted recognition of her territorial claims on Turkey, and the Porte's unwillingness to give effect to the Treaty's modest concessions, led the King of the Hellenes to renew his appeals for the aid which the Prince was loth to withhold. The Prince actively interested himself, too, in the fortunes of the youthful Prince Alexander of Battenberg, who was chosen under the terms of the Treaty to fill the newly established throne of Bulgaria. But greater anxieties were caused the Prince by events in Russia. There, not only did the bitter political rivalry with England alike in Europe and Asia continue unabated, but the assassination early in 1881 of Tsar Alexander II., with whom the Prince's differences had lately been acute, gave the Prince a lurid glimpse of the internal conditions of the country, and in the event provoked fresh perplexities as to Anglo-Russian association.

I

While the Berlin Congress was in session the Prince had, in correspondence with Lord Beaconsfield, earnestly pleaded the cause of Greece. Politicians in Paris credited him with seeking to exert an influence which he scarcely possessed.[1] Ultimately

[1] Hanotaux, *Contemporary France*, iv. 310.

the Treaty did nothing for Greece beyond promising some 1878
rectifications of the frontier in Thessaly and Epirus, to which Ætat. 36
obdurate Turkey delayed giving effect. The Prince made every
effort to reconcile his brother-in-law, the Greek King, to Turkey's
procrastination, and wrote assuring him that England had applied
to the reluctant Porte every practicable spur. On the 30th
August King George laid, with becoming restraint, his country's
grievance before the Prince:

> I should be sorry if you thought I had been complaining
> against England for its attitude in the Congress. I have never
> said anything like it. I am, on the contrary, very much satisfied
> with what has been done for Greece, and thankful to England
> for having accepted and agreed to the proposition made by the
> French Minister for Foreign Affairs in favour of Greece. If the
> proposition had been made by the English Plenipotentiaries—
> and I regret that they did not do it—it would have been of
> great use and immense effect, because it would have strengthened
> so much more the feeling of the Greeks that England had taken
> their future in hand. But I understand the delicate position in
> which England was in at the time vis-à-vis of Turkey, and that she
> preferred, therefore, to let M. Waddington propose the rectifica-
> tion of our frontier to those two rivers, instead of doing it
> herself. . . . Of course the Greeks will be in a ferment as long
> as Turkey refuses to sanction claims which have received the
> sanction of Europe.

In forwarding to the Prime Minister (September 9) the King's
letter, the Prince begged Lord Beaconsfield to send his correspondent some "encouraging lines"; but Lord Beaconsfield
could recommend only patience and the need of restraining
Greece from rash adventures. The Prince wrote in acknowledgement of Lord Beaconsfield's warnings (September 13):

> The King will, I am afraid, be disappointed at what you
> have written, but it is far better that there should be clearly laid
> before him and his Ministers the attitude of the British Govern-
> ment. Some allowances must be made for the difficulties the
> King has in keeping his inflammatory subjects quiet.

The deadlock continued, to the disappointment of the Prince.
Turkey employed every diplomatic device in order to shelve
negotiations, and the Greek King's further correspondence with
the Prince testified to an increasing impatience with England's
unwillingness to apply pressure to the Porte. At the end of

March the Prince consulted Sir Austen Layard, the British Ambassador at Constantinople, who happened to be in London. At the Prince's request Sir Austen "put into writing his views on the Greek question, in order that the Prince might communicate them to the King." Sir Austen's memorandum, which reached the Prince on 1st April 1879, merely recommended Greece to rely on a waiting policy. In acknowledging the rather ambiguous pronouncement, the Prince wrote (April 4): "I shall send it without delay to the King, my brother-in-law, and shall be curious to learn how far his views coincide with yours." [1] On 14th April Lord Beaconsfield sought to reassure the dissatisfied Prince. "The Porte and Austria," he remarked, "have settled their disputes and we are pressing the Greek affair." A few days later the King of Greece repeated to the Prince, with increased vehemence, his complaint that the English Government was failing to secure the delimitation of the frontier in accordance with the Berlin Treaty, and that in one of Lord Beaconsfield's letters to the Prince, the Prime Minister contemplated the withholding from Greece of the towns of Janina and Larissa, which the Treaty specifically promised to surrender. The Prince echoed his brother-in-law's irritation, and complained when he wrote to Lord Salisbury on the 1st May: "The Greek question seems to me less settled than ever, and there is no proper basis on which an understanding between the Porte and Greece can be arrived at."

The accession of the Liberal Government to power in April 1880 gave both King and Prince fresh hope. In the summer of that year the Prince entertained his brother-in-law and the Queen of Greece for three weeks (June 16–July 5) at Marlborough House, and at the Prince's suggestion the King received the high honour of the Freedom of the City of London. At Marlborough House the Prince introduced to his guest leading British statesmen, including Lord Beaconsfield and Sir Charles Dilke, the new Liberal Under-Secretary of Foreign Affairs. Both thought highly of the King's ability when, under the Prince's roof, he discussed with them his country's claims.

At length in 1881, to the Prince's relief, and to some extent through his personal intervention, a part of the Greek claim was satisfied. Russia had shown herself quite as unwilling as Turkey

[1] Layard Papers, British Mus., Addit. MSS. 39139, f. 56.

to encourage Greece's territorial expansion. But when, in
March 1881, the Prince went to St. Petersburg to attend the
funeral of the murdered Tsar Alexander II., Lord Granville,
the Foreign Secretary, urged him to persuade the new Tsar to
ease the situation.   Lord Granville wrote :

Y.R.H. feels so kindly about Greece that I hope you will
recommend the Emperor how much it will affect the position of
the King of Greece if the frontier line is settled in a manner not
entirely to disappoint the reasonable expectations of his subjects.
Not to mention, apart from any question of amour propre, how
much Europe must lose of power for good, if it is made manifest
that a slight opposition is sufficient to reverse the decisions
which all the Powers have taken. To divide Thessaly between
the Turks and the Greeks appears to be a certain way of creating
future difficulties.

The upshot was more satisfactory than the Prince hoped.   His
intervention at St. Petersburg bore good fruit.   Thessaly was
ceded to Greece by a Convention signed with Turkey on 2nd
July 1881.

But Greece deemed the concession inadequate, and the King
of the Hellenes' gratitude to the Prince took the not un-
common shape of pressing him for further favours.   He proceeded to invoke the Prince's influence with a view to securing
for his country larger advantages.   The Prince was indisposed
to humour indefinitely the habitual restlessness of his brother-
in-law's subjects.   When his friend Lord Rosebery was, in 1886,
for the first time in charge of the Foreign Office, the clamorous
Greeks, resentful of the recent incorporation of the Turkish
province of Eastern Roumelia within the boundaries of the
new Bulgarian State, resolved on an invasion of Turkey in
order to obtain some corresponding increase of territory.   The
King of the Hellenes communicated his embarrassment to the
Prince, who, although sympathetically perturbed, declined to
play any part in the new crisis.   The Powers summoned
the refractory country to disarm, and were met by a blunt
refusal.   On the 25th April Lord Rosebery informed the Prince
that a blockade of the Greek coast was needed to break Greek
defiance.   The Prince, who acknowledged the hopelessness of
the Greek position, learnt with natural concern that the
Ambassadors of Great Britain, Austria, Germany, and Italy left
Athens on the 7th May.   An effective blockade followed.   The

Prince's anxiety was relieved when, on the 1st June, the Greeks yielded to the pressure.

II

1895
—
Ætat. 53

The Prince's interest in the land of Greece was never entirely confined to the country's political embarrassments. He had inspected for himself the ancient monuments at Athens and elsewhere, and sympathised with the efforts in England, America, and Germany to promote the study of Hellenic art and architecture. King George was an active patron of archæological research, and the Prince was always ready to do what he could in the way of encouraging his brother-in-law's archæological zeal. The Prince identified himself with the first endeavour in England to found and endow the British School of Archæology at Athens. On 25th June 1883 he presided over a meeting which he summoned with this end in view to Marlborough House, and a sum of £4000 was there and then subscribed. Twelve years later he endeavoured to set the British School on a sound financial footing. Responding to the request of Mr. Charles Waldstein (afterwards Sir Charles Walston), who had made notable archæological discoveries in Greece as Director, from 1889 to 1893, of the American School at Athens, the Prince placed his influence at the disposal of the new effort.

"I am very glad," he wrote to Mr. Waldstein from Cannes early in 1895, "you have had some conversation with the Vice-Chancellor [of Cambridge] regarding the British School at Athens and if only Cambridge would take the matter up perhaps the other Universities would follow suit. After you have discussed the matter thoroughly with [Sir Edwin] Egerton [British Minister] at Athens, I shall be much interested in hearing what it is proposed to do. Our Universities ought to take it up if the State will not."

On the 29th July 1895 the Prince convened a meeting at St. James's Palace of Greek scholars and others interested in the history and the contemporary fortunes of Greece. The Prince occupied the chair and manifested complete sympathy with the general desire to make the British School permanent and efficient. He expressed special admiration for the eloquent plea to that effect, of the chief speaker, Professor Jebb, Regius Professor of Greek at Cambridge and the chief classical scholar

at the time. The promise of the meeting was well fulfilled
and the Prince served for life as Patron of the British School
which honourably distinguished itself by the new light which it
shed on the early developments of Hellenic art and architecture.

III

Meanwhile the political troubles of Greece, which no en-   1897
couragement of archæology could touch, remained acute.   Ætat. 55
Towards the end of the nineteenth century the King of the
Hellenes was faced by a more serious crisis than he had yet
known, and the Prince's interest in his welfare acquired fresh
energy. Their familiar intimacy was never long interrupted
throughout this trying period. Domestic incident brought them
together at brief intervals. The King was a guest at Marlborough House at the celebration of the Queen's Jubilee of 1887,
and two years later the Prince attended at Athens the marriage
of the King's eldest son, Constantine, with the Kaiser's sister.
The great family parties which assembled each autumn in Copenhagen or Fredensborg frequently included the two men and their
families. In conversation or in correspondence the King confided
to the Prince, as of old, his political embarrassments, and the
Prince continued to plead with English and foreign statesmen
for the due consideration of Greek national aspirations.

Early in 1897 Greece was involved in a fresh peril from which
it required all the benevolence of the Prince and others to extricate her. The centre of disturbance was once again the island
of Crete, whose inhabitants importuned the Greek government
with greater vehemence than before to rescue the island from
Turkish sway and annex it to the Greek kingdom. The Greek
people gave the Cretan appeal an enthusiastic reception. A
Greek fleet carried to Crete an army which on the 15th February
declared war on the Turkish garrison. The six European
Powers (England, Germany, Austria, France, Italy, and Russia)
taking concerted action, disapproved such precipitate conduct and
ordered the Greeks to abstain from hostilities. But Greece was
in its habitually refractory mood, and proceeded with its campaign. There was, however, much sympathy among the Powers
with the Cretans' desire for release from the Turkish yoke, and
they successfully urged the Porte to concede Cretan autonomy

under Turkish suzerainty (March 5). At the same time the
Greek troops were warned to evacuate the island within six days.
But the settlement, although fully approved by the Prince, was
unacceptable to the Greeks. The Greek government scouted
such terms, and resolved to attack Turkey on the mainland.
The puzzled Powers threatened Greece with a new blockade if
she persisted in defying their counsels. A dramatic change of
scene followed. The Porte, stung to fury by the Greek threats,
declared war on Greece on 17th April. Desperate fighting
straightway ensued. The Greek troops were quickly routed,
and on the 20th May the Greek government sued for peace.

The Prince, thoroughly perturbed by the danger which Greece
had courted, used such influence as he possessed to encourage
the six Powers to mediate between the combatants. His sympathy with his brother-in-law the King of the Hellenes was
profound. In April 1897, a recent acquaintance of his, Sir
Donald Mackenzie Wallace, Director of the Foreign Department
of *The Times*, who was intimately acquainted with Eastern
Europe, had visited Greece, and had reported to the Prince a
private interview with the Greek King, in which the King explained his complete inability to check the swelling tide of Greek
nationalism. When in the months that followed Greece lay
at Turkey's feet the Prince constantly implored Lord Salisbury
to protect her from the consequences of her rashness. In July
the ambassadors at Constantinople joined together in pressing
the Porte to treat its adversary mercifully. On the 17th the
Prince wrote hopefully to Lord Salisbury's secretary:

I rejoice to hear from your letter that the Sultan has given
way and accepted the principal demands of the Ambassadors.
If only England will lead the way "and put her foot down,"
Greece may yet be extricated from the terrible position in which
she is now placed.

In the result the Prince's hope was realised. After protracted
negotiations Greece was saved from Turkish vengeance. A
Treaty of Peace, which was at length signed at Constantinople
on the 4th November 1897, gave Turkey some very trifling
territorial advantages and the modest indemnity of £4,000,000.

Throughout this period the relations of the Prince with his
nephew, Kaiser William II., were uncomfortably strained, and
the Prince's activity in Greek affairs added fuel to the dissen-

sions between the two. Invidious comparisons were drawn at the 1897
Wilhelmstrasse between the Prince's interference on his Greek Ætat. 55
brother-in-law's behalf and the more correct conduct of the
Kaiser, who, although his sister was married to the Greek heir-
apparent, did not allow his domestic sentiment to influence the
attitude of his ministers towards the country of his sister's
husband.[1]

There was yet another phase of the pending Greek problem
in which the Prince played a prominent part, and thereby
intensified his nephew's irritation. Through the autumn of 1897
"our grave responsibilities in Crete," as the Prince wrote to his
friend Lady Londonderry on 27th September, occupied much
of his thought. After Turkey had ceded autonomy to the
island the Powers undertook to choose a Governor-General, and
the Kaiser fell foul of the candidate whom the Prince eagerly
favoured. The Tsar, Nicholas II., whose mother was sister of
the King of the Hellenes, was the first to suggest the name of
Prince George of Greece, second son of the King of the Hellenes,
who, now in his thirtieth year, had accompanied the Tsar on his
tour round the world before his accession. The Prince and
Princess enthusiastically backed the Tsar's selection, and Lord
Salisbury expressed approval. The Prince employed all his
energy in supporting Prince George's appointment. Towards
the end of January 1898 he invited the Russian Ambassador in
London, M. de Staal, to Sandringham for the day. Both Prince
and Princess spoke with frankness of their anxiety for a confirmation of the Tsar's choice. M. de Staal cautiously pointed
out that the Sultan's assent had yet to be invited, and that
opposition threatened from various quarters.[2]

M. de Staal spoke with knowledge. Germany induced
Austria to join her in violent opposition to the candidate of the
Tsar and the Prince. At both Berlin and Vienna the Prince's
support of Prince George was freely employed as an argument
against his selection. The Austrian Foreign Minister, Count
Goluchowski, complained that England and the Prince had
interested motives in pressing Prince George's nomination.[3]
But the Kaiser had soon to acknowledge the futility of resistance,

[1] *Die Grosse Politik*, xii. 310 a.
[2] M. de Staal to Mouravieff, 21st Jan./2nd Feb. 1898, Russian Archives.
[3] *Die Grosse Politik*, xii. 479.

1897
Ætat. 55

and to admit unwillingly that in the matter of the Cretan sovereignty his uncle had out-matched him. The central powers
discovered that France and Italy were ready to stand by Russia
and Great Britain. Thereupon Germany and Austria sulkily
withdrew from the European Concert. With great satisfaction
the Prince learnt that the four remaining Powers—Great Britain,
France, Russia, and Italy—formally agreed to nominate Prince
George Governor-General of Crete for a preliminary term of
three years.[1] On 21st December 1898 Prince George arrived
in Candia and took up his post for a three years' probationary
term. He was received with acclamation, and, despite premoni-
tions of a renewed agitation over union with Greece, tranquillity
prevailed for a time under his rule.

1900
Ætat. 58

The Prince of Wales continuously interested himself in the
Cretan fortunes of his wife's nephew. He sagaciously recommended the new Governor-General to hold aloof from party
strife, and to treat the rival races and religions of the island with
impartial favour. Towards the end of 1900 Prince George
reported his experience to the Prince of Wales in person. He
was paying a round of visits to the four guaranteeing Powers,
and in England he was the Prince's guest for some eleven days
(November 5–16), dividing his time between Marlborough House
and Sandringham. When he spoke despondingly to the Prince
of his difficulties in reconciling the discordant elements amongst
his subjects, the Prince repeated sympathetically his wise counsel.
After the Prince of Wales became King, his protégé disappointed
him by his failure to hold the balance even between the rival

---

[1] Before Prince George arrived in the Island the Turkish soldiers, who
were still in garrison there, broke out into open revolt, and the British Vice-
Consul in Candia was murdered. Lord Salisbury threatened that England
would, if need be, expel single-handed the Turkish troops. Russia and the
other two Powers, however, came to England's support and together they
compelled the Turkish troops to withdraw. The Kaiser, exasperated by the
Tsar's co-operation with the Prince in the election of Prince George to the
Governor-Generalship, sought, with customary perversity, to persuade the
Tsar in private letters that England and the Prince were pursuing a malignantly
selfish policy. On 20th October 1898, the Kaiser complained to the Tsar that
England was "using us all as catspaws to help her to take Crete or Suda Bay."
He pointed out somewhat wildly that it was incumbent on both himself and his
correspondent to conciliate the Sultan. The Sultan's friendship would prove
"a tremendous card in our game in case you or I were suddenly confronted
by a war with a certain meddlesome power." But the Kaiser was beating the
wind as far as the future of Crete was concerned. See *The Kaiser's Letters
to the Tsar*, pp. 60–62.

parties under his sway. King Edward acquiesced in 1906 in his compulsory withdrawal from his thankless post. However well-disposed to his brother-in-law, the King of the Hellenes, and to members of the King's family, and however desirous of serving their interests, King Edward, both as Prince and sovereign, many times found their political embarrassments beyond his power to permanently alleviate.

IV

It was not only in Greece that the provisions of the Berlin Treaty kept controversy fiercely astir in Eastern Europe from the autumn of 1878 onwards. Through the early months of 1879 the Prince saw with dismay Russia's strenuous efforts to evade the restraints which the Treaty placed on her ambitions in the Balkans and elsewhere. Writing to Lord Salisbury on 31st January 1879 he expressed anew his distrust of Russia's intentions, and pointedly cited a recent article from the *Neue Freie Presse* of Vienna, which prophesied that Russia's territorial advance in all directions was assured unless the revolutionary movement succeeded in putting an end to the existing régime. The Prince's fears were confirmed by the report which Lord Salisbury sent him (March 6) of the Tsar's farewell interview with the retiring British Ambassador, Lord Augustus Loftus. On that occasion the Tsar declared his profound dissatisfaction with England's endeavours to thwart Russia, and he foretold war in the near future as the certain outcome of the existing relations of the two countries. The Prince doubted Lord Augustus's capacity to uphold England's prestige at the Tsar's Court. He questioned whether he put the English point of view before the Tsar with adequate force. The appointment in his place of Lord Dufferin was welcome to the Prince. Of Lord Dufferin he had formed and retained a high opinion as a man of tact, vision, and perfect manner.

Russia's attitude to the Treaty's scheme for settling the Balkan difficulty especially provoked the Prince's misgivings. The grant of autonomy to Bulgaria under the suzerainty of Turkey dissatisfied the Tsar. A province to the south of Bulgaria, known as Eastern Roumelia, was constituted a separate independent State, also under Turkish suzerainty. Russia had been grievously disappointed of its hope that the two new States

1879
—
Ætat. 37

should be combined into one. At the time of the Treaty
Eastern Roumelia was in Russian occupation, and in the spring
of 1879 Russia, reluctant to abandon her hold, seemed bent on
making a fresh arrangement with Turkey, outside the Treaty,
for a joint occupation. The Prince judged that such a plan
gave Russia an advantage to which she was not entitled :

"I am indeed glad to hear," he wrote to Lord Beaconsfield
on the 13th April 1879, "that you are more sanguine about the
Roumelian difficulty, but I cannot help hoping that you will not
agree to a joint occupation. It would end in no satisfactory
results, and might lead to most serious difficulties and entanglements."

Lord Beaconsfield replied next day :

There is to be no joint occupation of Eastern Roumelia, to
my great relief. . . . I think if we be firm and stick to the
Treaty of Berlin we shall pull through.

The constitution of the new State of Bulgaria involved further
critical issues. Although it was to be nominally placed under
Turkish suzerainty, Russia was resolved on bringing it under
her substantive control. The choice of the first ruler awoke
some bitter jealousies. Nominally the election lay in the hands
of an assembly of notables at Tirnovo, the ancient capital city of
Bulgaria. Three candidates were proposed, viz. Prince Waldemar
of Denmark, the Princess of Wales's youngest brother ; and two
German princes, Prince von Reuss and Prince Alexander von
Battenberg. The candidate of Tsar Alexander II. was Prince
Alexander, who obtained a majority of votes and was duly
elected on the 29th May 1879. Russia's choice, a youth of
twenty-two of handsome appearance and attractive bearing, was
a nephew of the Tsaritza, and one of the Hesse circle which she
and her husband were in the habit of joining at Darmstadt. As
the youngest son of the Tsaritza's brother, Prince Alexander of
Hesse (by a morganatic marriage with a Polish countess), he
was regarded by the Tsar as a useful Russian pawn.

But the Tsar and his advisers would seem to have overlooked
Prince Alexander's own character as well as the ties which linked
him to the English royal family. Prince Louis of Hesse-
Darmstadt, Queen Victoria's son-in-law, was his first cousin, and
both the Queen and the Prince of Wales had already shown a
strong interest in the Battenberg family. Prince Alexander's

eldest brother, Prince Louis of Battenberg, had joined in boyhood the British navy, and was on the road to high rank in the service. The Prince of Wales's strong liking for Prince Louis, who had been his companion during the Indian tour, and the good opinion which he formed of his professional abilities, excited his interest in the fortunes of Prince Louis's two younger brothers, Prince Alexander and Prince Henry. The association of the Prince with the Battenberg brothers was soon strengthened by the marriages of two of them with his kinswomen. Prince Louis of Battenberg married in 1884 the Prince's niece, Princess Victoria of Hesse, the late Princess Alice's daughter, while next year Prince Henry of Battenberg married the Prince of Wales's youngest sister, Princess Beatrice.

1879
—
Ætat. 37

In May 1879 the Prince met Prince Alexander in Paris, where he awaited the news of his election to the Bulgarian throne by the notables of Tirnovo. In June Prince Alexander accepted an invitation from Queen Victoria to Balmoral, before proceeding to his Balkan principality. At Balmoral the Queen was most cordial in her greetings, bestowing on her guest the Order of the Bath, and bidding him consider himself "one of the family." The Prince of Wales improved the occasion by taking the youth, on his passage through England, under his wing. Thus the Prince thought that he might qualify that control which the Tsar looked forward to exerting over the young man in his new capacity. The Prince urged Lord Beaconsfield and Lord Salisbury to entertain Prince Alexander in London on his leaving Scotland. The youth, the Prince pointed out, was in an extremely difficult position, and it would be of service to him for the British government to show him attention. Both the Prime Minister and the Foreign Secretary took the Prince of Wales's hint. Prince Alexander was the recipient in London of abundant hospitality. Lord Beaconsfield invited him to Downing Street, while Lord Salisbury, the Foreign Secretary, at twenty-four hours' notice, summoned the whole diplomatic body in London to meet him at dinner in Arlington Street. Count Münster, the German Ambassador, was another host. When the Prince of Wales welcomed Prince Alexander to Marlborough House he impressively warned his guest against the perils of Russian domination, and reminded him of his obligation to respect the suzerainty of the Sultan in conformity with the

1879
Ætat. 37

Treaty of Berlin. From all his influential English hosts the young man received the counsel to remember that he was a vassal of the Sultan and no puppet of the Tsar.

The Russian Ambassador in London, Count Schouvaloff, was surprised and embarrassed by the warmth of the young man's reception, which he attributed to the maleficence of the Prince of Wales. One example of the Prince's influence over his young guest Count Schouvaloff cited in his letters to the Russian Chancellor with especial resentment. It was necessary for the young Prince, by way of prelude to his installation at Tirnovo, to pay formal homage at Constantinople to his suzerain, the Sultan. Before Prince Alexander arrived in England the Russian government had promised to convey him in a Russian man-of-war from Brindisi to the Turkish capital. This offer Count Schouvaloff understood to have been accepted. While in London, the young man received from the King of Italy a second offer of an Italian ship of war to carry him from Brindisi. Prince Alexander consulted the Prince of Wales, who advised him to travel by the Italian ship. Count Schouvaloff professed himself baffled. It was only after he had exerted all his power of persuasion that the youth consented to decline the Italian offer, and to respect his previous acceptance of the Russian ship.[1]

1883
Ætat. 41

Prince Alexander had no sooner settled in his new dominions than he showed a resolve to better the instruction which the Prince and English statesmen had given him. He identified himself with his subjects' nationalist aspirations to complete independence, alike of Turkey and Russia. The Prince continued to warn him that, however resolute he might be in resisting Russian dictation, he was bound to acknowledge the suzerainty of the Porte. In the summer of 1883 Alexander wrote to the Prince claiming the right to confer a decoration of his own creation "on an English Prince," to whom he wished to offer a mark of his esteem. The Prince consulted Lord Granville, who emphatically declared that Prince Alexander's suzerain, the Sultan of Turkey, could alone bestow decorations. The Prince acquiesced in the Foreign Secretary's view, which he pressed on his protégé in plain language.

The Prince remained steadfast in his objections to Russia's endeavour to treat the young Alexander as a catspaw in her

[1] Russian Archives, Chesham House.

Balkan game, and he fully approved the defiant attitude which
the Bulgarian ruler assumed to the Tsar Alexander III., son and
successor of Tsar Alexander II., to whom he owed his throne.
When the Prince met his sister, the Crown Princess of Prussia,
and her husband in the summer of 1884 he spoke to them with
much feeling of the Bulgarian ruler's peril from the estranged
Tsar. But it was not until the early autumn of 1886 that the
Tsar's long quarrel with Prince Alexander came to a head.
Then the ruler of Bulgaria was kidnapped by Russian officers,
and was soon afterwards forced to abdicate at the point of the
pistol. The Prince and his kinsfolk were roused to anger by
the indignities to which their friend was subjected. Their
strong feeling found expression in Queen Victoria's passionate message of sympathy with the victim of Russia's wrath:
"My indignation against your barbaric, Asiatic, tyrannical
cousin is so great that I cannot trust myself to write about it." [1]
But both the Queen and the Prince were in no position to retrieve
the situation. The English government reached the conclusion
that England had no direct interest in Prince Alexander's
wrongs, and they went unredressed.

The Prince's sympathy with the dethroned ruler was undiminished, and, to his discomposure and regret, storm and
stress pursued his protégé for some years longer. A promise of
an improvement in the young man's position in life only involved
him in further ignominy. With the approval of the Prince's
sister, the Crown Princess of Germany, Prince Alexander soon
engaged himself to her second daughter, Princess Victoria.
Thereby he caused a domestic and political crisis in Berlin, which
seriously involved the royal family of England. Prince Bismarck
professed to regard the engagement as a nefarious plot on the
part of the Crown Princess and her English kinsfolk to embroil
Germany with Prince Alexander's enemy, the Tsar. The young
lady's brother, Prince William, furiously denounced the proposed
mésalliance. The unedifying controversy reached its full height
after the accession to the throne of the Princess's father, the
Emperor Frederick, in March 1888. The mother still championed
Prince Alexander's suit for her daughter's hand. But Queen

1886
Ætat. 44

1888
Ætat. 46

---

[1] E. C. Corti, *Alexander von Battenberg, Sein Kampf mit den Zaren und
Bismarck* (Vienna, 1920), p. 267, where Queen Victoria's whole letter is given
in a facsimile reproduction.

Victoria and the Prince of Wales acknowledged the hopelessness of the young couple's situation, and the Prince welcomed the visit of Queen Victoria to Berlin, in April 1888, in order to employ her domestic influence in bringing the ill-fated engagement to an end. Queen Victoria's successful intervention dismissed the young Prince from the public stage of affairs. The Prince of Wales's association with Alexander of Battenberg's brief and chequered career ended with the young man's surrender of his claim to the hand of the Prince's German niece.[1]

V

Scarcely had the Prince reached home from Paris in March 1881, after notable intercourse with Gambetta, when he and the world were startled on the 13th of the month by the news that Tsar Alexander II. had that day been assassinated at St. Petersburg. The Tsar had been blown to pieces by a bomb flung at him in the open street while returning to the Winter Palace from a military review. The Prince learnt of the crime with natural horror and with profound pity for the fate of one from whom he was in matters of current politics widely divided. He had long known of the Tsar's danger. It was common knowledge that the Nihilists had destined him for a violent death, and the Prince's sympathies with the Tsar in his personal peril went hand-in-hand with his rooted mistrust of the Russian monarch's external and internal policy. The Prince hoped against hope for some liberal reform of the Tsarist autocracy which might qualify the rancours of the Tsar's domestic enemies. When Lord Beaconsfield informed the Prince (April 15, 1879) of an attempt to assassinate the Tsar the day before, the Prince wrote despairingly of "the deplorable state of things now extant in Russia." Hardly a year later, on the 17th February 1880, the Prince learned with consternation of an explosion in the Winter Palace, seriously damaging the room in which the Imperial family were accustomed to dine, and only missing the intended victims through an accidental postponement of the royal dinner hour. On that occasion the Prince of Wales proved his sympathy by inviting the Queen's permission to attend a Te Deum service in

[1] The dismissed suitor subsequently married an opera singer, and survived his marriage barely four years, dying at Graz on 17th February 1893, at the age of thirty-six.

the Russian Church in Welbeck Street, London. The Queen took the view that "it is never done here," in spite of the wish of the Duke of Edinburgh, the Tsar's son-in-law, for his brother's companionship. But the Queen raised no objection to the presence of both the Prince and Princess at a funeral ceremony in Welbeck Street on the day after the assassination. The Prince held a taper during the celebration of Mass.

The Prince promptly reached the conclusion that he ought personally to represent the Queen at the murdered Tsar's obsequies in St. Petersburg. His wife was sister of the new Tsaritza, and she was in no doubt as to her obligation to accompany her husband. "I feel firmly convinced that we *ought* to go to St. Petersburg," the Prince wrote to Lord Granville on the 16th. "Every one I have spoken to expects that I am going." The Duke of Edinburgh left London as soon as he heard of the tragedy, and, reaching St. Petersburg in three days, sent home word that the new Tsar and Tsaritza would appreciate the Prince and Princess's presence. From Berlin came the news that the Crown Prince of Prussia was going. Lord Dufferin, the English Ambassador in St. Petersburg, when his advice was invited, emphatically favoured the Prince's attendance at the funeral. The Queen hesitated, and then yielded. She laid stress on the risk, and in announcing to Lord Dufferin her reluctant assent, warned him that she would hold him responsible for any untoward incident.[1]

Lord Granville, the Foreign Secretary, strongly approved of the decision. He believed that despite the recent political friction between the two countries, the Prince might turn the tragic occasion to diplomatic account. The Liberal Government was seeking to relax the current political tension, and the Prince's good nature might, Lord Granville suggested, well be enlisted at such a juncture in forwarding the government's pacific purpose. Writing to the Prince on 21st March 1881, when the Prince was leaving London, Granville wrote:

I have no doubt that Y.R.H.'s visit will be productive of good. There can be no question that a good understanding and friendly relations between this country and Russia may be of immense advantage to both, while the hostility which is recommended by many good friends abroad can only be the cause

1881

Ætat. 39

---

[1] Sir Alfred Lyall's *Life of Lord Dufferin*.

of great evil. . . . The best course appears to be, to be perfectly frank, not to make undue concessions, but to avoid unnecessary complaints and petty acts of ill will.

The Prince, as his mother's representative, was desirous of giving his mission all possible dignity. He suggested to the Foreign Secretary that he should take with him the insignia of the Garter and invest the new Tsar with them after the funeral. Lord Granville, in spite of his strong approval of the Prince's visit, objected on the double ground of lack of precedent and of the ceremonial expenses. But the Prince questioned both arguments and gained the Queen's support. On the eve of his departure, the Prince wrote to Lord Granville :

"It would be a gracious act on the part of the Queen to give the son the first order in the world which the father and grandfather had. Precedents are all very well in their way, but there are surely occasions when they may be deviated from. I hope, therefore, that I may consider the matter as settled, and I will announce it to the Emperor on my arrival that the Queen intends conferring the Garter.—This instant (4.30) I receive a letter from the Queen that she announces my giving the Garter to the Emperor in a letter I take to St. Petersburg."
The Prince added by way of postscript "The Investiture will virtually be of a private nature, and it will *save* you a mission." [1]

The Prince and Princess set out from London on 21st March.[2] At Berlin they were met at the railway station by the Crown Princess, with her son William and her daughter Charlotte. St. Petersburg was reached on the 25th, and the party were lodged in the Anitchkoff Palace. The atmosphere was thick with gloom ;

[1] The question of expense was settled by a parliamentary grant of £2000 which was adopted by the House of Commons on the motion of Lord Frederick Cavendish, Financial Secretary to the Treasury. Sir Charles Dilke, Under-Secretary for Foreign Affairs, declined, in spite of his intimacy with the Prince, to father the resolution, on the ground of his objection, on principle, to all royal grants. The Prince took no exception to Sir Charles's inaction. In the event, the grant of £2000 was exceeded by £1500, and Lord Granville peremptorily refused a request for payment of the deficit out of public funds. The Prince vainly pointed out that the Crown Prince spent far more during four days in St. Petersburg than he spent in ten.

[2] They were accompanied by Lord Suffield, Sir Dighton Probyn, Col. Christopher Teesdale, Col. Stanley Clarke, and Miss Charlotte Knollys. The Prince deemed superfluous the Queen's proposal to add Lord Kenmare, the Lord Chamberlain, and he was left behind. Sir John Cowell, Master of the Queen's Household, however, joined the party and sent the Queen very full accounts of the Prince's experiences.

1881
Ætat. 39

suspicion was everywhere; the police force was reported to be honeycombed with conspirators, but all possible precautions were taken for the visitors' safety by Count Loris Melikoff, Minister of the Interior, in whom was vested supreme executive power to deal with the revolutionary agitation. Count Loris assured the Prince and Princess that, provided they did not go abroad in the Tsar's company, the Nihilists would do them no harm. The Prince and Princess attended the tedious funeral ceremonies under effective protection, and the Prince's companion, Sir Dighton Probyn, who was constantly sending wires to the Queen, was able to relieve her of anxiety.

After the obsequies were completed, the new Tsar and Tsaritza moved (on March 28) from the Winter Palace to the Anitchkoff Palace to enjoy the companionship of the Prince and Princess. The Duchess of Edinburgh, writing to the Queen on 18/30th March, said the Tsar and his wife felt much more at home at the Anitchkoff Palace, where "Bertie and Alex live with them." Two days later (March 20/April 1) the Tsar wrote to the Queen: "The presence [of the Prince and Princess] has been a great consolation for me and the Empress in our affliction." But the Tsar, who was pursued incessantly by Nihilist threats, lived the life of a prisoner whether at the Winter or the Anitchkoff Palace, and the Prince was dismayed by the narrow dimensions of the backyard of the latter residence, in which alone it was deemed safe for the new ruler to take exercise. The area would, the Prince declared, be unworthy of a London slum.

In such depressing conditions, within the heavily guarded palace, the Prince invested the Tsar with the Order of the Garter (March 28). Lord Dufferin was there, together with three princes besides the Prince of Wales, who already belonged to the Order: the Crown Prince of Denmark, the Duke of Hesse-Darmstadt, and the Duke of Edinburgh. The Prince of Wales's happily worded speech brought a ray of light into the dismal scene. "Nothing," wrote Dufferin to the Queen, "could have been in better taste, or more gracefully delivered" (March 31).

The St. Petersburg visit of the Prince and of his brother, the Duke of Edinburgh, ended on 31st March, the Princess staying on with her sister, the new Tsaritza, for another week. The train in which the brothers travelled to the frontier was guarded with exceptional rigour, and it was with great relief that Lord

Dufferin, on learning that the journey was safely completed,
sent the Queen his congratulations "on the fortunate way in
which the Prince of Wales's visit to this country has passed off."
"Now," the Ambassador added, "that the Prince is safe out of
the country, Lord Dufferin thinks it is a good thing that he should
have come. . . . H.R.H. has shown all Europe how ready he
had been to do a kindness to a near relative in spite of any
personal risk to himself."

VI

The Prince made some study in Russia of the internal situation into which the tragedy of the Tsar's death had introduced
new complications. He approached the intricate problem from
a Liberal point of view, and caught eagerly at some rather
elusive signs of a coming qualification of the Tsarist autocracy.
The late Tsar, shortly before his death, had acknowledged
reluctantly the need of reforming his mode of rule. His younger
son, the Grand Duke Constantine, had urged on him with some
success the need of concession to some of the revolutionary
demands. The last ministry of the murdered Tsar had adopted
a moderate Liberal policy. The Grand Duke filled in it the office
of Minister of Marine, but the guiding spirit was Count Loris
Melikoff, who had taken the office of Minister of the Interior on
an express understanding that a rigorous attitude towards the
Nihilists should be tempered by reforms tending towards constitutional government. On the morning of the day of the
Tsar's assassination he had signed a decree which his ministers
had drafted, granting a limited scheme of popular institutions.

The Prince, while in St. Petersburg, had the advantage of
confidential conversations with Count Loris Melikoff, and he was
confirmed by the Count in the view that the Russian monarchy
could hardly survive a blank refusal of constitutional reform.
He learnt that there was working against the Liberal Ministry a
Court coterie whose veteran faith in tyranny was ominously
intensified by the late Tsar's murder, and that these evil counsellors were urging on the new Tsar a blind policy of vengeance.
The new Tsar, while extending to the Prince every kindly
courtesy in the scene of sorrow, maintained in conversation with
him an impenetrable reserve in regard to the political situation.
The Prince cherished on slender grounds a sanguine hope that

Tsar Alexander III. was better disposed politically towards England than his late father had been, and he formed rather too hastily the impression that the new monarch would carry out the reforms to which the Liberal Ministry, in office at his accession, was committed. The Prince clung to such intuitions in spite of the lack of any positive information about the new Tsar's intentions. He tentatively accepted the vague opinion of his brother, the Duke of Edinburgh, that "if the villains would only give him time," the Tsar would remedy the faults of the old régime, "as circumstances permit." His wish was father to the thought when he wrote to Mr. Gladstone on his return to London (April 9):

Sad as our visit to St. Petersburg was, I was very glad that we went, and I think it was much appreciated on all sides, but I regret to say that we found everything in a most unsatisfactory state. The present Emperor—if his life is spared—is most anxious to be a liberal sovereign in every sense of the word, but the difficulty he finds is in obtaining those counsellors in whom he can trust.

Lord Dufferin showed a better insight in questioning whether the new Tsar had the energy or the character to take effective steps in any direction, whether with or without "good counsellors." [1]

In the months that followed, despairing letters, which enlightened observers of affairs in Russia addressed to the Prince, disillusioned him as to the Tsar's policy—both domestic and foreign. Count Loris Melikoff was soon dismissed from office, along with Grand Duke Constantine and other Liberal colleagues.

[1] Lord Dufferin, writing to Lord Granville on 24th March, described the new Emperor thus: "He is certainly neither clever nor intellectual, nor, like the late Emperor, a considerable man of business. But every one admits him to be frank, honest, and sensible. He is not a soldier, nor likely to be possessed by excessive military predilections beyond those imposed on him by his position. Neither is he much of a sportsman. In fact he is a very stay-at-home kind of person, devoted to his wife and children, fond of music, and has hitherto surrounded himself by a small circle of very insignificant persons. The only man of any eminence amongst his intimates is the newly-appointed Minister of Religion, M. Pobedonostseff, his former tutor." As events turned out, Pobedonostseff proved a reactionary of a very benighted kind, and his fanatical faith in autocracy of the most obsolete pattern, which, under his influence, Tsar Alexander III. assimilated, materially contributed to the ultimate overthrow of Tsardom. See *K. P. Pobedonostev and his Correspondents: Letters and Memoranda*, with preface by M. N. Pokrovsky, 2 vols. (Moscow: Government Publishing House); cf. *The Times Literary Supplement*, August 21, 1924.

The Tsar showed no greater disposition than his father to conciliate England. His personal predilections were for a firm
understanding with Germany, and at the outset he made advances
in that direction with the hope of embarrassing England. But
before he came to the throne Russian statesmen had favoured a
rapprochement with France to which his advisers lost little time
after his accession in giving effect. The Franco-Russian alliance
was not wholly to the Tsar's liking, and for some years its accomplishment remained a secret. In the meantime the Tsar continued his professions of goodwill for Germany, and showed keen
anxiety to keep England politically at arm's length. Despite
his personal abhorrence of war he readily encouraged Pan-Slavist
designs, alike on the Balkans and on India's north-west frontier.
At home the situation was signally unpromising. The Tsar fell
completely under the baleful influence of his former tutor,
M. Pobedonostseff, a convinced reactionary. According to one of
the Prince's Russian correspondents early in the new reign, the
Tsar grew impatient with all moderate counsels. He refused a
hearing to the plea that corruption and waste were poisoning
the autocratic bureaucracy. The suggestion of a Russian
Parliament with ministerial responsibility he dismissed as a
democratic chimera. When he was informed that the revolutionary party threatened to stir up the peasantry against the
nobles as well as against himself, he heatedly deprecated any
endeavour to allay the discontent.[1]

VII

In spite of the Prince's natural antipathy to the principles of
autocracy which Alexander III. followed with increasing blind-
ness, the Prince came before long to recognise, in the interests

---

[1] Feeling in English revolutionary circles ran high against the Tsar early
in the new reign. Threatening letters reached both the Queen and the Prince
of Wales in the course of April from self-styled friends of the Russian revolution, who wrongly believed both mother and son to sympathise with Russian
autocracy. No action was taken against the writers, although a German
socialist, Johann Most, editor of *Die Freiheit*, a paper published in London,
was convicted of a seditious libel on the late Tsar on 26th April, and was
sentenced to six months' hard labour. When the Russian Government rather
nervously asked whether the English Government would extradite Russian
refugees who were suspected of complicity in the recent regicide, the English
Government, after some hesitation, declined.

of his own country, the need of relaxing the long-continued
tension in Anglo-Russian relations. But the international
strain was destined to come near breaking-point before the
possibility of any improvement came within his vision. The
darkness which preceded any ray of light in the Anglo-Russian
atmosphere found the Prince in his sternest mood of resistance
to whatever savoured of Russian aggression.

The steady advances of Russia into Central Asia had always
excited the Prince's strong suspicion. Regarding India as
Russia's objective, he was long a careful student of up-to-date
maps of Central Asia.[1] During 1883 the Russians were moving
in a critical direction, and in February 1884 General Komaroff,
at the head of a Russian expedition, captured the fortress of
Merv in Turkestan. Mr. Gladstone's apparent indifference to
the incident was highly uncongenial to the Prince. A few months
later he met the expatriated Russian minister, Count Loris
Melikoff, at Wiesbaden, and made no concealment of his
annoyance at this display of Russia's Central Asian activities.[2]

The Prince was justified in this forecast of more threatening action on Russia's part. In the spring of 1884 General
Komaroff's force advanced southwards from Merv towards
the frontier of Afghanistan. The district of the Penjdeh
was reached in February 1885, although the Russians had
previously intimated to the English government that they had
no intention of moving in that direction. The breach of faith
exasperated the Prince, and he welcomed Mr. Gladstone's
announcement that the Prime Minister shared his resentment.
The British government promptly made it plain that if Russia
persisted in ignoring her engagements in regard to Penjdeh,
England was prepared to apply force. The government of India
took the politic step of indicating its interest in the fortunes of
Afghanistan by sending to the Amir an invitation, which he
accepted, to visit India at the end of March.

Writing, on 13th March 1885, to Lord Wolseley, then in the
Sudan, of General Komaroff's movements, the Prince said:

It is "touch and go" if we may not be in open hostility
with Russia regarding the Afghan frontier. The Government

[Margin: 1882 Ætat. 40]

[Margin: 1885 Ætat. 43]

---

[1] On the 21st March 1882 he asked Sir Charles Dilke to bring him a recent
map of the country and to explain the position of the Russians there (Gwynn
and Tuckwell, *Life of Sir Charles Dilke*, i. 427).

[2] A. Koni, *Reminiscences* (in Russian), iii. Pt. I. p. 10.

are very firm, and we cannot afford to be bullied by Russia, as our whole existence in India depends upon our resisting her aggression at a moment also when she knows we are so seriously occupied in Egypt.

Meanwhile the Prince's precocious nephew, Prince William of Prussia, was communicating by letter to the Tsar wild slanders of his uncle, whereby he foolishly thought to widen beyond cure the breach between Russia and England.[1] On the same day that the Prince was writing to Lord Wolseley, Prince William of Prussia, in continuance of his earlier ill-natured communications, sent to the Tsar intelligence from England which was designed to inflame discord :

I have given Dolgorouki [Russian Ambassador in Berlin] a few interesting little notes regarding the number of Indian and English regiments which they [the English] are preparing to concentrate at Rawul-Pindi for the Amir to pass in review on the 24th of this month. . . . The language and the cartoon on Russia in the latest *Punch* are insolent in the last degree ! All these things must be put together. They all form part of a whole. "Reader please note."

In Central Asia the worst quickly followed. On the 30th March the Russians violently dispersed, near Penjdeh, an Afghan army which was seeking to bar their progress. The full facts of the encounter only became known in England on the 14th April, and war between the two countries seemed inevitable. The Prince made no secret of his warlike convictions. M. de Staal, who had newly come to London as Russian Ambassador, and whose courteous bearing was soon to prove very attractive to the Prince, sought to calm English apprehension, but the Prince expressed to Lord Granville (April 18) the hope "that nobody will be taken in by Russia's promises and protestations." On 21st April the Prince was reassured by Mr. Gladstone's unexpected declaration in the House of Commons that England meant to resist by force Russian aggression on Afghanistan, and that the government proposed to ask the House on the 27th for a vote of £11,000,000 for the purpose. But the government failed to maintain their resolute tone. An appeal was made to diplomacy to settle the quarrel. The Prince questioned whether the situation permitted a peaceful settlement. "The Prince is very bellicose,"

[1] See pp. 485–6 *supra*.

wrote Count Münster from London to Count Herbert Bismarck 1885
in Berlin (May 1, 1885).[1] Three days later Prince William of Ætat. 43
Prussia, while maleficently forwarding to the Tsar his congratulations on General Komaroff's victory of Penjdeh, reported
Berlin gossip to the effect that both Queen Victoria and the
Prince were working against Mr. Gladstone's effort for a peaceful
accommodation.[2]

The governments of England and Russia were meanwhile
coming to terms. Both agreed to submit the dispute to the
arbitration of a neutral sovereign, and the Prince of Wales
strongly supported the choice of the King of Denmark—if any
arbitrator were to be chosen.[3] A settlement was, however,
reached without external aid. A commission of English and
Russian officers met on the scene of the trouble and agreed to
a delimitation of the Afghan boundary. The result went far to
justify the Prince's fear that England had failed to maintain her
ground. Penjdeh remained in Russian hands, and the Prince
saw with regret the British government acquiesce in an agreement whereby Russia gained rather than lost through her bold
menace of Afghan independence. He was confirmed in his
misgivings by a letter (dated April 25) from his frequent correspondent at Melbourne, Sir Henry Loch, Governor of Victoria,
who wrote that the people of Australia were convinced of the
hostile intentions of Russia, and that they expected a Russian
squadron before long to bombard Melbourne and Sydney. The
Tsar's quarrel with the Prince's young friend, Alexander of
Bulgaria, was through this period nearing its acutest stage, and
the Prince's feeling against the Tsar was thereby maintained at
full heat.

The end of the Prince's conflict with the Tsar seemed, in
1886, to be remote, but, despite the omens, a different spirit
was about to illumine the scene. The Prince's view of Anglo-
Russian relations was to undergo, in the course of 1887, a
pacific change, which memories of the Penjdeh dispute and of
Prince Alexander's wrongs failed to impede.

[1] *Die Grosse Politik*, iv. 120.
[2] A copy of General Komaroff's secret report of the action at Penjdeh was
forwarded to Prince William from St. Petersburg, and in acknowledging its
receipt the ill-natured young Prince repeated his warning that the war-fever
in England was as acute as ever (May 26).
[3] *Die Grosse Politik*, iv. 120–1.

CHAPTER XXVIII

HOME AFFAIRS—PERSONAL RELATIONS WITH POLITICAL LEADERS, 1880–1900

I

WITH much excitement the Prince watched the general election which Lord Beaconsfield suddenly invited in the spring of 1880— with results disastrous to himself. "It is impossible to foretell which side will win," wrote the Prince to Frere on the 24th March 1880; but at the end of the week the gain of numerous seats by the Liberal candidates foreshadowed the final result—a Liberal majority of 56 over Conservatives and Home Rulers combined.[1] Lord Beaconsfield acknowledged defeat before the next parliament assembled and tendered his resignation to the Queen on 18th April.

For the first time the Prince played behind the scenes an important part in the formation of a government. When Mr. Gladstone and Mr. Disraeli formed their ministries respectively in 1868 and 1874 the Prince was out of the country—in Denmark on the first occasion, and in Russia on the second. But he was now at home, and as an interested onlooker was to apply for the first of many times his maturing knowledge of public affairs and his growing intimacy with men in public life to the congenial task of tackling problems of Cabinet-making. Lord Beaconsfield was justified in describing him a year before as "one who has seen everything and knows everybody." In the political crisis which Lord Beaconsfield's fall occasioned, his range of outlook on men and things emboldened him to offer the Queen herself political

[1] The Liberals numbered 354, the Conservatives 236, and the Home Rulers 62.

counsel regarding the formation of her new government, and to make a variety of suggestions in less formidable quarters.

1880

Ætat. 38

The Queen regarded the overthrow of her favourite minister at the energetic call of his rival, Mr. Gladstone, as a personal calamity. The process of choosing a successor to Lord Beaconsfield provoked a delicate situation, to the easing of which the Prince devoted his tact and insight. He persuasively urged on his mother a view of her constitutional obligations which, however repugnant to her, was creditable to his judgement.

When the Liberal victory was assured and the Queen was faced with the duty of choosing a new Prime Minister, she wrote to Lord Beaconsfield on 9th April 1880: "Of course I shall not take any notice of Mr. Gladstone, who has done so much mischief. It is most essential that *that* should be known."[1] She justified the exclusion of Mr. Gladstone from her field of choice on the somewhat specious ground that he had nominally given up the leadership of the Liberal party soon after Lord Beaconsfield's accession to office. The Prince's friend, Lord Hartington, had then been chosen in his stead, and although Mr. Gladstone rapidly resumed those political activities to which the Queen rightly assigned Beaconsfield's defeat, he had not formally resumed the party leadership. The Queen resolved, therefore, to entrust Lord Hartington with the formation of a new ministry. If Lord Hartington failed her, she would fall back on Lord Granville, who was leader of the Liberal party in the House of Lords. In no event, she averred, would she invite Mr. Gladstone. The Prince soon learned of the Queen's resolve, and perceiving its impolicy bent himself to the embarrassing task of overcoming her objections to summoning Mr. Gladstone. Although he was as much out of sympathy as his mother with Mr. Gladstone's Turco-phobe and Russophil proclivities, his political dissent had failed to hamper his personal friendliness with the Liberal statesman.

With both Lord Hartington and Lord Granville, the Queen's alternative nominees, the Prince was also on terms of intimacy· From them he ascertained that neither would stand in Mr. Gladstone's light, and that in their view Mr. Gladstone was the only possible successor to Lord Beaconsfield. During three fateful days of mid-April (18th–21st), when the Queen was tenaciously resisting Mr. Gladstone's claim, the Prince was corre-

[1] Buckle, *Life of Disraeli*, vi. 528.

sponding with Lord Granville and was discussing in person with Lord Hartington the ways and means of breaking his mother's resistance.   In letters to Colonel Ponsonby, the Queen's private secretary, he sought assiduously to disabuse his mother's mind of her conception of Mr. Gladstone as of an ogre-like enemy who was incapable of either loyalty or courtesy.   To Lord Granville he wrote that the Queen was influenced by the Tory prejudices of her youngest son, Prince Leopold, who was constantly with her, and whose party zeal rendered "nugatory" his own broader counsels.

"The Prince of Wales feels sure," wrote Mr. Francis Knollys, his private secretary, to Lord Granville (April 1880) "that if the Queen would only look upon Mr. Gladstone as a friend instead of as the enemy of Her Majesty and the Royal Family, which Prince Leopold deliberately delights in persuading her he is, she will find him all she could wish."

Three long conversations with Lord Hartington in the privacy of the Turf Club, which the Prince reported to Colonel Ponsonby, convinced the Prince of the hopeless confusion in public affairs to which the Queen's obduracy might lead.   Lord Hartington, in the second interview of 20th April, proved "*more* anxious than ever" that the Queen should send for Mr. Gladstone to form a government instead of sending either for Lord Granville or himself.

"Both," the Prince of Wales wrote in what he called "a hurried scrawl," "are strongly of that opinion.   It would get over many difficulties, make the Queen most popular, and a stronger Government would be formed than the one Hartington would have to constitute, as the latter fears he could not form one that would last.   H. saw Mr. G. yesterday, and he told me that nothing could be nicer than the way the latter spoke of the Queen—how much he felt for her in the difficult position she was placed in, and having to part with her present Ministers, in whom she has so much confidence.   From what H. told me, Mr. G. will, I am sure, do all he can to meet the Queen's wishes and be conciliatory in every possible way. . . .   Depend upon it, it is a matter of the gravest import whom the Queen sends for to form a Government, and from what I hear I am strongly of the opinion that the Queen should send for Mr. Gladstone.   Far better that she should take the initiative than that it should be forced upon her."

On the evening of the 21st the Prince renewed the conversation with Lord Hartington at the Turf Club, and Lord Hartington declared with conviction that Mr. Gladstone must be sent for sooner or later, and the sooner the better. The Prince thereupon reiterated with added emphasis his appeal to the Queen to send for Gladstone without delay.

Under such pressure the Queen unwillingly retreated from her first position. Lord Hartington promptly refused her invitation to form a ministry (April 21), and she consented to discuss next day the situation with him and Lord Granville jointly. Yielding without much grace to their united representations, she followed the course which the Prince had recommended. Sending for Mr. Gladstone, she entrusted him with the formation of a new government (April 23), in which he assumed the double rôle of Prime Minister and Chancellor of the Exchequer.

II

Mr. Gladstone's second administration lasted for rather more than five years—until 8th June 1885. It was a period of strained relations between the sovereign and the Prime Minister. The Liberal leader was sincerely devoted to the monarchy and made many efforts to conciliate his royal mistress, but his manner continued to be antipathetic to her, his policy at home and abroad displeased her, and although she acknowledged the considerateness of the advice which he gave her regarding her family affairs, the gulf between them steadily widened. Meanwhile the Prince's personal relations with the new Prime Minister grew in cordiality, although in Mr. Gladstone's handling of foreign, of imperial, and ultimately of Irish questions the Prince usually found quite as much to condemn as did his mother. A shrewd friend and adviser of Mr. Gladstone, Lord Acton, advised him in 1881 to lose no opportunity of increasing his political hold on the Prince.[1] But Mr. Gladstone, while by no means undervaluing the Prince's political support and sympathy, made no deliberate endeavour to win them. He was content with the Prince's private friendship, and he always showed a readiness to serve the Prince's personal interests, whether in office or in opposition, as is amply attested by his part in the controversy over the

[1] Lord Acton's *Letters to Mary Gladstone*, p. 109.

1880
Ætat. 38

proposal to increase in 1889 the Prince's income from the State.[1]
The Prince on his part refrained from pressing his political
disagreements directly on the Liberal minister's notice. His
censure of Mr. Gladstone's policy he reserved for other eyes
and ears. Unlike Lord Beaconsfield, Mr. Gladstone left the
effective control of foreign affairs to the Foreign Minister,
Lord Granville, and it was to Lord Granville rather than
to the Prime Minister that the Prince addressed his eager
comments or criticisms on foreign policy which continued to
be his main political interest. His communications with Mr.
Gladstone chiefly dealt with recommendations of candidates for
honours and office, in which he displayed no lack of frankness or
of persistency. Nor was he on occasion diffident in urging on
Mr. Gladstone a rigid observance of etiquette in the relations of
the ministers with the Crown. When members of the cabinet
were "conspicuous by their absence" at a levée which the Prince
held in the Queen's name, he at once pointed out to the Prime
Minister with just a tinge of asperity "that the absence of the
greater part of Cabinet Ministers naturally excites comment"
(June 23, 1881). Mr. Gladstone submissively promised to bring
the matter to the attention of the next cabinet meeting.

The Prince welcomed the appointment to high places in the
new Liberal Government not only of Lord Granville but of other
members of his intimate social circle, in which the right wing of
the party was always amply represented. Lord Spencer became
President of the Council, and held the post until he resumed, in
critical conditions, the Irish Viceroyalty in 1882. Lord Hartington contented himself with the Indian Secretaryship. Another
social acquaintance, Sir Henry James, was made Attorney-
General. But the constitution of the ministry had, in his view,
some blemishes. He regretted the exclusion of Liberal friends
whom he thought to be deserving of at any rate minor office.
He recommended his lifelong ally, Lord Carrington, for the
Mastership of the Buckhounds, and was disappointed when
the Earl of Cork was chosen. He showed special anxiety
for the official recognition of another close friend, the Earl of
Rosebery, who had vigorously supported Mr. Gladstone throughout his strenuous fight in Midlothian, where the Earl's estates lay.
"He has," wrote the Prince, "every claim, especially after the

[1] See p. 602 infra.

Midlothian campaign."[1] But there was delay in the fulfilment
of the Prince's wish. In the summer of 1881 Lord Rosebery
received the modest post of Under-Secretary for Home Affairs
under Sir William Harcourt, but he found the work uncongenial
and resigned in June 1883. In the preceding March it was proposed to create a new post, that of Secretary of State for Scotland,
and the Prince urged Lord Rosebery's peculiar fitness for the
projected office.[2] Again, when Lord Spencer became Viceroy
of Ireland in May 1882, thereby vacating the Lord Presidency
of the Council, the Prince pressed Lord Rosebery's claim. By
way of alternative he suggested that if a more experienced
politician were needed for the Council, Lord Carlingford, the
Keeper of the Privy Seal, might receive the promotion, and Lord
Rosebery might take Lord Carlingford's place. The failure of
this scheme, like its predecessor, seemed to the Prince "very hard."
Not until Mr. Gladstone's ministry was nearing its close did Lord
Rosebery obtain any office of dignity. In February 1885 he at
length became Privy Seal and Chief Commissioner of Works with
a seat in the cabinet. The Prince had a belated satisfaction in
seeing one whose political abilities he justly rated higher than
those of any other of his close friends join the supreme Council
of the State.

It was not only friends of old standing among Mr. Gladstone's
colleagues with whom the Prince courted personal relations.
The new government included representatives of the Radical wing
of the party, and the society of these men, of whom he had
previously little personal knowledge, he cultivated with a broad-
minded prudence. The new Home Secretary was Sir William
Harcourt, whose wife was the daughter of the Prince's old guest at
Rome, J. L. Motley, the American diplomatist and historian. Sir
William's habits of invective on the political platform led the
Prince to dub him "Bombastes Furioso," yet he found his society
congenial and frequently exchanged hospitalities with him. But
a far profounder interest attached in the Prince's eyes to the two
acknowledged spokesmen in the government of Radical opinion
—the inseparable friends, Sir Charles Dilke and Mr. Joseph
Chamberlain. The Prince watched the first rise of both these

1881
Ætat. 39

[1] Gwynn and Tuckwell's *Life of Sir Charles Dilke*, i. 522.
[2] The plans for the new Secretaryship fell through at the time; they took
effect much later—on the 14th August 1885.

men to influence in the last House of Commons, and, despite their early leanings to republicanism, he had made them social advances.[1] In Mr. Gladstone's cabinet Mr. Chamberlain took his seat as President of the Board of Trade, while Dilke became, in the first instance, Under-Secretary for Foreign Affairs under Lord Granville, outside the cabinet. "I am glad to see that Dilke and Chamberlain accept office," the Prince wrote to Lord Granville (April 29, 1880).

In Dilke the Prince quickly found a congenial associate and an expert political instructor. Apart from his sturdy radicalism Dilke was a sedulous and enlightened student of foreign and imperial affairs, an expert on questions of military and naval defence, an intimate friend of M. Gambetta, a champion of the Anglo-French entente, and a believer in the future of Greece. The Prince soon discovered Dilke to be a storehouse of political information, which he was ready to place at the Prince's disposal. Throughout Dilke's official life, which just synchronised with the duration of Mr. Gladstone's second government, and was then unfortunately cut short by a personal scandal in which the statesman was involved, the Prince privately derived from him a fuller knowledge than he enjoyed before of the inner processes of government.

The five years' association of the Prince and Sir Charles, which was of educational advantage to the Prince, was creditable to both. There was no touch of the courtier about Sir Charles, and the Prince expected in their intercourse no dissembling of his friend's democratic sentiment. He tolerated Sir Charles's staunch opposition to grants of public money to members of the royal family. Dilke was somewhat cynical and cautious in his estimates of men, and he rather crudely characterised the Prince as "a strong Conservative and a still stronger Jingo, really agreeing with the Queen's politics," but he admitted that he found him always receptive to ideas which qualified what were, from Dilke's point of view, his untutored enthusiasms. "It is worth talking seriously to the Prince," wrote Dilke. "One seems to make no impression at the time . . . but he does listen all the same, and afterwards, when he is talking to somebody else, brings out everything that you have said." Contrasting the Queen with her son, Dilke credited the Prince with

[1] See p. 333 *supra*.

more sense and more usage of the modern world than his mother, whose long retirement has cut her off from that world, but less real brain power. He is very sharp in a way, the Queen not sharp at all, but she carries heavy metal, for her obstinacy constitutes power of a kind.[1]

Mr. Gladstone's government underwent reconstruction at the end of 1882 on the occasion of his resignation of the office of Chancellor of the Exchequer, which he had hitherto held with that of Prime Minister. Thereupon the Prince engaged with infinite zest in confidential negotiations with a view to Dilke's promotion to the cabinet. Dilke's services as Under-Secretary for Foreign Affairs justified such a reward, but the Queen, who took exception to Dilke's part in the republican agitation and his censure of royal grants, raised difficulties. She vetoed the first suggestion that he should take the Chancellorship of the Duchy of Lancester, which Mr. John Bright had vacated in July; the Duchy, she pointed out, was a "personal" office, and should be filled by a "moderate" politician. In November 1882 the Prince invited Sir Charles Dilke and his ally Mr. Chamberlain to Sandringham to discuss the situation, and for the best part of the succeeding month he busied himself with plans for effecting his purpose without offence to the Queen. He deprecated Mr. Chamberlain's threat of resignation if the Queen proved obdurate. It was essential that Dilke should receive a place which required no personal intercourse with the sovereign. Mr. Chamberlain, whom the Queen regarded with tolerance, was reluctant to fall in with the Prince's proposal that he should himself take the Duchy and leave to Dilke his office at the Board of Trade. The Prince, who was convinced of the exceptional versatility of his Radical friend, suggested that his sound views on service questions might find scope at the Admiralty. But Lord Northbrook, the First Lord, showed no readiness to retire. A general shuffling of other places in the cabinet, with which the Prince was unconcerned, finally landed Dilke in the Presidency of the Local Government Board. The post hardly seemed to the Prince worthy of his abilities, and he expressed a fear that Sir Charles was exchanging congenial for uncongenial work. In spite of the disappointing result, the Prince plumed himself on helping to bring Dilke into the cabinet.

1882

Ætat. 40

---

[1] Gwynn and Tuckwell's *Life of Sir Charles Dilke*, i. 500–1.

III

1884
Ætat. 42

The Prince found little satisfaction in the attempts of Mr. Gladstone and his ministry to solve the external problems which confronted them—the Transvaal, Egypt, the Sudan, continued ferment in the Balkans, Russia's advance in Central Asia[1]—nor did he withhold his sympathy from the Duke of Cambridge in his protest against the Army reforms which the Secretary for War, Mr. Childers, initiated in the early days of the administration.[2] The reforms of Indian administration in native interests which were carried out by the Liberal Viceroy, Lord Ripon, were scarcely congenial to the Prince ; but his friend, Lord Hartington, Secretary for India until 1882, whose judgement he respected, did what he could when they met privately to temper his suspicions.[3] But the government's chief domestic measure—the bill to extend the franchise in the counties which provoked, during the autumn of 1884, a struggle between the House of Commons and the House of Lords—the Prince viewed with a certain detachment. Mr. Gladstone's Franchise Bill was carried by a substantial majority in the House of Commons on the 27th June 1884, and was rejected by the House of Lords on the 9th July. The Conservative opposition in both Houses took the ground that a redistribution of seats was essential to any equitable enlargement of the electorate. Mr. Gladstone defiantly announced that his electoral Bill would be reintroduced into the House of Commons in an autumn session, and during the vacation, in speeches through the country, he and his Liberal colleagues threatened the House of Lords with a drastic reconstruction if it remained obdurate. The Prince did not lack sympathy with an extension of the franchise, but he shared Queen Victoria's dread of popular agitation against the House of Lords, which he regarded as a corner-stone of the Constitution. Earnestly did he share the Queen's hope of accommodation between the two parties and the two Houses, and he cautiously refrained from any word which might embitter the strife.[4] When

---

[1] See p. 509 *supra*.   [2] See pp. 555 *sq.*, *infra*.

[3] The Prince habitually invited at the time conversation with Lord Hartington on Indian topics, and was on some points quite ready to accept his guidance. On 9th September 1881 the Prince wrote to the Queen's secretary: "I had some talk yesterday with Hartington at Croxteth (Lord Sefton's) about the proposed changes in the Indian Army—he says that the matter will have to be looked into seriously soon, as Lord Ripon is strongly urging it."

[4] Canon Malcolm MacColl, an ardent political supporter of Mr. Gladstone,

the autumn session of Parliament opened in October, he and his
mother were relieved to learn that a compromise was in sight.
The Lords agreed to accept the Franchise Bill on the understanding that before they read it a third time Mr. Gladstone
should introduce a Redistribution Bill on acceptable lines into
the House of Commons. This programme was fulfilled. The
Redistribution Bill was read for the second time in the Commons
on the 4th December, and the next day the Lords finally passed
the Franchise Bill. The crisis thus ended, to the Prince's satisfaction. Writing to Lord Wolseley on 5th December 1884, he
gave free and easy vent to his feeling :

Parliament is up and we shall be able to go to our homes and
digest our Christmas dinners in peace and comfort. It is a great
blessing that the political crisis has been so satisfactorily settled,
as agitation on a question like the extension of the franchise and
against the House of Lords is much to be deplored.

IV

Mr. Gladstone's colleagues were well aware of the Prince's
profound political differences with their chief, but they were fully
conscious of the mutual regard which continued to inspire the
two men's personal relations. Consequently, while the franchise
question was in process of settlement, they sought, somewhat
paradoxically, to enlist the Prince's services in an endeavour to
induce the Queen to bestow an exceptional mark of honour on the
veteran Liberal statesman. There was an expectation that as
soon as he should succeed in carrying the Franchise Bill into law
the Prime Minister would, in view of his advanced age of seventy-
seven, withdraw from public life, and it was the wish of his friends
that the Queen should dignify his withdrawal in an unusual way
—by conferring on him the high decoration of the Knighthood of
the Garter. The Queen was known to be disinclined at the time
to show Mr. Gladstone any special attention. She had, with a
view to lightening his labours, offered him a peerage in the spring
of 1883 when he was temporarily disabled by illness, but he had

---

although a friend of Lord Salisbury, met the Prince at luncheon on 4th October
1884 at Aboyne Castle, Aberdeenshire, the seat of the Marquis of Huntly,
and wrote to Mr. Gladstone next day that the Prince "dropped a few cautious
observations which seemed to show that he disapproved of the action of the
Lords" (G. W. E. Russell's *Life of MacColl*, p. 101). Canon MacColl's words
attest the Prince's extreme care in avoiding any suspicion of partisanship.

1884
Ætat. 42

emphatically refused to entertain the proposal. The Queen was averse from courting a second rebuff of the kind. An offer of the Garter seemed to those who proposed it to raise, however, a different issue. Yet it was no easy task to bring, with any prospect of success, the novel suggestion to the Queen's notice.

Lord Granville appealed to the Prince's generosity to make the attempt. The Prince realised the difficulties in the road, but he amiably promised to face them. He told Lord Granville in September 1884 that he could not venture on sounding the Queen until he met her at Balmoral, where, he added, "she is always in a better way." Later in the autumn, in fulfilment of his undertaking, he spoke of the matter to his mother. He found her unresponsive, and confessed that he had chosen an inopportune time. He assured Lord Granville that he had done his best, but recommended that any further approach to the Queen should be postponed until the franchise legislation was finally disposed of. Nothing further was heard of the scheme, but on Gladstone's resignation in June 1885 the Queen showed that the Prince's persuasions were not wholly lost on her by her offer of an earldom to the outgoing minister. Although Mr. Gladstone declined the honour, he gratefully acknowledged the Queen's consideration.[1]

V

1885
Ætat. 43

A widening breach between the Whig and Radical elements in the Cabinet combined with the government's recent blunders in the Sudan[2] to hasten Mr. Gladstone's fall from power in June 1885. There were divided counsels, especially in regard to Ireland. Sir Charles Dilke and Mr. Chamberlain alienated many of their colleagues, and somewhat disconcerted the Prince by advocating the abandonment of coercion and the grant of a generous measure of local government. On 2nd June 1885 an adverse vote in the House of Commons on the Budget proposals brought about Mr. Gladstone's resignation, and Lord Salisbury, the Conservative leader, became for the first time Prime Minister. The recent franchise legislation compelled the postponement of a dissolution to the late autumn, and for the five succeeding months the new Conservative ministry held its own by the tacit indulgence of

[1] Morley's Life of Gladstone, iii. 209.
[2] See pp. 463 sq., infra.

the Liberals and with the support of the Irish Nationalist members. Before Mr. Gladstone's defeat the Prince had learnt with anxiety, from Lord Randolph Churchill, that it was Lord Salisbury's intention, should he come into power, to drop coercion.[1] The Prince's general satisfaction with the accession to office of the Conservative party was clouded by its reliance on the ordinary law in the administration of Ireland, where disaffection showed no sign of abating.

The Prince's main interest in the new government lay in his personal relation with its rising hope, Lord Randolph Churchill, who assumed the office of Secretary of State for India. The "forward" policy in India which Lord Randolph pursued during his brief tenure contrasted favourably in the Prince's eyes with the efforts of the Liberal Viceroy, Lord Ripon, to conciliate native pretensions and to ignore the Russian menace. But the links that united Lord Randolph and the Prince came only in subordinate degree from their political sentiments. Lord Randolph exerted on the Prince a personal fascination which created friendly ties between them in spite of rather than because of political issues. Their common enthusiasm for the turf furnished a subsidiary bond.

Lord Randolph, the younger son of the Duke of Marlborough, was known to the Prince in early days, but their intimacy only dated from 1883, and had been preceded by a long interval of estrangement. Lord Randolph had incurred social ostracism owing to his espousal of the cause of a brother whose dissolute conduct was the subject of notorious proceedings in the divorce court. The Prince's condemnation of the scandal had brought characteristically brusque retorts from Lord Randolph, and the Prince spoke openly of his "detestation" of his critic. But during Mr. Gladstone's ministry of 1880 Lord Randolph grew prominent in the political arena as the apostle of Tory democracy, and he pursued with dare-devil invective, both in the House of Commons and on the platform, not merely Mr. Gladstone and his colleagues, but the staid leaders of his own party, who questioned his principles and deplored his bitterness of tongue. On the country he made at this epoch a profound impression, and efficiently contributed to discredit Mr. Gladstone and his chief followers. The Prince watched with involuntary admiration

1885
Ætat. 43

1883
Ætat. 41

[1] Gwynn and Tuckwell's *Life of Sir Charles Dilke*, ii. 123.

1883
Ætat. 41

Lord Randolph's mounting repute. Many besides the Prince saw in Lord Randolph the man of the future, and the good offices of a common friend, Sir Henry James, brought about a reconciliation to which the social address of Lord Randolph's wife—an American—contributed. The breach was finally healed at a dinner which Lord and Lady Randolph gave to the Prince and Princess at their London residence in the winter of 1883, when the guests included the Prince's friends, Lord Rosebery and Mr. Henry Chaplin, as well as, strange to say, Mr. and Mrs. Gladstone, who bore Lord Randolph no resentment for his forcible attacks.[1] Thenceforth Lord Randolph was for a decade a notable figure in the Prince's circle. He charmed the Prince with his conversation, in which shrewdness mingled with irony, banter, and intemperate vituperation.[2] The Prince was fully alive to Lord Randolph's patent faults—his egotism and his quarrelsomeness. "He takes unfortunately strong likes and dislikes," the Prince wrote of him on one occasion to his mother, who disapproved of her son's association with Lord Randolph as warmly as she disliked that with Sir Charles Dilke. But the Prince was captivated by Lord Randolph's political audacity, and for the time had faith in his political prospects. When by his own impulsive indiscretion Lord Randolph brought his meteoric political career to an end, the Prince with characteristic fidelity continued to befriend him until his premature death of the nervous disease which long held him in its grip.

1885
Ætat. 43

In 1885, when the political intimacy between the Prince and Lord Randolph was ripening, the Prince was losing his political mentor of the past five years—Sir Charles Dilke—whose position in politics was suddenly prejudiced by proceedings against him in the divorce court. The Prince parted with Sir Charles on chivalric terms. When Sir Charles intimated to him that the charges were fabrications, the Prince expressed his confidence in him so promptly and considerately as to draw from Sir Charles a declaration that the Prince was one of his truest friends. Throughout Dilke's subsequent tribulation and loss of public repute the Prince gave private proofs of his good feeling, and after his accession to the throne he readmitted Sir Charles to

[1] Lady Randolph Churchill's *Reminiscences*, p. 130.
[2] Lord Rosebery, who shared the Prince's liking for Lord Randolph, published a graphic character sketch of him—*Lord Randolph Churchill*—in 1906.

Court, whence he had been long excluded. It was when Sir
Charles Dilke was giving up his rôle of the Prince's political tutor
that Lord Randolph began to play his part in the Prince's
political training. For a short time he bid fair, despite his
fitful temper, to fill Dilke's place of counsellor.

VI

The dissolution of Parliament in November 1885 resulted
in the return of the Liberals in numbers equalling the Conservatives and Irish Nationalists combined, and it was clear that the
Conservatives could not continue in office save with the support
of the Irish Nationalists. In December the rumour circulated that
Mr. Gladstone was contemplating concessions to the Irish demand
for Home Rule which would ensure him the Irish vote and thus
place the Conservative party in the House of Commons in a
hopeless minority. As soon as Parliament met in January 1886,
the Government were defeated by a united phalanx of Liberal
and Irish votes (331 to 252) on an agricultural issue which was
raised by a Liberal amendment to the address. Thereupon Lord
Salisbury's ministry resigned (January 26).

The Prince saw that the Queen had no option but to recall
Mr. Gladstone to power. He recognised the pain which the ordeal
would cause her. To her private secretary, Sir Henry Ponsonby,
he wrote, on 31st January 1886: "I purposely have not written
to her knowing how much she has to do and think of, and deeply
sympathise with her in the great difficulties she has to contend
with." The Prince was curious about Mr. Gladstone's rumoured
Irish plans. With the Queen's approval, her secretary informed
him of the minister's ambiguous disclosures to her when he took
office at her hands. But it was soon clear that Mr. Gladstone was
about to form a Government which would be committed to the
general principle of Home Rule.

The Prince was fertile in comment on Mr. Gladstone's embarrassments in constituting his new Cabinet. Most of the Prime
Minister's former colleagues were bound in his view to decline
office in a government committed to a policy of Home Rule.
On 31st January 1886 he wrote to the Queen's private secretary:
"Neither Lord Hartington, Mr. Goschen, nor Sir Henry James
can join a Home Rule Government, and I doubt Lord Spencer

or Lord Derby doing so. If Lord Spencer is talked over I lose for ever all the high opinion I have ever held of him as a politician and a man of honour."

On independent grounds the Prince was specially concerned about filling the posts of Foreign Secretary and Secretary for War. Lord Granville, he urged, had disqualified himself for the former office by his irresolution, to which the Prince assigned much past blundering. He thought that Lord Granville should be provided for elsewhere. He strongly deprecated the reappointment to the War Office of Mr. Childers, whose schemes of army reform had offended the Duke of Cambridge. He had his own candidates for both places :

I quite see that it would never do for Lord Granville to return as Foreign Secretary. Though I know that Lord Kimberley is not a *persona grata* to the Queen, still, in every department he has been in he has shown great capacity for hard work and ability. If he is an impossibility, how would Lord Rosebery do ? I cannot help thinking that he would be a good appointment. Should Mr. Campbell-Bannerman be moved up higher ? I know the Duke of Cambridge would gladly see him at the War Office, but Mr. (George) Trevelyan, for obvious reasons, would be very distasteful to him. As President of the Council Lord Granville would be perfect and still remain leader of the House of Lords. I shall indeed watch with the greatest interest and anxiety the formation of Mr. Gladstone's Government. If Lord Hartington cannot be induced to join the new Government (and for his sake I sincerely hope he will not) he will become the leader of the Liberal Party, while Mr. Gladstone becomes the head of the Radical one.

So exciting did the Prince find the process of cabinet-making that he postponed his departure from England on his customary visit to the south of France until the new government was formed.

Neither at this nor at other political crises did the Prince's censorious criticism of Mr. Gladstone's political action impair the cordiality of his relations with the statesman outside the sphere of politics. On 8th January 1885 he had been gratified by "the beautiful" letter of congratulation which the statesman had sent to his elder son on coming of age, and he had obtained Mr. Gladstone's permission to forward it to the press. Two months after Mr. Gladstone's resignation of the office of Prime Minister in the summer of 1885, the Prince, despite a thorough-paced dissatisfaction with his handling of current political problems, displayed all his geniality when they accidentally met on holiday. In the autumn of that year the Prince and Mr. Gladstone both happened to be touring independently in the Norwegian fiords. The Prince's yacht *Osborne* put into the harbour of Molde, where there lay by chance the yacht *Sunbeam*, belonging to Sir Thomas and Lady Brassey, whose guests included the statesman. The Prince at once invited himself to tea with Mr. Gladstone on the *Sunbeam*, and later in the afternoon carried Mr. Gladstone and all his companions to the royal yacht to dine and spend the evening. "The Prince," ran an entry in Lady Brassey's Diary, "was in great spirits," and the Prince writing to his friend, Alfred Montgomery, described "the G.O.M." as "in great form." Now, amid the heat of the political crises at the opening of the year 1886, with his usual complacence, the Prince and the Princess attended the marriage in London of Mr. Gladstone's second daughter, Mary, to Harry Drew, Rector of Hawarden, on the 1st February 1886. Throughout the ceremony the pending political excitement was uppermost in the Prince's mind. The wedding festivities did not deter him from asking the bride's father how he was faring in his distribution of posts. Mr. Gladstone had no qualms in replying that "he had made it all right with Lord Granville," who, to the Prince's surprise, was to go to the Colonial Office. "I should have thought," he wrote to Colonel Ponsonby next day, "that President of the Council would have been less of a come-down than the Colonies after the F.O."

Meanwhile the settlement of the War Office hung fire. "I am so glad the Queen is firm about Childers," the Prince wrote. "He really would never do at the W.O. How would Spencer do, with a strong Secretary in the House of Commons." Ultimately the post fell to the Prince's earlier choice, Mr. Campbell-Bannerman, while Lord Spencer became President of the Council. To a fresh suggestion that the Marquis of Lorne, the Prince's brother-in-law, should join the government, he declared himself firmly opposed.

With regard to Lorne, I hardly think the Queen's son-in-law should form part of the Government, no matter what party is in power. And how could he form part of a "Home Rule" Government? Fortunately he is not in the House of Commons, and he ought to be made a peer. I am very strong on that point, and

equally so that he ought *not* to join the present Government or
any other Government.   He would be in an utterly false position,
and I can hardly imagine that my sister would wish it.

At length Mr. Gladstone completed his difficult task. Mr.
Chamberlain, whom the Prince had incidentally suggested for the
Admiralty, became President of the Local Government Board,
with the proviso that he should retire if Mr. Gladstone's Home
Rule proposals proved, when drafted, to be unacceptable. Sir
William Harcourt became Chancellor of the Exchequer, and place
was found for Mr. Childers at the Home Office, while Mr. John
Morley, who, despite the differences in their temperaments, was
to win after the Prince's accession his full confidence as a
leading Minister of the Crown, first joined the cabinet as Chief
Secretary for Ireland.

But Mr. Gladstone's labour in forming his third cabinet—
a process in which the Prince had with some grave misgivings
actively interested himself—seemed in the event to be largely
thrown away. A Home Rule Bill was duly introduced into the
House of Commons, but was rejected, to the Prince's contentment, by a combination of Conservatives and dissentient Liberals.
Mr. Gladstone thereupon, against the Queen's advice, made a
new appeal to the country in July, with the result that the
Conservatives and Liberal Unionists were returned in a substantial
majority.

VII

Lord Salisbury's first tenure of the office of Prime Minister
had lasted only seven months. Now he was to retain his high
post for a six years' term, and then, after a three years' interval,
was to resume the office for a third and last term of seven years,
the concluding eighteen months of which coincided with a critical
stage in the Prince's career—the opening period of his reign.
With no other holder of Lord Salisbury's office were the Prince's
relations so prolonged. Through all but the last twenty months
of the thirteen years in which Salisbury was Prime Minister, he
held conjointly the Foreign Secretaryship, and the Prince's
perennial interest in foreign affairs quickened his quest of Lord
Salisbury's confidences.

Lord Salisbury, who was the Prince's senior by no more than
eleven years, belonged to a younger generation than Mr. Gladstone

and Lord Beaconsfield—the two Prime Ministers with whom the
Prince had hitherto been most closely associated. He had first
made Lord Salisbury's acquaintance when that statesman was at
the India Office in Lord Beaconsfield's ministry. Afterwards he
enjoyed much intercourse with him during his two years at the
Foreign Office as Lord Beaconsfield's understudy.

Lord Salisbury had none of Lord Beaconsfield's courtly
graces or of Mr. Gladstone's impressive fervour and long-
standing personal devotion to the Prince. Lord Salisbury's intellectual penetration and ironic habit of speech gave little play
to his feelings. Social diversions had no attraction for him. He
had no command of small talk, and was indifferent to fashionable
etiquette. His careless attire shocked the Prince. But in spite
of the aloofness in the two men's social relations which came of
the thoroughgoing differences in their social outlooks, they won
each other's regard. Lord Salisbury recognised the Prince's
common sense and knowledge of foreign affairs. He listened
patiently to the expression of views which did not always
concur with his own; while the Prince valued at their just
worth the statesman's mental grip, experienced judgement, and
imperturbability.

The Prince was even readier in the summer than in the early
spring of 1886 with advice on cabinet-making—on the formation
of Lord Salisbury's second cabinet. He highly approved the
appointment of his friend, Lord Randolph Churchill, to the high
posts of Chancellor of the Exchequer and Leader of the House of
Commons. But he pleaded the qualifications for responsible
office of three other intimate friends of Conservative convictions
—Lord Cadogan, his friend from boyhood; Lord Londonderry,
a more recent associate,[1] and Lord Charles Beresford.

Although of no outstanding political abilities Lord Cadogan
and Lord Londonderry as men of wealth and character, patrons
of the turf and generous hosts, were well fitted for political
careers. The Prince's third candidate, Lord Charles Beresford,
had less secure credentials. The Prince's suggestions in all three
instances bore fruit. Lord Cadogan was appointed Lord Privy

---

[1] Lord Londonderry was known till his succession to his father's peerage in
1884 as Lord Castlereagh, by which name the Prince always called him. His
wife, a daughter of Lord Shrewsbury, was a woman of brilliant social gifts with
active political interests; she stood high in the Prince's regard.

Seal, although Lord Salisbury did not admit him to the cabinet
until the April of next year, when the Prince was jubilant in his
congratulations to his friend "on what must be the zenith of
a man's ambition if he cares about politics" (April 19, 1887).
The Prince's recommendation of Lord Londonderry proved
peculiarly serviceable to the Prime Minister. Although Ireland
was not in the Prince's mind when he mentioned Lord Londonderry's name, Lord Salisbury promptly offered him the Irish
Viceroyalty, and appealed to the Prince's good offices in inducing him to accept the onerous post.[1] Lord Salisbury warmly
acknowledged "the kindness and efficiency with which you
have assisted me on the present occasion."

There was more difficulty in fitting the Prince's third candidate
into the political scheme. The breezy and impulsive Irish sailor,
Lord Charles Beresford, was an unsatisfactory politician compared with Lord Cadogan or Lord Londonderry. Lord Charles
had exchanged naval for parliamentary service as a high-flying
Tory.[2] The Prince took a justly modest view of his friend's
political insight when he wrote to the Prime Minister (July 27)
that his friend's political knowledge might not qualify him for the
difficult post of Chief Secretary for Ireland, but might fit him to
become "head of the Irish Police Force." "He is an admirable
organiser and hard worker. Being an Irishman and a well-known
man everywhere, his name would, I cannot help thinking, carry
considerable weight." Lord Salisbury responded not very
happily by bestowing on Lord Charles, "until some more agreeable offer becomes possible," the place of Fourth Lord of the
Admiralty. The experiment was hardly fortunate. Eager for
the reform and efficiency of the navy, Lord Charles rebelled
against what he deemed to be the slow bureaucratic methods of
the First Lord, Lord George Hamilton, and of Lord George's other
colleagues, while he seemed to them to be in closer touch with
the press than the tradition of the board sanctioned.[3] Much
internal friction at the Admiralty followed, and in spite of the
Prince's sympathy with his protégé's bold demands for strengthen-

---

[1] See p. 243 *supra*.

[2] Lord Charles first entered the House of Commons as Conservative member
for County Waterford in February 1874, and, after defeat at the General
Election of 1880, returned to the House in November 1885 as member for East
Marylebone. That seat he retained at the election of 1886.

[3] Lord George Hamilton, *Parliamentary Reminiscences*, p. 88 *seq.*

ing the Navy, he saw reason for advising him within two years   1886
to resume active service afloat.   "You should apply for a ship   Ætat. 44
before long (the Prince sagaciously wrote to Lord Charles, July
11, 1888) so that you may put in your sea time, and it will be a
change also after the House of Commons and London Society."
The Prince was none too well pleased that Lord Charles should
postpone, contrary to his counsel, his withdrawal from Parliament
for another year.

The prospect of security and tranquillity in domestic politics
which Lord Salisbury's accession to power in July 1886 seemed
to promise, was rudely disturbed six months later by the sudden
resignation of the Prince's ally, Lord Randolph Churchill, in what
seemed to be a fit of pique.   Lord Randolph found himself at
variance with his colleagues on the estimates for the Army and
Navy and, in the interests of an economical budget which he was
drafting, vainly urged a reduction.   In an over-confident hope
of bringing his fellow-ministers round to his view he resigned
abruptly on 23rd December.   Lord Salisbury promptly accepted
his resignation, and Mr. Goschen, whom Lord Randolph confessed
that he had forgotten, took his place as Chancellor of the Exchequer, while the conscientious Mr. W. H. Smith became First
Lord of the Treasury and Leader of the House of Commons.   The
Queen regarded Lord Randolph's withdrawal as an unforgivable
desertion.   The Prince admitted to her his friend's waywardness,
but he scarcely soothed her feelings by expressing a hope that
he might bring about a reconciliation between Lord Randolph
and Lord Salisbury and thereby arrange for his friend's re-admis-
sion to the cabinet.   The Prince's social relations with the
ex-minister grew closer.   At the chief race meetings, to which
Lord Randolph devoted much of his enforced leisure, they were
thenceforth inseparable companions, and the Prince ignored the
Queen's warning that intimacy with one "so changeable and
indiscreet" might prove compromising.   During the closing
years of Lord Randolph's life, when the steady development of
general paralysis rendered him a physical and intellectual wreck,
the Prince was assiduous in kindly attentions.[1]

[1] At the end of 1893 Lord Randolph, when scarcely able to speak or to hear,
was the Prince's guest at Sandringham.   He died on 24th January 1895

VIII

Lord Salisbury's ministry survived the crisis of Lord Randolph's withdrawal and remained in office until the summer of 1892. The Prince was in general sympathy with its Irish policy of "strong" government, with its strategic attitude to international rivalries and with its due assertion of England's authority abroad. The general election of July 1892, however, gave the Liberals with the Irish Nationalists a narrow majority of forty, and Lord Salisbury's second ministry came to an end.

Mr. Gladstone, then in his 83rd year, undertook for the fourth and last time, the office of Prime Minister (August 16, 1892). On some personal grounds the Prince welcomed Mr. Gladstone's return to power, although he regretted the Liberal leader's immovable devotion to Home Rule for Ireland. He was desirous that his friend Lord Rosebery should serve again as Foreign Secretary. Two years before, Lord Rosebery had suffered the loss of his wife, the daughter of Baron Meyer de Rothschild, and the bereavement had withdrawn him from public life. The Prince now joined other friends in persuading Lord Rosebery to resume his former office. Replying to the Prince's appeal, Lord Rosebery thanked him for this fresh proof of "constant friendship" and explained that his reluctance was solely due to private considerations; "however," he added, "the matter has now been practically taken out of my hands and settled in the way your Royal Highness wishes" (August 15, 1892). Lord Rosebery pursued in the main Lord Salisbury's foreign policy and well sustained English prestige in foreign eyes. In his attitude to both France and Germany he took an equally firm stand whenever either of those countries seemed to threaten English interests. But he disappointed the Prince by going somewhat further than his predecessor in his reliance on the principle of isolation.

The Prince greatly valued the intelligence which Mr. Gladstone now, for the first time, furnished him regarding the deliberations of the cabinet.[1] He was able to follow at first hand the course of the government's policy on domestic as well as on foreign affairs. In November 1893 he appreciated the accounts which reached him through the Prime Minister of Lord Rosebery's

---

[1] See p. 217 *supra*.

successful arbitration in the coal strike—a welcome confirmation of his estimate of his friend's statesmanlike qualities. But over all the operations of the ministry hung for the Prince the black pall of Mr. Gladstone's effort to solve the Irish problem on Home Rule lines, with the quarrel between the two Houses of Parliament which followed in its train. When the new Home Rule measure, after passing the House of Commons, was rejected by the House of Lords, the revived agitation against the Upper Chamber disturbed the Prince's equanimity. He resented the unbridled vigour of the oratory from Liberal platforms. When one of the junior ministers, Mr. Arthur Acland, fulminated against the Peers in a speech at Portsmouth, the Prince wrote to his old Oxford correspondent, Sir Henry Acland, the speaker's uncle: "It is a pity he should imitate the 'Bombastes Furioso' style of an older colleague of his." "Bombastes Furioso" was the Prince's sobriquet for Sir William Harcourt.

The growing infirmities of age compelled Mr. Gladstone's resignation of his great office in February 1894. The Queen's choice of Lord Rosebery as Mr. Gladstone's successor was entirely her own act. It won the Prince's full concurrence. For the first time in his life he found an old personal friend of his own generation at the head of a Government. Lord Rosebery ceased to be Foreign Secretary, and, in accordance with a former suggestion of the Prince, that post, in spite of the Queen's qualms, fell to Lord Kimberley. Lord Rosebery's position was no bed of roses. The government's majority in the House of Commons was dwindling. The Radical wing of the Liberal Party was not enthusiastic over a "peer-premier," and, owing to dissensions with his leading colleague and rival, Sir William Harcourt, the new Prime Minister suffered more than a common share of the worry incident to his office. The Prince keenly sympathised with his friend's embarrassments but he held aloof from the party controversy. The immediate conduct of foreign affairs had passed to other hands. There was indeed less intimate discussion of public affairs on the Prince's part with the new Prime Minister than with his predecessors. Lord Rosebery's precarious tenure of power lasted no more than fifteen months. He resigned after an adverse vote in the House of Commons on 21st June 1895.

In succession to Lord Rosebery, Lord Salisbury accepted the
Queen's invitation to form a new ministry for a third time
(June 25). "The formation of Lord Salisbury's government,"
the Prince wrote to Lady Londonderry the same day, "is being
watched with great interest by all." When its constitution was
completed, the Prince illustrated his impartial attitude to party
barriers by inviting all the out-going and in-coming ministers
to meet at dinner at Marlborough House. The chief guest was
the Shahzada, second son of the Amir of Afghanistan, who was
on a visit to this country. The entertainment proved thoroughly
harmonious under the cheerful sway of the Prince.[1]

Soon afterwards the new Prime Minister dissolved Parliament,
and at the general election the Conservatives and Liberal
Unionists gained the substantial majority of 152 over the Liberals
and Irish members. The Unionists were again returned to power
at the general election of September 1900, and the Prince found
them in office, when he became King four months later. A stable
government was thus in being during the last years of the Prince's
career as heir-apparent.

In Lord Salisbury's third ministry, of 1895, the Prince agreeably found an ampler representation of his personal coterie than
had befallen his earlier experience. The members were drawn
from both political parties. The Liberal-Unionist leaders now
joined the Conservatives in office and brought a strong infusion
of Liberalism to qualify veteran Conservative sentiment. The
Prince welcomed his close friends, the Duke of Devonshire,
(formerly Lord Hartington) and Sir Henry (now created Lord)
James, to Cabinet office under a Conservative chief ; the former
as President of the Council, and the latter as Chancellor of
the Duchy of Lancaster. A third Liberal-Unionist leader,
Mr. Joseph Chamberlain, with whom the Prince's more distant
acquaintance covered two decades, elected to go to the Colonial
Office. Mr. Chamberlain's powerful personality and the strong
imperial sentiment which he had recently developed gave
the new ministry its most distinctive feature. Another old
acquaintance of the Prince, Lord Lansdowne, also a Liberal-

[1] Sir Alfred Lyall's *Lord Dufferin*, ii. 285.

Unionist, who had served as Governor-General of Canada and
Viceroy of India, assumed the responsibilities of the War Office.
Conservative associates of old standing were also well represented
in the new ministry.   To the Prince's special satisfaction, Lord
Cadogan, for whom he had stood sponsor on his admission to Lord
Salisbury's former cabinet, now accepted the Lord Lieutenancy
of Ireland, and he soon renewed discussion with the Prince
regarding the enlistment of himself and his family in the conciliation of Irish sentiment.[1]   Mr. Henry Chaplin became President
of the Local Government Board.   Lord Londonderry, to the
Prince's regret, remained outside the government.   Lord Salisbury, as was his wont, combined the offices of Foreign Secretary
with that of Prime Minister, and from him or from his secretary,
Mr. Schomberg McDonnell, the Prince learnt confidentially of
cabinet decisions on important issues in home and foreign affairs.
On the critical foreign complications which faced Lord Salisbury
during his final term of office, the Prince confided to him his views
with no diminution of assurance and with added command of
the facts and of the personal equations attaching to foreign
problems.

When the general election of 1900 extended Lord Salisbury's
lease of power, he made some changes in the constitution of
his government.   The chief change was his withdrawal from
the Foreign Office in favour of Lord Lansdowne.   Minor modifications, which more immediately affected the Prince's circle, was
the ending of Mr. Chaplin's ministerial career and the return
of Lord Londonderry to office albeit in the unpretending position
of Postmaster-General.   On all branches of government the
Prince kept an alert eye in these closing years of Queen Victoria's
reign.   He proved as ready as ever in tendering the Prime
Minister advice on appointments to vacancies as they arose,
with varying results.   The important court office of Lord Chamberlain fell vacant on 19th November 1898 on the death of the
Earl of Lathom, who had long served in Conservative ministries.
The Prince proposed that Lord Pembroke, at the time Lord
Steward of the Household, should be promoted and that the
Lord Stewardship should be filled by Lord Denbigh.   But
on this occasion, Lord Salisbury ignored the Prince's advice
and nominated the Earl of Hopetoun, afterwards Marquis of

[1] See pp. 223-4, 244 *supra*.

Linlithgow, to the post of Lord Chamberlain and left Lord Pembroke where he was.

The Prince scrutinised, too, more narrowly than before, the choice by foreign governments of envoys to the British court as well as the filling of vacancies in the English diplomatic service. On the 7th August 1896, the Prince implored Lord Salisbury "to keep away" from London Count Tornielli, lately the Italian Ambassador there, who was reported to have been nominated by his government for a second term at the court of St. James. The Prince described the Count as "a great bore, very easily offended, and not friendly to England, especially as regards Egypt." Count Tornielli did not return to London. He was accredited to Paris, where he enjoyed a far higher reputation than the Prince acknowledged.[1]

There was no failure of the good relations during these years between the Prince and Lord Salisbury, in spite of the Prime Minister's distaste for the fashionable entertainments and sports which the Prince loved. The Prince and Prime Minister exchanged visits not only at their London and country houses, but when they were both on holiday on the Riviera, where Lord Salisbury had a villa at La Bastide. With Lord Salisbury's family, too, the Prince was on excellent terms. When, at the end of the century, Lady Salisbury's health failed, the Prince showed the anxious husband every solicitude, and on Lady Salisbury's death the Prince offered sympathy in very tender language : "I know," he wrote to Lord Salisbury (November 20, 1899), "from what Lady Salisbury was to you, and your intense devotion to her, that the blank must indeed be a terrible one for you. I shall always deeply mourn and regret her who has passed away, as she was always such a true and kind friend."

X

In the meantime, death, with slow approach, had stepped in finally to withdraw from the political stage the figure that had chiefly dominated it from the Prince's childhood.

---

[1] Count Tornielli remained a *persona grata* in France until his death in 1908. He helped to bring France and Italy into accord after a long estrangement.

Mr. Gladstone's delight in personal intercourse with the Prince remained as active during his last years as at previous eras. Early in 1887, when in his 78th year, he was the Prince's guest at Sandringham, and noted in his diary the pleasurable opportunity of "much conversation" with his host. Nine years later, when Mr. Gladstone was frankly discussing with a guest at Hawarden the character of Queen Victoria's predecessors, he denounced with moral indignation Charles II. and George IV. as "scoundrels," but he rounded off the talk with the pronouncement: "No royalty I have ever met had such charm and tact as the Prince of Wales."[1]

Very touching are the last records of the private harmony, undisturbed by any jarring note of politics, which characterised the relations of the Prince and Mr. Gladstone. The mutual fidelity is graphically reflected in the long series of Birthday or New Year felicitations, and in the messages of joy or sadness on domestic episodes which they continued to exchange with one another to the last. When the old statesman celebrated his golden wedding in July 1889, the Prince forwarded the gift of an inkstand with an autograph note of "most sincere congratulations," and effusive was Mr. Gladstone's acknowledgement of "this token of kindness" (July 25).

The sudden death of Gladstone's eldest son, William Henry, on the 4th July 1891, drew from the Prince next day affectionate reminiscences of his early companionship with the dead man.[2] He justified his prompt intrusion on his old friend's grief on the ground of "having known you ever since my childhood and your son Willy ever since our boyhood."

"I had not even heard," he continued, "of Willy's serious illness, and I cannot tell you what a shock it was to me to read the sad news in the newspapers. Never can I forget the days of my boyhood when your son came to see me here (*i.e.* Windsor) when he was at Eton—then the happy days we spent on the Rhine in the summer of '57 and our Oxford days at Ch. Ch.! I shall always deeply regret him from the kindliness and simplicity of his nature."

Retirement from political office served to tighten the bonds of affection. On the same day (February 28) that Mr. Gladstone

---

[1] Lord Ronald Gower, *Old Diaries* (May 20, 1896), p. 264.
[2] See pp. 16-17, 31 *supra*.

informed the Queen in an audience at Buckingham Palace of his intention to resign he sent the news to the Prince in a long autograph letter.

"In thus making [his retirement] known to your Royal Highness," he wrote, "I desire to convey, on my own and my wife's part our fervent thanks for the unbounded kindness which we have at all times received from your Royal Highness and not less from the beloved Princess of Wales. The devotion of an old man is little worth; but if at any time there be the smallest service which by information or suggestion your Royal Highness may believe me capable of rendering, I shall remain as much at your command as if I had continued to be an active and responsible servant of the Queen." [1]

The Prince promptly replied with a notable manifestation of right feeling (March 1):

Pray accept (his letter ran) my warmest thanks for the kind letter which I have received from you to-day—and for giving me after the Queen the important information that you are desirous of tendering your resignation of the Premiership. After your long and valuable services to the Crown and Country, I can well understand that you need the repose to which you are so fully entitled, but to those of your many friends and admirers amongst which I hope I may be counted, we shall naturally deeply regret the step you are about to take.

Both the Princess and myself are deeply touched by the kind words expressed by you concerning us. We have for a long number of years greatly valued your friendship and that of Mrs. Gladstone, and we sincerely hope that it may please God to grant you both many years yet of domestic happiness.

Let me also assure you how greatly we value your advice on all occasions as no one in this Realm has greater knowledge and experience in public affairs than yourself and we should never hesitate to ask it.

Although during the remaining four years of Mr. Gladstone's long life the Prince deprecated rumours of his resumption of political activities, he eagerly welcomed news of the old statesman. From Sandringham, on 29th December 1894, he wrote to his friend Acland: "To-day is Mr. Gladstone's 85th birthday. I am told he is in wonderfully good health, but I hardly imagine he will take any further active part in politics. *Requiescat in Pace*." Mr. Gladstone found it difficult to seclude

[1] Morley's *Gladstone*, iii. 510.

himself entirely from political controversy, and he caused Lord Rosebery, his successor in the Liberal leadership, some embarrassment by re-entering the political arena in 1896 with a fresh indictment against the Porte for its cruel usage of the Armenians. "I hope," a sympathising friend ingenuously wrote to the aged warrior (September 19, 1896), "you have written to the Prince to impress him with your point of view." [1]

1894
Ætat. 52

It was in a serener atmosphere that the two men held their final meetings before the inevitable parting. On 26th June 1896, the Prince opened at Aberystwyth the newly-created University of Wales, of which he had become Chancellor. In spite of infirmities, Mr. Gladstone came over from Hawarden to attend the ceremony, and at the lunch which followed it the veteran proposed the Prince's health. On New Year's Day, 1897, the statesman wrote to the Prince his customary letter of good wishes, to which the Prince promptly replied. Another meeting between the two followed within a few months in somewhat curious circumstances. In the spring the Prince was paying his customary visit to the Riviera while the Queen was at the Hotel Excelsior at Cimiez, near Nice. Both Mr. Gladstone and Lord Salisbury were staying in the neighbourhood ; Mr. Gladstone at Cannes, at the Palazzetto of Mr. Rendel, and Lord Salisbury, the Prime Minister, at his villa at La Bastide. The Prince made prolonged calls on both statesmen. But of greater interest was the Prince's presence at the Cimiez Hotel as his mother's guest when she received for the last time her aged minister, with whom her relations had grown very distant. The constraint on the part of both sovereign and subject rendered the interview painful, and significantly contrasted with the genial ease which characterised then as at all times the intercourse between the statesman and the sovereign's heir. The Prince met Mr. Gladstone for the last time a little later in the same year and then under the statesman's own roof. On his return to London from a short visit to the Duke of Westminster at Eaton Hall, near Chester, he paid his only visit to Mr. Gladstone at his home at Hawarden (May 9, 1897).

1897
Ætat. 55

A twelvemonth later on the 19th May 1898 Mr. Gladstone died at Hawarden. The Prince was assiduous in farewell tributes of respect. On 25th May he and his son, the Duke of York, acted as pall-bearers at the statesman's funeral in Westminster Abbey,

[1] Mr. G. W. E. Russell's *Malcolm MacColl*, p. 165.

1898
Ætat. 56
and when the coffin was lowered into the grave, he crossed to the place where Mrs. Gladstone was seated, and, after speaking a few sympathetic words, kissed her hand. The marked attention which the Prince paid the memory of the old Liberal leader caused some resentment among rigid party men on the Conservative side, who were unmindful of the ancient links. It was not as a political disciple, but as a sharer in a loyal friendship of half-a-century's duration that the Prince made his avowals of regard for the dead statesman. It was appropriate that the Prince should accept the post of President of the Committee which was at once formed to erect a national memorial in honour of the illustrious Victorian (July 1, 1898).

CHAPTER XXIX

CO-OPERATION IN SOCIAL REFORM, 1878–1895

I

DURING the last five-and-twenty years of Queen Victoria's reign both political parties acknowledged in steadily increasing degree the obligation of government to improve the social conditions of the people at large, and to palliate the discrepancies between the comforts of wealth and the discomforts and distresses of poverty. The *laissez faire* principles of the Manchester School of politicians were generally abandoned. The Prince's temperament stimulated his general sympathies with the newer conceptions of political duty. His breadth of outlook, his boundless curiosity, his experience as a benevolent landlord at Sandringham, his familiar intercourse with Sir Charles Dilke, rendered much current effort in social reform a congenial theme for observation and suggestion. The unceasing involutions of foreign affairs, the personal issues attaching to the distribution of honours and political office, combined as these interests always were with the calls of sport and social amusement, never succeeded in absorbing the whole of the Prince's attention.

There were sides of domestic legislation or administration which failed to interest him. He hastily identified with merely tiresome parochialism—with "the parish pump"—measures for the improvement either of local government or (save in the direction of music) of elementary education. But from the days of Lord Beaconsfield's supremacy onwards he canvassed, in conversation and correspondence, a wide range of social, industrial, and commercial questions, and he let Lord Beaconsfield and his successors know that he was prepared to take part in the quest of solutions. He acknowledged the national value of practical measures for the better housing of the artisan, for

1878

Ætat. 36

541

an efficient water supply, for due provision for the aged poor, for the reconciliation of capital and labour, for safeguards against depression of trade, for the amenities of London as the capital city of the Empire.   During the Prince's middle life fights were waged for some subsidiary social reforms which, under the early influence of his enlightened friend, Lord Houghton, appealed to his idiosyncrasy.   The warm controversies over marriage with a deceased wife's sister and over the Sunday opening of museums found him an avowed champion of change. His faith in the virtue of industrial and art exhibitions, which he inherited from his father, was notably whetted by his experiences in Paris in 1878, and he came with his growing years to regard such organisations not only as aids in promoting international peace, but as machinery capable of strengthening the bonds of Empire.

II

It was in the closing years of Lord Beaconsfield's ministry (1878–79) that the Prince first manifested a desire to play some personal part in the work of social or industrial reform, and although little came of his advances at the time, they bore practical fruit later when Lord Beaconsfield's successors gave him the opportunity of engaging in public inquiries into social problems.

Serious industrial and agricultural depression threatened the country before Lord Beaconsfield's tenure of office came to an end.   At the end of 1878 the Prime Minister contemplated the appointment of a Parliamentary Committee to investigate the causes of the decline in the country's commerce and industry, and Lord Beaconsfield entered into correspondence on the subject with the Prince.   The Prince agreed with the minister's pessimistic estimate of the state of affairs, and declared his readiness to take part in an investigation into its causes.   He was desirous that the proposed Committee should represent all parties so as to ensure its national character.   On Christmas Day, 1878, the Prince wrote to Lord Beaconsfield :

It is indeed sad to think in what a serious state the industrial condition of the country is at the present moment. . . . Your suggestion of a Committee seems to me an excellent one—and I need hardly say that I am entirely at your disposal and ready

to do anything you may think proper.   It certainly should not   1878
be a party move, but a national one, and I am very glad that   ‾‾
you propose that Mr. Goschen and Mr. Forster should be asked   Ætat. 36
to join the Committee.   I would also suggest that the names of
Lord Hartington and Mr. Gladstone, and perhaps also Lord
Granville, should be added—which.would show the country that,
if possible, there was one great national object in which both
Conservatives and Liberals acted in unanimity together.   For
my own part, I should be too glad to think—if our efforts prove
successful—that I had in some small way contributed towards mitigating the present unsatisfactory state of things in the country.

But the scheme fell through.   Two days later the Prince wrote
to the Prime Minister :

I am sorry to hear that the great project you had in view—
and concerning which you wrote to me a short time ago—"hangs
fire"; but I trust that something may yet be done to restore, if
possible, the present lamentable depression of trade.[1]

Another social or domestic question engaged public attention
at the time, namely, the improvement of the country's water
supply.   Here the Prince took action with a view to prompting
the government.   As President of the Society of Arts he, in
May 1878, summoned an influential conference to consider the
subject, and with his approval an appeal was made to the government to appoint at once "a small permanent scientific commission to investigate and collect" information.   On the 24th March   1879
1879 the Prince wrote at length to Lord Beaconsfield explain-   ‾‾
ing the aims of the conference and requesting him to receive a   Ætat. 37
deputation.   Lord Beaconsfield's reply evinced no desire personally to handle the matter.   The government, however, at the
opening of the next session announced its intention of dealing
with an important part of the theme, and a Bill was introduced
for superseding the private water companies of London by a
public Water Board.   The provisions of the Bill were adversely
criticised, and the dissolution of 8th March 1880 long postponed
any parliamentary enactment.[2]

[1] A Royal Commission of Inquiry into Agricultural Depression was appointed
on the 4th July 1879, and it reported in 1881.   But it concerned itself with a
portion only of the subject which the Prince deemed fitted for inquiry, and the
Prince did not serve upon it.
[2] In the course of the two following decades the water supply of London
was under frequent discussion, and as many as three royal commissions made
inquiries, but it was not until the Prince's accession to the throne that the
Act creating the Metropolitan Water Board was passed in 1902.

III

At the same period the Prince first publicly identified himself with the efforts of his friend Lord Houghton and other social reformers to redress the grievance attaching to the prohibition of marriage with a deceased wife's sister.[1] There was no faltering about his declaration of independence on this minor matter of social polity. On 6th May 1879, when Lord Houghton was announced to move the second reading of his Deceased Wife's Sister Bill, the Prince rose from his place on the cross-benches before the debate opened to present for the first time a petition to the House. The petition was signed by 3258 farmers of Norfolk, praying for the amendment of the law in question. On presenting the petition the Prince again established a fresh precedent by making a short speech. He declared that he acted

on local as well as on general grounds. . . . It is my firm conviction (he proceeded) that if this Bill passed, it would be of advantage to the community at large, and I shall, therefore, give my hearty support to the noble Lord who moves the second reading of the Bill to-night.

The Prince was present throughout the debate and voted with the "contents," who numbered 81. But 101 "noncontents" threw out the Bill.[2] The Prince, undaunted by defeat, remained a staunch supporter of the measure, and in
June 1882, when the Bill was reintroduced into the House of Lords, he again voted with the minority. While unchanging in his attitude he gave, in the course of this fresh skirmish in the Upper Chamber, attractive proof of his geniality in controversy. A chief feature of the debate was the powerful speech against the Bill by Dr. Magee, the eloquent Bishop of Peterborough. The Bishop, who was no puritan, had just before somewhat ruffled public opinion by a speech at Leicester in which he had announced that he would "rather see England free than sober." As the

[1] Such marriages had been long held by the Church to fall within the prohibited degrees; but it was only in 1835, at Lord Lyndhurst's initiative, that they had been forbidden by parliamentary enactment. In 1851 an agitation arose to annul the prohibition, and between that year and 1879 a Bill to that effect had seven times passed the House of Commons, but had on each occasion been rejected by the House of Lords.

[2] Fourteen Bishops were in the majority, together with Lords Beaconsfield and Salisbury. The Duke of Edinburgh, Lord Lansdowne, Lord Granville, Lord Spencer, Lord Carrington, and other Liberal peers, with one Bishop, Robert Bickersteth of Ripon, joined the Prince in the minority.

Prince passed the Bishop on his way to the division lobby, he told him that he liked his speech at Leicester "a great deal better" than his deliverance that afternoon, and would have preferred the Bishop to have made his Leicester speech over again. The Bishop's just comment on the sally was that the Prince took opposition "very good-naturedly."[1]

Three years later the Prince offered even less conven- 1885 tional proof than he had given previously of his sustained Ætat. 43 interest in the question. In 1885 he was invited to present to the Upper Chamber a petition for a second time in favour of the Deceased Wife's Sister Bill. The request came from a class of workers with whom the Prince was always on good terms— the cab-drivers of London, who knew him as a generous client. Lord Granville's counsel was invited as to the propriety of acceding to the cab-drivers' request. The minister pointed out the practical inconvenience which the Prince would incur if he yielded to the invitation. All manner of petitioners, Lord Granville warned him, on all manner of subjects would wish to present petitions through him. But the Prince took his own line, and while acknowledging the risk, sponsored the cab-drivers' appeal.[2]

Another eleven years passed before the House of Lords came round to the Prince's view, and then no more than a Pyrrhic victory was scored. In the session of 1896 the House of Lords accepted the Bill; it reached a third reading on 10th July, when the Prince voted in the majority of 142 against a minority of 104. Lord Dunraven was now Lord Houghton's successor as leading champion of the measure in the Upper House, and as soon as the last figures were announced the Prince wrote congratulating Lord Dunraven on "so good a majority."

"For so many years I hoped the Bill would pass that I am delighted at the result, and if in any small way I contributed towards it I am thoroughly content. You worked very hard for some time, and so did St. Albans, and must naturally be much pleased. If only we could get it through the House of Commons this session it would be a great triumph, but I much fear it will not be possible. But we must hope for the best."[3]

[1] Macdonnell's *Life of Magee*, p. 173.
[2] Mr. Knollys to Lord Granville, 5th and 9th June 1885. Lord Granville to the Prince, 6th June 1885.
[3] Lord Dunraven's *Memoirs*, vol. ii. p. 116.

The Prince's fears of the House of Commons were justified. The lower House failed to deal with the measure before the session closed and the triumph in the House of Lords proved abortive. It was not indeed until the Prince came to the throne that the long-controverted reform of the marriage law took legislative effect. Through the first three years of King Edward's reign (in 1901–3) Parliament treated the measure as unsympathetically as at earlier epochs. But better fortune attended it during 1907, when it was passed by both Houses. On 26th August in that year it received from King Edward the royal assent.[1] Twenty-eight years separated the final victory from the time when the Prince first identified himself with the agitation in favour of the reform. Through that long period he openly challenged conventional opinion in the interests of liberty and of what he deemed to be the general welfare.

IV

Mr. Gladstone, in the course of his second ministry, 1880–85, improved on his predecessor in his practical encouragement of the Prince's ambition to make himself useful in non-political spheres of public service. He was more anxious than Lord Beaconsfield to counteract the effect of the Queen's resolve to exclude her son from regular public employment. Mr. Gladstone's first step in this direction seemed to travel somewhat outside the scope of the Prince's interest. On 21st April 1881 the Prime Minister invited him to become a trustee of the British Museum "in the place of the late Sir Philip Egerton." He was duly appointed on the 6th May, and on the 14th May he was chosen to fill the late Lord Beaconsfield's place on the Standing Committee—the effective body of administrative control. Contrary to expectation, the Prince found the duties quite congenial. Whenever the agenda rose above mere routine he attended the meetings of the Standing Committee with fair regularity until he ascended the throne.[2]

---

[1] The Lords insisted on a proviso that no clergyman should be compelled to perform the ceremony of marriage when the bride was the sister of the bride-groom's deceased wife. On the 2nd December 1907 the Archbishop of Canterbury wrote to King Edward's private secretary that he adhered to the House of Lord's proviso, but was advising his clergy to accept the Act in all essentials.

[2] He always actively supported the authority of the Director of the Museum, Sir Edward Maunde Thompson. One of the services which he rendered

A majority of the British Museum trustees shared the
Prince's view of the advantage of opening that and similar institutions on Sunday, but the Sabbatarian sentiment of the country, which offered stout opposition to the innovation, postponed its adoption. Resolutions authorising Sunday opening were long introduced annually into both Houses of Parliament, only to be rejected. The Prince duly made his contribution to the movement's first parliamentary success. On the 20th March 1885, when the annual resolution in favour of Sunday opening was moved in the House of Lords by Lord Thurlow, the parliamentary tradition of defeat was first qualified by a tie—64 voting on each side. The Prince of Wales, who was in Berlin at the time, paired in favour of the motion. Next year, on the 19th March 1886, the motion was carried in the House of Lords by a majority of 14.

It took the House of Commons another ten years to assimilate the enlightenment of the House of Lords. It was not until 10th March 1896 that a substantial majority of the House of Commons, after many refusals to countenance the proposal, at length sanctioned the Sunday opening of the British Museum and other national collections, and gave practical effect to the Prince's long-cherished wish.

V

The most notable recognition, so far, in the Prince's career of
his desire to play his part in national social service belongs to the year 1884, when Mr. Gladstone, in February, nominated him for the first time a member of a Royal Commission of politico-social significance.[1] The subject of inquiry was a major theme

---

the museum was his suggestion of the appointment of his intimate friend, Baron Ferdinand de Rothschild, as a fellow-trustee (7th February 1896). The Baron proved his appreciation of the honour by bequeathing to the museum a valuable collection of objects of art. In behalf of his fellow-trustees the Prince unveiled a marble statue of Charles Darwin, the great naturalist, at the Natural History Museum, South Kensington, 9th June 1885.

[1] The Prince had already sat on two committees of the House of Lords— one on the Cattle Plague of 1866, and the other on the Scarcity of Horses in 1873, and had been President of the two Royal Commissions—for organising the British sections at the exhibitions of Vienna (1873) and of Paris (1878). To the Housing inquiry he brought expert knowledge. He had personally improved the housing accommodation of the labourers on his Sandringham estate, and as Duke of Cornwall he owned much property in poor districts of South London, where he acknowledged that the housing conditions were in crying need of amelioration.

of social reform—the Housing of the Working Classes. The appointment of the Commission has an historic importance as a joint acknowledgement by both parties of the claims of social reform to parliamentary attention. The Commission was suggested by Lord Salisbury and was adopted by the Liberal Government at the instance of the Prince's friend, Sir Charles Dilke, President of the Local Government Board. The Prince's inclusion was a fruit of his confidential relations with Sir Charles. A first suggestion to make the Prince the Chairman of the Commission was rejected on the score of his engagements elsewhere, and Sir Charles Dilke filled that post. But the Prince told Mr. Gladstone that he was "much flattered" by the invitation to join as an ordinary member.

When accepting the invitation on 22nd February, he pressed on Mr. Gladstone the inclusion among the Commissioners of two highly appropriate names, and in the second suggestion he proved himself more liberal and far-seeing than the Prime Minister and his colleagues. The Prince's nomination of Mr. Goschen— the first of his nominees (whom "I know" [the Prince wrote] "is most anxious to serve")—was accepted without discussion, but the Prince's recommendation of a woman as his second candidate was a startling challenge of precedent. Only the current fallacy of the inequality of the sexes in regard to public business could be urged against the Prince's nomination of Miss Octavia Hill, whose practical familiarity with housing conditions was unquestioned. The Prince by no means sympathised with the comprehensive movement in favour of "Women's Rights." He deprecated the grant to women of the political franchise, and viewed with active disapproval their claim to sit in Parliament. Yet he believed in women's qualifications for most branches of social service. On the other hand, Mr. Gladstone's innate conservatism, despite his political liberalism, indisposed him to break abruptly with any of the veteran prejudices against the participation of women in any department of public life. In reply to the prince's recommendation of Miss Hill, Mr. Gladstone, writing on the same day (February 22), fully admitted her "high qualifications," but, he added:

As a novelty the appointment may require careful consideration on grounds of prudence before the principle is adopted. It would be considered by many a serious innovation, and it

would perhaps be urged that Ministers ought not to advise the   1884
Crown to take up new ground on such subjects by administrative   ——
action.   I do not give this as my own deliberate conclusion, but   Ætat. 42
I think that the matter requires to be weighed.

Sir Charles Dilke approved Miss Hill's appointment,[1] but the
cabinet ultimately decided against it.   The Prince's plea of the
equal right of men and women to engage officially in social
inquiries instituted by the State was tentatively accepted some
eight years later.   A long twenty-one years were to pass before
it was fully recognised—not until the Prince had ascended the
throne.[2]

Another personal matter affecting the constitution of the
Commission was submitted to the Prince's arbitration, and his
judgement once again illustrated his faith in religious toleration.
Cardinal Manning, the Roman Catholic Archbishop of Westminster, accepted membership, as well as the Marquis of Salisbury
and two other peers—the Prince's old friend, Lord Carrington,
and Earl Brownlow.   The precedence of the Cardinal raised a
delicate issue.   Was his dignity as "a prince" of his Church to
be formally recognised?   If so, he would rank immediately after
the Prince of Wales and before the Marquis of Salisbury.   The
Prince promptly decided in the Cardinal's favour.

On 2nd March 1884 a formal motion authorising the enrolment of the Commission was brought before the House of Lords
by the originator of the design, the Marquis of Salisbury.   The
occasion proved of interest in the Prince's career.   He then
made the only full speech which he delivered as a member
of the Upper House of Parliament.   Some five years earlier
(on 6th May 1879) he had spoken a few words in the Upper
Chamber when presenting a petition from Norfolk farmers in

---

[1] Gwynn and Tuckwell's *Sir Charles Dilke*, ii. 17.

[2] The personnel of the Royal Commission on Labour (to inquire into the
relations of employers and employed), which was appointed on the 10th April
1891 under the chairmanship of the Marquis of Hartington (Duke of Devonshire), was supplemented in March 1892 by the addition of four women sub-
Commissioners (Misses Orme, Abraham, Collett, and Irwin).   In December 1905
Mr. Balfour, on the eve of his retirement from the office of Prime Minister,
admitted women for the first time to full membership of a Royal Commission in harmony with the Prince's recommendation of 1884.   A Royal Commission, which was appointed to inquire into the Poor Law, included three
women to take their place beside fifteen men.   Miss Octavia Hill, the Prince's
rejected nominee of 1884, was, after the long interval, one of the three women.
Mrs. Helen Bosanquet and Mrs. Sidney Webb were the other two.

favour of the Deceased Wife's Sister Bill. Now he dwelt at
length on the need of a searching inquiry into a subject in
which he claimed "the keenest and liveliest interest." He
spoke of his efforts at Sandringham, and described a recent
visit which he had paid to "two of the poorest courts and
districts in St. Pancras and in Holborn, where I can assure your
Lordships that the condition of the poor, or rather of their
dwellings, was perfectly disgraceful." In conclusion, he expressed
"an earnest hope" that the Commission would recommend to
Parliament "measures of a drastic and thorough character."
The Leader of the House, Lord Granville, in reporting the debate
to the Queen, wrote that "the Prince of Wales took a general
view of the subject with a happy allusion to what he had personally done in the matter." Lord Granville mentioned how later
in the debate the Lord Chancellor, "Lord Selborne, paid him a
great compliment."

The Commission was duly gazetted on the 4th March, and
the Prince attended the first meeting, which was held two days
later. Although the Prince's attendance subsequently was
somewhat fitful, he was present at 16 of the 38 meetings when
witnesses were examined. In May he cut short a visit to Royat
in order to attend. Liberal and Conservative members of the
House of Commons were evenly represented among his colleagues,
and with all of them he maintained throughout the proceedings
the most genial relations.[1] With Mr. Henry Broadhurst, a
working-man Liberal member and the only representative of
labour, and with Mr. E. Dwyer Gray, an Irish Nationalist representative who joined later, he was on the easiest terms. To the
witnesses he addressed pointed questions, and with the views of
trade-unionists and labourers he showed marked sympathy. His
Sandringham agent, Mr. Edmund Beck, gave detailed evidence
regarding the "sound cottages" which the Prince had substituted for "miserable hovels" on his own property.

In May 1885 the Prince signed the Commission's First Report,

[1] Besides the Prince and Sir Charles Dilke (the Chairman) the members
were: Cardinal Manning, Lord Salisbury, Earl Brownlow, Lord Carrington,
Mr. Goschen, Sir R. A. Cross, W. Walsham How (Bishop Suffragan of Bedford),
Messrs. E. Lyulph Stanley, W. T. McCullagh-Torrens, Henry Broadhurst,
Jesse Collings, Geo. Godwin, F.R.S., and Samuel Morley. On 16th August
there were added Sir Geo. Harrison (Lord Provost of Edinburgh) and Mr.
E. Dwyer Gray (Nationalist M.P. for Dublin). The secretary was J. E. C.
Bodley (Dilke's private secretary).

which dealt with the housing conditions of England and Wales, but he withheld his signature from an appendix signed by all his colleagues save five in favour of leasehold-enfranchisement, which was defined as "the acquisition on equitable terms of the freehold interest on the part of leaseholders."[1] The Commission subsequently pursued its investigations both in Edinburgh and Dublin, but the government deemed it undesirable that the Prince should travel to either place with his colleagues. The Prince, however, signed the reports which they issued in regard to both Scotland and Ireland. The Commission unanimously recommended, under the signature of the Prince, that local authorities should be empowered to compel owners to keep dwellings in healthy and habitable repair and to supply at their own outlay adequate accommodation. Public interest was quickened, and unlike many inquisitions of its kind, this Royal Commission early bore legislative fruit. A Bill embodying the principles of the report was promptly prepared by Sir Charles Dilke, and it became law in July 1885, under the auspices of Lord Salisbury, who then succeeded Mr. Gladstone as Prime Minister. But, owing to the slackness of local authorities, the measure worked ineffectually, and a fresh Act of Parliament of 1890 was needed to secure the practical operation of any of the Housing Commission proposals.

1885
Ætat. 43

VI

The Queen's persistent fear lest the Prince might intervene in politics was hardly silenced by his share in the Housing Commission, although she admitted that that theme of inquiry was only subsidiarily a party issue. His personal desire to repeat the experience was viewed by his mother with no particular favour. Early in 1891 an opportunity seemed at hand for the exercise of his interest in another phase of social polity. In April 1891 Lord Salisbury's government responded to growing social sentiment by appointing a Royal Commission to inquire into the relations of employers and employed and

1891
Ætat. 49

[1] Lords Salisbury and Brownlow, Sir R. A. Cross, and Bishop How— Conservative members of the Commission, together with Mr. Goschen, who was still a member of the Liberal party—also abstained from pronouncing in favour of leasehold-enfranchisement.

to consider whether legislation could usefully improve them. The Prince's friend, the Marquis of Hartington, who was to succeed his father as Duke of Devonshire at the end of the year (December 21), was nominated Chairman, and the Prince offered to serve on the Commission. But his offer was declined on the ground that the controversial issues at stake made it desirable that he should hold aloof. Late in the next year the new Liberal Government resolved to submit another branch of the social question to the consideration of a fresh Royal Commission, and Mr. Gladstone, taking a broader view of the Prince's position than Queen Victoria or his predecessor, enlisted his services in the inquiry. The subject of investigation was the relief which should, apart from the provisions of the Poor Law, be provided for destitute persons who were incapacitated from work by old age.

The Prince was anxious that the membership of the Aged Poor Commission should represent the working classes whose interests were chiefly involved. He welcomed co-operation for a second time with Mr. Henry Broadhurst, the working-man M.P., his colleague on the Housing inquiry, and strongly supported the addition of a second labour representative in the person of Mr. Joseph Arch, the founder of the National Agricultural Labourers' Union in 1872, who represented in the House of Commons in the Liberal interest the N.W. division of Norfolk, within the boundaries of which Sandringham lay. Mr. Arch claimed the Prince as one of his constituents, and spoke of himself as "The Prince's M.P." [1] The Prince's fellow-Commissioners, who numbered eighteen, included his old friend, Lord Playfair, as well as the Liberal-Unionist leader, Mr. Joseph Chamberlain. Lord Playfair became Chairman in place of Lord Aberdare, before the Commission ended its labours. With characteristic cordiality the Prince invited his colleagues, including Mr. Broadhurst and Mr. Arch, to spend week-ends with him at Sandringham.

The Prince took his duties as Commissioner very seriously. He attended 35 out of the 48 sessions in the course of the two years that the Commission sat, and he interrogated the

[1] With Mr. Arch the Prince's relations remained cordial to the last. When on a visit to the Countess of Warwick at Warwick Castle in May 1896, he paid him an unceremonious visit at his neighbouring home at The Cottage, Barford. Cf. *Joseph Arch: the Story of His Life, told by Himself and edited, with a Preface, by the Countess of Warwick*, 1898, p. 400.

witnesses with much pertinence. A fellow-Commissioner of strong radical convictions, Mr. James Stuart, thus described the part that the Prince played in the Commission's proceedings :

He attended very regularly, and asked, when his turn came, very good questions. I thought at first that he had probably been prompted to these, but I soon found out that they were of his own initiative, and that he really had a very considerable grasp of the subjects he dealt with. This was evident from the way in which the questions he asked followed on upon the evidence, and upon other questions which were interposed by one or other members of the Commission. He, like many other people when they are sitting on a committee, drew with a pencil on a piece of paper for a considerable part of the time. He drew Union Jacks, and he had two pencils, a red and a blue, besides his black one, which lay beside him always.[1]

The Prince especially sought in his interrogations to ascertain the grounds of the strong prejudice harboured by the aged poor against entering the workhouses. After visiting Lambeth workhouse in order to test for himself details of the current organisation, he asked one of the witnesses, Mr. George Lansbury, to explain the objection to workhouse dress and food. He also directed the Commission's attention to the discrepancies in the cost of outdoor relief in different districts, and laid stress on the need of precise particulars of the cost of Old Age Pensions for which his more advanced colleagues pressed. When Miss Octavia Hill pleaded in the witness chair for voluntary agencies as opposed to State organisation, he invited her to state her objections to "the Post Office Savings Bank or to deferred annuities purchased from the State." Throughout the inquiry he urged the prudence of encouraging thrift, and showed a lively interest in the working of the great friendly societies.

As the Commission proceeded with its task strong differences of opinion declared themselves between those who supported a system of non-contributory State pensions and those who believed that the friendly societies could adequately relieve the necessities of old age out of the contributions of would-be beneficiaries. At length the Commission reported—in March 1895. A halting conclusion was reached. The majority resisted State pensions, which the minority tentatively approved. Mr.

[1] James Stuart, *Reminiscences*, London, 1911 (privately printed), pp. 254-5.

1895
Ætat. 53

Broadhurst, in a separate memorandum, alone maintained with decisive vigour that the care of the aged poor should be a public charge to be borne by the whole community and not to be met by any contributory or insurance schemes.

The controversial temper which characterised the final deliberations of the Commission seemed to the Prince to preclude him from identifying himself with either side; he therefore refrained from signing either the majority or the minority report, and contented himself with a note which ran as follows:

I have taken the deepest interest in the long and laborious inquiry of the R. Comm. on the Aged Poor, the meetings of which I have attended as frequently as possible. In not attaching my signature to the Report I do not mean to express disapproval of it. I feel however that as the subject has now to a considerable extent become one of party controversy, both inside and outside of Parliament, it has assumed a phase inconsistent with my position of political neutrality.

ALBERT EDWARD P.

19 Feb. 1895.

The indecisive verdict of the Commission caused general dissatisfaction. Lord Salisbury's third ministry, which succeeded the Liberals in office in 1895, appointed during its term several committees to make further inquiries into the financial aspect of the question. But no progress was made with the project of Old Age Pensions until late in King Edward's own reign. Then, in 1908, another Liberal Government passed into law, on the proposal of Mr. Lloyd George, the Chancellor of the Exchequer, the first Old Age Pensions Act. To that primal measure of its kind King Edward gave his royal assent. With the arguments in its favour, his experience as member of the Commission of 1892–93 had familiarised him.

CHAPTER XXX

THE PRINCE AND THE FIGHTING SERVICES, 1880–1895

I

ARMY reform was an important plank in the Liberal programme from an early period of Queen Victoria's reign. The Liberal party sought to strengthen parliamentary control of the army, to abolish the influence of birth and privilege, and generally to modernise and democratise the military machinery.

Such aspirations ill tallied with the conceptions of military organisation in which the Prince had been trained. From youth he had regarded the army as his formal profession, and such military training as he had received was directed by his kinsman, the Duke of Cambridge, who became Commander-in-Chief as long ago as 1856. The Duke was a professional survival of an obsolescent military school. He set great store by parade drills and field days, and insisted with pedantic rigour on the etiquette of uniform. Promotion by seniority rather than by merit was a main article of his creed. At the same time he was jealous of his personal authority, which he claimed to exercise in the name of Queen Victoria, at once his sovereign and first cousin, well-nigh to the exclusion of Parliament. Never did the Duke submit willingly to the civilian control of the Secretary for War, and during the early days of Mr. Gladstone's second ministry there was much friction between him and Mr. Childers, who sought, as Secretary for War, to develop civilian control on the far-reaching lines which Mr. Cardwell had initiated in Mr. Gladstone's first government. Meanwhile the Duke found his antiquated outlook challenged by a band of enlightened and studious officers headed by General Wolseley, who urged, among other sweeping reforms, the creation of a

1880
Ætat. 38

555

General Staff on the lines of the Board of Admiralty. The Duke held that proposal to prejudice his own position of Commander-in-Chief, and he denounced it with warmth.

The Duke made every effort to keep the Prince loyal to his own old-fashioned standards, and with pathetic earnestness he frequently appealed to him to protect him from the threats of reforming officers and politicians. The Duke's persuasions were not without their effect. The Prince's affection for his kinsman and his sympathy with the Duke's fears of supersession inclined him for a long period to look askance on all changes in military organisation and administration. The Prince was impressed by "Uncle George's" nervous prognostications that promotion by selection would lead to jobbery, and that if the reformers had their way the sovereign's control of the army would be replaced by that of a political party. "Of this I feel convinced," he asserted (November 10, 1881), "and I know far cleverer and more long-sighted men than I can claim to be who think the same." Intercourse with his Prussian brother-in-law and his attendance in 1884 at the autumn manœuvres in Germany taught him that the Prussian military system gave many points in the way of fighting efficiency to the English system, but his knowledge of the Prussian army deepened his suspicions of civilian interference. In regard to the Indian army, too, he constantly questioned the prudence of subjecting military commanders to the authority of civilian councils, and when his brother, the Duke of Connaught, was Commander-in-Chief of the Bombay army (1886–1890) he expressed himself freely on the point. Despite a growing willingness to hear the other side, his attitude towards military reforms never lost the conservative bias which was mainly the fruit of the Duke of Cambridge's influence.

Queen Victoria, with her native shrewdness and her active sense of constitutional propriety, took a judicial view of her own relations with the army and of the Duke's position. She accepted ministerial advice on military matters without much demur. She even did what she could to reconcile her cousin to those military decisions of her government which were repugnant to him. Her son proved rather less pliable, but, however slowly, he came to yield to inevitable circumstance. Ultimately he seconded his mother's efforts to parry the Duke's obstructive attitude, and with kindly good-nature endeavoured to soften the incidence of the reforming blows which he saw that his kinsman could not escape.

II

General Wolseley, the leading champion among officers of military reform, was, from 1880 onwards, the Duke's *bête noire*. The Prince acknowledged the General's promise and ability, but he shared a touch of the Duke's unjustified suspicion that he was something of an upstart seeking notoriety. In the opening months of Mr. Gladstone's second government the Duke made an open avowal of his hostility to the General. On his return from South Africa, in May 1880, Wolseley had been made Quartermaster-General. But he was intended by Mr. Gladstone and Mr. Childers for higher rank. In the spring of 1881 Mr. Gladstone proposed to confer a peerage on him in order that the cause of military reform might have a spokesman in the House of Lords. The Duke let the Prince know that he would resign if the honour were bestowed, and the Prince sided with his kinsman. Largely owing to the Prince's representations, the Queen withheld her assent to the bestowal of a peerage at this stage of Wolseley's career. But the controversy over Wolseley's promotion was not ended. Later in the year Wolseley was nominated by Mr. Childers to the responsible office of Adjutant-General. The Duke protested that the appointment was prejudicial to his authority. The Prince again benevolently took up the Duke's cause. But here his intervention was unavailing. He vainly suggested to the Queen that Wolseley might be better employed as Governor-General of Canada in place of the Marquis of Lorne, who might be moved to Ireland. The Queen declined to take action, and public opinion gave neither the Duke nor the Prince any comfort. *The Times* newspaper pronounced itself emphatically in favour of General Wolseley's promotion. In a letter from Sandringham to the Queen on 10th November 1881 the Prince echoed the Duke's pessimistic view of the situation :

Uncle George is here, but worried to death by the Adjutant-General question. He sees that you are unable to support him in resisting Sir Garnet Wolseley. I sincerely hope he may yet be prevailed on not to resign, for if he does the War Office will become like the Board of Admiralty with Wolseley in the position of First Naval Lord.

Finally the Prince succeeded in inducing "Uncle George"

1880
—
Ætat. 38

to remain at his post with Wolseley as his chief colleague.   The
Prince was by no means blind to the weakness of the Duke's
case.   He recognised that his kinsman's retirement could not
be long delayed.   But the Prince believed it to be to the advantage of the monarchy still to associate the headship of the army
with the royal family when the Duke ceased to hold the office.
He cherished the hope that if the Duke's withdrawal could be
postponed for five or six years his brother, the Duke of
Connaught, might then be qualified for the succession.

The withdrawal of Mr. Childers from the War Office in favour
of Lord Hartington relieved the Prince of immediate embarrassment.   Lord Hartington favoured military reforms on the
accepted Liberal lines, but during his tenure of office as Secretary
of War he was too fully occupied with active military operations
in Egypt and the Sudan to find time for carrying Mr. Childers'
programme much further.   Lord Hartington's personal friendship
with the Prince, moreover, enabled him to soothe susceptibilities
which Mr. Childers had ruffled.

III

Army reform remained a theme of active controversy for the
rest of the Prince's life, and the obstruction in which the Duke
persisted at length found its natural end in his compulsory
retirement.   Military reformers were divided amongst themselves
as to whether or no the office of Commander-in-Chief should
form part of a reorganised administration of the army.   The
Prince urged the retention of the office in the interest of the
Duke of Connaught.   On other issues, the Prince's friend, Lord
Hartington, helped to persuade him of the need of reorganisation,
and his conservative doubts were diminished by the geniality
of Mr. Campbell-Bannerman, who was Secretary for War in both
the third and fourth ministries of Mr. Gladstone, and was pledged
to his party's policy of military reform.

Lord Hartington presided over a strong Royal Commission,
which inquired, between June 1888 and May 1890, into all the
broad issues of both naval and military administration.   One of
the Hartington Commission's findings was that the post of
Commander-in-Chief should be abolished when the Duke ceased
to hold it, and that he should be replaced by a Chief of the Staff,

with a number of colleagues, among whom various controlling
duties should be distributed. Mr. Campbell-Bannerman, on
becoming Secretary for War for the second time in 1892, sought
to give effect to some of the Commission's recommendations, but
he modified its findings in regard to the office of Commander-in-
Chief, which he proposed to retain, albeit with diminished powers.

Mr. Campbell-Bannerman's decision brought the vexed
question of the Duke of Cambridge's personal position to a final
issue. Before the Secretary for War took action Lord Rosebery
succeeded Mr. Gladstone as Liberal Prime Minister (on March 3,
1894). An essential preliminary of Mr. Campbell-Bannerman's
scheme was the Duke's supersession—a step in which Lord
Rosebery concurred. The old Commander-in-Chief was in no
compliant mood, and he announced that he would resist displacement to the last. Thereby he caused both Queen Victoria
and the Prince much grave embarrassment.

Queen Victoria calmly faced the inevitable situation. The
Prince at first showed sympathy with "Uncle George's" wounded
feelings, but he saw the futility of resistance and undertook the
unenviable task of inducing the Duke to yield. He pointed out
to him that the office of Commander-in-Chief, which both were
anxious to retain, would probably be abolished altogether if the
Duke proved obdurate. But the veteran was difficult to influence.
Much correspondence passed between the Prince and his mother
as to the form which effective pressure on their kinsman should
take. The Prince at first thought that an ultimatum would
come with better effect from the Prime Minister, Lord Rosebery,
than from Queen Victoria, and he suggested that Lord Rosebery
might gild the pill by allowing the Duke to retain office till the
end of the year. But Lord Rosebery was disinclined for half-
measures, and he made it clear that the resignation must take
effect at once. Finally the Prince urged his mother to invite
the Duke's retirement in a personal interview. He promised to
see the Duke a day earlier than that fixed for the Queen's
meeting, with a view to bringing him to a submissive frame of
mind. The Queen accepted her son's advice and help. But when
the Duke saw the Queen, on 16th May 1895, while he expressed
his readiness to follow her counsel, he showed a very inadequate
appreciation of the crucial situation; he suggested that he might
be allowed to remain at his post and be "assisted by a kind of

1894
—
Ætat. 52

board." The Prince, on hearing of the suggestion, declared with some impatience that nothing of the sort would be entertained. A day or two later the Duke made to Mr. Campbell-Bannerman much the same suggestion. At length, on the 21st, the Queen sent the Duke a letter which the Prince described as "excellent," explicitly requesting his unconditional resignation. Only then did the refractory Duke give way. Writing from Warwick Castle on 17th May to the Queen's Secretary, Sir Arthur Bigge, who had kept the Prince fully informed of the progress of events, the Prince deplored "the very difficult and disagreeable position in which the Queen finds herself placed" between the Duke, who objected to resigning, and the Government, who "wished him to go." He claimed to have convinced the Duke that "the position of Commander-in-Chief in the future would be at stake" unless he placed "his resignation in the Queen's hands." The Duke was disposed to claim a pension for his long service; but here again the government proved unsympathetic, and the Prince proved the soundness of his judgement by joining other relatives in dissuading the Duke from formulating such a request. Much of the Prince's action through the crisis went against the grain, but he sought, according to his lights, to treat with justice and consideration all parties in the struggle.

On 21st June Mr. Campbell-Bannerman was in a position, in part owing to the Prince's good offices, to announce to the House of Commons the withdrawal of the Duke from the office of Commander-in-Chief. His speech was a model of good feeling. Later in the sitting, by an unlooked-for coincidence, the ministry was defeated on a motion which came from the Conservative benches concerning the reserve supply of cordite. Lord Rosebery resigned office next day.

IV

The appointment of a successor to the Duke as Commander-in-Chief involved further delicate considerations. The duty fell to Lord Salisbury, the Conservative Prime Minister, who assumed office on Lord Rosebery's resignation. The Prince took the liveliest interest in the process of filling the Duke's place. He remained sanguine that his soldier brother, the Duke of Connaught, who at the time held the command at Aldershot,

might be chosen, but General Sir John McNeill, one of the
Queen's equerries, and other experienced military acquaintances,
convinced him that his brother, who was comparatively young in
the service, ought to wait for the supreme command. On such
a ground the Prince welcomed a proposal to limit the new
appointment to a term of five years, with the proviso that the
holder should not be reappointed.

Accepting his brother's temporary disqualification, the Prince
was at first inclined to push the claims of his friend Sir Redvers
Buller. But Lord Lansdowne, who became Secretary for War
in Lord Salisbury's new ministry, decided to appoint Lord
Wolseley. Neither Queen Victoria nor the Prince regarded Lord
Lansdowne's selection with much favour. Both thought that
Lord Wolseley might be advantageously provided for otherwise.
Kaiser William II. was at the moment pressing the Queen to
send Lord Wolseley to Berlin as British Ambassador in succession
to Sir Edward Malet. But the government carried their point,
and "Uncle George's" chief opponent through many preceding
years became, on a five years' tenure, the first Commander-in-
Chief under the new military régime.

With Lord Wolseley's accession to office there came into operation long-threatened changes of importance in the organisation of
the War Office and in the distribution of duties. Lord Lansdowne
readily sought the Prince's countenance for the alterations. He
forwarded to him the preliminary drafts of the requisite Orders in
Council, and the Prince invited the new Secretary for War, Lord
Lansdowne, to Sandringham to discuss them (November 1895).
The minister wrote to the Queen on 11th November 1895, "The
Prince of Wales was, Lord Lansdowne believed, fully satisfied by
his explanation of the papers." Lord Wolseley also was conscious
of the advantage of enlisting the Prince's support in behalf of his
reforms. "I am most anxious to work in all Army matters with
the Prince and under his orders," the new Commander-in-Chief
wrote in a rather courtly strain to the Prince's equerry, General
Ellis, in June 1896. Lord Wolseley made a special appeal to
the Prince to favour the adoption of a more practical uniform
and equipment for the troops than the Duke of Cambridge,
from his "parade point of view," had approved. The Prince
expressed sympathy with Lord Wolseley's suggestion.[1]

[1] Maurice and Arthur, *Life of Lord Wolseley*, 1924, p. 308.

1882
Ætat. 53

A subsidiary and unexpected result of the Duke of Cambridge's retirement from the army was to enhance the Prince's military prestige. By way of salving the Duke's injured feelings the Queen created him, on his retirement, her chief personal aide-de-camp and Colonel-in-Chief to the Forces, and in a letter to him on 3rd July 1895 accorded him the right of holding the parade on her birthday. But when the Queen's next birthday was approaching, Lord Wolseley, the new Commander-in-Chief, raised objection to his predecessor holding the parade. The Queen with reluctance endorsed Wolseley's protest. Thereupon she chose her eldest son to take the place which she had designed for her superannuated cousin. On the 5th May 1896 she wrote to the Duke: "Finding that there are some difficulties in the way of your taking the Command at the Parade on my birthday, I propose that Bertie should represent me and receive the Salute." Some days later, on 14th May, she expanded the compliment by directing the Prince to play as her representative the chief part not only at the forthcoming Birthday parade, but on all future occasions of the like kind.

V

1882
Ætat. 40

Although the Prince's relations with the navy and its administration were less intimate than with the army and its administration, he was unflagging in his advocacy of the maintenance of the fleet in a progressive strength, which should be adapted to future calls. The cheeseparing policy of a clique of Liberals and Radicals received no countenance from him. He was inclined to acquiesce in the most generous estimates of the country's naval needs. Successive popular agitations for increase in the naval establishment could always reckon on his support. During Mr. Gladstone's second ministry of 1880–85 the Prince frequently confessed doubts of the sufficiency of the Liberal naval programme. In the course of the reconstruction of the ministry of 1882 he suggested that his friend, Sir Charles Dilke, should take over the Admiralty from Lord Northbrook. He justly placed full confidence in Sir Charles's sound views, with which his fellow-Radicals showed scant sympathy, on questions of naval security. The Prince's suggestion failed of effect, but it well illustrated the trend of his thought. Some two years later journalistic allegations of the Liberal Government's neglect of the country's naval requirements excited a popular outcry, with which the Prince sympathised. "The deplorable state of our navy" he described as one of the "all-absorbing topics of the day," when writing on 15th October 1884 to a friend, Mr. Alfred Montgomery.

During the opening years of Lord Salisbury's second ministry (1886–92) public opinion was still disturbed by naval controversies. The Prince's interest was whetted by his close intimacy with Lord Charles Beresford, who was serving in the government as Fourth Lord of the Admiralty. With breezy indifference to ministerial conventions Lord Charles was urging on his colleagues, not only in the council-chamber but also in the press and on the platform, heroic developments of the navy, which the Treasury regarded as costly extravagances. The Prince was responsible for Lord Charles's admission to political office, and was inclined to pardon his protégé's indiscretions in what he believed to be a matter of urgency. When Lord Charles suddenly resigned his post at the Admiralty (January 1888) by way of protest against the niggardliness of the Treasury, the Prince for the time stood privately by him. Lord Charles, as a private member of Parliament, initiated a vigorous crusade against the government and the Board of the Admiralty. But the pugnacious impetuosity of his attack soon caused the Prince some qualms. He harboured no doubt of the justice of his friend's aims but questioned his tactics. "You will *never* get any *real* reforms with the *present* Board of Admiralty," he wrote to him, 9th July 1888, "and nobody knows that better than yourself." The Prince advised Lord Charles to retire from the House of Commons and from party polemics and complete his service at sea. Lord Charles's postponement of that step for a year was hardly congenial to the Prince. Lord Charles urged in justification of the delay his wish to stiffen the provisions of the government's Naval Defence Bill which was promised for the session of 1889. The Bill provided for the addition to the fleet of as many as ten battleships, forty-two cruisers, and eighteen torpedo-boats, to be completed in four and a half years at a cost of £21,500,000. The Prince admitted that his protégé's efforts to strengthen the measure during its passage through the House of Commons were useful, but he continued to urge Lord Charles to abandon politics for naval service.

1886
—
Ætat. 44

1888
—
Ætat. 46

"I was much interested," the Prince wrote to him from the Marlborough Club, 2nd April 1889, "in hearing your speech last night and staying for part of the debate on the Naval programme. The subject is indeed one of vital interest to the country, and I was sorry to see how empty the Government Bench was. However, I have little doubt that public opinion will be in your favour and that our fleet will be strengthened and improved as it ought to have been long ago. You have done all that is in your power in that direction, and I hope that by the time you go to sea this summer you will have been rewarded for your efforts."

Lord Charles was scarcely satisfied with the final shape which the Naval Defence Bill took, but the Prince was relieved by his retirement from the House of Commons in the summer, and by his appointment in December to the command of H.M.S. *Undaunted*. The fascination which the House of Commons exerted on Lord Charles was, however, unexhausted, and he returned to it eight years later in as aggressive a temper as ever. In the interval he had forfeited his long tenure of the Prince's confidence, and a breach on private grounds alienated the Prince's interest in Lord Charles's future achievements, whether political or professional.

In the Prince's view, far more still required doing in regard to naval defence when Lord Salisbury's second ministry came to an end. Lord George Hamilton, the Conservative First Lord, was succeeded in 1892, when Mr. Gladstone resumed office, by the Prince's old friend Lord Spencer. There were fresh public demands for a strengthening of the fleet in view of early indications of Germany's ambition to challenge England's naval supremacy. The Prince believed Lord Spencer to be well alive to the situation, and, despite the Treasury's warnings against large expenditure, hoped for the best.

"Our Admiralty is, I think," he wrote to Sir Henry Acland on 17th December 1893, "fully alive to the importance of strengthening our Navy, but the Government (with a bad Budget) hesitate about voting the necessary supplies. I hope, however, that all will be right. Our position as a great Power *entirely* depends on the efficiency and preponderance of our Navy."

The view which the Prince expressed in the last sentence was one of his profoundest convictions.

Bastien-Lepage pinxit

Emery Walker ph sc

King Edward VII in his thirty eighth year

CHAPTER XXXI

SOCIAL TIES AND RECREATIONS, 1877–1900

I

ON the 9th November 1881 the Prince celebrated his fortieth
birthday. Replying to his mother's congratulations, he wrote:
"Forty certainly sounds formidable, but (*unberufen*) I am feeling
well and strong, as if I were twenty-five, and trust I may still
have some years of usefulness before me." He was bearing his
years well, and the buoyancy of youth was slow to desert him.
He did not aspire to great length of days. When good accounts
reached him in 1885 of his old Oxford chief, the septuagenarian
Dean Liddell of Christ Church, he wrote to their common friend,
Dr. Acland (November 15): "But when one reaches seventy-
five it makes one feel serious. As far as I am concerned, though
I feel (*unberufen*) strong and well, I do not aspire to reach that
age." The Prince was shrewd enough to perceive the surest way
to health. "The best plan to maintain health is, I am sure, to
be careful of your diet and take as much exercise as possible,"
was the simple counsel of perfection which he communicated to
Dr. Acland on completing his fifty-third year (October 25, 1894).
A robust constitution, which knew very occasional disablement
by illness in middle age, tempted him at times to qualify the
personal application of his precept, and yet to conserve rich
stores of vitality. He was thus able to face with unresting
spirit the immense variety of calls on his energy. Of a restless
temperament, he was in no danger of dulling his faculties by
inertia, and he only acknowledged with some reluctance that
there were limits to the scope of his exertions. When, in March
1880, Sir Bartle Frere suggested a visit to the Cape, the Prince
expressed complete willingness to fall in with Frere's suggestion

"if it were possible." "But," he added, "there are so many 'ifs.' It is such a long way off, and our various occupations and vocations keep us nearer home." There was no exaggeration in his remark to Acland (December 18, 1889), "I am rather hard worked in the summer, and people are very exacting in their demands on one's time and strength."

The energy and verve with which he fulfilled multifarious engagements in London and in the country may be gauged from a typical chronicle of his activities at the close of a busy season, which he sent to his friend, Alfred Montgomery, in 1885.

"There has been a good deal going on in society," he wrote on 15th July from Studley Royal, where he was making a two days' stay with the Marquis of Ripon. "Last week I was at Newmarket, and the weather was splendid. On Monday the Westminsters gave a ball. We [*i.e.* the Prince and Princess] came here yesterday [from London], and our function at Leeds [the opening of the Yorkshire College, after-wards Leeds University] to-day went off admirably. We met with a most enthusiastic reception. To-morrow I go to Preston for the Royal Agricultural Show, staying the night at Lathom, and returning to town the following day. From Saturday to Monday I shall be at Ferdy Rothschild's palatial residence of Waddesdon. This day week we go to Cowes for my sister Beatrice's wedding [with Prince Henry of Battenberg] the day after. The following week we go to Goodwood, and on August 1 till 17th we expect to be at Cowes."

Within these five weeks he, in agreement with his usual habit, was gyrating on divers errands between London and seven places at a distance.

Among some observers there was complaint of a lack of serious aim in the social rotations of his seasonal programme. A critical sociologist pointed out in 1891 that according to the evidence of daily newspapers of the previous year, the Prince attended, between 1st January and 30th September, 28 race meetings, 30 theatrical performances, 43 dinner-parties, banquets, balls, and garden parties, together with 45 official and phil-anthropic ceremonies, and 11 sittings of the House of Lords.[1] The deduction was drawn that pursuits of pleasure figured dis-proportionately in the lists of the Prince's engagements to the injury of the prestige of the monarchy. The Prince's secretary,

---

[1] Arnold White, *Tries at Truth*, p. 119.

Francis Knollys, took up the challenge and pointed out, in a
letter to the writer, that much of the routine which social custom
expected of the Prince brought him anything but amusement:
"His position demands that he should every year go through a
certain round of social duties which constantly bore him to death."
The private secretary discreetly refrained from filling in the
numerous gaps in his correspondent's story. If, on the one
hand, Mr. Knollys naturally ignored the private diversions inseparable from the Prince's hedonistic temperament, he, on the
other hand, withheld any hint of his untiring interest in domestic
and especially in international politics, which lay beyond the
range of public knowledge. Nor was reference made to the
exceptional range of "the philanthropic and official ceremonies"
in which the Prince took part. Colleges, schools, libraries, art
galleries, parks, municipal buildings, docks, as well as hospitals,
were inaugurated by him in person in all parts of the country.[1]

The Prince regarded social calls, in spite of their monotony
which tried his patience, as obligations which it would be a
dereliction of duty in him as a social leader to evade. Their
irksomeness, which grew more oppressive with his years, never
impaired his devotion to the social round. He occasionally felt
himself estranged from the younger generation with whom he
deemed himself bound to keep in near social touch. He sometimes imputed to his juniors a frowardness which jarred on him
when his spirits flagged. In 1887 he wrote to his friend Mr.
Alfred Montgomery: "Refinement of feeling in the younger
generation does not exist in the nineteenth century!" To
Dr. Acland, he wrote next year in a like mood (December 31):

We are, I suppose, becoming more and more civilised, and,
I presume, acquiring more knowledge, but I doubt whether
either is turned to as good an account as would be expected and
desired. The age of chivalry has, alas, passed, and one sees it

[1] The Prince illustrated the comprehensive liberalism of his philanthropy
by presiding, somewhat to the scandal of the temperance party in the
country, at the Jubilee celebrations of the Licensed Victuallers' Benevolent
Institution in 1877. He explained that he was present not as an advocate of
the sale of strong drink but from a wish to support a deserving charity.
Two engagements which he fulfilled in the year 1886 illustrate the general
importance attaching to many of the structures which he formally dedicated
to public uses. On 28th April he inaugurated the working of the Mersey tunnel
at Liverpool, and on 21st June he laid the foundation stone of the Tower
Bridge, which he opened eight years later, on 30th June 1894.

daily, both in political and social life—but one must go with the times and try and pick out the good and discard the bad!

Those who accused him in later life of sympathy with irresponsible frivolity and of blind devotion to "ceremony," the traditional "idol" of princes, spoke without book.

II

⌐One of the serious interests which grew upon the Prince in middle life was freemasonry, which powerfully appealed to his fraternal and philanthropic instincts. He had been initiated into the Order by King Charles XV. of Sweden, when on a visit to Stockholm in December 1868.[1] On the 1st September of the following year he had received in London the rank of Past Grand Master of England at a meeting of Grand Lodge, and in September 1875, after the resignation of his friend the Marquis of Ripon on his conversion to Roman Catholicism, he was installed in great splendour at the Albert Hall in the supreme office of Grand Master. In his speech on accepting the office he impressively denied that freemasons had any political aims. "The great object of our Order," he declared, "is to strengthen the bonds of fraternal affection. . . . Our masonic principles and hopes are essential parts of our attachment to the Constitution and loyalty to the Crown." The masonic ritual appealed to his idiosyncrasy. During the twenty-six years that he filled the post of Grand Master, he presided over many brilliant concourses of masons, notably those which voted an address to Queen Victoria on her escape from an attempt at assassination in 1882 and on the occasions of her Jubilee and of her Diamond Jubilee. With full masonic rites he performed the laying of foundation stones of many notable buildings. Especially noteworthy were the formularies of the masonic ritual which distinguished, despite clerical misgivings, his laying of the foundation stone, on 20th May 1880, of Truro Cathedral—the first Anglican cathedral erected in England since St. Paul's Cathedral was rebuilt in 1697.[2] In the charitable side of freemasonry the Prince was likewise characteristically

[1] See p. 291 *supra.*
[2] A. C. Benson's *Life of Archbishop Benson.* The Prince returned to Truro seven years later to attend the consecration of the eastern portion of the cathedral (November 3, 1887).

active.   He did what he could to promote the welfare of the three   1881
great charitable institutions of freemasons, the Boys' School, the   Ætat. 40
Girls' School, and the Benevolent Institution, presiding at
festival dinners and opening extensions of the buildings.   His
faith in the Order was attested by his introduction into it of his
brothers, the Duke of Connaught and the Duke of Albany, and
of his eldest son, the Duke of Clarence.   On his accession to the
throne he relinquished the Grand Mastership, and assumed the
title of Protector of the Craft of England.   His interest in
freemasonry never slackened to the end of his life.

III

The wider life which the Prince lived outside the social en-
clave of which he was the accredited sovereign furnished very
numerous correctives of its tiresome routine.

The Prince's recreative resources were abundant, although
his temperament allowed him to find little or no solace in literature
in which most men of notable activity in public affairs have
discovered refreshment.   Books never played any appreciable
part among the Prince's diversions.   If he mentions one at all
in the familiar correspondence of his maturity, it is to announce
that he looks forward to reading it, but there are few signs that
his anticipation was fulfilled.   "As soon as I have some quiet
hours I shall certainly read the Croker Papers with the greatest
interest," he tells his friend Montgomery on the 29th September
1884.   To Mr. Gladstone he confides, on 2nd January 1897:

Mr. Brett [afterwards, as Lord Esher, an intimate friend of
King Edward] has been kind enough to send me his book, *The
Yoke of Empire*, which I look forward to read—especially after
having been recommended to me by you.

To Lady Londonderry the Prince writes from Mar Lodge
on 27th September 1898: "I have not yet seen Busch's book
(*i.e. Conversations of Bismarck*), but it will be unsatisfactory
reading."   The Prince rarely speaks of the few books which
he attempted to read with much approval.   He asked Lady
Castlereagh (September 27, 1898) whether she had read two
recently published novels, one of them Hall Caine's *The
Christian*, and added the comment, "Neither of them is a
satisfactory book."

Music and the drama always stood with the Prince on a footing very different from literature. In the opera and the play he found through life one of the most effectual means of relief from the monotonies of ceremonial routine. In his leisure hours at home and abroad he welcomed, too, the society of leading members of both the dramatic and musical professions.

The Prince's theatrical tastes, while they inclined to the lighter forms of entertainment, were, in middle life, comprehensive. Alike in London and in Paris he made trial of many kinds of theatrical endeavour. He witnessed in Paris well-nigh every piece which enjoyed a vogue in his day, and the leading French performers were among his familiar French acquaintances. The famous French actress, Madame Sarah Bernhardt, won his admiration, and he welcomed her many visits to London.

In England the Prince personally interested himself in a wide range of drama and in its leading interpreters. On Sir Henry Irving, the serious-minded chieftain of the English stage through the later half of Queen Victoria's reign, the Prince bestowed much attention. He witnessed most of Irving's Shakespearian productions at the Lyceum Theatre from 1872 onwards, and maintained with him friendly social relations. He supped with Irving and his friends on the Lyceum stage after the performance of *Much Ado About Nothing* (May 8, 1883); and when Queen Victoria, who eschewed the theatre in her widowhood, was on a visit to Sandringham on 26th April 1889, he invited Irving to perform in her presence *The Bells*, a melodrama in which the actor made his first fame, as well as the trial scene from *The Merchant of Venice*, to which the rendering of Miss Ellen Terry as Portia added distinction. After their performance the two artists supped with the Prince and Princess.[1] This was the second dramatic entertainment which the Queen had witnessed since her husband's death. The first had also been provided by her son when she was his guest at Abergeldie Castle eight years before (October 11, 1881). His choice, which then fell on *The Colonel*, a satirical farce by his friend of Cambridge days, Francis Burnand, well illustrates the versatility of his theatrical tastes.

With well-nigh every London theatre was the Prince familiar, and his widespread patronage left its mark on theatrical history.

[1] Bram Stoker, *Personal Reminiscences of Henry Irving*, ii. 212 *et seq.*, 1906.

The Prince of Wales's Theatre, off Tottenham Court Road, which   1881
from 1865 to 1880 obeyed new standards in the interpretation of   Ætat. 40
domestic comedy, was christened after him by the fertile and
popular playwright, H. J. Byron, and the brilliant comedy
actress, Marie Wilton (afterwards Lady Bancroft), when they
became, in 1865, the joint-lessees, and set the little playhouse
on its road to fame.[1]   In 1880 Marie Wilton and her husband,
Mr. Squire Bancroft, leaving the Prince of Wales's, developed
their fame as actors and managers at the Haymarket Theatre,
where the Prince was a frequent visitor.   Under different control
their earlier house, the Prince of Wales's, achieved a record run
of a year and a half with Burnand's *The Colonel*.   The Prince
often joined the audience at Drury Lane and the Adelphi
theatres while they were identified with sensational melodrama,
under the managements, respectively, of Augustus Harris and
of the actor William Terriss.[2]   The drollery of the most popular
comedian of the epoch, J. L. Toole, also potently appealed
to the Prince's sense of humour.   Thrice Toole appeared, on
the Prince's invitation, in characteristic parts on visits to
Sandringham.   On one of these occasions the comedian enlivened
the celebration of Prince Albert Victor's coming of age (January 8, 1885).

The social standing of actors was sensibly raised by the   1891
Prince's theatrical zeal.   Besides Irving and Toole, he occasion-   Ætat. 50
ally entertained at Marlborough House other members of the
profession—(Sir) Charles Wyndham, (Sir) Squire Bancroft, and
(Sir) John Hare; and when at Homburg in the August of many
successive years, during the last decade of the century, he welcomed the society of these and other actors who happened to be
fellow-visitors.   The dramatic world generously acknowledged
the Prince's sympathy.   On 10th November 1891, the day after
his fiftieth birthday, Sir Augustus Harris, Herbert Beerbohm
Tree, Squire Bancroft, John Hare, and D'Oyly Carte travelled
to Sandringham and, in behalf of the whole body of London actors
and managers, presented to the Prince a solid gold cigar-box.

---

[1] The Prince of Wales's Theatre, off Tottenham Court Road, after 1881
lost its vogue, and the building ceased to be used for theatrical purposes,
being afterwards demolished and replaced in 1905 by the Scala Theatre.   The
Prince of Wales's name was meanwhile bestowed on a new theatre in Coventry
Street, which was originally opened in 1883 as the Prince's.

[2] Cf. Jesse Millward, *Myself and Others*, ch. vi. (1923).

1891
Ætat. 50

To the Prince's influence may be attributed the bestowal of official honours on leading actors. The new precedent was inaugurated by the grant of a knighthood to Henry Irving in 1895. A like dignity was conferred two years later on Squire Bancroft, who belonged, like Irving, to the Prince's histrionic circle. The practice thus instituted was maintained by the Prince when he came to the throne, and he himself knighted two other actors with whom he was on social terms—John Hare in 1907, and Beerbohm Tree in 1909. The dramatic author, Arthur Pinero, was similarly decorated by him in the latter year.

'The Prince's persistence as a playgoer and his interest in actors could not fail to provoke unfavourable remark in some old-fashioned quarters, but the theatre in England and elsewhere was a national institution and a purveyor of amusement for the people at large, which deserved in unprejudiced minds all the encouragement that the Prince gave it.

IV

1885
Ætat. 43

It was in foreign travel and in sport that the Prince found, in a growing degree with increase of years, the most efficient antidote to the weariness of formal social and public functions. Under foreign skies his transparent incognitos of Baron Renfrew or Earl of Chester did not always protect him against invasions of his privacy, but the freedom which he sought always required for its full enjoyment congenial social intercourse, albeit in unceremonious conditions. Neither abroad nor at home did he find solace in solitude. The spontaneous remark of a gillie in attendance on him when deer-stalking in the Scottish Highlands, that he enjoyed "the privacy of the public road," had a very wide application. The Prince remained faithful to his habit of sojourning in early spring on the crowded Riviera, making his headquarters at Cannes. A few days in Paris on the outward and return journeys always formed an important part of his prophylactic against the fatigues of the coming season. But more prolonged trials of the foreign corrective were usually made in the late autumn after the season ended. His three weeks' "cure" at a German watering-place—he preferred Homburg in the later years of the century to his earlier choice of Wiesbaden—was frequently a prelude to tours through scenes

which were little frequented by his English associates, and
where he could count on a warm welcome from foreign hosts and
often on indulgence in exceptional forms of sport.   His youthful
delight never diminished in the large family parties which his
wife's Danish parents were wont to assemble in September at
the Castle of Fredensborg.   The polyglot environment and the
vast numbers of the assembled kinsfolk gratified him.   "We are
an immense family gathering—quite a Babel, as seven different
languages are spoken," he wrote to a friend from Fredensborg
on 18th September 1885.   "We are an immense family party,
never sitting down to dinner less than fifty or sixty," was
his comment two years later on the hospitalities of his wife's
family.

The autumn visit to Denmark was often the starting-point of
a more extended tour.   A typical example belongs to September
1885.   He left Denmark to stay with King Oscar of Sweden at
the picturesquely situated Castle of Drottningholm, whence he
explored in the royal yacht *Osborne* the fiords of Norway.   "The
scenery in the fiords quite surpassed my expectations," he wrote
elatedly on 11th September, but he was more impressed by the
sport which his host offered him.   "We have had most extra-
ordinarily good sport elk shooting this week, and got sixty of
those antediluvian-looking animals in three days."   From the
northern kingdoms he went through Vienna to Hungary.   There
he enjoyed some stag-hunting as the guest of his friend, Count
Tassilo Festetics, at his country seat of Bezeneze.   Before turning
homewards through Paris he satisfied a different predilection by
visiting the International Exhibition at Buda-Pesth.   There he
was very pleasantly entertained by Countess Karolyi, wife of the
Austrian Ambassador in London, who was a favourite member
of the diplomatic corps at the Court of St. James's.[1]

Another example of a distant autumn tour belongs to 1888,
when he interrupted a month's travel in Austria and Hungary

---

[1] During the eighties the Prince's intimacies among members of the
diplomatic corps in London notably increased.   Very congenial was his
intercourse with many ambassadors who made at this period long stays in this
country, notably with M. Waddington, French Ambassador from 1883 to 1893,
and his American wife; with Count Karolyi, Austrian Ambassador from 1878
to 1888; with M. de Staal, Russian Ambassador from 1884 to 1902.   M. Falbe,
the Danish Minister from 1880 and his English wife became close friends of the
Prince, and he described their country house at Luton Hoo, where he was a
frequent guest, as "one of the most comfortable houses I know of."

in order to pay a week's visit to the King and Queen of Rumania at their summer palace at Sinaia in the Carpathian Mountains. One evening Queen Elizabeth (of the German Wied family), who was well known as a poetess under the pseudonym of Carmen Sylva, presented for the Prince's entertainment a series of thirteen *tableaux vivants* of scenes from Shakespeare's plays. In the course of this tour the Prince revisited Buda-Pesth and again enjoyed the hospitality of Count Festetics, who introduced him to Keszthely, another of his shooting estates—"a charming place and a palatial residence" as the Prince described it. There the Prince engaged for four days in August in varied sport. A year later, in 1889, after a fortnight's stay at Fredensborg, he passed by way of Vienna and Venice to Athens to attend the marriage of his niece, the Empress Frederick's daughter Sophie, to Constantine, the Duke of Sparta, his wife's nephew, and heir to the Greek throne. From Athens he proceeded to Egypt to enjoy a fresh experience of Khedivial hospitalities.[1]

Austria and Hungary offered to the Prince, when bent on holiday far afield, much attraction in the ways alike of sport and of adventurous social intercourse. His creed of social liberty was at times conspicuously illustrated on his visits to the Dual Monarchy by his close social relations with men of such contrasted status as Crown Prince Rudolph and Baron Hirsch, the Hungarian-Jewish millionaire. The Prince showed complete indifference to the objections taken on very different grounds to his association with both these companions. With Crown Prince Rudolph, Emperor Francis Joseph's heir, the Prince had first come into intimate touch when the Crown Prince visited London as a youth of nineteen in February 1878. The young man was lavishly entertained, and the Prince gave on 10th February a dinner in his honour at which the Prime Minister, Lord Beaconsfield, was a fellow-guest. The Prince was unsuccessful in persuading the Queen to confer on the visitor the Order of the Garter. When the Crown Prince married at Vienna on 10th May 1881 Princess Stephanie, second daughter of King Leopold II. of Belgium, the Prince was desirous of attending the wedding, but the Queen withheld her permission. Reports of the Crown Prince's dissolute life, which the Prince of Wales discredited, failed to slacken their intimacy. The Crown Prince attended

---

[1] See p. 461 *supra*.

Queen Victoria's Jubilee in 1887, and in the autumn of the
following year the Prince of Wales spent much time abroad in
the Crown Prince's society, joining him and his father at the
autumn manœuvres in Croatia, and engaging with the Austrian
heir-apparent in hunting stags, bears, and chamoix elsewhere
in Austria. The Crown Prince's death at Mayerling by suicide
in scandalous circumstances on the 30th January 1889 shocked
the Prince, who took a characteristically chivalrous view of the
episode, but the hope of the Viennese Court that the Prince of
Wales would attend the funeral was unfulfilled.

It was in 1891 that the Prince once again visited Austria and
Hungary mainly to enjoy the hospitality of Baron Hirsch,
thereby ruffling the susceptibilities of the Austrian Court, which
looked askance on the Prince's host. The Baron had made most
of his immense fortune by financing railways in the Balkans and
in Turkey, and he devoted a large part of it to improving the
conditions of members of his race in Russia, where he endowed
schools and facilitated emigration to America and Asia Minor.
But despite his munificent charities, high birth on the Continent
steadily held aloof from him. The Prince, who had been introduced to the Baron in Paris, was, however, attracted by the
Baron's philanthropic ardour, and by his enthusiasm for sport
and for the turf. Very readily did he accept the Baron's invitation to join, in 1891, a shooting-party on his Hungarian estate at
St. Johann. The Prince spent twelve days there (October 6–18),
besides enjoying his host's company in Vienna while passing
to and from Hungary. The Baron was a good shot and the birds
flew high and well, but the sport at St. Johann, organised on a
great scale, was something of a battue, and in five days 11,300 head
of game, chiefly partridges, were bagged.[1] The Prince, in the best
of humours, cemented his friendship with his host, and was by no
means disconcerted by the criticisms passed in strait-laced circles

[1] "No fewer than 200 beaters were employed. They started in a circle of
about seven miles in circumference, driving the birds to the guns, who stood
about sixty yards in a circle which perhaps extended over three acres. Each
gun was stationed in a box walled in with branches of fir, so that all the shots
must be directed upwards, for the birds fly high. It is thus impossible that a
neighbour or beater could be struck. The movements of the beaters were
directed by a head keeper posted in a high tower, from which he had an extensive view of the country, and notes on a horn indicated to the leaders of the
beat when to advance and what they were required to do" (A. E. T. Watson
King Edward VII. as a Sportsman, p. 338, 1911).

1885
Ætat. 43

1891
Ætat. 50

on the display of his broad-minded sympathies. In spite of the responsibility of the Baron, who was excluded from the Austrian Court, for the Prince's presence in the Austrian capital, the Prince exchanged visits with Emperor Francis Joseph. The interests of this vacation were enhanced by the opportunities which he found in Vienna of discussing some urgent political problems with Count Kalnoky, Austrian Minister for Foreign Affairs, and with Prince Lobanoff, the Russian Ambassador.

Of his regard for his Hungarian-Jewish host he continued to make frank demonstration at home as well as abroad. The Baron was, under the Prince's auspices, a familiar figure in English society on his visits to London, until near his death in 1896. He was encouraged by the Prince in an active patronage of the English turf. The Prince introduced him to his friend and counsellor in racing matters, Lord Marcus Beresford, and Lord Marcus bought, in 1890, for the Baron, at the Prince's prompting, the yearling filly La Flèche, which in 1892 scored the rare triumph of winning the four classic prizes—the One Thousand Guineas, the Cambridgeshire, the Oaks, and the St. Leger. The Prince rejoiced in the triumph of one who in his view was disparaged by unworthy prejudice, and had thoroughly gratified, at least on one notable occasion, his love of variety in his vacation tours abroad.

V

Sport at home offered the Prince a relief from the formal social routine more readily accessible than travel abroad. Until he turned forty he remained true to his early hunting proclivities. From the date of his settlement at Sandringham he constantly hunted with the West Norfolk hounds, and on occasion followed the more famous packs of the Midland shires—the Quorn, the Cottesmore, the Pytchley, and the Belvoir. But increasing bulk and the superior facilities which the county of Norfolk offered for shooting led him by degrees to give up following the hounds and to devote to the gun most of his hours of outdoor exercise at Sandringham or elsewhere. One of his latest experiences in the hunting field was on 7th January 1882, when he stayed with his Yorkshire friend, Christopher Sykes, at Brantingham Thorpe, to hunt with the Holderness. His withdrawal from fox-hunting practically coincided with his genial presentation at Sandringham,

on behalf of the hunt, of a testimonial to the retiring Master of the   1889
West Norfolk hounds (Mr. Anthony Hammond) in March 1883.   Ætat. 47

The Prince always acknowledged the superiority of fox-
hunting over stag-hunting, but did not eschew the latter form
of sport. Through the seventies he enjoyed many excellent
runs in the Windsor district with the royal buckhounds, the maintenance of which by the State harmonised with his early conceptions of Court ceremonial. During Mr. Gladstone's fourth
ministry (1892–95) a strong popular agitation sought the abolition
of the royal pack—mainly on humanitarian grounds. The
Prince discussed, in 1893, with the then Master of the Buckhounds, Lord Ribblesdale, the possibility of converting the royal
buckhounds into fox-hounds, in accordance with a suggestion
of his earlier years. The Prince, who cherished memories of the
resplendent uniform of the official *Grand Veneur* at Napoleon
III.'s Court at Fontainebleau and Compiègne, deprecated a
complete divorce of hunting from the State. But he was unable
to resist the trend of popular opinion and acquiesced in the suppression, near the end of his mother's reign, of the mastership of
the buckhounds, and therewith the final dissociation of the Court
from hunting. Nor, when he reconstituted the Court on succeeding
to the throne, did he make any effort to revive the office.

The sandy soil of the Sandringham estate well rewarded the
Prince's strenuous effort to perfect its shooting facilities by
developing the coverts and adding to the stock of game. Grouse
hardly flourished there, but partridges and pheasants multiplied,
and marshy ground and good pools were attractive homes for
snipe, woodcock, and wild duck. The Prince was always on the
alert for changes in the organisation of sport. Muzzle loaders
were soon replaced by breech loaders, and the woods were
adapted to the modern system of beating. The Prince, on his
return from his visit to Baron Hirsch at St. Johann, adopted
the Baron's system of "remises" (or shelters) for partridges or
pheasants, where the birds might nest and feed, and be ready in
the season for the method of driving them over the guns. His
shooting-parties at Sandringham, the chief of which assembled
just before his birthday in November, rarely consisted of more
than eight guns, and commonly included the best shots of the
day, such as Earl de Grey, heir of the Marquis of Ripon,
Lord Walsingham, and Hon. Henry Stonor. The Prince's own

performances remained to the last variable. He had an exceptional knack of killing birds behind him at an angle which most
people find very difficult.

From friends, in Norfolk or elsewhere, the Prince was
always ready to accept invitations to shooting-parties. "We
had yesterday a capital day's partridge driving, and got nearly
two hundred brace," he wrote from Melton Constable, the seat
of Lord and Lady Hastings, on 15th October 1884. From
1892 until the year of his death, with two exceptions, he was
the guest of Edward Lawson (afterwards Lord Burnham), the
proprietor of the London newspaper, the *Daily Telegraph*, for a
day or two each year in January at Hall Barn, near Beaconsfield. A week at the end of each November from 1895
onwards was spent at Castle Rising with Horace (afterwards
Lord) Farquhar, while he was an annual visitor to the Duke
of Devonshire's shoot at Chatsworth in January.

The Prince long retained his zest for deer-stalking on his
autumn vacations in Scotland, and was for many years equal
to all the fatigues. But as age began to tell he resorted to the
less exacting practice of driving deer.

As a shot the Prince enjoyed his foreign experiences of pursuing animals unknown to England. But one exceptional quarry
came under the fire of his gun at home. In 1876, after his return
from India where he had engaged in the pursuit of big game, he,
while the guest of Lord Tankerville at Chillingham Castle,
Northumberland, brought down one of the herd of wild bulls in
the park there.

VI

Racing became, after middle life, the most absorbing of
the Prince's sporting interests. The "glorious uncertainty of the
turf," to use his own phrase, fascinated his mature years. The
gambler's thrills were neither unknown nor unwelcome to him.
He yielded readily to the alternations of excitement attaching to
racing ownership—the anxieties of the training stable, the
depression following defeat on the course, the exhilaration that
comes of victory. At the same time the camaraderie of the
turf gratified, to an extent increasing with his age, his social
instinct. From 1880 he rejoiced in the occupancy during the
Newmarket meetings of a suite of rooms in the house of the

Jockey Club. From 1885, on the night of each Derby day, he entertained all the members of the club at dinner at Marlborough House and, during his reign, at Buckingham Palace. With trainers and jockeys he was always on sociable terms. He thoroughly enjoyed the visits which he regularly paid to great houses in the neighbourhood of the courses where the classic races were run. For many successive years he was the guest of Lord Sefton at Sefton Park for the Grand National at Aintree, near Liverpool, and of the Duke of Richmond at Goodwood. He stayed with the Duke of Westminster at Eaton Hall for the Chester races. In later life he invariably spent a week with Lord Savile at Rufford Abbey, in order to witness the St. Leger at Doncaster. The annual sojourn there was especially congenial, and the Prince spoke of it as "like coming home." Through the decade preceding his accession, his popularity with the great sporting democracy was vastly enhanced by his prominence as a racing owner, and by his punctual attendance at all the principal and at several of the secondary meetings in diverse parts of the country. When out of England, too, he rarely missed an opportunity of frequenting race meetings of repute. He was often seen on the courses at Auteuil, near Paris, and at Nice. In 1883 he ran a horse, The Scot, for the great steeplechase at Baden Baden. He was "hail fellow well met" in the racing society of the continent, almost equally with that of England. His insistence on decorum in dress, which was a characteristic of him in all relations of life, did not desert him on the race-course, nor indeed in the hunting field. He was severe in rebuke of any infringement in either place of accepted conventions.

Although he was elected a member of the Jockey Club in 1864, and was thenceforth a familiar figure at Newmarket and other racing centres, he played no part on the turf as an owner of race-horses until after his return from India in 1876. His career of ownership opened with the purchase of a few yearlings at an extravagant price, and the royal colours—purple, gold braid, scarlet sleeves, black velvet cap with gold fringe—were first seen at the July meeting at Newmarket in 1877, when he matched unsuccessfully his Arab horse Alep against another Arab horse Avowal, belonging to the veteran General, Lord Strathnairn.[1]

---

[1] Cf. A. E. T. Watson's *King Edward VII. as a Sportsman* (1911), which supplies, on good authority, the main facts of the Prince's racing career.

Lord Marcus Beresford, younger brother of Lord Charles, who, while an officer of the 7th Hussars, acquired a rarely rivalled knowledge of all that pertained to the turf, soon gave the Prince good counsel, and proved his oracle in racing matters for the rest of his life. Lord Marcus, in wit and sagacity, was far superior to his brother Charles, and there was no break in the long stretch of the Prince's intimacy with him.[1] In 1878, on Lord Marcus's advice, the Prince turned his attention to steeplechasing, and purchased, in partnership with Lord Marcus, two promising jumpers, Jackal and Congress, the former of which, bearing Lord Marcus's colours, won the Craven Steeplechase at the Liverpool meeting of that year.[2] Regimental race meetings were always congenial to the Prince, and under Lord Marcus's guidance he, in the years that followed, achieved at such meetings some success with Jackal and other steeple-chasers which Lord Marcus procured for him. The Prince's earliest experience of victory on his own account was at the Aldershot Regimental Meeting on 14th April 1880, with his steeplechaser Leonidas, which he soon disposed of.[3] The Prince's sole classic victory in steeplechasing came in 1900, when his horse Ambush II. won the Grand National at Liverpool. Expectations ran high in later years with regard to the winner, but his subsequent performances proved disappointing.

Meanwhile, the Prince rapidly developed, as an owner, lasting ties with flat-racing. In 1883, on Lord Marcus's introduction, he opened a ten years' association with John Porter, the famous trainer at Kingsclere, near Basingstoke. He committed to Porter's charge two fillies, Geheimniss and Junket, which he leased from Lady Stamford jointly with the well-known sportsman, Lord Alington. Two years later, on the advice of Lord Marcus, the Prince went a notable step further in his racing

[1] For Lord Marcus Beresford's relations with the Prince see A. E. T. Watson's book *ut supra* and the obituary notice of Lord Marcus in *The Times* of 18th December 1922, two days after his death.

[2] Congress was disabled by an accident before its racing qualities could be tested.

[3] Lord Marcus's steeplechasing "finds" for the Prince made a good show at various regimental meetings. Fair Play won the Household Brigade Cup at Sandown in 1882. In 1887, the Prince's jumper, Hohenlinden, came in first for the Gold Cup at the Grand Military Meeting at Sandown, but was disqualified owing to his owner not being, in accordance with the conditions, an officer on full pay. Another steeplechaser, Magic, which the Prince acquired in 1888, twice failed for the Grand National.

1889
Ætat. 47

career, and inaugurated a breeding stud at Sandringham, stocking it at first with a few purchases that he personally made at a yearling sale at Newmarket in July. But little good fortune for the time came the Prince's way, in the way either of breeding or racing, and he often bemoaned his disappointments to his trainer, John Porter, with whom, none the less, his personal relations were invariably cordial.[1]

The tide of failure was in time triumphantly stemmed. In 1887 Porter did the Prince a service which put him on the road to vast success. The trainer bought for the Sandringham stud the mare Perdita II. The mare's earliest progeny was hardly reassuring, but in 1891 she became the dam by the sire St. Simon of the notable thoroughbred Florizel II., and in 1893 and in 1897, respectively, by the same sire, she gave birth to the two more notable thoroughbreds, Persimmon and Diamond Jubilee. Florizel II. started a new era in the Prince's racing career by winning five races of second rank in the season of 1894.

By that date some notable changes had been made in the Prince's racing establishment. Lord Marcus, in 1890, was appointed manager of the stud at Sandringham, becoming at the same time an Extra Equerry, and in 1893 the Prince was induced by Lord Marcus to transfer his horses for training from John Porter's stable at Kingsclere to that of Richard Marsh at Egerton House, Newmarket. Lord Marcus and Richard Marsh retained their positions for the rest of the Prince's career, and well deserved their secure place in his confidence.

From 1893 until Queen Victoria's death, the Prince's achievements on the turf steadily soared. Persimmon, Perdita II.'s foal of 1893, proved the best thoroughbred of the era, and with him the Prince became for the first time victor in the classic races. In 1896 Persimmon won both the Derby and the St. Leger. The Prince's first triumph at Epsom was acclaimed through the length and breadth of the Empire, and the excitement was long remembered. Earl Grey, when Governor-General of Canada, recalled in a letter to King Edward on 5th May 1909:

When Your Majesty won the Derby with Persimmon, I was at Bulawayo. I can remember as if it were yesterday the

---

[1] Cf. *John Porter of Kingsclere*, an autobiography written in collaboration with E. Moorhouse (1919).

thrilling pleasure that vibrated through that small but big-hearted community, when the cable that the Prince of Wales had won the Derby arrived.

Persimmon followed up his triumphs of 1896 by winning next year the Eclipse Stakes and the Gold Cup at Ascot, thus setting the seal on his racing fame. Other progeny of the Sandringham stud now promised well, but for a time they increased the Prince's victories only in smaller contests. The triumphs of Persimmon were, however, eclipsed at the end of the century by his brother, Diamond Jubilee, who arrived at Newmarket from Sandringham for training in 1899. In 1900 Diamond Jubilee won the five classic races: the Two Thousand Guineas, the Newmarket Stakes (for three-year-olds), the Eclipse Stakes, the Derby, and the St. Leger.[1] The Prince's excitement ran high at Diamond Jubilee's triumphal progress through the season. "Thanks for wishing me further good luck with 'D. Jubilee'," he wrote to Lady Londonderry on 12th August. "He will, I hope, win the Leger, though I shall not be there to see it." The death of his brother, the Duke of Saxe-Coburg-Gotha, prevented his attendance at Doncaster to witness Diamond Jubilee's victory.

In the year 1900 the Prince's racing career thus reached its zenith. His winning stakes, which totalled £29,586, set him at the head, for the only time, of the list of winning owners. In that list he had been twice previously placed second: in 1896 with £26,573, and in 1897 with £14,295. In the same year (1900) his steeplechaser Ambush II. won the Grand National. So imposing a series of victories for an owner in one year was without precedent (nor has it been repeated), and the Prince ascended the throne early next year before the popular enthusiasm had spent itself. Although he pursued the sport with his old energy throughout his reign, and although the number of his horses in training increased, no conspicuous prosperity attended his racing ventures as King until he won the Derby for the third time with Minoru in 1909. In that—the last racing season of his life,—he was placed second in the list of winning owners.

On the whole, the Prince's racing experience, in spite of vicissitudes, proved profitable. He reckoned that the purchase of Perdita II. in 1887 brought him within twenty years a quarter

---

[1] Diamond Jubilee came in second for the Princess of Wales's Stakes at Newmarket, but was unplaced in the Jockey Club Stakes.

of a million.   Perdita's son, Diamond Jubilee, after his racing
career was closed, was sold to an Argentine dealer for £31,500.
Diamond Jubilee's elder brother, Persimmon, was justly reckoned
the brightest jewel in the crown of the Sandringham stable.
There he ended his days, through an accident, on the 18th
February 1908.   Of the tragedy the Prince (then King) wrote
feelingly to his friend Lady Londonderry :

In Persimmon I have lost a trusty friend.   We hoped he
might have lived eight or ten years more.   He is a great loss
also to the racing community.   The damage was more serious
than we thought, and he died from exhaustion.[1]

VII

Yachting was another form of recreation and sport to which   1886
the Prince was faithful from boyhood.   His career as a racing   Ætat. 44
yachtsman did not open till 1876—just a year before he first
acquired a race-horse.   From that date, for some twenty years,
he pursued yacht-racing with much the same ardour as horse-
racing, frequently sailing on racing craft of his own both on the
Solent and on the Mediterranean, off the Riviera.   But after
1897, while remaining an enthusiast for yachting, his zeal for
yacht-racing declined, while that for horse-racing continued
active till his death.

The Prince's frequent residence in youth at Osborne had
early interested him in the yachting activities at Cowes.   Of the
Royal Yacht Squadron there, the most distinguished yachting
club of the world, the Prince Consort had been patron, and in
1863 the Prince accepted that office in succession to his father,
presenting, at the same time, an annual cup for competition at
the Cowes Regatta.   Two years later, on the 8th July, he was
elected an active member, and in 1882, when his interest in
yacht-racing had matured, he was invested with the blue ribbon
of the yachting fraternity by being admitted to the office of
Commodore of the Squadron.   Although his racing interests as
a yachtsman were mainly centred in the Solent, he became, in
1874, Commodore also of the Royal Thames Yacht Club.[2]

[1] The skeleton of Persimmon the King presented to the Natural History
Museum, South Kensington.
[2] The Prince's yachting career may be traced in Montague Guest and
William B. Boulton's *Memorials of the Royal Yacht Squadron* (1903), pp. 350

1889
Ætat. 47

In 1866 the Prince first acquired a yacht of his own, the *Dagmar*—a cutter of 37 tons. But it was ten years later that he first bought a racing boat—the schooner-yacht *Hildegarde*. In 1877 the Prince won for the first time, with this vessel, the Queen's Cup at Cowes. The race was run in very heavy weather and, as was his habit, he himself sailed on his craft. With his second racing cutter, the *Formosa*, which he bought in 1879, he won the Queen's Cup for the second time, in 1880. A year later he acquired the schooner *Aline*, of 216 tons, which had been built some fifteen years earlier and already had achieved some fame. But the *Aline* did comparatively little for the Prince's racing reputation during the twelve years of his ownership. In Queen Victoria's jubilee year of 1887, the Prince entered her for two races which attracted attention —the Jubilee race round the United Kingdom, which was organised by the Royal Thames Yacht Club (June 15–29), and the Royal Yacht Squadron Jubilee race in the Channel, over a course of 330 miles (August 8–10). The Prince's yacht was unsuccessful in both competitions, but came in third out of thirteen competitors in the Channel race.

It was not till 1892 that the Prince had a racing cutter built for him. The vessel, known as the *Britannia* (300 tons), was designed by George Lennox Watson, a marine architect of high repute, and proved "the most successful cutter-yacht that had been raced in European waters since the days of the almost invincible *Arrow*." It was a roomy craft, accommodating, with a crew of twenty-eight, her owner and two or three guests. When on the Riviera he made the *Britannia* his home for many years, from 1894 onwards, sailing in her from one Mediterranean port to another.

The exploits of the *Britannia* gave a new impetus to the pursuit of yachting in France as well as in England. During her first season (May–September 1893) she started in 43 races off the British Isles, and won 24 first prizes and 9 second or third. She began her career on the Riviera in the spring of 1894, when she scored a record success, and in the three following seasons she well maintained her high position in the Mediterranean. Before

---

et seq., and in Watson's *King Edward as a Sportsman*, where the chapter on yachting is from the efficient pen of King Edward's Equerry, Captain Sir Seymour Fortescue, K.C.V.O.

her racing career came to an end in 1897, the aggregate of her first
prizes in all waters had risen to 122, with 25 second or third
prizes out of 219 starts. Throughout the *Britannia's* racing
days the Prince sailed on her every day of the Cowes Regatta.

The Prince's enthusiasm for yacht-racing was destined to
wane in presence of an unlooked-for challenge. His activity in
the sport was one of the many fields which was to provoke the
rivalry of his all-aspiring nephew, the Kaiser William II. A
visit of the Kaiser, then recently crowned, to Cowes during the
regatta season of 1889 bred in him the ambition to prove himself the equal, or rather superior, of his uncle in competitions on
the Solent. With hospitable courtesy, his uncle at once proposed him for membership of the Royal Yacht Squadron. Two
years later the Kaiser entered his yacht *Meteor I.* for a race.
Next year the versatile monarch returned to witness the Cowes
Regatta in the newly assumed rôle of a yachting enthusiast.
During the three following seasons he ostentatiously sustained
the character, openly contesting the Prince's rightful place of
social prominence during the regatta week. It was in 1895 that
the ambitious Kaiser commissioned George Lennox Watson, the
architect of the *Britannia,* to build for him a new yacht, *Meteor II.,*
on the same lines as the *Britannia,* but on a larger scale. Next
season the Kaiser tried, on the Solent, conclusions with the
Britannia, which hitherto had held her own against well-nigh all
comers at home and on the Riviera. *Meteor II.* soon proved that
the *Britannia* had been outbuilt. The success of the new-comer
quickly put the *Britannia's* achievements in the shade. The
intrusion of the jealous Kaiser into the Prince's own domain
at Cowes, where, as Commodore of the Royal Yacht Squadron,
he enjoyed great authority, tended to cool his zeal for yacht-
racing. After 1897 the Prince continued to sail in the *Britannia*
on the Solent, but she took part in no more races. She was the
last of the racing cutters which the Prince owned. The Prince
remained faithful to Cowes Regatta and the Royal Yacht
Squadron till the end of his life. On his accession to the throne
he combined with the office of Commodore of the Royal Yacht
Squadron the higher dignity of Admiral of the Squadron. But
for the last thirteen years of his career he sought satisfaction for
his sporting instincts elsewhere than in the proprietorship of a
racing yacht.

VIII

1891　　　Cards formed, from the Prince's early days, a recreative
Ætat. 49　solace. He was always ready from boyhood to take a hand of
an evening at whist. But a love of adventure led him from time
to time to experiment in card games in which chance predominated over skill. He had tried his luck on holiday at
gaming in fashionable clubs—on the Riviera and in Germany—
and almost all forms of card games became familiar to him in
course of time. Irresponsible social gossip, which found a home
in the scandalous press at home and abroad, frequently imputed
to the Prince sensational gambling adventures.[1] For a short
period after 1890 he was attracted by the hazardous game of
baccarat, and an incident attending his indulgence in that
diversion while on a private visit in the early autumn of 1891
came, through an accident, into public notice and ruffled public
opinion by a specious confirmation of the journalistic innuendoes.

In the second week of September of that year he was the
guest, for the Doncaster races (September 8 and 9), of Mr.
Arthur Wilson, a wealthy shipowner of Hull, who resided at
Tranby Croft, near Doncaster. The company included sporting
friends of the Prince—Lord Coventry, General Owen Williams,
and Sir William Gordon-Cumming, Colonel of the Scots Guards—
besides members of the host's family. Baccarat was played by
the party at comparatively low stakes. Some of the Prince's
fellow-players saw cause to charge Sir William Gordon-Cumming
with cheating. The Prince, after due inquiries, reluctantly came
to the conclusion that the charge was well-founded, and the
offending player was induced to sign a paper acknowledging his
guilt and promising not to touch cards again. There the unhappy business seemed to end. But subsequently the story
leaked out, and Sir William brought an action for slander against
his hostess, her son, daughter, and son-in-law, and a fifth guest.
The case came before Lord Chief Justice Lord Coleridge on the

---

[1] The Prince was well aware of the habitual insinuations of certain organs
of the press. "I am happiest," he wrote in a confession album, "when . . .
I can, like plain Mr. Jones, go to a race meeting without it being chronicled
in the papers next day that His Royal Highness the Prince of Wales has
taken to gambling very seriously, and yesterday lost more money than ever
he can afford to pay" (Alfred E. T. Watson's *King Edward as a Sportsman*,
p. 120).

1st June 1891, and lasted for seven days. The Prince, who was in court the whole time, appeared unwillingly as a witness for the defence. He frankly related all that he knew of the affair. A verdict for the defendants was returned.

1891
Ætat. 49

In the result a violent storm beat about the Prince's head. A renewal threatened of the puritanic suspicions of twenty years ago, which had never been wholly silenced. The trial and its incidents shocked conventional middle-class sentiment. *The Times* newspaper, in a leading article on the 10th June, assumed a pontifical tone. The writer fulminated against the Prince for his part in a sordid business, condemning him for mixing in questionable society, for indulging in "questionable pleasures," and for giving thereby a shock to "the monarchical principle." [1]

The Prince was profoundly disturbed by the outcry. The Queen's distress of mind, which was acute, especially grieved her son. To her he promptly gave assurances that he would abstain from gambling games thenceforth and never suffer baccarat to be played in his presence. For complaint of extravagance in the popular denunciation, he had good ground. He resented the allegation that the affair at Tranby Croft reflected his habitual practice. His manifold activities of a serious kind, only a few of which were known to the public, sufficiently confuted the insinuation that undignified distraction so dominated his life as to justify misgivings of his fitness for the throne. In a letter to Dr. Benson, Archbishop of Canterbury, who was long on intimate terms with himself and his family (August 13, 1891), he sought to clear up prevailing misconceptions at the same time as he protested against the indiscriminate detraction.

"A recent trial," the Prince's letter to the Archbishop ran, "which no one deplores more than I do, and which I was powerless to prevent, gave occasion for the Press to make most bitter and unjust attacks upon me, knowing that I was defenceless, and I am not sure that politics were not mixed up in it. The whole matter has now died out, and I think, therefore, it would be

---

[1] In the House of Commons on 15th June attention was called to the Prince's breach of the Queen's regulations (No. 41), which laid on all officers on the active list the obligation of requiring a fellow-officer suspected of dishonourable conduct to submit his case to his commanding officer. The Prince, who had suffered Sir William Gordon-Cumming to atone for his offence by a private confession, admitted to the House, through the Secretary of State for War, Mr. Edward Stanhope, "an error in judgement" (Hansard, 3rd series, cccliv. 394).

inopportune for me in any public manner to allude again to
the painful subject which brought such a torrent of abuse
upon me, not only by the Press, but by the Low Church, and
especially the Nonconformists.

"They have a perfect right, I am well aware, in a free country
like our own, to express their opinions, but I do not consider
that they have a just right to jump at conclusions regarding
myself, without knowing the facts.

"I have a horror of gambling, and should always do my
utmost to discourage others who have an inclination for it, as I
consider that gambling, like intemperance, is one of the greatest
curses which a country could be afflicted with.

"Horse-racing may produce gambling, or it may not, but I
have always looked upon it as a manly sport which is popular
with Englishmen of all classes; and there is no reason why it
should be looked upon as a gambling transaction. Alas! those
who gamble will gamble at anything. I have written quite
openly to you, my dear Archbishop, whom I have had the
advantage of knowing for so many years." [1]

Level-headed observers, who could not be suspected of any
special tenderness for royalty, were at one with the Prince in
regarding the public attack as overdone. "All this clatter,"
Mr. John Morley remarked to Sir William Harcourt, "about the
Prince of Wales and the baccarat, which no doubt raises some
curious points in manners and in ethics, is beginning to make me
sick. I really think of taking his part." [2] Mr. Morley's detached
point of view found many sympathisers. The ugly censure soon,
as the Prince foretold, subsided. Its purport was not, however,
wholly lost on the Prince. He set himself to discourage, as far
as he could, the vogue of gambling, which was always threatening
to grow in fashionable circles. Personally he gradually abandoned other games of cards for the newer game of bridge, in
which, though he played regularly and successfully, he developed
no more than a moderate skill.

[1] A. C. Benson's *Life of Archbishop Benson.*
[2] Viscount Morley's *Recollections*, i. 273-4.

Frank Holl R.A. pinxit   Emery Walker ph.sc.

Bencher of the Middle Temple

1884

CHAPTER XXXII

DOMESTIC VICISSITUDES, 1878–1900

I

In the later as in the earlier years of his adult life the Prince 1878
was fortunate in the chief officers of his household. It was not Ætat. 36
in his nature to abnegate control of any of his manifold affairs,
but he sought and found, from youth upwards, highly efficient
and loyal assistance in the management of his diverse interests.
He was constant in his devotion to those in whom he placed his
confidence, and most of the men who filled responsible posts in
his household scored record years of service. He rarely parted
with an equerry until age or ill-health incapacitated him, and
Colonel Arthur Ellis and General Stanley Clarke, who were his
invariable companions abroad, were close friends. But the most
notable instances of the mutual fidelity which characterised his
relations with those in his service were furnished by the two
men who filled, through an almost unprecedented length of time,
the all-important posts, respectively, of Private Secretary and
Comptroller and Treasurer of his household. Mr. Francis
Knollys, successor since 1870 of Mr. Herbert Fisher, the Prince's
first private secretary, developed during his prolonged service
a well-nigh marvellous tact, industry, and knowledge of men and
matters, preserving, in his attitude to his master throughout the
long period, the ideal mean between self-assertion and self-
suppression.[1] In Sir Dighton Probyn the same characteristics
were combined with a faculty for rigorous finance. Sir Dighton
had achieved a brilliant reputation as a cavalry officer in the
Indian army before he first joined the Prince's household as an
equerry in 1872. The Prince at once recognised his promise as an
administrator in addition to his fine military aptitudes. He and

---

[1] See p. 155 *supra*.

589

Knollys both accompanied the Prince on his Indian tour. After
their return home, when the Prince's first Comptroller and
Treasurer, Sir William Knollys, retired at the age of eighty (March
16, 1877), the Prince had no hesitation in appointing Probyn to
the vacancy. At the time, the Prince described him as "the only
man I know who could succeed him" (*i.e.* Sir William Knollys).
Sir Dighton justified the choice by the efficient performance of
the duties of the office so long as the Prince lived, becoming, on
the Prince's accession to the throne, Keeper of the Privy Purse.
In course of time he acquired, in addition to his other qualifications, command of the work of land-agent and horticulturist, and
thus he ably seconded his master's efforts in developing the
Sandringham estate. Both Knollys and Probyn were the
Prince's seniors, and were unusually long-lived. Both died near
the same date in the same year, 1924, more than fourteen years
after their master had passed away.[1]

II

Amid all the multifarious calls on the Prince's time and
thought, in answering which he could count on the unceasing
assistance of Knollys and Probyn—amid his social and public
functions, his engagements of sport and pleasure, his political
study and observation, his business transactions as a man of
property—he was never unmindful of the personal services which
he owed his kinsfolk. To every member of his family, notably to
his brothers and sisters and to his children, he gave practical proof
of his affection at all turns of his career, following their fortunes
with his characteristically alert interest and sympathy. He
was the confidant, so long as they lived, of his two sisters who on
marriage settled in Germany—the Crown Princess, his eldest
sister, and Princess Alice of Darmstadt, his second sister. He
followed with close attention the progress in their professions of
his sailor brother, Alfred, Duke of Edinburgh, and of his soldier
brother, Arthur, Duke of Connaught, and he sympathised with
the cultured avocations of his youngest brother, Prince Leopold,

---

[1] Sir Dighton Probyn, born on 21st January 1833, died at Sandringham on
20th June 1924; after King Edward's death he became Comptroller of Queen
Alexandra's household and held that post until the end. Lord Knollys, born
on 16th July 1837, died on 15th August 1924; he remained for three years,
1910–13, Private Secretary to King Edward's son and successor, King George.

Duke of Albany. To the husbands of his younger sisters he paid all fraternal attentions. He encouraged them to engage in fitting spheres of public life, and was ready with detached advice. He felt some compunction with regard to the presence in the House of Commons of the Marquis of Lorne, son and heir of the Duke of Argyll, who married, in 1871, his fourth sister, Princess Louise.[1] He thought the royal family ran thereby a risk of identification with a political party. He deemed it more fitting that the Marquis should be called up to the House of Lords in the Duke of Argyll's lifetime. He always strongly deprecated the Marquis's admission to a ministry. But he warmly welcomed his appointment, in September 1878, to the dignified post of Governor-General of Canada. "He has a fine career open to him" (he wrote to Frere on 8th September 1878), "and my sister living in one of our most important colonies cannot fail to have a most excellent effect." To like effect he wrote to Acland (October 11): "I trust that my sister's sojourn in Canada and her husband's position as Governor-General may be productive of good both there and at home. It is indeed a fine, useful, and important position." The Prince's anticipations of the good effect of the Marquis's presence in Canada were satisfactorily fulfilled, and he was disappointed that the Marquis was entrusted with no further responsibilities of the kind. The field of Empire was always one in which the Prince deemed that the energies of members of the royal family might be employed to advantage.

III

Death dealt the Prince's large domestic circle inevitable blows, which affected him profoundly. The close of the year 1878 involved him and his kindred in a grief which vividly recalled earlier trials. Princess Alice, wife of Prince Louis of Hesse-Darmstadt, fell ill of diphtheria at the Palace at Darmstadt while nursing her children. She died on the 14th December 1878, the seventeenth anniversary of the Prince Consort's death, and the eighth anniversary of the Prince of Wales's own recovery from what seemed to be a mortal malady. The

[1] The Marquis of Lorne represented Argyllshire as a Liberal from 1868 to 1878. He joined the Liberal-Unionists in 1886, and after some defeats as a candidate, sat for South Manchester from 1895 to 1900, when he succeeded to the Dukedom of Argyll on his father's death.

1878
Ætat. 36

1878
Ætat. 37

Princess had attended her father during his last illness, and she had aided in nursing her eldest brother through the crisis of 1871. A simple sincerity of phrase marked the Prince's avowals of distress in his bereavement. To Lord Beaconsfield he wrote: "The love and affection we bore towards one another . . . increased as years went by"; to Mr. Gladstone: "She sacrificed her life to the duties of a mother and wife"; to Lord Granville: "She was my favourite sister, so good, so kind, so clever; we had gone through much together—my father's illness, then my own."

The Prince hastened to the house of mourning at Darmstadt, where he was already a familiar figure. In his dead sister's children, especially in her four daughters, he showed thenceforth a paternal interest. The fortunes of his nieces in their married lives strengthened the bond between him and them. The two eldest of Princess Alice's daughters, Princess Victoria and Princess Elizabeth, both married in 1884. Princess Victoria became the wife of Queen Victoria's protégé and the Prince's friend, Prince Louis of Battenberg (afterwards Marquis of Milford Haven); while the Princess Elizabeth became the wife of the Grand Duke Serge, the younger brother of the Tsar Alexander III. A little later the Prince rejoiced in the marriages of the two youngest daughters, which seemed at the time of good augury for international goodwill. Fate was, in the years to come, to dissolve that promise in tragedy. Princess Irene married her first cousin, Prince Henry of Prussia, only brother of Kaiser William II., while Princess Alix became the wife of the Tsar Nicholas II.[1]

1884
Ætat. 42

The Prince suffered a second severe domestic bereavement—in the death of a brother—in 1884. On 28th March the youngest of Queen Victoria's sons, Prince Leopold, Duke of Albany, died suddenly at Cannes. Always of frail health, he had been the special care of his mother, and had been constantly in her society, at any rate until his marriage on 27th April 1882. The Prince

[1] The Prince lived long enough to see only the first of the dark shadows which in time involved the careers of three of the daughters of his sister Alice. The Grand Duke Serge was slain by revolutionaries at St. Petersburg on the 4th February 1905. After the Prince's death came the alienation through war of Prince Henry of Prussia and his wife from their English kindred, as well as the crowning tragedy which overtook the widowed Grand Duchess Serge and her sister, the Tsaritza, who both fell victims to the brutal fury of the Russian Bolshevik revolution in 1918.

of Wales thought at times that Prince Leopold exerted a somewhat reactionary influence on their mother's political opinions.
While mainly devoted to literature and art, Prince Leopold was
ambitious of public employment, and the Prince of Wales
encouraged the aspiration.   Two months before Prince Leopold's
death the Prince expressed approval of Sir Charles Dilke's
suggestion that his youngest brother should be appointed
Governor of Victoria in succession to the Prince's frequent
correspondent, Sir Henry Loch.

Prince Leopold's unexpected death at Cannes was a severe
shock.   On receipt of the news the Prince of Wales hurried out
to superintend the funeral arrangements.

"I had indeed a long and sad journey to Cannes and back,"
the Prince wrote to Mrs. Liddell, who had known Prince Leopold
as an undergraduate at Christchurch, "but I had the mournful
satisfaction of bringing him home to his last resting-place.   I
could not bear the thought of his returning home without a
relative to look after him in death as they had so often done in
life."   (12th April.)

To another of Prince Leopold's Oxford friends, Dr. Acland,
he wrote :

The University has lost a true friend in him.   If it had
pleased God to spare his life, what a bright and useful life he
had before him.   (14th April.)

The funeral took place at St. George's Chapel, Windsor, on
6th April, and next day the Prince wrote to Lord Granville of
the mental and physical strain which the whole episode had
caused him.   A little later, in February 1886, he travelled to
Cannes to lay the foundation stone of a memorial church of
which Prince Leopold's friends defrayed the cost.

Death made no further breach in the circle of the Prince's
brothers and sisters for some sixteen years.   His brother Alfred,
Duke of Edinburgh, three years his junior, who had been the close
companion of his youth, succeeded to the Duchy of Saxe-Coburg-
Gotha in November 1893.   The Duke's succession brought to
fruition that arrangement of 1863 whereby the Prince himself
had renounced his heirship to the German principality.[1]   The
new Duke of Saxe-Coburg-Gotha died unexpectedly of paralysis
of the heart at Rosenau on 30th July 1900.   He was already

---

[1] See pp. 246-7 supra.

threatened by another disease, incurable and painful, whose
progress was commonly slow. The Prince attended the funeral
in the cemetery at Coburg, together with his nephew, the Kaiser.

"My brother and I," the Prince wrote to Lady Londonderry
from Cowes (August 12, 1900), on his return to England, "were
devoted to one another, but we had no idea until quite lately
that he was so seriously ill, as he kept it from everybody. I had
so hoped to have seen him again this month that when the
terrible news reached me that he had 'passed away' it came
like a thunderbolt upon me. For him it was a mercy that his
life was not prolonged, as his sufferings would have been intense.
But, thank God, he died in his sleep."

A more poignant distress was caused by the hopeless illness
at the time of his eldest sister, the Empress Frederick. Her
death, six months after he had ascended the throne, deprived the
Prince of the kinswoman with whom he was longest in intimate
touch.

IV

The Prince fulfilled with kindly complacence his parental
responsibilities. The education of the two sons, Albert Victor
and George, naturally invited careful consideration. The Prince
had little wish to subject them to a repetition of his own strict discipline and elaborate training. Personal experience gave him no
sympathy with excessive restraint of youthful exuberance at any
educational stage. "Young men at college are not schoolboys,
and should not be treated as such," he wrote to Mrs. Liddell
(December 14, 1893). Nor had he much faith in a literary
education for youths in his sons' station.

The shape which his sons' training took had at any rate the
merit of originality. Queen Victoria had her own views on the
subject, with which the Prince found himself in disagreement.
The Queen welcomed a suggestion that her grandsons should
go to a public school — to Wellington College — but the Prince
dissented and entered them as naval cadets on the *Britannia*
training-ship at Dartmouth. The Queen argued that a training-
ship scarcely provided an adequate curriculum. The Prince
replied that the step was experimental. His plan was carried
into effect on the 17th May 1877. He sent his mother a report,
"which" (he added) "I am glad to say is satisfactory," on the

boys' entrance examination. They joined the training-ship, in
charge of a tutor, the Rev. J. N. Dalton, who retained the post
throughout the period of their education. Mr. Dalton took his
obligations seriously, and the Prince encouraged him in his
deprecation of uncovenanted interruptions of their working
time. In May 1878 the Prince, on Mr. Dalton's advice, refused
the Queen's urgent request to allow the boys leave from the
Britannia in order to stay with her at Balmoral over her birthday. The Prince often visited the *Britannia* to watch the boys'
progress, with which he professed himself satisfied, and they
remained there till the summer of 1879, when he determined
to test comprehensively his faith in the educational value of
travel by sending them, under Mr. Dalton's care, on a world-
wide cruise in H.M.S. *Bacchante*.

The cruise was planned on a great scale. Embarking at
Portsmouth on 17th September 1879, the Prince's sons first
spent some eight months in the West Indies. He met them off
Spithead on their return on 3rd May 1880, but he did not keep
them long at home. On the 19th July following they started
in the same ship on a second cruise, which was planned on a
larger scale. It lasted fully two years. Australia, Japan, the
Holy Land, Egypt, and Greece were all included in the itinerary.[1]

The Prince had much correspondence with the Queen and
Lord Granville as to the status which his sons were to claim on
visits to rulers of foreign states. The Queen thought that official
hospitalities and official receptions might turn the boys' heads.
The Prince argued that his sons ought not to be received with
smaller honours than had been tendered recently to two foreign
princes—Prince Henry of Prussia, younger son of the Crown
Princess, and the Duke of Genoa, first cousin of King Humbert
of Italy—who had both made tours of the world not long before.

The Japanese government, whose country had only recently
assimilated the spirit of Western civilisation, devised an elaborate
programme of entertainment which the Prince approved and the
Queen deprecated. But the Prince had his way, and his sons
were formally welcomed by the Japanese government on their
arrival at Tokyo on 24th October 1881. The Mikado received

1878
Ætat. 36

[1] The two cruises are fully described in *The Cruise of H.M.S. "Bacchante,"*
1879–82, compiled from the private Journals, Letters, and Notebooks of Prince
Albert Victor and Prince George of Wales, with Additions by John N. Dalton.
London, 2 vols., 1886.

them next day. The Prince had at first favoured a suggestion that his sons should, on Queen Victoria's behalf, hand an Order to the Mikado, but he finally reached the conclusion that it would be sufficient for them to present a portrait of their grandmother. Insistent were the appeals which he made to Lord Granville to despatch the picture to Tokyo in good time. His warning was neglected, and his sons, in their interview with the Mikado, could only assure him that Queen Victoria's portrait would arrive later.

The Queen further demurred to the acceptance of the Khedive's offer of a palace for the boys' accommodation during their stay at Cairo, though she approved their passage up the Nile in the Khedive's steamer. The Prince begged Lord Granville to induce her to reconsider her decision. "I have been four times to Egypt during the last twenty years," he wrote (February 17, 1882), "and always stayed at a palace, knowing how impossible it was to refuse, and all members of the different royal families have done the same. I therefore fear the Khedive would be offended if his offer on this occasion was refused." Sir Edward Malet, the English representative in Egypt, deemed the visit inopportune, owing to threat of internal disturbance; but it took place none the less. The boys reached Egypt in March 1882, and in the event received from the Khedive Tewfik the same lavish kind of hospitality as his father, Khedive Ismail, had offered their father some fourteen years before.

On his sons' return from their long cruise, in August 1882, the Prince arranged for further training on more normal lines. The younger son, George, following in his uncle Alfred's steps, made the navy his profession, and passed through all the normal stages of naval preparation and promotion. The elder son, Albert Victor, who was in the direct succession, had more varied educational experiences. The Prince regarded the army as the accepted profession of an heir to the throne, and he arranged for Prince Albert Victor to join his own regiment, the 10th Hussars. But at the same time the Prince judged it wise to provide him with a rather belated opportunity of more general education. In the autumn of 1883 the Prince accompanied him to Trinity College, Cambridge, which he had himself joined in youth, and he witnessed his son's matriculation as an undergraduate.

With every later episode of importance in his elder son's

career the Prince personally associated himself. In all the celebrations of the youth's coming of age (January 8, 1885) the Prince was an elated and prominent figure. He was profuse in thanks to Mr. Gladstone, then Prime Minister, for a "beautiful letter" in which good counsel was offered his heir in somewhat turgid strains. In the following spring the youth accompanied his parents on their adventurous tour through Ireland.[1] Through the succeeding years the Prince spared no effort to stimulate his heir's interest in public and social life, making him his constant companion at public and social functions. He wished him to follow in his own footsteps as a man of affairs. In the interest of the young man's enlightenment, the Prince devised for him a tour through India in the winter season of 1889–90 on the lines of his own expedition of 1875–76. Father and son travelled together as far as Ismailia, where the young Prince embarked for Bombay (December 8, 1889). After his return from the East, Prince Albert Victor was created, on Queen Victoria's birthday, 24th May 1890, Earl of Athlone and Duke of Clarence,[2] and he took his seat in the House of Lords. But the new Duke's opportunities of public service were destined to be few. Within a year his career was prematurely closed by death.

1885
Ætat. 43

V

General interest in the Prince's domestic life was meanwhile whetted by other episodes which happened during Prince Albert Victor's early manhood. There fell on the 10th March 1888 the twenty-fifth anniversary of the Prince's marriage, and the Prince's arrival at this matrimonial milestone was celebrated impressively. He had witnessed with sympathetic interest, five years before, the celebration at Berlin, in accordance with German custom, of the silver wedding of his eldest sister, the Crown Princess.

1888
Ætat. 46

[1] On 10th June the Prince dined in Middle Temple Hall, when his son was admitted a Bencher. Mr. Gladstone's government had been defeated two days before, and the presence at the banquet of the Conservative leaders in the House of Commons—Sir Stafford Northcote, and Lord Randolph Churchill who claimed the glory of the victory—lent the occasion, in the Prince's eyes, an extra zest (see Lang, *Life of Sir Stafford Northcote*, p. 356). When the young Prince received the Freedom of the City of London (June 29, 1885) his father was the chief guest at the luncheon in the Guildhall which the Corporation gave in honour of the event.

[2] The ducal title had been borne by William IV., the young man's great-grand-uncle, before his accession to the throne.

The German custom was as yet imperfectly acclimatised in England. But the Prince and Princess decided to follow it. The occasion was unique in English history. No opportunity for the celebration of a silver wedding had arisen before in the life of an English heir-apparent. The incident appealed to the domestic sentiment of Queen Victoria, her family, and her people.

Unluckily, the day before the anniversary came round, a shadow fell on the royal circle, in the death of the old German Emperor, William I. The event was politically of no good omen. It was to carry in its train perilous changes in the relations between the dynasties of England and Germany. For the moment, the respect due to the memory of the dead Kaiser, to whom the Prince's attachment had not been impaired by political differences, demanded curtailment of the silver wedding programme. Queen Victoria, although she reckoned the widowed Empress Augusta among her oldest closest friends and correspondents, was reluctant to ignore the celebration, and she suspended Court mourning for the day. A family banquet at Marlborough House was, in the circumstances, the chief festivity. Guests from abroad included the King of the Belgians and the Crown Prince and Princess of Denmark. Queen Victoria broke her habit of widowed seclusion by coming to London for the evening to dine with her son and daughter-in-law. On the night, London was brilliantly illuminated and Queen Victoria, before returning to Windsor, drove through the principal streets to witness the display. The general enthusiasm testified to the Prince and Princess's popularity. Gifts of silver ornaments reached them from all quarters. A sum of £2000, collected in small amounts in the Colonies, including the Transvaal and native settlements, was expended by the Prince on a silver candelabrum adapted to electric light, which was then a novelty. Amid the flow of congratulations the Prince was especially gratified, as he informed the Prime Minister, Lord Salisbury, by a message from M. Carnot, President of the French Republic, and the members of his Cabinet in Paris. At the close of the abbreviated ceremonial of the silver wedding, the Prince, with Prince Albert Victor, left for Berlin to attend the obsequies of the dead Kaiser.

The year following the Prince's silver wedding saw a fresh and

promising development in the Prince's domestic experiences—
the first wedding in his family. The event caused him much
exhilaration. In the summer of 1889 his eldest daughter was
betrothed to his friend and comrade, the Earl of Fife. "They
are devoted to each other," the Prince wrote in announcing the
engagement to Mr. Gladstone (June 27, 1889), "and it meets
with our entire approval and with the Queen's sanction." "Our
daughter's marriage makes us very happy," he confided to
another intimate (July 13). Conventional opinion was somewhat
critical of an alliance of the Prince's youthful daughter with one
below royal rank and much her senior in years. But the union of
Queen Victoria's fourth daughter, the bride's aunt, to the Marquis
of Lorne, offered an adequate precedent, if one were needed.
To the Prince, with his broad social views, the criticism made
scant appeal. The marriage of the Princess Louise and the Earl
of Fife, who was raised to the dignity of a Dukedom in honour
of the occasion, took place with appropriate ceremony in the
private chapel of Buckingham Palace on the 27th July 1889.

"I think it was a very pretty sight," the Prince wrote
(July 30), "and the departure of the 'happy couple' from
Marlborough House Gardens in an open carriage and four—
amidst the showers of rice and a dense concourse of people—
very effective."

VI

The passage of his children from youth to maturity involved
the Prince in increased pecuniary responsibilities, and a delicate
constitutional controversy arose over the means of providing for
his fresh domestic expenses. In spite of Sir Dighton Probyn's
careful control of his finances, the Prince's annual income had
of late barely met the varied calls on his purse. Gossip continued grossly to exaggerate the normal deficit, but the Prince's
resources were clearly unequal to the provision of separate
establishments for his sons on reaching manhood, or of dowries
for his daughters on marriage. The hereditary Duchy of Cornwall still provided him with some £60,000 a year, which formed
the bulk of his revenues. An additional sum of £40,000 a year
was supplied him by the State, in agreement with the parliamentary settlement of 1863. The Prince cherished the view that
the State owed it to the heir-apparent to increase the parlia-

mentary grant in proportion to his growing needs, and friends of his had raised the point with both Mr. Disraeli and with Mr. Gladstone while his children were yet young. But at this period neither statesman lent any encouragement to the suggestion of an additional allowance from the State. Democratic misgivings of the costs of royalty remained alive long after the subsidence of the republican agitation of 1870–71, and they gained in strength between 1879 and 1885. In course of those years the Queen's three youngest children married, and an appeal was made by the sovereign in each case for their endowment by the State.[1]

Sir Charles Dilke, with whom the Prince maintained a close intimacy while he held office in Mr. Gladstone's second ministry, was the chief spokesman, both in the House of Commons and in the country, of the Radical hostility to grants of public money to the royal family. He had moved the rejection of the proposal of Lord Beaconsfield's ministry to make a grant to the Duke of Connaught on his marriage in 1879, and, though he was a member of Mr. Gladstone's government, had declined to vote for Mr. Gladstone's motion to make a grant to Prince Leopold in similar circumstances in 1882. The Prince viewed Sir Charles's attitude on these occasions with a composure which Queen Victoria did not share. He did not despair, by exercise of tact, of overcoming the objections of Sir Charles and his political allies to some increase of his own income in his domestic interests.

The Prince's sociable relations with Sir Charles encouraged him frankly to discuss with him the position of his children, who were entitled, in the Prince's view, to some parliamentary provision. Sir Charles somewhat mellowed under the Prince's confidences. The critic of royalty agreed that the Prince's elder son, who was in direct succession to the throne, was placed rather differently from the rest of the Queen's family. But he expressed doubt whether the other children of the Prince were qualified for the financial consideration of Parliament. To piecemeal grants he was rigidly opposed. Ultimately, he

[1] In 1879, on the proposal of Lord Beaconsfield's government, the House of Commons settled an annual grant on the Duke of Connaught on his marriage. In 1882 and 1885 respectively Mr. Gladstone's government was equally complaisant in the cases of Prince Leopold and Princess Beatrice. On each of the three occasions objection was taken by Radical members in the House and by their followers in the country.

favoured the appointment of a Select Committee, representative of all parties, to formulate principles which should govern henceforward the Crown's Civil List. Accordingly, on the 9th May 1882, Sir Charles forwarded to the Prince a draft plan of the procedure which he recommended.

Nothing immediately followed, but the Prince was unwilling to let the matter sleep. A year later, when Dilke was dining at Marlborough House (May 7, 1883), the Prince raised afresh the position of his two sons, and he found Sir Charles in quite a conciliatory mood.

"The Prince," Sir Charles wrote in his diary at the time, "spoke to me about the allowance for his sons as they came of age, and told me that he thought the money might be given to him as head of the family. My own view is very much the same, but I would give it all to the Crown, and let the King for the time being distribute it so that we should not deal with any other members of the family."[1]

The Government, however, showed no eagerness to take up the matter, and the Prince prudently refrained from pressing it. In December 1884, on the eve of his elder son's twenty-first birthday, he let Lord Granville know, to the Government's relief, that he had no intention of applying for an allowance for the young man until he should marry.

The Queen's request to the government, in 1885, to make the customary provision for Princess Beatrice on her approaching marriage with Prince Henry of Battenberg, gave a new fillip to the discussion. On pressure from Sir Charles Dilke, the cabinet, while they acceded to the Queen's wish to submit the usual motion to the House of Commons, decided at the same time to move for the appointment of a Select Committee on the lines of Sir Charles's proposal to the Prince of 1882. The Prince was quite favourable to such procedure, and when the Queen raised objection, he undertook to persuade her of its reasonableness. On the 14th May 1885, Mr. Gladstone moved in the House of Commons the grant to Princess Beatrice, and he announced at the same time that a representative Select Committee would be appointed at an early opportunity to devise a scheme for adapting the Civil List to future requirements. Mr. Labouchere, a Radical malcontent, together with prominent members of the Irish Nationalist party,

1882
Ætat. 40

1885
Ætat. 43

---

[1] Gwynn and Tuckwell, *Life of Sir Charles Dilke*, i. 523.

argued that the deliberations of the Select Committee should
precede any debate about the grant to Princess Beatrice, and
in course of the sitting some disrespectful references were made
to the Prince. The grant to the Princess was, however, carried,
and the resignation of the government immediately afterwards
on a different issue suspended consideration of the Select
Committee or of the Prince's income. The Prince was ill-
pleased by the tone of the minority's opposition to his sister's
grant, but he was gratified by the publication of a letter from
Mr. John Bright, in which the Radical orator announced to
some disaffected constituents his complete approval of a suitable
maintenance of royalty by the State. The Prince, although Mr.
Bright's political opinions usually made small appeal to him,
at once wrote to him in his own hand : "I send my warmest
thanks to you for the kind expressions you made use of on that
occasion, and I know they will be deeply appreciated by the
Queen and every member of my family" (May 19, 1885).[1]

It was not until the betrothal of the Prince's eldest daughter
in 1889 that the Prince deemed it opportune to raise again the
controverted question of his children's financial position. Lord
Salisbury, who was then Prime Minister, was known to be
apprehensive of the state of public opinion on the subject. Sir
Charles Dilke had retired from public life. The Prince therefore
resolved to invite his old friend, Mr. Gladstone, then leader of
the opposition, to bring the matter to an issue which might be
satisfactory and final. Mr. Gladstone was ready to discuss the
subject with the Prince, but he warned him by letter (June 19,
1889) of the widespread objection to any "piecemeal" treatment
of it. He recalled Sir Robert Peel's nervousness when questions
of the kind arose, and pointed out that proposals should "come
from the Government on the responsibility of the leaders of the
Government and Opposition." The Prince agreed that the
question ought to be settled once for all and ought not to be
raised again, at any rate while Queen Victoria lived.
 The Prince at once entered into practical details. He
suggested, in a memorandum dated 5th July 1889, which he
handed to Mr. Gladstone, that each of his daughters should

---

[1] This letter belonged to the late John Albert Bright, John Bright's eldest
son.

receive either a permanent annuity of £5000 for life, or £3000 at   1889
the present time and £6000 after the death of the Queen. In the   Ætat. 47
former case a dowry of £20,000 should be provided : in the latter,
one of £15,000. With regard to the sons, he wished the elder,
Prince Albert Victor, to receive not less than £10,000 nor more
than £15,000 a year, to be raised to £25,000 on his marriage.
As for his younger son, George, he asked that on his own accession the young man might be granted £25,000 a year, the same
sum as was allowed to his uncles, Queen Victoria's younger sons.

Lord Salisbury, relying on Mr. Gladstone's support, acceded
to the Prince's request to bring the matter before Parliament.
Accordingly, on 4th July the Leader of the House of Commons,
Mr. W. H. Smith, moved the appointment of a Select Committee
to inquire into former practice touching provision by the State
for the sovereign's grandchildren, and to report upon the principle which it was expedient to follow now and hereafter. The
motion was seconded by Mr. Gladstone. Signs of opposition
from the Radicals at once manifested themselves. Mr. Bradlaugh, member for Northampton, who had been prominent in
the republican agitation of earlier years, proposed an amendment
extending the inquiry to the whole of the Civil List, but this
was rejected by 313 to 125. A Committee of twenty-three, representing all parties in the House, was straightway nominated.[1]

The government submitted to the Committee proposals
which very slightly modified the Prince's own suggestions. The
elder son of the heir-apparent was to receive an annuity of
£10,000, to be increased on his marriage to £25,000 ; for every
other son there should be provided an annuity of £8000, to be
increased on marriage to £15,000 ; and for each daughter, an
annuity of £3000 with a dowry of £10,000.[2]

[1] There were ten Conservatives, including Mr. W. H. Smith, who was made
Chairman; three Liberal Unionists—Mr. Chamberlain, Mr. Goschen, and the
Marquis of Hartington; eight Liberal Home Rulers, including Mr. Gladstone;
and three spokesmen of the Radicals (who viewed all royal grants with misgiving), viz. Mr. John Morley, Mr. Labouchere, and Mr. Burt, the miners'
representative. The Nationalist contingent consisted of Mr. Parnell and Mr.
Sexton.

[2] At the same time the government acknowledged the right to public
provision of the children of other than the eldest son of the Queen, excepting
only such as might succeed to foreign thrones. Against this acknowledgement
there were ominous murmurings. The Queen had already agreed to provide
out of her own resources for the children of her daughters, and she promptly
announced that she waived any provision for the children of her younger sons.

Mr. Gladstone's position was not an easy one. On personal
grounds he could count on the support of the Irish Nationalists,
but his earnest conviction of the need of maintaining the
monarchy in due dignity was not shared by his Radical followers.
Recognising an obligation of meeting Radical criticism, he
moved, in the Committee, that the sovereign had no *absolute*
right to call on her people to provide for any of her grandchildren, at the same time as he claimed that the sons and
daughters of the heir-apparent were entitled to special consideration. Mr. Gladstone's qualifying motion was narrowly
rejected by the Conservative element in the Committee (by 12
votes to 10). The Radical members of the Committee—Mr.
John Morley, Mr. Labouchere, and Mr. Burt, the miners' spokesman—all declared themselves hostile to any reservation in the
Prince's favour. Mr. Gladstone lost no time in explaining fully
to the Prince his difficulty with his followers. Together they
came to the conclusion that the Prince's proposal should be
modified. The scheme of separate allowances to the Prince's
children should be dropped, and for it should be substituted a
plan whereby a quarterly payment out of the Consolidated Fund,
amounting to £36,000 a year, should be made directly to the
Prince of Wales, out of which "he would be empowered to make
such assignments and in such manner to his children as his Royal
Highness should in his discretion think fit." The Committee
adopted the change and embodied it in its report to the House
of Commons.

When the government's resolution for the adoption of the
report came before the House, amendments were vainly moved
by Mr. Labouchere and Mr. John Morley. Mr. Labouchere
proposed retrenchments in the existing Civil List, while Mr.
Morley refused to entertain any new grant to the Prince on the
ground that the report provided no condition of finality. Sir
William Harcourt supported Mr. Morley, and drew from Mr.
Chamberlain the remark that opponents of the grant were "the
Nihilists of English politics." But with the defeat of Mr. Morley's
amendment by 385 to 154 the Committee's report was adopted
by the House, and the Prince of Wales's Children Bill, which
gave it a statutory form, was introduced. The Bill provided
for the lapse of the arrangement on Queen Victoria's death.
The Radicals continued to fight, but the Bill passed its

final reading in the Lower House on 5th August 1889, and in
the Upper House four days later. Mr. Gladstone's action
throughout the controversy moved the Prince's warmest gratitude. Nor did he bear malice against those who had sedulously
obstructed the passage of the measure through Parliament.
Mr. John Morley, Mr. Labouchere, and Mr. Thomas Burt had
no ground for complaining in later years of his attitude towards
them.

1889
Ætat. 47

VII

The opening years of the last decade of the Prince's career
as heir-apparent saw some rapid alternations of light and shadow
in his home environment. In the autumn of the year 1891
domestic considerations led the Princess, accompanied by her two
unmarried daughters, to join, early in October, her family in
Copenhagen ; subsequently she accompanied the Tsar and her
sister, the Tsaritza, to the Tsar's Crimean home at Livadia,
on what promised to be a long stay. The Prince's fiftieth
birthday, 9th November, was thus celebrated at Sandringham
in the Princess's absence.[1] Unexpected domestic trouble was at
the moment impending. The day before the Prince's birthday
the younger son, George, fell ill. A few days later the Prince
brought the young man from Sandringham to Marlborough
House to receive expert attention. The illness was diagnosed as
enteric fever. Through the anxious time, the father showed the
utmost solicitude, spending many hours in the sick-room. As
soon as the news reached the Princess in the Crimea, she travelled
home at all possible speed, arriving at Marlborough House on
the 22nd November. The parents shared the anxiety together
over the sick-bed. Not until 3rd December was Prince George
pronounced to be out of danger.

An incident of happy augury, which proved delusive, meanwhile supervened. There was unqualified rejoicing in the royal
circle when announcement was made on 7th December 1891 that
the Duke of Clarence had betrothed himself to Princess Mary,

1891
Ætat. 50

---

[1] The Prince's family was represented by his two sons, his married daughter,
the Duchess of Fife, and his son-in-law, the Duke of Fife, and his two brothers,
the Dukes of Edinburgh and Connaught. Among a few other guests was the
Prince's special friend among diplomatists of the period, the Russian Ambassador, M. de Staal.

only daughter of the Duke and Duchess of Teck, and niece of the Duke of Cambridge. "We are delighted," the Prince wrote, "at the choice he has made of so charming a young lady, and he will, I am sure, be very happy." "It is also a great satisfaction to feel," he informed Earl Spencer, "that the marriage will be popular in the country." The Prince's nephew, the Kaiser, was prompt in his congratulations. "What happy and interesting news," he wrote to the Queen on 8th December 1891; "Eddy is engaged! I am very glad for Uncle Bertie. This will be a ray of light after the troubles of Sandringham and poor George's illness." But when the Kaiser offered to attend the coming wedding and received an intimation that his presence was not desired, his enthusiasm suffered some abatement.

Unexpectedly, death stepped in to forbid the auspicious union. The Duke of Clarence was never strong. An attack of typhoid fever in boyhood had weakened his constitution, and the doctor, Sir William Broadbent, who had recently attended his brother George, had expressed concern for the Duke's health. Early in the new year, 1892, he fell a victim to an epidemic of influenza, and died at Sandringham on the 14th January.

The blow was the heaviest that the Prince and Princess had yet encountered in their married life. Telegraphing the sad tidings to Mr. Gladstone, who was at Biarritz, the Prince described his wife and himself as "heart-broken." A little later, he wrote to his Oxford friend, Mrs. Liddell, 4th February 1892:

"To lose our eldest son at the age of twenty-eight after only a few days' illness and on the eve of his marriage is one of those calamities that one can never really get over, and though, as time goes on, our duties and occupations will have to be followed, everything in our daily life will remind me of the gap made amongst our children."

The tragedy evoked an immense outburst of national grief. Mr. Gladstone, writing to Sir William Harcourt, 6th February 1892, compared the public manifestation of sorrow to "that on the death of Princess Charlotte," and he greeted it as "a remarkable evidence of national attachment to the Queen and the royal family." The Prince and Princess issued from Windsor Castle, 20th January, an impressive acknowledgement "of their deep gratitude for the universal feeling of sympathy." Time very slowly healed the wound in the Prince's and the Princess's hearts.

The Duke of Clarence's death raised the Prince's second son George to the position of heir to the Crown after himself, and on Queen Victoria's next birthday, 24th May 1892, he was created Duke of York. Less than a year later, on 3rd May 1893, the betrothal took place between the Duke and Princess Mary of Teck. Two days later the Prince announced the engagement to Mr. Gladstone: "The choice he has made," the Prince wrote, "is one which gives me great gratification." The marriage took place in the Chapel Royal at St. James's Palace on the following 6th July. The event lay outside the sphere of politics. It was essentially a domestic concern. But the presence of certain wedding guests at Marlborough House seemed to justify the Prince's hope that the reign of international peace was brought a step nearer by the marriage of his son. The Kaiser was represented by his brother, Prince Henry, and the Tsar of Russia by the Tsarevitch Nicholas. The Russian heir-apparent formed a brotherly attachment to the bridegroom — his first cousin. Next year he was to ascend his father's throne, and to enter on that anxious career of rule which ended in ghastly tragedy. His cousin's wedding always loomed large among the few happy memories of his later life. Four years later he was writing to his host, the Prince of Wales, "I always look back with such pleasure to my charming stay at Marlborough House for Georgie's wedding" (June 1/13, 1897). The Russian Prince proved his tender interests in the fortunes of Prince George by coming back to England the year after the marriage to stand sponsor at the baptism of the first child— Prince Edward.

A third and last marriage among the Prince's children followed after a three years' interval. On 28th October 1895 the Prince wrote to Mr. Gladstone:

You have always taken such a kind interest in our family that I wish to be one of the first to announce to you that our youngest daughter Maud is engaged to be married to her cousin Charles, the second son of [Frederick] the Crown Prince of Denmark.

"It is an event which gives us great pleasure," the Prince informed another friend (Mrs. Liddell) on 15th November 1895;

Margin note: 1893 / Ætat. 51

"in her cousin she has made an excellent choice, as he is both charming and good looking." The marriage was celebrated at Buckingham Palace on 22nd July 1896. This was the only marriage of a child of the Prince which came into touch with foreign politics. No political association was anticipated at the time that Princess Maud's marriage took place. But twelve years later, when Norway dissolved the union with Sweden, there was much international controversy over the choice of ruler of the newly established State. Princess Maud's father, then King Edward, intervened with success in the endeavour to persuade the Norwegians to make his son-in-law their King, under the title of King Haakon VII.

The Prince's second daughter, Princess Victoria, remained unmarried, and was the constant companion of her mother. In her fortunes the Prince maintained to the last as lively a paternal interest as in those of her married brother and sisters.

The Prince assumed for the first time the rôle of grandfather on the birth of a daughter to his eldest daughter, the Duchess of Fife, on 17th May 1891. The Duchess bore a second daughter on 3rd April 1893. His eldest grandson, Edward, first child of Prince George, was born 23rd June 1894 ; and while the Prince of Wales was yet heir-apparent two other sons—Prince Albert (December 14, 1895) and Prince Henry (March 31, 1900)—were added to the family of his son Prince George. The birth of his first grandson, to whom he stood sponsor together with Queen Victoria, Princess Alexandra's parents, the King and Queen of Denmark, and the Tsarevitch Nicholas, gave, before the Prince came to the throne, added stability to the monarchy by making the direct succession to the Crown trebly secure. There were many phases of the Prince's career which were unique in the experiences of English heir-apparents. No earlier English heir-apparent had become a grandfather during the life of the sovereign. In his relations with his grandchildren the Prince filled to admiration the rôle of a genial and indulgent grandfather. He instinctively acquired *l'art d'être grandpère*.

CHAPTER XXXIII

THE JUBILEE (1887) AND DIAMOND JUBILEE (1897) OF QUEEN VICTORIA; THE PRINCE'S COMMEMORATIVE EFFORTS—THE IMPERIAL INSTITUTE AND HIS HOSPITAL FUND

I

ON 20th June 1887 Queen Victoria completed the exceptional span of fifty years of rule. Through forty-six years of that extended period the Prince, her heir, had been her chief subject. The criticism to which the seclusion of her widowhood exposed her was dwindling, and her length of days had evoked in her people a sense of veneration which was destined to grow steadily during the rest of her life. A recent development of the imperial sentiment had given the English monarchy by 1887 a new strength in the popular mind. It helped to make of the sovereign a living symbol of the unity not merely of the British nation, but of the British Empire. Although Queen Victoria was still holding her heir aloof from her regal responsibilities, circumstance was enhancing the lustre of his heritage.

The celebration of Queen Victoria's Jubilee in the summer of 1887 was designed on an impressive scale which corresponded with the developing consciousness of the Crown's place in the national and imperial economy. The Prince, in his dual capacity of son and heir-apparent, took an energetic part in planning a celebration of appropriate splendour. Subject to the Queen's supreme authority, he was untiring in supervision of ceremonial details and in hospitable greetings of the numerous representative visitors from abroad—kings and princes of Europe, ruling princes of India, and envoys from the Colonies—among whom his tact was useful in settling some vexed questions of precedence. Marlborough House was as crowded as Buckingham Palace with

1887

Ætat. 45

foreign guests of royal rank. The King of Denmark, the Prince's father-in-law, and the King of Greece, his brother-in-law, were among those who stayed under his roof.

When Queen Victoria passed in procession from Buckingham Palace to Westminster Abbey on 21st June to attend there a service of thanksgiving, a cortège of princes of her own house, thirty-two in all, including her sons, her sons-in-law, and her grandsons, preceded her carriage. At its head rode the Prince. But a shadow was threatening the bright scene. Towering above Queen Victoria's kindred in the princely escort was the Prince's brother-in-law, the Crown Prince of Germany, in the white uniform of the Pomeranian Cuirassiers, his gilded helmet shining in the bright sunlight. The stalwart heir to the Imperial crown of Germany was already in the grip of a fatal disease, which had well-nigh deprived him of the power of speech, and his condition raised privately an apprehension which qualified the joy of the Prince and his family.[1]

At the close of the Thanksgiving Service in the Abbey the Prince was first to greet his mother. Approaching her, he raised her hand to his lips, and she returned his salute with a motherly kiss.

In all the public functions of succeeding weeks the Prince was his mother's companion, or, in her absence, he served as her deputy. He was with her at a great military review at Aldershot on 9th July. At the naval review off Spithead on 29th July he stood at her side as the royal yacht passed between the long lines of battleships. The Prince had a special interest in this demonstration of England's naval strength. The Queen, by way of acknowledging his place in the nation's life as well as the national importance of the country's first line of defence, promoted him on the occasion to the rank of Admiral of the Fleet.

II

A decade later, in 1897, a like demonstration welcomed the conclusion of Queen Victoria's sixty years of sovereignty. Her

---

[1] In a second procession which accompanied the Queen on her passage through London, there rode four kings—of Saxony, Belgium, Greece, and Denmark—with the heirs-apparent of Austria, Portugal, and Sweden, as well as of Greece. In other processions there figured ruling princes of India in dazzling array and special envoys from the British colonies, to all of whom the Prince gave welcome proofs of his cordiality.

reign was now the longest known to English history,[1] and the 1897
veneration in which she was held by the nation and Empire far Ætat. 55
excelled all previous experience. Under the influence of the
Colonial Secretary, Mr. Joseph Chamberlain, the ministry of Lord
Salisbury decided to give the celebration of the Queen's Diamond
Jubilee a predominantly imperialist tone. There were invited
to London not only a larger detachment than before of ruling
princes and other representatives of India, but also the Prime
Ministers of all the Colonies, Governors and Ministers of the
dependencies, and delegations of all the armed forces of the
Empire—mounted riflemen from Australia, New Zealand, South
Africa, and Canada, Indian sepoys, native soldiers from the West
Indies, West Africa, Hong Kong, Borneo, and elsewhere.
Although sovereigns of the great European powers were not
included among Queen Victoria's guests, the princes of Europe
and rulers of small states assembled in imposing number on her
invitation. Her grandson, the Kaiser, had written to her as
early as 2nd January 1897 asking her advice as to whether he
should attend; but she deprecated his coming, and he was
represented by his brother, Prince Henry of Prussia, and by his
mother, the Empress Frederick, who joined the rest of the
Queen's children. The order of precedence among the foreign
royalty caused heartburnings, which the Prince, as in 1887,
helped to allay. But it was found impossible to satisfy the claims
of Prince Ferdinand of Bulgaria, a distant kinsman of the Queen,
who had succeeded to the uneasy throne of the ill-fated Prince
Alexander of Battenberg. The sensitive guest long cherished
a grievance on this score against both the Queen and the
Prince.

The official programme of the Diamond Jubilee, which the
Prince aided in formulating, was long and impressive. Although
the Queen nerved herself to play a prominent part, her age set
limits to her activities. The Prince showed a filial anxiety to
save her fatigue by filling her place as often as she would allow.
"I shall be delighted," he modestly wrote to her on 19th June,
"to undertake in your name such duties as the reception of
addresses or the distribution of medals to the Indian and Colonial

---

[1] Her grandfather, George III., who had worn the British crown for the
longest previous period, reigned 59 years 96 days, but through 20 years of his
reign he was disabled from the exercise of royal functions by mental illness.

troops." The Queen willingly accepted her son's offer and he became the leading figure in many of the ceremonial observances. On the eve of the celebrations the Queen cogently testified to the harmony of her relations with her heir-apparent. She conferred upon him the Grand Mastership of the Bath, an honour which she had created for her husband near half a century before and had suffered to lapse when she became a widow. At the same time she decorated the chief members of his household.

"I cannot describe," the Prince wrote to her in simple terms of filial affection on 19th June, "how touched I am by your great kindness in appointing me, on the occasion of your Jubilee, Grand Master of your great and distinguished Order of the Bath. I feel it as a very high honour having succeeded dear Papa after an interval of so many years. . . . The honours you intend conferring on my gentlemen have greatly gratified me and will please them immensely."

Throughout the celebrations the Prince made unsparing contribution to their success. On the 19th June he presided at the Imperial Institute at a banquet given in honour of the Colonial premiers, and his speech of welcome was seconded by Lord Salisbury, the Prime Minister, by Lord Rosebery, and by Mr. Chamberlain. On the evening of the 21st the Queen entertained her family and her chief guests at a banquet at Buckingham Palace, when the Prince feelingly proposed the health both of his mother and of his sister, the Empress Frederick. Next morning the outstanding episode of the Diamond Jubilee demonstration took place. The Queen, amid a brilliant cavalcade of princes and soldiers, drove from Buckingham Palace to St. Paul's Cathedral, where, on the pavement outside the west entrance, a short service of thanksgiving was held. Thence the royal procession passed by way of London Bridge through the poorer districts of London on the south side of the Thames. The Prince in his Field-Marshal's uniform rode through the six miles' route beside the Queen's carriage, and he shared with his mother in the public eye the honours of the exhilarating day. Two days later the Queen returned to Windsor, and the full burden of entertaining foreign princes and envoys fell on the Prince's shoulders. The most impressive function which he performed in the sovereign's absence and on her behalf was to review the fleet at Spithead on the 26th, when the display of England's naval power outran all record; 173 vessels of war were drawn up in four lines, stretching over a course of thirty miles.

At no point in the protracted programme did the Prince's efforts slacken. The Princess of Wales had inaugurated a fund to entertain at dinner 330,000 poor people in honour of the Diamond Jubilee, and on the 24th and 30th June the Prince and the Princess visited their humble guests in course of their entertainment, which was provided in public buildings scattered throughout London. On the 3rd July the Prince again, in the Queen's name, presented, in the gardens of Buckingham Palace, Jubilee medals to the Indian and Colonial troops. Seventeen days later, in his new rôle of Grand Master of the Order of the Bath, he gave a banquet at St. James's Palace to all G.C.B.'s. Of the private entertainments which celebrated the Diamond Jubilee, the most spectacular was a fancy-dress ball which was given at Devonshire House by the Prince's friends the Duke and Duchess of Devonshire. The Prince wore the costume of the Grand Prior of St. John of Jerusalem, and the Princess appeared as Marguerite de Valois. The event recalled the splendours of a similar entertainment which the Prince had devised at Marlborough House in 1874.[1]

The Prince's prominence in the proceedings of the Diamond Jubilee drew towards him something of the peculiarly earnest sentiment of loyalty which at the close of her reign was focussed on his mother. Widespread as was the Prince's personal popularity at home and abroad, it rested on foundations very different from those which sustained the reverence felt for Queen Victoria. When, after little more than three years, he succeeded to her throne, not the least important portion of his inheritance was that impassioned devotion to the throne of which the Diamond Jubilee gave the paramount manifestation.

III

There was a confident hope that the sentiment, of which the plaudits and the pageantry of the Jubilee demonstrations of 1887 and 1897 were the outward perishable signs, would endure. The Prince shared the view that as historic landmarks they warranted commemoration in a form which would permanently link them

[1] Lady Randolph Churchill's *Reminiscences*, pp. 301 *seq.*

with work of public usefulness.   In 1887 he actively joined others in establishing in memory of the Jubilee of that year an institution in London which was designed to teach the English people the range of the Empire's productive resources and to provide a meeting-place for colonists visiting the mother country. Ten years later he made an effort to commemorate the Diamond Jubilee by devising a new philanthropic scheme for the secure endowment, by means of private charity, of the London hospitals. The earlier design, which issued in the Imperial Institute, failed to answer the Prince's expectations. The later and less expansive scheme, which took shape as the Prince of Wales's (afterwards King Edward's) Hospital Fund, came nearer the fulfilment of his hope.

The Prince's commemorative plan of 1887 was an outgrowth of his early enthusiasm for industrial and art exhibitions.[1] His disappointment over the annual series of exhibitions at South Kensington of 1871–74 had only temporarily diminished his ardour in the cause. In 1881 his interest had been reawakened by the successful endeavour of a Norfolk neighbour, Sir Edward Birkbeck, of Norwich, to give a new application of the principle of exhibitions. Sir Edward, who was seeking to improve the fishing industry of the country, organised at Norwich a National Fisheries Exhibition, which the Prince opened in April 1881.[2] Its success encouraged the Prince to develop the experiment by supervising an International Fisheries Exhibition at South Kensington two years later. This venture he opened and closed in person on 14th May and 31st October respectively, and he gave distinction to the ceremonies by inviting the attendance of the Diplomatic Corps and a distinguished array of other guests. The enterprise proved attractive enough to warrant the Prince in promoting sequels of a cognate character in the three succeeding years. An International Health Exhibition was opened on 8th May 1884 in his behalf during his absence from England, by the Duke of Cambridge. The medical profession, with leading members of which the Prince was in close touch, helped to make the Exhibition a serious

[1] See p. 191 *supra*.
[2] The first International Fish and Fishing Exhibition was opened in Berlin by the Crown Prince on 20th April 1880. A similar International Exhibition opened at Edinburgh on 11th April 1882.

effort to promote popularly sound medical knowledge of the latest kind. Sir James Paget, the eminent surgeon, who enjoyed the Prince's intimacy, actively co-operated, and the Prince, writing to his medical friend Dr. Acland, described the result as "very interesting and instructive." [1] An International Inventions and Music Exhibition followed, under the Prince's auspices, and was opened by him on 4th May. The public showed less interest in this effort than in its predecessors, and it resulted in a small pecuniary loss.

But the Prince had already in mind a more ambitious addition to this series of exhibitions, which should be ready for the following year and triumphantly retrieve the situation. The aim was to illustrate the products, manufactures, and arts of India and the Colonies. The importance of the design led to an application to the government to appoint a Royal Commission for purposes of organisation and control. No such assistance had been asked in connection with any of the recent undertakings. A representative Commission was formed, with the Prince as President (October 8, 1884). The Prince threw himself with energy into the organising work in a confident belief that the scheme would stimulate goodwill between the home country and the Empire overseas. He enlisted the Queen's interest, and co-operated vigorously with fellow-Commissioners, who included his Canadian friend, Sir John Rose, Sir Philip Cunliffe Owen, and many fellow-workers in similar enterprises of much earlier date. The Colonies and India Exhibition was opened on 4th May 1886 by Queen Victoria, with much pomp, which the Prince had a main hand in devising. He induced the Poet Laureate, Lord Tennyson, to write for the occasion an Ode which his friend Sir Arthur Sullivan set to music. The Queen, in reply to an address by the Prince on the general aim, described the Exhibition as "an impressive development of the idea which the Prince Consort had originated in 1851." The Prince manifested in lavish hospitalities his friendly sentiment for his fellow-Commissioners from India and the Colonies. He celebrated the Queen's Birthday that year (May 29, 1886) by entertaining them at dinner at Marlborough House. On the same night the Prime Minister, Mr. Gladstone, gave his prescriptive Birthday dinner, which the

[1] The Prince to Acland, Royat, 18th May 1884; cf. Stephen Paget's *Life of Sir James Paget*, p. 84.

Prince had been of late in the habit of attending, but he excused his presence on the ground that "the Colonial and Indian Commissioners . . . have so ably supported me in making the present important Exhibition a success."[1] During the summer he importuned the Prime Minister with more than usual pertinacity for titular honours on behalf of his numerous co-workers. Mr. Gladstone proved conciliatory as far as precedent allowed; he refused the Prince's request of a peerage for Sir John Rose.[2]

The Colonial and Indian Exhibition fascinated the public, who christened it colloquially the "Colinderies." Popular patronage was so liberal as to furnish a surplus profit of well over £30,000. By spreading in England a knowledge not only of the extent of the British Empire, but also of its productive possibilities, the enterprise proved one of the historic milestones in the development during Queen Victoria's reign of the imperial consciousness.

IV

When the "Colinderies" was drawing to a close, the Prince proposed that the design should be re-embodied in a shape which might permanently commemorate Queen Victoria's Jubilee of 1887. In response to a letter which he sent from Marlborough House on 13th September 1886, the Lord Mayor of London opened a fund at the Mansion House for the endowment of "an Institute which should represent the arts, manufactures, and commerce of the Queen's Colonial and Indian Empire." In the months that followed the Prince spared himself no effort to win support, soliciting subscriptions in his own hand from friends at home and abroad. On 12th January 1887 he presided over an influential meeting which he summoned at St. James's Palace, and sketched out a scheme for an Imperial Institute which

[1] The Prince to Mr. Gladstone, 5th March 1886. The Prince was represented at Mr. Gladstone's table by his elder son. His absence was not wholly unwelcome to the statesman, who was greatly embarrassed by many distinguished followers' repudiation of his leadership over his recent adoption of Home Rule for Ireland, and he confessed to Lord Granville his reluctance to expose to the Prince at the official Birthday dinner "the great nakedness of the land" (Morley, *Life of Gladstone*, iii. p. 322).

[2] On 6th June 1886 the Prince sent a long list of names to Mr. Gladstone, appealing to him to arrange for the announcement of the decorations on the following coronation day (June 19). "Though I understand," he added, "that there are no vacancies in the K.C.B.'s and C.B.'s, I believe the Queen has the power of creating extra members of the Order on exceptional occasions."

should be at once a place of study and a social resort for producers and consumers of all parts of the Empire. On the motion of the Prince's friend Lord Spencer the meeting resolved to establish such a foundation by way of a national memorial of the Queen's Jubilee.

Although the final fruits of the Prince's activity in the matter were disappointing, the initial stage promised well. He was gratified to receive from his French royalist friend the Duc d'Aumale on 17th March a cheque for £500. Lord Dufferin, Viceroy of India, one of the friends whom the Prince approached earliest, was doubtful whether the Indian government could render any appreciable help. There were agitators in India, Lord Dufferin reminded the Prince (October 11, 1886), who were always denouncing British greed and injustice, and public opinion in India might misinterpret the appropriation of public money to the Prince's project. But Lord Dufferin promised to encourage the formation of voluntary committees who might raise funds privately. The native princes yielded more readily than the Viceroy to the Prince's persuasion. Munificent donations came from many of them.[1]

In the practical work of organisation the Prince relied largely on the counsel of his old associate Sir Lyon Playfair. The Prince pleaded eagerly for the allocation of the reserve funds of the Exhibition of 1851 Commission, of which he was still President, but Playfair deprecated that course,[2] raising, however, no objection to the Prince's more modest suggestion that the Royal Commission which controlled the recent Colonies and India Exhibition should hand over to the new enterprise the greater part—£25,000—of its profits (April 30, 1887). A public site in South Kensington, adjoining some existing public premises which were capable of adaptation, was readily appropriated for the main building. Some expansion of the original scheme was soon adopted. Provision was made not only for the illustration of the commercial and natural resources of the Colonies and India, but also of the natural products and manufactures of the United Kingdom.

---

[1] The Maharajah of Jodhpore sent £10,000 (June 1887), and subsequently the Maharajah Holkar of Indore gave 100,000 rupees, and the Maharajah of Jeypore £20,000.

[2] Reid, *Life of Lord Playfair*, pp. 449–52.

By the time that the celebration of the Jubilee arrived, all was ready for the inauguration. On 4th July 1887 the Queen laid the foundation stone of the new building, and the ceremony, which the Prince supervised, ranked among the more notable features of the Jubilee programme.

But signs were soon apparent that in spite of the Prince's solicitude the Institute excited no great popular enthusiasm. The flow of contributions slackened. There were consequent delays in completing both the building and the organisation. Not until 28th April 1891 was a constitution for the Institute promulgated. The Prince of Wales was appointed President, with a large governing body, of which twelve members were nominees of the Crown. A portion of the new building was completed in the summer of 1892, when the governing body, with the Prince's approval, but somewhat to the prejudice, as it proved, of the serious aims of the project, announced the addition to the Institute's attractions of concerts and other amusements. The formal opening by the Queen took place with elaborate ritual on 10th May 1893. Military contingents from Canada, Australia, and India escorted the royal cortège from Buckingham Palace. The Prince, undaunted by the growing difficulties, eloquently foretold the position which the Institute was destined to fill in the economy of the Empire. The Queen, in reply, earnestly prayed "that it may never cease to flourish as a lasting emblem of the unity and loyalty of her Empire." None the less the Institute failed to progress. To the Prince's disappointment popular interest continued to decline. Ultimately the Prince came reluctantly to acknowledge the virtual failure of his enterprise. In 1899 he readily consented to the government's offer to convert the main building into a new home for the University of London. That conversion took effect on the 5th July. The Imperial Institute retained adjacent galleries in which to exhibit products of the Empire, and its corporate existence was maintained. But the spacious aims, with which the Prince had launched the Institute on its career, were unrealised. The Institute embodied a sound educational principle which made only a limited appeal. The imperial sentiment sought popular expression in other ways.

V

Greater success attended the Prince's effort permanently to commemorate Queen Victoria's Diamond Jubilee of 1897. The purpose differed widely from that of the Imperial Institute. An endeavour was made under the Prince's supervision to found a memorial of the Queen's sixty years' reign by helping in perpetuity to assuage the sufferings and sickness of the people of her capital.[1] Not all the original hopes of the venture were fulfilled. It did not preserve its initial commemorative associations. But the movement inaugurated an era of promise in the embarrassed history of London hospitals, and lent the organisation of philanthropic effort a new efficiency.

Practical philanthropy always appealed to both the Prince and the Princess. From early years the Prince had interested himself in the adequacy and efficiency of hospital accommodation throughout the country. Since his appointment in 1867 to the office of President of St. Bartholomew's Hospital, hospital management became an object of his study and of his discerning criticism. As far as his other engagements permitted, he was always willing to preside at dinners which were organised to raise funds for hospitals in financial distress, or to lay foundation stones, or to open new or additional buildings. He showed concern for the welfare of the General Hospital of Norwich, where he laid the foundation stone of a new building on 27th June 1889. But the hospitals of London claimed the lion's share of his philanthropic attention. He was always ready to lend his influence to improve the fortunes of the London Hospital, which serves poor dwellers in the eastern districts of the capital. A smaller east end hospital, the Poplar Hospital, of which he opened a new wing on 11th June 1894, also came well within the range of his sympathies. When Guy's Hospital in south London was, in 1896, in acute pecuniary distress and was seeking to raise an

[1] A movement in the interest of the staffs of hospitals throughout the country had been initiated under the auspices of Queen Victoria and of the Princess of Wales in connection with the Queen's Jubilee of 1887. There was then established a national pension fund for nurses and hospital officers which became, it is said, the largest voluntary women's thrift society in the world. The Princess of Wales accepted the office of President and, until 1900, she annually presented pension certificates at Marlborough House.

endowment fund of half a million, he presided at a dinner at which £150,000 was collected.[1]

It was in harmony with a lifelong interest that the Prince, after due consideration, identified himself in 1897 with a bold scheme for promoting the welfare of hospitals of London by way of commemorating the Diamond Jubilee. It was a critical period in the history of the London hospitals, the expenses of which were defrayed by voluntary contributions. The uncertainties attaching to the voluntary mode of support constantly involved the risks of bankruptcy or the reduction or extinction of the hospitals' services. The Prince was persuaded that the voluntary system was superior to that of endowment by the State. Organised effort to stimulate the voluntary system had been made without conspicuous success by two existing organisations—the Hospital Sunday Fund and the Hospital Saturday Fund. It was with the object of putting the voluntary system on more secure foundations that the Prince fathered a new and vigorous movement in 1897.

Some misgivings arose in the Prince's mind at the outset. The first suggestion of the new scheme was made to him by Mr. (afterwards Sir) Henry Burdett, who had long devoted himself with great energy to urging on the public its obligation of making more adequate provision for the hospitals, and on hospital managers the need of a more efficient equipment. Mr. Burdett's general argument carried weight with the Prince, but at the first blush he questioned the propriety of connecting Mr. Burdett's plan with the commemoration of the Diamond Jubilee. Nor was he convinced that a member of the royal family should lead the proposed effort. Another preliminary difficulty which presented itself to the Prince was that the Hospital Sunday Fund had since 1873 been seeking to cover, under the sanction of the churches, something of the same ground. A suggestion to meet possible rivalry with the Hospital Sunday Fund by secularising the new movement and excluding the clergy from any control, the Prince promptly vetoed. It was undesirable, too, to discourage the Hospital Saturday Fund, which addressed its appeal mainly to industrial workers. The proposed scheme, the Prince

---

[1] On 21st June 1898 the Prince laid the foundation stone of the new University College Hospital, which was erected at the cost of Sir John Blundell Maple, one of his associates on the turf.

contended, must rest on a thoroughly comprehensive basis, and the support of the leaders of every religious denomination and every industrial interest was to his mind essential to its launching. At length he summoned to Marlborough House on 21st January 1897 a representative meeting to consider ways and means of establishing in the interests of the London hospitals a new fund to be called, in view of the Diamond Jubilee, Queen Victoria's Commemoration Fund. Men of position in the spheres of medicine, surgery, commerce, industry, administration, and religions of all creeds accepted the Prince's invitation and agreed to work together for the scheme. His friend Lord Rothschild consented, at his request, to serve as treasurer. Subsequently the Prince drafted an explanatory letter, which was published in the London press on 5th February.

1897
Ætat. 55

"Having ascertained from the Queen," he wrote, "that she has no wish to express a preference for any one of the many proposals loyally suggested for commemorating nationally or locally the sixtieth year of her reign, I feel at liberty to bring to the notice of the inhabitants of the metropolis a project lying very near my heart, its object being to attach the sentiment of gratitude for the blessings which the country has enjoyed during the last sixty years to a scheme of permanent beneficence."

The expenditure of London hospitals and convalescent homes fell, he pointed out, far below their receipts, yet of the five hundred thousand households in London only fifty thousand contributed anything towards the support of hospitals. It was therefore necessary, if the voluntary principle were to continue, "to enlarge the area from which annual subscriptions were gathered." There was no intention to trench upon the ground occupied by the Hospital Sunday and Saturday Funds. An endeavour would be made to secure from £100,000 to £150,000 in annual subscriptions from those who had not hitherto regularly contributed.

In all the details of organisation the Prince played a characteristically active part. He personally invited contributions from his friends and acquaintances. He was much gratified by the receipt of £200 from Mr. Cecil Rhodes. His applications for help did not always meet with a prompt response. The Duke of Westminster, who was consulted, declined assistance on the ground that he had pledged himself to obtain £100,000 for the

better endowment of the Queen's Jubilee Nursing Institute, and
of this sum only £22,000 had yet reached him (January 20, 1897).
However, the Duke contributed £100 and joined the General
Council in virtue of his office of Lord-Lieutenant of the County
of London. Before the end of the year a sum of £227,551 was
collected, of which a tenth part was promised as a recurring
annual subscription.

In the administration of the fund the Prince encouraged the
Committee to keep two points in view: firstly, the need of
building up a substantial reserve fund, the interest of which
should form a permanent endowment; and secondly, the
desirability of enforcing on hospitals which should receive grants,
the obligation of maintaining a high standard of efficiency in
organisation and equipment. A suggestion which he personally
approved, that some part of the fund's receipts should be
applied to medical research or medical education, was found to
be unworkable. A first distribution of grants to institutions
which satisfied conditions of efficiency was made during the first
year, under the direction of Lord Lister, to the amount of nearly
£60,000, while some £167,000 was invested.

The Prince's prominent identification with the fund led early
to the shelving of its original purpose of a memorial of the
Diamond Jubilee. It was finally christened "The Prince of
Wales's Hospital Fund." [1] In large measure the movement
realised its ends. A fresh lease of life was assured the voluntary
system. To the original promotor of the scheme, Mr. Henry
Burdett, the Prince always assigned a large share of the success,
and he pressed on Lord Salisbury in 1897 the justice of conferring on him the honour of the K.C.B., raising objections to
the Prime Minister's first proposal to confine the honour to a
knighthood.

So long as Queen Victoria reigned the Prince remained the
active President of the Prince of Wales's Hospital Fund, holding
the annual meetings at Marlborough House. After the Queen's
death the fund was rechristened "King Edward's Hospital
Fund" (January 1, 1902). He then exchanged the office of
President for that of Patron, and the presidency was assumed

---

[1] A subsidiary movement called the League of Mercy, which aimed at
drawing small subscriptions from young persons, was inaugurated by the Prince
at a meeting at Marlborough House on 18th December 1899.

by his son. Throughout King Edward's reign his interest in the movement remained alert. In the year of his coronation his services to the fund were publicly recognised by a record contribution of £605,000, of which a sixth part was at once distributed, and the rest, in conformity with his policy, invested.[1]

1898
Ætat. 56

VI

Although endowment of research was finally excluded from the scope of the Prince of Wales's Hospital Fund the Prince always cherished profound interest in the improvement of medical and surgical practice, and in the increase of medical and surgical knowledge. He watched with enlightened curiosity the progress of curative science throughout his adult years, and he encouraged, as far as he could, all scientific research which was likely to promote health. He cultivated the society of eminent physicians and surgeons, and listened with attention to their talk of the processes of disease and of fresh means of arresting them. The cause and cure of scourges like consumption, cancer, and leprosy were to his mind most urgent themes of study, and he followed eagerly the important investigations in this direction, which were pursued in hospitals and laboratories abroad as well as at home. When the International Congress of Medicine first met in London in August 1881,[2] under the presidency of the Prince's close acquaintance Sir James Paget, the eminent surgeon, he took part in the proceedings. It was an impressive gathering of scientific experts from all quarters. Charles Darwin, with Professors Tyndall and Huxley, were among the English delegates; Pasteur and Charcot among the French, and Virchow and Koch among the German. The Prince, who was accompanied by his brother-in-law, the Crown Prince of Prussia, then on a visit to England, opened the Congress (August 3) in St. James's Hall with a speech of greeting, in which he anticipated great international benefit from conferences of students of medicine

[1] In the year of the King's death, 1910, the receipts exceeded £205,000, of which £77,000 came from investments, and the sum distributed reached a total of £155,000. The success of the fund is now assured, and in 1921 over £228,000 was distributed, the income from investments amounting to over £107,000. The capital of the fund now exceeds £1,500,000.

[2] Six preceding conferences at triennial intervals had taken place at different cities on the continent. The latest had taken place at Amsterdam in 1878.

and surgery, welcomed the promised "discussion of important
questions relating to public health, to the cure of sick in hospitals
and in the houses of the poor, and to the welfare of the Army
and Navy," and warmly acknowledged the services of men who
sought not only the remedy but the prevention of disease.
After the morning session he and his brother-in-law lunched
privately with Sir James Paget, and he talked familiarly
with Sir James's fellow-guests, Koch, Pasteur, Virchow, and
Darwin.[1]

It was from early continental experimenters—from Koch and
Pasteur—that the Prince learned at first hand of the germ theory
of disease, which revolutionised medical science during his epoch.
He visited the Pasteur Institute in Paris in the summer of 1888
just before its completion, and learnt from M. Pasteur's lips
much about his work. At the outset he was cautious in his
attitude to the new theory, but he became an enthusiastic
believer, under the influence of his medical acquaintances at
home and of his sister, the Crown Princess of Germany, who
sedulously followed German advances in the field and reported
them to her brother. The riddle of well-nigh all diseases—notably
consumption, cancer, and leprosy—was, he grew convinced, in
process of solution, and he energetically set himself to spread the
faith by active support of movements for bacteriological research.
The contemporary growth of the ignorant prejudice against
compulsory vaccination, which showed a fatuous disbelief in
the value of bacteriology, met with his outspoken scorn. He
had little patience with the Parliament which passed a measure
in 1898 legalising the conscientious objections of the anti-
vaccinators.

When he laid the new wing of Brompton Consumption Hospital as early as 1881 he had shrewdly asked, if the disease were
preventable, why was it not prevented. On 21st December 1888
he called a meeting of men of science and others at Marlborough
House to found a National Association for the Prevention of
Consumption, which was designed to forward bacteriological
inquiry. When in 1900 the Second International Tuberculosis
Congress was appointed to be held in London in the following
year, the Prince accepted the office of President, although, owing
to his accession to the throne in January 1901 he resigned

[1] *Memoirs and Letters of Sir James Paget*, ed. Stephen Paget, pp. 308 seq.

the post to the Duke of Cambridge.[1] At the same time he
greatly valued improvements in the therapeutics of consumption, and he persuaded more than one rich acquaintance to
found the sanatoria for consumptives which were required by
new methods of treatment.

A movement for the bacteriological investigation into the
cause, prevention, and cure of leprosy received similar encouragement from the Prince. The death of Father Damien, the Belgian
missionary, who heroically sacrificed his life to the lepers of the
Sandwich Islands, 10th April 1889, excited world-wide sympathy
with the martyr and a resolve in the medical profession to
grapple anew with the disease. In England the recognition of
Father Damien's heroism and the fresh study of leprosy were
actively promoted by the Prince. With vehemence he at once
denounced unchivalrous slanders which were circulated in regard
to Father Damien's morals and evoked next year a triumphant
vindication from the pen of Robert Louis Stevenson. There was
formed in London on 18th June 1889, under the Prince's auspices,
a fund which ultimately provided a statue of the hero at Kalawao,
where he ended his days, and a National Leprosy Fund for the
treatment and study of the disease, especially in India. On the
13th January 1890 the Prince presided at a dinner in London in
support of the National Leprosy Fund. He warmly approved
of the foundation in the same cause of the Prince Albert Victor
Hospital for Leprosy at Calcutta, which was named after his
elder son.

The most comprehensive effort which the Prince made in the
way of promoting bacteriological research in England also
belongs to the year 1890. His sister, the Empress Frederick, in
a letter to him on 30th September 1890, pointed out how little
attention was paid to bacteriology in England compared with
Germany, and she urged the foundation of a bacteriological
institute on the model of one already in existence in Berlin.
The English surgeon and bacteriologist, Sir Joseph Lister, was
already meditating a foundation of like aims. The Prince, on
learning of Sir Joseph's concurrence with his sister's view, lent
him all his influence in bringing the idea to fruition.[2] After
much negotiation the Prince had the satisfaction of seeing the

[1] The First Congress had been held in Berlin, 24th–27th May 1899.
[2] Sir R. J. Godlee, *Life of Lord Lister*, p. 503 (1917).

British Institute of Preventive Medicine established in July 1891.[1]

1897
Ætat. 55 The Prince's medical friends were highly appreciative of his zeal in behalf of their profession and science, and in the year of the Queen's Diamond Jubilee they gave him a unique proof of their regard. On the proposition of one of the Prince's oldest medical associates, Sir Joseph Fayrer, who had accompanied him through India, he was offered and accepted the unusual compliment of an honorary fellowship of the Royal College of Physicians (July 19, 1897). He received from the College not only the diploma, but a model of its prized gold-headed cane—the physician's ancient badge—whose line of successive owners included Dr. John Radcliffe, of London and Oxford, and the chief physicians of the eighteenth century.

[1] Mr. Lister was the first chairman. Some time afterwards the name of the institution was altered to the Jenner Institute, and in 1903 to the Lister Institute.

CHAPTER XXXIV

APPEALS FOR POLITICAL SUPPORT FROM RULERS OF MINOR STATES OF WESTERN EUROPE, 1876–1891

I

THE Great Powers of Europe took frequent observation of the Prince's views. In Germany and Russia statesmen and diplomatists as well as the crowned heads and their families sedulously sought to keep themselves informed of his political inclinations. Lineal ties with the ruling families of both countries account for something of the apparent importance which attached to his opinions. Shrewd heads in the chancelleries of St. Petersburg and Berlin, conscious of the stern limitations which the English constitution and the Prince's relations with Queen Victoria set at home on his political power, were not disposed to overrate his political influence. But even in their sight his word was far from negligible.

The peoples of the great nations of Europe knew him from his foreign travel or from repeated mentions of him in their press as a familiar symbol of England's standing in the world. In Italy, where he could claim no family connections, popular sentiment treated signs of his interest in Italian affairs as a national asset. The Triple Alliance, inaugurated in 1882 by Germany, Austria, and Italy, was never quite congenial to the Italian irredentists, who resented Austria's continued occupation of territory which had once been Italian.[1] In 1891, when a

[1] Italy's object in joining the Triple Alliance was to protect herself against France's Mediterranean ambitions. The periodical renewals of the Alliance lightened Italy's obligations to the other members of the Alliance, and the resentment of Italian nationalism was to some extent appeased in 1887, when the second renewal of the Alliance was followed by a Convention of Italy with England, Austria, and ultimately with Spain, which promised to maintain the *status quo* of Italy and the other powers in the Mediterranean, and to check any further development of French pretensions. But the Austrian connection still grated on nationalist nerves.

1891
Ætat. 49 third renewal of the Triple Alliance was in course of negotiation, the Italian Prime Minister, the Marquis de Rudini, sought to sweeten the pill for the Italian nationalists by inducing some public demonstration of England's goodwill towards Italy. The Marquis looked to the Prince to facilitate his purpose. An interchange of personal courtesies between leading members of the royal families of the two countries appeared to the Italian statesman the best means of reconciling advanced public opinion in Italy to the Austro-German alignment. In May 1891 the Marquis de Rudini let it be known that he desired an early meeting of the King of Italy either with Queen Victoria or with the Prince.[1] The Prince lent a ready ear to the suggestion, but he reckoned the most convenient way of satisfying the Marquis's wish was to bring the King of Italy's heir, the young Prince of Naples (afterwards King Victor Emanuel II.) to England on a State visit. This plan was duly carried out, and the Prince played a foremost part in the hospitalities which were offered the Italian heir-apparent in England for some three weeks in the summer of 1891. The Prince received him in person on his arrival in London on the 22nd July, showed him continuous attentions during his stay, and was present at Osborne on the 3rd August when the young man was invested with the Garter by the Queen. Italian sentiment was gratified. While Italy continued her association with the two Central Powers, popular Italian feeling which regarded England as the veteran friend of national aspirations was fortified in its distant hope of recovering the Trentino and Trieste.

II

Rulers of the smaller States of Europe, especially those who claimed kinship with the Prince, went far beyond the governments of the Great Powers in their conception of his political status. There he was often regarded as an Olympian of unmeasured potentialities. They believed that appeals to him might succeed in modifying English policy in their interests at critical junctures. The King of Greece was never entirely disabused of this misapprehension.[2] In Western Europe similar illusions were through the Prince's middle years cherished by the

---

[1] *Die Grosse Politik*, viii. 53.   [2] See pp. 489 sq. supra.

kinsmen who occupied the thrones of Belgium and of Portugal.
The Prince's native benevolence and his constant wish "to be
of use" did something to foster the prevalent impression.
Occasions arose when in matters outside the range of crucial
controversy he was able to serve his royal kinsmen who ruled
small kingdoms, at any rate by putting their case in a favourable
light before ministerial friends.   At the same time he necessarily
disappointed many expectations.

The King of the Belgians, Leopold II., the Prince's second
cousin and his intimate associate from youth, fell early under
the sway of colonial ambitions which were soon infecting, to the
prejudice of the world's peace, the Great Powers of Europe.
King Leopold sought the Prince's countenance for his initial
advance into the colonial field, and the encouragement which he
eagerly solicited was not withheld.   It was Central Africa, where
international rivalries were about to rage with violence, that the
King of the Belgians made his colonial objective.

As early as 3rd August 1876 the King invited the Prince's help
and suggestion in regard to a conference which he proposed
summoning to Brussels to discuss "the settlement by Europeans
of unexplored Africa and the encouragement of exploration with
a view to spreading civilisation."   The Prince lent a complacent
ear to the proposal.   He consulted Sir Bartle Frere, and suggested
to the King that the three explorers—his friend Sir Samuel
Baker, Colonel Grant ("Speke's companion"), and Lieutenant
Cameron—should, with a few persons "with handles to their
names," be invited to Brussels to represent England at the
conference.   The Prince's advice was adopted and the conference
duly took place on 12th September 1876.   The King volubly
professed to the Prince that his sole motive was philanthropy—
an altruistic profession to which the subsequent course of events
gave an ironic significance.   The Prince, with worldly prevision,
expressed a doubt if much would come of the project of colonising
"unexplored Africa" if philanthropy were to be its only inspiration.   On 14th October 1876 he wrote to Sir Bartle Frere:

The question is whether the public who represent money
will take the same interest that he (*i.e.* King Leopold) does.
Philanthropy is all very well, but unless it is practical and gives
a practical result it will not find that favour in the eyes of the
English public that it deserves.

However, the Prince was quite willing to aid the King on his own lines and, at the King's invitation, he accepted the Presidency of "the English National Committee for Civilising Africa Internationally." The King, in thanking the Prince for accepting the office (October 12, 1876), told him that he was encouraged by the Prince's compliance to solicit the like co-operation from the sovereigns of Germany, Austria, Russia, Portugal, Spain, and Sweden.

King Leopold's original African design made little progress either in England or on the Continent. The English traveller, H. M. Stanley, who was already familiar with Equatorial Africa, formed plans for a thorough exploration of the region of the Congo. Finding no encouragement in this country, Stanley in August 1878 offered his services to King Leopold and induced the King to transform his abortive organisation into the "Association International du Congo." Under King Leopold's auspices Stanley revisited Central Africa, and in negotiations with the natives laid the foundations of the Congo State in the King's behalf. The Prince, who was always interested in explorers and exploration, followed Stanley's efforts apprecia-tively. The King kept the Prince fully informed of the develop-ment of his African schemes, and was not backward in soliciting the Prince's assistance in securing England's formal recognition of his personal right to ownership of the spacious territories which Stanley had placed at his disposal.

The Prince's doubts of the cogency of the King's philan-thropic professions were justified, and he was in no position to give the King much further effective assistance. The King's claims to the Congo territory were at once disputed by France and Portugal, both of which asserted rival titles. In the Upper Congo the French traveller De Brazza competed with Stanley for the native chiefs' allegiance, and to King Leopold's dismay the Frenchman succeeded in securing for France a large slice of the enviable region.

Portugal already held Angola, an expansive territory to the south of the Congo State, and, apprehensive of Belgian encroach-ment, asked England to guarantee her rights by treaty. King Leopold confided his anxieties to the Prince. He implored him to use his influence with Mr. Gladstone's Government to prevent any robbery by Portugal of his new African possessions (March

1883). The King begged the Prince to make sure that any 1884
arrangement which England might make with Portugal should Ætat. 42
leave his Congo State untouched. The Prince, although not
unfavourable to the King's view, saw the likelihood of misunderstandings and took counsel with Lord Granville, the
Foreign Minister.

The English government, while refusing Portugal active
support in Central Africa, offered her in February 1884 a convention which recognised her claim to both banks of the mouth
of the river Congo. France and Germany joined Belgium in
protest against this recognition. The British government
looked, in fact, with small favour on the invasion of Central
Africa by either King Leopold or the French. They were especially suspicious of King Leopold's genuine intentions, while the
boldness of France's colonial aspirations was causing them alarm.
When, late in 1884, the rumour ran that King Leopold was
mysteriously meditating the sale to France of the Congo State,
the English government deemed it necessary to warn him plainly
of their objections to any such step. The Prince was forwarding
regularly to Lord Granville the letters which reached him from
King Leopold, and the Foreign Secretary now deemed it prudent
to employ him as a confidential intermediary. Lord Granville
requested the Prince to inform his royal correspondent that
England had interests of her own to protect in Central Africa.
Accordingly, the Prince warned King Leopold that the sale to
France of the Congo State "would be viewed with great dissatisfaction by Her Majesty's Government." The King replied
that it was quite contrary to his wish to hand the Congo over to
the French. He had merely negotiated with France the right of
pre-emption, but he had no present intention of sale.[1]

In November a Conference of the Powers was summoned to
Berlin to consider the relations of Europe to the Congo and to
secure commercial equality for all European nations and conditions of good government within the region. The deliberations
ended in a triumph for the Belgian King. The Belgian Congo
State was formally recognised by the Powers, and King Leopold
assumed the title of "independent sovereign." The Prince
welcomed the arrangement, to which England's jealousy of
French colonial expansion made her a party. He sent warm

[1] The Prince to Granville, 14th December 1884.

congratulations to the King, who assigned to the Prince some credit for his victory. By way of foiling the menacing advance of France into Equatorial Africa, the English government gave much subsequent support to the King in his rôle of sovereign of the Congo, and the policy met with the Prince's approval. But the King's later associations with the Congo alienated the Prince's sympathy. Before the century ended the Prince suffered disillusionment regarding the moral character of King Leopold in many regards—notably in his capacity of promoter of colonial enterprise. Charges were brought against the King of sanctioning brutal persecution of the Congo natives in his own mercantile interests. The King cynically defended his agents. In the event the Prince's friendly relations with his cousin, whose colonial fortunes stood indebted to his initial encouragement, changed to distrust and dislike.

III

A curious instance of the faith in the Prince's political influence which was cherished in the remoter haunts of Central Europe was furnished by an invitation which he received in the summer of 1884 to solve personally a minor dynastic problem. While staying with the Princess and her parents in June at Wiesbaden, the Prince was the guest for a day (June 10) at the neighbouring palace of Königstein, of Adolph, Duke of Nassau, a kinsman of King William III. of Holland. The Prince knew little of the Duke, although his sister Sophia, wife of King Oscar II. of Sweden and Norway, had entertained him more than once at Stockholm; but he sympathised with the Duke's sufferings at the hands of Prussia, which had deprived him of his principality for siding with Austria in the war of 1866. Duke Adolph's dominant interest in life lay in a presumptive claim which he was preferring to the Grand Duchy of Luxemburg. The dynastic law of the Grand Duchy, an appanage of the Crown of Holland, disallowed female sovereignty. King William's only son, William, Prince of Orange, was nearing the end of a dissipated life at Paris, and the Dutch King's only remaining child was a daughter, Wilhelmina. Duke Adolph, as the head of the elder branch of the family of Nassau to which the Dutch King belonged, held that he was rightful heir to the Grand Duchy on the death of the Dutch heir-apparent, the Prince of Orange.

The Prince of Wales had barely parted with Duke Adolph at Königstein when the Prince of Orange died (June 21, 1884). Thereupon Duke Adolph forwarded to the Prince a full statement of his case and earnestly requested his correspondent to bring the British government to the support of his pretensions. The Prince took counsel with Lord Granville, the Foreign Secretary (August 16). Lord Granville replied that the Powers of Europe would have to be consulted before any decision could be reached, and that the present moment was inopportune for raising the topic. The Prince, who resented the evasive answer, retorted that his "very sensitive" correspondent ought not to be kept waiting for a reply. He asked Lord Granville's advice as to the view that he should adopt in writing to Duke Adolph. Lord Granville warned the Prince against committing himself. The Prince took the hint but contrived discreetly to encourage Duke Adolph's hopes. Duke Adolph's aspirations were before long realised, and he was persuaded that his appeal to the Prince had had its effect. On 29th October 1890, when King William of Holland, with no male heir, was pronounced insane and incapable of rule, Duke Adolph became Regent of the Grand Duchy of Luxemburg, and on the King's death a few weeks later (November 23, 1890) he was installed as Grand Duke, with the approval of Great Britain and other Powers. He was confirmed in the impression that he owed much to the goodwill of the Prince when the Prince welcomed him to England on the occasion of Queen Victoria's Diamond Jubilee in the summer of 1897.[1]

[1] A paradoxical situation in the dynastic history of Luxemburg ensued when the Prince of Wales had become King Edward. Grand Duke Adolph lived to the great age of eighty-eight, dying on 17th November 1905. He was succeeded by his only son, William—a mature married man with a family consisting only of daughters to the number of six. The new ruler's children were, by the constitution of the Grand Duchy, barred from the succession. King Edward watched with ironic detachment the Grand Duke William's dynastic dilemma. Soon, in 1907, the Grand Duke cut the knot by cancelling the old Grand Ducal law which prohibited female succession. After his death in 1912 two of his daughters were in turn sovereigns of the Grand Duchy—in rather shameless defiance of a law which the Prince of Wales's influence, at Duke Adolph's prompting in 1884, had helped to keep operative in Duke Adolph's interest.

IV

A supplication in 1890 from another royal kinsman to intervene on his behalf with the British government caused the
Prince much embarrassment. Central Africa was once again
a main cause of trouble. The Prince was gravely perplexed
by the warm competition for African territory which was waging
between his own countrymen and the people of Portugal whose
king pleaded for his countenance.

Dom Carlos, King of Portugal, a kinsman of Queen Victoria,
succeeded on the 19th October 1889 to the throne of his father,
Dom Luis, whose guest at Lisbon the Prince was on his return
from India in April 1876. Both the new King and Queen of
Portugal were on terms of intimacy with the Prince and his
family. The Prince had known from childhood not the new
King only, but also his consort, Princess Amélie, the Comte
de Paris's daughter, whom Dom Carlos married at Lisbon on
22nd May 1886.

The new King's political acumen was scarcely equal to his
social accomplishments, and he found his country at his accession
in a mood which severely tried his political temper and capacities.
A republican party was growing formidable. The government
was financially embarrassed and there were signs of disloyalty
in the army. Portugal's national feeling, which prided itself on
its African colonies of veteran standing, was at the same time
deeply affronted by Lord Salisbury's grant of a Charter to the
British South Africa Company, of which Cecil Rhodes was
chairman and the Prince's son-in-law, the Duke of Fife, was a
director. Broad stretches of territory, long in Portuguese
occupation—Angola on the west and Mozambique on the east—
bounded the Chartered Company's spacious estate (afterwards
known as the province of Rhodesia). The absence of well-
defined boundaries rendered dispute inevitable between Portuguese explorers or settlers and the Chartered Company's agents.

No sooner had Dom Carlos become King than Lord Salisbury
pressed the Portuguese government for a settlement of the
quarrel, and the two governments signed an agreement as to
the boundaries of their properties on the 20th August 1890. But
the agreement was summarily repudiated by the Cortes, and a
storm threatened the relations of the two countries. The King,

at his wits' end, turned to the Prince of Wales. With a view to
soothing his subjects' wounded feelings, he sought the Prince's
good offices in moderating England's action. At the Portuguese
Legation in London the King had a representative who was well
qualified to promote efficiently such an appeal. Senhor Luis de
Soveral had already been for some six years Secretary of the
Portuguese Legation at the Court of St. James, and his vivacious personality had won the Prince's regard. M. de Soveral
was directed by Dom Carlos to deliver to the Prince an autograph supplication for assistance. A second missive of like tenor
addressed to Queen Victoria was enclosed, with a request that
the Prince should forward it to her. Both letters plaintively
begged the British sovereign and her heir to let Portugal off
lightly. On 1st November Soveral arrived on his errand at
Wynyard Park, the residence of Lord Londonderry, where the
Prince was staying. The Prince gave the emissary a kindly
welcome and showed every sympathy with the Portuguese King's
embarrassments. While sending on to his mother Dom Carlos's
appeal to her he explained, in a covering letter, dated 2nd
November, his view of the situation :

1890
Ætat. 48

I know Carlos is most anxious for some reasonable solution
of the present difficulties. His position is a most difficult one,
as he fears a Republic may be established in Portugal, and
probably Spain would follow suit, which would be a great disaster.
Count Kalnoky spoke most seriously to me on the subject at
Vienna last month. I fear the Powers will put pressure to bear
upon us, which would be regrettable and disagreeable, and it
would, I am sure, be far more satisfactory if your Government
and Portugal could settle the matter without the interference of
the Powers. But I assure you the situation is very grave, and
far more so than you have any idea of.

The Queen took the Prince's view and urged Lord Salisbury
to accept terms which might prove agreeable to the Portuguese.
She feared, she wrote, "the overthrow of the Portuguese government." The Prince, with his mother's approval, wrote to the
Prime Minister in the same sense. Lord Salisbury was complaisant and suggested a six months' *modus vivendi* which, by
accepting the *status quo ante*, might calm the susceptibilities of
the Portuguese. An agreement on these lines was signed on 14th
November. Two days later both the Queen and the Prince
wrote to Dom Carlos explaining that the British government was

bound to protect the rights of its subjects in the disputed African area, but they personally anticipated a final friendly settlement.

Yet the smooth words of the Queen and her son did not enable King Carlos to allay the irritation of his subjects. On 12th December M. de Soveral wrote excitedly to the Prince that the situation was worse than ever. The British South Africa Company, at the instigation of Cecil Rhodes, was bent on further encroachments on Portuguese colonies. The Company was claiming the Portuguese district of Manica, in Mashonaland, on the borders of Mozambique.

Early in 1891 the government of Lisbon in a state of desperation despatched a military expedition to hold Manica against all comers. The British government sought to avoid a breach of the peace. It warned the Chartered Company to qualify its pretensions. But the Company's tone was defiant, and hostilities with the Portuguese followed. In spite of his sympathy with the harassed King, the Prince was well disposed to the Chartered Company, and he deplored the pertinacity of the Portuguese. The Queen's patience was strained by the obduracy of both sides, but she inclined like her son to the Chartered Company. Although a new convention attempted to define with impartiality the disputed boundaries and was ratified by both sides on 11th June, the local unrest continued and Portuguese relations with England, to the Prince's profound regret, remained stormy. At length in March 1894 the dispute was referred to the arbitration of the King of Italy, and the delimitation was settled after much delay on 30th January 1897.

Meanwhile the Prince's perturbation was increased by the King of Portugal's growing troubles at home. Early in 1892, in order to alleviate the financial embarrassments of his government, he surrendered a fifth part of his revenues. But popular discontent was scarcely appeased, and next year an attempt was made on his life in the streets of Lisbon. Amid such perils the King showed greater anxiety than before to retain the personal goodwill of Queen Victoria and the Prince. In his efforts to that end he was zealously seconded by Senhor de Soveral, now Portuguese Minister in London.

In October 1895 the King wrote to the Prince offering to pay England a first visit since his accession. M. de Soveral took advantage of his growing intimacy with the Prince to

point out that a cordial reception of his master in England 1895
would greatly improve the King's position in his own country. Ætat. 53
His appeal for the Prince's good offices was not made in vain.
The Prince was in full sympathy with his kinsman, and the
knowledge that Dom Carlos was proposing to call at Berlin on
his way to England spurred the Prince to persuade his mother
to lend adequate dignity to the Portuguese King's welcome.
The Prince pressed for the bestowal of the Garter on the royal
guest. The Queen was somewhat apathetic, and the Prince
found in his path difficulties of which he had had earlier
experience. There was a general feeling in English political
circles that Portugal's colonial policy in Africa was vexatious and
troublesome. Dom Carlos, moreover, pointed out to the Prince
that owing to a binding engagement to be back in Lisbon on
17th November for the opening of the Cortes, his visit to England
could only take place in the early part of November—a period
of the year which the Prince usually spent at Sandringham and
the Queen invariably at Balmoral. The Prince therefore requested
the Queen to return a few days earlier than was her wont to
Windsor in order to receive the King there and confer the Garter
upon him. But the Queen, after considering the suggestion
benevolently, decided against it, to M. de Soveral's confusion.
The King's presence in Scotland would be necessary if he were
to receive the decoration at the Queen's hand. The Prince was
compelled to adapt the programme to the Queen's decision.

All things considered, the King's visit passed off satisfactorily.
He spent his first two days (November 6 to 8) at Sandringham,
where Lord Rosebery and Lord Lansdowne were fellow-guests.
Thence he took the long journey to Balmoral, where the Queen
invested him with the Garter. During his subsequent three
days' stay (from the 11th to 14th), at Buckingham Palace where
the Queen allotted him rooms, he was formally entertained at
the Mansion House and was visited by the Prince as well as by
Lord Salisbury, the Prime Minister. The Prince had brought
tact to bear on a delicate situation. The King's reception in
England added to his prestige on his return to Lisbon, and there
was an improvement in the relations of the two countries.

King Carlos's faith in the Prince's political helpfulness was
increased rather than diminished by the somewhat tortuous
course of events of 1890–95. Portugal's representative in London,

M. de Soveral, who became a very prominent figure in the Prince's social circle, kept him well informed of Portuguese affairs and confirmed his interest in them ; but the Prince's capacity to aid foreign monarchs in distress was circumscribed. It was beyond his power to solve the internal difficulties of the kingdom of Portugal, which continued to bring external complications in their train. The special favour which the Prince showed King Carlos by making his court the first in Europe to receive a visit from him after his accession, failed to stem the tide of fate which decreed Dom Carlos's assassination in 1908 and the inauguration of a republic at Lisbon in place of the monarchy on 5th October 1910, five months after King Edward passed away.

CHAPTER XXXV

THE ACCESSION OF KAISER WILLIAM II. WITH ITS
CONSEQUENCES—POLITICAL AND DOMESTIC, 1888–1895

I

IN the year 1888 the Prince's relations with Germany were to enter a troubled phase which lasted for the rest of his life. From his youth the Prince had viewed German policy, both domestic and foreign, with misgivings. He had deplored many times Prince Bismarck's resolute hostility to constitutional principles of government at home and his cynical policy of aggressiveness abroad. His sister, the Crown Princess, had, in correspondence and in conversation, kept well alive his suspicions on such scores. But family ties counselled the avoidance of a definite breach between England and Germany, and the Prince cherished the hope that the accession to the German throne of his brother-in-law, the Crown Prince, whose liberal tendencies reflected his wife's sentiment, would bring about a comprehensive purification of German policy. The swelling ambitions of France and the internal signs of political instability and fickleness which developed in her after the death of his friend, M. Gambetta, in 1881 for a time damped, though they far from quenched, the Prince's French ardours, and he therefore came shrewdly to entertain the notion of an improved understanding with Germany, which might beneficially take effect when the Crown Prince became Emperor Frederick III.

The illness of the Crown Prince—the throat ailment which caused disquiet in the English royal family when the Crown Prince came to England to take part in the Jubilee festivities of 1887—now overcast the Prince's outlook on the future. The prospect of the Crown Prince's early death was rendered, for the

Prince, especially dark by the knowledge that the Crown Prince's elder son, Prince William of Prussia, next heir to German sovereignty, was forming perilously exalted conceptions of his destiny and was treating his parents and his uncle with insolent contempt. In the Prince's forecast, the young man's temperament promised, when he entered on his inheritance, not only family disturbances, but a reckless encouragement of Germany's militarism and autocracy on lines which went beyond Prince Bismarck's range.

The ill-conditioned slanders of his parents and uncle which Prince William had lately lavished on the Tsar were by no means the only evil presages of his future conduct. The old Kaiser and Prince Bismarck encouraged in the young man that scorn for his father's pacifism and Anglophilism with which his Junker comrades first infected him. The inevitable breach with his father was widened by the willing ear which the old Emperor lent to his grandson's impatient appeals to take a premature part in affairs of State. Prince Bismarck, although he soon viewed Prince William's growing self-sufficiency with misgivings, sanctioned in the autumn of 1886, at the old Emperor's request, his access to confidential Foreign Office despatches by way of gaining experience. The father vehemently protested against the step. In a letter to Prince Bismarck he pointed out his son's lack of judgement or sound knowledge, his unripeness in experience, "together with his leaning towards vanity and presumption and his overweening estimate of himself." Such defects might, his father declared, easily render him a public danger in any position of responsibility.[1]

II

The Crown Prince of Germany at the close of the Jubilee festivities spent three months in England—at first at Norwood, near London, and then in the Isle of Wight—and Scotland. He was seeking medical treatment which might arrest the progress of the disease. The Prince and his family saw much of him during that period, and their anxieties were not removed. The following autumn and winter were passed by the doomed man in Italy, chiefly in a villa at San Remo. In the spring of 1888 the Prince of Wales spent his customary vacation at Cannes,

[1] Crown Prince Frederick to Bismarck, 26th September 1886. *New Chapters of Bismarck's Autobiography*, English translation, 1920, pp. 4-6.

(February 10–March 3), going over to San Remo to visit his stricken brother-in-law.

Scarcely had the Prince returned to London from France than the first stage in the ominous series of coming events in Germany was reached. The Crown Prince's father, Kaiser William I., breathed his last in his ninetieth year at Berlin on 7th March. The celebration of the Prince's silver wedding was cut short to allow him to attend the dead sovereign's obsequies. He and his elder son reached Berlin on 14th March, putting up at the British Embassy with Sir Edward Malet. Next day the Chancellor, Bismarck, paid the Prince a visit of ceremony, and the popular demonstration in the street in the Chancellor's honour while the short interview was in progress brought home to the Prince the conviction that the German people relied on Prince Bismarck's masterful guidance, in the difficult days that were at hand.[1]

In the mournful surroundings the Prince abstained from political discussion, and his sympathetic bearing was appreciated by the German public. Crown Prince Frederick, now Kaiser Frederick III., at once, on receipt of the news of his father's death, left San Remo for Charlottenburg, near Berlin, but ill health confined him to his room there, and he could not join his heir and the Prince of Wales in the funeral procession from Berlin cathedral to the royal mausoleum at Charlottenburg. He was, however, able to receive his brother-in-law, and although his voice was gone and he could only communicate his thoughts in writing, he gave his visitor an illusive impression of improved general health. On his arrival in London on 20th March the Prince at once went to Windsor to report on the situation to the Queen.

A month later, in May, the Prince was in Berlin on a second domestic errand, giving Germany further outward proof of his kindly feeling. A daughter of his late sister Alice, Princess Irene of Hesse, was to marry her first cousin, Henry, the second son of the new Emperor and Empress, and Crown Prince William's only brother. The marriage took place at Charlottenburg in gloom (May 24). By a heroic exercise of will the Emperor Frederick, with the marks of death upon him, attended the ceremony. The Prince conciliated German sentiment by donning

[1] Rennell-Rodd, *Diplomatic Reminiscences*, i. 130–31.

his red-coated uniform of the Blücher (5th Pomeranian) Hussars, of which he had been made Colonel-in-Chief some five years before.[1] After the wedding he met in friendly mood at the British Embassy Count Herbert Bismarck, and he accentuated his desire for harmony by travelling to Stolp, in Pomerania, in order to inspect his Prussian regiment. But in spite of the Prince's outward complacence he was perturbed not alone by the Emperor's precarious state, but by the attitude of his nephew and Prince Bismarck to his sister. She bitterly resented their efforts to anticipate the inevitable end of her husband's sufferings by urging his immediate withdrawal from State affairs in favour of his heir, and they intensified her griefs by citing the Prince of Wales as supporting their design.[2] Prince Bismarck was pressing on the dying man confirmation of a policy of which he disapproved, while the Crown Prince's unfilial arrogance led his mother to exclude him from his father's presence.

At Prince Henry's marriage the Prince saw his brother-in-law for the last time. Shortly afterwards the dying Kaiser was removed to his favourite palace at Potsdam, and there he died on 13th June. His reign had lasted a hundred days. On 14th June the news of his brother-in-law's death reached the Prince on Ascot race-course. The Prince, when acknowledging the condolence of friends, paid liberal tribute to the noble character of the late Emperor, and described his death as a disaster, not only for his family and the country, but for the world.

With the Princess and his elder son he hurried to Berlin on the day following the receipt of the sad news, thus visiting Germany for a third time within three months. Rooms were allotted the party at the royal palace at Charlottenburg. The Prince on arrival hastened to the palace of Potsdam, where he sought to console his widowed sister. During the full week which he stayed at Charlottenburg he spent some hours with her each day. The funeral took place at Potsdam on the 18th, the Prince again wearing his Prussian uniform.

[1] See p. 477 *supra*.   [2] Waldersee, *A Field-Marshal's Memoirs*, p. 139.

III

The position of affairs which confronted the Prince at the German Court on the occasion of his brother-in-law's funeral proved far more disconcerting than his forebodings suggested. His nephew, with the approval, if not at the instigation of, Prince Bismarck and of his son, Count Herbert, was heaping on his bereaved mother brutal humiliations. A cordon of soldiers surrounded the Potsdam Palace, and the Prince found his sister virtually a prisoner. He learnt with dismay how the name of Friedrichskron, which his brother-in-law had bestowed on his latest residence, was by the new Emperor's order summarily replaced by its old title of Neues Palais. Such intercourse as was vouchsafed him by the new Kaiser gave him no comfort. All his tendencies to self-assertion were accentuated by his entry on his great office. He claimed a divine right to his throne which justified truculence in his attitude to men. He could scarcely bring himself to express sorrow for his loss, and gave his uncle the impression that he held his father's memory in small esteem. The Bismarcks, father and son, at the same time shocked the Prince by heaping disparagements in his hearing on the dead man's name. Count Herbert excelled his father in offensiveness and spoke of the Emperor Frederick as an "incubus" and "ineffectual visionary."[1] When Count Herbert bluntly added in his conversation with the Prince that "an Emperor who could not talk was unfit to reign," the Prince of Wales's patience gave way, as he confessed to Prince von Hohenlohe (afterwards the German Chancellor).[2]

In spite of all the portents the Prince somewhat blindly clung to his cherished hope that some of his late brother-in-law's and his sister's liberal ideals of German policy might yet be realised. He was loth to abandon a delusive expectation that the intentions imputed to his late brother-in-law of redressing past wrongs, which in the Prince's mind blackened the fame of Prussia, would meet with the new Emperor's respectful consideration. He knew the theme to be delicate, but his regard for his brother-in-law's memory led him in somewhat strained talk with Count Herbert to trench on the treacherous ground. His remarks, wantonly exaggerated, reached the Kaiser's ear, with the result that a storm was raised

[1] *Die Grosse Politik*, vi. 326.   [2] *Memoirs of Prince von Hohenlohe*, ii. 391.

in their mutual relations which it proved difficult to allay. The
opening days of the reign, in fact, brought to a head between uncle
and nephew an antagonism which had already threatened and,
though it was speciously assuaged hereafter by periodic exchanges
of professions of family affection and of desire for political co-
operation, continued until King Edward died. Some public
danger attached to the private feud in view of the vociferous
development of chauvinist sentiment during the new Kaiser's
reign in sections of both the English and the German peoples.
The Prince was conscious of the risk of aggravating international
friction by pursuit of domestic broils, and he often, in the interest
of international goodwill, overlooked, at some expense to his
pride, his nephew's defiant acts and demeanour.

It is on the Kaiser's shoulders that history must lay the
responsibility for the untoward personal relations between him and
the Prince. The insolence of the Kaiser's young manhood grew in
his middle years into a rarely paralleled egotism which made short
work of family affection. Only in the case of his grandmother,
Queen Victoria, among his English kinsfolk, did he show in his
maturity a domestic sentiment which could be credited with
sincerity. He would recall the simple pleasures of his childish
visits to her at Osborne House or Balmoral, but even of Queen
Victoria he could on occasion speak and write abusively. In all
relations of life, whether public or private, he sought recognition
of his personal primacy. With grotesque blasphemy he cited
God as approving his pretension. Any of his kinsfolk or subjects
who questioned it received from him short shrift. Prince
Bismarck himself was among his early victims, and he would
willingly have made, if he could, his uncle another. The Prince
of Wales stirred in excessive degree his passion of jealousy. On
his theatrical tours to foreign courts and peoples, on which his
vanity laid immense stress, the Kaiser soon found that his less
assertive uncle, in whose footsteps he followed, usually received a
warmer welcome than himself. He saw in the Prince of Wales,
both while heir-apparent and while King, the most formidable
rival to the place of predominance which his magnified self-
consciousness led him to claim in the world.

In the Kaiser's philosophy of life, force tempered by cunning
was the decisive controller of human affairs. The militarism of
the German army, and the aggressiveness of Pan-Germanism and

Welt-politik satisfied his political and moral ideals. If presentiments of the danger of imitating Louis XIV. or Napoleon I. in their wild schemes of territorial aggrandisement awakened in him at critical moments, he gloried in the attention which he drew to himself from friend and foe by his habit of invoking "the mailed fist." Counsellors more cautious than himself, who had difficulty in restraining his rash utterances, long prevented him from taking the fatal plunge into war. They managed to postpone the shattering European conflict which, under the influence of his braggart faith in the brute strength of his adult army and of his infant navy, he many times, to his uncle's perturbation, threatened to provoke. The devastating world war, of which he was the prime mover, broke out after his uncle's death.

The Kaiser's diplomacy, in which threats mingled with blandishments, was as ill-conditioned a weapon as his gesticulation in shining armour. Alike in political diplomacy and in personal controversy he resorted to subterfuge and tergiversation, of which he had given signs in boyhood. His habit of imputing the blankest stupidity or all degrees of Machiavellianism to his uncle as to every one else with whom he differed reflects his tortuous idiosyncrasy and the variability of his moods. He constantly oscillated between the two paths of co-operation with England and of defiance of her. He would one day profess in sugared accents the conviction that an alliance between the two nations was the only guarantee of the world's peace, and would next day viciously impute every infamy to England and Englishmen, and avow devotion to their enemies. His uncle and English statesmen on whom he at times lavished his schemingly pacific assurances were shrewd enough to distrust them.

The Kaiser's interests, though focussed throughout his reign on the development of his fighting forces and on the exaltation of his country's prestige, ranged superficially and feverishly over a far wider field. He looked at all phases of life through the distorting medium of his colossal self-confidence. Omniscience grew to be his foible.[1] Art, music, science, religion, technology

---

[1] A judgement passed by an acute French observer on his claims to supreme authority in artistic matters may be found in De Goncourt's *Journal* (ed. Julius West, pp. 366–7): "March 23, 1890—This young German Emperor, this neurotic mystic, this enthusiast for the religious and warlike operas of Wagner, this man who, in his dreams, wears the white armour of Parsifal, with his sleepless nights, his sickly activity, his feverish brain, seems to be a monarch who will be very troublesome in the future.

1888
Ætat. 46

1888   were worlds which he thought to rule.   There were at his command
Ætat. 46   some social gifts, to which his expansive superficiality lent a
flickering glamour.   The high spirits which congenial company
excited in him could break into frolic and into practical joking
which was liable to degenerate into bullying.   The impression left
on strangers whom he met in society was at times delusively
favourable.   Mr. John (afterwards Viscount) Morley, who lunched
with him and a distinguished party at Londonderry House in
London on 9th July 1891, wrote of him thus:

He is rather short; pale, but sunburnt; carries himself
well; walks into the room with the stiff stride of the Prussian
soldier; speaks with a good deal of intense and energetic gesture,
not like a Frenchman, but staccato; his voice strong but pleasant;
his eye bright, clear and full; mouth resolute; the cast of face
grave or almost stern in repose, but as he sat between two pretty
women he lighted up with gaiety, and a genial laugh.   Energy,
rapidity, restlessness in every movement from his short, quick
inclinations of the head to the planting of the foot.

But Lord Morley closes his too generous catalogue of outwardly
attractive traits on a comprehensive note of warning.   "I
should," the observer concludes, "be disposed strongly to doubt
whether it is all sound, steady, and the result of a—what Herbert
Spencer could call—rightly co-ordinated organisation." [1]

IV

The first of the long series of quarrels between the Kaiser
and his uncle sprang out of the inquiries of delicate import
which the Prince made of Count Herbert Bismarck at the time
of the Emperor Frederick's funeral.   The episode illustrates the
Prince's faith in his brother-in-law's sense of justice and the
endurance of his own sympathy with Denmark and France
in regard to the injuries which Prussia had inflicted on those
countries in the wars respectively of 1864–66 and 1870–71, and
also his persistent resentment at the vengeance which Prussia

[1] Viscount Morley's *Recollections*, i. 272-3. The estimate, in these pages, of
the character and conduct of Kaiser William II., which is the fruit of independent
study of published and unpublished evidence, tallies with that recently published in
the diaries or memoirs of men in closest personal intercourse with him at the Imperial Court;   see the Reminiscences of Baron von Eckardstein (1920), of Field-
Marshal von Waldersee (1922), of Count Philipp zu Eulenburg, Court Chamberlain
(1923), of Count Robert von Zedlitz-Trüschler, Court Marshal (1924), and of Admiral von Tirpitz (*Political Documents*, ed. Professor Kerns, 1924).

wreaked on his kinsfolk of Hanover in the war of 1866. The
Prince had reason for crediting the late Kaiser with a design of
reversing German policy in all three directions. He believed,
rightly or wrongly, that the Emperor Frederick contemplated the
restoration of Alsace-Lorraine to France and of Schleswig to
Denmark, as well as the surrender to the Duke of Cumberland,
who had married the Princess of Wales's youngest sister, of the
private property of the expelled royal family of Hanover, which
Prussia had sequestrated. Prince Bismarck's responsibility for
these three acts of spoliation hardly made it discreet on the
Prince's part to seek from the Chancellor's son information as to
the Emperor Frederick's rumoured designs of reparation. But
he yielded to his generous impulse.

Count Herbert promptly reported to the Kaiser and to his
father the Prince's conversation, recklessly misinterpreting the
tone and range of the Prince's questionnaire. The Prince was
falsely represented as having personally suggested that the new
Kaiser ought to commemorate his accession by putting into
effect the alleged pacific intentions of his father. Count Herbert's
statement exasperated the Prince's nephew. Especially did the
Prince's reference to France's lost provinces rankle in the Kaiser's
mind. Count Herbert contrived to complicate the situation
by communicating his version of the Prince's Alsace-Lorraine
proposal to Tsar Alexander III., when the Kaiser was the
Tsar's guest at St. Petersburg in July.

The Prince gave his own version a little later of what took
place. He stigmatised Count Herbert's story as "a positive
lie." As for the matter of Alsace-Lorraine, he declared that he
did no more than ask Count Herbert "whether Fritz would have
wished to give back the provinces of Alsace and Lorraine if
possible"; that Count Herbert replied, "there was no foundation for such a rumour," and that "there the matter ended."
Of Schleswig and the royal family of Hanover he had spoken
quite vaguely (Prince of Wales to Prince Christian, 3rd April
1889).

Neither Prince Bismarck nor the Kaiser was disposed to let
the matter sleep. Prince Bismarck promptly set on foot a bitter
campaign against the Prince in the *Deutsche Zeitung* and in
other newspapers which he influenced, as well as in Austrian
newspapers through their Berlin correspondents. The Prince

was charged with offending German pride. The Kaiser might as justifiably, it was argued, criticise English internal affairs—notably her troubles in Ireland.[1]

The Kaiser chose his own time for crossing swords with his uncle. He parted with him after his father's funeral with a specious amiability. He acceded to the Prince's request that he should receive at the coming German manœuvres three English officers who were the Prince's personal friends—Colonel Oliver Montagu, A. Prinsep, and Count Gleichen. He showed irritation only when the Prince inquired as to the arrangements which he was making for his mother's future. He subsequently complained to Queen Victoria (July 6) that the Prince was misrepresenting his intentions, which he assured his grandmother were quite considerate. The widowed Empress Frederick had yet much to suffer at her son's hands, and the Prince's solicitude was well justified. But there was at this moment no open breach between the Prince and his nephew on this score.[2]

The Kaiser's reprimands of his uncle for the grave offence which he imputed to him on Count Herbert's testimony, were promulgated with no undue delay. His first protest against the Prince's reported allegations of the Emperor Frederick's pacific attitude to France, Denmark, and Hanover was launched in mid-August. When he unveiled at Frankfort-on-the-Oder on 16th August 1888 the monument to his cousin, Prince Friedrich Karl, a prominent Prussian commander in the war of 1870, he closed a boastful speech with this thinly veiled rebuke of his uncle: "There are people who have the audacity to maintain that my father was willing to part with what he, in conjunction with the late Prince, gained on the battlefield. We, who knew him so well, cannot quietly tolerate, even for a single moment, such an insult to his memory. He assuredly cherished the same idea as we do, namely, that nothing should be surrendered of what had been gained in those great days. . . . On this point there can be only one opinion, namely, that we would rather sacrifice our eighteen army corps and our forty-two millions of

[1] *Die Grosse Politik*, vi. 326–33.

[2] Sir Rennel Rodd, who was on intimate terms with the Empress Frederick, accepted her invitation to prepare a memoir of her late husband, and the Prince of Wales urged Rodd to comply. The new Kaiser looked on such a project with disfavour, and when the book was published later in 1888 treated the writer with scant courtesy (*Memoirs, 1884–93*, pp. 143–89).

inhabitants on the field of battle than surrender a single stone of
what my father and Prince Frederick Charles gained." [1]

The Prince was soon to discover that his nephew's speech
at Frankfort-on-the-Oder was merely the prelude to a more
wounding admonition.

Immediately after he had ascended his throne, the Kaiser
invited himself to the courts of St. Petersburg and Vienna.
Queen Victoria wrote deprecatingly to her grandson of his foreign
project on the ground that he was in mourning. The Kaiser
replied that his grandmother must no longer treat him as a boy,
and that he was travelling in the interests of peace and of his
country. "We Emperors," he told Queen Victoria, "must
stand together." [2]   He contemplated pursuing the flirtation with
Russia to which he inclined before his father's death, thereby
thinking to give England cause for anxiety. His tour gave him
the opportunity of putting on the Prince of Wales a deliberate
affront, by way of avenging his uncle's alleged offences.

The Prince had accepted an invitation from the Austrian
Emperor to join him in mid-September at the military manœuvres
and afterwards to shoot with him and Crown Prince Rudolph
his son in Hungary. The Prince was on the previous 5th
March appointed, to his gratification, by Emperor Francis Joseph,
Honorary Colonel of the Austro-Hungarian 12th (Palatinate)
Hussars, and he was anxious to thank the Austrian Emperor
in person for the honour. On hearing that the Kaiser was to
be entertained at Vienna at much the same time, the Prince,
miscalculating his nephew's mood, wrote to him on 15th August
from Homburg, expressing his pleasure at the prospect of their
meeting under the Austrian Emperor's roof. He innocently

---

[1] *The German Emperor's Speeches*, translated by Louis Elkind, p. 17. In a
more benevolent mood the Kaiser, however, yielded the domestic point about
Hanover which the Prince, in June 1888, had raised in Berlin, together with
more crucial themes. In exchange for a written assurance from the Duke of
Cumberland that he would engage in no undertaking against the peace of the
German Empire, and would withdraw his protest against the annexation of his
father's kingdom, the Kaiser, by rescript, restored to the Duke the disputed
Welf Fond on 12th March 1892 (*Die Grosse Politik*, vi. 331, and footnote). A
complete reconciliation between the Kaiser and the Duke of Cumberland
followed on 24th May 1913, when the Kaiser's only daughter, Victoria Louise,
married Ernest Augustus, Duke of Brunswick and Lüneburg, the Duke of
Cumberland's only son.

[2] Cf. Ex-Kaiser William's *Memoirs*, pp. 25–6; Kaiser to Queen Victoria,
6th July 1888.

inquired the date of his nephew's arrival. The Kaiser sent no reply.

After a short call on the Duke of Cumberland at Gmünden, on leaving Homburg, the Prince on 10th September reached Vienna, where he donned for the first time the resplendent uniform of his new Austro-Hungarian regiment of Hussars—gold-frogged tunic, red breeches, Hessian boots and shako. From his host's lips he at once learnt to his mortification that his nephew had stipulated that no royal guest save himself should be present at the Viennese Court during his forthcoming stay. No doubt as to the Kaiser's meaning was permissible. Sir Augustus Paget, the British Ambassador at Vienna, informed the Prince on the authority of his German colleague, Prince Reuss, that the Kaiser refused to meet his uncle. Corroboration of the Kaiser's intentional insult reached the Prince from both the Crown Prince Rudolph, who had no love for the Kaiser, and from Count Kalnoky, the Austrian Foreign Minister. The Prince took the rebuff to heart and vainly sought some way out. By his direction his equerry, General Ellis, wrote to Colonel Swaine, the British Military Attaché at Berlin, a letter for his nephew's eye, stating that the Prince proposed to welcome the Kaiser at the Vienna railway station in Prussian uniform. Colonel Swaine, who at the time was with the Kaiser at the German manœuvres, had hitherto been on the friendliest terms with him, but after he left at the Kaiser's quarters General Ellis's letter, together with a covering one of his own, he received from the Kaiser the cut direct. To add to the Prince's embarrassment, baseless rumours spread in the press of both Berlin and Vienna that he was bent on a foolish busybodying intervention in the coming conference between the German and Austrian Emperors. He was credited with the wild hope of alienating them both from Russia, and of initiating some kind of agreement between them and his favourite country, France.

Emperor Francis Joseph, although he feared the displeasure of his young imperial and imperious colleague, showed the Prince on his arrival hospitable attentions at Vienna and at the military manœuvres in Croatia. Count Kalnoky, the veteran Minister of Foreign Affairs, entertained him and spoke to him of the need of an assertion of Austria's influence in the Balkans against the designs of Russia. At Miskolcz in Hungary the Prince inspected

two squadrons of his regiment of Hussars, and to a telegram
expressing his satisfaction at the soldiers' rousing welcome which
he addressed to the Emperor Francis in the second person
singular, he received a cordial reply reciprocating the Prince's
tutoiement. The Prince enjoyed much sport, chiefly in the
society of Crown Prince Rudolph, the current rumours of whose
dissoluteness (he always said) escaped his ears.

But there was no escape from the humiliation of withdrawing
from Austro-Hungarian territory for the eight days of Kaiser
William's stay in Vienna. On the eve of his nephew's arrival
(October 3), the Prince sought refuge in the hospitalities of the
King and Queen of Rumania at their country palace of Sinaia in
the Carpathians. On 12th October, the day after his nephew
left Vienna, he returned to the city to bid the Austrian Emperor
farewell.

V

A reconciliation between uncle and nephew was not easy to
effect. The situation was scarcely relieved by a three months'
visit of the Empress Frederick to her English kinsfolk (November
1888–February 1889) on the Queen's invitation. Lord Salisbury,
the Prime Minister and Foreign Secretary, who was seeking at
the time to fathom the Kaiser's intentions in regard to England,
suggested a postponement of the Empress's visit; but the Prince
pointed out (October 25) that it was useless to try to change the
Queen's mind on the subject. The Queen's desire that there
should be some public demonstration of English sympathy with
her eldest daughter in her distresses was unfulfilled. The Prince
showed his sister every brotherly attention. He crossed to
Flushing to "bring her over" to Port Victoria, where the
Queen awaited her arrival on 18th November. It was for the
Empress "a sad return to her old home," the Prince wrote to
Mrs. Liddell. In the following January his sister joined him at
Sandringham.

Early next year the history of the Kaiser's estrangement from
his uncle entered a new phase with the nephew's proposal to visit
England for the first time in his newly acquired dignity. He
would come to Cowes in August. Queen Victoria welcomed her
grandson's proffer of amity. Lord Salisbury's government agreed
with the Queen that good relations with Germany were to this

country's advantage, and that, despite the new ruler's caprices, a way might be found of satisfying mutual interests. The Prince, avoiding questions of policy, promptly announced that he could not take part in the reception of the Kaiser until he had received from him an apology for what had taken place at Vienna.

Both Queen Victoria and Lord Salisbury expressed sympathy with the Prince, but persuaded him of the political necessity of ending the quarrel before the Emperor came to England. The Prince was by no means implacable. With the Queen's approval he deputed his brother-in-law, Prince Christian, the uncle of the Kaiserin, who was visiting Berlin in April, to invite his nephew to express his regrets in writing. "Most sincerely do I hope," the Prince wrote to Lord Salisbury on 11th April after Prince Christian had reached Berlin, "that the young Emperor will accept the olive branch which I offer him. I do not think I could write or ask less, and I have no wish to ask for more. It will certainly be a great relief to my mind if this matter could now be amicably settled once and for all."

The Kaiser was not the man to admit a fault. He treated Prince Christian's mediation lightly and impenitently. He declined to descend to details and breezily denied the whole of his uncle's allegations, suggesting that Prince Reuss, the German Ambassador at Vienna, had shown a lack of tact, or that the officials of the Austrian Court had taken too literally a vague suggestion of his wishes. The Prince, in commenting on Prince Christian's report, remarked that the Kaiser had a bad memory, but repeated his hope that his nephew might yet show a more conciliatory spirit. The negotiation hung fire for some months, and anxious doubts filled Lord Salisbury's and the Queen's minds over the arrangements for the Kaiser's reception in England. In June, at Queen Victoria's request, Sir Augustus Paget, the British Ambassador at Vienna, arrived in London to supply her with full details of the contretemps at the Austrian Court. The Queen resolved to act as arbitrator in the dispute, the main responsibility for which she assigned to the ill-will of Prince Bismarck and his son.

The Kaiser had set his heart on his English visit, and recognised the imprudence of ruffling English opinion. The Queen, tactfully avoiding thorny particulars, wrote pressing on him the need of treating the Prince with the consideration due

from a nephew to an uncle. She invited assurances from her
grandson that he would not offend again. The Kaiser replied in
gentle if somewhat evasive terms that he felt happy at learning "that you regard the Vienna affair as concluded, in which I
heartily concur." "I shall be happy," he added, "to meet
Uncle Bertie at Osborne" (June 23, 1889). The Prince, whom
Sir Augustus Paget found "much calmer than he had been led to
expect," yielded with some reluctance to the Queen's persuasion
to press the matter no further and meet his nephew at Osborne.[1]
The Prime Minister still discovered in the Prince at the end of
June "a most Rehoboam humour." Happily a more amiable
mood ultimately prevailed. The Prince acknowledged the
obligation of doing what he could to further Lord Salisbury's
policy of conciliating Germany, and he agreed to pay the Kaiser
in England the attention due to a European potentate. The
discord between uncle and nephew sprang from fundamental
causes which circumstance might qualify but could not remove.
For the time the differences between the two apparently fell into
abeyance, but they were to recur many times hereafter.

VI

The Queen and her government left no stone unturned to
gratify the Kaiser's vanity and to humour his idiosyncrasies, in
view of his coming visit. The Kaiser had lately assimilated the
grandiose ambition of his Pan-German friends to convert Germany
into a great naval Power. The future was to declare the full
significance of that aspiration. At present neither the Prince
nor Queen Victoria nor her government was disposed to take
seriously the Kaiser's flamboyant prophecies. Hitherto Germany
had been content with a "baby fleet," and it was not easy for
English opinion to realise that with time and strenuous effort the
German navy might acquire formidable proportions.[2]

[1] Lady Paget, *Embassies of Other Days*, ii.
[2] Prussia had created a miniature navy early in the fifties. It consisted
in 1851 of fifty-one vessels, chiefly small gunboats, under sail, of two guns each.
Between 1854 and 1869 the port of Wilhelmshaven was constructed on territory
purchased from Oldenburg, and Prussia added to her fleet two ironclads and
some eighty-seven small craft under steam or sail. In England the early naval
aspirations of Germany excited ridicule. A cartoon in *Punch* on 19th October
1861, entitled "The German Fleet," depicts Mr. Punch offering a diminutive
German a toy-ship with the words: "There's a ship for you, my little man; now
cut away and don't get in a mess." In November 1865, Lord Russell, then

To the Queen and the Prince, the Kaiser tortuously represented his country's plan of naval expansion as a compliment to
England.   For their benefit he traced its origin to that admiration
of the English fleet which had been roused in him as a boy on his
visits to his grandmother in the Isle of Wight, when his uncle,
the Duke of Edinburgh, a naval officer, had often shown him over
Portsmouth Dockyard.   But he frankly acknowledged that one
motive of his forthcoming visit to Cowes was to improve his
knowledge of England's naval equipment.   The Queen and her
government decided that her grandson's developing interest in
naval matters might, in the cause of general harmony, be indulged
by the bestowal on him in the course of his stay of the honorary
dignity of British admiral.   The Prince had been promoted to
the rank of Admiral of the Fleet only two years before on the
occasion of the Queen's Jubilee.   But he offered no opposition.
The news of the Queen's decision was received by the Kaiser with
an outburst of boylike ecstasy.   "Fancy wearing the same
uniform as St. Vincent and Nelson," he wrote exultingly to Sir
Edward Malet (June 14, 1889).   "It is enough to make me quite
giddy."   By way of acknowledgement the Kaiser conferred on
his grandmother the rank of honorary colonel of the 1st Dragoon
Guards, which was thenceforth known as "The Queen of England's
Own Regiment."   At the same time a naval review in the Solent
was arranged in his honour.[1]

The Prince, with characteristic complacence, seconded the
Queen and the Prime Minister's efforts to conciliate German
sentiment in all directions.   Lord Salisbury thought that a
friendly gesture on the Queen's part to Prince Bismarck might
be helpful.   An order was reckoned inappropriate.   The Prince

---

Prime Minister, wrote to Lord Clarendon, "Bismarck is very amusing with his
baby fleet."   Prince Bismarck's annexation of Schleswig-Holstein to Prussia
in 1866 greatly extended Germany's seaboard, and the acquisition of the port
of Kiel gave her a naval advantage capable of development.   The Kaiser on
his accession encouraged the Pan-German dream of a colossal navy.   Until his
reign opened, the German navy was under the control of the Minister of War.
The Kaiser gave the first indication of his naval intentions by creating an
independent Admiralty Department (Reichsmarineamt).

[1] The Kaiser eagerly assented to reach Cowes a day earlier than was at first
arranged in order to meet the convenience of members of the two Houses of
Parliament who wished to be present at the naval review.   "This participation," the Kaiser wrote to the Queen, "shows the world that the country fully
concurs and sympathises with their illustrious sovereign in tightening the bonds
of friendship between our two families and countries" (June 14, 1889).

undertook to consult Count von Hatzfeldt, the German
Ambassador in London, with whom he was personally on good
terms.   Together they arranged for the despatch to the hitherto
all-powerful Chancellor of a copy of the earliest painting of the
Queen which came from the brush of the German artist, von
Angeli.

The Kaiser duly arrived at Spithead on 1st August,
escorted by twelve German ships of war, of one of which, the
Irene, his brother, Prince Henry, was in command.   The Prince,
wearing the uniform of an admiral of the fleet, accompanied by
the Duke of Cambridge and his son Prince George, awaited his
nephew's arrival on the royal yacht *Osborne*.   The British ships
which were to take part in the coming naval review were already
in position, and the English and German royal yachts steamed
down the long lines side by side before the Prince boarded the
Hohenzollern.   Subsequently uncle and nephew landed at Cowes
and drove to Osborne House, where the Queen and Lord Salisbury awaited them.   On four of the five days during which the
Kaiser's visit lasted, he dined with his grandmother and the
Prince, and through the whole period the Prince was almost continuously in his nephew's society.   The naval review took place
on 5th August.   The Prince escorted the Kaiser and his
brother, Prince Henry, on board the royal yacht, the *Victoria and
Albert*, where the Queen handed to her grandson the coveted
commission of Admiral of the Fleet.

On the surface all went well, but beneath lurked symptoms
which disquieted the Prince.   The Kaiser displayed for the Cowes
Regatta, which was in progress during his stay, an enthusiasm
which the Prince regarded as unduly obtrusive.   He set, however, a strict guard on his feelings.   As Commodore of the Royal
Yacht Squadron he proposed his nephew for membership, and
on the evening of 6th August entertained him at a banquet
at the Royal Yacht Club, where high-flown speeches were exchanged between host and guest.   The Prince, in proposing his
nephew's health, expressed the hope that the German army and
navy might guarantee the peace of the world.   The Kaiser replied
"in terms of respectful affection," dithyrambically hailing the
British fleet as the finest in the world.   Yet when the Kaiser in
the Prince's company made a minute inspection of the assembled
British men-of-war, the Prince's patience was taxed by the

1889

Ætat. 47

visitor's claims to expert knowledge of naval guns and armaments. The Kaiser plied all about him with random technical
suggestions, and hinted not obscurely that the time was coming
when his own fleet would excel that of England, at any rate in
scientific equipment. On 7th August, when a review was held
at Aldershot in the Kaiser's honour, the Prince excused his
presence on the ground of a bad knee.

In spite of the Prince's disquietudes, he and the Kaiser
exchanged on parting warm professions of amity. The Prince
took leave of his nephew on board his yacht the *Hohenzollern*
on 8th August, as she was starting for Wilhelmshaven. On his
arrival in Berlin the Kaiser spoke buoyantly of the "cordiality
and affection" shown him both by the Queen and the Prince of
Wales, and of the profound impression which the British fleet
left on his mind. He acknowledged the pleasure which he
derived from the Cowes Regatta, and promised himself an early
renewal of the experience. But the Prince's misgivings found
echoes in many quarters. *The Times* newspaper questioned the
prudence of stimulating the Kaiser's naval ambitions by allowing
him to make so free a study of England's naval organisation.
The tones in which the Kaiser expressed to the Queen his
gratitude for the bestowal on him of admiral's rank were hardly
reassuring :

"Thanks," he wrote to the Queen from Bayreuth on 17th
August, "for all kindness to Henry and me during the visit,
and for the commission as Admiral of the Fleet. It really gave
me such an immense pleasure that I now am able to feel and
take interest in your Fleet as if it were my own, and with
keenest sympathy shall I watch every phase of its further
development, knowing that the British ironclads, coupled with
mine and my army, are the strongest guarantees of peace,
which may Heaven help us to preserve! Should, however, the
will of providence lay the heavy burden on us of fighting for our
homes and destinies, then may the British Fleet be seen forging
ahead side by side with the German, and the 'Red Coat'
marching to victory with the 'Pomeranian Grenadier.' " [1]

[1] Through many subsequent years the Kaiser took occasion to repeat in
varied notes of extravagance his admiration for the British fleet and its heroes.
When he entertained his fellow-admiral and uncle, the Duke of Edinburgh,
at Berlin (January 22, 1893), he described British naval heroes, and especially
Nelson, as the "guiding stars of German naval officers and crews." "And
should it ever happen," he continued, "that the British and German navies
have to fight side by side against a common foe, then the famous signal, 'England

VII

The Kaiser, with characteristic self-assurance, thenceforth
interpreted his honorary commission of British admiral as justifying him in tendering advice to the Queen, the Prince, and British
Ministers on all manner of points touching the British navy.   A
meeting in foreign waters of the Prince and the Kaiser little more
than two months after their parting in the Solent gave the Kaiser
an opportunity of further disturbing his uncle's equanimity by
airing, ostensibly for the Prince's benefit, his critical views of the
present state of England's fleet.   A marriage had been arranged
between the Kaiser's third sister, Sophie, and Constantine, Duke
of Sparta, eldest son and heir of the King of Greece.   The union
promised to all appearances to confirm the good domestic relations
of as many as four royal families of Europe.   The bride was the
niece of the Prince as well as the Kaiser's sister, while the bridegroom was the nephew of the Princess of Wales and grandson of
the King of Denmark, as well as heir to the Greek throne.   The
wedding, which took place at Athens on 22nd October 1889, was
attended by the sovereigns of Germany, Denmark, and Greece,
together with the Prince of Wales and all his family.   The ceremonial assumed something of the character of a naval as well as
of a domestic demonstration.   The Prince reached the Piraeus in
the royal yacht *Osborne* escorted by the Mediterranean squadron
under Admiral Sir Anthony Hoskins.   The Kaiser, the Kaiserin,
and a large suite, including Count Herbert Bismarck, then
minister of foreign affairs under his father, came in the imperial
yacht *Hohenzollern*, which flew the British Admiral's flag as well
as the German.   The Kaiser, wearing the uniform of a British
admiral, straightway inspected the Prince's escort in Phaleron
Bay, and lunched on board the British Admiral's ship, the
Dreadnought, on which he caused his admiral's flag to be hoisted.
The experience, he declared later, made the day one of the happiest

1889

Ætat. 47

---

expects that every man will do his duty,' which England's greatest naval hero
gave out before the battle of Trafalgar, will find an echo in the patriotic heart
of the German navy" (*The German Emperor's Speeches*, trans. by Louis
Elkind, pp. 100 and 101). Again on 24th June 1895, when dining with
Admiral Lord Walter Kerr on board the flagship *The Royal Sovereign* of the
Channel squadron which was present at the opening of the Kiel Canal, he
claimed that German sailors were faithful disciples of the English, and that
the history of the British navy was as familiar to German as to British naval
officers and seamen.

in his life. While uncle and nephew were together at Athens, the Kaiser took occasion to confide to the Prince his doubts as to whether the strength of Admiral Hoskins's fleet was adequate for the purposes which it might be called upon to fulfil.[1]

Happily the Prince was able to escape betimes from his nephew's fertility of criticism. The *Osborne* conveyed him and his elder son, Prince Albert Victor, to Ismailia, where the young man embarked on the steamship *Oceania* for his Indian tour, and the Prince took the opportunity of renewing his previous acquaintance with Egypt—now settling down under English control. Meanwhile the Kaiser left Athens to be the guest of the Sultan Abdul-Hamid at Constantinople and to initiate that understanding between Germany and Turkey which was to bear fruit of peril to England.

VIII

Various reasons, political and personal, impelled the Kaiser to make conspicuous show of the good relations which he had re-established with his uncle. Russia's attitude to Germany roused his misgivings. Signs were multiplying of Russia's rapprochement with France and the Kaiser's professed enthusiasm for the Tsar was waning. Prince Bismarck, still faithful to his old policy of "keeping two irons on the fire," was seeking to maintain a passable show of friendliness to both England and Russia. He was thinking, without consulting his master, of renewing the secret three years' agreement of 1887 between Russia and Germany, which he called the "Reinsurance Treaty."[2] The Kaiser was of another opinion, and believed in a substantive understanding

[1] Later in the year he wrote to Queen Victoria from Potsdam (December 22, 1889) that the British Mediterranean squadron included only five first-class battleships, whereas in his opinion it should consist of twelve. France had in commission nine first-class battleships at Toulon. "Admiral Hoskins," he added *tout court*, "must be reinforced." Some time before he had drafted a scheme of reinforcements which he forwarded through Lord Charles Beresford to Lord Salisbury. He now sent the Queen "a copy of a scheme as it is worked out for my navy. It shows the British navy and the French navy told off in squadrons for war." Next year (February 24, 1890), when an increase in the American fleet was threatened, he issued to the Queen another set of orders: "Your navy must now be trebled to be able to meet the Mounseers and Yankees on equal terms. . . . This is the humble notion of a simple Admiral of the Fleet."

[2] This instrument provided that the two Powers should observe a benevolent neutrality if either should engage in war with other Powers, but it excluded from the provision of neutrality the event of an attack either by Germany on France or by Russia on Austria.

with England as a useful corrective of possible trouble with Russia. The Kaiser's self-will was indeed provoking a sensational crisis in his political environment at home. Prince Bismarck, the Chancellor, was proving himself impatient of his new master's assertion of personal authority. There was disagreement in domestic as well as foreign affairs. The veteran statesman was regarded with no friendly eyes by the English royal family, but the Kaiser, with a volatile inconsistency, desired his English relatives to acknowledge the reasonableness of the step which he was meditating of driving the Chancellor from office. Motives of this kind led the Kaiser at the New Year of 1890 to send, through the Queen, to the Prince and his second son, George—the elder son was in India—an invitation to the Imperial court for next March. He promised his uncle the same splendours of reception which had attended his entertainment the year before of three reigning monarchs—the Emperor of Austria, the King of Italy, and the Shah of Persia. He would invest his cousin, Prince George, in the Prince's presence, with the insignia of the Order of the Black Eagle. The Queen demurred to an ostentatious programme, and the Prince confessed small enthusiasm for it. The death, on 7th January, of the Kaiser's grandmother, the Empress Augusta, the Queen's intimate friend of forty years, seemed to her to impose on the Kaiser the restraints of mourning. But when the Queen suggested that the Prince should pay his nephew a private visit at an earlier date than had been proposed, merely "to congratulate him on his thirty-first birthday" (January 27), the Kaiser retorted that the first appearance in Berlin during his reign of the English heir-apparent called for a welcome of elaborate ceremony. The Queen and Prince accepted the argument.

On 21st March 1890 the Prince and his son arrived in Berlin as the Kaiser's state guests. They were met at Lehrter station by the Kaiser with his mother, his two sisters, Victoria and Margaret, and a brilliant suite. An imposing military escort conducted them in procession to the Schloss. The programme of hospitalities was designed on a great scale. The Kaiser was in his blithest humour and treated the Prince with all the distinctions due to a reigning sovereign. At a banquet in the Prince's honour the Kaiser, wearing his British Admiral's uniform, spoke once more, on proposing the health of the Prince and of his son, of his pride in his new rank of British Admiral, and descanted on the historic brotherhood of British and Prussian arms on the field of Waterloo. The Prince in reply expressed his pleasure in wearing the uniform of the Prussian Hussars. At a Chapter and Ordens-fest of the Order of the Black Eagle Prince George was cere-moniously invested with the Collar and Robes by his Imperial cousin in his father's presence. The reception at many points wore a military complexion. On the 24th October the whole garrison of Berlin took part in honour of the Kaiser's guests in a sham fight on Tempelhof-Common, where the Kaiser himself was in command of the "invading" force. On the 25th the Kaiser conducted the Prince over the School of Musketry at Spandau, where opportunities were given him of inspecting a new rifle and the practical uses of smokeless powder.

The state visit ended with a concert at the Schloss, but the Prince remained privately in Berlin for a further three days, which he distributed between intercourse with his sister, who was absent from the state festivities, and informal visits in political or social quarters outside the Kaiser's immediate range of vision. During the Prince's presence in Berlin a Congress of International Workers was meeting there on the Kaiser's impulsive initiative and in defiance of Prince Bismarck's advice. The object was to consider means of ameliorating the conditions of the working classes in all European countries. The Prince's sister, the Empress Frederick, who was in thorough sympathy with efforts at social reform, invited him to meet the delegates at dinner. The Prince was cordial in his greetings of the English delegates, who included Sir John Gorst and Thomas Burt, the miner M.P. He showed interest in the measures, framed on the model of earlier English enactments, which the Congress was considering for the regulation of labour in mines and for protecting women and children employed in factories.

There were more exciting events in the political arena of the Prussian capital to invite the Prince's attention after he ceased to be a state guest. The Kaiser's political aim in entertaining his uncle was attested by the presence at the official festivities of General von Schweinitz, the German Ambassador from St. Peters-burg. The General was to furnish the Tsar at first hand on his return to Russia with warning hints of the triumphant success of the Prince's reception, and to give the Russian Chancellor, M. de Giers, the impression that Germany and England were

hand in glove.[1] After the Prince's official welcome in Berlin   1890
ended he paid Count Paul Schouvaloff, the Russian Ambassador   Ætat. 48
there (brother of the former Russian Ambassador in London), a
long visit, which gave him a serviceable insight into his nephew's
serpentine policy.

But a startling crisis in German domestic politics offered the
Prince at the moment more piquant diet. Two days before his
arrival in Berlin the Kaiser had "dropped his pilot." On
19th March Prince Bismarck received the Kaiser's notice to quit
office. The dismissed statesman, though in his seventy-fifth
year, had shown no diminution of vigour in the conduct of public
business, but the limits which he set to the new ruler's independence had grown intolerable to the arrogant Kaiser. As soon as
the Chancellor's compulsory resignation took effect the Kaiser
telegraphed to his grandmother that Prince Bismarck had
retired on account of failing health. In a letter written eight
days later he qualified this disingenuous explanation with the
revealing words : "I have been educated politically by the Prince
(*i.e.* Bismarck), and now I must show what I can do." The Prince
of Wales was puzzled. His nephew repeated, for his benefit, his
message to Queen Victoria. When the Kaiser's formal hospitality
ended, the Prince of Wales's eager curiosity led him to call on the
ex-Chancellor (March 26). He found the fallen minister overflowing with rage, and he listened to the old man's heated protests
against his humiliation and to his liberal abuse of the Kaiser's character and capacity. "The old Prince," he wrote to his mother
(March 31), "was terribly hurt and pained at being forced to resign,
but seemed in excellent health." Prince Bismarck was grateful
for the note of sympathy which he imputed to his visitor's tones,
and Count Herbert Bismarck, foreign minister under his father,
invited the Prince to dinner. In spite of recent differences, the
Prince accepted the invitation. From Count Herbert he learnt
more of Prince Bismarck's bitter resentment and of the Kaiser's
resolve to rule alone.[2] The Prince saw that the removal of

---

[1] *Die Grosse Politik*, vii. 10, 12, 16.

[2] Prince Bismarck himself invited Lord Londonderry, General Ellis, and
other members of the Prince's suite to luncheon with him during the Prince of
Wales's stay in Berlin, and to them he denounced the Kaiser in unmeasured
terms. His fury reached its highest point when in the course of the meal a
letter arrived from the Kaiser conferring on the ex-Chancellor the unwanted
title of Duke of Lauenberg.

Bismarck loosened all restraint on his nephew's headstrong and ill-balanced will. He inclined, with qualifications, to the verdict of Sir William Harcourt, who wrote at the time to John Morley : "What do you say to the removal of the great German Panjandrum himself ? It is not a pleasant prospect to have Europe left at the mercy of a hothead who seems also to be a fool." [1]

IX

"Our visit to Berlin," wrote the Prince to his mother after its close (March 31), "I may consider as a great success in every way, and certainly William did all in his power to make it very agreeable and interesting : he treated me quite like a sovereign, and considered my visit as in your name, and, in fact, your representative." Similarly Sir Edward Malet wrote (March 29) : "Nothing could have gone off better. . . . There were no contretemps of any kind. The Emperor and H.R.H. appeared to be equally satisfied and pleased." When, on his return home, the Prince dined with the Prime Minister, Lord Salisbury, in London on 11th April, he declared himself to be "much impressed with the strong desire of the Emperor William to be on good terms with this country." In reporting the Prince's conversation to the Queen, Lord Salisbury made the prudent comment : "So long as it lasts, this mood is very valuable, but will it last ?"

Lord Salisbury, however, deemed it politic, in view of the Kaiser's benevolent mood, to take a definite step towards an Anglo-German understanding. Soon after the Prince quitted Berlin the Prime Minister suggested a territorial bargain between the two countries, which he believed to be to their mutual advantage. He proposed the cession of the island of Heligoland, in the North Sea (in agreement with an earlier suggestion on the part of Germany), in exchange for the East African protectorates which Germany claimed over Zanzibar, Witu, and Somaliland. The British Admiralty approved the cession of Heligoland on the ground that unless immense sums of money were spent upon its fortification in order to render it self-defending, it would be of no use in case of war with Germany. The acquisition of Zanzibar and the neighbouring region was reckoned of value to

---

[1] Gardiner, *Life of Sir William Harcourt*.

England not only materially, but sentimentally, owing to the 1890
increased influence which the ownership would give her in Ætat. 48
suppressing the East African slave trade. The Kaiser was
enthusiastic over the proposed exchange of territory.

In the eyes of the Kaiser's new Chancellor, Count von Caprivi,
and of his new Foreign Minister (in succession to Count Herbert
Bismarck), the chauvinist Marschall von Bieberstein, the opportunity of acquiring the island of Heligoland was a stroke of the
best possible fortune. Lord Salisbury's predecessor in office, Lord
Granville, had deemed it imperative to maintain England's
hold on the island,[1] and Lord Salisbury's change of view was
unexpected. The Pan-Germans coveted the island in order to
convert it into a strongly fortified post which might effectually
protect from attack the long-projected Kiel Canal. Count von
Hatzfeldt, the German Ambassador in London and the chief
German negotiator, avoided all mention of the Pan-German
point of view in the discussions with Lord Salisbury, and this
issue would seem to have escaped the Prime Minister's attention.

The Queen was doubtful of the prudence of the negotiation,
and the Prince, though approving the spirit of Lord Salisbury's
friendly effort, echoed his mother's view. "The conditions you
enumerate," she wrote to the Prime Minister when he laid the
detailed proposals before her, 23rd May 1890, "are sound,
and the alliance with Germany valuable, but that any of my
possessions should be thus bartered away causes me great uneasiness, and I can only consent on receiving a positive assurance
from you that the present arrangement constitutes no precedent."

[1] Already in 1884 Count Münster, Count von Hatzfeldt's predecessor in
the German Embassy, pointed out to Lord Granville, the Foreign Secretary,
that possession of the island was essential for the protection of the contemplated
Kiel Canal. The cession of Heligoland would strengthen, Count Münster added,
the good feeling of Germany towards England to an extraordinary degree.
Lord Granville replied that the surrender of Gibraltar to Spain would strengthen
the good feeling of Spain towards England in quite as extraordinary a degree.
Count Münster thereupon dropped the subject (*Die Grosse Politik*, iv.; Fitzmaurice's *Life of Granville*, ii. 425). Lord George Hamilton, First Lord of the
Admiralty at the time of the cession of Heligoland in 1890, deemed Lord
Salisbury's action well justified on the ground of the uselessness to England of
the island in its then condition. Lord George subsequently asserted that in
the Great War of 1914–18 Heligoland, if in English hands, must have been captured readily by the Germans, and would not, owing to the action of submarines
and torpedo destroyers, have aided in the blockade of the Kiel Canal. Lord
George admits that the main purpose of the cession, which was to conciliate
Germany, failed egregiously (*Parliamentary Reminiscences and Reflections, 1880–
1903*, pp. 140 *seq.* 1922).

"Giving up what one has," she added a few days later, "is always a bad thing." Among politicians Sir Charles Dilke, the Prince's former friend, stood almost alone in protesting against the bargain. In the event the Anglo-German Convention was duly signed at Berlin by the British Ambassador, Sir Edward Malet, and the German Chancellor, von Caprivi, on 1st July 1890.

The signing of the Convention had in England an unexpected constitutional sequel, which profoundly interested the Prince. Lord Salisbury, contrary to precedent, resolved to apply to Parliament for its ratification. He thereby raised a constitutional issue which, however academic at bottom, nearly touched the Queen's and the Prince's sense of dignity. Admittedly the sovereign could authorise territorial cession or acquisition only on ministerial advice, but it had been hitherto held by constitutional authorities that the prerogative of ceding or acquiring territory still adhered to the Crown, and that such exercise of the prerogative with ministerial sanction needed no parliamentary confirmation. Lord Salisbury, the Conservative Prime Minister, ironically argued that it was safer to submit the Anglo-German agreement to Parliament in the form of a bill than to leave its sanction solely to a formal act of the Crown. It was Mr. Gladstone, the Liberal leader, who came on this occasion to the defence of the prerogative, which he charged his political opponents with disparaging. In a speech of energetic eloquence he opposed in the House of Commons the new departure. The Prince approved Mr. Gladstone's view and deplored Lord Salisbury's appeal to Parliament. The government, however, was unmoved by criticism. The cession of Heligoland, with the compensating acquisition of influence and territory in East Africa, was embodied in a parliamentary bill, which, after passing rapidly through both Houses, received the royal assent on the 4th August 1890.

The precedent was irrevocable. In similar circumstances of perhaps greater historic importance the Prince, when King Edward VII., strenuously but vainly sought to reverse Lord Salisbury's ruling of 1890. Early in his reign King Edward urged that it lay within the scope of the prerogative to sanction the far-famed Anglo-French agreement which Mr. Balfour, the Prime Minister, and his colleagues reached with France in 1904. Exchanges of territory were involved, together with the recog-

nition of the two countries' spheres of influence in distant parts
of the world. Mr. Balfour questioned the cogency of the King's
plea, and the Anglo-French *entente*, like the Anglo-German
agreement of 1890, was ratified by a parliamentary bill. No
claim of personal sovereignty on either occasion was at stake.
The point at issue was the sufficiency of ministerial power to
authorise the sovereign's exercise of his prerogative in a manner
which was historically justified. In the result, despite Mr.
Gladstone's protests and the Prince's demurs, the prerogative in
dispute passed from the Crown to Parliament.

The Heligoland agreement seemed to set on firm foundations
an understanding between Germany and England, and to all
appearances an added guarantee of its fair promise was furnished
by the arrival of the Kaiser on a fresh visit to Cowes (the second
after his accession) on the very day, 4th August, that the Queen
gave her assent to the Anglo-German Convention Bill. The royal
yacht, the *Victoria and Albert*, with the Prince on board, met in
the Solent the Imperial yacht, the *Hohenzollern*, with the Kaiser
on board. The Prince accompanied his nephew, who wore the
uniform of a British Admiral, to Osborne, where the Queen
awaited them. Whatever doubts the Heligoland cession had
roused in the mind of the Queen and the Prince, they exchanged
cordial congratulations with their guest. Naturally the Kaiser's
spirits ran high. Although his visit to England was formally
represented as a purely family affair without political significance,
Lord Salisbury was summoned to Osborne to meet him. The
Kaiser buoyantly urged the Prime Minister to bestow on the
Triple Alliance a greater benevolence than he had yet evinced.[1]

The Prince spent much time with his nephew during the five
days of the Kaiser's stay. On the evening of 5th August the
Kaiser, as before, was the chief guest at the annual banquet of the
Royal Yacht Squadron, over which the Prince presided. In
toasting one another's health, uncle and nephew pledged themselves in unexceptionable terms to paths of peace and friendship.
Next morning the Prince accompanied the Kaiser to Eastney,
near Portsmouth, where they watched a sham fight. On the 7th,
at the Kaiser's request, the two made together a tour of inspection
of Portsmouth Dockyard. On the 8th, after dining with the
Prince on board the yacht *Osborne*, the Kaiser took a friendly

[1] Schwertfeger, *Zur Europäischen Politik*, v. 267.

leave. He proceeded in the *Hohenzollern* to Heligoland, his newly acquired possession. There he publicly assumed the coveted sovereignty. "Without a battle, without the shedding of a tear," he boasted in an exuberant speech, "this beautiful island has passed into my possession. We have acquired it by a treaty freely concluded with a country to which we are related by blood. I drink to the illustrious lady to whom we are indebted for the transfer."

X

In the retrospect the Kaiser's words strike a hollow note. On the English side the hopes of the Heligoland agreement were not realised. The friendly negotiation remained *in vacuo*. The Kaiser continued to importune England to join the Triple Alliance which Germany dominated, and to convert it into a Quadruple Alliance. But his importunities and those of his ministers were indistinguishable from threats, and were received coldly by England. Germany's colonial ambitions were growing steadily and her fleet was making substantial progress. The Kaiser's demeanour to his uncle was more offensive and provocative than before. His dithyrambic assurances of goodwill sounded to English kinsfolk and their fellow-countrymen insincere. From 1894 to the end of the century the relations alike of uncle and nephew and of the governments of the two countries were enveloped in mist and storm.

Each of the five years, 1891 to 1895, found the Kaiser, by his own wish, revisiting England and his English relatives in order to air, often with unseasonable vehemence, his professed ambitions to bring England "into line" with his own country. The five visits saw a progessive decline in the cordiality of uncle and nephew, until they came at the last near open breach.

In 1891 Queen Victoria and her government deemed it politic to invite the Kaiser and Kaiserin to pay her and her country, for the first time since their accession, a state visit. The Kaiser accepted the invitation with abundant professions of satisfaction. During the four opening days of their stay (July 4 to 8) the imperial couple were the Queen's guests at Windsor, and for the remaining days (8th to 13th) they were lodged at Buckingham Palace. The Prince figured prominently in the reception of his

nephew and the Kaiserin.   At a state banquet in St. George's
Hall, Windsor, 7th July, he with genial tact toasted the guests in
his mother's name.   He bore the Kaiser company when the visitor
received in the Guildhall on 10th July the freedom of the City of
London, and he heard the Kaiser on the occasion give the well-
worn assurances: "As far as it is in my power, I intend to
maintain the historical friendship between these our two nations.
My aim is, above all, the maintenance of peace."

In the imperial retinue was the Pan-German Foreign Minister,
Marschall von Bieberstein, who had political conversation with
Lord Salisbury, the Prime Minister.   Lord Salisbury showed no
inclination to draw tighter the bonds between the two countries.
The Kaiser's design of an Anglo-German alliance received no
substantive encouragement.   But his hopes still ran high.   His
vanity did not allow him to envisage failure.   The Prince parted
with him on amiable terms at King's Cross railway station,
whence the Kaiser proceeded by train to Leith to join his yacht
for a Norwegian cruise.

A disconcerting incident next month served to sharpen the
Kaiser's appetite for Anglo-German co-operation.   In August his
brother, Prince Henry, with Princess Henry, daughter of the late
Princess Alice, and their son, Prince Waldemar, were, to his
satisfaction, the Queen's guests at Osborne.   But the fair promise
of this visit was soon clouded by the announcement that the
French fleet, under Admiral Gervais, was to arrive at Portsmouth
on the invitation of the British government, while the Kaiser's
brother and his family were enjoying the Queen's hospitality.
Their hostess regretted, in the circumstances, the obligation
which her government imposed on her of entertaining the French
naval officers at Osborne and of reviewing the French fleet off
Spithead.   The Prince, who was away at Homburg, was perplexed.
He, however, relieved his mother of a personal embarrassment by
putting at the disposal of her German guests his yacht *Aline* for
a cruise in the Channel during the time that the Queen was
showing attention to the French visitors.[1]   German observers
could scarcely view Lord Salisbury's move with equanimity.
The French fleet had come from Russia, where the Tsar had
entertained them at Cronstadt.   Startled Europe saw in that

---

[1] Admiral Gervais and his fellow-officers dined with the Queen at Osborne
on the 20th August; and next day she reviewed the French ships off Spithead.

episode a confirmation of the vague rumour of a secret Franco-Russian alliance. Lord Salisbury had no intention of joining forces with the new allies, but his reception of the French fleet fresh from Russian waters indicated, at any rate, that he viewed foreign entanglements with impartial detachment. The Prince had no liking for a policy of isolation, but acknowledged at this juncture the difficulty of choosing allies. The self-confident Kaiser saw the need of putting insidious pressure on England in order that his vision of a Quadruple Alliance should materialise.

XI

On the four annual visits which he paid to Cowes (1892–95) the Kaiser was careful to disclaim a political errand. He came, he averred, to pay his respects to his grandmother at Osborne, and to make holiday in the company of his uncle at the Cowes Regatta. The programme of his week at Cowes varied little year by year. He arrived near the beginning of August on the imperial yacht *Hohenzollern*, escorted by a small squadron of battleships and cruisers usually under the command of his brother, Prince Henry of Prussia.[1] His yacht remained his headquarters during his stay, and that circumstance provoked the criticism in Germany that there was no great anxiety on the part of his English kinsfolk to make him their guest. Two visits were, however, annually paid to Queen Victoria at Osborne, where she entertained her grandson at dinner, *en famille* on one occasion and in state on the other. His uncle, on board the royal yacht *Osborne*, exchanged with him much hospitality, and uncle and nephew from 1893 onwards often cruised together on the Prince's cutter, the *Britannia*. The Prince invariably presided at a banquet in honour of the imperial visitor at the Royal Yacht Squadron Clubhouse, when they toasted each other's health in conventional oratory. Unaccompanied by the Prince, the Kaiser inspected the warships in Portsmouth Dockyard in 1893, and, two years later, he camped at Aldershot for a field day.

There were elements which caused the Prince and others a progressive disquiet in the professedly innocent purposes of his nephew's visits to Cowes. The Kaiser, under the cloak of privacy,

---

[1] His companions included his favourite attendants, Count Philip von Eulenberg and Major-General von Plessen.

lost no opportunity of pressing forward his political designs. He
summoned Count von Hatzfeldt from London to attend him
while he was in English waters, and he sought interviews with the
English Foreign Minister of the day. In the result, Cowes became,
while the Kaiser stayed there, a political wrestling ground. The
English government was discovering each year fresh reasons to
distrust the Kaiser. Germany's colonial policy in the Samoan
Archipelago of the Pacific and in various parts of Africa, and her
discordant attitude to problems of the Near and Far East were,
from 1893 onwards, straining English forbearance.[1] The Kaiser
was soon discovering disrespect towards himself and disparagement of Germany in English statesmen's hesitation to fall in with
German colonial and other political proposals which he made in
the course of his holiday conversations. Lord Salisbury, whose
cold demeanour the Kaiser resented, was succeeded in 1892 at the
Foreign Office, on the formation of Mr. Gladstone's fourth and
last ministry, by the Prince's friend, Lord Rosebery. But Lord
Rosebery gave the Kaiser rather less comfort than his predecessor by his stern refusal of well-nigh all concessions to German
demands. The Kaiser, who was prone to catch, while at Cowes,
at any straw as a sign that the wind was setting in a direction
congenial to his pride, was slow to credit the low estimate which
the Prince and English ministers set on his political offers.[2]

1893
——
Ætat. 51

[1] The Kaiser in 1895 ridiculed as sentimental vapouring English sympathy
with the cruel fate of the Armenians at the hands of his friend the Sultan of
Turkey, and he deprecated English encouragement of the ambitions of Japan,
after that progressive state had routed China in war. A change in the Chancellorship and in the control of German foreign policy in 1894 explains the Kaiser's
growing impatience with England during his Cowes visit of that year. After
leaving the Solent (October 28, 1894) the Kaiser wired to the Queen the news of
Chancellor von Caprivi's resignation, and the succession to the office of the
septuagenarian Prince von Hohenlohe, "Uncle Chlodwig Hohenlohe," a friend
of his grandmother's youth and a kinsman by marriage of the Queen's half-sister,
Princess Feodora von Leiningen, the wife of Prince von Hohenlohe-Langenburg.
The Prince, too, had known the new Chancellor from boyhood. But Prince von
Hohenlohe proved a cipher in affairs of state. His accession to office coincided
with the Kaiser's assignment of the full direction of Germany's foreign policy
to the aggressive Baron Marschall von Bieberstein, the Foreign Minister, and
the mysterious Director of the Political Section of the Foreign Office, Geheim-
rath Fritz von Holstein. Under these men's influence the Kaiser's Anglophobic
jealousies steadily developed.

[2] The Kaiser's vanity always encouraged his tendency to distortion. The
Queen communicated to her grandson at Cowes in August 1893 a confidential
telegram from Lord Rosebery intimating a grave (but temporary) crisis between
France and England in regard to French claims on Siam. The Kaiser treated
the Queen's courtesy as an invitation to him to join England in war with France.

1894   Before 1894 ended there came nearly complete disillusionment.
Ætat. 52 Of no pending political issue within Europe or beyond it did
the English and German governments hold the same view.   The
comprehensive misunderstandings personally involved the Prince.
He had lately made a serious bid for the goodwill of Russia and
had given, in 1894, plain proofs of his friendly regard for the new
Tsar Nicholas II.[1]   His German nephew, who was well versed
in the art of coquetting with Russia in the hope of injuring
England and the Prince, deemed his uncle to be taking unfairly
a leaf out of his own book.   He wildly charged the Prince with
fomenting at St. Petersburg an insidious plot against Germany
and himself.

1895   The Kaiser's last August sojourn off Cowes in 1895 lost all
Ætat. 53 touch of holiday calm.   Lord Salisbury had resumed control of
the Foreign Office in July.   The Kaiser now summoned him to
an interview on his yacht in the Solent (August 8, 1895).   The
imperial yachtsman loaded his political visitor with insults for
his alleged unwillingness to propitiate German sentiment.[2]   The
Prince protested against his nephew's effrontery in seeking to
bully the Prime Minister of England.   But the Kaiser was in no
mood to curb his political and personal rancours.   Queen Victoria
took a charitable view of her grandson's tempestuous humours
at this time when she wrote of him as "this impetuous and con-
ceited youth" (January 22, 1895).   The grandmother might well
be excused for forgetting that the Kaiser was just closing his
thirty-seventh year.

   [1] See p. 692 *infra.*
   [2] The interview abounded in untoward incident. The Prime Minister and
Foreign Minister, Lord Salisbury, who had just assumed office, accepted the
Kaiser's invitation to visit him on the *Hohenzollern* on 8th August to discuss the
brutal offences of Turkey against her Armenian subjects. (The Kaiser had
already scouted Lord Salisbury's plan of joint coercion of the Porte by the
Great Powers—the six "impuissances" as he called them in a flippant letter
of the date to Queen Victoria on the subject.) Lord Salisbury was by accident
an hour late for his appointment with the Kaiser. The Kaiser treated him
with a frigidity which put friendly intercourse out of the question. The Kaiser
ridiculed Lord Salisbury's alleged purpose of dismembering the Ottoman
Empire. After leaving the Kaiser, Lord Salisbury remarked to a friend
that the Kaiser forgot that as Prime Minister of England he could not work
for the King of Prussia. According to the Kaiser's story, when the two men
parted, he offered to renew the conversation next morning. Lord Salisbury
misunderstood the Kaiser's offer, and did not keep the appointment. The
Kaiser's irritation was scarcely allayed by an apology which Lord Salisbury
sent to Count von Hatzfeldt on learning that the Kaiser had proposed a second
interview (Eckardstein, *Ten Years at the Court of St. James's,* pp. 57-60).

The worst of the many offences which the Prince laid to his nephew's charge when he visited Cowes in August 1895 came of his inclusion in his naval escort of two new cruisers, the *Wörth* and the *Weissenburg*. Both vessels were named after places in Alsace where, in 1870, the invading Prussian army had won conspicuous victories over the French. The twenty-fifth anniversary of those victories fell respectively on 4th and 6th August. On the intervening day the Kaiser arrived in the Solent, and on the 6th, the anniversary of the battle of Wörth, he made on board the cruiser of that name a bellicose harangue to the sailors, which could not fail to outrage French susceptibilities. The Prince denounced his nephew's provocative utterance as an affront to his hosts. The English Conservative press charged the orator with infringing accredited rules of hospitality. The German press made a virulent reply, and a journalistic warfare between the two countries was waged with intense heat.[1] Some five months later the Kaiser was writing plaintively to Queen Victoria (January 8, 1896): "Our press is still angered by the *Standard* articles which appeared when I was at Cowes and which were very unkind to me personally, and which wounded Germany's *amour propre* more deeply than the authors might have thought." The Kaiser acknowledged no fault on his part. He affected to regard himself as the innocent victim of English malevolence. On arriving in Berlin from Cowes in August 1895 he registered a vow that he had done with England. A seven years' endeavour to bring the two countries politically into line with one another had been, he declared, foiled by England's "selfishness and lying."[2]

It was not only political dissensions that renewed ancient grudges between the uncle and nephew at Cowes in August 1895. The Kaiser challenged in the Solent the Prince's forbearance

[1] On leaving Cowes the Kaiser spent five days (August 11-15) with his friend the Earl of Lonsdale at Lowther Castle, Cumberland. Thence he returned home to conduct an oratorical campaign against France, delivering in Berlin two vainglorious declamations on Germany's military triumphs of 1870. There followed a tour with the Empress through the conquered provinces of Alsace and Lorraine; and on the battlefield of Wörth, in the presence of his mother, he unveiled a monument to his father, when he declared in tones of brass, with one eye on his uncle, that he would hold Alsace and Lorraine against all comers for ever.

[2] *Die Grosse Politik*, xi. 8 *seq*. (Report of conservation with his friend Colonel Swaine, the British Military Attaché, 25th October 1895.)

1893
Ætat. 51 on other and more personal grounds. The Prince's recent successes in yacht-racing spurred the Kaiser to rival his uncle's exploits at the Cowes Regatta. When, in 1893, the Prince's new racing yacht, the *Britannia*, took the water in the Solent, the Kaiser promptly entered a yacht of his own, *Meteor I.*, to race against her, and on 1st August the Kaiser had the satisfaction of defeating his uncle's vessel in the race for the Queen's Cup. Each owner sailed on board his own craft. The Kaiser further showed his zeal by offering a "Meteor Challenge Shield" for annual competition. On the surface no reproach attached to the Kaiser for challenging his uncle in the yacht-racing field, but the Kaiser's jealous and overbearing temper imparted to his interposition unpleasing features which could not fail to try the Prince's temper.

One episode in the regatta of 1893 illustrates the difficulties in which the Kaiser's self-assertion was prone to place the Prince. On 2nd August the Prince matched his yacht *Britannia*, with himself and the Duke of York on board, against Mr. A. D. Clarke's *Satanita*. The course was a circuit of the Isle of Wight from Cowes to Cowes. The Kaiser resolved to accompany the racing yachts on board the *Meteor I*. There was a delay in the start, which was not made until 8 o'clock in the evening. For the same evening, the Queen had arranged a state dinner at Osborne in honour of the Kaiser which the Prince and his son were to attend. Early in the race the Prince recognised that it would be impossible to reach Osborne in time for the Queen's dinner if the course were to be covered. He was anxious to spare his mother the inconvenience which the unpunctuality of her chief guest and himself would occasion her. Accordingly he signalled from the *Britannia* to the Kaiser on the *Meteor I.* an urgent request to abandon the race, and, by taking train from the nearest point on land, to keep the engagement at Osborne. The Kaiser's gunboat *Blitz* had been ordered to escort the yachts to meet such an emergency. But the Kaiser peremptorily declined to act on the Prince's suggestion. In the result, uncle and nephew reached Osborne after the Queen's dinner was over.[1]

[1] Eckardstein, *Ten Years at the Court of St. James's*, pp. 45–6; *The Times*, 3rd August 1893. The present writer is assured by eye-witnesses of the Queen's placid reception of her son and grandson at Osborne on the occasion that the description given of the scene by Eckardstein, which is repeated with embellishments by Mr. Lytton Strachey in his *Queen Victoria*, p. 282, is not to be trusted.

On the concluding visit to Cowes in August 1895, the Kaiser's spirit of racing rivalry developed darker features than before. He sought to take the control of the regatta out of the hands of his uncle, the Commodore of the Royal Yacht Squadron, and when he was rebuffed for his presumption, tried to prejudice the success of the meeting. He once again entered his yacht *Meteor I.* against his uncle's cutter in the race for the Queen's Cup, but, dissatisfied with the handicapping, refused to sail, derisively leaving his uncle's *Britannia* to sail the course alone (August 6). Although the customary hospitalities were exchanged on board the *Osborne* and the *Hohenzollern*, the Kaiser spoke to and of his uncle in terms of insult. He taunted him to his face with never having engaged in active military service, and in private conversation with his suite, dubbed him, "the old peacock." [1] The Prince plaintively protested to Baron von Eckardstein, secretary to the German Embassy in London, with whom he was on friendly terms: "The regatta used to be a pleasant recreation for me, but now, since the Kaiser takes command, it is a vexation."

Happily, the Kaiser did not again put in a personal appearance at the regatta and the Prince was able to continue his attendance in peace. But the Kaiser still contributed from afar to the excitement of the racing and kept his name to the fore in the chief contests. His love of competing with his uncle in the Solent was not quenched. Before he bade farewell to Cowes in August 1895, he commissioned the accomplished architect of his uncle's cutter *Britannia* to design a racing yacht on similar lines but of superior racing quality. The result was *Meteor II.*, which in the Kaiser's absence, appeared in the Solent in the season of 1896, and soon showed by her exploits that the *Britannia* was outbuilt. The Prince silently accepted the defeat, and in 1897 the *Britannia* was withdrawn from the yacht-racing field.

XII

Warmly as the Prince resented the Kaiser's unmannerly bombast alike in his domestic and his political character, he still cherished a hope that concessions to his nephew's vanity might

[1] Eckardstein, *Ten Years at the Court of St. James's*, pp. 55–56.

put some check on his unpromising humours and serve the general interests of peace. The Prince's faith in the expedience of such experiments was hardly shared by his mother or her ministers, and events proved in the long run that their judgement herein was the sounder. Early in 1894 the Prince sought a practical trial of his politic benevolence and challenged a conflict with his mother and her government. By dint of the pertinacity with which he usually pursued controversy, he carried his point, but the outcome of his victory scarcely answered his expectation.

The Kaiser was to celebrate on his thirty-fifth birthday, 27th January 1894, his "military jubilee." In anticipation of the event, he gratified his uncle by appointing him à la suite of the Prussian Dragoon Guards, of which Queen Victoria was already Honorary Colonel. The Kaiser was no quite disinterested giver. He nursed the hope of a new British honour in exchange. To the British Military Attaché in Berlin, Colonel Leopold Swaine, whom he described to his grandmother as "a personal friend of mine and much liked by Papa and Grandpapa," he confided his wish for an honorary rank in the British Army, preferably the Colonelcy-in-Chief of a Highland regiment, so that he might wear the Highland uniform, which had delighted him in boyhood. When the suggestion was reported to the Queen she invited the Prince's view without indicating her own. The Prince deemed it an occasion for a soothing draught. He doubted whether the military recognition should take the precise form that the Kaiser suggested, and privately ridiculed his nephew's presumptuous conceit in making the request. But at some expense of his consistency, he eagerly strained arguments in favour of the gratification of his nephew's desire in some shape or other. To the Queen he wrote from Sandringham on 16th January:

I would strongly urge you to make him a general in our Army on the occasion of his military jubilee. It would please him immensely—he is very much attached to England, and as your eldest grandson I think you might perfectly well do so. Making him hon. colonel of a regiment might be difficult, as it has never been done before.

The Prince further suggested that Prince Edward of Saxe-Weimar, "one of the oldest officers in our Army," might bear the Queen's congratulations to the Kaiser on his military jubilee, with

a letter announcing his appointment as general. But the Queen
consulted other advisers and considered the question for herself.
She was still resentful of the ungainly criticism of the English
royal family which had been provoked in Germany by the Duke
of Edinburgh's accession to the duchy of Saxe-Coburg-Gotha in
the autumn of 1893, and she announced her resolve to refuse
the Kaiser's request.

1894
Ætat. 52

The Prince, however, persisted in his plea. He urged on the
Queen that it was worth while paying a compliment to "the
finest army in the world," and he cited the precedent of the late
King of the Belgians, who was made a British field-marshal. The
Prince sought support in all quarters. The Secretary of State
for War, Mr. Campbell-Bannerman, cautiously allowed that
there was no objection to creating the Kaiser an honorary
general, or even a field-marshal, although there was no precedent
for making a foreign sovereign an honorary colonel of a regiment.
The chief objection in the mind of the Secretary for War was that
other foreign sovereigns might expect a like compliment which
political considerations might not allow the Government to
entertain. The Prince brought the Duke of Cambridge and
his brother, the Duke of Connaught, round to his point of
view. The Duke of Cambridge deprecated an honorary
colonelcy, especially of a Highland regiment, but he quoted
the case of "the old King of Holland" by way of a second
precedent for the appointment of a foreign sovereign as
field-marshal. The Duke further argued that the naval rank
which had already been bestowed on the Kaiser justified
military rank, and the Queen's acceptance at her grandson's
hands of an honorary colonelcy in the German army called for
reciprocity. The Queen for the time stood her ground. She
declared that the naval rank of admiral was quite sufficient; that
the honour had been deliberately given in preference to military
rank; that were her nephew a general or a field-marshal, "he will
be interfering with our Army"; that the whole suggestion was
a "new departure" and would "offend other sovereigns";
and if all honours were showered on him now, "what is left for
him when he is older?" (January 20 and 22, 1894). On 24th
January the Queen perturbed the Prince by assuring him
that her refusal was final. Three days later Lord Rosebery,
the Foreign Secretary, ratified the Queen's decision. The

Emperor, he pointed out on 27th January 1894, had already
received from a naval nation the unique distinction of honorary
Admiral; the bestowal within four years of high military rank
would be misinterpreted as "a declaration of a policy which just
now is neither desirable nor desired"; France and Russia would
both be seriously puzzled, while German jealousy of England,
which deprecated English influence on German sovereigns or
princes, would be excited anew, and would prejudice rather than
promote co-operation between the two nations.

Yet the Prince's influence with the ageing Queen was growing,
and his defeat proved only temporary. In April he and the Duke
of Cambridge reopened the question. They made a direct appeal
to Lord Rosebery, who had become Prime Minister on 3rd
March. The new Prime Minister replied that he saw no reason
to alter his former opinion:

So marked an additional honour should only be given at a time
when it is necessary to display either signal gratitude or signal
friendship. Now there is at the present moment no necessity for
the display of any extraordinary friendship, still less for the
demonstration of any extraordinary gratitude.

But the Queen, apparently exhausted by her son's importunities, exercised a woman's right of changing her mind
and suddenly gave way. She consented to make her grandson
honorary Colonel of the 1st Royal Dragoons (the Royals), of
which Prince Francis Teck, the younger brother of the Duchess
of York, was the commanding officer. Although the military
honour did not take the precise form which the Kaiser designed,
he received the Queen's offer with ecstatic professions of
gratitude:

"I am moved, deeply moved," he wrote to the Queen on
24th April, "at the idea that I now, too, can wear, beside the
naval uniform, the traditional British 'Red Coat.' How many
brave and brilliant soldiers have worn it? And, before all, my
beloved Grandpapa. The congratulations I receive from all
parts show me how much this token of your kindness is valued
here, and how glad they are here that the bonds of friendship
between our countries and armies have received a new addition."

The Queen's surrender to her son was indeed complete. In June
Prince Francis Teck, with a few other officers of the regiment,
proceeded, with her approval, to Berlin to offer formal congratula-

tion to the Kaiser.   Moreover, when the Kaiser revisited Cowes   1894
for the Regatta in August 1894, and was invited to attend in his   Ætat. 52
new military rank a field day at Aldershot, the Queen ignored
the hesitations of Sir Henry Campbell-Bannerman, the Secretary
for War, and of Sir Redvers Buller, Adjutant-General, and she
directed a detachment of the Kaiser's regiment, "The Royals,"
to take part in the operations.   The Kaiser's boisterous elation
over this proof of the Queen's complacence hardly contributed to
the harmony of the Prince's relations with the Kaiser at the Cowes
Regatta.   In spite of his responsibilities in the matter, the Prince
omitted to bear his nephew company at the Aldershot field day.
The Prince's effort to conciliate his nephew's self-esteem bore
disappointing fruit.

XIII

The Kaiser, in June 1894, celebrated with much pomp and
circumstance the opening of the Kiel Canal, to which his acquisition of Heligoland lent in his mind security.   He informed Queen
Victoria that the canal was designed "to promote the union of
nations and the peaceful development of their wealth."   Every
foreign country sent a naval squadron to join the' procession
which the Kaiser led through the new waterway in the *Hohenzollern* (June 20).   France, at the persuasion of her ally Russia,
reluctantly joined in the demonstration.   The Prince refrained
from attending this illusory carnival of peace, but his son, the
Duke of York, represented his mother and himself on board the
royal yacht *Osborne*.

The distasteful demeanour of the Kaiser at Cowes which   1895
reached a climax in 1895, strengthened rather than weakened the   Ætat. 53
Prince's sense of the need of handling his nephew with care.
Critical importance attached, in the Prince's eyes, to the choice
of a successor to Sir Edward Malet, whose retirement from the
British Embassy at Berlin was due at the end of that year.
Although Sir Edward had in earlier years done much to conciliate
the Kaiser and German public opinion, Germany's growing
jealousy of England had recently embarrassed his relations with
the German Court and with the Wilhelmstrasse.   Diplomatic
appointments always interested the Prince, but he discovered in
the one now at issue exceptional fascination.   The selection, he
averred, should propitiate his nephew, and Lord Salisbury would

find the task intricate and difficult. The question was broached before the Kaiser left Cowes in August 1895. He let the Queen and the Prince know that he desired a British soldier at the Berlin Embassy, and urged the choice of Lord Wolseley. The Prince was doubtful. The long rivalry between Lord Wolseley and the Duke of Cambridge was raging at the moment. Neither the Queen nor Lord Salisbury was unfavourable, but the Queen finally wrote to her grandson that Lord Wolseley was unavailable in view of the fact that he was succeeding the Duke of Cambridge as Commander-in-Chief (August 28). Other names were tentatively proposed by the Queen, the Prince, or Lord Salisbury. Lord Londonderry, the Prince's friend, Lord Jersey, Sir Francis Grenfell, and Lord Cromer were all suggested. Sir Francis Grenfell alone possessed the military qualifications for which the Kaiser yearned. But all these names the Kaiser regarded coldly, and on Lord Cromer he laid a peremptory veto. Lord Salisbury thereupon fell back on professional diplomatists. He was divided in his mind between Sir Edmund Monson, then at Vienna, and Sir Frank Lascelles, then at St. Petersburg. The Prince had long been on friendly terms with Sir Frank, and he intervened strongly in his favour, at the same time suggesting that Lord Cromer should be Sir Frank's successor at St. Petersburg. This ancillary suggestion came to nothing, but Sir Frank Lascelles finally carried the day. The Queen explained to the Kaiser that he was of good family, with a wife "clever and agreeable though not good-looking," and might be relied upon to maintain good relations between the two countries. The Kaiser repressed his misgivings, and promised to do his "best to help Lascelles." The settlement of the thorny question gave general relief. While the controversy was at its last stage the Prince went over, as was his wont, from Homburg to dine with his sister, the Empress Frederick, at Friedrichshof, and there he met his nephew, who, in spite of their embarrassed relations at Cowes, received him cordially. The Kaiser reported the friendly meeting by telegram to the Queen (August 27).

Lascelles, to whose victory the Prince contributed, took up his post at Berlin in November. He arrived on the eve of the acute crisis which disturbances in the Transvaal provoked in the relations of the two countries. The tension was hardly favourable to the Kaiser's reception of the new Ambassador. Yet before

many months had passed, the two men were on terms of genial
familiarity. The Prince's intimacy with Lascelles also developed,
and they were soon corresponding regularly and confidentially.
The Prince's knowledge of the Kaiser's and of the German
ministers' fluctuating attitude to himself and to his country
grew fuller and more precise. It was often Sir Frank's
unenviable duty to report to uncle and nephew the free
criticisms which the one passed on the other, and the delicate
communications of which he was the transmitter put heavy
strains on his tact and peace of mind. His anxiety to avoid
giving offence in either quarter at the same time as he endeavoured to be scrupulously accurate, was bound to involve
him in misunderstandings, especially with the Prince, both before
and after his accession. The Kaiser's regard for Sir Frank was
proof against the differences between England and Germany
which steadily increased during his tenure of the Berlin Embassy.
It was inevitable that the future should raise doubts in the minds
of King Edward and others whether the choice of 1895 fully
justified itself—whether Sir Frank's temperament was sufficiently
robust to allow him to hold his own against the Kaiser's blandishments when international differences required him to assume an
attitude of resolute firmness towards the wayward monarch to
whom he was accredited.

CHAPTER XXXVI

RUSSIA, 1886-1898—THE TENSION RELAXED

I

1886
———
Ætat. 44

THE Prince's bitter political feeling against Russia, which in boyhood Lord Palmerston and in manhood Lord Beaconsfield kept well alive, had been occasionally assuaged but not materially diminished by domestic association with the Russian royal family. Tsar Alexander III., although he was the husband of the Princess of Wales's sister, had, by his treatment of Prince Alexander of Bulgaria and by the defiant advances of his troops in Central Asia, stirred the Prince's wrath as potently as his father, Alexander II., had done by his menaces of Turkey in 1876-80. In June 1886 the Prince's anger against the Tsar blazed as fiercely as ever when Russia suddenly repudiated the clause of the Treaty of Berlin which had, on Lord Beaconsfield's urgent plea, made Batoum on the Black Sea a free port; and though during the same month he showed the Tsar's pleasant-mannered cousin and aide-de-camp, Grand Duke Michael Michaelovitch, marked social attentions while the Grand Duke was on a visit to England, he was indisposed to qualify his condemnation of what he regarded as Russia's political perfidy.[1]

The Prince's Liberal friends had often pleaded for an accommodation between Russia and England on crucial points of estrangement in both Asia and Europe. The Prince treated the argument with brief spells of tolerance, but some fresh manifestation of Russia's aggressiveness always intervened to revive in force his traditional distrust. Influences, however, developed in the Prince's personal environment from 1886 onwards to moderate his Russian rancours and even to urge him to explore the possi-

[1] Russian Archives, M. de Staal to M. de Giers, 26th May/7th June 1886.

680

bilities of an Anglo-Russian *entente*. At the Russian Embassy
in London there was, from 1884 until 1902, a representative of
Russia, M. de Staal, whose charm of personality caught the
Prince's notice.   None of M. de Staal's recent predecessors, Count
Schouvaloff (1874–79), Count Lobanoff (1879–82), and Baron
Mohrenheim (1882–84), had found much favour in the Prince's
sight.   M. de Staal's attractive manner made him a popular
figure in English society, and intimacy with the Prince
developed steadily during the Russian Ambassador's nineteen
years' tenure of office.   From M. de Staal the Prince could
at least learn Russia's point of view in accents which were
pleasant to his ear.   But an English counsellor in whom he
put much faith was also at hand to help in qualifying the
Prince's anti-Russian prejudice.   Towards the end of 1886
Sir Robert Morier, his friend and protégé, who at the end
of 1884 had been appointed, largely by his influence, British
Ambassador at St. Petersburg, was persuading him that an
effort to cultivate Russia's friendship might prove to England's
advantage.   Sir Robert was no friend of Prince Bismarck's policy,
which sought to make Russia Germany's tool.   Sir Robert seized
the opportunity of a visit to Sandringham over New Year's Day,
1887, to lay his views before the Prince.   The Prince was cautious
in comment, but on leaving Sandringham Morier wrote restrainedly
to the Prince (January 7) of his "great satisfaction at having had
the opportunity of stating my views to Y.R.H., and explaining
some of the prevailing misconceptions."   Sir Robert admitted
the "dangers and difficulties of the relations between us and
Russia," but he added "the alternative of maintaining peace and
of steering out of troubled into smooth waters should not be lost
sight of."   Morier's argument had its effect on the Prince.

Other incidents rapidly followed to stimulate the Prince's sympathies in the new direction.   In the autumn of 1887 (September 6)
both the Prince and the Tsar joined one of those large family
parties which the King and Queen of Denmark loved to assemble
at Fredensborg.   The King and Queen of Greece were of the
company.   The Tsar and the Prince had not met of late, but the
sympathetic atmosphere encouraged friendly intercourse in spite
of current political dissension.   The thorny phases of Anglo-
Russian relations were avoided.   But the Tsar and the Prince
found in the dubious character and aims of Prince William of

1887
Ætat. 45

Prussia, who was nearing his accession to the German throne, a theme on which they found themselves in agreement. The Prussian Prince had already courted the Tsar's favour by slandering his uncle and by pandering to the Tsar's political suspicions and dislike of England. The Prince had no difficulty in dispelling the equivocal impressions which Prince William had sought to leave on the Tsar's mind, by pointing to the dangers lurking in his nephew's wild militarist ambitions. Those ambitions might, the Prince suggested, in spite of all Prince William's fair words to the Russian ruler, find a vent in an attack on Russia as readily as on England or France.[1]

The meeting of the Prince and the Tsar had a curious sequel which lent it point. Rumours of their friendly talk reached Prince William in Berlin and caused him concern. The cunning plot, on which he prided himself, of driving a wedge between the Tsar and his uncle seemed to be encountering an unexpected check. The disconcerted intriguer took a prompt and farcical step with a view to recovering any lost ground. The Tsar travelled home from Denmark through Germany, and at Wittenberg, on the way to Berlin, Prince William before daybreak boarded the Tsar's train. He thought to repeat to the Tsar his insincere flatteries and to discover precisely what had passed in Denmark. But the Tsar professed himself too sleepy to gratify the curiosity of his impetuous and inopportune visitor, and the future Kaiser, baffled in his vain manœuvre, returned to Berlin to lend a ready ear to the anti-Russian growlings of his military coterie.[2]

II

Later in the year a fertilising breeze, coming from a very different quarter, played on the Prince's nascent Russian sympathies. Lord Randolph Churchill, after his sudden retirement from Lord Salisbury's ministry in December 1886, became, despite Queen Victoria's protests, one of the Prince's most constant companions in society and on the turf. The Prince discussed politics with Lord Randolph almost as freely as in former days he had discussed them with Sir Charles Dilke, and he fancied that he discovered in Lord Randolph's haphazard and often malevolent

---

[1] *Die Grosse Politik*, vi. 326–33.
[2] Bismarck, *New Chapters of Autobiography*, p. 263.

judgements, some promising intuitions. In November 1887 Lord
Randolph told the Prince of his intention to take a holiday in
Russia. Lady Randolph had never visited Russia, and Lord
Randolph was anxious to show his wife the country. The Prince
was encouraging. At his suggestion the Princess gave Lord
Randolph a private letter of introduction to her sister the
Tsaritza. The Prince warned his friend, who since his desertion
of Lord Salisbury's government had shown no kindness for it,
against presenting the letter through M. de Giers, the Russian
Chancellor, or of giving his visit any sort of official colour.

At Berlin Lord Randolph met Sir Robert Morier on leave
from St. Petersburg, and Sir Robert reinforced the Prince's
warning, bidding him avoid any discussion of the international
situation with the authorities at St. Petersburg. But such
prudent counsels were lost on Lord Randolph. No sooner did he
arrive in the Russian capital then he threw discretion to the winds.
He succeeded in interviewing not only the Russian Chancellor,
but the Tsar himself, and aired opinions on foreign policy which
were anathema to Queen Victoria and her Prime Minister. He
acknowledged the Prince's responsibility for his Russian visit, and
implicitly made him a party to his Russian advances by sending
him detailed reports of them. The Prince, although he communicated Lord Randolph's letters to his mother and Lord Salisbury,
incurred the suspicions of both. Lord Randolph, according to
his communications to the Prince, proclaimed in all Russian
quarters—official and social—a complete identity of interest
between England and Russia. The Tsar, Lord Randolph informed
the Prince, was anticipating early war with Austria, and if Germany
stood by her ally, with that Power as well. He was filled with
"an extreme desire" for an Anglo-Russian understanding "une
fois pour tout." Lord Randolph assured the Tsar that he was
working to the same end. Rumours spread through the chancelleries of Europe that Lord Randolph was revolutionising British
policy in regard to Russia, and that Anglo-Russian dissensions
would soon be things of the past. Protests against Lord Randolph's unauthorised representations came from the Foreign
Office in London and from the British Embassies in foreign
capitals. Sir Robert Morier described Lord Randolph as "a
dangerous man." Lord Lytton, the British Ambassador in
Paris, heatedly denounced his recklessness. Berlin affected to

regard the episode as a Machiavellian move on England's part against Germany.

The Prince was well-nigh alone among onlookers in taking a detached view of his incautious friend's sympathetic attitude to Russia. His acknowledgements of Lord Randolph's letters showed no abatement of confidence or cordiality. When Lord Randolph returned to London in January 1888, the Prince was absent at Cannes. But he wrote to Lord Randolph bidding him call upon Lord Salisbury and come to terms with him. The Prime Minister consented to receive the prodigal, but he confined his remarks, Lord Randolph reported to the Prince, to the prospects of the Unionist party, which he pronounced to be "very fair."

The Prince found Queen Victoria's irritation more difficult to placate. She reproached her son with his "high opinion of a man devoid of all principle, who holds the most insular and dangerous doctrines on foreign affairs, and who is impulsive and utterly unreliable" (Queen to Prince, January 3, 1888). She entreated her son to cease to correspond with Lord Randolph, or at any rate, if they met, to open his eyes to the perils attaching to his conduct.

"We must try," she wrote to the Prince (Feb. 6, 1888), "and not alienate all our best allies, and we are, I am thankful to say, on the best of terms with Germany, Austria, and Italy [i.e. with the Triple Alliance], which is, as you know well, of the utmost importance and the only means of keeping Russian aggressiveness in check. If Lord Randolph Churchill should begin in this dangerous strain, you will be prepared to meet it. . . . And if you can keep him from publicly holding such very dangerous doctrines, you will be doing great good."[1]

But the Prince remained impenitent. The need of relaxing the old tension with Russia was becoming a fixed belief. He not only continued to treat Lord Randolph with the same friendliness as

[1] The episode of Lord Randolph's Russian visit is narrated in long letters from Lord Randolph Churchill to the Prince, dated 29th and 30th December 1887; 11th January and 11th February 1888, and in correspondence between the Queen and the Prince, dated 1st and 3rd January, and 6th February. There are interesting communications from M. de Staal to M. de Giers on the subject in the Russian Archives at Chesham House, dated respectively January 23/February 4, 31 January/12 February, and 6/18 February 1888. See also Winston Churchill's *Life of Lord Randolph Churchill*, ii. 360 *et seq.*

before, but sought other opportunities of probing the possibilities
of political friendship with the Tsar and Russia.

III

Lord Randolph's friend and close parliamentary ally Sir Henry
Drummond Wolff had been introduced by Lord Randolph to the
Prince's circle.   The cynical frankness of Wolff's conversation
and his lively epistolary style made him welcome to the Prince
as a companion and a correspondent.   On abandoning the House
of Commons in 1885 he had rejoined the Diplomatic service in
which he began his career, and was soon appointed Minister at
Teheran (December 1887).   Persia was a lively battle-ground for
Anglo-Russian rivalry.   Russia and England were hotly competing against one another for commercial domination of the
country.   At Teheran, Drummond Wolff narrowly studied
Russian policy, and in vivacious letters to the Prince he kept
him informed of all the intrigues at the Shah's court.   With
infinite spirit he narrated his good-humoured skirmishes with the
Russian envoy, Prince Nicholas Dolgorouky.   Yet Wolff came
before long to share Lord Randolph's hopes of an Anglo-Russian
entente.   He conceived a plan of reconciling the two countries'
respective interests in Persia.   The Shah, Nasr-ul-Din, although
he was finding it hard to resist Russia's importunities, still
cherished the view which he had formed in early life, that his
country would benefit by closer commercial relations, not with
Russia alone, but with the other mercantile powers of the west.
While always loyal to oriental habits and to oriental conceptions
of autocracy, he had shown his interest in European civilisation
by his continental tours, one of which, in 1873, had included
England.   Early in 1889 he proposed to revisit Europe and to
bring England within his itinerary.   In the summer of 1889
Drummond Wolff temporarily returned to London in order
to make preparations for the Shah's reception.

The English government and the Prince favoured the Shah's
visit.   In the ceremonial programme which was arranged by the
Foreign Office in consultation with Drummond Wolff, the Prince
agreed to play a prominent part.   Visits to the nobility alike in
their town mansions and their country residences were admitted
to the scheme of hospitality.   The Prince encouraged many

1889
―
Ætat. 47

intimate friends—Lord Cadogan, Lord Rosebery, and the
Rothschilds among them—to offer the Shah elaborate
entertainment.

The Persian monarch arrived in the Thames on 1st July in
the royal yacht, the *Victoria and Albert*, which conveyed him
from Antwerp, where he had been the guest of the King of
the Belgians. The Prince and his two sons awaited him at
Tilbury and accompanied him to Westminster Bridge, where
he disembarked. The Shah was lodged in Buckingham Palace.
For a week the Prince was assiduous in personal attendance.
He went with the Shah to the Guildhall, where the Lord Mayor
and Corporation of London presented him with an address (July 3).
The Prince gave a garden party on the 4th July at Marlborough
House in the visitor's honour at which Queen Victoria made one
of her rare appearances. He accompanied the Shah to Kempton
Park Races on the 5th, and to a Crystal Palace Fête next day.
On the 7th and 8th of July the Prince and Princess stayed with
Lord Salisbury at Hatfield to meet the Shah. There the Prince
and he took leave of one another.[1]

The Prince, through the Shah's capable interpreter, Aboul
Kassem Khan (Nasr-ul-Mulk), who had been educated at
Balliol College, Oxford, and spoke English perfectly, found
opportunity for much conversation with the Persian monarch.
He professed sympathy with the Shah's wish to develop his
country's natural resources and to introduce foreign capital,
and he assented to his view that both England and Russia
might prove of service to him in his economic aims. Drummond
Wolff, too, discussed the Persian question with the Prince, and
easily convinced him that Persia offered propitious scope for
the promotion of Anglo-Russian goodwill. The Prince was an
attentive listener to Drummond Wolff's scheme of an economic
partition of Persia into two spheres of influence, one to be
regulated by England and the other by Russia. The Prince
advised Drummond Wolff to lay his plans before the Tsar. The
diplomatist caught eagerly at the suggestion. The Prince advised
him to return to Teheran through Berlin, where the Tsar was

---

[1] From Hatfield the Shah made a tour through the manufacturing towns
of Birmingham, Sheffield, Manchester, Glasgow and Newcastle, and visited
many noblemen in Scotland. He quitted England for France on the 29th
July. A few years later he met his death at the hands of a Persian assassin
(May 1, 1896).

expected in October on a visit to the German Court.[1]   The Prince
not merely furnished Drummond Wolff with an introduction to
the Tsar, but on meeting the Tsar once more in the early autumn
at Fredensborg at another party of his wife's family, he requested
the Russian ruler to give Drummond Wolff an attentive hearing.

Drummond Wolff omitted to communicate with the Foreign
Office before he confided to the Prince the details of his Persian
scheme.   Lord Salisbury complained to Queen Victoria that he
heard the whole story, including the Prince's personal intervention
with the Tsar, for the first time from the Prince's lips.   The
Prime Minister resented the direct appeal to the Tsar over his
head, but he was not averse from Drummond Wolff's general
principles, though he deprecated precipitate action and judged
Wolff's Persian dream unlikely to come true for at least a
generation.

Drummond Wolff left England on his return to Persia in
October 1889, and at Berlin he presented to the Tsar the Prince's
letter of introduction.   At the audience which the Russian ruler
readily accorded him, the Tsar seemed to Drummond Wolff to be
favourably impressed by his proposal.

"I am most desirous," the Tsar said, according to Drummond
Wolff's report to Lord Salisbury, "to come to an understanding
with England in Persia.   We have no interests in common in
Europe.   Our common interests lie in Asia.   There I desire to
live in friendship with her, and to establish an understanding
which will enable us to be friends."

In the course of the interview the Tsar expressed a strong personal
affection for the Prince and Princess of Wales, and added that
" one of his greatest wishes was to welcome them in Russia, where
everything was always prepared for their reception." [2]

The Prince, by bringing the Tsar into direct touch with
Drummond Wolff and his Persian project, was moving ahead of
the current goal of diplomacy.   The immediate outcome of
Wolff's effort was negligible.   The Tsar's advisers held that the
Prince's friend underrated the obstacles which the Persian government, in spite of the Shah's amiable professions, was certain to
place in the way of his plan.[3]   While, in British interests,

[1] Drummond Wolff's *Rambling Recollections*, ii. 366 *seq.*
[2] *Ibid.*, ii. 360-70.
[3] M. de Staal to Giers, 23rd October/4th November 1889; Lord Salisbury
to Queen, 8th November 1889.

1889
Ætat. 47

Drummond Wolff helped to establish the Imperial Bank at Teheran, Russian influence over Persia continued to grow—to the disparagement of British influence. Yet the seed which Drummond Wolff sowed, with the Prince's encouragement, in due time blossomed. In 1907, in the sixth year of King Edward's reign, Russia and England made that partition of their respective interests in Persia the desirability of which Drummond Wolff brought to the Prince's approving notice eighteen years before.

IV

The Prince's pro-Russian predilections saw no immediate development after his open-minded discussions with Lord Randolph and Sir Henry Drummond Wolff. The Russian Government reverted in the next few years to its traditional attitude and showed little inclination to conciliate English goodwill. In 1891 she gave a fresh display of her intractability by a defiant advance on the Pamirs to the north of Afghanistan which drove the Prince's friend, Sir Robert Morier, almost to despair of a favourable change in Anglo-Russian relations. The consummation of the long-threatened Franco-Russian alliance, which the Kaiser regarded as aimed at the Triple Alliance and other observers as aimed at England, evoked no enthusiasm in the latter country in view of the growing friction between England and France. Yet despite the unpromising diplomatic atmosphere the Prince was drawing closer his domestic ties with the Tsar, and he remained sanguine that political advantages might yet come of the personal bond. The Tsar and the Prince met at the family gatherings of the Danish royal family in 1889, 1891, and 1892, and though the Tsar refrained from political conversation, he tacitly assented to the Prince's protestations of his wish to work for the general peace of Europe. In May 1892, when they both attended the celebration of the King and Queen of Denmark's golden wedding, the Prince commended the Tsar's intention of visiting his nephew the Kaiser at Kiel on leaving Denmark. The meeting was a desirable pledge of peace, he told the German Minister at the Danish Court—Freiherr von den Brücken—the only diplomatist whom he received owing to mourning for the Duke of Clarence.[1]

[1] *Die Grosse Politik*, vii. 407.

Matrimonial events in the Tsar's family during 1894 favoured the growth of personal amity. In July 1894 the Princess of Wales and her daughters attended at St. Petersburg the wedding of her niece the Grand Duchess Xenia, the Tsar's e dest daughter, to her cousin the Grand Duke Alexander Michaelovitch, whose father, Grand Duke Michael Nicolaievitch, was long one of the Prince's cosmopolitan circle on the Riviera. But of more significant promise was the betrothal (in April) of the Tsar's heir, the Tsarevitch Nicholas, to the Princess Alix of Hesse, daughter of the Prince's favourite sister, the late Princess Alice. A little later the Prince urged on the Queen as "an excellent idea" the bestowal on the Tsar of an Honorary Colonelcy of an English cavalry regiment. The Prince reported to his mother the information which reached him from St. Petersburg that the Tsar welcomed the suggestion, adding that a light cavalry regiment or the 16th Lancers would be an appropriate choice. But this precise effort at conciliation was frustrated by news in September of Tsar Alexander III.'s illness. On 30th September the Tsar was removed in a serious condition from St. Petersburg to Livadia in the Crimea. No improvement followed, and on the 31st October the Prince and Princess hurried from London to their brother-in-law's deathbed. The Tsar died the next day at the premature age of forty-nine. The Prince and Princess reached Livadia on 3rd November when all was over, and when the new Tsar Nicholas II. had succeeded to his father's place. The Prince prolonged his stay in Russia for more than a month. He seized the mournful opportunity of pressing forward his design of an Anglo-Russian political rapprochement.

The Prince travelled with the funeral cortège of the dead ruler from Livadia to Moscow (November 8 to 11), and on the sad journey spent his fifty-third birthday. Crowds of kneeling peasants in tears made a profound impression on the English visitors. The Prince was at the side of the new Tsar Nicholas through the long funeral ceremonies—first at the Archangel Church in the Kremlin at Moscow (November 11), and finally in the fortress cathedral of St. Peter and Paul at St. Petersburg, where the dead Tsar was interred in the Imperial vault (November 19). In St. Petersburg, to the satisfaction of the Russian Court, the Duke of York joined his parents.

The Prince, on arriving at the Russian capital, described

his recent experience in a letter to Lady Londonderry (November 14):

> "Our visit to Russia," he wrote, "has indeed been a very sad one, and though, alas, we arrived too late to find the Emperor alive, I am glad we came here, as we have, I think, given consolation to the Empress, the Princess especially, who is so devoted to her sister, as you know. We have indeed had immense deal of travelling since a fortnight, first from north to south and then the reverse. At Livadia the weather was lovely, like on the Riviera and in very similar scenery. Then on our way to Moscow it got bitterly cold, but now it is dull and gloomy just like our atmosphere in London at this time of year. We have continual services every day, which are most impressive, and the singing is beautiful."

The Russian people, as well as the imperial family, were gratefully impressed by the Prince and Princess's practical marks of sympathy with them in their season of grief. According to a report to the Foreign Office from Sir Frank Lascelles, then English Ambassador in St. Petersburg (November 9), the international relations sensibly improved as soon as the Prince reached the country. The favourable impression was deepened by the ready assent of the Prince to stay on after the obsequies were completed (November 19).

An event of great import in the life of the new Tsar was impending. Just a week after the close of the funeral ceremonies, on the 26th, the Prince, with his wife and son, was present at the marriage, in the private chapel in the Winter Palace, of the new Tsar with the Prince's niece, Princess Alix of Hesse. In agreement with the Prince's recommendation, Queen Victoria offered the bridegroom on his wedding-day the Honorary Colonelcy of the Scots Greys. The Tsar reciprocated the honour by creating the Prince Honorary Colonel of the Kieff (27th) Regiment of Russian Dragoons.

On 2nd December the Prince and his son, after taking part in the main nuptial festivities, left on their homeward journey. The Princess remained with her widowed sister for another two months. *En route* the Prince and his son paused at Berlin to call on the new German Chancellor, Prince von Hohenlohe, and to visit the Empress Frederick at Friedrichshof, where his nephew the Kaiser made him a complimentary call. The Prince was jubilant over the political promise of his Russian sojourn, but the Kaiser moodily credited his uncle with insidiously working in St. Petersburg against Germany and himself. The Prince's satisfaction was not clouded by his nephew's suspicion. He reached London from Berlin at noon on 6th December and proceeded in the afternoon to Windsor to acquaint his mother with what had come under his notice during his month's absence from home.

The Prince's energetic display of sympathy with the Russian Crown in its vicissitudes was approved by the English people and by the government of which Lord Rosebery was then the head. The belief spread that the convincing evidence which the Prince had given of his personal attachment to Russia might prove a new guarantee of European peace by linking Russia and England in friendly bonds. The Queen's ministers laid emphatic stress on the sound public service which the Prince was rendering—in a degree without obvious precedent in his career.

Lord Rosebery, the Prime Minister, wrote to him from 10 Downing Street on the day of his arrival in London :

I am anxious to be among the first to welcome your Royal Highness home, and to express my deep sense of the good and patriotic work that you have accomplished since you left England. Never has your Royal Highness stood so high in the national esteem as to-day, for never have you had such an opportunity. That at last has come and has enabled you to justify the highest anticipations, and to render a signal service to your country as well as to Russia and the peace of the world.

Sir William Harcourt on the same date wrote in equally appreciative terms. The Prince's Russian visit had, Sir William averred, established "not only in fact, but (what is not less important) in public opinion and sentiment, the most intimate and friendly relations with Russia. This is an experiment," he added, "which has never been yet fairly tried in foreign affairs, and it is my humble opinion that there is none which is more likely to minister to the cause of peace and good-will." [1] From humbler quarters came like congratulations. William Rogers, Rector of Bishopsgate, a genial philanthropist with whom the Prince was always on friendly terms, wrote : "You have done your work manfully and well" (December 6).

[1] This letter is printed at length in Gardiner's *Life of Sir William Harcourt*, ii. 326.

V

The change of ruler in Russia—the death of Alexander III. and the accession of Nicholas II.—thus seemed to favour that rapprochement between England and Russia to which the Prince had been for some years inclining. Tsar Alexander III., though he loved peace and quiet and found his chief happiness at his domestic hearth, reconciled himself sluggishly to new turns of policy even when he approved them. The new Tsar, by nature modest and retiring, had committed himself to no well-defined political views during his father's lifetime. At his accession his liking for the English royal family, and his wife's kinship with Queen Victoria and the Prince, seemed to the Prince a promising foundation on which to rear a political union between England and Russia. The Prince regarded the new ruler as a trustworthy auxiliary in the formation of an Anglo-Russian *entente*. To an Austrian friend the Prince wrote hopefully during his stay at St. Petersburg: "The character and personality of the new Tsar give assurance of the benefits which would come of an alliance (*Verbindung*) between England and Russia."

Politicians, at a greater distance, read the portents in a similar light. Count Kalnoky, the Austrian Foreign Minister, who was no friend of Russia, confessed to Count von Eulenberg, the German Ambassador in Vienna, a fear that the Prince's influence with the Tsar and the popular acceptance in England of the Prince's professions of tenderness for Russia, might easily issue in a political combination. If the new Tsar should adopt Liberal principles in his domestic affairs, the English people, Kalnoky prophesied, would, under the Prince's influence, welcome with open arms an Anglo-Russian *entente*. The two English political parties were agreed in their distrust of Germany. There was consequently every prospect in the Austrian statesman's view of the fruition, under Nicholas II.'s auspices, of the Prince's endeavour to weld England and Russia together.[1]

Count Kalnoky's forecast came true—but more slowly than he or the Prince anticipated. Neither the Austrian statesman nor the Prince took into adequate account the stubborn conservatism

[1] See reports of Count von Eulenberg, German Ambassador at Vienna, to the German Chancellor, Prince von Hohenlohe, 14th December 1894, of conversations with Count Kalnoky, in *Die Grosse Politik*, vol. ix. p. 181.

of Russian bureaucracy or the new Tsar's weakness of will and his reactionary leanings. Though Tsar Nicholas possessed all the domestic virtues and cherished to the last the affection which he formed for the Prince in early years, his character was vitiated by a lack of education and of political insight. In both home and foreign affairs he yielded easily to pressure from one quarter or another. In no direction was he capable of taking a firm stand. He was soon wavering between political friendship and political enmity with England. His intellectual helplessness invited the terrible tragedy which ultimately ended his inglorious career.

1895
Ætat. 53

The Prince was by no means oblivious of the Tsar's infirmity of purpose. He viewed with dismay early manifestations of the Tsar's autocratic idiosyncrasies.[1] Yet the checks which the Tsar's character and conduct promised to impose on the design of an Anglo-Russian *entente* failed to daunt the Prince in his pursuit of it. Before the end of 1895, the veteran note of hostility to England was sounded afresh in the Russian press, and Queen Victoria was moved to write in protest to the Tsar. There was a difference of view between the two governments as to the handling of uncompliant Turkey, and France was pressing her new ally to help her to the recovery of Egypt. But the political differences failed to deter the Prince from giving the Tsar proof of his personal goodwill in the hope that the Russian ruler might prove amenable to arguments in favour of political co-operation.

Very cordial were the Prince's congratulations to the Tsar on the birth of his first child, the Grand Duchess Olga. Although the Prince declared himself disappointed that the child was not a boy, he sought in the Tsar's new paternal rôle a means of strengthening the domestic solidarity of the royal houses with a view to political friendship.

VI

Meanwhile the Prince was scanning attentively the sort of influence which the Tsar's ministers exerted on their master and on their country's policy. When in Russia he had treated

[1] Within little more than a month after the Prince's departure from Russia, the Tsar shocked English political sentiment by a speech in which he replied at the Winter Palace to various addresses of congratulation on his accession. He then denounced in emphatic tones as "senseless dreams" all schemes of popular government, and declared his deliberate resolve "to maintain for the good of the whole nation the principle of absolute autocracy as firmly and as strongly as did my lamented father."

1896
Ætat. 54 M. de Giers, the Chancellor and Minister of Foreign Affairs, with much cordiality, and when that Russian statesman died soon after they parted (March 1895), he sent through Sir Frank Lascelles, the British Ambassador at St. Petersburg, a message of condolence to his widow in which he described her husband's death as "a loss to Europe." To the Prince's satisfaction the new Tsar Nicholas offered the vacant post to the Prince's friend, M. de Staal, the Russian Ambassador in London, but M. de Staal declined the offer on the ground of his long absence from home. The post was thereupon conferred, to the Prince's disappointment, on Prince Lobanoff, who for a short time, 1879–82, had been Russian Ambassador in London and whose attitude to England was one of ill-concealed jealousy. It was therefore with no profound regret that the Prince learnt of Prince Lobanoff's premature and unexpected death on 31st August 1896, within some sixteen months of his high appointment. In the Prince's view there was more imperative need than ever of the presence at the Russian foreign office of a friend to England. In spite of M. de Staal's recent refusal, the Prince's thought promptly reverted to him. Without a moment's delay he telegraphed (September 1, 1896) to Queen Victoria asking her "to try her best to appoint as Lobanoff's successor, if only for a short time," that "charming and popular" diplomatist. The Prince knew that he could thoroughly rely on M. de Staal for the encouragement of Anglo-Russian amity. His appointment, he adjured the Queen, "was absolutely necessary for the maintenance of better relations between England and Russia." The Queen brought the Prince's message to the notice of Lord Salisbury, but the Prime Minister replied that there was no justification for interfering in any way with the Tsar's choice of Prince Lobanoff's successor.[1]

[1] After some delay Count Muravieff, a man of shrewdness if of limited ability, who had been brought up in the school of Prince Gortschakoff, was selected for the vacant office on the suggestion of the Tsar's mother. After holding subordinate diplomatic posts in Berlin, Stockholm, and Paris, the Count had, since 1893, been Russian Minister at Copenhagen, where he enjoyed opportunities of close intercourse with the Danish royal family and came into occasional touch with the Prince on his frequent visits to Denmark. But Count Muravieff, as the Prince well knew, was no friend of England. He hungered for Russian expansion in the Far East at the expense of China. An admirer of Prince Bismarck, he preferred the German connection to the English, and at the Kaiser's prompting played with the fancy of a European coalition against the British Empire in the dark days of the Boer war. His tenure of his new office however was, to the advantage of England, cut short by death on 21st June 1900.

VII

Meanwhile the Queen had invited the Tsar and the Tsaritza, 1896 with their infant daughter, to visit her privately at Balmoral in the Ætat. 54 autumn of 1896. The invitation was promptly accepted. The Prince welcomed the coming presence of the Tsar and his family in his own country. But his conceptions of the situation made him impatient with the Queen's offer of a merely domestic reception. He saw in the visit, if fitly contrived, a fresh guarantee of an Anglo-Russian political agreement. A ceremonial welcome was to his mind essential. At Homburg, where he was taking his customary cure in August, he heard of the Queen's intentions. With prompt energy he drafted an elaborately detailed programme which would lend the occasion befitting pomp. In forwarding his plan to his mother's private secretary (Sir Arthur Bigge), he wrote (August 29, 1896) :

Though I know the Queen expects the visit to Balmoral to be a private one, still, as it is the first time that the Emperor and Empress visit our shores in the high position they occupy, she would, I am sure, wish all honour to be done to them in the eyes of the world, especially in those of Russia. I am so anxious that the arrival should be marked with every possible compliment for the Emperor.

At Leith, the port of debarkation, the Prince recommended that the visitors should be received in full state by guards of honour with the Duke of Connaught in the uniform of the Scots Guards, by the Lord Provost of Edinburgh, and by Lord Rosebery as Lord Lieutenant of the County. Guards of honour should also be stationed at Aberdeen and at Ballater stations, and "even one of a Highland regiment, or, if the worst comes to the worst, a volunteer one, at Balmoral itself." Among the suite appointed to attend upon the Tsar there should be a general officer of distinction, such as Sir John McNeill, "as the Russians, like the Austrians and Germans, think so much more of military rank than that of a civilian, however great his position may be." He further recommended that M. de Staal, the Russian Ambassador, should be the Tsar's fellow-guest at Balmoral, and that Lord Salisbury's presence would "have the best possible effect." The Queen was complacent. She wired to the Prince her acquiescence

1896
Ætat. 54

in his proposals. She acknowledged that they would make a good impression on Russia.

On 22nd September 1896 the Tsar and his family arrived at Leith in his yacht *Standart*. The Prince had been Lord Rosebery's guest at Dalmeny during the three previous days, and he now boarded the imperial yacht with his host and M. de Staal. After luncheon the Prince accompanied the imperial visitors to Balmoral, where they stayed twelve days. Lord Salisbury, the Prime Minister, in conformity with the Prince's suggestion, arrived as minister in attendance on the Queen. Amid the domestic festivities opportunity was found for much political discussion which satisfied the Prince that his friendly attitude to Russia might yet bear fruit.

The Tsar acknowledged a general wish to work with England. He deprecated any difficulty in regard to India but he sedulously avoided mention of Egypt. He admitted only a single theme of friction between the two countries—the opening of the Dardanelles to Russian ships, which he deemed a matter of primary importance. "He regretted William's injudicious policy and Germany's inimicality towards us (*i.e.* England)." Of the Franco-Russian alliance he spoke to the Queen with great frankness. She still cherished, in contrast with her eldest son, moral as well as political prejudices against France. She questioned the Tsar as to the reason of Russia's friendship. The young ruler ingenuously replied that the Triple Alliance was aimed at Russia and that Russia's request to join it was refused.[1] The Tsar conciliated his hostess by confessing that he had no liking for the current irreligion of France and had no personal enthusiasm for the French people. To Lord Salisbury the Tsar, at a private interview between the two, spoke in much the same strain, and the Prime Minister forwarded to the Prince a memorandum of what passed.

From Balmoral the Tsar proceeded to Portsmouth to pay a visit to France, which was made, according to Lascelles, "on his own initiative." The Queen, at the parting at Balmoral on 5th October, expressed the hope that her imperial guest and

---

[1] The Tsar seemed here to be scarcely accurate. According to a despatch of Sir Frank Lascelles (Nov. 20, 1896), Russia resented the Kaiser's refusal in 1890 to sanction Prince Bismarck's proposal to renew with Russia "the Reinsurance Treaty" of 1887 (see p. 658 *supra*). It was only after the rejection of her advance to Germany in 1890 that Russia signed the alliance with France.

kinsman would "tell France not to be so hostile to England." In conformity with the Prince's wish to extend to the Tsar all the formalities due to his rank, a British squadron convoyed the Tsar from Portsmouth. In mid-Channel a detachment of the French fleet replaced the British escort. The warmth of the French people's reception of the Tsar brought home to the Prince, and indeed to the world at large, the stability of the Franco-Russian alliance. The demonstration inspired a sagacious correspondent to urge shortly afterwards on Lord Salisbury the "great gain" it would be "to the world, and to England not least, if England could come to a friendly understanding" not with Russia alone but with France as well.[1] It was that twin goal which England was to reach under the auspices of the Prince as King Edward before many years had passed.

1896
Ætat. 54

VIII

The Prince did all he could in the years that followed the Tsar's visit to England to foster the affection which he had stirred in the young ruler. The Tsar's growing dependence on his wife, the Prince's niece, deepened, as time went on, the Tsar's tender interest in the fortunes of "the dear family," as he came to call the Prince's household. Intimate autograph letters in English constantly passed between the two. To "Dearest Uncle Bertie" the Tsar regularly reported his family affairs, always bringing his communications to a close "with Alix's and my tenderest love," and signing himself "Ever your most loving Nephew, Nicky." Shortly after his return to St. Petersburg from his foreign tour (February 3/15, 1896), the Tsar wrote confidingly to the Prince of his delight in wearing his new uniform of the Scots Greys on the occasion of his reception of a visiting delegation of officers of the regiment. On 1st/13th June 1897, when the Tsar announced to the Prince the birth of a second daughter, Tatiana, he added that he envied the good fortune of his uncle, the Grand Duke Serge, and of the Grand Duke's wife, Princess Elizabeth of Hesse, the Tsaritza's sister, in going to England for the celebration of Queen Victoria's Diamond Jubilee ("Serge and Ella must be envied, as they are going to witness all the jubilee festivities"). Politics

---

[1] G. W. E. Russell's *Life of Malcolm MacColl*, pp. 207-8. MacColl to Lord Salisbury, 27th August 1897.

1896
Ætat. 54

filled a subsidiary place in the correspondence, and the Tsar cautiously invited the views of his ministers before replying to the Prince's inquiries on any matters which touched politics. Rather characteristic are some sentences in a letter from the Tsar to his uncle, which bears date 14th/26th June 1898 :

"I regret," the Tsar wrote, "the delay in answering your inquiry concerning the Caucasian affair. Herewith I send you a short memorandum of Mr. Witte [Russian Minister of Finance] explaining briefly the reason why the proposition of the English capitalists cannot be accepted."

Unfortunately the Prince was not the only kinsman in high place with whom the Tsar was, through the greater part of his ill-starred reign, in regular communication. The Prince's nephew, the Kaiser, was all the time pestering the Russian monarch with letters which slandered his uncle and abounded in self-interested and menacing political advice or in false political rumours calculated to alienate Russia from England. Very striking is the contrast between the good-natured ease of the Prince and the laboured insincerity of the Kaiser in their epistolary intercourse with the luckless Tsar.

IX

1898
Ætat. 56

The Tsar gave in the course of 1898 striking proof of the discrepant mingling in his character of a pacific idealism with an obscurantist faith in autocracy and brute force. In that year he endorsed with every appearance of enthusiasm Count Muravieff's suggestion of a Utopian scheme for the abolition of war.[1] To the general surprise, Count Muravieff, on behalf of the Tsar, issued on August 24, 1898 a circular to all the Powers of the Old and New Worlds inviting representatives to a conference to consider the

---

[1] According to Count Witte, the Tsar's astute Finance Minister, the peace scheme was a rather cynical result of Russia's financial embarrassments, which did not allow her to bring the equipment of her army up to contemporary standards. In the summer of 1898, General Kuropatkin, Russia's Minister of War, demanded the re-arming of the Russian artillery on the ground that Austria was completing such a reform. Count Witte, when explaining to Count Muravieff that no money was available for the purpose, expressed a merely pious wish that the European Powers might agree to slacken their pace in improving and increasing their armaments. Count Muravieff took Count Witte's remark literally, and to Count Witte's surprise and annoyance straightway proposed the Hague Conference. The Tsar was influenced far more profoundly than his Foreign Minister by the idealist promise of the proposal (Count Witte's *Memoirs*, 96–97).

possibility of securing universal peace by means of an agreed
disarmament. Save among a pacifist minority which made itself
very audible in England and elsewhere, there was small faith in
the practical value of the Russian project. But Great Britain
and twenty-five other Powers accepted, in terms more or less
sympathetic, the Tsar's invitation to send envoys to the Hague,
there to discuss the theme in the following May. The suggested
agenda included not only the question of disarmament but also
the merciful relaxation of the laws of war and the creation of
efficient machinery of arbitration. The Prince, despite his desire
for peace, was for once in substantial accord with his nephew, the
Kaiser, in questioning whether much would come of the Tsar's
scheme. The Tsar's zeal was unaffected by the prevalent doubts.
Meeting the Duke of York at Copenhagen in October, on the
occasion of the funeral of their maternal grandmother, the Queen
of Denmark, the Tsar endeavoured to enlist the sympathies of the
Prince's son in a crusade against war. Meanwhile an enterprising
journalist of London, Mr. W. T. Stead, strenuously identified
himself with the Tsar's purpose. Hastening to Copenhagen,
Stead succeeded in obtaining an audience with the Tsar, who
talked eagerly to his interviewer of his Utopian hopes. Mr.
Stead, on his return home, organised a propagandist movement
throughout England. With characteristic assurance, he appealed
to the Prince of Wales to permit his son to head the agitation.
"The Duke," wrote the impulsive journalist to the Prince
(December 6, 1898), "is the only Englishman besides myself to
whom the Tsar has spoken freely on the subject of his desire for
the success of the Peace Conference." But the Prince declined
to allow his son to intervene. He deprecated his own or his
son's association with Mr. Stead's propagandism.

The Peace Conference met at the Hague on the date appointed
by the Tsar—18th May 1899. The Prince's friend, M. de Staal,
the Russian Ambassador in London, was elected President. But
the Tsar's expectations were doomed to disappointment. None
of the Great Powers were willing to entertain the suggestion of a
general disarmament, and Russia's scheme for a limitation of
armaments was decisively rejected. All that was effected was
the adoption by a majority of the delegates of resolutions in favour
of diminishing the brutalities of warfare, and for the establishment of a permanent Court of Arbitration. At the end of July

1898
Ætat. 56

1899
Ætat. 57

1899
Ætat. 57   the Conference dissolved after an agreement on these points was
reached.   The Kaiser wrote sceptically to Queen Victoria of the
result of "The Tsar's Peace Conference" (December 29, 1899).
He described the final conclusions as "not very lucid, and far
from reassuring."   The Kaiser's judgement coincided with that
of the Prince.   Events were to justify the scepticism of both
uncle and nephew.

CHAPTER XXXVII

THE CLASH WITH FRANCE, 1886–1900

FRANCE'S colonial ambitions, which involved continuous rivalry with England, put out of the question until the century was well ended any good understanding between the two countries. Internal political ferment, which gave an impression of France's instability, helped, too, to dishearten English friends who wished to see the international friction abate. Through the long series of Anglo-French colonial disputes the obvious interests of England came in the Prince's mind before all else, and he was always resolute in deprecation of anything like undue concession on the British government's part. But even when the clouds were blackest, the Prince never despaired of such an understanding with France as he had championed in his early years, and was to help to fruition subsequently. The Prince was slow to interrupt his visits to Paris or the Riviera where his personal popularity was long proof against the slanders with which the French press assailed his country and her government. In the spring of 1887 the Prince was at Cannes when an alarming earthquake took place, and his cool and courageous behaviour during the peril enhanced his fame in Southern France.

The French monarchist aristocracy continued to figure largely among his hosts and guests on the Riviera, and at times he impetuously flattered such society by disparaging the bourgeois manners of the leaders of the Republic whom he held responsible for the hostility to England   Only when the Anglophobic fury of the Paris mob descended to the lowest depths of malevolence at the extreme end of the century was the Prince's name dragged through French mud. His resentment was fierce, and for a time he absented himself from France, but even then he was solaced by signs that the Quai d'Orsay was seeking to conjure up a new spirit of harmony in Anglo-French relations, and his memories of his many efforts to promote an Anglo-French *entente*, after a brief interval, hopefully revived.

I

From 1887 to 1889 the peace of Europe seemed threatened by delusive menace of a Royalist reaction in France. A traitor was lurking in the Republican camp. General Boulanger, Minister of War in M. de Freycinet's cabinet, courted popular favour by vowing early vengeance on Germany. Prince Bismarck threatened reprisals, and a new Prime Minister, M. Rouvier, in May 1887, removed the General from office. The General replied with a declaration of war on the French government, raising a cry for the revision of the constitution. There soon gathered under his banner a horde of malcontent politicians—Royalists and Communists alike—who were joined by the roughest elements of the Paris mob. The General appeared to be aiming at a military dictatorship which should make the running for a monarchy and bring a rupture with Germany in its train. The more responsible members of the Royalist party deprecated the identification of their cause with a leader of such ambiguous character. But the Prince's friend, the Comte de Paris, with some of his incautious followers, showed the General favour. For a moment the Republic seemed to stagger under the attack.

The Prince was well alive to the situation. Germany's attitude to the General's agitation was very threatening and the Prince responded to a call from France to help in appeasing the internal discord. Information from Germany as well as from France convinced him that a European conflagration could best be averted by a substantial vote of confidence, on the part of the Chamber of Deputies, in M. Rouvier, who alone seemed at the time capable of restraining the General's baleful activities. Accordingly, in June, the Prince made a private effort to protect M. Rouvier from overthrow. M. Floquet, an influential rival, was credited with the intention of defeating the ministry almost as soon as it was formed. Without the support of the Royalist deputies of the Right, M. Rouvier's fate was sealed. The Prince's intimacy with the Comte de Paris allowed him to direct the exile's attention to the ministry's peril. The Prince urged the Comte to relive the immediate tension in both France and Europe by rallying his followers in the Chamber to the aid of M. Rouvier. The story ran in Paris that the Comte accepted the Prince's counsel.[1] At any rate the members of the Right came to M. Rouvier's rescue, and a vote of confidence was passed by a substantial majority consisting largely of Royalists. "If the Right had wished it, M. Rouvier would have had against him a majority of more than 300 votes and would have found himself *sur la terre.*"[2] The Prince viewed the matter from the international point of view, and regarded M. Rouvier's victory as a check alike on Prince Bismarck's aggressive temper and on General Boulanger's malignancy. But General Boulanger's power for evil was not yet destroyed.

M. Rouvier remained in office until near the end of the year (December 2, 1887), when he gave place to M. Tirard, an old acquaintance of the Prince. A fresh complication had arisen. Financial scandals affecting the son-in-law of President Grévy and other public men came to a head, and President Grévy was forced to resign in favour of M. Carnot. The presidential crisis gave General Boulanger a fresh advantage, and through the early months of 1888 he was the idol of the Paris mob.

French friends kept the Prince informed of the developments of the General's unhallowed agitation. The Prince's old comrade, General Galliffet, sent him from Paris, early in 1888, a detailed estimate of the General's position, wittily dating his letter "An premier de la Boulangerie."[3] Galliffet made clear to the Prince that "Germany will profit more than any other country from the humiliating turmoil." Another French correspondent, the Marquis de Breteuil, gratified the Prince with the report that Galliffet was to become Minister of War and was to take the severest measures against the General, who would, when captured, be sent to New Caledonia. But the Prince was again disturbed

[1] Taine, *Life and Letters*, 1908, iii. 271, where the story of the Prince's intervention is told.
[2] Freycinet, *Souvenirs, 1878–1893*, p. 378. M. de Freycinet's account of the critical incident makes no mention of the Prince's intervention.
[3] General Galliffet in his letter to the Prince scornfully estimated the number of the Boulangists at no more than 240,000, of whom 160,000 were Socialists, Communists, ticket-of-leave men, women's bullies, and the rest were servants, cab-drivers, restaurant touts, scavengers, women-workers who believed that Boulanger would raise their pay, a few students, and people without a sou.

by the rashness of the incorrigible Comte de Paris, who at this stage intervened with one more anti-Republican manifesto (July 6, 1888). The Prince's Royalist acquaintances in Paris confessed to him a fear that the Republicans might wreak on them a brutal retaliation.

1889

Ætat. 47 The end was not long delayed. Deprived of his military command, the General was cited on 2nd April 1889 to stand his trial before the Senate on a charge of conspiracy against the State. His bubble was thereupon pricked. "Le brav' Général" fled to London, and on 14th August was sentenced, in his absence, to imprisonment in a fortress. In London the charlatan found a better welcome than he deserved. The Prince, with his cyclopædic zest for personal study of French notoriety, was curious to meet the man who had kept France, and indeed Europe, effervescing for two years. The Prince's friends, Lord and Lady Randolph Churchill, gave him the opportunity, and he dined with the General at their London house with a few personal intimates. The General talked little, and that little proved to the Prince flat and without interest.[1] The General thenceforth passed out of notice and came to an appropriately squalid end by committing suicide, near Brussels, on 30th September 1891.

II

While France was writhing under General Boulanger's mockheroics, the Republican government and authentic Republican sentiment sought of the Prince an overt sign of his sympathy. The Prince's response was hardly reassuring. The request took a form which ran counter to his monarchical predilections, and he risked offending French Republican feeling by a resolute refusal. Despite all internal embarrassments, France resolved to organise on a great scale a new International Exhibition in 1889. The project was intended to satisfy three aims—firstly, the commemoration of the centenary of the French Revolution of 1789; secondly, the unification of divided national sentiment; and, thirdly, the encouragement of industrial activity and international trade. Notification of the coming Exhibition was sent to the English government early in 1888, and hope ran high in

[1] Lady Randolph Churchill's *Reminiscences*, p. 200. The party included the Duchess of Manchester, Lord Hardwicke, Lord Hartington, Sir George Lewis, and Mr. and Mrs. Leopold de Rothschild.

France that the Prince, whose favour seemed at the moment to be a national asset, would play the same responsible part in the projected Exhibition as he had felicitously filled in that of 1878. But France was doomed to disappointment. The Queen insisted that no member of her family could officially take part in a design whose main intention was anti-monarchical. On international grounds, Lord Salisbury pleaded for a broader view. He urged the Prince to follow the precedent of 1878 and become again President of a Royal Commission which should organise a British section. But the Prince preferred his mother's injunction to the advice of her Prime Minister. He declined all aid to the forthcoming Exhibition, which he seconded his mother in pronouncing to be a revolutionary demonstration. President Carnot and M. Tirard, now Prime Minister, were emphatic in regret at the Prince's decision. The President was reluctant to treat a first refusal as final. But the Prince stood firm. In the event, no British Royal Commission was appointed. The French organisers, on the advice of the British Ambassador in Paris, Lord Lytton, applied to the Lord Mayor of London, Sir Polydore de Keyser, and the Lord Mayor formed, in March 1888, an influential committee which undertook the organisation of a British section.[1]

The French people resented the official aloofness of the English government more warmly than that of the other Powers. But the bitterest blow of all was the Prince's official disapprobation. The Prince had, however, no intention of pressing the situation to extremes, and in a private capacity he made some effort to appease wounded French susceptibility. While he adhered to his official abstention, he gave private signs of interest in the Exhibition's success. On a visit to Paris in September 1888 he inspected the Champ de Mars and the other extensive sites which were allotted to the Exhibition buildings, and during

1889
Ætat. 47

---

[1] The expenses were defrayed by public subscription. There was no Government grant. See a full account of the Paris Exhibition of 1889 by (Sir) H. Trueman Wood, in *Journal of the Society of Arts*, 9th March 1888, and 13th December 1889. The monarchical rulers of Russia, Italy, Austria, and Germany shared Queen Victoria's and the Prince's suspicions of the aim of the "Revolution" Exhibition. They also abstained from official recognition. Before President Carnot opened the Exhibition, on the 6th May 1889, all the monarchical Ambassadors followed the example of the British Ambassador, Lord Lytton, in taking temporary leave of Paris. Only their *chargés d'affaires* represented the kingdoms of Europe at the inaugural ceremony.

June 1889, after the opening, he perceptibly assuaged French discontent by visiting the Exhibition unofficially with the Princess and all his children. In the course of this family excursion, during which he stayed, as was his custom, at the Hôtel Bristol, M. Eiffel conducted the party up the Eiffel tower. The Prince received at his hotel the President of the Republic, M. Carnot, with all his charm of courtesy, and he returned the visit at the Elysée.

III

The years following the "Revolution" Exhibition saw a succession of acute crises between England and France over their rival pretensions to supremacy in various parts of the world. The Franco-Russian alliance stimulated French national pride. She no longer stood alone in the world. Other Powers besides England, notably Italy and Belgium, looked askance at the wide-flung claims of France, while Germany, always bent on overwhelming France at the psychological moment, sardonically scrutinised every turn in the situation with a view to a tactical advantage. Everywhere France seemed to be threatening English interests. In Australian waters she was seeking exclusive control of the New Hebrides Islands. In Africa, where England's continued occupation of Egypt was a rankling sore, she was converting her protectorate over Tunis into full sovereignty, thereby impelling Italy to appeal to Lord Salisbury for England's aid in preventing France from turning the Mediterranean into a French lake. In Central Africa she was stirring fresh turmoil in the Sudan at the same time as she was perturbing Belgium by her challenges of the peace of the Belgian Congo state. Off the east coast of Africa she was maintaining her grip on the island of Madagascar and rigorously suppressing native unrest. In Asia her aims of territorial expansion were imposingly illustrated by her successful effort to create under her sway a new and vast Indo-Chinese empire. There she was not only challenging the English hold on Burma, a kingdom which had recently been annexed to India, but was menacing the independence of the kingdom of Siam and was provoking the active protests of China.

The Prince's equanimity was disturbed by the accumulating proofs of France's assertive imperialism, and the Kaiser lost no

opportunity of fanning his uncle's anxiety on that score. French
feeling against Germany grew in bitterness with the growth
of France's imperialistic programme. In February 1891, the
Prince's sister, the Empress Frederick, with doubtful prudence
paid Paris a private visit. An unmannerly demonstration
against her presence in the French capital offended the English
royal family, and the Kaiser threw out the suggestion that the
Prince, by way of protest, should make a tour with him through
Alsace-Lorraine (February 1891). But the Prince was not to be
caught in so simple a trap.

At the end of July 1893 an alarming but happily momentary
crisis suddenly developed between France and England. French
warships were flaunting England by blockading Bangkok, the
capital of the kingdom of Siam which England was protecting,
and when two English gunboats were told off to watch French
action the French admiral peremptorily ordered the British
vessels to withdraw. Thereupon Lord Rosebery, the English
Foreign Secretary, sent to Paris an ultimatum (30th July). The
day before, the Kaiser had arrived on his annual visit to Cowes,
and the Queen courteously apprised him of Lord Rosebery's
telegraphic intimation to her of the perturbing incident. The
Kaiser irritated the Prince by affecting to regard Queen Victoria's
confidential communication as an invitation to join England in
war on France.[1] The strained situation was quickly relieved by
the Quai d'Orsay's prompt disclaimer of the order given by the
French admiral to the English gunboats off Bangkok.

The episode quickened the Prince's hope that cautious
diplomacy might yet compose the quarrels with France and
restore the possibility of an Anglo-French understanding.
Lord Dufferin, the British Ambassador in Paris, was doing his
best to calm public opinion on both sides of the Channel.
In March 1894, when feeling again ran dangerously high in
the two countries over French defiance of both English and
Belgian claims in Equatorial Africa, Lord Dufferin in an address
to the British Chamber of Commerce at Paris gave an impressive
warning against exaggerating the significance of the pending
dissensions. The Prince at the moment was taking his annual
spring holiday at Cannes. He at once wrote to Lord Dufferin,

[1] *Die Grosse Politik*, vol. viii., where the Bangkok crisis is greatly exaggerated.
Cf. Admiral Ballard's letter in *The Times*, 9th January 1924.

warmly commending his prudent utterance; he reported how favourably the ambassador's remarks had impressed the Russian Grand Dukes and even the German princes with whom he was passing his time.

Three months later, on 24th June 1894, M. Carnot, the French President, was assassinated at Lyons, and the Prince seized the tragic opportunity of manifesting his sympathy with France. As soon as the news reached the Prince, he called in person on Baron de Courcel, the French Ambassador in London, to offer his condolences. M. de Staal, the Russian Ambassador in London, in a despatch to the Russian Chancellor, M. de Giers, laid stress on the Prince's performance in person of an attention which Queen Victoria was content to pay vicariously.[1] On 2nd July 1894 the Prince with his son, the Duke of York, attended a requiem Mass for the dead President at the French Chapel in Leicester Square.

IV

The Anglo-French dispute over Equatorial Africa proved, however, more stubborn than either the Prince or Lord Dufferin foresaw. France was pursuing her quarrel with Belgium over the respective pretensions of the two countries in the region of the Congo, and the differences tended to stimulate French ambition to improve her position in Central Africa. While evincing sympathy with Belgium, England was willing to meet French demands in another quarter of Central Africa, and agreed to a delimitation by a joint Anglo-French Commission of disputed boundaries in the region of the Lower Niger.[2] But France's ill humours were not to be readily appeased. England was, in 1894, meditating the reconquest of the Sudan as a logical corollary of her continued occupation of Egypt. French ill-will against England was thereby inflamed anew, and the Belgian imbroglio in the Congo helped to fan the French resentment. M. Hanotaux, who entered on a long tenure of office as Foreign Minister of France on 19th May 1894,[3] thought to steal a march on England in her

[1] Russian Archives, M. de Staal to M. de Giers, 15/27 June 1894.

[2] The Commission met in Paris. Early in 1898 a settlement, which was satisfactory to France, was reached, and was confirmed by a pact between the two Governments signed at Paris on 14th June.

[3] M. Hanotaux remained in office until the 28th June 1898 with a short interval 31st October 1895–28th March 1896.

designs on the Sudan. On assuming office he secretly authorised
the despatch of small expeditions of French explorers from the
French Congo across the continent in order to protect what he
asserted were French interests in the Sudan. The British
Government learnt vaguely of M. Hanotaux's programme, and
warned France that they regarded it as a threat against England.

In March 1896 Lord Salisbury's Government began their
attack on the Sudan.[1] The Sirdar of Egypt, Sir Herbert
Kitchener, was ordered to invade Dongola, a Sudanese province.
The Prince, when he learnt of the decision, warned the government, in view of past experience, against taking any undue risks.
On a written notification of the official order to Sir Herbert
Kitchener he wrote: "I sincerely hope that sufficient Anglo-
Egyptian troops may be sent, so that we may risk no reverses"
(March 16). France warmly protested against the British
government's action, and watched Kitchener's advance with
jealous eyes. By September 1896 the English General suc-
ceeded in reuniting the province of Dongola to the dominion
of Egypt. The whole of the next year he devoted, with an
exemplary caution and completeness which appealed to the
Prince's business instincts, to the organisation of a larger expedition for the recovery of the rest of the Sudan from the
sway of native insurgents. French opinion continued disturbed.
The Kaiser, who rejoiced in the fresh prospect of a breach between
France and England, wrote blusteringly to an English friend
(January 11, 1898) that England in her "new expedition to
the Sudan" was likely to meet "suddenly beside the Mahdi
and Menelik of Abyssinian 'connaissance,' France, for all that
I know."[2]

The Prince did what he could to allay French irritation. On
his way out to Cannes in March 1898 for his usual spring visit,
he paused at Paris to exchange visits with President Faure, and
at luncheon at the British Embassy he met the main fomenter

1896
Ætat. 54

---

[1] According to German testimony, the time was chosen at the instance of
Count von Hatzfeldt, the German Ambassador in London. Early in 1896
there was a threatening native rising against the Italian occupation of Abyssinia
—to the east of the Sudan, and serious turmoil arose among the Sudanese under
the leadership of the Khalifa, a successor of the Mahdi. Count von Hatzfeldt
urged on Lord Salisbury a military expedition into the Sudan from Egypt in
order to relieve the native pressure in Abyssinia on Germany's ally, Italy
(Eckardstein, *Ten Years at the Court of St. James's*, p. 87).

[2] Repington's *Vestigia*, p. 100.

of strife—M. Hanotaux—as well as the Russian Ambassador in
Paris, Prince Urusoff (March 3). His fellow-guests were not
unimpressed by his blandishments. A week later—on the 10th
March—soon after his arrival at Cannes, he laid the foundation
stone of a new jetty, and in speeches on the occasion, earnestly
pleaded for international amity and comity.

"I hope with you," he remarked in a reply to the address
from the Mayor of Cannes, "that this ceremony may well be a
fresh pledge of cordial relations between France and Great
Britain." "I sincerely hope," he told M. Leroux, the Prefet
of the Alpes Maritimes, "that France may long enjoy the benefits
of the Government which you represent, and that the cordial
relations between France and Great Britain may continue for
the good of humanity."

He added the expression of a wish that "this hospitable country,"
with which he was always ready to co-operate, might enjoy "the
greatest prosperity."

V

Kitchener won a first victory over the Sudanese at the battle
of Atbara on the 6th April 1898, and after further fighting his
campaign ended in the decisive battle of Omdurman, on the bank
of the Nile opposite Khartoum, on 2nd September following.
That action finally restored the Sudan to Egyptian rule, and the
disasters of 1884–86, which embraced the death of Gordon at
Khartoum, were largely retrieved. Lord Salisbury made it
plain to France that all the Sudanese territories recently subject
to the rebellious Khalifa passed by right of conquest to the
Egyptian government and its British controllers. "The fact,"
Lord Salisbury declared, "was not open to discussion." The
Prince was jubilant in congratulations on "Kitchener's brilliant
success."[1]

At the very moment, however, that Kitchener was earning
his plaudits at home from the Prince and others, the French
menace of Equatorial Africa was fulfilling itself in a fashion
that brought France and England to the verge of war. A
cabinet minute of 27th July 1898, which was communicated to
the Prince, enjoined Kitchener to hoist throughout the Sudan
the British and Egyptian flags and to permit no other. Yet a

[1] Letter to Lady Londonderry, 27th September 1898.

few days after the battle of Omdurman—on 7th September— 1898
news reached Kitchener that, under a permit of the French Ætat. 56
Colonial Office dated 24th February 1896, Captain Marchand, a
French explorer, had, with a party of 5 officers and 120 Sengalese,
crossed the centre of the continent from the French Congo and,
having entered the southern regions of the Sudan, had on 10th
July 1898 planted the French flag at a place called Fashoda
on the White Nile, five hundred miles south of Omdurman.
Kitchener took immediate action.   Within three days he started
down the White Nile with five gunboats.   On the voyage he
received from Captain Marchand a brief notice of his refusal to
budge.   For a few days the two men faced each other at Fashoda,
each under his own flag.   "Our occupying of Fashoda," wrote
the Prince on 27th September, "may produce grave results."
Lord Salisbury instructed Kitchener to insist on the French
captain's unconditional surrender.   France proposed a conditional evacuation.   Neither Government seemed ready to give
way, and the worst was feared on both sides of the Channel—
when suddenly the scene changed and France yielded to the
English demands (November 4).   Captain Marchand hauled
down his flag and retired from Fashoda.

France's submission was due to a recent change in the control
of the French Foreign Office, where, on the 28th June 1898, a
few weeks before the battle of Omdurman, M. Hanotaux had
been succeeded by M. Delcassé—a statesman of very different
mettle.   During the seven eventful years that M. Delcassé
remained at the Quai D'Orsay, he set himself to effect, ultimately in willing co-operation with the Prince of Wales as King
Edward VII., a complete revolution in the relations of England
and France.   "I do not wish," he told a friend on taking office,
"to leave this desk without having restored the good understanding with England." [1]

Near the opening of his long tenure of the post of French
Foreign Minister, M. Delcassé recalled Baron de Courcel, the
French Ambassador in London, and replaced him by M. Paul
Cambon (November 1898), who was well qualified to advance
the cause of Anglo-French friendship.   In the Prince, M. Cambon,
despite his bourgeois manner, at once found a warm friend.
M. Cambon's first duty, after Captain Marchand's withdrawal,

[1] Lémonon, *L'Europe et la Politique Britannique, 1882–1911*, p. 136.

was to aid in the delimitation of the boundaries of French and
English territory in Central Africa, and under his conciliatory
auspices the work went through quickly and smoothly. There
were many other rocks of stumbling to be removed before an
Anglo-French understanding could rest on sure foundations, and
Lord Salisbury was sceptical of the possibility for the time of
attempting more than was now in course of achievement in
Central Africa. Lord Salisbury had good ground for pointing
to the uncertainty of French public opinion. The *amour propre*
of the French people was wounded by what they regarded as
the humiliation of Fashoda, and despite the courteous professions of French diplomatists, the popular anger with England was
long in abating. The Prince, as the Englishman whose name was
most familiar to the Paris mob and to writers in the Parisian
press, was to suffer much contumely from the affronted national
pride. None the less the way was cleared at Fashoda for the
accomplishment of his early hope, to which he clung in spite of
all ill-omens, of an effective and durable Anglo-French *entente*.

M. Delcassé's attitude to Germany as well as to England was
unmistakable from the first. His accession to power was a keen
disappointment to the German Emperor, the Prince's nephew,
and before long the Kaiser, to the disturbance of the peace of
Europe and to the resentment of his uncle, was to cross swords
with this new friend of England.[1] With his usual duplicity,
he sent congratulations to Queen Victoria and the Prince on
Lord Kitchener's victories over the Sudanese—after the battle
of Atbara, and again after the battle of Omdurman, which he
described as avenging General Gordon's death. But at the
same time he voiced his disappointment at what he described
as France's fatuous surrender to England. At the time of the
Fashoda settlement the Kaiser was making a theatrical progress
through Palestine. In writing to the Tsar Nicholas, from
Damascus on 9th November, he described the news of the French
submission, "after such a first-rate, well-planned, and plucky
expedition of poor and brave Marchand," as falling like a thunder-

---

[1] Just before M. Hanotaux left office he had been approached by Count
Münster, German Ambassador formerly in London and now in Paris, with
vague proposals to join Germany in foiling alleged designs of England on the
Portuguese colonies. Count Münster's note on the subject was almost the first
official letter which came before Delcassé in his new office. He left it unacknow-
ledged (Lémonon, *L'Europe et la Politique Britannique, 1882–1911*, p. 135).

bolt on the people of the East. On the strength of a hearsay 1898
report, he blamed the Russian Foreign Minister, Count Muravieff, Ætat. 56
for having "counselled France to take this foolish step." "The
Moslems call it 'France's second Sedan,'" he added, and he
prophesied that France was hardly likely to forgive Russia for
her fatal advice. The Kaiser's wish was father to his thought
and his disillusionment was not long in coming. What he
malevolently called "France's second Sedan" proved a substantive stepping-stone to that understanding between France
and England which he credited his uncle with jealously contriving
to the injury of himself and his country.[1]

[1] *The Kaiser's Letters to Tsar,* p. 69.

CHAPTER XXXVIII

I

1895
Ætat. 53

Two foreign crises of far more sensational tenor than England had recently experienced followed hard on Lord Salisbury's resumption of the double office of Prime Minister and Foreign Secretary in July 1895, and the Prince watched the stirring course of events with more than his customary critical ardour. With the first crisis, which involved English relations with the United States, the Kaiser had no direct concern, although he welcomed the embarrassment which it caused England. The second crisis was provoked by Germany and further embittered the Prince's relations with his nephew.

An acute controversy suddenly arose between the English government and the great kindred power across the Atlantic in the closing days of the year 1895. For a long period England had been at odds with the little Republic of Venezuela on the north-east coast of South America. The dispute arose out of a question of boundaries between that state and its neighbour, the colony of British Guiana. The Venezuelan republic, which was in a chronic state of revolution, long defied British appeals for a settlement. Early in 1895 a handful of Venezuelans sought to occupy a strip of territory which England regarded as part of British Guiana. Lord Salisbury, on entering office in July 1895, contented himself for the time with pacific remonstrance. The British public was therefore the more startled by the publication of a despatch dated 7th August from the United States Secretary of State, Mr. Olney, in which the boundary issue was held to lie

At Homburg
1896

within the ambit of the Monroe Doctrine, and declaration was
made that it should be settled independently of England by impartial arbitration, resistance to which on England's part must seriously embarrass Anglo-American goodwill. Lord Salisbury at once addressed an ultimatum to Venezuela requiring her to meet the British demands, while in reply to Mr. Olney he questioned the American interpretation of the Monroe Doctrine and declined the Secretary of State's one-sided scheme of arbitration. A startling retort to the British argument followed on 17th December, when President Cleveland sent to Congress a defiant message, announcing that he was about to send a commission to delimit the borders between Venezuela and British Guiana, and that if the need arose he should impose by force on Great Britain the acceptance of the Commission's report.

The blustering terms of the Presidential message roused strong feeling in England, and for some days war looked imminent. But in both countries influential opinion sought means of averting such a calamity. The Prince openly associated himself with the peace-makers. Since his tour as a boy in the United States, he had done much to cultivate the good feeling of Americans. He had entertained at home and on the continent of Europe numerous American visitors—both men and women of many classes—and their unconventional conversation gave him pleasure. Amid the varied company which he was wont to admit to his society on his visits to Homburg was Mr. Joseph Pulitzer, who was proprietor of the *New York World*. Six days after the delivery of President Cleveland's message, Mr. Pulitzer took the bold step of cabling to the Prince and to his son, the Duke of York, a request for an expression of their views of the critical issue. The Prince at once did what he could to pour oil on the troubled waters by drafting a vague but reassuring reply in the following terms :

I thank you for tgm. I earnestly trust and cannot but believe present crisis will be arranged in a manner satisfactory to both countries, and will be succeeded by same warm feeling of friendship which has existed between them for so many years (December 23, 1895).

Before telegraphing his message the Prince invited Lord Salisbury's opinion as to the propriety of its despatch. The Prime Minister deprecated the Prince's intervention. But the

Prince decided to take his own line. His telegram was forwarded despite Lord Salisbury's warning and was promptly published in the *New York World* on Christmas Eve. The Prince's conciliatory words had the best effect on American public opinion, and aided the pacific efforts of Lord Salisbury and of Sir Julian Pauncefote, the British Ambassador at Washington. American sentiment soon repudiated the President's aggressive tones. In accordance with an agreement quickly reached between the British and American governments, the British quarrel with Venezuela was remitted for settlement to a commission on which two Englishmen and two Americans served under a neutral chairman.[1] The outcome of the explosion of 1895 was a strong reinforcement of the sense of mutual repugnance to war between England and America. The Prince continued to do what he could to promote good Anglo-American relations both socially and politically.[2] In the course of the Diamond Jubilee festivities, 1897, he accepted an invitation to dine with the special American plenipotentiary, Mr. Whitelaw Reid, a man of great wealth and of polished manner, and he formed with him an acquaintance which ripened into intimacy when Mr. Reid succeeded to the American Embassy in London in 1905. The Prince's relations with Mr. Reid were closer than with any other representative of the United States at the Court of St. James's, and helped to deepen the Prince's American sympathies.

II

While English public opinion was recovering from the first shock of President Cleveland's defiant manifesto, another blow to English national pride was dealt by the Kaiser with the vociferous approval of his fellow-countrymen. However the historical evidence now accessible may distribute the precise shares in the concoction of the Kaiser's telegram to President Kruger of 3rd January 1896, that inflammatory document

---

[1] This Commission, after a thorough investigation, settled the debated boundaries between Venezuela and British Guiana in October 1899.

[2] At the end of 1896 a first treaty of arbitration between England and the United States bore witness to the good intentions of both countries, but it failed to secure ratification by the American Senate. The first Anglo-American Arbitration Treaty, albeit of modest purport, which was enacted with the Senate's ratification, belonged to King Edward's reign (April 8, 1908).

remains an authentic demonstration of the Kaiser's mischievous jealousy of England, and of the resentments which the recent visit to Cowes had warmed to fever-heat. The Kaiser's Kruger telegram gave fresh assurance of the coming cleavage between England and Germany, and the episode justly confirmed the Prince's mistrust of his nephew.

The circumstances which provoked the Kaiser's incautious challenge of English sentiment at the opening of the year 1896 concern the old-standing friction between English settlers in South Africa and the Boers of the Transvaal Republic.[1] In 1895 there came to a head the long-growing exasperation of English settlers—Uitlanders as they were locally called—in the Transvaal mining district of the Witwatersrand. Mr. Cecil Rhodes, a leading mining capitalist on the Transvaal rand, and director of the British South Africa (Chartered) Company, which controlled the territory on the Transvaal border known as Rhodesia, had become Prime Minister of the Cape government. Mr. Rhodes secretly engineered an insurrection against President Kruger's rule. His friend, Dr. Jameson, Administrator of Rhodesia, collected, in December 1895, with Rhodes' connivance, a force of 600 irregular troops in the service of the British South Africa Company in order to invade the Transvaal, and, with the aid of the Uitlanders of Johannesburg, to overthrow President Kruger's government.[2] The plan miscarried. By the 29th December Dr. Jameson was on the march. Next day he and his irregular

[1] Mr. Gladstone's conditional restoration, which the Prince disapproved, of the independence of the Transvaal Republic in 1881 (confirmed by a definitive treaty of 1884), failed to abate the Boers' racial dislike of the English. President Kruger always looked to the Germans, with whom he felt himself to be of closer kin, for sympathy and, in an emergency, for practical help. He welcomed German traders to the Transvaal. In 1887 the discovery of the Witwatersrand gold mines within the Transvaal brought a new element into Boer history. Crowds of European miners, chiefly English, crowded into the Transvaal and founded the mining town of Johannesburg. President Kruger treated the Uitlanders (i.e. the foreign mining settlers), among whom the English preponderated, with the utmost rigour, taxing them heavily and refusing them the franchise. In 1889 the British South Africa (Chartered) Company was formed to settle an immense area of Central Africa to the north of the Transvaal. Under the powerful direction of Cecil Rhodes, one of the Johannesburg settlers, the Company's operations intensified President Kruger and the Boers' jealousy of the English.

[2] Before Dr. Jameson's expedition started the Johannesburg Uitlanders announced a resolve to set up in the Transvaal an international republic, and professed unwillingness to fight under the Union Jack. Cecil Rhodes, on receiving this intelligence, made a belated and vain attempt to revoke Dr. Jameson's advance.

1896
Ætat. 54

following entered Transvaal territory. No Uitlanders joined him, and the Boer government summoned troops of burghers to stop the raiders' progress.

As soon as rumours of Dr. Jameson's proceedings reached Mr. Chamberlain, the Colonial Secretary, he telegraphed to Dr. Jameson to quit the Transvaal territory. The Prince had met Dr. Jameson earlier in the year. He presided at a lecture which the Doctor had given at the Imperial Institute on the history and prospects of the new province of Rhodesia (January 28, 1895).[1] The reports of Dr. Jameson's present action perturbed him, and he echoed an opinion general in England when he wrote to a friend on 2nd January 1896: "The accounts from the Transvaal have been an unpleasant New Year's Card! Matters look grave, and our position is quite unfortunate." Dr. Jameson and his companions were meanwhile surrounded by armed Boers, and, surrendering on the day that the Prince was writing, were made prisoners.

A fabricated letter, purporting to be an appeal from the women and children of Johannesburg to Dr. Jameson and his friends to rescue them from Boer oppression had been published in the London newspapers on the 29th December. This forged appeal startled the British public, and misled the unthinking portion of it. Mr. Alfred Austin, who had just been appointed Poet Laureate, based upon the concoction a set of jingling verses applauding the heroism of the raiders in undertaking at a moment's notice a mission of mercy. The "effusion" appeared in *The Times* on 31st December, and was the poet's first performance in his new capacity. On New Year's Day the arrival of more accurate information covered the Poet Laureate with ridicule. The Prince had condemned Lord Salisbury's appointment of Mr. Austin to an office which had last been held and had been dignified by Lord Tennyson, and he joined in the outcry against the new Poet Laureate's blunder. "I always thought," he wrote a little later (March 26, 1901), "that Mr. Austin's appointment was not a good one," and he called the Prime Minister's attention to "the trash which the Poet Laureate writes" (November 3, 1901).[2]

[1] Ian Colvin's *Life of Dr. Jameson*, ii. 18.
[2] The Queen wrote to Lord Salisbury about Mr. Austin's unfortunate verses on the Johannesburg appeal a few days after their publication. Lord Salisbury replied in scorn that he had "missed Mr. Austin's poem, but he has

III

From the beginning of 1895, the Kaiser and his ministers had watched the quarrel between President Kruger and the English in South Africa with close attention, in the Machiavellian hope that it might turn out to England's injury. According to the Kaiser's own account, "for the last two years" Germany had been vainly pressing on the notice of Downing Street the important interests which Germany possessed in the Transvaal.[1]

In the autumn of 1895 the Transvaal government sent its Secretary of State, Dr. Leyds, to Berlin to dilate on the wrongs of the Boers, and to fan German sympathy. He was received with open arms by the Kaiser and his ministers. The Kaiser took the Boer emissary into his confidence, suggesting to him that one means of checking English designs in South Africa would be for either Germany or the Boers to acquire from the Portuguese the important South African port of Lorenzo Marques.

When the first news of Dr. Jameson's raid reached Berlin, the Kaiser and his ministers grew busy.[2] On the 31st von Marschall, the Foreign Secretary, in a written review of the situation asserted that Germany would not brook the annexation by

1896
Ætat. 54

---

heard it strongly condemned by many persons, both from a political and a literary point of view. It is a pity that this effusion was his first performance. Unluckily it is to the taste of the galleries in the lower class of theatres, and they sing it with vehemence."

[1] The Kaiser to Sir Edward Sullivan, 3rd February 1896 in Colonel Repington's *Vestigia*, pp. 191-2. The German Consul at Pretoria, Herr von Herff, had completely won the Boer President's ear and stimulated the jealous rancours which the President cherished against Cecil Rhodes and his associates. At the end of October, Sir Edward Malet, the retiring British Ambassador in Berlin, complained to Baron von Marschall, the German Foreign Minister, that the Germans were encouraging the Boers in their resistance to the English demands. The Minister retorted that the reckless filibustering of Cecil Rhodes and English jealousy of Germany were at the root of the evil, that Germany's economic interests demanded the maintenance of the Transvaal Republic, and that if the Republic were in danger Germany might come to its rescue. The Kaiser, who irresponsibly asserted that "Rhodes had nothing more to do with the Transvaal (*i.e.* had no more right to interfere in Transvaal affairs) than he himself," wildly distorted Sir Edward Malet's remarks into a threat that the continuance of German ill-will would drive England into the arms of France and bring on war. The British Ambassador's words were spoken without instructions, and Lord Salisbury promptly repudiated the Kaiser's interpretation of them.

[2] On the 30th December, Herr von Herff, in a telegram from Pretoria, announced to the Wilhelmstrasse that the raid had begun, and asked for a company of marines to protect Germans in Johannesburg.

England of the Transvaal. At the same time he instructed
Count von Hatzfeldt, the German Ambassador in London, to ask
Lord Salisbury whether the English government approved the
raid, and in case of an affirmative reply to demand his passports.
Simultaneously a telegram from German settlers in Pretoria
invited the Kaiser to come to their aid. Lord Salisbury, in
conversation with Count von Hatzfeldt, who personally sought a
pacific solution, as well as in instructions to Sir Frank Lascelles
at Berlin, did what was possible to allay German disquietude.
On New Year's Day, Sir Frank Lascelles told the Kaiser,
according to the Kaiser's story, that the raiders were "filibusters
or rebels," and the Kaiser said that he hinted in reply that "we
(*i.e.* Germany) ought to join and co-operate in keeping them
from doing mischief." [1] The British Ambassador informed von
Marschall on the same day that Mr. Chamberlain, Secretary of
State for the Colonies, had no previous knowledge of the raid,
and had no intention of condoning it. The German Foreign
Office professed incredulity.[2]

German public opinion ran high in President Kruger's favour,
and the Kaiser sailed recklessly near the winds of war. He
sounded the French Ambassador in Berlin, and the Tsar at St.
Petersburg, as to whether they would join him in "common
defence of our endangered interests." Admiral von Tirpitz, the
chauvinist champion of a great German fleet, was at the time
preparing a report in favour of a vast naval expansion, and the
Kaiser impulsively spoke of the Transvaal imbroglio as justifying
the immediate adoption of von Tirpitz's proposals. His ministers
at first gave the Kaiser's rashness some encouragement, but the
wisest of them soon saw the need of tacking. They were ready
to flout England by verbal encouragement of the Boers, but
they shrank from direct action. At best, the Chancellor and the
Foreign Secretary, von Marschall, believed that a threatening

---

[1] The Kaiser to Queen, 8th January 1896.

[2] On the 2nd January, Count von Hatzfeldt was directed to forward to
Lord Salisbury an ultimatum affirming Germany's determination to uphold the
status quo in South Africa. Count von Hatzfeldt obeyed his orders, but owing
to Lord Salisbury's absence from the Foreign Office his note remained there
unopened. Next day the news reached London and the world that Dr. Jameson's plot had miscarried. Thereupon the German government changed their
tactics, and Count von Hatzfeldt, acting under instructions, managed to recover
his ultimatum before any one in the Foreign Office had read it (*Die Grosse
Politik*, Bd. xi. p. 27).

demeanour on Germany's part might alarm England, and that a sense of fear might incline her to reconsider that invitation to join the Triple Alliance which the Kaiser vainly suggested to her some years before.

A momentous step was taken by the authorities in Berlin on 3rd January, on receipt of the news of Dr. Jameson's capture. At 10 o'clock on the morning of that day the Kaiser took the chair at a conference at the Foreign Office. He was supported by the Chancellor, the Foreign Minister, von Marschall, and three representatives of the Germany navy—Admiral von Hollmann, Freiherr von Senden und Bibran, the Kaiser's naval aide-de-camp, and Admiral von Knorr.   (Kayser, the Colonial Secretary, and von Holstein, the chief secretary of the Foreign Office, followed the proceedings from an adjoining room.)   General satisfaction was expressed at the failure of Dr. Jameson's raid. The Kaiser opened the debate with proposals to declare a German protectorate over the Transvaal, to mobilise the marine infantry and to send troops to Pretoria.   The Chancellor objected that "that would mean war with England."   The Kaiser retorted, not very coherently, "Yes, but only on land."   Baron von Marschall and his colleagues condemned the Kaiser's suggestions, but anxious to placate their master, they vaguely countenanced another of his proposals, viz. the despatch of his aide-de-camp, Colonel Schele, to the Transvaal to make observations.[1]   The debate continued indecisively, and when there seemed small hope of unanimity, the Colonial Secretary, Kayser, suggested to von Marschall that a congratulatory telegram to President Kruger should be drafted in the Kaiser's name.   According to a statement attributed to Admiral Hollmann, the Kaiser at first refused his assent, remarking that the world would treat such a communication as his own impulsive act, and not as the work of his elderly advisers.   In any case he quickly changed his tone and eagerly seconded Kayser's suggestion.   The Colonial Secretary drafted the message on von Marschall's instructions.   Von Marschall stiffened the wording by the Emperor's order.   For the milder phrase "the prestige of your government" ("das Ansehen Ihrer Regierung"), on which Kayser in the original draft congratulated President Kruger, von Marschall substituted

[1] Prince von Hohenlohe led the Kaiser to abandon this proposal three days later.

1896
Ætat. 54 the bolder words, "the independence of your country" ("die
Unabhängigkeit des Landes").[1] The evidence is clear, in spite
of the Kaiser's belated assertions to the contrary, that he was
disposed to go further than the Foreign Minister in strength of
language. To the last, some members of the conference earnestly
deprecated the sending of the telegram as likely to provoke war
with England, but they yielded their doubts to the assurances
of the Chancellor and the Foreign Minister that there was no
other way of deflecting the Kaiser's will from more perilous
action.

The Kaiser's telegram to President Kruger (January 3, 1896)
was finally couched in the following terms :

I express my sincere congratulations that, supported by your
people without appealing for the help of friendly Powers, you
have succeeded by your own energetic action against armed bands
which invaded your country as disturbers of the peace and have
thus been enabled to restore peace and safeguard the independence
of the country against attacks from the outside.

President Kruger replied at once :

I express to Your Majesty my deepest gratitude for Your
Majesty's congratulations. With God's help we hope to continue
to do everything possible for the existence of the Republic.

As soon as his telegram to President Kruger was published
the Kaiser wrote and spoke of it vaingloriously, as if he were
its sole author. Many years later, after his fall from power,
he sought contradictorily to lay the whole blame on his ministers.
But whatever their executive part in the transaction the moral
responsibility rests on the Kaiser's shoulders.[2]

[1] *Die Grosse Politik*, xi. p. 32, *n*.

[2] Many documents concerning the events leading up to and following from
the Kaiser's telegram to Kruger are published in *Die Grosse Politik*, vol. xi.
chapter 63 (1923). A statement minimising the Kaiser's responsibility, attributed
to Admiral Hollmann, appears in Baron von Eckardstein's *Ten Years at the
Court of St. James's*, pp. 62–63. The Kaiser in his *Memoirs*, pp. 79–82 (1922)
writes that he yielded under compulsion to the Chancellor's warning that his
constitutional advisers would brook no refusal of his signature to the telegram.
Von Marschall told Sir Valentine Chirol, at the time correspondent of *The
Times* in Berlin, that the telegram was "Eine Staats-Aktion," for which the
German government assumed responsibility, but he added that the Emperor
"had only with great difficulty been induced to allow some of the terms used
in his original draft telegram to be softened down" after both the Chancellor
and von Marschall had pointed out to him that they were needlessly provocative

1896
Ætat. 54

The Kaiser's telegram roused in England a tempestuous outcry against him and his country. "The nation will never forget this telegram," wrote the *Morning Post*, "and it will always bear it in mind in the future orientation of its policy." An article in the *Saturday Review* declared "Germania delenda est." The brunt of England's anger fell on the Kaiser. The England press heaped upon him every kind of vituperation. There is no need to question his story that he received a flood of insulting letters from English correspondents. In Germany, on the other hand, the telegram was received with uproarious applause, and von Marschall, in the Reichstag, helped to inflame German feeling by declaring anew that the independence of the Transvaal was a vital German interest. At the same time, the Kaiser himself and some of his Ministers, Admiral von Hollmann among them, professed innocent surprise at the explosion of English wrath.

For three or four days after the publication of the telegram, war between the two countries looked imminent. The English government put a flying squadron in immediate commission, and proclaimed that by the Convention of 1884 the foreign relations of the Transvaal were under the supervision of the British Foreign Office. The German government proposed to ship several hundred colonial troops from German East Africa to Delagoa Bay, and thence, with a naval detachment from three German cruisers already lying off Lorenzo Marques, the port of the Bay, to march to Pretoria, where the little army was to place itself at President Kruger's disposal. "War," said Lord Salisbury three years later, "would have been inevitable from the moment that the first German soldier set foot on Transvaal soil. No Government in England could have withstood the pressure of public opinion; and, if it had come to a war between us, then

---

(Sir V. Chirol's letter to *The Times*, October 14, 1922). The fullest light on the history of the telegram, and of the part played in it by the Kaiser, is shed by the German Archivist, Friedrich Thimme, in "Die Kruger-Depesche, Genesis und historische Bedeutung," *Europäische Gespräche*, Hamburger Monatshefte für auswärtige Politik, Mai/Juni, 1924, No. 3, pp. 201, 244. Herr Thimme cites the unpublished diaries of von Marschall and of von Senden, besides correspondence and verbal statements from those in close contact with the other members of the conference of 3rd January. (Save the Kaiser, all who were present are now dead.) Herr Thimme's documents show a practical unanimity as to the Kaiser's responsibility. The narrative in the text takes into account all the accessible evidence and seeks to reconcile its discrepancies.

1896
—
Ætat. 54

a general European war must have developed."[1]   Happily,
Delagoa Bay and Lorenzo Marques were Portuguese possessions,
and Portugal's assent had to be obtained before the German plan
could be carried out.   M. de Soveral, the friend of the Prince,
was then Foreign Minister at Lisbon, and he peremptorily
announced that no German troops would be allowed in Portuguese
territory.

IV

The Prince eagerly watched the crisis and was well supplied
with information.   The Queen forwarded to him all communications on the theme which reached her from Germany,[2] and he
kept in close touch with both Lord Salisbury and Mr. Chamberlain.
With the rest of his family he laid on his nephew's shoulders
the whole responsibility for "that shameful telegram," and he
took the general view that the Kaiser had wilfully forfeited
England's respect and friendship.   As soon as he read the
Kruger message he appealed to Queen Victoria to rebuke her
grandson sharply—to administer to him (in his own phrase) "a
good snubbing."   But the Queen recognised more clearly than
her heir the need of self-restraint.   "Those sharp, cutting
answers and remarks," she pointed out to the Prince (January 15),
"only irritate and do harm, which one is sorry for.   Passion
should be most carefully guarded against.   William's faults come
from impulsiveness, as well as conceit.   Calmness and firmness
are the most powerful weapons in such cases."

The Queen contented herself with the following gentle protest
which she addressed from Osborne on 5th January to "My dear
William":

[1] According to Baron Eckardstein (pp. 85–86), who reports the remarks
of Lord Salisbury at length, the Prime Minister continued thus: "Courcel
had already told me on behalf of his Government, that in the event of an
Anglo-German war France would observe a most benevolent neutrality towards us, and would moreover probably in the end take an active part in
the war.   Further, Petersburg gave us to understand that, in the case of a
war with Germany, England would have nothing to fear from Russia in
Central Asia or elsewhere.   Any one in his senses must have seen that
Germany had everything to lose and nothing to gain by such a war."

[2] A batch of original letters, bearing on the telegram, from the Kaiser, the
Empress Frederick, and others was forwarded to the Prince at Marlborough
House by Queen Victoria.   These papers are still preserved at Marlborough
House in the large envelope which the Queen addressed to the Prince in her
own hand.

I must now also touch upon a subject which causes me much pain and astonishment. It is the Telegram you sent to President Kruger, which is considered very unfriendly towards this country, not that you intended it as such I am sure—but I grieve to say it has made a most unfortunate impression here.

The action of Dr. Jameson was, of course, very wrong and totally unwarranted, but considering the very peculiar position in which the Transvaal stands towards Great Britain, I think it would have been far better to have said nothing. Our great wish has always been to keep on the best of terms with Germany, trying to act together, but I fear your agents in the Colonies do the very reverse, which deeply grieves us. Let me hope you will try to check this.

You will, I am sure, take my remarks in good part, and believe that they are entirely dictated by my desire for your good.

Lord Salisbury, on receiving a copy of the Queen's letter, remarked (January 16) : "It is entirely suited, in Lord Salisbury's judgement, to the occasion, and hopes it will produce a valuable effect."

The Kaiser, in reply to his grandmother's appeal, illustrated alike an unwillingness to incur her open displeasure and his casuistry and disingenuousness in self-defence. Representing that the telegram was his unassisted performance, he asserted that he designed it in the interests of his grandmother and of her country. His duplicity takes a lurid hue when one compares with the excuses which he offered Queen Victoria a confidential comment on the situation in South Africa which he sent six days earlier to Tsar Nicholas II. On 2nd January—the eve of the despatch of the telegram—he had written to the Tsar thus :

Now suddenly the Transvaal Republic has been attacked in a most foul way as it seems not without England's knowledge. I have used very severe language in London, and have opened communications with Paris for common defence of our endangered interests, as French and German colonists have immediately joined hands of their own accord to help the outraged Boers. I hope you will also kindly consider the question, as it is one of principle of upholding treaties once concluded. I hope all will come right, but, come what may, I shall never allow the British to stamp out the Transvaal.[1]

"Most beloved Grandmama" the apologetic grandson wrote

[1] *The Kaiser's Letters to Tsar* (1920), p. 30.

in quite a different strain of wheedling from "Neues Palais, 8/1/96":

Never was the Telegram intended as a step against England or your Government. By Sir Frank as well as by the Embassy in London we knew that Government had done everything in its power to stop the Freebooters, but that the latter had flatly refused to obey and in a most unprecedented manner went and surprised a neighbouring country in deep peace. . . .

The reasons for the Telegram were 3-fold—First, in the name of peace as such which had been suddenly violated, and which I always, following your glorious example, try to maintain everywhere. This course of action has till now so often carried your so valuable approval. Secondly, for our Germans in Transvaal and our Bondholders at home with our invested capital of 250–300 millions and the local commerce of the Coast of 10–12 millions, which were in danger in case fighting broke out in the towns. Thirdly, as your Government and Ambassador had both made clear that the men were acting in open disobedience to your orders, they were rebels. I, of course, thought that they were a mixed mob of gold diggers quickly summoned together, who are generally known to be strongly mixed with the scum of all nations, never suspecting there were real Englishmen or Officers among them.

Now to me Rebels against the will of the most gracious Majesty the Queen, are to me the most execrable beings in the world, and I was so incensed at the idea of your orders having been disobeyed, and thereby Peace and the security also of my Fellow Countrymen endangered, that I thought it necessary to show that publicly. It has, I am sorry to say, been totally misunderstood by the British Press. I was standing up for law, order, and obedience to a Sovereign whom I revere and adore, and whom to obey I thought paramount for her subjects. Those were my motives, and I challenge anybody who is a Gentleman to point out where there is anything hostile to England in this. The Secretary of Transvaal was even at his audience the day before yesterday cautioned by me to warn his Government on no account to do anything that could be interpreted as being hostile to England. The Gunboat in Delagoa Bay was only to land in case street fights and incendiarism broke out, to protect the German Consulate as they do in China or elsewhere, but was forbidden to take any active part in the row : nothing more. As to the silly idea in the Press that I was or wanted to behave hostilely to England, I with a clear conscience refer to Lord Salisbury, who has material enough in his hands from the last years to know my thoughts and what I do for England. But the English Press has been rather rash in its conjectures, and having since some months freely lavished its displeasure on our devoted heads, the Home Press are still sore. . . . This made people rather hot and rash. But I hope and trust this will soon pass away, as it is simply nonsense that two great nations, nearly related in kinsmanship and religion, should stand aside and view each other askance with the rest of Europe as lookers-on. What would the Duke of Wellington and old Blücher say if they saw this?[1]

The prince read his nephew's apologia with impatience, and desired more information. While accepting the Kaiser's pretension to entire responsibility, he was curious to discover how far the German Ministers went in approval of their master's rash act. The Empress Frederick let her mother and brother know that, to the best of her information, the telegram was no "mere hasty and ill-advised action of his (*i.e.* the Kaiser's) own." On the 4th January the Chancellor lunched with the Empress, who sent the same day an account of what passed between them for her mother's and her brother's benefit:

"I slightly touched," the Empress wrote, "on the question of the Transvaal, and I asked whether a certain telegram was to be rejoiced at. He [*i.e.* the Chancellor] answered that it certainly was in accordance with German public feeling at this moment, from which answer I gather that the telegram was approved. Prince Hohenlohe, who is so cautious and gentle and courteous, did not say much on the subject, but told me he had seen a great deal of President Kruger's Secretary of State, a Dr. Leyds, and the latter had made a most excellent impression on him. Evidently this Dr. Leyds has influenced the German Government a good deal, and most likely German public opinion."

But the Queen and the Prince remained firm in the belief that the full onus of blame lay on the Kaiser. The Queen confirmed the Prince in this conviction by writing to him on 11th January: "I have now heard that the Government (William's)

[1] These extracts follow the original text of the letter, which is among the papers at Marlborough House. A copy in the State Archives at Berlin has been printed in full by Herr Friedrich Thimme in *Europäische Gespräche*, May/June 1924, No. III. p. 243. To his friend Sir Edward Sullivan, the Kaiser wrote from Berlin on 3rd February 1896 to much the same casuistical effect. To Sir Edward he protested his ignorance that Englishmen and officers were among the raiders. He thought they were "a pack of gold diggers." His telegram was merely a "thankful outcry" that German "men and money had been saved from loss and ruin" at the hands of "Jameson and his marauders" (Colonel Repington's *Vestigia*, pp. 191–2).

had nothing to do with this outrage which has created such a
sensation." Lord Salisbury's government finally adopted the
view that the telegram was not "an official document," and
was mainly the fruit of the Kaiser's waywardness.

On 11th January the Queen remarked to her son that
the excitement in England "fortunately is cooling down."
The Queen's forecast was justified. On 7th January the
Transvaal government handed over the arrested raiders to
the Governor of the Cape (Sir Hercules Robinson), and they
were ordered to London to stand their trial on the charge
of making war on a friendly State. President Kruger grew
doubtful of active assistance from Germany and grudgingly
consented to negotiate a settlement with England. On 20th
February 1896 Mr. Chamberlain sent to the Prince a review of
the situation, and wrote that he was sanguine of making terms
with Kruger. The Kaiser's vague appeals for the co-operation
of France and Russia in reducing England's power over the
Transvaal misfired, and he recognised the prudence of placating
English feeling. On 18th June 1896, the anniversary of Waterloo,
he commissioned Baron von Eckardstein of the German Embassy
in London to place on his behalf a wreath on the colours of his
English regiment, the Royal Dragoons, then stationed at The
Curragh. The military authorities of the camp arranged a
picturesque ceremonial. The Prince acknowledged the futility
of pursuing the Kruger telegram controversy further, and the
perturbation in England abated. But there was no genuine
slackening in the mutual rancours of the peoples and the press
of the two countries, and the Prince's resentment against his
nephew was unappeased.

In July there were signs of a renewed outbreak of German
feeling against England. Loud complaint was then made of
the inadequacy of the punishment meted out for their offences
to Dr. Jameson and five of his companions, who were military
officers.[1] The Prince showed sympathy with the officers who,
after their trial, were deprived by the War Office of their commissions. He admitted the necessity of this step. "I am
very much obliged to you," he wrote to the Queen's private

[1] Dr. Jameson and five military officers (Sir John Willoughby, Major
Robert White, Colonel Henry White, Colonel Grey, and Major Coventry) were
tried in London, 20th–28th July, for infringement of the Foreign Enlistment
Act, were found guilty, and were sentenced to short terms of imprisonment.

secretary, Sir Arthur Bigge, from Homburg, 29th August, "for
telling me the fate of the Jameson raiders. I always thought
they would not keep their commissions." But he looked forward
to the officers' early restoration, and he expressed disappointment
that no action was taken when the question came on two occasions
before the Cabinet (July 27, 1897, and May 10, 1898). At the
end of the year (1896) he received from Sir Schomberg Macdonnell,
Lord Salisbury's private secretary, a copy of a Cabinet memorandum (dated December 11), to the effect "that no further
official notice was to be taken of the German Emperor's telegram
to Kruger, as that unfortunate communication was not in itself
an official document, and as all the assurances which the Government is now receiving from Germany are of a pacific nature."
The Prince's confidence in Germany's change of mind was
scarcely complete, but he was willing to await events.

V

It was solely as a rigorous and incisive critic of the Kaiser
in private that the Prince came into relation with the heated
episode of the Kruger telegram. Another sequel of the Jameson
raid brought him into more open touch with South African
controversy. Dr. Jameson's ill-advised action provoked party
conflict at home. Liberal politicians warmly pleaded that the
causes of the raid on the Transvaal demanded searching investigation. Mr. Cecil Rhodes, who filled the three authoritative offices
of director of the British South Africa Chartered Company,
Chairman of the De Beers Mining Company on the Rand, and
Prime Minister at the Cape, had admitted responsibility for Dr.
Jameson's design. The spokesmen of the Liberal Party argued
that Rhodes's fellow-directors of the De Beers and the Chartered
Companies were implicated equally with himself, and all ought
to be called to strict account. There was a hope, too, among
political opponents of proving, if inquiries were pressed far
enough, that Mr. Chamberlain, the Unionist Colonial Secretary,
was personally privy to the rash exploit. Popular rumour,
moreover, mentioned the Prince as being well disposed to the
Chartered Company and as deprecating the Liberals' effort to
scrutinise the initiation of the raid too closely. The directors
of the Company included his son-in-law, the Duke of Fife, and

his old friend the Duke of Abercorn. Nor did the Prince make any secret of his sympathy with Mr. Rhodes's imperial ambitions. Sir William Harcourt, the Radical leader, who engaged with zest in the political agitation, reckoned the Prince among the active patrons of Mr. Rhodes and his colleagues. On the 6th of May 1896 Sir William was the Prince's guest at dinner at Marlborough House. Writing to his wife in the afternoon, Sir William expressed impatience with the financial forces rallying round the Prince and his friends of the Chartered Company. "The language of *The Times* and the stock-jobbing Press is most disgraceful," he wrote. "I dine with H.R.H. at Marlborough House to-night, when I suppose we shall be in the midst of the enemy." [1] Sir William discovered nothing in his intercourse with his host to lend substance to his own and to the popular suspicions that the Prince had confidential knowledge of Transvaal affairs.

Yielding to popular pressure, the government appointed on 14th August 1896 a Select Committee of the House of Commons to inquire into all the circumstances connected with the origin of the raid. The Committee, of which Sir William Harcourt was a member, was slow in getting to work, and not until its re-appointment next year did it sit to take evidence (January 14, 1897). Witnesses were numerous. Mr. Cecil Rhodes, one of the first, was searchingly examined by Sir William. The Duke of Fife and the Duke of Abercorn denied all knowledge of the intended raid. Mr. Chamberlain testified to like effect. The Select Committee reported on 15th July, and gave absolution to well-nigh all the suspected persons. They attributed the raid to the discontent of the Uitlanders in Johannesburg, but while they censured Cecil Rhodes, alike as Prime Minister of the Cape and as acting manager of the De Beers Mining Company on the Rand, for grave breaches of duty, and reproved two fellow-directors, Mr. Alfred Beit and Mr. Rochfort Maguire, they exonerated from complicity the imperial and colonial govern-ments and the rest of the directors and officials of the Chartered Company. The evidence fully justified the wholesale exculpa-tion, but it disappointed many who had taken part in the hue and cry.

Some incredulity persisted in Radical quarters as to the

[1] Gardiner's *Sir William Harcourt*, ii. p. 389.

Prince's detachment from the main issues. Popular rumours now took the shape of charging the Prince with influencing the terms of the Report in the interests of his friends. The allegation was unfounded. Sir William Harcourt, one of the signatories of the Report, publicly countered the insinuation by asserting that the verdict accorded with the facts as they were proved in evidence.

The Prince's signs of sympathy with Mr. Rhodes's heroic plans for the expansion of British influence in South Africa alone gave plausibility to the Radical allegations. The Prince deplored Rhodes's indiscretions, but after his wont he reckoned that they were out-balanced by his imperial services in the past, and by his future programme of work for South Africa. His friendly relations with the South African magnate were not interrupted by the events of 1896, and continued until Rhodes's premature death six years later. The Prince deprecated the coolness with which Lord Salisbury habitually regarded him. Early in 1897 the Prince wrote asking Schomberg Macdonnell, Lord Salisbury's private secretary, to explain the grounds on which Lord Salisbury declined to give Rhodes an interview while he was on a visit to London (February 10). The Prince was especially attracted by Rhodes's scheme for continuous telegraphic communication between Cairo and the Cape, and he welcomed intimate reports from Rhodes on the progress of his preliminary negotiations. Those negotiations brought Rhodes early in 1899 into personal touch with the Kaiser. From him and from his associates Rhodes learned how the estrangement between uncle and nephew prejudiced the good relations between their two countries. He took advantage (as he said) of the friendly sentiment which the Prince had long cherished for him, to direct the Prince's attention to that critical fact.

VI

During the three years 1897–1898–1899 much fuel fed the dissensions alike between England and Germany and between the Kaiser and the Prince. Now and then within the period, when the flames seemed to droop, they suddenly shot higher. Not before the close of 1899 was there any assurance of their subsiding. The wayward disposition of the Kaiser seemed to deny him for the time all self-control. His utterances were a tumult of glaring contradictions. Towards his English relatives his attitude was like that of an ill-trained and ill-tempered child. He professed alternately a desire to re-visit England on friendly family terms and a resolve to stay away from a country which was bent on his humiliation. As far as one can draw order out of chaos, one may trace through the Kaiser's vagaries a wild dream of an Anglo-German alliance on terms of his own devising and imposing. Disapproval on England's part of his arrogant advances provoked unmannerly language from his lips and pen, as well as a dishevelled tangle of underhand efforts to damage her power and prestige. To the Prince and to Lord Salisbury he assigned the chief responsibility for the rejection of his high-handed offers. Catching at straws, he put on occasion the flattering unction to his soul that the English government was yielding to his dictation and that an Anglo-German alliance was about to take shape. He gloated over the anticipated discomfiture which his triumph would cause his uncle.[1]

The political controversies of the period between the English and German governments ranged over a wide field. There was the long-standing quarrel over the Samoan Archipelago, and there were new wrangles over affairs of the Near East and of the Far East.[2] German endeavours to obtain a foothold in China were viewed with suspicion by Russia, as well as by England. The Kaiser played with fresh energy his former game of seeking to embroil these two countries by pouring into the ears of both

---

[1] *Die Grosse Politik*, xiv. pt. i. 218.

[2] The grant of autonomy to Crete in 1897, with the sanction of the six Powers—England, France, Italy, Russia, Germany, and Austria—led to a bitter quarrel between the Kaiser and both England and Russia. The Prince and the Tsar contrived that their kinsman, Prince George of Greece, son of the King of the Hellenes, should become first Governor-General of the autonomous island. The Kaiser regarded the choice as a personal affront, and in dudgeon induced his own country and Austria to withdraw from the European concert which was supervising the settlement of Crete (see p. 495, *supra*). German occupation of Chinese territory, another rock of stumbling, began early in 1898, when Kiao-chau was occupied by a German squadron under the command of the Kaiser's brother, Prince Henry. At the same date the Kaiser was encouraging Tsar Nicholas to annex, by way of challenging England, the Liao-tung Peninsula and the harbour of Port Arthur on the coast of China. "We two will make a good pair of sentinels," the Kaiser wrote to the Tsar, 28th March 1898. Lord Salisbury retaliated in May by leasing from China the port and district of Wei-hai-wei on the mainland, lying midway between Kiao-chau and Port Arthur (May 20, 1898). Furthermore, early in 1898, owing largely to the Kaiser's urgency, the German Reichstag adopted the first Naval Act (March 26) which Admiral von Tirpitz, lately become Secretary of the Naval Department, devised in consultation with the Kaiser.

Tsar Nicholas at St. Petersburg and of the English Ambassador at Berlin malevolent hints of the enmity of the one government for the other. The knowledge that his uncle was befriending the new Tsar, Nicholas II., imparted an added venom to the Kaiser's confidential appeals to the Russian ruler to thwart England at all turns.[1] At the same time the Kaiser was constantly challenging England's self-respect by blustering prophecy of the coming world-predominance of the German navy. Many times he indulged in the brazen boasts that "the trident is in German hands," and that "our future lies on the water." To the meaning of the Kaiser's naval ambitions the Prince was especially well alive. On 21st March 1897 the well-travelled and well-informed Sir Donald Mackenzie Wallace, formerly foreign editor of *The Times*, who was now sending the Prince confidential reports on foreign affairs, forwarded to him from Berlin the information that his nephew had in naval matters "taken the bit between his teeth," and had "tabled proposals" for a vast increase of the German fleet "without the consent of the Chancellor."

1897
Ætat. 55

VII

The Kaiser, while he professed despair of his uncle, made flickering efforts to keep Queen Victoria and the rest of the royal family in good humour. Queen Victoria, although she doubted her grandson's sincerity, was always careful to reciprocate every show of courtesy. She sent her third son, the Duke of Connaught, to represent her when the Kaiser unveiled

[1] The Kaiser repeatedly pointed out to the Tsar that China, where "the German Michael was firmly planting his shield," offered promising ground for Russian activities which might injure England's prestige in the Far East. He especially congratulated the Tsar in 1898 on England's perturbation over Count Muravieff's designs on the Province of Manchuria in Northern China. A threat to the integrity of China was certain to agitate England. At the end of 1897 Baron von Marschall left the Wilhelmstrasse for the German Embassy at Constantinople, there to consolidate the German understanding with the Sultan to which the Kaiser was committed. Count von Bülow, a disciple of Prince Bismarck, was recalled to Berlin from the Embassy at Rome to fill the office which von Marschall vacated. Von Bülow was a master of finesse, and was as fully convinced as his old master Bismarck of the advantage of playing off England and Russia against one another. That device was always congenial to the Kaiser, and, encouraged by von Bülow's example, he now worked it with an impulsive defiance of truth and honesty which at times disconcerted von Bülow himself.

a statue in Berlin of his grandfather, William I. (March 22, 1897). In the autumn of 1897 the Queen's cousin, the Duke of Cambridge, accepted the Kaiser's invitation to attend the manœuvres. The Duke reported to the Princess Beatrice for the information of her mother :

Nothing could exceed the friendliness and amiability of both Emperor and Empress. . . . Not an unkind expression of any sort or kind was uttered by H.M. with reference to England, and he evidently was anxious to avoid any subject that would evince any other feeling than a friendly one in the several conversations with him.

Some English politicians, too, deprecated a continuance of England's isolation, and, despite the prevalent distrust of the Kaiser, they were not unwilling to consider dispassionately his equivocal proposals for co-operation between the two countries. Russian aggressiveness in China and the shrewish temper of France led Mr. Chamberlain, the Colonial Secretary in Lord Salisbury's government, in the spring of 1898, to explore the possibilities of some kind of Anglo-German understanding. Count von Hatzfeldt, the German Ambassador in London, was encouraging. The capricious Kaiser, who coolly disclaimed all faith in Lord Salisbury, assumed an air of unconcern. A new personal difficulty had arisen between the Kaiser and the Prince to feed the Kaiser's animosity towards England.

The new quarrel between uncle and nephew rested on a trivial ground. Among the Kaiser's confidants was Admiral von Senden und Bibran, his naval A.D.C. and chief of his Naval Cabinet—a Junker in manner and speech. The admiral had always accompanied the Kaiser to Cowes, where his aggressive bearing was good-naturedly tolerated by the Prince. When the Kaiser's visits to Cowes ceased, he was entrusted by his master with the duty of bringing to England the Kaiser's letters to Queen Victoria. It was his hand which carried to the Queen the Kaiser's letter containing his casuistical defence of the Kruger telegram. On such missions the German admiral was in the habit of calling informally on the equerries at Marlborough House. Occasionally he met the Prince there. The rumour ran that he usually returned to the Kaiser with some spiteful gossip about the Prince.

Early in February 1898 the Prince met by chance his

nephew's messenger at Marlborough House in the room of his equerry, Sir Stanley Clarke. Little passed between them. The Prince inquired after the health of the Kaiser and the Kaiserin. The admiral offered to perform commissions for him in Berlin ; the Prince replied that the only letter which he was sending to Germany was one to the Empress Frederick which would be carried by royal messenger. The admiral, taking offence at the Prince's curtness, retaliated characteristically. He told the Kaiser on his return to Berlin that the Prince had spoken disparagingly of Germany and of its ruler. The Kaiser, who accepted the statement without seeking confirmation, treated it as a deliberate affront. Calling on Sir Frank Lascelles at the Embassy, he bade the Ambassador report his grievance to Lord Salisbury. Sir Frank invited the Prince's view of the situation. The Prince promptly replied (February 23, 1898) :

I have always been on most friendly terms with Admiral Senden, and whenever we have met have treated him as an old acquaintance. It was through me that he was made an honorary member of the R.Y. Squadron, as I thought it would please the Emperor and be agreeable to the Admiral during his frequent visits to England. Why, therefore, he should have deliberately tried to make mischief between me and the Emperor, and made statements which are not true, is simply incomprehensible to me. . . . I deny *in toto* that I was uncivil in my usage ; his statements are positively untrue, and I greatly resent them as a positive insult to myself. Nobody is more anxious for friendly relations with the Emperor than I am, though on more than one occasion I have been sorely tried.

In accordance with the Prince's direction, Lascelles communicated to the Kaiser the contents of this letter. The Kaiser testily remarked that the Prince always looked upon him as "a silly boy," and "that this continued hostility evinced towards him by the Prince of Wales would possibly have serious results upon the relations between the two countries." [1] The Prince had no wish to carry the matter further, but asked Lascelles to let the admiral know that he wished to have no more to do with him (March 10, 1898). The Kaiser declined to side with his uncle against his A.D.C., but circumstances soon led him to desire an accommodation.

[1] Lascelles to Salisbury, 14th March 1898.

VIII

1898
Ætat. 56

On second thoughts, the Kaiser inclined to bestow on Mr. Chamberlain's friendly gesture toward Germany greater favour than was his first intention. He therefore sought in a clumsy way to compose or at least to side-track the fresh dissension with his uncle. Again approaching Sir Frank Lascelles, he proposed that his mother should arbitrate between his uncle and himself over the Senden squabble and the causes of their alienation. With doubtful relevance he complained that political and family misunderstandings kept him away from England; he had no quarrel with Queen Victoria; he looked forward to an improvement in Anglo-German relations; he proposed to visit his grandmother in the summer.

The Prince's reasonable comment on the Kaiser's utterance, which Lascelles reported to him, ran as follows : [1]

If only the son could see more of his mother and could get under her influence, how different everything would be, and I am sure he would be far happier himself. . . . His remark that he hoped that an "improvement in the relations of the two courts would soon take place" seems to me to be quite unnecessary. All his English relations wish him well and desire to be on the best of terms with him. But they will *not* stand being misrepresented or having things said about *them* which are not true. *Voilà tout!* The whole matter rests in the German Emperor's hands and there is really no need for his mother's good offices. . . . The idea of the German Emperor visiting the Queen in Scotland seems an excellent one and might perhaps be suggested, but would it be in the summer or autumn?

The immediate sequel was not reassuring. The Kaiser took in July the unusual course of confiding to his mother his wish to reconnoitre English political feeling in regard to his scheme of a dictated alliance. He believed her to be in a better position than himself to sound both her mother and brother in matters touching Anglo-German relations. In her eagerness to promote international goodwill the Empress probably went a little further than her son intended. On 15th July 1898 she wrote to Queen Victoria of the desirability of an Anglo-German pact. Amid some rhapsodising she gave her mother and brother

---

[1] It was dated from Nice on 30th March.

clear hints of the lie of the land. No insuperable obstacle, she pointed out, would be raised by the German Chancellor, von Hohenlohe, by the German Foreign Minister, von Bülow, or by the Kaiser, if Lord Salisbury would make a concrete proposal.

"I do know for a fact," the Empress proceeded, "that William is most anxious for a rapprochment with England, and hopes with all his heart that England *will* come forward in some sort of way and meet him half-way. Chamberlain's utterances have made the most favourable impression on W., but he fears that Salisbury does not endorse them." [1]

Neither on Queen Victoria nor on the Prince did the Empress Frederick's benevolent impetuosity make much impression. Lord Salisbury, when Queen Victoria showed him her daughter's letter, replied that he was indisposed to take any action.

But the Kaiser declined to be put off quite summarily. He pressed his government to make a further trial of England's sentiment by making her a substantive offer of a fresh exchange of colonial possessions. The proposal was duly delivered.[2] The Prince agreed with the government in regarding it as illusory, and he was relieved to learn from Lord Salisbury's secretary, Mr. Schomberg Macdonnell, that "the territorial demands of Germany were too extensive to be acceptable, and that the project had therefore fallen through." All the Kaiser's wrath against both the Prince and Lord Salisbury flamed up anew on learning that his government's offer was rejected. On 8th August 1898 he wrote to Queen Victoria that his overtures were received "with something between a joke and a snub." To the Tsar he declared in his blustering vein (August 18) that

[1] The letter continues: "Alas, such a thing as an alliance is too good to be true! English Govts. are dependent on the House of Commons—ministries change so—a continuous foreign policy with a *plan* to be followed up cannot exist in England. Bülow seemed to think a good understanding could only be the work of time, and of slow growth, whilst I imagine Wm. thinks the moment propitious—and would be anxious for the idea to take shape and form. If I may say—I also think it would be wise to treat and consider the matter without too much delay. I tried myself to improve the opportunity— and told Wm. what I thought, which you know I *very* rarely do. I also once wrote to Hatzfeldt—quite confidentially (6 weeks or more ago)—but he never answered or took *any notice*."

[2] Germany offered to surrender her claims on Tonga Islands and the Samoan Archipelago in the Pacific and any claim she might acquire to Delagoa Bay if England would cede to her Blantyre (Nyasaland) in Central Africa and Walfisch Bay, a strong strategic position which England valued in South-West Africa.

the English reply was dictated by the lowest instincts of self-interest. "They are trying hard," he added mysteriously and incoherently, "as far as I can make out, to find a continental army to fight for their interests, but I fancy they will not easily find one, at least not *mine*." [1]

IX

For another full year the Kaiser continued to storm against England, of which he regarded the Prince and Lord Salisbury as the evil geniuses. When on occasion the clouds seemed to be breaking and better weather to promise, he grew louder in his imprecations on the English royal family and on English statesmen. A more sinister spirit coloured the warnings of England's and of his uncle's trickery which he addressed to the Tsar Nicholas, while in order, as he thought, to keep England on tenterhooks he drew lurid pictures, for the benefit of the English Ambassador in Berlin, of the ruin which Russia was preparing for England.

In the summer of 1898 a new issue, the financial embarrassments of Portugal, brought a fresh complication into the relations of England and Germany. The episode opened badly, but its development suggested a possibility of reconciling, at one point at any rate, the two countries' interests,—a prospect which was very imperfectly fulfilled. Portugal had applied to England for a loan. Germany protested against English assent to the application. The Prince, who was anxious to assist his friend and kinsman, Dom Carlos, endorsed a Cabinet Minute reporting Germany's protest (19th June 1898), with the words: "Why should Germany object to our making a loan to Portugal?" Germany replied that Portugal was as much in arrears with the interest due on debts to German investors as with that due to English investors. But the attitude of France to Portugal's troubles soon put the situation in a new light, and England deemed it prudent to seek Germany's co-operation in a joint arrangement with Portugal. France was reported to be promising Portugal substantial aid on the security of her African possessions. England had no wish for France to strengthen her position in Africa. She had less at the moment

[1] *The Kaiser's Letters to the Tsar*, pp. 57-58.

to fear in that quarter from Germany. Germany, too, was   1898
anxious to thwart every ambition of France, colonial or other.   Ætat. 56
In the event, England and Germany based on Portugal's difficulties a secret pact with one another (October 1898). On
the assumption that Portugal was willing to accept financial
assistance from both England and Germany, the two powers
agreed that they would jointly grant Portugal the financial
relief she needed, provided that she either ceded to them her
colonial possessions in Africa, and in the Sunda Archipelago
(Indian Ocean), or granted them rights of pre-emption. There
was no specification of how the rich territories were to be divided
in case of a joint ownership, but the contracting parties were
satisfied that they were precluding Portugal from mortgaging
any of her colonies to France. The secret arrangement proved
abortive, but the Kaiser welcomed it with a premature and a
fantastic elation.[1]

The secret treaty brought anything rather than reconciliation
of England and Germany in its train. In November 1898 the
Kaiser spoke of it to Sir Frank Lascelles in terms of wild exaggeration. He described it as the corner-stone of an Anglo-German
"alliance." The Ambassador expressed a cautious satisfaction.
The Kaiser, however, perversely informed his mother that a full
understanding with England had been reached at the interview.
"Everything," he declared, "was coming out right." England
and Germany together could render Russia helpless, and if
England would only adopt reasonable views he would enter into
an alliance with her within twenty-four hours.[2] To his friends
in Berlin he talked exultingly of his "Lascelles arrangement."
Lord Salisbury, on hearing of the Kaiser's inflated misapprehension, instructed Sir Frank Lascelles to disabuse the German
government and the Kaiser of the notion that any alliance was
in the wind. There followed a stormy meeting of Sir Frank

[1] Rumours of completion of the secret Anglo-German treaty put Portugal
on her mettle, and she met her financial embarrassments without contracting
the obligations which the treaty had in view. The illness of Lord Salisbury
had withdrawn him temporarily from the Foreign Office, and the transaction,
for which he had little enthusiasm, was carried out in his absence by his nephew
Mr. Balfour, with Mr. Chamberlain's assistance. Count von Hatzfeldt, at the end
of the year, inquired of Lord Salisbury whether the Azores fell within the scope
of the treaty. The Count had heard that France had designs in that quarter.
Lord Salisbury disconcerted the German Ambassador by a blunt statement
that the future of the Azores was not involved in the negotiations.

[2] Eckardstein, p. 214.

1898
Ætat. 56

with the Kaiser at the palace of the Empress Frederick at Cronberg on 9th December 1898. The Kaiser denounced with heat the pusillanimity of the British ministry.

X

The incalculable Kaiser immediately afterwards struck another note. He affected a wish to placate Queen Victoria, and his action mystified public opinion in England and elsewhere. He sent his grandmother a congratulatory telegram on Lord Kitchener's victory over the Sudanese at Atbara (April 5, 1898). In the autumn (September 4) he claimed credit of his grandmother for having celebrated Lord Kitchener's decisive victory of Omdurman (September 2) at a camp-service at the Waterloo-Platz at Hanover (September 4), when, in an address to the troops, he recalled how British and German fought shoulder to shoulder at Waterloo. He felicitated Queen Victoria on Kitchener's success in avenging Gordon's death.

Queen Victoria was gratified by such friendly professions, and she sought to persuade her son to accept them at their face value. They suggested to her and others a desire on the Kaiser's part to make amends for the Kruger telegram, and the Queen readily reciprocated them in the interests of political and domestic peace. Towards the close of 1898 the Queen accordingly asked Sir Frank Lascelles not only to broach with the Kaiser the question of a visit to England, for which the Kaiser seemed to yearn, but also to assure him that the Prince of Wales had spoken of him to the Queen quite amiably. The Kaiser appeared for the moment to welcome these friendly intimations. When he celebrated his fortieth birthday (January 28, 1899), he wrote to the Queen in tones of ingenuous humility (Feb. 5, 1899) :

How extraordinary the fact must seem to you that the tiny weeny little brat you often had in your arms, and dear Grandpapa swung about in his napkin, has reached the forties, just the half of your prosperous and successful life.

He struck a half-penitent note in his confession that the strain upon him was "often too heavy to bear," but he trusted to the good and genial heart of his grandmother to view with compassion the failures of "her queer and impetuous colleague."

But the prospect of calm was again quickly overcast.   Fresh storms were brewing. The Kaiser's bad temper broke loose once more, and Queen Victoria's irritation with her grandson almost equalled that of the Prince. The first of the new rifts came in February 1899 over the affairs of the duchy of Saxe-Coburg. The present Duke's only son and heir died on 5th February—"a terrible blow to his parents, being their only son," as the Prince wrote to Lord Spencer (February 9). Once again, the succession to the family duchy occupied the Queen's mind. She took the view that her third son, the Duke of Connaught, was entitled to the succession, and that his name ought to be submitted to the local Diets of the two duchies. Unfortunately, she omitted to consult the Kaiser before venturing on the suggestion. When the news reached her grandson he ridiculed her choice, and threatened her and Lord Salisbury with the veto of the German Reichstag. The local Diets favoured the election of the Duke of Connaught, but the Queen was unwilling to add fuel to her grandson's wrath, and the Duke, at his mother's request, renounced his candidature for the duchies in his own behalf; subsequently he made a like refusal in behalf of his son, Prince Arthur of Connaught. The Duke of Albany, the posthumous son of the Queen's youngest son, Leopold, was finally adopted on 30th June as heir-presumptive to the principality with which were entwined all Queen Victoria's wifely affections.

Worse followed in the long story of the Kaiser's antagonisms. The English government's refusal to accept his solution of the persistent Samoan problem whetted his fury against England and his English kinsfolk. Samoa seemed now to work on his brain like a corrosive acid. He denounced to the Tsar with increased virulence England's perfidious policy, at the same time as he overwhelmed Sir Frank Lascelles with allegations of the Tsar's treachery to England.[1] Through the spring and

[1] The Queen, although she had no direct knowledge of the Kaiser's letters to the Tsar, was aware of the Kaiser's slanders on the Tsar which he communicated to Sir Frank Lascelles, and she shrewdly suspected the tone of her grandson's comments, in his correspondence with the Tsar, on herself, and her country. She was moved to warn the Tsar against the Kaiser's recklessness. "I feel," she wrote to the Tsar on 2nd March 1899, "I must write and tell you something which you *ought* to know and perhaps do not. It is, I am sorry to say, that William takes every opportunity of impressing upon Sir F. Lascelles that Russia is doing all in her power to work against us; that she offers alliances to other Powers and has made one with the Amir of Afghanistan, against us. I need not say that I do not believe a word of this, neither do Ld. Salisbury nor Sir F. Lascelles. But I am afraid William may go and tell things against us

early summer his grandmother came under the lash of the Kaiser's tongue or pen equally with the Prince and Lord Salisbury. Yet, with blind obliviousness to the offence that he was giving, he suggested that he should visit the Queen on her forthcoming eightieth birthday (May 24, 1899). Her deprecation of the proposal was a fresh wound to his pride, especially, as he pointed out, it was his filial intention to present to his grandmother on the occasion the whole of his family.

XI

In his unbalanced temper, the Kaiser was always ready to blame his uncle for what he described as England's intransigeance. However misconceived the Kaiser's grievance against the Prince, there was among peace-lovers in both countries a strong wish that the friction between uncle and nephew might abate. In March 1899 a peace-making effort was volunteered from an unexpected quarter. The Kaiser accorded an interview in Berlin to Mr. Cecil Rhodes. The King of the Belgians, who was at odds with both England and France in regard to his claims on Central Africa, had refused Mr. Rhodes's application to carry his proposed telegraph line from Cairo to the Cape through the Belgian Congo State. He was therefore bent on obtaining the Kaiser's permission to carry the line through German East Africa. But the conversation between the Kaiser and the South African leader covered far wider ground than the telegraph scheme. Relations not only of England and Germany, but of the Kaiser and the Prince, came into the discussion. The Kaiser professed himself willing, on conditions, to work with England, but he made a general complaint that his uncle's rooted dislike of him prejudiced his pacific inclinations.

Mr. Rhodes at once wrote in full to the Prince on both the political and the personal issue. Mr. Rhodes frankly admitted the offence which the Kaiser had given the Prince by his telegram to President Kruger, but he ventured to urge that the telegram should be treated as past history. The Kaiser's suspicion that

---

to you, just as he does about you to us. If so, pray tell me openly and confidentially. It is so important that we should understand each other, and that such mischievous and unstraightforward proceedings should be put a stop to. You are so true yourself, that I am sure you will be shocked at this."

his uncle hated him ought to be removed in the interests of Anglo-German peace. "In view of the complications in the world," Rhodes asserted, "we must work with some nation, and Germany seems the best." The Prince, Rhodes concluded, had it in his power to remove any personal difficulty which militated against a political accommodation.

The Prince took in good part Rhodes's frank assumption of the rôle of peacemaker, but nothing immediately came of the intervention. Only a small part of the case lay within Mr. Rhodes's vision, and the Kaiser's mood in the weeks following his interview with Rhodes was scarcely calculated to encourage the Prince to pursue Mr. Rhodes's well-meaning, if imperfectly informed, counsel.

The next three months saw the Kaiser's Anglophobic indignation in full blast. At the end of March the Kaiser angrily complained to Lascelles that English policy was "incomprehensible" to him. For years he had been the one true friend of Great Britain on the Continent of Europe, and he had done everything to help her policy and assist her. Ingratitude had been his reward. Lord Salisbury was his "consistent enemy." He distrusted Mr. Chamberlain's professions of friendship.[1]

In a subsequent interview with Lascelles [2] he characterised the English government's unconciliatory treatment of the Samoan dispute as a deliberate personal affront. Although on 26th May 1899 he deemed it a point of etiquette to give a banquet at Berlin in honour of Queen Victoria's eightieth birthday, he talked the same day of the possibilities of England having to face the German fleet. "Tell your people to behave themselves properly," he remarked to Lascelles; and by way of illustrating his sentiment towards the English people he cited with a grim effort at sarcasm Dean Liddell's remark to an undergraduate, "You have not only imperilled your immortal soul, but you have incurred my serious displeasure." [3]

[1] Lascelles to Salisbury, 31st March 1899.   [2] *Ibid.* 3rd May.
[3] *Ibid.* 26th May 1899. The Kaiser's exasperation also vainly manifested itself in the spring of 1899, in a conversation with the Marquis de Noailles, the French Ambassador in Berlin, in which he warned France of the dangers to which British assertiveness and acquisitiveness exposed the common interests of France and Germany in different parts of the world. M. Delcassé, the French Foreign Minister, who was biding his time for an Anglo-French under-

1899
—
Ætat. 57

On 27th June 1899 the Kaiser informed his grandmother that German public opinion "is very much agitated and stirred to its depths by the most unhappy way in which Lord Salisbury has treated Germany in the Samoan business." Germany was despised by Lord Salisbury. Samoa, the Kaiser remarked, was "a stupid island which is a hairpin to England compared to the thousands of square miles she is amassing right and left unopposed every year." Lord Salisbury saw in the Kaiser's fresh outburst the influence of the jealousy excited by the Prince's intervention in the Cretan business.[1] At the same time the Prime Minister protested that it was unprecedented for a foreign sovereign to attack the minister of another country. The Queen, in a frank reply to her grandson (July 3), took the charitable view that the Kaiser was the victim of temporary irritation, "for I do not think you would otherwise have written in such a strain, which I doubt whether any sovereign ever employed in writing to another sovereign—and that sovereign his own grandmother —about her Prime Minister. I never attacked Bismarck personally, though he was a bitter enemy of England." To this reproof the Kaiser irrelevantly retorted that Russia was doing all she could to injure England.

XII

The storm had now reached its height. The Kaiser mercurially acknowledged that his estrangement from Queen Victoria and the Prince had gone far enough. The German government discovered in some fresh proposals from England a way out of the Samoan *impasse*. There was, too, a growing wish on the part of an influential section of the English people to see England and Germany make up their differences. Mr. Chamberlain, who was facing a critical situation in South Africa where the Boers were spoiling for a fight, was meditating a fresh approach to Germany. Although the Kaiser clung privily to the hope that Germany might reap advantage from England's difficulties, he checked the display of his rancour and resolved on

---

standing, in spite of the popular French outcry over Fashoda, bade his French representative in Berlin request of Count von Bülow "categorical proposals" for France to consider with a view to Franco-German co-operation. The Kaiser was suspicious of M. Delcassé's temper, and no reply was made to the French request.   [1] See p. 495 *supra*.

a demonstration of friendship with his English kinsfolk. The Prince viewed the Kaiser's change of tone in a very detached frame of mind, but he courted peace.

Four years had passed since the Kaiser had visited England. Throughout the acute period of personal dissensions between him and his English kinsfolk, he had often mad capricious complaint that his wish to see England again was thwarted by the ill-will of the Prince and Lord Salisbury. He now took the line that all differences between England and Germany might be composed if he came again to England as his grandmother's guest. In the season of his anger he had threatened never to see Cowes and Osborne again. Now, when the political sky was clearing, he indicated his altered mind by wiring to Queen Victoria (July 22, 1899) that an accident to the Empress alone prevented him from visiting Osborne in August. No invitation had been sent him. The Queen and the Prince were both ready to fall in with the Kaiser's amicable mood. In his absence the Kaiser was represented at Cowes Regatta by his yacht *Meteor II.*, and his benevolent temper gathered strength when his yacht won the race for the Queen's Cup. The Prince, in sportsmanlike fashion, congratulated him on his success.

The Kaiser now concentrated his effort on obtaining an invitation from the Queen to Balmoral in the autumn. The Queen hesitated. Count von Hatzfeldt addressed himself to the Prince of Wales. The Prince was scarcely enthusiastic, but in the public interest he promised the German Ambassador his aid. In the result, the Queen invited the Kaiser to pay her a visit not indeed at Balmoral, but at Windsor in the following November. Some hitch in the protracted Samoan negotiations threatened for a moment the Kaiser's purpose. But, finally, he not merely accepted the Queen's invitation on his own behalf, but proposed to bring with him the Empress and two of his sons.[1]

The final settlement in October of the Samoan conflict lent plausibility to prophecies of the good effect of the coming

[1] Some growls in the pan-German press suggested that the chauvinists preferred the Kaiser to be on bad rather than on good terms with his English relations. The Kaiser, however, asserted that the Chancellor, von Hohenlohe, set great store by the coming visit; it was calculated, in the Chancellor's opinion, to give the final blow to the English people's irritation over the Kruger telegram; the Kaiser's personal conversation with English statesmen might well preclude future misunderstanding.

visit.[1] "This fact" (*i.e.* the Samoan agreement), the Kaiser wired to Queen Victoria on 9th October, "will help to promote good feeling and peace between our two countries." The Queen replied, "It is always my great wish, as well as that of my government, to be on the most friendly terms with Germany."

The date of this exchange of friendly messages between the Queen and her grandson coincided with a critical event in the history of the British Empire. On the same day, the prolonged negotiation for a settlement of the veteran differences between England and the Transvaal republic came to an end with the Boers' appeal to the arbitrament of the sword. The Boer War, which was to last nearly three years, broke out on 11th October. Before a month had passed, a series of "regrettable incidents" on the field of battle showed that the English authorities had gravely underrated the strength of the enemy. There followed a season of gloom and anxiety for the English people. But no thought was entertained by guest or host of postponing the Kaiser's visit.

The outbreak of the Boer War absorbed most of the Prince's attention. But he lent his well-seasoned energies to the task of organising the Kaiser's reception. In view of the uneasiness which events in South Africa were provoking, the programme was shorn of brilliant spectacle, and the Kaiser readily acquiesced in a modest scale of entertainment. The Prince had the impression that his nephew would, however, desire a reception by the City of London, and he supported the view that if the Kaiser went in procession to the Guildhall "there should be as much military display as possible." But the Kaiser solved any difficulty which might arise on this score by informing the Prince that he had no intention of appearing in London at all (November 10, 1899). Unfortunately, the most recent of the personal differences between the Prince and his nephew threatened, on the eve of the visit, to break out anew, and the incident illustrated how treacherous was the ground which the two men were treading. The Prince discovered in the list of the Kaiser's suite

---

[1] England at length adopted Germany's proposal that she should take over the two chief islands of the Samoan group with the adjacent islets, while the other islands farther east should pass to the United States, and England should be compensated for her withdrawal from any part of the Samoan Archipelago by receiving the neighbouring Tonga group of Pacific Islands.

the name of Admiral von Senden und Bibran, whose offence of February 1898 he had not forgiven. The Prince requested Baron von Eckardstein, Secretary of the German Embassy, who was leaving for Berlin, to protest against the Admiral's presence in England. To Eckardstein's protest the Kaiser retorted : "If I go to England at all this autumn, I shall take whom I like with me." Eckardstein reported to the Prince the Kaiser's uncompromising words.[1] The Prince was slow to give way, and the Kaiser threatened at the eleventh hour to cancel his visit. Happily, the Prince's friends, the Duke and Duchess of Devonshire, intervened to persuade him, on terms of an apology from the offender, to withdraw his veto on the Admiral.

At length, on 19th November, the Kaiser, accompanied by the Kaiserin and two of his younger sons, arrived at Portsmouth on his way to Windsor for a five days' stay there. He was attended by his Foreign Secretary, Count von Bülow, and the favourite members of his personal suite, Count von Plessen and Count von Eulenburg as well as Admiral Senden und Bibran, the fomenter of strife who, on arriving at Windsor, made a full *amende* in writing.[2] The Kaiser and the Prince greeted each other cordially. The Kaiser expressed his sympathy with the South African troubles. Political discussion did not go very far. Lord Salisbury, the Prime Minister and Foreign Secretary, was in retirement. His wife had died on the day of the Kaiser's arrival, and immediately afterwards he was attacked by influenza. Mr. Balfour, First Lord of the Treasury who was acting Prime Minister, and Mr. Chamberlain, Colonial Secretary, came, however, to Windsor to hold political conversation with von Bülow. He told them that it was the desire of the Kaiser "to be on the best of terms with England." The lines of the Samoan settlement might well, he amicably suggested, be followed when other questions of the sort arose. He scarcely thought alliances were in vogue in England, but he would always be ready for friendly discussions. Goodwill on his part would not be wanting. He deplored the growing friction between Russia and Japan and feared the threatened encroachments of Russia on China.

[1] Eckardstein, *Ten Years at the Court of St. James's*, pp. 97, 100, 121-4.

[2] Sir Frank Lascelles was summoned from Berlin for the occasion. Count von Hatzfeldt, the German Ambassador in London, was too ill to stay at Windsor more than a day.

South Africa was unmentioned by the German Foreign Minister in his colloquies with English statesmen.[1]

The Prince's reconciliation with the Kaiser seemed outwardly consummated when his nephew and the Kaiserin left Windsor on the 25th, with von Bülow, for a three days' stay at Sandringham. It was nineteen years since the Kaiser had set foot in the Prince's country house. His nephew's self-sufficiency was always prone to cause his uncle especial irritation when they were informally in each other's company, but on this occasion there was no disturbance of the general harmony. The Prince's friend at the German Embassy, Baron von Eckardstein, with Sir Frank Lascelles and Lord Wolseley, the Commander-in-Chief, were among the Kaiser's fellow-guests. When the conversation touched politics, nothing but peaceful professions were exchanged. On his return to Germany [2] the Kaiser wrote to the Prince of the "delightful" time which they had spent together, while in a letter to Queen Victoria he grew ecstatic over his "lovely days" at Windsor. He was, he declared a month later, "still under the charm of all the kindly impressions" (December 21).

Great as was the importance attached at the time in the Chancelleries of Europe to the Kaiser's visit, and to the outward signs of reconciliation with the Prince, the whole episode proves in the retrospect to have been delusive. The political discussions at Windsor or Sandringham, in spite of their friendly tone, were indefinite and superficial. Mr. Chamberlain vainly sought to give them a greater significance than they deserved in a speech which he delivered at Leicester on the day after the Kaiser's departure. In a comprehensive survey of the political situation at home and abroad, he expounded afresh his former plea for an understanding with Germany,[3] and the Utopian touch about the statesman's

---

[1] Report by Sir Frank Bertie, Under-Secretary of State for the Foreign Office, of a conversation with von Bülow at Windsor dated 26th November 1899 (Foreign Office Archives).

[2] From Sandringham the Kaiser travelled to Port Victoria, where he embarked for Germany (November 29), after his ten days in England.

[3] No "far-seeing English statesman could be content," Mr. Chamberlain said, "with England's permanent isolation on the continent of Europe. . . . The natural alliance is between ourselves and the great German Empire." The differences which had arisen between the two nations, he sanguinely explained, had been "one by one gradually removed" until nothing remained that was likely to cause antagonism. Both interest and racial sentiment united the two peoples, and a new Triple Alliance between Germany, England, and the United States would correspond with the sentimental tie that already bound

utterance did not check the popular fancy that it rested on solid 1899
Ætat. 57 foundations which had been laid at Windsor. But Mr. Chamberlain was building on sand. The fair words which the Kaiser and his Foreign Minister spoke to their English hosts came only from the lips. Before the year ended the Kaiser, while still pursuing Queen Victoria and the Prince with professions of friendship, was setting on foot an insidious plot which aimed at England's serious injury. In underground negotiations with Russia, he was seeking to use the embarrassment which the Boer War was causing England as a lever to overthrow her. The reckless scheme failed; but its history, the details of which are revealed in the following chapter, presents the Kaiser in a light which proves the Prince and Lord Salisbury to be better judges than Mr. Chamberlain of his real character, and of his real attitude towards England. In his letters to Queen Victoria and the Prince during the next year he masked, with Pecksniffian art, his sinister tone behind vows of fulsome affection and overstrained expressions of sympathy with the anxieties of the Boer War. Yet the evidence of his duplicity is complete. In the autumn of 1908 (27th October), the Kaiser sanctioned the publication in a London newspaper, the *Daily Telegraph*, of an interview with himself in which he thought to refute the prevalent belief in England that he had worked in the course of the Boer War against the interests of this country. In that statement he declared that documents at Windsor Castle, "awaiting the serenely impartial verdict of history," exist to relieve him, once for all, of the charge of seeking England's injury. The investigation has now been made at Windsor and elsewhere, with the result that the Kaiser's plea of innocence meets its doom.

Teutons and Anglo-Saxons together. He attached no dogmatic value to the word "alliance": "an understanding, a determination to look favourably on the motives of those with whom we desire to be on terms of friendship—a feeling of that kind, cultivated and confirmed by all these three countries" would bring about the millennium quite as well or better. This speech of Mr. Chamberlain was omitted from the collection of his speeches edited by C. W. Boyd, 1914.

CHAPTER XXXIX

THE SOUTH AFRICAN WAR, 1899-1900—THE KAISER'S TWO VOICES

THROUGH the summer and autumn of 1899 Mr. Chamberlain postponed, as long as conditions of honour allowed, that full pressure on the Boers which the misgovernment of the Transvaal Republic was inviting. The Prince in June showed some impatience with the Colonial Secretary's deliberate procedure, and characterised his policy as "somewhat ambiguous" (June 13). But early in October the Prince was reassured by Mr. Chamberlain's quickened pace. In the result President Kruger, on 9th October, delivered an ultimatum to the British government which rendered war inevitable. Hostilities broke out two days later.

The Prince was not among the few who foresaw that the warfare was to wind its weary way through two years and seven months. From beginning to end of that period England suffered a harassing series of anxieties which no foreign sympathies solaced. The cause of the enemy was indeed favoured by well-nigh all foreign peoples, who saw in the struggle only the brutal oppression by a strong of a weak nation. In every great capital of Europe the press virulently traduced the British name, and the Queen and the Prince, as the most conspicuous of British nationals, were exposed to a raking fire of abuse. All the while, too, the Kaiser was busily occupied in penning for his uncle's eye comments on the anxious course of events, in which he incongruously wove together cajoling caresses and mystifying threats. Of strange fashions were the misshapen kites which the Kaiser flew in the diplomatic sky during the year 1900.

England's South African War cannot in the retrospect excite national pride. If the lessons which the British armies learnt

on the African veldt proved of future benefit to the country, 1899
the protracted war brought little glory to British arms.

With the latter half of the stubborn conflict it was the Prince's
fate to be prominently identified. After the fighting had dragged
its slow length through fifteen months, Queen Victoria passed
away, and the Prince duly fulfilled his belated destiny of succeeding to his mother's throne. It was not until King Edward's
reign had reached its sixteenth month that the warfare ceased,
and that peace was at length proclaimed under his royal auspices.

I

The opening months of the South African campaign, October–
December 1899, presented a succession of disquieting reverses
to British arms, and a very critical situation was created. One
"black week" in December embraced the signal defeats of
Lord Methuen at Magersfontein, 10th–11th December; of Sir
William Gatacre at Stormberg, 10th December; and of the
Prince's friend, Sir Redvers Buller, at Colenso, 15th December.
The Prince, surprised and shocked, privately acknowledged his
misgivings of the country's military organisation. Nor did he
measure his language in condemning the Generals who were
responsible for the "regrettable incidents." Stronger steps
than had yet been contemplated were clearly called for. With
relief the Prince learnt from Lord Lansdowne, the Secretary
for War, on 17th December (before the information was made
public), that Lord Roberts was appointed Commander-in-Chief,
with Lord Kitchener as his Chief of the Staff. The Prince
cordially welcomed the partnership of the two men who enjoyed
the highest reputation in the British Army. At the same time
he laid stress on the need of large reinforcements, strenuously
seconding in conversation and correspondence with the authorities, Queen Victoria's appeals to like effect. The Queen urged
on Lord Salisbury the calling out of the whole of the Militia,
which she described as "the constitutional force of the country."
The government deemed it more prudent to raise a large
volunteer army by special enlistment of the county yeomanry
and the volunteers. A great part of the new levies was organised
under the designation of Imperial Yeomanry. The City of
London independently equipped a regiment of City Imperial

Volunteers, popularly known as the C.I.V. The Prince was indefatigable in inspecting contingents of these reinforcements on their departure for South Africa, bidding them "God speed and a safe return."

II

In the early months of the war the philanthropic ardours which the war excited in England offered the Prince a promising if somewhat embarrassing field for the exercise of his organising aptitudes. Numerous independent volunteer agencies came into being in various parts of the country to collect funds for the relief of soldiers and sailors on active service, their wives, widows, and families. Many newspapers started funds among their readers, and each large town instituted one or more relief organisations. The scattered efforts tended to overlap and largely to defeat their purpose. The need of co-ordination and centralisations grew imperative during the winter of 1899–1900. Appeal was made to the Prince to aid in checking the confusion, and he brought to bear on the problem his tact and influence. On 1st March 1900 he called a representative meeting at Marlborough House to consider the situation, and a sub-committee was appointed under the chairmanship of the Duke of York to draft a scheme of unification. Eleven days later, 12th March, a second conference at Marlborough House created "The Prince of Wales's Committee" with the Prince as Chairman, to exercise consultative and advisory functions and control over all existing relief agencies. The task of effective co-ordination proved difficult, and it was hardly possible to banish all the elements of disorder which sprang from the original separatism. The government came to the aid of the Prince of Wales's Committee, and after due inquiry formally authorised it to pursue its unifying efforts. But the problem of consolidation was not yet solved. A fresh step was taken in July, when the Lord Mayor of London, by direction of the Prince, arranged for a further conference at the Mansion House on 31st July, with a view to creating a Central Council on thoroughly representative lines to take over the work of the Prince of Wales's Committee. In each county and county borough, committees were to be formed to work under the Central Council. The scheme was adopted, and it continued in effective operation until the end of the war. The Prince had

faith in the Council and sought to secure for it statutory
permanence, so that all funds which should be collected now
and hereafter for the relief of soldiers and sailors should be at
its command.   The government, however, took another view.
After the Prince's accession there was passed the Patriotic Fund
Reorganisation Act which, superseding the Central Council,
came into operation on 1st January 1904. On the consequent
dissolution of the Central Council, King Edward expressed his
satisfaction at the work which it had done, and testified to the
hope that its labours would be efficiently continued by the
reorganised Patriotic Fund under the authority of his government. If his anticipations were not completely realised the
public generally had learnt the lesson, which he had a large part
in teaching, of the need of unified, rather than detached, efforts
in movements of the kind.   On the outbreak of the Great War
in August 1914 the formation of the Prince of Wales's Fund, in
the name of King Edward's grandson, carried out with substantial success the unifying principle of patriotic benevolence
which King Edward advocated at the opening of the South
African War.

III

Throughout the long struggle full information of its vicissitudes was at the Prince's disposal. Lord Wolseley, the Commander-in-Chief at home, sent him from time to time elaborate
reviews of the military situation. Official intelligence reached
him regularly from Lord Lansdowne at the War Office and from
Mr. Chamberlain at the Colonial Office. In his acknowledgements of ministerial communications he was lavish in comment
and inquiry, now asking for estimates as to the strength of the
enemy, and now for particulars of the provisions which were
made for prisoners of war. The Prince also encouraged friends
and acquaintances on active service to write to him fully and
frequently. He highly valued the letters from the front of "his
old friend," Sir Arthur Paget, who was in command of the Scots
Guards, and of Colonel W. H. H. Waters of the Royal Artillery.
"The most perfect freedom" of Sir Arthur's correspondence
was a source of satisfaction to him, and during the second year
of the war he wrote of Sir Arthur to Mr. St. John Brodrick, who
had then succeeded Lord Lansdowne as Secretary of War:

I have great confidence in his judgment and the honesty of his opinions, and he has seen more fighting and perhaps gained more experience almost than any officer during the present war (January 6, 1901).

Mr. Winston Churchill, the son of his old friend, Lord Randolph, sent the Prince graphic descriptions of his capture by the Boers at an early stage in the fighting and of his imprisonment at Pretoria, whence he made a daring escape (November 30, 1899). Subsequently the Prince heard constantly from Lady Randolph Churchill, Mr. Winston Churchill's mother, who was in charge of the hospital ship *Maine*, provided by American women for the relief of the wounded.[1]

But not all the Prince's correspondence about the war proved quite welcome. From one quarter he was besieged by expressions of sympathy uncannily mingled with somewhat ambiguous comments and counsels on the varying military developments and with dark hints of a continental coalition against England. To both the Queen and the Prince the Kaiser was sending from the early days of the war elaborately phrased condolences on the heavy losses in the field and on the military repulses. The Kaiser assured his grandmother and his uncle on paper that the "Black Week" of December caused him as much concern as those to whom he was writing. The Prince quickly detected a grating double edge in his nephew's commiserations.

On 21st December the Kaiser sent his uncle greetings for Christmas and the New Year, and grew rhapsodical in lamentation :

What days of sad news and anxiety have passed over the country since we spent our delightful days at Sandringham. Many brave officers and men have fallen or are disabled after showing pluck, courage, and determined bravery ! How many homes will be sad this year and how many sufferers will feel agonising pain morally and physically in these days of holy pleasure and peace ! What an amount of bloodshed has been going on and is to be expected for the next months to come ! Instead of the Angels' song "Peace on Earth and Goodwill to Men" the new century will be greeted by shrieks of dying men, killed and maimed by lyddite shells and balls from Quickfirers. Truly *fin de siècle !* Let us hope that Christmas itself will, for

[1] Other correspondents on active service, with whom the Prince kept in close touch, included Prince Adolphus of Teck, afterwards Marquis of Cambridge; Count Gleichen, and Captain (Sir) Seymour Fortescue, his naval A.D.C.

those few days at least, remain unpolluted by the shedding of
human blood, and that out of it may arise the ray of some sort
of light which may bring the two white fighting Brothers together
ere too much harm and waste of lives is done! Your losses, as
they are made known little by little, are quite appalling, and find
every sympathy with our Army here, as well as the gallant dash
of the men and officers. Especially the losses of the Highlanders
created a sensation, as they are much admired by my soldiers
over here! May we soon hear of a good end and Peace in that
part of the globe, so that every one can again breathe more
freely! For the sight of white man killing white is not good
for the Blacks to look on for too long; the simple suspicion
that they might find it practical to fall on the whites in general
is enough to make one's blood run cold.

In a postscript the Kaiser dropped his sentimentalities and
announced that he had invited comments from his military
advisers, and had compiled from their statements a brief series
(in German) of impartial reflections—"Gedankensplitter," he
called them—on the military situation. Those he enclosed:

"Should it interest you," he wrote to his uncle, "to know
what is the gist of conversations in military circles over here,
I have made a sort of extract for you, in form of reflections,
which are only made as 'orientierung' for you what the men
of the Services and forces here think and say. I put it down
without any comment and without expressing any opinion whatever, so you may burn the thing or use it just as you think fit."

The Prince circulated the Kaiser's "Gedankensplitter"
among the authorities and some English friends in an English
translation. Their tone was the reverse of optimistic, and the
Prince, who resented the Kaiser's interposition, acknowledged
them with a cold courtesy, which implied a very qualified gratitude.
But the Kaiser was not easily repressed. When, with the entry
of Lord Roberts on the field, the tide of battle in South Africa
was beginning to turn in favour of the English, the Kaiser
forwarded to the Prince on 4th February 1900 a second set of
"Aphorismen" or "Gedankensplitter," which could not easily
be absolved of deliberate intention to give offence.

"Dearest Uncle," the Kaiser wrote, "the kind way in which
you were so good as to accept my aphorisms on the war in
December encourages me to venture to submit a new series of
them for your kind perusal. They may perhaps be interesting
to you, or possibly of some use even if you think so. They are
to show you how interestedly and closely I try to study and

follow the operations of the Army through all their different phases. At the same time, they are written down by one who has seen active military life since now 23 years, and who commands and directs the training of the German Army since 88, *i.e.* 12 years.

"I hope and trust that the Royals have come out all right from the last fights, and that we may have no deaths to deplore. The losses of the Lancastrian Brigade are indeed tremendous, and show how valiantly they fought.

"I so hope that dear Grandmama may not be too agitated or emotioned by the news ! For the rest patience, and a lot of it, will be required, if no end can be made beforehand. Though the Prayer for Victory in the Service of St. Paul's has not been fulfilled, provided Providence is willing to grant this wish . . .

"Pray make any use you like of my memorandum according to your pleasure; perhaps it would interest Grandmama."[1]

The enclosed "Notes" suggested a suspension of the British advance in South Africa until further reinforcements had rendered possible the concentration of an overwhelming army on various objectives in the enemy's lines. "It might be essential," the Kaiser ominously added, "to postpone such operations until the autumn," and, meanwhile, England would have to consider whether her relations with other powers would justify so long "a respite." The alternative was a negotiated peace with the enemy. For the last paragraph of his notes the Kaiser reserved a malicious sting, which bore witness to his genuine state of mind. After all, he argued, for England to accept defeat meant no disgrace. Her experience of contests in the football and cricket fields had taught her how to take beatings with chivalrous equanimity. "Last year," the Kaiser's concluding words ran, "in the great cricket match of England *v.* Australia, the former took the latter's victory quietly, with chivalrous acknowledgement of her opponent."[2]

---

[1] The original of this letter is at Windsor. A copy in the Berlin Foreign Office was published in *Die Grosse Politik*, Band 15, p. 553.

[2] The Kaiser first gave his own account of the preparation of his advisory "Notes" on 11th August 1908 in a long conversation at Cronberg with Sir Charles Hardinge (afterwards Lord Hardinge of Penshurst), who was at the time in attendance on King Edward VII. The Kaiser incidentally mentioned to Sir Charles how he had sent to Queen Victoria, after the early reverses in the South African War, "a plan of campaign," drawn up at his request by his General Staff (*The Times*, 10th November 1924). The Kaiser repeated in fuller detail his version of the transaction in the interview with him published in the *Daily Telegraph* of the 27th October 1908, in which he generally defended himself from a charge that he ever showed England ill-will. His statement in the

The Prince again sent copies of an English translation of his nephew's second series of "Notes" to Queen Victoria and to some personal friends.   Lord Rosebery, when acknowledging receipt of one of these copies (February 19, 1900), remarked on the sinister strain.

Other ostentatious proofs which the Kaiser gave at home of his zealous scrutiny of England's embarrassments disquieted the Prince.[1]   "We are expecting Henry home soon, and Mama

1900

Ætat. 58

Daily Telegraph ran as follows: "Just at the time of your Black Week, in the December of 1899, when disasters followed one another in rapid succession, I received a letter from Queen Victoria, my revered grandmother, written in sorrow and affliction, and bearing manifest traces of the anxieties which were preying upon her mind and health.   I at once returned a sympathetic reply.   Nay, I did more.   I bade one of my officers procure for me as exact an account as he could obtain of the number of combatants in South Africa on both sides, and of the actual position of the opposing forces.   With the figures before me, I worked out what I considered to be the best plan of campaign under the circumstances, and submitted it to my General Staff for their criticism.   Then I despatched it to England, and that document is among the State papers at Windsor Castle, awaiting the serenely impartial verdict of history.   And, as a matter of curious coincidence, let me add that the plan which I formulated ran very much on the same lines as that which was actually adopted by Lord Roberts and carried by him into successful operation.   Was that, I repeat, the act of one who wished England ill?   Let Englishmen be just and say!"   The Kaiser's story is inaccurate in many particulars.   His "Notes" were forwarded, not to Queen Victoria, but to the Prince, and were in two sections, the first being dated 21st December 1899, and the second the 4th February 1900.   Neither section quite corresponds with the Kaiser's description.   Both series, with the Kaiser's covering letters addressed to the Prince, are in the Windsor Archives.   A copy in the Berlin Foreign Office of the second series, with the Kaiser's covering letter, is printed in *Die Grosse Politik*, Band 15, pp. 553–57.   The full text of the English translations, which the Prince caused to be prepared, of both series is printed in an appendix to this volume.

[1] In December 1899 Germany had discovered a grievance against England's Navy, of which she made the most.   Three German merchant ships, the *Bundesrath*, the *Herzog*, and the *Marie*, had been seized by an English cruiser on their voyage to South Africa.   The *Herzog* and the *Marie* were soon released, but the *Bundesrath* was taken before a Prize Court at Durban on a charge of carrying contraband of war.   The German government's protest was couched in vehement language, and an ultimatum from Berlin was expected in London. But Lord Salisbury promptly cleared away this rock of offence by setting the *Bundesrath* free, by offering compensation, and by promising not to trouble German ships again (January 19, 1900).   So generous a surrender on the part of the British government failed to diminish anti-English agitation in Germany, and a cry for a further increase in the German navy rapidly yielded fruit in Admiral von Tirpitz's second Navy Bill.   That Bill, which was openly described as an imperative safeguard against English arrogance and aggression, doubled the naval programme of 1898.   It was introduced into the Reichstag on 8th February 1900 and became law on the 12th June.   The Kaiser was eloquent in public expressions of satisfaction with a measure for which he claimed personal credit.   "The ocean is essential for Germany's greatness," he declared, "but the ocean proves that on it and beyond it no great decision can be taken without the German Kaiser."

will be the first to welcome him," the Kaiser had written
with apparent simplicity to his uncle on the 4th February.
The Kaiser's brother was expected home in a few days with his
squadron from China, whither the Kaiser had despatched him
in 1897 to demonstrate the significance of Germany's naval
ambitions. But Prince Henry's home-coming was not the
simple domestic ceremony which the Kaiser's remark to the
Prince suggested. Prince Henry's return to Berlin on 13th
February afforded the Kaiser an opportunity of sounding a
fresh trumpet-call to his people to hasten on with their preparations of a colossal navy in order to compete with that of
Great Britain.

To the Prince's especial irritation Dr. Leyds, the Secretary
of State to the Transvaal government, who had already won
his disapprobation by his earlier activities in Berlin at the date
of the Kaiser's Kruger telegram, now reappeared in that city
(December 1899). The Prince learnt with disgust that Chancellor von Hohenlohe invited the official representative of
England's foe to the banquet which he gave on 27th January
1900 in honour of the Kaiser's birthday. It was obligatory on
Sir Frank Lascelles, the British Ambassador in Berlin, to join
the Chancellor's guests. The Prince warmly resented this
challenging courtesy to Dr. Leyds. To Lascelles he pointed out
(February 6) that Dr. Leyds was "the most bitter, dangerous,
and unscrupulous enemy we have. He goes about from one
place to another telling lies, trying to do us all the harm he can."
The Prince expressed the hope that when the British Ambassador
returned home from the Chancellor's dinner, he washed his hands
with carbolic soap after having shaken hands with the Boer
representative.

There was no beating about the bush in the Prince's reply
(February 8) to his nephew's letter with its accompanying
"Gedankensplitter" of the 4th February. Dr. Leyds's reception
in Berlin was not overlooked.

I have read, with the greatest possible interest, your memo.,
and according to your suggestion will send it on to Grandmamma
with an English translation. She is naturally very anxious about
every movement of our Troops, but bears up, as our whole
Nation does, at the different reverses our arms have sustained.
We, however, feel confident that in the end the result will be

successful, though that opinion is not shared on the Continent or by Dr. Leyds, who, I perceive, has been received with open arms by all classes of Society in Berlin!

By your Memo. I see how closely you follow the movements of our troops and their vicissitudes. You ask me if I have heard anything of the "Royals." No, I have not, but feel sure you take a deep interest in their welfare.

I am afraid I am unable to share your opinions expressed in the last Paragraph of your Memo., in which you liken our conflict with the Boers to our Cricket Matches with the Australians, in which the latter were victorious and we accepted our defeat.

The British Empire is now fighting for its very existence, as you know full well, and for our superiority in S. Africa. We must therefore use every effort in our power to prove victorious in the end!

The Kaiser quickly took up his uncle's challenge. His defence hardly mended matters. His exhortation to maintain the British fleet at full strength was not quite easy to reconcile with some of his recent pronouncements in Berlin on the growth of the German navy:

"My last paragraph in the 'Gedankensplitter,'" he wrote, 23rd February 1900, "seems to have given you some umbrage! But I think that I can easily dispel your doubts about it! The allusion to Football and Cricket matches was meant to show that I do not belong to those People, who, when the British Army suffers reverses, or is unable at a given time to master the enemy, then immediately cry out that British Prestige is in danger or lost! Forsooth! Great Britain has bravely fought for and lost the whole of North America against France and the Rebels, and yet has become the greatest Power in the World! Because her fleet remained unimpaired and by this the Command of the Sea! As long as you keep your fleet in good fighting trim, and as long as it is looked upon as the first and feared as invincible, I don't care a fiddlestick for a few lost fights in Africa. But the Fleet must be up-to-date in guns and officers and men and on the 'Qui vive,' and should it ever be necessary to fall back upon it, may a second Trafalgar be awarded to it! I shall be the first to wish it luck and God-speed!"[1]

The Prince, indisposed to carry the matter further, wrote to his nephew on 28th February:

[1] The originals of this and the Kaiser's previously cited letter are at Windsor. Copies of both at the Berlin Foreign Office are printed in *Die Grosse Politik* (1924), Band 15, pp. 358, 359–60.

I am glad that I misunderstand your allusion to the cricket matches, as I was under the impression that you thought to make peace with the Boers in spite of our successes.　That would have been a simple impossibility, and the Government that proposed it would not have remained in office for 24 hours![1]

Meanwhile the Kaiser was voluble in congratulations to the Queen and the Prince, as British successes followed rapidly one upon another during February and March.　His greetings to the Queen on the relief of Kimberley on the 15th February concluded with the words: "How happy Mr. Rhodes will be." While commenting in a letter to the Prince on the strategy of Lord Roberts, of which the relief of Kimberley was an early outcome, he claimed credit for the happy foresight of his second series of "Notes."　On the 23rd February he wrote to the Prince:

Lord Roberts has *at last*, in a masterful way, *concentrated* all the troops he could lay hands on, and has then, by a well-designed scheme, outflanked the enemy, made him fall back, and relieved Kimberley!　This clearly shows the correctness of my calculations in my last "Gedankensplitter," that the main point is *concentration of the available forces* on *one part* of the Field of Operations for a great blow, and that this is the main road to success.

The brave old soldier will, of course, be effectively helped by his valiant troops, who are admirable in the way they march after fatigues and privations, confident in their Leader and in the ultimate success of the cause they are suffering and bleeding for.　Also a word of praise ought to be said for the most effective manner in which the Army Transport and Commissariat Dep. have worked, coping with almost incredible difficulties.　The despatch of Lord Roberts relating to the German Hospital at Jacobsdal has created an excellent impression in Germany and given the Empress much pleasure as she is Patroness of this Column.

General Cronje's surrender to General Roberts at Paardeberg on 27th February was welcomed in England with great enthusiasm, and the Kaiser sent the Prince a telegram of congratulation. Next day the Prince, in reply to the Kaiser's last letter, wrote:

I am glad that you give our gallant friend, Lord Roberts, such praise in the way he retained Kimberley and has since "hemmed in" the redoubtable Cronje—which forced the latter

---

[1] *Die Grosse Politik*, Band 15, p. 561.

1900
—
Ætat. 58

to surrender with his army. Every military man will, I think, admit that not only is the Field Marshal a brave soldier, but has also shown considerable strategical qualities—in which he has found Lord Kitchener an able coadjutor.   I am most grateful and deeply appreciated your telegram of yesterday, which was a day of rejoicing throughout the Country. . . .   From Sir R. Buller's telegrams the difficulties he encounters in reaching Ladysmith are very great, but in to-day's telegram he has had entire success, and does not think he can now be prevented from retaining the town.

The relief of Ladysmith was completed on the day that the Prince was writing. The entry of Lord Roberts into Bloemfontein followed on 13th March. The stream of the Kaiser's congratulations continued in full flood.

"I can well imagine," he wrote to the Prince on 3rd March, "the feeling of general relief at the news of the relief of Ladysmith. General Sir G. White has bravely borne up with, and struggled against, all adversities, and England has to thank him that he managed to keep the Garrison in good spirits, and to keep the flame of hope alive in their hearts. If it had not been for his indomitable energy and his sturdy will the Troops would have given out long since."

The Prince replied (March 7) :

Your eulogy on Sir G. White will be greatly appreciated by him, and indeed I think it is well merited, as it cannot have been an easy task to have held out during these long and weary months.

IV

But the Kaiser was pursuing a very tortuous path. The congratulatory rhetoric which flowed from his pen in his correspondence with his uncle disguised an insidious design. He was playing a game of greater perfidy than he had yet essayed. His nefarious plan was secretly to persuade Russia to initiate a coalition of the Powers which should take advantage of England's difficulties in South Africa by making war upon her during her time of stress. The Kaiser fancied that he could play upon the specious humanitarianism of the weak-willed Tsar, and he had no doubt that he would find a willing instrument in Count Muravieff —the Tsar's foreign minister—who was disappointing all the Prince's hopes of an Anglo-Russian *entente* by his aggressive

diplomacy in China and elsewhere. Having obtained the ear
of the Russian Minister, the Kaiser deemed it easy to draw
France, Russia's close ally, into the conspiracy. The bitter
pro-Boer tendencies of popular feeling, alike in Russia and
France, convinced him that a concerted attack on England
would make a warm appeal to the French and Russian peoples.
When the Russian and French governments had fallen into his
trap he meditated the assumption of the proud rôle of deliverer
of Europe from the shackles of England's colonial supremacy.
He had at his call in his own country the same inflammatory
Anglophobism as was fermenting in Russia and France. He
gloated over the near prospect of bringing his uncle's country
to her knees.

But the Kaiser's impetuous duplicity on this, as on all other
occasions during his reign, woefully miscalculated his personal
influence and the means at his disposal. He took no account of
the mistrust which his character provoked in St. Petersburg, no
less than in Paris and London. He misapprehended the operative
efficiency of the Tsar's pro-Boer sympathies, which might induce
the Russian government mildly to protest against England's
persistence in the South African War, but were hardly the stuff
out of which ultimatums are made.

The Kaiser's plot missed fire, and when the fact of failure
was too patent for him to ignore it he brazenly represented to
Queen Victoria and his uncle that their country owed to his
magnanimous interposition their escape from overwhelming
peril. The alleged peril had no existence outside his sordid
imagination. France turned a deaf ear to the Kaiser's base
promptings. Russia listened supinely and distrustfully, and
a tardy and somewhat hesitating assent on the part of the
Tsar's foreign minister was hurriedly cancelled on an unexpected
disclosure of the shuffling workings of the Kaiser's mind.

The confidential correspondence of Russian diplomatists
preserves the main incriminating evidence of the Kaiser's
Machiavellian activity. On the 1st January 1900, while he was
penning his elegiac consolations for the consumption of his
English relatives over the military disasters which befell their
armies in the early stages of the South African War, the Kaiser
visited the Russian Ambassador in Berlin, Count Osten-Sacken,
and surprised his auditor by suddenly suggesting an attack on

England.[1] After an exchange of New Year's greetings the
Kaiser expressed high praise of some recent experiments in
mobilisation on the Afghan border.

"The Kaiser saw in it" (according to Count Osten-Sacken's
report to Count Muravieff) "confirmation of his cherished opinion
that Russia alone could paralyse the power of England and deal it
if need be a mortal blow.   This subject led the Emperor to declare
with ardour that if ever our august master [the Tsar] should be
moved to order his armies against India, he himself [the Kaiser]
would guarantee that none should stir in Europe.   He [the
Kaiser] would mount guard over our frontiers.   'They are well
aware of it in England,' His Majesty added.   'I have never
concealed from them the fact that in the Far East they would
not have me on their side.'   This spontaneous declaration had
[the Russian Ambassador proceeds] taken me so much by surprise
that I asked the Emperor if he desired me to convey it to our
august master.   'Certainly,' replied His Majesty, 'the Emperor
Nicholas has, indeed, only to reread my letters at the time of
our intervention in the Chino-Japanese War and the Kiau-chau
expedition.   I have already given him this assurance more than
once.'"

The Kaiser left no doubt on the Russian Ambassador's mind
that, in spite of his recent reconciliation with the Prince of Wales
and of his reception at Windsor in the previous November, his
grudge against England was as lively as ever, and that, although
his language was guarded, he was ready to make common cause
with Russia against her.   The German Foreign Minister, von
Bülow, confirmed the impression.   In Count Osten-Sacken's
view both the Kaiser and von Bülow thought that England's
decisive victory over the Boers would seriously prejudice the
Colonial fortunes of the other European Powers, and that so good
an opportunity as the present would not recur for checking
England's "imperialist cupidity."   The Kaiser's omission to
specify the precise hostile action which Germany contemplated
against England, Count Osten-Sacken assigned to the Kaiser's
doubts of France's readiness, despite the French popular Anglo-

---

[1] Copies of Count Osten-Sacken's despatches to M. Muravieff from Berlin
during January and February 1900, which are the authorities for the statements
in the text, are among the Archives of the Russian Embassy at Chesham
House, London. They have been consulted by the present writer by the
courtesy of M. Eugène Sablin, formerly Russian chargé d'affaires.

phobia, to co-operate honestly and heartily with Germany.   The
Kaiser was

> Letting " I dare not " wait upon " I would,"
> Like the poor cat i' the adage.

But he hugged the hope that Russia would screw French
rancour to the sticking point.

The Kaiser, in pursuit of his intrigue, threw all scruples of
veracity to the winds.   In a second conversation with Count
Osten-Sacken on the 9th January, he communicated to him an
invented rumour that the pressure in South Africa was compelling
England to denude Egypt of troops, and that the British govern-
ment was inviting Italy to occupy that country in her place.
He artfully added that although Italy belonged to the Triple
Alliance he could not advise her against a design so congenial
to her ambition, because the terms of the Triple Alliance left
Italy free to make any arrangement with England that she chose.
The Kaiser intended that this clumsy fabrication should reach
France through Russian channels.   Thus French rancour against
England, of which dislike of the English occupation of Egypt
was a motive-force, might be stimulated, and French jealousy
of Italy be whetted.   The Kaiser thought that he was making
play with an unerring weapon which would drive France into
his snare.   But this reckless hit signally missed its mark.   The
false rumour was at once discredited in France, and was promptly
nailed by Italy to the counter as a lie.

Count Muravieff, on learning from Berlin of the Kaiser's
conversations with Osten-Sacken, sent the unexpected information to all the Russian Ambassadors abroad (St. Petersburg,
January 13/25).   Count Muravieff had visited M. Delcassé in
the previous October on returning from a holiday at Biarritz, but
no notion of joint action against England had been breathed.
Nor when the Tsar was entertained by the Kaiser at Berlin
(November 8, 1899) on the eve of the Kaiser's visit to Windsor,
had any question of the kind been raised.   "The overtures,"
Count Muravieff now wrote in a covering letter to his representatives at foreign courts, "made by the Emperor William
and Count von Bülow to our Ambassador, reveal a tendency on
the part of the German government to take the initiative in
concerted action against the designs of England both in South

Africa and with regard to Egypt, and especially a desire to associate us with that action as much as possible." The Russian Foreign Minister added that Russia had no direct interest in the questions at issue, but would watch events. In certain undefined eventualities Russia might possibly follow the Kaiser's lead.

1900
Ætat. 58

The news of the Kaiser's plotting reached M. Delcassé in Paris through M. Nelidoff, the Russian Ambassador there. M. Delcassé pointed out that if Russia and France should deem it prudent to take any action at all against England, the ' had no need of the assistance of another Power. He suggested that the Kaiser was in point of fact seeking an alliance with England, and was merely laying traps for France and Russia. If the Kaiser could be trusted—a large proviso—and were openly to take the initiative in forming a coalition against England, France's attitude might perhaps change. Count Osten-Sacken on 27th January/8th February expressed to Count Muravieff his belief that the Kaiser was recommending to the other Powers hazardous enterprises from which Germany would be the first and the last to benefit, although he shrank from sharing the risk. Count Muravieff advised the Russian Ambassador in Berlin to invite continued confidences from the Kaiser and from von Bülow, and by no means to discourage Germany from taking the initiative in embarrassing England alike in South Africa and Egypt; but Russia was to be committed to nothing but "a waiting attitude."

The Kaiser's plot was a sickly plant doomed to an early and a squalid death. France had clearly no appetite for the conjoint adventure, and the Kaiser soon showed signs of nervousness as to what was in M. Delcassé's mind. Russia was in no forth-coming mood. If that Power were unable or unwilling to bring France into the conspiracy, the Kaiser's purpose was clearly foiled.

In the middle of February a somewhat shadowy offer of co-operation reached him from St. Petersburg, but the delay had cooled his ardour for his scheme. The new British offensive in South Africa was lending new vigour to the Tsar's and to his peoples' pro-Boer sympathies. According to a statement which the Tsar made to King Edward some fifteen months later, he was receiving at this time "addresses, letters, telegrams, etc.

in masses, begging me to interfere even by adopting strong measures." [1] He thought of writing to Queen Victoria "to ask her quite privately whether there was any possibility of stopping the war," but he abstained from a fear of hurting her feelings. His conscience, he told King Edward, was troubled by his passiveness.

Count Muravieff, with some reluctance and still cherishing doubt alike of the Kaiser's sincerity and of the prudence of making the Boers' troubles a Russian concern, deemed it his duty to take some step towards satisfying his master's scruples. He would, at any rate, test the meaning of the Kaiser's incitements. Accordingly, on 15th/27th February, the Count sent simultaneously to the Russian Ambassadors in Berlin and Paris an invitation to the governments to which they were accredited to join the Tsar in approaching the Court of St. James, with the expression of a hope that the British government would bring to an end "the unequal struggle between the small republics and mighty England." Count Muravieff reminded the Russian Ambassador in Berlin of "the considerations advanced by the Emperor William and communicated by you in several secret letters, with regard to the disadvantageous consequences for the whole of continental Europe to which the military operations in South Africa might lead."

Count Muravieff's kite was flown rather wildly. Russia's ally—France—was unimpressed. M. Delcassé avowed vague sympathy with the Russian Minister's suggestion (February 19/ March 3), but pleaded the consequences of possible failure. It would be needful to persuade the United States of America to join Russia, France, and Germany before any step could be safely taken. Count Muravieff's purpose of putting the Kaiser's sincerity to the test was better served. The German Emperor's untrustworthiness was completely revealed. The Kaiser authorised an equivocal acknowledgement, which plainly showed Count Muravieff that his design was to prompt others behind the scenes rather than figure on the stage himself. The Kaiser informed Count Osten-Sacken on 3rd March of his general approval of the Russian proposal, but with mystifying coolness he declared himself compelled to sound London in advance as to the spirit in which the British government would

[1] Tsar to King Edward, May 22/June 4, 1901.

receive the suggested approach. His own policy was to avoid complications with other great Powers, particularly with the maritime Powers. His uncertainty about France required him to ask as a preliminary condition of any far-reaching combination the execution of an agreement by which the contracting Powers should mutually guarantee their European possessions for a fixed number of years. Count Muravieff, on reading Count Osten-Sacken's despatch from Berlin, complained that the Kaiser had played him false. He recalled to the Kaiser's memory (February 21/March 5) that his project was an outcome of that monarch's personal overtures to the Russian Ambassador in Berlin. No separate representation to London by Germany, he added, could he entertain. The three Powers must act together or not at all. The Kaiser's proposal for a mutual guarantee of the Powers in regard to their European possessions was a new issue without relevance to the Kaiser's personal suggestion of a coalition which should work for England's downfall.

The Kaiser's intimation of his pusillanimous retreat from a position of his own creating, and the virtual refusal of support from France, compelled Count Muravieff to abandon his proposed interpellation of England. He showed no sign of regret, and during his few remaining months of life—he died 24th June —he became one of the objects of the Kaiser's most furious vituperation. There was a faint echo of the abortive words which Count Muravieff addressed to Berlin and Paris some sixteen months later, on 22nd May/4th June 1901, when the Prince had become King Edward. The Tsar then addressed to him a respectfully worded plea for the cessation of the Boer War. There was little affinity between the Tsar's appeal and Count Muravieff's beating of the wind sixteen months before.

V

The Kaiser's plot had failed, and he boldly masked his defeat to his own perverted satisfaction by unprincipled representations to his uncle that he had successfully foiled a desperate conspiracy on the part of France and Russia against England's very existence. Before his reckless scheme proved altogether unworkable, the Kaiser thought to rack English nerves by vague hints of mysterious perils which threatened her. When he

urged on the Prince on 4th February 1900, England's imperative
need of a breathing space wherein to reconstruct her military
arm, he expressed a pharisaical concern whether diplomacy
would be able to guarantee England *"absolute safety"* against
foreign Powers during the passive period. Nineteen days later,
he harped on the same string in more rasping accents. France,
he falsely hinted, was about to spring on her prey across the
Channel.

"It is to be fervently hoped," he wrote to his uncle on 23rd
February, "that the situation in South Africa may soon be
cleared and the decisive blow, if possible, soon delivered so that
England may soon end this war and have leisure to look about
and see what is going on around her. For I am afraid that
'Sundry Peoples' are quietly preparing to take liberties and
foster intrigues and surprises in other parts of the world. This
is beginning to be instinctively felt in Europe and is consequently
causing much uneasiness in the Political World. I want a strong,
unhampered England. It is eminently necessary for the Peace
of Europe.
"Be on the look out! The concentration of the Reserve
Squadron at Portland is most wise, and will, I hope, create a
quieting impression in 'certain neighbouring quarters.' To
my opinion this measure ought always to be taken as soon as
the Channel Fleet leaves for its ordinary trip to Gib. &c. By
the way, this name is most inappropriate to the Fleet, as the
Channel is the place where it is the least met or seen!"

In the same letter, in tones of rhapsodical bluster, he claimed
to have checked the pro-Boer virulence of the German press,
which he alleged was corrupted by French and Russian money.

With superhuman efforts Bülow and I slowly got the better
of the German Press, swamped as it was with articles, news,
canards, and last, not least, roubles and francs from both sides,
with a view of creating a so-called anti-English feeling, which
was to be denounced by my kind neighbours to England, this
being accompanied by Pharisaical protestations of good faith
and friendship! Humbugs! Ware wolf! We must both keep
our weather eye open!

The Prince stood on his guard in his acknowledgement of the
Kaiser's ecstatic warning, and there was a home-thrust in his
reference to the preparedness of the British Navy to meet all
emergencies.

"All you say," he wrote to his nephew on 28th February,

"concerning our continental friends (?) I entirely agree with and we must indeed 'Keep one another's eyes open!' We are, however, obliged to believe official assurances given by certain countries of friendship towards us. . . . For any eventualities which may occur, our Fleet is ready to be mobilised at any moment."

As soon as the Kaiser received Count Muravieff's very qualified and belated assent to a modest fragment of his own suggestions of hostile action against England, the imperial plotter with characteristic effrontery lost no time in revealing to his uncle Count Muravieff's proposal in a garbled version of his own concocting.

The Kaiser rarely made a more egregious exposure of his hypocrisy. Along with his misleading summary of Count Muravieff's communication, he confided to the Prince his own claim, often to be repeated later with progressive emphasis, to have given England's arch-foe his *coup-de-grace*, and to be acting at all points as champion of England's interests.

"My warnings have not been too soon," the Kaiser wrote to the Prince (March 3, 1900). "Yesterday evening I received a note from St. Petersburg in which Count Mouravieff formally invites me to take part in a Collective action with France and Russia against England for the enforcing of Peace and the help of the Boers!

"I have declined. I have answered that I thought it best that the Organiser of the European Peace Conference at the Hague—H.I.M. the Tzar—were to inform himself directly in London whether the British Government and People were in a mood to listen to such proposals as His I.M.'s Government was thinking of making.

"I had my doubts about it, and personally thought I knew pretty sure what the answer would be from London. After inquiring what Russia would do in case of a 'refus' from England, the very reassuring answer was given 'Nothing'!

"Sir Frank has been informed by me of this preposterous step in a *very confidential* manner."

The Prince acknowledged the Kaiser's revelation in sympathetic phrases. Some politic blandishments masked the suspicion which the Prince shared with Lord Salisbury that the Kaiser had a larger responsibility for Count Muravieff's action than he wished his English relatives to know.[1]

---

[1] Eckardstein, p. 164.

"What you tell me about Mouravieff's conduct," the Prince wrote on 7th March 1900, "does not surprise me, as I believe there is nothing he would not do in conjunction with France to annoy us in every possible way.

"The Peace Conference at the Hague is always a very useful peg to hang any political hat on! What your answer was I had little doubt of—you have no idea, my dear William, how all of us in England appreciate the loyal friendship which you manifest towards us on every possible occasion. We hope always to look upon Germany as our best friend as long as you are at the helm. It is of course deeply to be regretted that the feeling throughout Germany is not, alas! very friendly towards us. One can only hope that it may improve in time, and when both countries become thoroughly satisfied, that to go hand in hand together in friendly rivalry is the mutual benefit of us both!"[1]

To Sir Frank Lascelles the Prince wrote in a less sanguine strain:

I am glad the Kaiser gave such a decided answer to Russia when the latter hoped that Germany and France would support her in interfering with our proceedings in S. Africa. This outside interference may be one of our greatest difficulties, and they are fostered by that villain Leyds, who is now without mercy and is, in fact, the real originator of the crisis!

The Kaiser's "very confidential" conversation with Lascelles, respecting his retort to Count Muravieff, took place on 9th March, and a report of it reached the Prince from Lord Salisbury. With equivocal vehemence the Kaiser blew his trumpet as England's saviour, at the same time seeking to keep English fears alive by saturnine warnings that England was not yet out of the wood.[2] "The Emperor of Russia," the Kaiser told Sir Frank, "had now become pro-Boer," and was entirely under the control of a perfectly unscrupulous minister, Muravieff, who was ready to plunge Europe into war in order to keep himself in power. Owing

[1] Die Grosse Politik, Band 15, pp. 523–24.

[2] According to Sir Frank Lascelles's report, dated 9th March, the Kaiser added to the remarks cited from it above the allegations that he had promptly circulated the Russian note proposing intervention in South Africa among German diplomatists abroad. From Vienna, he had learned that the French Ambassador remarked that "if England were allowed to achieve a complete success, her power would be increased, and her arrogance would render her absolutely insupportable," while the Russian Ambassador at Vienna "had insisted that it was advisable to take advantage of opportunities which might not recur; and both were strongly of opinion that the German Emperor was the proper person to take the initiative."

to the impossibility of influencing the Tsar, the Kaiser had ceased
to correspond with him. The Kaiser mischievously laid stress on
Russia's recent action in Persia, which he stigmatised as "a
triumph of Russian over English diplomacy." War between
England and France, he continued in the malignant tones which
he had already employed for his uncle's benefit, was well-nigh inevitable, but he would "keep his bayonets fixed on the land side."
"The present war," he concluded with unpleasing insinuation,
"had set many stones rolling, and no one could say where they
would stop, and had raised many questions which had much better
have remained latent." Finally, with more prophetic insight
than he knew, he asked what the position of Germany would be
if she found herself confronted by a coalition of France, England,
and Russia. He answered his question with the remark that she
would have to fight for her very existence. The Kaiser, while
persisting in his claim to England's abiding gratitude, intended
to keep her susceptibilities ruffled by a vision of the early and
inevitable approach of a conflict between her and the world.[1]

1900
Ætat. 58

---

[1] The Kaiser in later years repeated his claim to have rescued England
from the perils of a formidable European coalition in the early days of the
South African war, and to be entitled on that account to England's abiding
gratitude. Four statements which he made on the subject are good examples
of his habits alike of self-deception and of inaccuracy. In conversation
with Mr. Alfred Beit in Berlin at the end of 1905 the Kaiser remarked that
at the time of the Boer War "he was approached *twice* by France and Russia
to invade England, but he declined and wired to the Queen and was thanked
for his effort" (Lord Esher's Memorandum to the King, January 17, 1906).
No *second* approach to the Kaiser on the part of Russia or France in any way
comparable with the first is identifiable. On 11th August 1908, in a conversation at Cornberg with Sir Charles Hardinge (afterwards Lord Hardinge of
Penshurst) who was at the time in attendance on King Edward VII., the
Kaiser said that he had declined the approaches of France and Russia to
make a coalition against England, and "had threatened to make war on any
Power that dared to make an unprovoked attack on England at that time"
(*The Times*, 10th November 1924). The third version given by the Kaiser
of his alleged successful rescue of England appeared in the *Daily Telegraph*
interview of 27th October 1908 and ran as follows: "When the struggle
was at its height, the German Government was invited by the Governments
of France and Russia to join with them in calling upon England to put
an end to the war. The moment had come, they said, not only to save
the Boer Republics, but also to humiliate England to the dust. What was
my reply? I said that so far from Germany joining in any concerted European
action to put pressure upon England and bring about her downfall, Germany
would always keep aloof from politics that could bring her into complications
with a Sea Power like England. Posterity will one day read the exact terms
of the telegram—now in the archives of Windsor Castle—in which I informed
the Sovereign of England of the answer I had returned to the Powers which
then sought to compass her fall. Englishmen who now insult me by doubting

1900
Ætat. 58

The Kaiser's fund of disingenuous benevolence towards England was not yet exhausted. The Boer government—the Transvaal and the Orange Free State—were playing with fancies of peace. They tentatively aired the suggestion of an agreement with England on the basis of maintaining the Republics' independence. With a view to forwarding the rather hopeless project, the Boers approached the German Consul at Pretoria, who telegraphed to the Foreign Office of Berlin on 11th March a request on the part of the Boers for mediation. The Kaiser promptly replied in outwardly correct form that the Boer governments had better discover before going further whether the English government would accept mediation, that Germany's material interests in the Transvaal would not allow her to be the intermediary, and that some other Power which was thoroughly disinterested as to the future of the Transvaal and the Orange Free State should be asked to serve in that capacity. The Kaiser telegraphed to both Queen Victoria and her son the terms of his reply, and made fresh claim to their grateful thanks. The German *chargé d'affaires* in London, Count Metternich, talked with both Lord Salisbury and the Prince of the Kaiser's answer to the Boer governments' appeal as well as of the prospects of peace. Both professed appreciation of the Kaiser's attitude. But the Prince made it clear that there was no chance of the Boer Republics

---

my word should know what were my actions in the hour of their adversity." The Kaiser's fourth version appears in his Memoirs (1922, pp. 83 *seq.*) which were written in exile and solely from memory. Errors in detail abound. He represents, with a deplorable defiance of chronology, that in February 1900, while he was receiving the oaths of naval recruits at Wilhelmshaven, after attending the naval manœuvres off Heligoland, he received from the Wilhelmstrasse a telegram announcing that Russia and France proposed to Germany to make a combined attack on England. As a matter of fact, Count Muravieff's announcement reached the Kaiser in Berlin before he set out for Heligoland. He proceeds to state that he at once directed that the proposal should be declined. He foresaw (he remarks) that, when the news got about Europe, Paris and St. Petersburg would misrepresent the scheme as originating in Berlin. In order to anticipate such a misrepresentation he immediately telegraphed both to Queen Victoria and the Prince the true facts of the Russo-French proposal, and his refusal of it. The Queen expressed her hearty thanks; the Prince professed astonishment. Subsequently, the Kaiser adds, the Queen was able to convince her government that Germany had no hand in devising the plan, and finally she declared that she would not forget the service her grandson had rendered England in troublous times. The Kaiser here woefully garbles the accounts which he sent to the Queen and the Prince of Count Muravieff's suggestion of the 27th February (new style). The documents quoted in the text show the falsity of the Kaiser's assertion that Russia and France jointly proposed to Germany any kind of fighting coalition against England.

retaining their independence. He pointed out to Count Metternich "that England could not engage in the repetition of a war such as the present one, and for that reason the Republics must not, and would not, be granted independence." [1]

At the same time Queen Victoria, in a letter to the Kaiser, spoke for her son as well as for herself, when she plainly warned her grandson that on no account would the mediation of himself or of any other ruler be entertained. "All interference," the Queen wrote, "will be resisted by my country, which has suffered from so cruel a sacrifice of precious lives." The Kaiser acknowledged the Queen's notification in the sentence : "Just as I thought." [2]

The Queen's language roused in the Kaiser's mind a passing doubt as to whether his pretension to be honoured as England's deliverer was fully accepted by his English kinsfolk at his own valuation. He thought to convince them by louder boasts of his past service and more emphatic professions of his present devotion to their country's interest. Writing to the Queen on 31st March he reiterated in exultant tones how he had saved

your country from a most dangerous situation in warding off a combination aiming a blow at England in a moment which was vital to her. May your Government see in my action a renewed proof of my firm friendship and a sign of my determination to see that you should have fair play. For I am sure that South Africa once under the British flag, order, thrift, life, commerce and peace, with goodwill towards all men, will be assured.

VI

The Kaiser's ill-conditioned impulses were inclining him, as M. Delcassé shrewdly suspected, to a fresh effort to draw England into the Triple Alliance on his own terms. France and Russia had rejected his bait. England, the prey of South African embarrassments, might well be induced to follow his lead. In February 1900 the Kaiser took a step which seemed to him to favour his new purpose. The continued illness of his Ambassador in London, Count von Hatzfeldt, rendered it

---

[1] Count Metternich to the Berlin Foreign Office, 11th March, *Die Grosse Politik*, Band 15, p. 527.

[2] President Kruger sent a similar appeal to Vienna, and Lord Salisbury informed the Queen as early as 15th March 1900 (on the report to him of Count Deym, the Austrian Ambassador in London) that Kruger's request to the Austrian government had been promptly met by "a simple refusal."

1900
Ætat. 58
necessary to choose a successor. His choice fell on an intimate associate, Count Paul Wolff Metternich, a man of charming address, on whom the Kaiser could rely to give effect to his every wish. Count Metternich had already served in subordinate positions at the German Embassy in London, and was reckoned well disposed to this country. When his name was first suggested to the English Foreign Office as German *chargé d'affaires* and Ambassador-elect, Lord Salisbury invited the Prince's opinion. The Prince guardedly replied that he had no objection to raise. Metternich arrived in London in the middle of February, and was at once genially received by the Prince. The Kaiser lost no time in expressing to his uncle effusive thanks "for the cordiality and open frankness" of the Prince's reception of his representative.

"You have placed your confidence," the Kaiser wrote 23rd February 1900, "in no ordinary man. He is by conviction a staunch friend of England, and was chosen by me as my représentant on that account. But he is at the same time a trusted and true friend of mine, enjoying my fullest confidence, who will, I am sure, always faithfully repeat all you honour him by telling him to me, the same as he will in all I have to let you know. He will do all in his power to tighten the relations between our two countries and to smooth over and alleviate frictions and roughness that will turn up, as much as he can, and in this work he will, I am sure, find his best and strongest support in you."[1]

The Prince replied to his nephew on 28th February:

Knowing that Count Metternich possessed your entire confidence and friendship, I spoke to him most unreservedly, and expressed a hope that his presence in charge of the German Embassy would prove conducive to the good relations between our two countries. Being a perfect, upright and straightforward man, and being fond of England, which he knows so well, I have but little doubt that his position will not only be an excellent one, but one pleasing to himself. I most heartily say that at any time he wishes to see me I shall be only too happy to receive him and talk over any matter which is always more difficult to express or discuss by letter.

Before long Count von Hatzfeldt sufficiently recovered to enable him to resume some of the duties of his office, and Count Metternich served in a subordinate position. It was only on

---

[1] Printed from the original at Windsor. A copy in the Berlin archives appears in *Die Grosse Politik*, xv. 559.

Count von Hatzfeldt's death on 24th November 1901 that Metternich was installed as Ambassador. Already the fair promise of his first interview with the Prince had become clouded. As a faithful echo of his master he was soon making representations to the British Foreign Office which had a grating cadence.

Meanwhile, the Kaiser persisted in his blandishments in the hope of driving England into his scheme of a quadruple alliance. With that end in view he was scrupulous in his attentions to both his grandmother and his uncle. In May he invited his uncle to the annual autumn German manœuvres at Stettin, promising that Queen Victoria's regiment of Dragoons should take part in the operations. Complacently accepting a refusal on the ground of health, he transferred the invitation to the Prince's son, the Duke of York. On 3rd May he informed the Queen that he was raising a fund to relieve sufferers from the Indian famine. At Vienna he let it be known that he attached the greatest importance to the maintenance of thoroughly cordial relations with England. On 23rd May he sent to Queen Victoria an unusually effusive greeting on her birthday :

The whole of us will to-morrow be assembled with dear Mama at Friedrichshof to drink your health with all our hearts.

The Prince, without qualifying his ingrained doubts of the Kaiser's motives, wisely reciprocated the Kaiser's advances. He suggested that his nephew should once again join him at Cowes in August. The Kaiser responded favourably, but public affairs so developed in the autumn as to keep him at home. Lord Salisbury congratulated himself on the harmony which for the time prevailed between uncle and nephew. He told the Prince that "all who value the peace of Europe and cherish the interests of England" desired the good relations between him and the Kaiser to continue. But all the time the Kaiser's capacity for honest dealing was none the less questioned by shrewd English minds. The Prime Minister told the Queen of his conviction, although the evidence was not then available, that the Kaiser's allegation that France and Russia had proposed to him a plan of combined action against England was a figment of his fertile imagination, and that his claims on

England's gratitude for having preserved her from an immense peril rested on fictitious foundations.

VII

The popular animosity on the Continent against England showed in the spring no signs of abating. Prominent Englishmen on their travels abroad received unwelcome attentions from infuriated partisans of the Boer cause. "Vive les Boers" was the constant cry of mobs when English travellers were within hearing. The full brunt of the ugly agitation fell on the Prince and Princess in April while they were passing by train through a foreign country.

The Prince had hitherto been free from any of those attempts at assassination which commonly dog the steps of royalty. Queen Victoria had suffered five attempts on her life, none happily of a very serious kind. The Prince occasionally received threatening letters, chiefly from lunatics. During the Fenian agitation of 1884–85, leading Fenians promulgated, both in Ireland and the United States, an offer of £2000 reward for the body of the Prince, dead or alive.[1] Nothing followed this wild announcement. Not until April 1900 did he suffer any risk at an assassin's hand. Luckily it was the only experience of the kind which befell him, and did him no injury.

On the 3rd April the Prince and Princess left London on one of their customary three weeks' visits to Copenhagen. They went by way of Ostend and Brussels. As the train in which they travelled was steaming out of the Gare du Nord at Brussels

---

[1] *The Times*, 12th February 1885. The Prince treated such threats lightly. In November 1882 a man named Charles Brookshaw wrote threatening to kill the Prince if he did not receive £10. Sir Henry Hawkins, the judge, sentenced the prisoner to ten years' penal servitude (November 21, 1882). On 26th November the Prince wrote to the Home Secretary, Sir William Harcourt, asking for a mitigation of the heavy sentence on the ground of the man's probable insanity. The Queen thought a reduction of the sentence would have a bad effect. Sir William Harcourt took no action (Gardiner's *Harcourt*, i. p. 408). Again, when the Prince visited Bristol while on his way to Leigh Court to be the guest for three days of Sir Philip Miles, M.P., at the end of January 1884, he was escorted through the city by a strong force of police owing to threats that had reached Marlborough House of a Fenian attempt on his life. In the result, the police arrested in lodgings at Clifton, Bristol, a gentleman farmer of Herefordshire, William Cook Doune, who admitted that he had come to Bristol to shoot the Prince, and had bought a gun in the city for the purpose. He turned out to be insane and was sent to a lunatic asylum.

on 4th April, a Belgian youth of fifteen named Sipido jumped on
the footboard of the carriage in which the Prince and Princess
were seated, and, pointing a pistol at them, fired wildly four
times. The weapon twice missed fire; one bullet went wide of
the mark, but the fourth lodged in the partition wall of the
compartment between the heads of the Prince and Princess.
Fortunately neither was hit. The Prince showed the utmost
coolness, bidding the bystanders on the platform, who seized the
assailant, do him no harm. The journey was scarcely interrupted.
With the would-be assassin, the boy Sipido, there were also
arrested three adult companions. All proved to be members of
an anarchist club cherishing anti-British and pro-Boer sentiments. Sipido explained that he regarded the Prince as "an
accomplice of Chamberlain in killing the Boers."

The congratulations on the Prince's escape were numerous,
and the Prince's acknowledgements took a complacent view of
"the untoward incident." To Sir Frank Lascelles he wrote on
his arrival at Copenhagen on the 6th April:

The bullet was found in our carriage to-day; though a small
one it was quite capable of doing serious mischief if it had struck
a vital part.[1] Fortunately Anarchists are bad shots. The
dagger is far more to be feared than the pistol. . . . The Princess
is none the worse, and bore everything with the greatest courage
and fortitude.

To Lady Londonderry he also wrote from Copenhagen in
the like strain on the 8th April: "Fortunately 'all's well that
ends well'." On the 13th April, in reply to congratulations
from Lord Spencer, he wrote:

It was fortunate that the miscreant was so bad a shot, as it
seemed inconceivable that he should have missed me at two
yards. Dr. Leyds's propaganda has borne fruit in the Anglophobism he has produced in the Foreign Press, and the anarchists
are profiting by it, as they look on England and the English as
the enemies of mankind in oppressing the poor Boers!

Abroad, marks of sympathy were as abundant as at home.
The Kaiser and Count von Bülow were both profuse in their

[1] This bullet was forwarded the Prince, and it is still preserved at Windsor
Castle in a cabinet in the Souvenir Room. It is kept in an envelope labelled
outside in the Prince of Wales's handwriting: "Sipido's Bullet, Brussels,
April 1900."

1900
Ætat. 58

felicitations to Sir Frank Lascelles at Berlin.   The Kaiser, indeed, called upon Sir Frank immediately on hearing the news early next morning, and roused him from his bed.   The Prince declared himself "touched" by the Kaiser's promptitude.   To the Prince's surprise the Kaiser, moreover, intercepted him at Altona railway station on his return journey from Denmark at the end of the month, and repeated his congratulations in person.   Sir Frank Lascelles and Baron von Eckardstein were the Kaiser's companions on the occasion.   On the way back to Berlin the Kaiser deemed it a favourable occasion to air for Sir Frank's benefit his Anglophilism.   He was, he told the Ambassador, England's firm friend, and would brook no interference with her on the part of any European Power while the South African War lasted.[1]

While congratulations were pouring in, the Prince remarked on the omission of any expression of sympathy from one dignified quarter.   He confessed himself "a little surprised and hurt" that the British Parliament ignored the episode altogether and refrained from any offer of formal congratulations.   He reminded Lord Salisbury that a congratulatory vote had been passed by both Houses of Parliament when the Fenians attempted the assassination of his brother, the Duke of Edinburgh, on his visit to Jackson, N.S.W., in April 1870.   The Duke was then slightly wounded.   The Prince pointed out that he had received votes of congratulations from the Parliaments of Portugal and Greece. Lord Salisbury scarcely took the Prince's view of the situation. He explained on 26th April the omission of parliamentary notice thus :

The matter was raised in Cabinet [on the day after the attempted assassination] and the precedents considered, but the adjournment of the House of Lords had already been fixed for that day, and it would have been necessary to have had a special sitting with proper notice.   It was thought better not to take that course, especially as it was not then known that the pistol contained a bullet, which the extreme youth of the culprit rendered doubtful.

The sequel of the Brussels outrage gave the Prince small satisfaction.   The Belgian Courts took too lenient a view of the offence to be reassuring.   Sipido with his three alleged instigators

[1] Eckardstein, pp. 163–64.

or accomplices were tried by a jury at the Cour d'Assises at
Brussels, 5th July. The three men were acquitted, and while
Sipido was found guilty, he was absolved of any intention to
kill. The Court declared him, in view of his youth, to be incapable of receiving a penal sentence, and ordered him to be
detained in a House of Correction till he came of age. He was
released, pending an appeal which he was allowed three days to
prepare. The boy at once escaped into French territory. The
Prince was not well pleased with the course of events, but he
easily yielded the palm to his nephew, who was seeking every
means of propitiating him, in vehemence of denunciation of
Belgian "justice."

"The behaviour of the Belgians," the Kaiser wrote to the
Prince on 18th July 1900, "in the Sipido affair is simply outrageous, and people in Germany are utterly at a loss to understand
the meaning. Either their laws are ridiculous, or the jury are a
set of d——d, bl——dy scoundrels. Which is the case I am
unable to decide."

The Belgian authorities made little effort to capture the
fugitive. At the end of July the British government protested
against the facilities of escape of which Sipido had taken
advantage. The Belgian government replied that they regretted
the incident, but denied that the prisoner had received any
preferential treatment. Such search for Sipido as Belgian, with
the aid of French, detectives made in Paris during the late
summer, produced no result. In October a more influential
personage, Leopold II., King of the Belgians, descended into the
arena to engage in the hunt. The Prince's relations with his
Belgian kinsman had of late been strained by differences over
the King's questionable treatment of the Central African
problems, and over scandals in the King's household. The King
was anxious to dispel the coolness, and to that end took the
strange step of visiting Paris with the object of himself discovering Sipido's whereabouts. On 19th October he wrote to Queen
Victoria from the French capital that he had enlisted the French
government's help in his quest. He had visited President
Loubet, M. Delcassé, and other ministers, and while they promised
him friendly aid, assured him that Sipido was not in Paris. The
King, however, discredited that information, and made feverish
efforts to get on the boy's track. He advised Queen Victoria

to order her Ambassador in Paris to let the French government know that she would regard the surrender of Sipido to Belgium as a friendly act.   At the same time he prayed the Queen to keep his activities dark, because if the hunted boy learned of them he would probably get away to America.   From Balmoral on 22nd October the Queen forwarded King Leopold's account of his detective endeavours to the Prince.   In a covering letter she said, "I wrote to Leopold that we were rather shocked by Sipido's escape," and she added that it was very lame to excuse the Brussels verdict on the ground that the Prince's freedom from injury implied no intention to wound.   King Leopold's effort meanwhile bore fruit.   The fugitive was arrested in Paris a week after the King wrote to Queen Victoria (October 26).   He was handed over to the Belgian government, which placed him under surveillance until he came of age.   After the Prince's accession to the throne, both the boy's mother and the boy himself appealed to King Edward for his forgiveness, and for the exertion of his influence so as to relieve the lad from further detention.   The Foreign Office dealt with both letters, and sent merely formal acknowledgements.

From another point of view King Leopold's adventure failed of its purpose.   The reconciliation with the Prince which the Belgian King hoped for, did not follow.   The relations between the two men during King Edward's reign were strained to breaking-point, and the King of the Belgians made it a specific grievance that his strenuous exertions to recapture Sipido in Paris were never adequately recognised by King Edward, and that he himself was unfairly blamed for his country's criminal code, which prohibited the penal treatment of offenders under age.[1]

VIII

In spite of M. Delcassé's resolve to bring to fruition that Anglo-French *entente* of which the Prince had long dreamed, the French government was powerless to check the pro-Boer sympathies of the French populace, and good relations between the countries seemed past praying for.   The Prince rightly resented the brutal violence of the attack on England by the

[1] Constantine Phipps, British Minister at Brussels, to King Edward, 31st October 1903.

French press, and his long-cherished faith in France appeared

to be nearing shipwreck.   His personal popularity was no longer
proof against the rancorous mood of Parisian journalists and
caricaturists, and during the progress of the South African War
he was repeatedly held up to savage ridicule in widely circulated
French prints, while Queen Victoria suffered greater indignities.

One result of the rabid storm was that the Prince absented
himself throughout the year 1900 from France, the country
which had fascinated him all his adult life and had hitherto been
the scene of his vacations year by year.   A visit to Denmark
replaced the customary spring sojourn in the French Riviera.
Lord Salisbury, who valued as an international asset the sympathetic sentiment linking in happier days the Prince and
France, vainly persuaded him to take a gentler view of French
insolence, but though the Prince's anger was quickly to pass
away, he could not bring himself for the time to treat the French
insults lightly.

Even some of the Prince's royalist friends caught the con-
tagion of abuse or showed sympathy with the slanderous
epidemic.   In March 1900 there came a burst of French venom
from a quarter which old ties might well have been expected
to free from sympathy with ribald attacks on the Queen or the
Prince.   A letter, approving the campaign against the Queen
in the French press, was published in Paris over the signature
of Philippe, Duc d'Orléans, the head of the old royal family of
France, the heir of the Comte de Paris, and great-grandson of
King Louis Philippe.

The Duc d'Orléans, who was born at Twickenham while his
parents were in exile, had passed most of his life in England,
and from his boyhood had received from both the Queen and
the Prince every kindly courtesy.   But he had always treated
the Prince with a challenging pomposity.   The Prince and the
Queen now showed natural indignation at his conduct.   The
Queen caused inquiries to be made of the Duc as to the authenticity of the discreditable letter.   The Duc was found to have
lately left England for Lisbon on a visit to his sister Amélie,
Queen of Portugal.   He replied from Lisbon to Queen Victoria,
evasively asking to be supplied with the evidence against him.
The Queen consulted the Prince as to further steps.

"It is a somewhat pompous effusion," the Prince replied to

his mother on 13th March 1900, "similar to those I occasionally receive from him. If the story, which is believed in England and France, of his having written that letter is not true, he had better deny it, but I doubt his being able to do so. You will, I hope, not answer his letter till you have had more authentic information. It seems strange that he should have thought it necessary to write to you from Lisbon instead of from England."

The correspondence was laid before Lord Salisbury, who pointed out to the Queen (March 15) that it was impossible to seek the truth through diplomatic channels, but that the Queen of Portugal might be willing to discover it. The Prince thought it desirable to obtain authentic testimony. Lord Salisbury deemed it strange that the Duc, should he be innocent, did not directly contradict the charge, which was widely circulating. Happily this unpleasing episode reached a more satisfying conclusion than at first seemed likely. The Duc confessed to the Queen that he had extended some favour to her French detractors, but he regretfully apologised for his ill-considered action. Queen Victoria magnanimously forgave the Duc for what she charitably treated as an indiscretion.

The Prince was not in the mood to be quite so readily placated. An opportunity offered him of bringing his irritation with the excesses of the French press home to France in a way that might well wound her susceptibilities. As early as 1897 the French Government had announced its intention to organise yet another International Exhibition in Paris for the year 1900. There was a general wish on both sides of the Channel that the Prince should, as in 1878, fill, in connection with the project, the office of President of the British Commission. On 22nd January 1897 Lord Salisbury wrote requesting the Prince to accept the position.

"It will be a great occasion," the Prime Minister pointed out, "and one which the French will desire earnestly that we should do our best to support. We can gratify them in this respect in no way more surely than by securing your Royal Highness's assistance as President of the Commission, for the appointment will conciliate the French and will act as a strong spur and encouragement to the British exhibitors."

The Prince promptly acceded, and he approved Lord Salisbury's subsequent suggestion that his son the Duke of

York, his brother-in-law the Marquis of Lorne, and his friend the Duke of Devonshire should serve as vice-presidents.

During the next two years the Prince performed his presidential functions with his wonted activity, and while in Paris early in 1899 watched the Exhibition buildings rising from their foundations. But at the end of 1899 his ardour was damped by the rising tide of French malevolence. In December he contemplated withdrawal from his presidential office. The Government, however, deprecated any step which should increase the tension with France. The Queen took her Government's point of view, and persuaded her son to continue:

"It is important," she wrote to him (December 18, 1899), "that no difficulty should be made about the Paris Exhibition. It is an affair between the two Governments, and the French Government is well disposed."

As the day of opening, which was fixed for 15th April 1900, came in sight, the Prime Minister appealed to the Prince to attend the inaugural ceremony. Lord Salisbury deemed that his presence would tend to improve Anglo-French relations, but against this appeal the Prince took a firm stand. He frankly rejected the Prime Minister's counsel. He might, he wrote, visit Paris some time during the Exhibition, but it would be impossible for him to attend the opening. The campaign of personal abuse of the Queen was far from over, although he himself was now the main target. He called Lord Salisbury's particular attention to a specially scurrilous article in *La Patrie*. There was a likelihood that the Paris mob might insult the British uniform which he would wear if he attended the opening ceremony. His presence, he represented, would be a slight to the Queen, and a proof of indifference to the vile lampoons of her. Many British exhibitors had marked their disgust at the excesses of the Parisian press by withdrawing their exhibits. Lord Salisbury accepted the emphatic declaration with regret, and he pencilled on the Prince's note the words: "No more to be said."

In the result the Prince saw nothing of the Paris Exhibition of 1900. It was the only Paris Exhibition of his time which he failed to visit. Although he had played no official part in the organisation of the Exhibition of 1889, he had fully inspected it as soon as it was in working order.

The Queen was in substantial agreement with the Prince's attitude towards the ugly phase of French animosity. She had abandoned an intended spring hol day in Italy, owing to the scurrilities which threatened her on her journey through France. She had heroically substituted a visit to Ireland. It was anomalous, she declared, for the Prince to go to Paris when she could not even pass through France *en route* for Italy. But although the Prince's quarrel with France had unpromising and ungainly features, it proved in the end a lovers' quarrel which, having run its course, served to intensify the old mutual affection.

IX

The ugly temper of the French press and people towards England throughout the year 1900 prejudiced M. Delcassé's project of an *entente*, and immensely stimulated the Kaiser's efforts to bring off his long-meditated coup of a quadruple alliance which should include England. The Prince's resentment of French virulence led him the more readily to reciprocate the Kaiser's professions of sympathy. His disappointment, too, over the renewal of Russia's intractable attitude towards England in Asian affairs under Count Muravieff's direction inclined him favourably to entertain the friendly advances of Germany. Yet discordant elements always lay very near the surface of the ground which the Prince and his nephew trod together. Signs of the Kaiser's untrustworthy temper and disingenuous instinct continued to make heavy calls on his uncle's forbearance. Events in the Far East, which led to concerted military operation by Germany, England, and other Powers, excited defiant displays of the Kaiser's arrogance which repelled the Prince.

From time to time rumours reached the Prince that the Kaiser was still bent, in spite of his professions, on stirring up France and Russia against England. While he was staying with his wife's family at Copenhagen in the spring of 1900, an anonymous paper in French, which was addressed to him there, warned him that Germany was still tempting the cupidity of both Russia and France by fancy pictures of the territorial acquisitions which would come their way in Asia and Africa if they joined a Franco-Russian-German coalition against England. A German

general, it was stated, had devised a plan of campaign for a com-   1900
bined attack by German and Russian troops on both India and   Ætat. 58
Egypt.[1]   On his return to London the Prince inquired of Baron
von Eckardstein of the German Embassy as to the meaning
of the anonymous communication.   The Baron denied it any
authenticity, but he admitted the possibility that some Pan-
German general or admiral might have indulged his Anglophobism by devising a plan of assault on England's position
overseas.   Yet the Prince, while he knew the footing to be
treacherous, maintained through 1900 good outward relations
with his nephew, and the general amiability was on the surface
unimpaired when Queen Victoria died on 22nd January 1901.

A great part of the month of August 1900 was spent by the
Prince in Germany in circumstances of much domestic depression.
The Prince's next brother, Alfred, Duke of Saxe-Coburg-Gotha,
died suddenly at Rosenau on 30th July, and the Prince attended
the funeral there on 4th August.   The Kaiser joined the concourse
of mourners.   After returning home for eight days, the Prince
set out for his annual "cure" at Homburg, and there he came
under the shadow of another domestic calamity.   The health
of his sister, the Empress Frederick, who was residing in the
neighbourhood at her palace of Friedrichshof (near Cronberg),
was causing acute anxiety.   She was known to be suffering from
cancer, and her days were numbered.   The Prince had now the
melancholy satisfaction of passing much time with her.   On
his way out, he lunched with her at her palace (August 17), and
he repeated the visit three days later.   Opportunities were also
offered the Prince of intercourse with his nephew, the Empress's
eldest son, who was staying in the same district at his castle of
Wilhelmshöhe.   He seemed to share the Prince's concern in his
mother's condition, and his demeanour towards her and towards
her brother was unusually considerate.   The Kaiser invited his
uncle to lunch with him at Wilhelmshöhe on the 21st, and at the
Prince's request Sir Frank Lascelles, the German Ambassador in
Berlin, who was staying at Homburg, accompanied him.[2]   There
was some political talk, which Lascelles reported to Lord Salisbury.
The Kaiser aired, for his uncle's benefit, suspicion of Russian

[1] Eckardstein, pp. 164–67.
[2] See, on the opposite page, the facsimile of the Prince's letter to Sir
Frank Lascelles making the appointment.

designs in China. But the conversation mainly turned on innocuous issues. The Kaiser asked his uncle to convey to General Sir Francis Grenfell, who was another visitor at Homburg, an invitation to attend the German army manœuvres as the Kaiser's guest. On the 24th August uncle and nephew met again under the Empress Frederick's roof, and the Kaiser returned with the Prince to his hotel (Ritters Park) at Homburg. The next time that the two men met was in England, when Queen Victoria lay on her deathbed.

The day before the Prince left Homburg, on 9th September, his sister's health allowed her to come over to Homburg to bid her brother farewell. But the Empress Frederick's strength was gradually declining, and no sooner had the Prince ascended the throne early next year than he paid her a last visit before her death, which followed on the 5th August 1901.

X

The position of Russia in China, to which the Kaiser directed his uncle's attention at the Wilhelmshöhe luncheon, had a material bearing on the relations of England with Germany and other Powers. Long-pending difficulties, caused by China's hostile attitude to foreign settlers, reached an acute crisis early in 1900.[1] China was making irregular war impartially on Englishmen, Frenchmen, Germans, Italians, and Russians, as well as on Americans and Japanese within her borders. The seven Powers whose nationals were threatened decided on joint efforts to repel the assault, and ordered small bodies of marines to Tientsin. The little composite army rapidly curbed the enemy's activities in that quarter. But the siege in June of the Foreign Legations at Pekin by the Chinese incendiaries convinced the Powers that more drastic steps were necessary. The Kaiser was stung to fury by the murder of his Minister at Pekin, and in letters to the Prince and in oratory at home pointed out the obligation of all the Powers to wreak together condign vengeance on Chinese barbarism. The situation appealed to the Kaiser's chauvinist

---

[1] A secret society known as the Boxers, whose members numbered many thousands, led attacks on all foreign settlers in the spring and summer of 1900. The campaign of outrage was openly favored by the Dowager Empress who ruled the country. In June 1900 all the foreign Legations of Pekin were threatened by the Boxers, and the Chancellor of the Japanese Legation and the Envoy of Germany were both killed.

vanity. It was to his mind an occasion in which Germany might well play the dominant part, and might give the rest of the world a taste of Germany's coming supremacy both on sea and land. In negotiating a joint punitive expedition he displayed an egotistical arrogance which was calculated to provoke English irritation. Russia, under Count Muravieff's guidance, was also following defiant courses, and the English government, in view of England's isolation, deemed it prudent to humour the Kaiser's bluster.

1900

Ætat. 58

The despatch of German troops in a German fleet to co-operate in distant China with a military contingent sent out by sea from England peculiarly excited the Kaiser's spirit of bravado. With self-assertive energy he sought to imbue the German troops, before setting out, with his boastful feeling. In July, while yachting off the fiords of Norway on his way home to inspect the German expeditionary force, he announced to the Prince that the urgent calls upon him compelled him to abandon his contemplated visit to Cowes.

"The regiments destined for China are leaving," he wrote from Trondhjem on 20th July, "at the beginning of August, and I want to see some of the troops off—the first German troops that leave for an oversea campaign since the troops which the Great Elector sent to William of Orange to help him to win the throne of England. I am so glad that Tientsin has at last been retaken, though it cost four weeks' hard fighting and I am sorry to say many officers and men. The Chinese have learned how to use European arms, and fight like demons; they want to get rid of all foreigners once and for all. There is no mistake about that. So it is supremely necessary that all the Powers should keep firmly together and to well prepare the campaign in Pekin, which will cost at least 80,000–90,000 men, the Chinese having at least 60,000 before Tientsin and 50,000–60,000 before Pekin. Our bluejackets and marines had their 'baptême de feu' and I am happy to say have behaved splendidly, which has been kindly acknowledged by all under whom they fought."

The Kaiser's historical reference to the last occasion on which German soldiers had crossed the ocean for purposes of war hardly seemed happy to the Prince. There was something sinister in the comparison of the present German expedition to China with the despatch of Hanoverian troops to England in 1689 to help William of Orange to win the English throne. But

the Kaiser's egotism knew no restraint. With an offensive air
of superiority he heaped advice on the English government in
regard to the organisation of the allies' army, and bitterly complained to his uncle of the English government's unwillingness
to follow his counsels. In irritated tones he called his uncle's
attention to the "great difficulties in pulling together," and
"the lack of . . . eagerness to receive suggestions in Downing
Street."

"I wish to see my way more clearly," he continued, "as to
the motives and aims which actuate the souls of the great men
dwelling there. Their answers are so enigmatic as to give the
impression that their origin is not far from the tripod of Pythia :
in the long run this won't do in Politics, though animated by the
best intentions."

Russia was suspected by England of designs on China which
were irreconcilable with the proposed concerted action, and
there was good reason to believe that the Kaiser was resorting
to his customary tactics of playing off Russia against England.
On the latter point the Kaiser sought to reassure the Prince.

There is nothing in the reported "agreement" between
Russia and Germany. The difficulty of co-operation does *not*
lie there. The Tsar's policy in China is founded on principles
in general identical to mine. We both want China to remain
whole and undivided, not split up in spheres of interest and open
doors.

The Kaiser's affected confidence in Russia was misplaced,
and when he met his uncle at Homburg at the end of August he
hinted in accents that might well stir suspicion of his own
sincerity that Russia was intending to seize Manchuria, to make
peace with China on her own account, and by ignoring the other
Powers to place them in a critical dilemma.

The Kaiser's bombastic ambition now declared itself in the
demand that the European forces destined for China should be
placed under the control of a German Commander-in-Chief.
For that office he nominated his close friend Field-Marshal Count
von Waldersee, from whom he had, from his youth upwards,
imbibed much of his Pan-German truculence. He misrepresented the suggestion as coming from the Tsar. The Powers
yielded to the Kaiser's request without enthusiasm. The Prince
acknowledged the wisdom of a conciliatory reply. The English

government, while raising no objection to the German Field-   1900
Marshal's appointment, proved rather more backward than the   Ætat. 58
other Powers in carrying out the complemental arrangements.
The Kaiser appealed to his uncle to use his influence in that
direction.   He pointed out to the Prince that it was essential
for the British government to nominate a British officer to
serve on Count Waldersee's staff.

"It would be most practical and the best means," the Kaiser
wired to the Prince on 10th August, "for ensuring the clearness
of communication between C.-in-C. of the Allied Forces, Count
Waldersee and the British Troops if a British Officer were attached
to his Staff in the same manner as the other Powers have done."

The Queen approved the proposal, and the Kaiser had his
way.   The Queen sagaciously recommended that the selected
officer should speak French and German.   The Prince suggested
Colonel Charles Swaine, "who has had experience with the Indian
Army," but in the event Lord Wolseley, the Commander-in-Chief,
appointed Colonel James Grierson (August 13).

The Kaiser's overbearing mood showed all its extravagance
in the dithyrambic harangue which he addressed to German
troops on 27th July at Bremerhaven on their embarkation for
the Far East.   He there employed an historic reference, this
time to early German history, which had an ominous bearing
on the reputation of German arms in the future.

"You know well," the Kaiser told his soldiers in bidding
them farewell, "that you are to fight a cunning, fearless, well-
armed and cruel foe.   When you meet him, understand, pardon
will not be given, prisoners will not be taken.   Whoever falls
into your hands is doomed.   As a thousand years ago the Huns
under King Etzel [Attila] made a name for themselves which
renders them still terrible in tradition and story, in like manner
may the name 'German' in China through you be so famed
that for a thousand years to come no Chinese may venture to
look askance at a German." [1]

With blind assurance the Kaiser on 1st August wrote to his
uncle of his triumphant performance at Bremerhaven, and laid

[1] A verbatim report of the Kaiser's speech appeared in the Bremen news-
papers before von Bülow knew of its delivery.   On learning the fact, the
Foreign Minister made vain efforts to suppress the speech's circulation.   See
Zurlinden, *Der Weltkrieg* (Zurich, 1917), vol. i. p. 315, and David Jayne Hill,
Impressions of the Kaiser, p. 142.

new stress on Germany's glorious first attempt "to transport
troops and masses of military stores across the seas." But the
Kaiser was once more deceiving himself. Count von Waldersee
declared later that well-nigh every mistake that was possible was
made in loading the ships with arms and stores.[1] Nor, indeed,
were any of the Kaiser's magnified expectations of exalting
Germany's prestige on Chinese soil realised. There was little
need of much military effort. The allied contingents already
in the Far East captured Pekin before Count Waldersee arrived
on the scene at the head of the newly despatched expeditionary
force. Little remained for him to do, save to terrorise a defenceless population with rapine and plunder and await the result
of negotiations for peace between China and the Powers. The
German Commander's claim to supreme authority proved a
futility. It was disputed on the field by most of the allied
commanders. The Russian army from the first declined to serve
under him. General Gaselee, the British Commander, rendered
him little assistance, and in revenge Waldersee reported to Berlin
that the British troops were "hated by all the contingents."
Nevertheless, in his despatches, he misled the Kaiser by giving
him the impression that "the respect for Germans in the Far East
unquestionably increased, and that for the British fell pro-
portionately." [2] The Kaiser adopted the sanguine view that as
a result of the international military combination under German
leadership "the other nations will recognise the superiority of
our system, and the wish to stand up against us in a war will
weaken. As a guarantee of peace it is better than the Hague
Conference." The Kaiser's egotism led him into misconceptions
which ultimately proved his ruin.

Yet in spite of all unpromising signs Germany and England
reached for the time an apparent agreement on one important
point. The Kaiser professed sympathy with the British government in their suspicion of Russia's attitude to Manchuria, China's
northern province. Lord Salisbury and von Bülow concluded
on 18th October the Yangtse Agreement which provided for the
opening of China's doors impartially to every nation, and for
the guaranteeing at the same time of the integrity of Chinese
territory. The Yangtse Agreement stipulated that should a
third Power defy its principles, the two signatories should discuss

[1] Waldersee, *Denkwürdigkeiten* (1900–4), Band iii.   [2] *Ibid.*

1900
Ætat. 58

common action against the challenger. But Germany was hardly playing an honest game. As far as the integrity of China was concerned, the Yangtse Agreement proved waste paper. Russia after disingenuously declaring herself in its favour, seized Manchuria. Thereupon England appealed to Germany to defend China against Russian aggression, but Germany refused, on the specious ground that Manchuria did not fall within the scope of the Yangtse Agreement. The Prince acknowledged that Russia's action was indefensible, but he still sanguinely cherished the illusory hope that the wrong might be repaired by the Tsar's peace-loving beneficence, and a breach between England and that country might be avoided.[1] The episode effectually served to confirm the Prince's conviction that his German nephew's purposes required most careful watching.

XI

The advance of the British Army in the conflict with the Boer Republics of South Africa continued through the summer and autumn with a success more apparent than real. The war had still to run its course for nearly two years longer. But from May onwards Lord Roberts was establishing what looked like complete ascendancy over the enemy. After successes in the field which were reckoned at the moment to be decisive, he proclaimed the annexation of the Orange Free State on 28th May, and that of the Transvaal on 1st September. President Kruger fled from his capital into Portuguese territory on the approach of British troops, and next month (November) he sailed for Europe in a Dutch cruiser. On the surface, the South African War appeared to be near its end. But the Boer leaders were not yet defeated. They were initiating a guerilla warfare which the English were unable to master for another twenty months.

Popular sentiment in England was for the most part steadfast in the resolved quest of a final and a decisive victory. At the

[1] Germany's relations with England in regard to China were to the end uneasy. In December, a difference arose as to the punishment to be allotted to Prince Tuan and the ringleaders of the anti-foreign rebellion. Germany insisted on their execution as an indispensable condition of peace. England and the other Powers successfully resisted this demand, and were content with the imprisonment for life of Prince Tuan, the banishment of two of his companions, and the execution of five others.

general election, dubbed "the Khaki Election," which followed Lord Salisbury's dissolution of Parliament on 25th September 1900,[1] the main issues raised by the Unionists were the necessity of consummating the South African triumph which was mistakenly believed to be close at hand. The Liberal party was divided on the justice of protracting the conflict, and a section of the party, who won the sobriquet of "pro-Boers," urged the immediate making of peace. But the Unionists were returned in a vast majority, numbering 402 against 186 Liberal and Labour members and 82 Irish Nationalists. The Prince was well satisfied with the Unionist majority of 134 over all parties, which was only 9 below that of the previous General Election.

Lord Salisbury, while continuing in office, made some changes, which especially interested the Prince, in the personal constitution of his government. The Prime Minister was in his seventy-first year, and he relieved himself of part of his heavy responsibilities by handing over the Foreign Secretaryship, which he had hitherto combined with the office of Prime Minister, to Lord Lansdowne, who had hitherto been Secretary of State for War. Lord Salisbury took over from the veteran Lord Cross the sinecure office of the Privy Seal. Lord Lansdowne's place at the War Office was filled by the appointment of Mr. St. John Brodrick, who, in spite of some demur on the Queen's part, had become Parliamentary Secretary to the War Office in 1895, and had since 1898 been Under-Secretary of State for Foreign Affairs. With Lord Lansdowne the Prince's relations had long been familiar, although they had failed to see eye to eye on many matters. On the minister's transference to the Foreign Office they came into closer association than before. The Prince welcomed the accession to his new office of the new War Secretary, and for the time their intercourse was exceptionally cordial. A member of the Prince's intimate social circle also joined the reconstructed ministry. Lord Londonderry became Postmaster-General in place of the Duke of Norfolk. Another close friend, Lord Cadogan, remained, to the Prince's satisfaction, Lord-Lieutenant of Ireland. But a third friend of old standing, Mr. Chaplin, was somewhat unceremoniously given his *congé*. The Presidency of the Local Government Board which

[1] The ministry had held office for five years and a quarter.

Mr. Chaplin had filled passed to Mr. Walter Long.[1] It was
Lord Salisbury's ministry in the shape which it now assumed
that welcomed the Prince to the throne.

1900
—
Ætat. 58

XII

There was much in the conduct of the war during the
latter part of 1900, despite specious signs of an early termination, to increase the misgivings with which the opening
operations had inspired the Prince.   The inefficiency of the army
medical service was for him, and others, an especially disturbing
feature, and he welcomed in July the appointment of a Royal
Commission of Enquiry, but he was disappointed by the half-
hearted schemes of reform which it recommended in a Report
which was issued on the last day of Queen Victoria's reign.   A
more drastic reorganisation was initiated after he ascended the
throne.   Nor was the Prince well satisfied with the conduct of
the War Office in the last months of the Marquis of Lansdowne's
tenure of the Secretaryship of State.   He was always suspicious
of the civilian administration of the Army, and he regarded
Lord Lansdowne as pressing unduly his civilian authority.   He
formed the opinion that Lord Wolseley, the Commander-in-Chief,
was not taken adequately into the Secretary of State's confidence.
The Prince indeed expressed the opinion (September 26) that
the Commander-in-Chief was "virtually a cipher."   There was
much to justify the Prince's doubts of the success of that
reorganisation of the War Office which Lord Wolseley's
appointment in 1895 had been designed to promote.

Until the close of the war, the Prince continued a severe critic
of incapacity on the part of commanding officers in the field, and
he professed much discontent with what he deemed the vacillating
attitude of the War Office towards incompetence.   He shared
with the Queen a strong dislike of the publication by the War
Office of formal censures on officers for failures in the field,
especially when the soldiers who suffered reprimand were allowed

[1] Two other ministers besides the two mentioned above, Lord Cross and
Mr. Chaplin, retired, viz. Sir Matthew White Ridley, Home Secretary, and Mr.
Goschen, First Lord of the Admiralty.   Lord Selborne became First Lord of the
Admiralty in succession to Mr. Goschen; Mr. Ritchie became Home Secretary
in place of Sir Matthew White Ridley and was succeeded at the Board of Trade
by Mr. Gerald Balfour, formerly Irish Secretary; Mr. George Wyndham took
the Irish Secretaryship.

to retain their command. Against the practice of "washing one's dirty linen in public" he always inveighed with vehemence. In April he shared the Queen's irritation at the publication by the War Office, six months after the events, of Sir Redvers Buller's despatch regarding his defeat at Spion Kop, and of Lord Methuen's despatch regarding his defeat on Modder River. To the published despatches there were appended scathing censures of both Generals from the pen of Lord Roberts. Objection was taken by the Queen and her son to the issue of such a disquieting manifesto at an ill-chosen moment, and to the failure of the War Office to take any action against officers who, according to the language of Lord Roberts, scarcely deserved to remain in the army. With special heat, too, the Prince denounced the two humiliating disasters which befell Sir Henry Colvile at Sanna's Post, 31st March, and at Lindley on 31st May respectively. He insisted that the well-being and discipline of the army required the exemplary punishment of every serious error, although as far as was possible, all public advertisement should be avoided. The Prince took the general view that the misadventures of the South African War made imperative a thoroughgoing reform of the army, even if the moment for overhauling the War Office and the army had not yet arrived. It was scarcely possible until the current war was closed that the far-reaching inquiries essential to a complete scheme of reform should be undertaken. The reconstruction of the War Office and of the army was one of the obligations which remained to be fulfilled under the Prince's own auspices as sovereign.

In the autumn of 1900, however, a personal issue directed the Prince's special attention to the office of Commander-in-Chief for an increase of whose "power and responsibility" he was urgently pleading. Lord Wolseley's five years' appointment was nearing its end, and the choice of a successor was imminent. There was some difference in the matter between Queen Victoria and the Prime Minister, Lord Salisbury. The Queen thought the time had come for the appointment to the supreme military command of her son, the Duke of Connaught. She had recommended him for the post when the Duke of Cambridge had retired in 1895 and Lord Wolseley had been nominated by the ministry. Lord Salisbury now declined to support the Queen's recommendation. He held the opinion that Lord

Roberts's eminent services in South Africa entitled him alone to
the post.[1] The Queen consulted the Prince, and he stood by
the Prime Minister. He deemed Lord Roberts's claim superior
to that of his brother. For the present, too, the Prince argued
that the terms of tenure should remain unchanged. Accordingly,
on the fallacious assumption that Lord Roberts's work in South
Africa was done he was recalled to England in November. On
the 29th of that month he handed over the South African
Command to his colleague, Lord Kitchener, and, leaving Cape
Town for England on 11th December, landed at Cowes in order
to visit the Queen at Osborne on 2nd January 1901. His
installation in Lord Wolseley's place followed immediately.

Although Lord Roberts's fitness for the functions of Commander-in-Chief was (as the event amply proved) open to
question, the Prince adopted the government's plea that
he had rendered in South Africa great national service, and
that he deserved on his arrival home an imposing public
welcome with the award of high honours, and a substantial
pecuniary recognition. The moment seemed hardly well-chosen
for a triumphal celebration, and the Prince allowed that objections might fairly be taken against it. He shared the justifiable
misgivings which were rife in many quarters respecting the
completeness of Lord Roberts's work in South Africa. "There
cannot be any doubt," he wrote to Mr. Brodrick, Lord Lansdowne's successor at the War Office (January 6, 1901), "that
the generals and C.O.'s are getting stale. I cannot see how
it could be otherwise, and we want fresh blood and capable
men." He pressed his argument personally on Lord Roberts
on his arrival, and urged with success the despatch of Sir
Laurence Oliphant, of the Grenadier Guards. Lord Roberts
himself openly admitted that much remained to be done, and
that admission confirmed doubts in the public mind of the
justice of a reception and of rewards which seemed only due
to a victorious General after peace was won.

None the less, the recognition of such a trend of public
opinion did not preclude the Prince from playing a prominent
part in the ceremonies of Lord Roberts's home-coming. At
Osborne on 2nd January the Queen had bestowed on the General
an earldom and the blue ribbon of the Garter. Arriving in

[1] Lord Salisbury to the Queen, 28th September,

London next day Lord Roberts was met at Paddington Station
by the Prince and Princess, and they entertained him on behalf
of the Queen at a luncheon at Buckingham Palace. In the
evening the Prince joined the dinner which Mr. Brodrick, the
new Secretary of State for War, gave in Lord Roberts's honour
at his house in Portland Place.

The grant of money which the cabinet first proposed to make
Lord Roberts was a sum of £50,000. But the Prince thought, in
view of Lord Roberts's small private resources, and the high
dignity of an earldom which had been conferred on him, that a
larger generosity should be shown him by the State. On the
6th January 1901 he wrote to Mr. Brodrick, the Secretary of
State:

Most earnestly do I hope that H.M.'s Government will
reconsider the grant to be made to Lord Roberts. It is the
universal opinion that £50,000 is too little, as he has been created
an earl. £100,000 seems to me to be the least he could receive.
I feel sure the House of Commons will not grudge it him and
will vote anything. I know that the Queen feels as strongly
as I do on the subject and has communicated her views to the
Prime Minister.

Lord Salisbury accepted the Prince's suggestion, and a sum
of £100,000 was duly voted to Lord Roberts by the House
of Commons on the 30th July 1901, on the proposition of
Mr. Balfour, leader of the House of Commons, seconded by
Mr. Campbell-Bannerman, leader of the opposition.

XIII

Meanwhile President Kruger's arrival in Europe had provoked on the continent fresh demonstrations of popular animosity
towards England. The government of France proved unable to
resist the popular cry that the refugee should be offered a welcome
by the State. The President landed at Marseilles on 22nd November, and was accorded a popular ovation. In Paris on 24th
November he was received by President Loubet, and a resolution
of sympathy with him was passed by the Chamber of Deputies,
29th November, and by the Senate, 30th November. In Holland,
where the President made up his mind to settle, an equally
warm welcome was offered him on his arrival in the country,

and the Queen of the Netherlands received him in audience, 1900
(December 8). In Germany, the refugee was greeted by the Ætat. 58
people with a like enthusiasm as he passed from Paris on his
way to the Hague.

The Kaiser, however, continued to pursue England with
conciliatory favour. The flow of his felicitations to his English
kinsfolk on Lord Roberts's operations in the summer and autumn
had not ceased, even if they came at somewhat rarer intervals
than similar messages in the early months of the year. The
attitude of the French Government to President Kruger stimulated
him to take a line which should be more grateful to English
feeling. He announced on 1st December his refusal to receive
the exiled President in Berlin. The Kaiser was hopeful of some
practical recognition of his complaisance from the English
Government, and deprecated the pessimism of Count von Bülow,
who had become Chancellor in succession to Prince von Hohenlohe on 16th October, and had small faith in the likelihood of
permanent Anglo-German friendship.

The Prince, like many members of Lord Salisbury's cabinet,
was growing more confirmed than ever in his doubts of the
wisdom of the policy of "splendid isolation." Some of the
Ministers were too mistrustful of the Kaiser to entertain the
notion of any co-operation with him, and believed despite unpromising omens of the moment that England might benefit by
an alignment with France or with Russia, or with those two allied
countries together. But certain of Lord Salisbury's most influential colleagues deemed it more prudent to encourage the Kaiser's
apparently benevolent advances. On the 7th of January 1901
the Prince paid a five days' visit, as had been his wont of past
years, to the Duke and Duchess of Devonshire at Chatsworth.
The Duke, one of the Prince's oldest friends, was President of
the Council in Lord Salisbury's cabinet. It was a large party
of the Prince's intimate friends, and the time was spent for the
most part in pleasurable recreation. "The theatricals were
excellent," the Prince wrote to his friend Lady Londonderry
on 14th January. Among the company were the Secretary of
the Austrian Embassy, Count Albert Mensdorff, who was soon
himself to become Ambassador, and Mr. Balfour, leader of the
House of Commons, who was before long to succeed his uncle,
Lord Salisbury, as Prime Minister. There was under the Duke

of Devonshire's roof some political discussion, and from his host
the Prince learnt of the Government's developing disposition
to consider the possibilities of some general understanding with
Germany.[1]   Although the Prince's distrust of his nephew was
far from dispelled, he appreciated the reasons which inclined his
host towards a German *entente*.

Meanwhile, the Kaiser was redoubling his efforts to keep
his royal English kinsfolk in good humour.   Early in January 1901 he confided to Sir Frank Lascelles his intention of
shortly paying with his elder sons another visit to the Queen.
Simultaneously he let the Prince know that he was to
celebrate in Berlin, on 18th January, the 200th anniversary
of the foundation of the Prussian Monarchy.   He invited his
uncle to attend the ceremony, or, if that were impossible, to
send a member of his family.   Sir Frank, who knew that the
Prince would be scarcely willing to attend in person, pointed out
that the Kaiser expected the presence of other foreign princes.
Sir Frank urged the Prince to permit the Duke of York to represent him at the approaching celebration.   But the Prince saw
in the invitation one of his nephew's familiar projects of self-
glorification.   Reluctant to flatter the Kaiser's vanity, he
questioned the propriety of Sir Frank's suggestion.   He had
already proposed that the Duke of York should bear his
congratulations to the Kaiser on the Kaiser's birthday on
January 27th, and that he should, at the same time, present, on
the Queen's behalf, the insignia of the Garter to the Crown
Prince of Germany, the Kaiser's eldest son.   Ultimately the
Prince compromised the matter by asking his brother the Duke
of Connaught to represent him in Berlin at the commemorative
ceremonies.[2]

[1] Immediately on the Prince's departure from Chatsworth Mr. Chamberlain
arrived, together with Baron von Eckardstein of the German Embassy, and
they conferred with the Duke of Devonshire on England's international relations.
Mr. Chamberlain insisted that England's need of allies on the continent would
best be met by an agreement with Germany, although, if Lord Salisbury and
other colleagues remained averse, it would be well to sound Russia (Eckardstein,
p. 185).

[2] Sir Frank Lascelles to the Prince, 5th January 1901; the Prince to Sir
Frank Lascelles, 8th January 1901.

CHAPTER XL

THE DEATH OF QUEEN VICTORIA

I

THE hostile feeling of the French people and the anxieties of the pending war led Queen Victoria to abandon in 1900 her usual spring sojourn in the Riviera. The Prince deprecated her absence from her own dominions at so critical a period, and he commended her decision against going "abroad when her presence at home is so much needed, so that she might keep in touch with her Ministers." It was a grievous disappointment to the Queen to be deprived of the opportunity of visiting her stricken eldest daughter, the Empress Frederick, at whose residence she had intended to break her journey on her anticipated continental tour. Finally, the Queen resolved to seek change during the spring of 1900 in Ireland.

It was with great satisfaction that the Prince learnt of his mother's decision to substitute for her customary stay on the continent a three weeks' sojourn in Ireland. It was nearly forty years since she had visited that country. Of late she had declined to renew the experience on the ground of the Nationalist clamour against the English connection. The Prince spoke with fervour of the Queen's heroic resolution to repair neglect of so long a standing. The ground which moved her to take the step was the admiration which she conceived for the conduct of Irish troops in South Africa. She desired to show sympathy with her Irish soldiers' suffering in the field. The reception of the Queen by the Irish people in Dublin left on the surface nothing to be desired, and the Prince saw in the success of the visit good promise of the future.

There was much to depress the Queen's spirit as the year

1900

Ætat. 58

799

advanced. The death of her second son, the Duke of Saxe-Coburg-Gotha, and the grave illness of her eldest daughter, the Empress Frederick, intensified the anxieties which came of the military operations in South Africa. "We have been deceived by the Boers and are suffering accordingly," she had written on 11th February. A severe blow followed on 29th October in the death of her grandson, Prince Christian Victor of Schleswig-Holstein, elder son of Princess Helena, the Queen's second daughter, who fell a victim to enteric fever contracted on the battlefield of South Africa. The young man was buried by the Queen's direction in St. George's Chapel, Windsor, on 1st November, and the Prince attended his nephew's funeral.

II

During the summer of 1900 the health of Queen Victoria, who then entered her eighty-second year, showed signs of failure. The trials of the war helped to sap her strength, but the disabilities of old age had long been telling on her. For some five years a rheumatic stiffening of the joints had rendered walking difficult, and from 1898 onwards incipient cataract greatly affected her eyesight. A tendency to aphasia showed that her powerful memory, on which she had so long and justly prided herself, was decaying. She was, too, losing weight and suffering from sleeplessness. None the less, she and her son both had confidence that the indications of physical decay might be checked by a visit to the Riviera, which was designed for the following spring. She was still interesting herself with something of her old pertinacity, not merely in the war, but in all phases of public affairs, continually pressing advice on the Government and complaining if any action were taken without her knowledge. But as the autumn wore on it was recognised that although no immediate crisis was apprehended, the end could not be very far distant.

On 18th December 1900 the Queen travelled from Windsor to Osborne, which she was not to quit alive. At Osborne her health betrayed no genuine improvement, yet her will could still respond to the calls made upon it. On 2nd January 1901 she nerved herself to welcome Lord Roberts from South Africa. She was greatly affected by the interview, and her weakness was perceptible. Through the next fortnight her condition somewhat varied from day to day, but was not judged to be on the whole unfavourable. On the 11th January she gave a brief audience to Mr. Chamberlain, the Colonial Secretary, and on the 14th she again summoned Lord Roberts to her side to learn further particulars of the progress of the war. Next day she drove out for the last time. Not until the 18th did her physicians inform the Prince and the other members of her family that her condition had become precarious. On that date the Court Circular announced : "The Queen had not lately been in her usual health and is unable for the present to take her customary drives." The Prince travelled next day to Osborne, and at once cancelled all his pending engagements. That afternoon a further bulletin stated that the Queen was "suffering from great physical prostration, accompanied by symptoms that cause anxiety."

A telegram from Baron von Eckardstein of the German Embassy in London informed the Kaiser on the 18th of his grandmother's serious state. He was, as his uncle had already learned from him, engaged in celebrating the two hundredth anniversary of the foundation of the Prussian Monarchy. The Duke of Connaught was attending the ceremonies as the Prince's representative. The Kaiser, on receipt of the news from England, immediately broke off the celebrations and made hasty preparation to attend his grandmother's deathbed. With his uncle, the Duke of Connaught, he hurried the same night to England by way of Holland.

There was embarrassment among the Kaiser's English relatives at his sudden and unexpected arrival. It was not a moment when they were in the mood to pay him ceremonious attention. But the Prince of Wales, in the uniform of the Prussian First Dragoon Guards, met him at Victoria station, and drove with him to Buckingham Palace, where the Kaiser spent the night. Next morning, the 20th, the Prince accompanied his nephew to Osborne where the Queen was nearing the last stage of her long pilgrimage. She barely recognised her grandson; she seemed to mistake him for his father.

The Prince and the Kaiser, with the Duke of Connaught and the Queen's three daughters, Princess Helena, Princess Louise, and Princess Beatrice, and her other grandchildren, watched at her bedside during her last hours. The Kaiser was, indeed,

1901
Ætat. 59

a prominent and busy figure in the chamber of death, and when, in the coming years, the relations of uncle and nephew were more than usually strained the Kaiser often recalled the scene to King Edward's memory somewhat more intrusively than was always congenial.

Let us rather remember the silent hour when we watched and prayed at her bedside, when the spirit of that great Sovereign Lady passed away as she drew her last breath in my arms.[1]

At half-past six on the evening of Tuesday, 22nd January, Queen Victoria passed away. Her last articulate word was her eldest son's Christian name. A quarter of an hour later the Prince of Wales in accordance with precedent telegraphed to the Lord Mayor of London : "My beloved mother, the Queen, has just passed away, surrounded by her children and grand-children."

This was the first official and public intimation of Queen Victoria's death, and of the Prince's accession to her throne.[2]

III

It was at the mature age of fifty-nine years, two months, and thirteen days, that the Prince came into his heritage. For nearly six decades he had been the first in rank among his mother's subjects, but she had shared little or nothing of her sovereign rights with her heir-apparent. Her prolonged tenure of royal place and of such royal power as the British constitution allowed her fed the popular fancy that death would never claim her, and that her reign was unending. In the first shock of her demise, none seemed able to foretell what would follow so startling a breach with the past. Doubts were cherished in many quarters whether the Prince was fitly prepared for his new responsibilities. Few

[1] Kaiser to King Edward, 1st February 1906.

[2] The Queen was eighty-one years and eight months old, less two days. Her reign had lasted sixty-three years, seven months, and two days. She had lived three days longer than George III., the longest-lived sovereign of England before her. Her reign exceeded his, the longest yet known to English history, by nearly four years. Only two European sovereigns reigned longer than Queen Victoria, a predecessor, Louis XIV. of France, who reigned seventy-one years, and a contemporary and survivor, Emperor Francis Joseph of Austria, who reigned sixty-eight years. Francis Joseph, Emperor of Austria, Queen Victoria's junior in age by eleven years, ascended his throne in 1848, eleven years after her accession. He died on 21st November 1916.

knew the breadth of interest, the knowledge of men and affairs which he had surely and steadily assimilated, as this record shows in full detail for the first time, during the long years that he was standing on the steps of the throne. When his hour struck, experience had given him exceptional qualifications for the hereditary burden. Despite his pleasure-loving temperament he had never ignored the significance of the Prince of Wales's motto, "Ich Dien" ("I serve"). From his boyhood he had wished "to be of use," and although limits had been set in political directions to the fulfilment of this boyish aspiration, he had succeeded throughout his manhood in rendering much useful political service and in amassing valuable political information, while he had taken an active lead in social and philanthropic movements of most varied range. Lord Beaconsfield's description of him in 1880 as a Prince "who really has seen everything and knows everybody" was truer of him twenty years later than when the words were written. He had become in a supreme degree a man of the world, in whom shrewdness mingled with benignity. He still retained touches of early prejudice and impetuosity, which at times clouded his judgement. If it could not be quite truthfully said of him what an eminent Victorian critic said of a Greek dramatist, that "he saw life steadily and saw it whole," he could justly claim to know life more comprehensively than commonly falls to the lot of humanity. His vitality was not effectually impaired when his mother died, and he was physically fitted to take advantage of the enhanced repute which the English monarchy had acquired under her sway. To his career there is applicable the apophthegm, which has obvious limits in its ordinary application, that the last ten years of life are the best, because they are fullest of experience and freest from illusion. Although fate decreed that the Prince's term of rule should scarcely pass beyond nine years — little more than a seventh part of his mother's span — he was to leave as King an impression on the history of his country, and on the popular mind at home and abroad, out of all proportion to the brevity of his tenure of the predestined dignity.

APPENDIX

TWO SETS OF NOTES ON THE EARLY STAGES OF THE SOUTH AFRICAN
WAR, SENT TO THE PRINCE OF WALES BY HIS NEPHEW, KAISER
WILLIAM II., ON 21ST DECEMBER 1899 AND 2ND FEBRUARY
1900 RESPECTIVELY

THE following are English translations, which the Prince caused
to be made, of the two sets of the Kaiser's advisory "Notes" on
the South African War, which he forwarded in German to his uncle
at early stages of the military operations, on 21st December 1899
and 2nd February 1900 respectively.[1] These translations were
prepared for the Prince immediately after his receipt of the papers
from the Kaiser. The Prince sent copies to the Queen and to a few
intimate friends. The original German version of the second set of
notes has been printed by the German Government in *Die Grosse
Politik*, Band 15 (1924), pp. 554-57. Of the first set, nothing has
been published before. The earlier paper ran thus:

I

NOTES ON THE WAR IN THE TRANSVAAL

NEW PALACE, POTSDAM,
21/12/'99.

A rapid mobilisation of the active regiments intended for service
abroad, and an excellent organisation of the transport service by
sea, has allowed of the despatch of the troops in quick succession,
and brought in six weeks about 40,000 men to Africa.

There the landing and proceeding by railway and marching to
the seat of war was well and smoothly effected. The operations have
been carried out along the railways which ensured regular supply
of ammunition, provisions, and reinforcements, as well as the clearing
off of the wounded, for so long as the lines were not destroyed.

[1] For the circumstances attending the receipt of the papers by the Prince
of Wales and the Kaiser's inaccurate descriptions of them in after years, see
pp. 755 *sq., supra.*

The aim of the operations appears to have been :

On the seat of war in *the East* the relief of Ladysmith, and with it the setting free of the 4th Division and of Natal, in *the West* the relief of Kimberley, in *the centre* the march on Bloemfontein and the linking with the two other fields of action.

The troops were distributed as shown on the accompanying "Ordre de bataille."

The fighting has, notwithstanding heroic bravery and efforts, not led to reaching the aims indicated.

There have been employed in Natal, including the 4th Division, 30,000 men, in the centre and the West 32,000 men, together 62,000 men.

The losses which have unfortunately been sustained amount *approximately* to 350 officers and 10,000 men in killed, wounded, prisoners, and missing, not counting the sick from other natural causes.

Hence there are now at disposal about 52,000 men of partly much-diminished or shaken troops. Replacement of the losses by the despatch of reinforcements will have taken place at the end of January by the arrival of the 5th and 6th Divisions. Then the whole Army will again be just as strong as at the beginning of November, that is to say, about 60,000 to 65,000 men. That number, however, is apparently not sufficient for the task, as shown by the course of the campaign.

To overcome the resistance much larger numbers are required, about 60,000 men with 550 to 600 officers.

The numbers are sought to be formed from volunteers, militia, and yeomanry who can arrive at the theatre of war about spring-time. It is doubtful and remains to be seen whether this material of men which is totally unaccustomed to tropical warfare and un-trained in shooting, led by inexperienced officers, will succeed where "seasoned" and trained active troops, accustomed to warfare, have been unable to succeed.

At any rate the war, which is now passing through a momentary period of rest, will after the arrival of the above reinforcements enter on a second stage, to which not improbably will have to be added the struggle with the rebellious population.

The second set of the Kaiser's "Notes" on the Boer War which he sent to the Prince of Wales ran as follows :

II

FURTHER NOTES ON THE TRANSVAAL WAR

BERLIN,
4/2/1900.

(1) After the engagement at Colenso the operations in Natal were to some extent suspended, the time being utilised for restoring organisation and for clearing away the wounded, etc.

(2) Gradually the 5th Division, under General Sir C. Warren (6 Battalions), arrived.

(3) At the beginning of January preparations for resuming the offensive were made. As the position of the enemy at Colenso had proved to be too strong, it was intended to outflank the enemy's *right*.

(4) For this purpose the Tugela was to be crossed in its upper course, and about the 10th January the Cavalry Brigade Dundonald started in the direction of Springfield. The main body followed under the command of Sir Redvers Buller on the 11th January.

(5) The operation was planned as a surprise, but this was frustrated in consequence of the great heat, the defective state of the roads, and the magnitude of the transport which considerably retarded the march. A column of 5000 wheeled vehicles of every description, distributed over a line of several English miles, reduced the rate of progress, according to Sir R. Buller's statements, to 5 miles per day. The "dash for Ladysmith" required 5 days for reaching the Tugela.

(6) On the 15th January the head of the Division Clery reached Potgieter's Drift; the Division Warren and the Brigade Dundonald Trichard's Drift, and Buller himself Spearman's Camp.

(7) The Brigade Dundonald crossed the Tugela without hindrance and cleared with unimportant skirmishes the country up to and beyond Acton Homes.

(8) The position of the enemy opposite Potgieter's Drift was soon found to be so strong as to show that debouching under the enemy's fire would be impracticable. To overcome the enemy, Zwart's Kop and Mount Alice were occupied with heavy artillery, and that position, as well as Spearman's Camp, strongly fortified.

(9) It was now resolved to outflank and if possible to get round to the north-west of the enemy's right, which was supposed to be on Spion Kop. For that purpose the Brigade Dundonald advanced up the valley of Venterspruit, followed by the Division Warren and the Brigades Hildyard and Hart of Clery's Division, whilst the Brigade Lyttelton held the ground north of Potgieter's Drift, and the Brigade Barton made a demonstration opposite Colenso.

(10) In the course of the outflanking attempt by the valley of Venterspruit it was seen, however, that the enemy occupied a second position stretching from Spion Kop in north-west direction on to Taba Myama and down to the valley. His right wing was on the 20th January successfully attacked by Warren with his Division and with the two Brigades of Clery's Division, and the enemy was in 3 days' fighting slowly driven back uphill.

(11) During the night of the 24th, part of Warren's Division occupied Spion Kop, and being reinforced held it gallantly under heavy losses during the 24th. In the night of the 25th, however, Spion Kop was lost again, notwithstanding heroic resistance entailing heavy losses. With the loss of Spion Kop the outflanking movement has collapsed, and on the 27th the troops are again concentrated on the south side of the Tugela.

(12) The very incomplete reports do not at present enable the distant critic to estimate the strength of the troops which were employed to storm and defend Spion Kop. So far as may be concluded from the very imperfect lists of losses, the Division Warren and more especially Woodgate's Brigade appear to have taken part therein. How far the Brigades Hart and Hildyard participated, or whether these were only held in reserve, cannot be ascertained here. In the reports on Spion Kop they are not mentioned at all. Warren had crossed the Tugela with about 17,000 combatants, and had finally attempted, apparently with only 5000 or at the utmost 7000 men, to reach and to hold Spion Kop, the goal of his march and attack. Lyttelton helped with 2000 men.

(13) The extent of the front of all the troops under Buller's command beyond the Tugela reached during the fighting 10 English miles, a situation which, with an enemy adopting the offensive, might undoubtedly have become fatal, and could eventually have made a retreat across the Tugela impossible.

(14) So long as considerable reinforcements do not reach the Army in Natal, it will hardly be in the condition to force the position of the enemy.

(15) In the other fields of operation no very important changes have taken place since the middle of December. General French has on the whole concentrated more in northern direction round Colesberg, where parts of the newly arrived 6th Infantry Division Kelly-Kenny (Brigade Clement) were apparently involved in an unfavourable skirmish, whilst other parts of this Division have joined General Gatacre.

(16) The 7th Infantry Division has with 5 Battalions reached Cape Town. After arrival of the remaining Battalions the supply of regular Active troops will for the present be finished, as the 8th Division, now being mobilised, is, according to the decision of the Government, not to leave England for the present.

(17) On the way out or about to arrive are some formations of Volunteers and Yeomanry, designed to serve as Mounted Infantry. Their main advantages, good marksmanship and excellent horsemanship, will materially depend on the description of the carbines and horses which can be placed at their disposal. Owing to their slight training in field-and-reconnoitering-service and in fighting with large tactical units, it will be possible to estimate their tactical value on the field of battle only where particularly the question of discipline, in the event of a protraction of the war, will also play a certain part.

(18) Altogether, including the troops about to arrive, but deducting killed, wounded, missing, and sick, the Commander-in-Chief, Field-Marshal Lord Roberts, will have about 86,000 combatants at his disposal. The statement of the Secretary of State for War in Parliament that 180,000 men were assembled in South Africa is based apparently on including into the account Engineers, the Army Medical Corps, and the transport and supply services. Should the report be well founded that Lord Roberts had asked for a reinforcement of 90,000 combatants, it would prove the correctness of my figures above mentioned, as the Army would thereby be raised to 176,000 men. This number was already at the beginning of the campaign (*October*) contemplated here as indispensable for its assured victorious termination, but in *February 1900*, after the loss of about 13,000 men and officers, it has not yet been reached.

(19) Assuming, therefore, that extensive far-reaching operations were suspended until the arrival of such reinforcements and the collection of the required numbers (which in every respect would be most advisable), and that the delay were thoroughly utilised to rest and reorganise the active troops of the first line, to make the Volunteers and Yeomanry acquainted with the country, and to accustom men and horses to the climate, it would then be possible to concentrate the British forces at any point of the theatre of war and to attempt under one command the solution of the task.

(20) Unity in the command and in the direction of the different columns towards one fixed point of the extensive field of operations are, however, the indispensable preliminary conditions of success. To keep in view the main object, with the neglect of all secondary considerations, however important these may appear, must be the firm aim of the Commander. Representations or even directions of Civil Governors, who may be alarmed about their territories or provinces, must of course remain unheeded.

(21) The course sketched under (19) requires much time, perhaps till next autumn, but it might be of advantage to the Army and extricate it from its present unfavourable situation. Of course it would be wise policy to place such a *respite* for the Army *in absolute safety* against foreign Powers, the attainment of which in the present situation of the world appears somewhat doubtful. The present

position of the war does not allow of doing anything decisive from the military point of view. If, therefore, diplomacy *cannot guarantee* absolutely to secure the respite just referred to, it would certainly be better to bring matters to a settlement.

(22) Even the best football club, if it is beaten notwithstanding the most gallant defence, accepts finally its defeat with equanimity. Last year in the great cricket match of England *v.* Australia the former took the victory of the latter quietly with chivalrous acknowledgement of her opponent.

WILHELM.

INDEX

811

END OF VOL. I.